Environmental Economics

New Horizons in Environmental Economics

General Editor: Wallace E. Oates, Professor of Economics, University of Maryland

This important new series is designed to make a significant contribution to the development of the principles and practices of environmental economics. It will include both theoretical and empirical work. International in scope, it will address issues of current and future concern in both East and West and in developed and developing countries.

The main purpose of the series is to create a forum for the publication of high quality work and to show how economic analysis can make a contribution to understanding and resolving the environmental problems confronting the world in the late 20th century.

Innovation in Environmental Policy
Edited by T.H. Tietenberg

Environmental Economics
Policies for Environmental Management and Sustainable Development
Clem Tisdell

The Economics of Solid Waste Reduction
The Impact of User Fees
Robin R. Jenkins

Environmental Economics:

Policies for Environmental Management and Sustainable Development

Clem Tisdell
Professor of Economics
University of Queensland
Australia, 4072

Edward Elgar

Published by
Edward Elgar Publishing Limited
Gower House
Croft Road
Aldershot
Hants GU11 3HR
England

Edward Elgar Publishing Company
Old Post Road
Brookfield
Vermont 05036
USA

A CIP catalogue record for this book
is available from the British Library

LIBRARY OF CONGRESS CATALOGING-IN-PUBLICATION DATA

Tisdell, C. A. (Clement Allan)
    Environmental economics: policies for environmental management and sustainable
development/Clem Tisdell.
        p.   cm. — (New horizons in environmental economics)
    1. Economic development—Environmental aspects. 2. Environmental policy.
I. Title.   II. Series.
HD75.8.T5633 1992   92–21370
333.7'2—dc20   CIP

ISBN 1 85278 639 6

Printed in Great Britain at the University Press, Cambridge

Contents

Figures and Tables

List of Figures

List of Tables

Preface

Appropriate policies for environmental management and for sustainable development are being sought by many in the present era. However, as highlighted by the World Conference on Environment and Development held in Rio de Janiero in 1992, political processes of searching for workable solutions to environmental problems face many obstacles. But in any case political processes must also be supplemented by in–depth economic analysis and careful identification of issues and workable policies. Unless this is done, concern is likely to degenerate into rhetoric and policy proposals may lack solid foundations.

The purpose of this book is to make a contribution to the debate about appropriate policies for environmental management and sustainable development by concentrating on conceptual issues and by following analytical arguments to their logical conclusions even when their results are at variance with preconceptions. New horizons in environmental economics and other fields can be opened up by careful attention to the meaning and definition of concepts, which in consequence become useful tools for analysis and policy formulation. When concepts are poorly defined, policies using these concepts rest on insecure foundations.

This book is intended to strengthen and extend the foundations of environmental economics and its policy applications. The book is based upon a selection of my essays written in the period 1970–1992, as acknowledged at the end of this volume. The original essays have been revised as appropriate and the text has been presented in an integrated way rather than as a mere collection of reprinted essays. Because of the common themes present in the original essays, connecting them together in book form has not been a difficult task. It has also been a satisfying one because it has enabled the common themes and interconnections inherent in the earlier essays, published in diverse journals, to be highlighted specifically. The reader should find this feature of value.

Production of a book involves a co–operative effort and especially in this case since research and writings on which this book is based occurred over a long period of time. Consequently, it is impossible to acknowledge specifically all those who deserve to be mentioned. However, I am grateful to Edward Elgar for encouraging me to produce the manuscript for this book and for making positive suggestions about the type of presentation needed and also to the staff of Edward Elgar for their assistance. The final manuscript was prepared by Jeannine Fowler and Susan Tooth and the diagrams were drawn professionally by Sue Gray. Adrian Foster and Thea Vinnicombe helped with the proofreading and preparation of the index. My thanks to them all for their contribution and to the staff in the Department of Economics at the University of Queensland for their general encouragement with this project. Once again my family has had to forgo my time with them to enable me to play my role in this creative process and I wish to thank Mariel, Ann–Marie and Christopher for this and for their support.

Clem Tisdell
Brisbane

PART I

Environmental Economics and Sustainability –
The Setting

1. Background to Environmental Economics and Sustainable Development

In less than two decades, environmental economics has become a major focus in economic studies and most universities in developed countries offering degrees in economics now include at least one course on environmental economics. This is so in the USA, many European countries, Canada and Australia, for example. Japan has been slower in introducing such courses but there is growing interest in them. These developments reflect increased public concern about the natural environment and may also be a response of economists to the growing involvement of natural scientists in such issues.

The development of environmental economics has opened up new academic vistas, encouraged interdisciplinary work and resulted in cross–fertilization of ideas. In many respects, environmental economics has been able to free itself of the constraints of orthodox economics. In this climate, diverse new theories and models have been developed and continue to be developed. Because of these developments, an issue can be examined from varied points of view using different theories, thereby improving our understanding of it. In turn, this diversity is an antidote to dogmatism, and therefore is likely to foster further progress in economic thought.

WHAT IS ENVIRONMENTAL ECONOMICS?

Environmental economics is concerned with economic interrelationships between mankind and the environment, that is with the environs or surroundings of human beings. It involves, amongst other things, study of the impact of economic activity on the environment as well as the influence of the environment on economic activity and human welfare. Its coverage is not restricted to the natural environment, although at present this is its main focus. Man–made environments such as urban environments, historical and cultural environments and modified natural

3

environments all fall within the domain of environmental economics. In general the environment surrounding economic entities is the main concern of environmental economics. It tends, therefore, to leave the environment within these entities out of consideration. It does not, for example, usually study the workplace environment or the environment within the household or home for these are mainly internal rather than external in creation. Nevertheless, even here one can see areas of relevance to environmental economics, e.g. questions concerning the use of noisy machinery, the noise of which is restricted to the economic unit but which may in the long term induce deafness. The borderline is also not so clear in relation to matters involving environmental health. In these cases, health may be influenced not only by environmental factors originating outside an economic unit but also by environmental conditions within it.

It is appropriate to give considerable attention to natural resources in studying environmental economics. This is because the state of the natural environment is an important surrounding directly affecting the welfare of human beings. To a large extent the natural environment is the foundation on which man–made environments rely for their sustainability and is an important receptor or sink for wastes from human activity such as air and water pollutants and solid wastes. With massive economic growth, demands on the natural environment to provide its myriad of 'free' services have increased, thereby overloading it and in some cases this has led to or threatens environmental disasters. Furthermore, there are fears that man–made environments will be threatened by the depletion of non-renewable natural resources and that mankind is irreversibly losing natural environments that are worth preserving in themselves as a source of human enjoyment and/or for higher ends. For all these reasons, and possibly others, natural resource economics has become the single largest area of concentration in studies of environmental economics.

However, the coverage of environmental economics and natural resource economics is not the same even though they overlap considerably in coverage. It could even be argued that the domain of natural resource economics is basically a subset of environmental economics.

EXTERNALITIES AND SUSTAINABILITY

From what has been said above, there are clearly two important factors that need to be studied in environmental economics: (1) environmental externalities or spillovers between economic entities – that is, the effect of the economic activities of one set of economic entities on the environment of others and vice versa, and (2) environmental sustainability – that is, our ability to sustain particular environments (man–made and natural) which in turn will depend amongst other things on the availability and quality of natural resources. Other things will include the stock of knowledge, man–made capital and so on.

Because of the central importance of externalities and sustainability of environments for environmental economics these twin concepts, and policies associated with these, are given considerable attention in this book. Externalities are the central theme of Part II. Part III focuses on project evaluation and the environment and is a 'transitional' part in which externalities, lack of information and the presence of uncertainty and sustainability are all considered in relation to project evaluation. Part IV concentrates on sustainability in relation to the environment and economic activity. Although there are many different concepts of sustainability and sustainable economic development, these concepts are useful in providing new dimensions to economic analysis and the basic economic problem of scarcity. Today environmental changes affect the whole globe either directly or indirectly. Direct effects are possible from ozone layer depletion and from the emission of greenhouse gases for example, and even from loss of genetic diversity. Indirect effects can also arise for instance through changes in patterns of international trade as a result of environmental changes in particular regions, and through a depletion in the pool of genes (due to extinction of wild varieties of a species for example) important for commercially cultivated or husbanded species. Furthermore, in so far as environmental degradation is a source of poverty or of unsustainable economic growth in any part of the world, it is of concern to the whole world community because modern communications have helped to increase worldwide empathy. Therefore, Part V of this book concentrates on the global environment and conservation, and policies proposed to prevent a serious deterioration in this environment. In this context, considerations involving externalities, public goods, the existence of unpriced natural resources, sustainable resource use and economic development are intertwined.

By way of general background to the main text, it may be useful to review in broad terms the failure of market systems to conserve nature (animals, plants and natural areas) optimally from society's viewpoint, the role of economics in decisions about nature conservation, the deterioration of the world's stock of living resources and the consequences of this for sustaining economic development and maintaining living standards. It is appropriate to pay particular attention to the market system, since it is the dominant means of social organization in the world today, and with the demise of centralized communism in the former USSR can be expected to increase its dominance.

Since mankind's existence depends ultimately on the living or biological world (for example, through the food chain) it is difficult to overestimate the importance of nature to mankind. Mankind's economic welfare, indeed its very survival, depends upon other living resources and although issues such as unemployment and inflation are significant, they are more transient and less fundamental than issues involved in conserving the world's living resources and their life supports.

Man's relationship with nature has changed greatly over the centuries. In early times, man had little control over nature but as a result of scientific and technological progress as well as growth in human populations, mankind controls or determines the destiny of the natural world (including the continuing existence of species) to an ever increasing extent. This magnified power of man over nature has come at a time when bonds or direct relationships of most of the human population with nature have been weakened by industrialization and urbanization. Mankind has to give greater consideration to its relationship with nature and the natural environment than in the past and economics has an important part to play in such deliberations. This is clear from the *World Conservation Strategy* (IUCN, 1980) and the revised and extended version of it, *Caring for the Earth* (IUCN–UNEP–WWF, 1991).

MARKETS AND MARKET FAILURE

The *World Conservation Strategy* (IUCN, 1980) suggested greater government involvement in decisions about resource use and less reliance on the market system, a stand significantly modified in the follow–up to this strategy (IUCN–UNEP–WWF, 1991). Dependence on markets to determine what is to be produced and preserved, how, where and when, was believed not to achieve socially acceptable conservational goals. How is this stance to be reconciled with the view that the market system is an efficient, possibly an ideal, system for allocating the use of scarce resources in society? Many economic textbooks claim (at least as a first rough rule) that businesses by maximizing their profits and consumers by maximizing their utility or satisfaction can bring about an economic optimum through the operation of the price mechanism (cf. Brown, 1975, secs 3.5 and 3.6; Tisdell, 1979, Ch.1). It is also frequently suggested that through the operation of the price mechanism consumers tend to be sovereign (Brown, 1975, p.43; Tisdell, 1979, Ch.1).

While the market system is a powerful, relatively inexpensive and responsive mechanism for allocating resources, in practice it is less than perfect. Market failure occurs. Market failure is said to occur when the price mechanism or the market system, the so-called invisible hand, fails to bring about a social optimum. Economists have specifically identified a number of factors that can cause market failure. One of the most important sources of market failure is the presence of externalities or spillovers. Basically these occur when the private decisions of individuals or firms about resource use result in unpaid-for benefits or costs. Externalities can be an important source of market failure in natural resource use. For example, the destruction of mangroves may benefit a housing/canal development but have an unfavourable externality on fishing because breeding areas for prawns (shrimp) and certain fish are destroyed as well as important food sources for these (Hamilton and Snedaker, 1984). Some general aspects of externalities are discussed later in this chapter and also some other sources of market failure in nature conservation and management are considered such as public goods or collective goods and common property or common access to natural resources.

However, is market failure a sufficient reason for government intervention in natural resource conservation? While economists are agreed that market failure does occur, there are differences of opinion about the extent of such failure. Some members of the Chicago School of Economics (who mostly favour free trade and small government) argue that the extent of market failure is exaggerated and furthermore that in many cases market failure can be overcome by creating conditions more favourable to market operations, for example, by creating private property rights rather than by say permitting common or open access to a resource. In addition, they point out that even idealistic government intervention involves a cost and government intervention is subject to 'political and administrative failure' (cf. Tisdell, 1982, Ch.16). Political and administrative mechanisms of resource allocation can have serious shortcomings. Thus there is no simple universal means for attaining the best allocation of resources. We cannot rely purely on market mechanisms nor trust entirely to political and administrative approaches. We need to weigh up the alternatives rationally in each circumstance and monitor the operation of adopted resource allocation mechanisms. The best approach is likely to involve a blending of market, political and administrative mechanisms.

THE ECONOMIC PROBLEM AND THE CONSERVATION OF NATURAL RESOURCES

Economics is sometimes said to be the science of the allocation of scarce resources in society. A widely accepted view in our society is that these resources should be allocated so as to maximize human happiness or satisfaction or minimize human want in relation to available resources. Defining what constitutes a maximum of human or social welfare has proven to be a difficult problem. Nevertheless, putting such difficulties to one side, the basic view in our society reflected in neoclassical economics is that mankind alone is the purpose for economizing. Only the wants of humanity are considered. The feelings of all other living things or their possible rights to existence count for nought unless these influence the desire of individual humans.

Even on the basis of a rather narrow man–centred approach, conservation of the natural environment is important in solving the economic problem. Up to a point, it is necessary to conserve the natural environment in order to increase or to maintain the production of man–made or transformed goods. Even if man–made or transformed goods only are valued by humans, the natural environment must be conserved to the extent necessary to maintain production of these.

This can be illustrated by Figure 1.1. In Figure 1.1 the curve ABC represents a possible hypothetical relationship between the output of man–made or transformed goods and the extent of conservation of the natural environment. If only man–made or transformed goods are valued, human satisfaction is maximized when the level of production corresponding to point B occurs. This requires the conservation of the natural environment to the extent x'. A smaller amount of conservation will reduce production and reduce human happiness.

However, individuals derive satisfaction not only from man–made or transformed goods but also directly from natural environments such as beaches, undisturbed forests, animals in the wild and so on. Taking this into account, greater preservation of the natural environment than that corresponding to point B in Figure 1.1 may be called for. For instance, a level of conservation corresponding to point K may be optimal.

Some conservationists argue that mankind has a moral obligation to conserve nature to a greater extent than might be dictated by humanity's own selfish desires, e.g. Worster (1985, Ch.13). They argue that man should act as a steward for nature and take care not to exterminate species. Hence a level of conservation greater than that corresponding to point K in Figure 1.1 may be called for. Such a view does not mean that the economic problem disappears. Rather the economic problem becomes a constrained one: for example, to maximize human welfare or satisfaction subject to constraints on preserving species, conserving natural areas and so on. A number of complex issues are involved particularly in specifying the constraints but these will not be considered here.

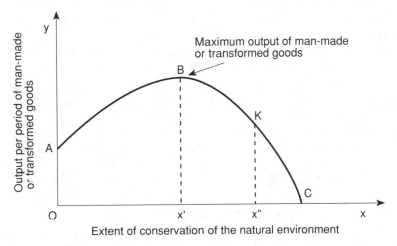

Figure 1.1   Up to a point conservation of the natural environment is necessary to increase or maintain the output of man−made or transformed goods.

EXTERNALITIES AND RELATED MARKET FAILURES IN CONSERVATION

As mentioned earlier, various factors may result in the market system conserving less of the natural environment than is socially optimal. These market failures may not only reduce the volume of produced goods available but also prevent humans obtaining adequate achievable satisfaction from natural environments. Let us consider externalities in this regard and give consideration to public goods or collective goods supplied through the conservation of nature.

Externalities

Externalities can be of many types, favourable or unfavourable. An unfavourable externality arises from the activity of an individual or firm when this imposes costs or losses on others for which they are not compensated. Hence, the individual or firm undertaking the activity does not bear the full cost to society of the activity. Even though the activity involves a net loss for society, it may nevertheless go ahead and/or be carried out on a greater scale than is optimal from society's point of view. For instance, swampy or marshy land or mangrove areas may be developed but this may reduce fish and prawn (shrimp) stocks because such areas provide breeding areas and food for such species. The developers do not bear the cost of reduced fish and prawn (shrimp) stocks. The development of such natural areas may also reduce recreational opportunities, for example, the access of amateur fishermen to water bodies for fishing, and reduce birdlife and this will be regarded as a loss by nature lovers. The external costs may well be so high that the area should remain undeveloped, or the external costs may dictate less development from a social viewpoint than would occur privately.

The last point can be illustrated by reference to Figure 1.2. Here, the curve *ABC* represents the extra or marginal net value to the owner of developing the land holding, say for a housing estate. The extra or marginal external costs imposed by this development are indicated by curve *OBF*. Hence, it is socially optimal to develop 1,000 hectares of this estate and leave 1,000 hectares undeveloped. At point B, the extra net value to the developer of developing an extra hectare of land just equals the extra external cost or losses imposed on others by doing this. If more than 1,000 hectares of the property are developed extra external costs exceed the additional net value obtained by the developer. However, since the extra net value to the developer remains positive, the developer finds it worthwhile to develop the whole 2,000 hectares. Consequently, there is an overall loss to society indicated by the hatched area in Figure 1.2 (that is, by the area of the triangle *BCF*).

In a case such as this the government may elect to place legal restrictions on the quantity of land that may be developed, impose a tax on the quantity of land developed or purchase a quantity of the land, e.g. 1,000 hectares, and leave this undeveloped. By such means it could bring about a socially optimal amount of development and of conservation of the land area.

Many other examples could be considered. For instance the clearing of trees on farms may benefit an individual farmer but involve a cost to others because water run–off is increased adding to chances of flash–flooding downstream, the rate of siltation of waterways may increase, in some areas neighbouring properties may be damaged by salting of the soil, visitors to the countryside may find the scenery less attractive if there is considerable removal of tree–cover and there may be wildlife losses that are regretted by some individuals in society. It may therefore by socially optimal for an individual farmer to remove fewer trees than is profitable from his/her own point of view (cf. Tisdell, 1985).

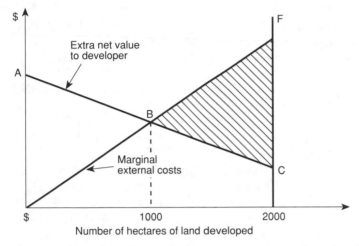

Figure 1.2   From a social viewpoint it is optimal to develop only 1,000 ha. of this land but it will all be developed by a private owner or owners.

Collective or Public Goods Supplied by the Existence of Nature

Some goods or services can be enjoyed by all if they exist and our enjoyment or consumption of these does not reduce the available supply for other individuals. These are called pure public or collective goods. Some natural resources, for instance species such as whales and kangaroos, have existence value. Some individuals value the existence of these species as such and would in principle be prepared to pay something to ensure their continued existence. The fact that one individual enjoys the existence of a species in no way reduces the opportunity of others to enjoy its existence. The conservation of the species at least up to a point satisfies a collective demand. This should be taken into account in decisions about the management of the species. This factor may support greater conservation of the species than would be the case in the absence of government intervention. The fact, for example, that individuals who really do not expect to see these animals have donated considerable sums to save the Lord Howe Island wood hen (in excess of $200,000) and the hairy-nosed wombat in Australia is evidence of existence value.

COMMON PROPERTY OR COMMON ACCESS TO NATURAL RESOURCES

Common or open access to natural resources such as fish can lead to their excessive exploitation and in some cases to their disappearance. When there is common access to a resource (when it is common property) there is no incentive to conserve it (see Hardin and Baden, 1977; Tisdell, 1982, Ch. 15, Tisdell, 1991, Ch. 6). Failure by an individual to harvest or gather common property may merely result in its being taken by someone else. For example if fish or animals are left by an individual to grow large in size, someone else may harvest these. This is not a problem when resources are private property.

One might think that the answer to this problem is to make all resources private property. However, this is not always practical or economical. Mobile resources such as kangaroos and whales cannot easily be made private property since they cannot easily be confined or herded.

In relation to mobile resources which cannot economically be made private property, some government intervention to control access to and the rate of exploitation of the resource may be called for. This for instance has happened in Australia in the lobster fishery, in the southern blue fin tuna industry and in kangaroo harvesting. In many states, commercial fishermen and hunters must be licensed and quotas in some cases limit the catch. Access of users to different zones in the Great Barrier Reef is now controlled according to type of use so as to satisfy conservation goals and minimize conflicts between different users. This is also a recognition of the fact that open access does not result in optimal resolution of conflict about resource use.

GLOBAL ENVIRONMENTAL TRENDS

The above may seem to be too microeconomic in focus because it ignores macro–environmental and macroeconomic changes which have important implications for economic sustainability. There is a need both for microeconomic analysis which mostly addresses the question of optimal balance between competing demands for resource use and macro–analysis which is concerned with aggregate demands on resource use, that is the absolute level of resource use by humans. Changes have occurred and are occurring in living resources and their life–support systems e.g. air and water quality (in the biosphere) which are a matter of concern. The main reason for these changes has been the rapid rise in the world's human population and growing levels of consumption, made possible largely by investment and new technology. In short, several environmental problems are growing because the world as a whole has experienced considerable economic growth.

The question has been raised of whether economic growth can continue as in the past and whether high rates of economic growth are desirable and in fact sustainable in view of the environmental impacts of economic growth. In the 1950s and especially in the 1960s, economic growth was considered to be a most desirable national objective. In the 1960s however several economists, most notably Mishan (1967) and Boulding (1966), began to warn about the environmental costs of economic growth and its possible long–term consequences. Boulding in particular pointed to the need to consider the relationship between economic activity and the environment by likening the Earth to a self–contained spaceship. In 1972, Meadows and others created considerable controversy when they published *The Limits to Growth: A Report for the Club of Rome's Project on the Predicament of Mankind.*

On the basis of then current growth trends, the Report predicted an economic and environmental crisis for the world by early in the 21st century. In particular there was concern about the rate of depletion of non–renewable resources, especially energy resources such as oil, and about growing levels of pollution, particularly air pollution. The report recommended that economic growth and population growth should be slowed down, or even stopped, and that immediate government action be taken to control pollution and conserve non–renewable resources such as minerals. Biologists such as Ehrlich (1970) and economists such as Daly (1980) reinforced this view by arguing in favour of steady state economies with zero population growth.

In comparison with the Report for the Club of Rome, *The Global 2000 Report to the President of the U.S.* (Barney, 1980) paid much more attention to living resources and the environments needed to support these. Most living resources have the property that they are renewable but become non–renewable under unfavourable environmental conditions.

The Global 2000 Report expressed concern about huge increases in the level of human population to be expected in the future, most of which will be concentrated in less developed countries, the possibility of growing shortages of energy resources, likely deterioration in the quality of water supplies and growing scarcity of water, continuing loss of forests especially in tropical areas which may add to the greenhouse effect and which will definitely reduce biodiversity, and loss of agricultural land and other economically productive land due to human–induced increases in soil erosion, salinization of soil and desertification.

The report predicted a dramatic loss in species as a result of economic change (a loss of half to two million species in the span of about 20 years) of which more than half will be lost as a result of the despoliation of tropical forests. Loss of biodiversity may mean the loss of potentially useful new sources of food, of pharmaceuticals and so on, as well as genetic stocks important for maintaining the productivity of our cultivated crops. These are to all intents and purposes irreversible losses. The report points out that 'extinction, of course, is the normal fate of virtually all species, but the extinctions projected for the coming decades will be largely human–generated and on a scale that renders natural extinction trivial by comparison' (Barney, 1980, p.149).

Similar views about global environmental and natural resource trends were expressed in the *World Conservation Strategy* (IUCN, 1980), *Our Common Future* (WCED, 1987) and more recently in *Caring for the Earth* (IUCN–UNEP–WWF, 1991). All these documents warn that current living standards may decline unless strategies for conserving natural resources and for maintaining environmental quality and existing ecological systems are improved.

In response to *The Global 2000 Report* and similar views about limits to growth, Julian Simon published an optimistic view of the prospects for growth, namely *The Ultimate Resource* (1981). Basically he argues that people are the most important resource and the more people there are the more scope there is for new ideas and for increases in productive knowledge. Improvements in technology, productivity and education are seen as overcoming limits to growth. He argues that we can look 'toward a beautiful resource future' and that the supply of natural resources is really infinite.

Debates about the limits to growth are in fact quite old (see Tisdell 1990, Chs 3 and 4). Thomas Robert Malthus (1798) was one of the earliest economists to raise this matter. Applying the principle of diminishing returns in production, he pointed out that an increase in per capita income levels above subsistence levels might be frittered away by population increases. David Ricardo (1817) pointed out this could be staved off by technological progress. Frederick Engels, Karl Marx's benefactor and friend, argued that because of scientific progress there is no need to fear overpopulation. He suggests that 'science advances in proportion to the knowledge bequeathed to it by the previous generation, and thus under the most ordinary conditions also in geometrical progression. And what is impossible to science!' (1959, p.204, first published 1844). Thus Engels is as optimistic as Julian Simon (1981). The result all depends on how optimistic we are about continuing scientific progress (cf. Tisdell, 1981, p.23). How sure can we be about these prospects?   Furthermore, even if considerable scientific progress occurs, it may be powerless to reverse major environmental changes, such as the greenhouse effect or to recreate pre–existing biodiversity.

That economic growth might be limited by insufficiency of natural resources was already well recognized in the early part of the 19th century. Limitations to expansion of food supply because of diminishing marginal productivity of land suitable for agriculture and limitations due to depletion of more productive deposits of minerals were seen as the main constraints to increased economic growth with rising population. But today several new possible limits to economic growth have been recognized. These include the limited ability of the natural environment to absorb wastes from human activity, the environmental risks and uncertainty, sometimes of a global nature, associated with high levels of human economic activity such as release or possible release of pollutants into the atmosphere and loss of biodiversity and living natural resources with consequent difficulties for maintaining economic production and/or human welfare.

COMMENT

We should be concerned more now than ever before about the effect of mankind on the natural environment. Mankind's power to alter the natural environment is greater than ever before. Even if humanity is not on the verge of economic and ecological disaster because of its failure to conscrve nature and preserve natural environments, the environmental risks from activities of humans have grown and can be expected to do so further as science and technology progress. We are at a stage in historical development where the economic, scientific and technological ability of mankind could lead to economic and ecological disaster. But the exact relationships remain uncertain, a factor that greatly complicates rational policy formulation. Many important policy issues of our time require simultaneous consideration of environmental factors involving externalities or spillovers, uncertainty and sustainability. These factors are, therefore, given particular attention in this book.

Economics has an important role to play in helping to improve decisions about conserving the living world and the natural resources on which life depends. Sustainable economic prosperity and human happiness require mankind to achieve a lasting balance with nature and the natural environment. This is true locally as well as globally. Nevertheless, human welfare does not solely depend on natural environments but also on man–made environments. But to a certain extent, the maintenance of man–made environments requircs natural environments to be sustained. For this reason and for others, the provision of both types of environments needs to be studied. Environmental economics is well placed to contribute to this study.

REFERENCES

Barney, G.O. (1980), *The Global 2000 Report to the President of the U.S.* Vol 1, Pergamon, New York.

Boulding, K.E. (1966), 'The Economics for the Coming Spaceship Earth' in H. Jarrett (ed.), *Environmental Quality in a Growing World*, Johns Hopkins University Press, Baltimore.

Brown, R.J. (1975), *Student Economics*, 6th ed., Pt 1, William Brooks, Sydney.

Daly, H.E. (1980), *Economics, Ecology and Ethics: Essays Towards a Steady–state Economy*, Freeman, San Francisco.

Ehrlich, P.R. (1970), *The Population Bomb,* Ballantine Books, New York.

Engels, Frederick (1959), 'Outline of a critique of Political Economy' in Karl Marx, *Economic and Philosophical Manuscripts of 1844*, Foreign Languages Publishing House, Moscow.

Hamilton, L.S. and Snedaker, S.C. (1984), *Handbook for Mangrove Area Management*, East–West Center, Honolulu.

Hardin, G and Baden, J. (1977), *Managing the Commons*, Freeman, San Francisco.

IUCN (1980), *World Conservation Strategy*, International Union for the Conservation of Nature and Natural Resources, Gland, Switzerland.

IUCN–UNEP–WWF (1991), *Caring for the Earth: a Strategy for Sustainable Living,* IUCN, Gland, Switzerland.

Malthus, T.R. (1798), *An Essay on the Principle of Population as it Affects the Future Improvement of Mankind,* J. Johnson, London.

Meadows, D.H. et al. (1972), *The Limits to Growth: A Report for the Club of Rome's Project on the Predicament of Mankind*, Universe Books, New York.

Mishan, E.J. (1967), *The Costs of Economic Growth*, Staples Press, London.

Ricardo, D (1817), *The Principles of Political Economy and Taxation*, London.

Simon, J. (1981), *The Ultimate Resource*, Martin Robertson, Oxford.

Tisdell, C.A. (1991), *Economics of Environmental Conservation.* Elsevier Science Publishers, Amsterdam.

Tisdell, C.A. (1990), *Natural Resources, Growth and Development,* Praeger, New York.

Tisdell, C.A. (1985), 'Conserving and Planting Trees on Farms: Lessons from Australian Cases', *Review of Marketing and Agricultural Economics*, 53(3), pp. 185–94.

Tisdell, C.A. (1982), *Microeconomics of Markets*, John Wiley, Brisbane.

Tisdell, C.A. (1981), *Science and Technology Policy: Priorities of Government*, Chapman and Hall, London.

Tisdell, C.A. (1979), *Economics in Our Society*, Jacaranda Press, Brisbane.

WCED (World Commission on Environment and Development) (1987), *Our Common Future*, Oxford University Press, New York.

Worster, D. (1985), *Nature's Economy: A History of Ecological Ideas*, Cambridge University Press, Cambridge.

PART II

Externalities and Policies to Control
Environmental Spillovers

2. On the Theory of Externalities: Relevant and Irrelevant Externalities

As economies grow externalities become more pervading and a matter of increasing concern for policy. In technologically advanced economies in particular, developments in the economic theory of externalities are of much more than academic interest. While literature on the theory of externalities is extensive, discussions of Pareto irrelevant externalities are infrequent. Despite earlier discussions of this subject (Meade, 1952; Buchanan and Stubblebine, 1962; Mishan, 1965) its significance has not been as widely appreciated as it deserves to be. Consequently, to redress this situation it is intended to use simple production models to illustrate and discuss cases of Pareto irrelevant externalities. First, cases will be considered in which the private choice of techniques is also the socially optimal choice and externalities are generated through variations in the level of activity. Secondly, cases will be considered – possibly most common – in which the choice of techniques is not socially optimal.

The analysis proceeds as follows: First, it is shown for the simple model used that in the absence of externalities perfect competition results in a Pareto optimum. Then, on the assumption that externalities vary only with the level of activity, infra–marginally irrelevant and marginally irrelevant externalities are considered. Next, externalities which vary with changes of techniques are discussed; and finally the cost of government intervention is taken into account. The theory is also shown to have implications for cost–benefit analysis and the allocation of investible funds.

OPTIMALITY OF PERFECT COMPETITION IN THE ABSENCE OF EXTERNALITIES

The model employed is very 'artificial': its merit is that it is one of the simplest for illustrating the main points. Furthermore, as shown later, it can also be modified to fit other cases. Let us first use it to indicate that in the absence of external economies and diseconomies, a perfectly competitive equilibrium satisfies the conditions of Pareto optimality.

The model assumes one relevant product, Y, which is produced by one variable but specific factor, X, whose aggregate supply is inelastic. Within the economy X, by assumption, has a positive marginal product up to at least its full employment level and no feasible distributions of Y can satisfy the desires of all; that is, for every feasible distribution, Y remains a scarce product (for at least one person).   Under these conditions, a Pareto optimum requires the X be fully employed and that the output of Y be maximized. Our aim is to show that these conditions will be met by a perfectly competitive equilibrium, given the model below.

Assume that there are n producing units in the economy and represent the production restraints on the $i-th$ unit by the strictly concave and differentiable function:

$$y_i = f_i(x_i) \tag{2.1}$$

where y_i denotes its output of Y, and x_i its employment of X.   In other words, diminishing marginal productivity is assumed to be the case. If a Pareto optimum is to occur, then

$$Y = \sum_{i=1}^{n} f_i(x_i) \tag{2.2}$$

must be maximized subject to

$$\sum_{i=1}^{n} x_i = X \tag{2.3}$$

Y and X represent respectively the aggregate output of product Y and the aggregate supply of factor X. Where λ is a Lagrange multiplier, an optimal allocation of X must simultaneously satisfy the following set of equations:

$$\frac{df_i}{dx_i} = \lambda \qquad (i=1,....,n) \tag{2.4a}$$

$$\sum_{i=1}^{n} x_i = X \tag{2.4b}$$

In other words, the marginal physical productivity of X must be the same for all firms and X must be fully employed if Y is to be maximized.

The strict concavity restrictions on the production functions ensure that the solution of the equations in (2.4) is unique and yields an absolute maximum of Y and not a minimum nor an inflection value. The necessary conditions for a Pareto optimum of production having been stated, let us see whether they are satisfied in a perfectly competitive equilibrium.

In a perfectly competitive equilibrium, all markets are cleared and this implies that condition (2.4b) above is met. Secondly, the price of Y is the same for all firms and so is the factor's price. This, in conjunction with the profit–maximization hypothesis, implies that condition (2.4a) is satisfied. Where w represents the factor's price and p the product's price, the perfectly competitive equilibrium conditions are:

$$\frac{df_i}{dx_i} = \frac{w}{p} \qquad (i=1,...,n) \tag{2.5a}$$

$$\sum_{i=1}^{n} x_i = X \tag{2.5b}$$

Expressions (2.5a) indicate that firms, in order to maximize their profit, equate the value of the factor's marginal product to its price, and since w and p are the same for all firms the marginal physical productivity of X will be the same for all. The strict concavity of the production functions ensures that the solution of (2.5) is unique and that Y reaches an absolute maximum. In expressions (2.5), w/p corresponds to λ in (2.4). On the production side, the necessary conditions for a Pareto optimum are satisfied by a perfectly competitive equilibrium if externalities are absent.

INFRA–MARGINAL EXTERNALITIES MAY NOT CAUSE MARKET FAILURE

If externalities are present, perfect competition may but need not lead to a Pareto optimum. Let us consider this proposition in terms of a one–way dependence case in which the externality varies with the level of activity. With one–way dependence, the external effects are not reciprocal – firms affected by externalities have no external effects. Within the bounds of this assumption, a great many cross–effects are possible but it is unprofitable to explore the whole range of cases. The essential factors will be brought out if attention is restricted to two firms one of which is dependent, the other independent.

Assume that the assumptions of the previous section apply *mutatis mutandis* and let the concave and differentiable production functions of the firms be represented respectively as

$$y_1 = f_1(x_1, x_2) \tag{2.6}$$

and

$$y_2 = f_2(x_2) \tag{2.7}$$

If a Pareto optimum is to be achieved,

$$Y = f_1(x_1, x_2) + f_2(x_2) \tag{2.8}$$

Let $(\bar{x}_1, \bar{x}_2)$ represent the allocation imposed in the perfectly competitive equilibrium. Then, only if

$$\frac{\partial f_1(\bar{x}_1, \bar{x}_2)}{\partial x_2} = 0 \tag{2.9}$$

will the necessary conditions for a maximum of Y be satisfied in this equilibrium.

It is possible for condition (2.9) to be satisfied and for

$$\int_0^{\bar{x}_2} f_1(\bar{x}_1, x_2) dx_2 > 0 \tag{2.10}$$

i.e. for an infra–marginal external economy to occur on balance, or for this expression to be negative in which case an external infra–marginal diseconomy occurs on balance. In these circumstances, the perfectly competitive equilibrium is Pareto optimal despite the externality.

In order to illustrate the infra–marginal case, assume the following production functions for firms one and two:

$$y_1 = g_1(x_1) + h_1(x_2) \tag{2.11}$$

and

$$y_2 = g_2(x_2) \tag{2.12}$$

where $g_1''<0, g_2''<0,$ and $g_2''+h_1<0.$

The necessary conditions for a maximum are:

$$\frac{dg_1}{dx_1}=\frac{dh_1}{dx_2}+\frac{dg_2}{dx_2}=\lambda \tag{2.13}$$

and

$$x_1+x_2=X \tag{2.14}$$

While the additive production function (2.11) is useful for illustrative purposes it is not very realistic because the cross–effect of x_2 on one's production does not depend on the level of firm one's activity.

This case can be given a diagrammatic interpretation like that in Figure 2.1. In Figure 2.1, the marginal product of x_1 is shown to the right and that of x_2 is shown to the left for arbitrary functions based upon functions (2.11) and (2.12).

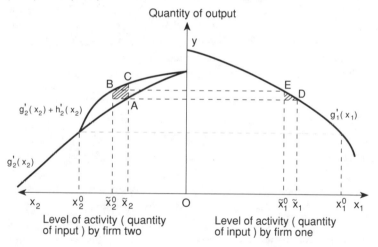

Figure 2.1 A Pareto irrelevant externality illustrated.

In the case illustrated, the marginal external economy generated by firm two, $h_1'(x_2)$ falls to zero for $x_2 \geq x_2^o$. Clearly, if $X \geq x_1^o+x_2^o$, the perfectly competitive equilibrium will result in Y being maximized and an infra–marginal external economy will exist. But if $X < x_1^o$, then a Pareto relevant marginal economy will occur and the perfectly competitive equilibrium will not maximize the output of Y. Too little of X will be allocated to firm two. To illustrate this, imagine that $X=\tilde{X}<x_1^0+x_2^0$. Since

under perfect competition each firm maximizes its profit by equating its private marginal product from the factor to its real price per unit, w/p, the factor is allocated so as to equate private marginal products. In this case the equilibrium private marginal product of the factor for each firm is D, and $\tilde{x}_1$ of it is allocated to firm one and $\tilde{x}_2$ of it to firm two. But in the perfectly competitive equilibrium, total output is not at a maximum because the social marginal product of x_2 (i.e. C) exceeds the social marginal product of x_1 (i.e. D). By re-allocating $\tilde{X}$, it is possible to increase the output of Y. To maximize output, it is necessary to equate the social marginal product of each firm and this will be achieved by allocating $\tilde{x}_1^0$ to firm one and $\tilde{x}_2^0$ to firm two. Employment of the factor by firm two needs to be increased at the expense of firm one. After the re-allocation the social marginal product of the factor will be E for both firms but the private marginal product of the factor in firm two's employment will be lower than for that in firm one's. The gain in total output as a result is equal to the shaded area in the neighbourhood of C less that in the neighbourhood of E. The gain may also be found by sliding $g_1{'}(x_1)$ to the left so that D corresponds to A and E to B. The gain is given by the shaded area in the neighbourhood of C above the transposed curve which passes through AB.) While for this case the externality is Pareto relevant, for a great enough level of activity (viz., $X \geq x_1^o + x_2^o$) the external economy becomes infra-marginal and Pareto irrelevant, since social and private marginal products coincide in this range.

MARGINAL EXTERNALITIES PARETO IRRELEVANT IN SPECIAL CASES

As in the one-way dependence case, Pareto irrelevant externalities may arise in the general interdependence case due to the presence of infra-marginalities. But unlike in the former case, Pareto irrelevance may also arise if marginal externalities are non-zero. At least this is so in this illustrative model in which X is specific and is in inelastic supply.

To illustrate the point, assume two firms only and represent their respective production functions by

$$y_1 = f_1(x_1, x_2) \tag{2.15}$$

and

$$y_2 = f_2(x_1, x_2) \tag{2.16}$$

If X is in inelastic supply, the necessary conditions for a maximum of Y are

$$\frac{\partial y_1}{\partial x_1} + \frac{\partial y_2}{\partial x_1} = \frac{\partial y_1}{\partial x_2} + \frac{\partial y_2}{\partial x_2} = \lambda \tag{2.17}$$

and

$$x_1 + x_2 = X \tag{2.18}$$

While perfectly competitive equilibrium ensures the full employment of X, it does not ensure that equation (2.17) is satisfied. In this equilibrium $\partial y_1/\partial x_1 = \partial y_2/\partial x_2$ but the cross-marginal effects may differ. If they do, then Y will not be maximized and the allocation of X will be less than optimal.

Although this is true generally, it is convenient to illustrate it by a simple but not very realistic case because of the additive nature of the production functions. Assume that the production functions of the two firms are

$$y_1 = g_1(x_1) + ax_2 \tag{2.19}$$

and

$$y_2 = g_2(x_2) + bx_1 \tag{2.20}$$

If $g_1(x_1)$ and $g_2(x_2)$ are strictly concave functions, the solution of these equations yields the absolute maximum of Y.

Allowing a and b to be of any sign, then in perfectly competitive equilibrium too few resources are allocated to firm two if $a>b$ and too many if the inequality is reversed. However, if $a=b$, Y will be maximized in the perfectly competitive equilibrium. Even if $a=b\neq0$, the externality is Pareto irrelevant.

This Pareto irrelevant case may be illustrated by the example in Figure 2.2. Here, $a=b>0$; mutual external economies occur. The total supply of X is shown as $x_2^o + x_1^o$. Perfectly competitive equilibrium will ensure that $g_1'(x_1) = g_2'(x_2) = OA$. But coincidentally, since

$a=b, g'(x_2)+a=g_1'(x_1)+b=OB$, and the output of Y is maximized.   The marginal externality is Pareto irrelevant.

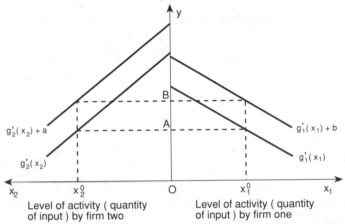

Figure 2.2 An irrelevant marginal externality – a special case.

Although the illustrated case is a particular one, equality of the cross–effects can occur at the margin under a wider range of conditions. However, the conclusion still depends on inelasticity of the factor's aggregate supply. If supply of the factor is not perfectly inelastic, then in this case, the factor is underemployed in the production of Y if external economies exist (overemployed if external diseconomies occur) even though the balance of employment of the factor by productive units is socially optimal relative to the level of Y produced.

Note that the theory discussed here can easily be applied to the optimal allocation of investible funds and to cost–benefit analysis. To do so, interpret X as the total quantity of available funds. The productivity functions now become discounted present return functions and the firms become divisions of a firm or individual investment projects.

RELEVANT   INFRA–MARGINAL   EXTERNALITIES AND CHOICE OF TECHNIQUES

So far the argument has rested on the assumption that the technique adopted under perfect competition is socially optimal and that all relevant externalities are generated by differences in the level of activity. But in practice alternative techniques may generate different externalities and their private and social returns may differ in such a way that socially optimal techniques are not adopted. Situations which appear on the basis of the preceding analysis to involve Pareto irrelevant externalities may after all involve Pareto relevant externalities. This is so for seemingly irrelevant infra–marginal externalities and for marginal ones and consequently this new possibility reduces the likelihood of Pareto irrelevant externalities.

Once the assumption about the adoption of socially optimal techniques is relaxed, a range of new possibilities is opened up. The magnitude of externalities may vary with the whole gamut of techniques adopted by interdependent firms. If we take one firm, its external influence may vary not only with its own technique but with those adopted by others. While it is not profitable for us to explore the whole range of possibilities, it is interesting to illustrate the proposition that in these new circumstances externalities which appear on first sight to be Pareto irrelevant may not really be irrelevant at all.

First, consider the infra–marginal case centring on Figure 2.1, but assume now that firm two has an alternative technique to the one whose marginal productivity function is shown in that figure and that firm one has no alternative technique. Represent firm two's first technique by g_2 and its alternative technique by G_2. Furthermore, assume that one–way externality continues but that its magnitude varies with firm two's technique. Specifically, suppose that with technique G_2 the production functions of the two firms are

$$y_1 = g_1(x_1) + H_1(x_2) \tag{2.21}$$

$$y_2 = G_2(x_2) \tag{2.22}$$

and that with g_2 they are represented in (2.11) and (2.12). Imagine that $G_2(x_2) < g_2(x_2)$ so that firm two's private product is least for technique G_2 but that

$$\int_0^{x_2^o} H'(x_2) \, d \, x_2 > \int_0^{x_2^o} h'(x_2) \, d \, x_2 > 0$$

i.e. the favourable external effect is greater for technique G_2. Under perfect competition firm two will adopt technique g_2. However, if the favourable externality of G_2 is sufficiently greater than that for g_2, G_2 may be socially optimal. The output of Y may be increased although firm two's private output declines. It follows in these circumstances that the externality which appeared to be Pareto irrelevant for $X \neq x_2{}^o + x_1{}^o$ is not Pareto irrelevant at all.

Even if no externality occurs in a perfectly competitive equilibrium, there may be a Pareto relevant alternative to it. To illustrate, assume the conditions immediately above but that now firm two's technique, g_2, has no external effect so that the alternative faced by the productive system is that expressed in (2.21) and (2.22) (using technique G_2) or the following:

$$y_1 = g_1(x_1) \tag{2.23}$$

$$y_2 = g_2(x_2) \tag{2.24}$$

Again, assume that $G_2(x_2) < g_2(x_2)$. Consequently, under perfect competition firm two adopts technique g_2, and the equilibrium solution does not involve an externality. However, if the favourable externality of technique G_2 is great enough, society may gain if firm two adopts G_2 even though it lowers that firm's private productivity.

A case in which Y increases if G_2 is adopted rather than g_2 is represented in Figure 2.3 in which the appropriate marginal productivity functions are shown. The figure is similar to the previous ones and the total supply of X is assumed to be equal to $X = x_1{}^o + x_2{}^o$.

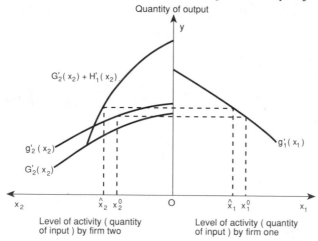

Figure 2.3 Externalities dependent on choice of techniques complicate rules for Pareto optimality.

As indicated in Figure 2.3, in perfectly competitive equilibrium x_1^o of X is employed by firm one and x_2^o by firm two; technique g_2 is adopted and consequently private and social marginal productivities are equal. However, the output of Y is increased if firm two adopts technique G_2 and $\hat{x}_2$ of X is allocated to it and the remainder of X (namely $\hat{x}_1$) is allocated to firm one. In this optimal situation, the private marginal productivity of x_2 differs from its social marginal productivity and an (optimal) externality exists.

It follows that if externalities are possible, neither the mere absence of externalities nor the mere presence of Pareto irrelevant externalities is evidence that production is conducted in a socially optimal way. Disconcertingly, we see that simple allocation rules fail in this area and that policy decisions can become immensely complicated.

So far it has been shown that if a perfectly competitive equilibrium involves no externality at the margin, either because no externalities exist or the externality is infra-marginal, there may nevertheless be a Pareto relevant and superior alternative to it. Further, a perfectly competitive equilibrium, such as indicated in Figure 2.2 in which the marginal externalities are Pareto irrelevant from the point of view of the allocation of X, may nevertheless be inferior to one which involves the adoption of alternative techniques. Since the illustration of this is clear from the previous discussion, it is unnecessary to give a specific example. To repeat, if in the economy, externalities are infra-marginal or in other ways apparently Pareto irrelevant or even if they are absent altogether, this is not evidence that production is conducted in an optimal way. A different choice of techniques may lead to greater overall output and in the new situation Pareto relevant externalities may exist.

STATE INTERVENTION COSTS

We have now reached the conclusion that, if Pareto irrelevant externalities occur in production, production nevertheless may not be conducted in an optimal fashion. While this seems to strengthen the case for state intervention in the productive system if externalities are important, there are other factors to take into account. So far the direct costs of state intervention have been ignored and these must be offset against any gain which might otherwise eventuate. The direct costs of policing, supervising and administering changes in production may be considerable even if imperfections of administration are absent. There is also the psychic cost of bureaucratic control to consider.

The way in which the state intervenes influences these costs and its procedures affect the optimality of solutions. Mishan has, for example, pointed out the importance of the law in this respect (Mishan, 1967; see also Chapter 5). He states: 'In cases of conflicting interest, according as the law, deliberately or by default, places the burden of reaching optimal arrangements on one party or group rather than on the other, both the characteristics of the optimal outcome and the costs of its attainment are altered. And the more important, as a component of welfare, are the external effects in question the greater, in these respects, is the impact of the law', (Mishan, 1967, p. 255).

Frequently it is better for government to bring about a reallocation or a change in economic procedures not by direct intervention but by promoting the co-operation of the parties who are affected by the externality. How can a government promote such co-operation? To answer this it is necessary to consider the reasons why groups may fail to co-operate when it is to their Pareto advantage to do so. Since many of these reasons have been discussed elsewhere, e.g. Tisdell (1966), only a few will be listed. Reasons why a group may fail to co-operate when it is to their Pareto advantage to do so include the following:

(i)   The optimal co-operative solution may be of the unstable prisoner-dilemma type (Luce and Raiffa, 1957, Chapter 5).

(ii)   The information of members of the group may be defective.

(iii) An externality may be involved in the organization of social change, and this may be of considerable importance. It may occur if the initiators of change must bear an organizational cost which exceeds their private gain or if their organizational cost does not exceed their private gain but is positive. In the latter case, everyone may wait for others to initiate the change.

(iv)   Bargaining may prove to be an insuperable barrier.

The government may help to remedy these barriers. It may overcome a prisoner-dilemma type problem by enforcing agreed solutions; it may provide improved information to members of the group; it may take some of the initiative to reduce the cost of social change, either lightening the burden on individuals or shifting it (e.g. by a change of the law) so that the importance of the externalities previously mentioned are reduced; and it may arbitrate in negotiations. But no matter whether the government, in order to deal with externalities, adopts a direct or indirect method of interference in the economic system, its intervention costs may exceed the gains to be had from pushing the system to or towards a state which involves a Pareto improvement in the absence of such costs.

CONCLUDING COMMENTS

While externalities may justify interference in the productive system, their mere presence does not. Both in infra–marginal cases and in various marginal cases the externalities may be Pareto irrelevant or the costs of government intervention may exceed the anticipated gains to the community.

Unfortunately, moreover, the fact that in an (equilibrium) situation externalities are Pareto irrelevant or are absent altogether does not imply that the economy has reached a global Pareto optimum. It may have, but it need not have. If different techniques give rise to a suitable array of externalities, the economy may well reach a preferred position by adopting techniques which are different to those which would be adopted under free competition. The different techniques, of course, may require a rather different Pareto optimal allocation of resources to that for perfect competition.

This theory has policy implications, not in the sense that it gives any global rule of thumb but in the sense that it underlines the inadequacy of the marginalist approach in this area. One must in many cases compare the absolute social and private effects of different techniques. There is no short way. Given the widespread externalities in our system, marginal analysis and rules of thumb based on it are becoming increasingly deficient and there is little hope that they will be more adequate in the near future.

Because a simplified special theory has been used to illustrate consequences of relevant and irrelevant externalities, this may give the impression that the theory is of limited relevance. This is however, far from the case. Similar models can be constructed, for example, taking industry output as the variable giving rise to externalities, or the area conserved or retained in forest cover (Tisdell, 1991, p. 48), or quantity of emission of a pollutant (see Chapter 3) as the independent variable resulting in an externality. Even cases involving public goods or collective goods can give rise to similar relationships. (See for instance, Tisdell, 1991, sec. 5.2 for an example dealing with the economics of wildlife conservation.) A further application also of the type of model outlined here can be considered: it is, for example, often claimed that research and development activity gives rise to favourable external economies. Expenditure on research and development (R & D) may be treated as the input and private and social returns to such expenditure as the outputs (Tisdell, 1973). It follows that cases can occur in which an infra–marginal favourable externality from research and development expenditure exists and subsidization of such expenditure is not justified on Pareto efficiency grounds. However, there are also other complications to consider, e.g. whether different methods of conducting R & D give rise to differing externalities. So actually, the theory has a wide range of possible applications to environmental and other matters.

REFERENCES

Buchanan, J. M. and Stubblebine, W. C. (1962) 'Externality', *Economics*, 29, November.

Luce, R. D. and Raiffa, H. (1957), *Games and Decisions*, John Wiley, New York.

Meade, J. E. (1952), 'External Economies and Diseconomies in a Competitive Situation', *Economics Journal*, 62, March.

Mishan, E.J. (1965), 'Reflections on Recent Developments in the Concept of External Effects', *Canadian Journal of Economics and Political Science*, 31, February.

Mishan, E.J. (1967), 'Pareto Optimality and the Law', *Oxford Economic Papers*, 19, November.

Tisdell, C.A. (1966), 'Some Bounds on the Pareto Optimality of Group Behaviour', *Kyklos*, 19(1).

Tisdell, C.A. (1973), 'The Australian Research Subsidy to Overseas Firms and Other Aspects of the Distribution of Research Grants', *Economic Research*, 17(2), August, pp. 194–210.

Tisdell, C.A. (1991), *Economics of Environmental Conservation*, Elsevier Science Publishers, Amsterdam.

3. Relevance of Non–Marginal Externalities: Allowing for Extra–Marginal External Economies

The previous chapter concentrated on infra–marginal externalities, particularly external economies. Infra–marginal external economies were shown to be Pareto irrelevant unless the externality varied materially with the type of technique adopted. Since in many cases material variation is likely, even infra–marginal external economies may be Pareto relevant. However, special attention was not given to infra–marginal external diseconomies and the possibility of extra–marginal externalities was not discussed. This chapter is intended to remedy this situation.

Buchanan and Stubblebine (1962)[1] introduced the notion of infra–marginal externalities, and clearly indicated their belief that such externalities could be Pareto relevant. However, their analysis contains two important omissions. In the first place, they do not investigate the circumstances under which infra–marginal externalities become Pareto relevant; nor, in the second place, does their analysis encompass the case of the extra–marginal externality. Building on Chapter 2, the present chapter offers a diagrammatic exposition of Buchanan and Stubblebine's infra–marginal case, which enables us to clarify some of the circumstances in which the infra–marginal externality becomes Pareto relevant. Moreover, in a similar manner, we are able to extend the technique to the often neglected extra–marginal case, and thereby to focus attention on a striking symmetry between the extra–marginal and infra–marginal cases.

To keep the presentation as manageable as possible, while illuminating the crucial aspects of non–marginal effects, we restrict our attention to a simple production model involving non–reciprocal (i.e. one–way) external effects, in a perfectly competitive environment. This was introduced in the previous chapter. Moreover, we assume throughout that each firm adopts the socially best technique of production. As shown in the previous chapter, this is an important assumption. Although the techniques of production chosen by firms at the non–competitive equilibrium may, for instance, generate neither marginal nor non–marginal external effects, there may exist socially preferable techniques of production which, if adopted, may generate Pareto relevant externalities.

The qualitative nature of the results we derive concerning the relevance or otherwise of non–marginal effects can be applied equally to consumption externalities, or to mixed consumption–production externalities if we retain the assumptions of non–reciprocity and a competitive environment.

First the production model, with external effects, is presented, that is, employed in this analysis and infra–marginal and extra–marginal externalities are defined in terms of the model. The next two sections consider infra–marginal externality situations, demonstrating that infra-marginal external diseconomies (but not economies) may be Pareto relevant. Then it is demonstrated that in the extra–marginal externality case, external economies (but not diseconomies) can be Pareto relevant. Policy areas including environmental and educational ones, are indicated for which these analytical results have importance.

EXISTENCE OF MARGINAL, INFRA–MARGINAL AND EXTRA–MARGINAL EXTERNALITIES

The analysis is presented in terms of the simple production model employed in Chapter 2. Assume two firms, one and two, which both produce a single product Y with inputs of a single factor X, the aggregate supply of which is fixed. Denoting the output of Y by firms one and two respectively by y_1 and y_2, and their inputs of X by x_1 and x_2, we assume the following production functions:

$$y_1 = g_1(x_1) + h_1(x_1) \tag{3.1}$$

$$y_2 = g_2(x_2) \tag{3.2}$$

where $g_1'' < 0$ and $g_2'' 0$. Firm two's employment of factor X thus imposes an external effect on firm one's production possibilities. Note that the additive form of the production function employed here is obviously greatly oversimplified and it is adopted merely to allow us to illustrate our central argument diagrammatically. In general, we might expect that the effect of x_2 on firm one's production would also depend on the level of firm one's activity.

A Pareto optimal allocation of factor X between the two firms requires that the marginal social product of X be the same in both. In the case of production functions (3.1) and (3.2), we require that

$$\frac{dg_1}{dx_1} = \frac{dg_2}{dx_2} + \frac{dh_1}{dx_2} \tag{3.3}$$

The assumptions of perfect competition, however, only ensure equality of marginal private products

$$\frac{dg_1}{dx_1} = \frac{dg_2}{dx_2} \qquad (3.4)$$

which translates into condition (3.3) only if, at the competitive equilibrium allocation of factor X, $(\bar{x}_1, \bar{x}_2)$,

$$\left.\frac{dh_1}{dx_2}\right|_{x_2 = \bar{x}_2} = 0 \qquad (3.5)$$

In short, if an externality does not exert an influence at the relevant margin, perfectly competitive production can result in Pareto optimality.

However, Pareto optimality is ensured only if the total impact of the externality is Pareto irrelevant. Suppose that (3.5) is true, but that

$$\int_0^{\bar{x}_2} \frac{dh_1}{dx_2} dx_2 \neq 0 \qquad (3.6)$$

Then an infra–marginal externality exists which is a diseconomy if (3.6) is of negative sign, but an economy if it is of positive sign. On the other hand, if (3.5) holds an extra–marginal externality arises if

$$\int_{x_2}^{\infty} \frac{dh_1}{dx_2} dx_2 \neq 0 \qquad (3.7)$$

being an economy if this expression is positive, and a diseconomy if the expression is negative. The crucial point is that in both the extra–marginal and infra–marginal externality cases the fact that the externality exerts no influence at the margin does not necessarily imply its total irrelevance. Our subsequent analysis is concerned with illustrating this fact, and with illuminating the circumstances which can make such externalities relevant. We begin by considering the infra–marginal case.

AN INFRA–MARGINAL EXTERNAL DISECONOMY MAY BE PARETO RELEVANT

In the previous chapter, infra–marginal external economies were shown to be Pareto irrelevant, if technological choice does not involve externality problems. However, the case of the infra–marginal external diseconomy remains to be discussed, and can, in fact, be shown to be different because it can be Pareto relevant. This possibility can be illustrated with the aid of Figure 3.1.

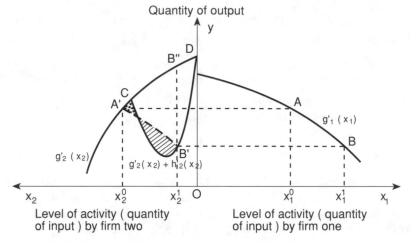

Figure 3.1 Infra–marginal external diseconomies can be Pareto relevant.

The marginal product of x_1 is shown in quadrant I, and that of x_2 in quadrant II. Note that the marginal product of x_2 consists of two components: first, the marginal product of x_2 in production of y_2, as shown by the curve $g'_2(x_2)$ which passes through D, C and A'; but also the marginal product of x_2 in production of y_1, $h'_1(x_2)$, which is negative for employment of x_2 up to point C. The negative influence of x_2 on production of y_1 causes the social marginal product of x_2 to take the loop $DB'C$ before the external diseconomy is exhausted at C.

Suppose that initially the total supply of X is $X=x^\circ_2+x^\circ_1$. Perfectly competitive equilibrium will result in firms one and two producing at A and A' respectively where

$$g_2{'}(x_2)=g_1{'}(X_1) \tag{3.8}$$

Since at A', $h_1{'}(x_2)$ is zero, the conditions for a local Pareto optimum are satisfied.[2] But

$$\int_0^{x^0_2} h_1{'}(x_2)dx_2<0 \tag{3.9}$$

–external diseconomy is infra–marginal.

If we were now to transfer a unit of X from firm two to firm one, the marginal product of x_2 rises and that of x_1 falls, causing a reduction in aggregate output of $y_1 + y_2$.   However, suppose that we transfer an amount of $x_2^0 - x_2^1$ a factor X from firm two to firm one. The fall in the total product of x_2 is measures by the area $x^0A'CB'x_2^1$:   this represents a fall in output of y_2 of $x_2^0 A' B'' x_2^1$, but an increase in output of y_1, through the reduction in the performance of the diseconomy generating activity, of $CB'' B'$. At the same time, the increased factor inputs to firm one increase the total product of x_1 by the area $x_1^0 ABx_1^1 (= x_2^0 A' B' x_2^1)$.

It is clear that in this case, the fall in output of y_2 is exceeded by the increased output of y_1 and so aggregate output of Y is increased by the factor reallocation.[3] The move is thus Pareto desirable, and the infra–marginal externality which exists at the competitive equilibrium is Pareto relevant. Moreover with the factor allocation (x_1^1, x_2^1)

$$g_1'(x_1) = g_2'(x_2) + h_1'(x_2) \tag{3.10}$$

The necessary conditions for Pareto optimality are satisfied, and there is no further reallocation of the fixed supply of factor inputs that will further increase total output.

REASONS FOR RELEVANCE OR IRRELEVANCE OF INFRA–MARGINAL EXTERNALITIES

The example in the previous section illustrates the general proposition that infra–marginal external diseconomies can be Pareto relevant. It may be useful at this point to explain intuitively what gives rise to this possibility, and to explain why infra–marginal external economies are irrelevant when variation of externalities with choice of techniques does not raise complications.

Perfectly competitive equilibrium is achieved when the total supply of factor X is allocated so as to equalize its marginal product in the two firms, one and two. In the absence of externalities, and under the normal assumption of diminishing marginal productivity, the competitive equilibrium is also Pareto optimal: any reallocation of the fixed factor X between the firms would raise the marginal product of X in the contracting firm, and lower its marginal product in the expanding firm relative to the initial position of equality, necessarily lowering aggregate output of Y.

In the case where at the competitive equilibrium one firm imposes an infra–marginal external economy on the production of others, the qualitative change in the marginal products of the factors used by the firms is not altered. If, say, we reduce the amount of X employed by the externality generating firm, then the existence of the external economy may simply cause the marginal product of X employed by that firm to rise further, or faster, than otherwise. The conclusion that the aggregate output of the two firms will fall is confirmed, and may indeed be intensified by the fact that we may in the reallocation process also destroy some of the beneficial influences of the external economy. Infra–marginal external economies are thus not Pareto relevant.

However, what makes the infra–marginal external diseconomy case potentially relevant is the fact that the 'normal' behaviour of the marginal products may be reversed. Observe in Figure 3.1 that as we reduce the quantity of X available to firm two, a point arises (at C) where the marginal product of x_2 begins to fall. Moreover, the marginal product of x_2 falls below its initial competitive value at A', and falls at a faster rate than the marginal product of x_1 diminishes as quantities of X are transferred to y_1 production. This pattern of behaviour of the marginal product of x_2 appears to be necessary to ensure Pareto relevance of the infra–marginal diseconomy generated by employment of x_2. Unfortunately, examination of the behaviour of the marginal products alone is not sufficient to determine the relevance or otherwise of the diseconomy. For example, it could be shown in Figure 3.1 that for some initial supply of $X > x^o_2 + x^o_1$ the infra–marginal diseconomy would be irrelevant relative to the competitive equilibrium allocation of X.

In summary, infra–marginal external economies are not Pareto relevant, but infra–marginal external diseconomies can be. The potential relevance of the diseconomy case depends crucially upon the magnitude of the diseconomy over its range of influence, but also upon the initial competitive allocation of resources.

EXTRA–MARGINAL EXTERNALITIES – THEIR EFFECTS

We turn now to a case not considered in the previous chapter – the case of the extra–marginal external effect. When competitive equilibrium is reached, such externalities exert no influence on current production either at the margin, or below the margin. In fact, they would exert an influence only if the level of the externality generating activity were expanded. The important question, then, is that of whether it would be Pareto desirable to expand the extra–marginal externality generating activity. It turns out, in fact, that there is an interesting symmetry between the infra–marginal and extra–marginal cases. That is, while infra–marginal economies are irrelevant, extra–marginal economies can be relevant, and while infra–marginal external diseconomies can be relevant, extra–marginal diseconomies are irrelevant.

The possibility of extra–marginal external economies being relevant is illustrated with the aid of Figure 3.2. As in Figure 3.1, the marginal product of x_1 is shown on the right side and that of x_2 on the left side. However, in this case, employment of X by firm two yields an external economy to firm one $(h'_1(x_2)>0)$ represented by the addition of the loop $CB'D'$ to the curve of the marginal product of x_2 in production of y_2. Note also that the external economy arises only when employment of x_2 reaches some critical level, as shown by the point C.

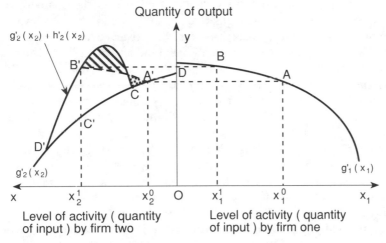

Figure 3.2 Extra–marginal external economies may be Pareto irrelevant.

Assuming an initial (fixed) supply of $X = x_2^o + x_1^o$, competitive equilibrium is achieved with the factor allocation (x_2^o, x_1^o): at this point the marginal products of x_1 and x_2 are equal. Since $h_1'(x_2) = 0$, the necessary conditions for a Pareto optimum are satisfied at this equilibrium. The external effect is clearly extra–marginal: it exerts no influence on current production, and would be brought into effect only by increasing firm two's allocation of factor X. Would a reallocation of factor X in firm two's favour be Pareto desirable?

Clearly a marginal reallocation of X to firm two would decrease total product, the marginal product of x_2 falling and that of x_1 rising. However, consider the following non–marginal reallocation. Remove from firm one an amount $x_1^o - x_1^1$ of X, and employ it in firm two. The total product of x_1 falls by $x_1^1BAx_1^o(= x_2^1B'A'x_2^o)$, while the total product of x_2 rises by $x_2^oA'CB'x_2^1$. The rise in x_2's product has two components. First, production of y_2 is increased by $x_2^oA'C'x_2^1$ as a result of increased factor inputs; and, secondly, production of y_1 is increased by $CB'C'$ as a result of the external economy generated by employment of x_2.

It is evident that in the case illustrated total Y production is increased.[4] That is, area $x_2^oA'CB'x_2^1$ exceeds area $x_1^1BAx_1^o$. Moreover, at the new factor allocation (x_2^1,x_1^1), the necessary conditions for Pareto optimality are fulfilled. Relative to the initial competitive equilibrium the extra−marginal external economy is Pareto relevant.

As with the infra−marginal diseconomy case, this example is intended to illustrate only that extra−marginal economies can be Pareto relevant, not that they are always relevant. Even in the case illustrated there exists some initial supply of $X < x_2^o + x_1^1$ such that relative to the competitive allocation of X the extra−marginal economy would be irrelevant. Furthermore, it is obviously necessary for the existence of the external economy to cause the (social) marginal product of x_2 to behave 'abnormally' for the situation to have potential Paretian relevance. The marginal product of x_2 must rise over some range as inputs of x_2 are increased and, moreover, it must rise above its initial competitive value, and rise further, or faster, than the marginal product of x_1 increases as x_1 is reduced.

These latter comments obviously indicate the perfect symmetry between the infra−marginal diseconomy and the extra−marginal economy cases. The general symmetry between the infra−marginal and extra−marginal externality situations can be completed by showing that, like infra−marginal economies, extra−marginal diseconomies are Pareto irrelevant.

Diagrammatically, the extra−marginal diseconomy case could be shown by redrawing the loop $CB'D'$ (or one like it) below the $g'_2(x_2)$ curve in Figure 3.2. Intuitively, the reason for the diseconomy's irrelevance is quite simple. Like the infra−marginal external economy, the extra−marginal diseconomy does not alter qualitatively the behaviour of the marginal product of x_2 in the relevant range. That is, as x_2 is increased, the diseconomy simply causes the marginal product of x_2 to fall further than otherwise in the appropriate range. The argument that a reallocation of inputs in firm two's favour from the competitive equilibrium will, in the absence of externalities, cause a fall in total product carries over completely, but more dramatically, to the extra−marginal external diseconomy situation.

ENVIRONMENTAL AND OTHER EXAMPLES OF INFRA–MARGINAL AND EXTRA–MARGINAL EXTERNALITIES

Infra–marginal and extra–marginal externalities are not mere academic curiosities. Several illustrative examples spring to mind which are of particular interest in relation to the ecology/pollution debate. For example, consider productive processes which pollute streams and impose external diseconomies on those who wish to use the streams for commercial or recreational purposes.[5] Beyond some point, outpourings of effluents render the streams completely valueless for these other uses and once this 'threshold' level of outpourings is exceeded, marginal adjustments in the pollution level are Pareto irrelevant in relation to the commercial or recreational uses. None the less, it is conceivable (though by no means assured) that some non–marginal reduction in pollution, such as lowering of outpourings to a level below the threshold, would be Pareto relevant. Similarly, once deterioration of the environment passes beyond a critical point, some species of flora and fauna may entirely disappear from an area. At this point, the marginal effects of further environmental deterioration on the species are zero, but the total effect may be Pareto relevant.

An interesting extra–marginal externality corresponds to this latter case. Many ecologists have observed that some species cannot survive unless their natural habitats are of some minimum size. Given that landowners do not obtain (or could not enforce) property rights in the native species concerned, and given that these species have social value, expansion of the size of suitable habitats beyond that chosen by landowners in the freely operating market may give rise to favourable externality. It may well be in the interest of society to provide subsidies to landowners designed to induce them to maintain at least the minimum–sized habitats suitable for the preservation of selected species.

On the other hand, one could also point to clear–cut examples of irrelevant non–marginal externalities. A producer who claims a subsidy, or tariff protection, on the grounds that his/her activity generates favourable externalities ought to have his/her claim denied if the favourable effects are exhausted at the competitive margin: the external economy he/she generates is then infra–marginal. Similarly, the case for subsidizing higher education because of the external economies generated rests on it being shown that economies have a marginal effect at the higher education level. To the extent that the external effects usually quoted can be attributable to education in general, rather than higher education in particular, they are, for individuals who have reached the higher education level, infra–marginal and hence Pareto irrelevant.

CONCLUSIONS FROM THIS ANALYSIS

The conclusions of our analysis may now be stated as follows: If, at the competitive equilibrium, an infra–marginal external economy or an extramarginal external diseconomy is exerted by one economic agent upon another, that externality is Pareto irrelevant (i.e. there are no mutual gains from readjustment of the activity). On the other hand, if an inframarginal external diseconomy or an extra–marginal external economy exists at the competitive equilibrium, the externality may be Pareto relevant.

If we add to this statement the by now well established result that nonreciprocal externalities which exert a marginal influence at the competitive equilibrium are Pareto relevant, we can conveniently tabulate the results concerning non–reciprocal externalities under competitive conditions so as to illustrate the symmetry between the economy and diseconomy case, as in Table 3.1. As mentioned previously, it is assumed that variations of externalities with choice of techniques are not a complicating factor.

Table 3.1   Implications for Pareto optimality of non–reciprocal externalities for the model outlined.

Extra–marginal	Infra–marginal	Marginal
ECONOMY ?	NR	R
DISECONOMY NR	?	R

R   =   Pareto relevant
NR =   not relevant
?   =   can be relevant

As indicated in the previous chapter, complications arise where choice of techniques with significantly differing external effects are available. In that case the social optimality of alternative arrays of techniques must be evaluated – one cannot rely on the tabulations in Table 3.1 as a guide to whether or not state intervention may be justified. This complicates policy making because total rather than marginal effects must be considered and considered not only for the techniques actually adopted but in comparison with alternative techniques which could be adopted.

As indicated in the previous section and in the previous chapter, the theory has a wide range of applications. It can be applied to cases where externalities depend upon variables other than quantities of inputs used by productive units, e.g. the quantity of emission of pollutants, conservation of nature, provision of educational services, research and development expenditures. Some of these applications are considered in the next chapter.[6]

NOTES

1. For details see references for Chapter 2, p. 34.
2. Explicit reference to a local Pareto optimum is made here because the central point of this analysis is essentially to show that when non–marginal externalities exist multiple optima may be generated, and the local Pareto optimum identified at the competitive equilibrium may not be the global optimum. That is, an alternative allocation of resources may exist which, in Paretian terms, dominates the competitive allocation.
3. The net output gain is the difference between the cross–hatched area and the dotted area in Figure 3.1. This is confirmed by comparing the various areas mentioned in the previous paragraph.
4. As with the infra–marginal case (see note 2) the output gain is measured by the differences between the cross–hatched and dotted areas in Figure 3.2.
5. It might be objected that the diagrammatic approach used is not sufficiently flexible to analyse such examples. Because we live in a multi–commodity world, practical application of the above analysis may require us to recast it in money terms. Assuming that a monetary index of social welfare is to be maximized, this can be done simply if marginal net private and marginal net social returns curves are defined and replace the productivity curves in our diagrams. The social return function should allow for any externalities which are generated by the activities under consideration. However, it is clear from cost–benefit analysis that there are considerable practical and philosophical difficulties in evaluating social return functions. Nevertheless, as the examples indicate, our principles are relevant to a wider context than that encompassed by the particular model in this chapter.
6. This chapter is based upon material originally published in conjuction with Cliff Walsh and I wish to thank him for permission to make use of this joint work. The material was published in C. Walsh and C. Tisdell (1973) 'Non–Marginal Externalities: as Relevant as Not', *Economic Record*, 49, pp. 447–55.

4. Pollution Control Policies: Proposals by Economists

Although the discipline of economics or political economy developed several centuries earlier, the mainstream of economic thought ignored spillover effects or externalities from economic activity until the 1930s when Pigou published *The Economics of Welfare* (Pigou, 1932). Until then and conveniently for liberal philosophy, the need for government to regulate pollution by private individuals and companies was, with the exception of a few radical economists such as Engels, scarcely considered by economists (Engels, 1845). Even then the subject of spillovers and pollution control did not achieve prominence in economics until after the mid–1960s.

Economists are interested in the effects which pollution has on the level of satisfaction or welfare which citizens obtain from their resources, and with the effectiveness and value of various means for regulating pollution such as taxes on pollution or subsidies for pollution reduction and pollution rights and quotas. They are not concerned with the discovery of engineering and natural scientific relationships involved in the control of pollution although these relationships are essential data in any pollution control problem.

Economic models which are used for discussing the social effects and control of pollution abstract considerably from variations which appear to occur in the world. Consequently, these models may only be able to capture the essence of a particular pollution problem if they are significantly modified. Nevertheless, they provide benchmarks and many economists use these abstract models to support various means of pollution control in principle.

Simple models are used in this chapter to discuss pollution control by the taxation approach of Pigou (1932), by the bargaining method of Coase (1960), by the sale of pollution rights as suggested by Dales (1968) and by the enforcement of environmental standards as discussed for instance by Baumol (1972). Particular attention is paid to the relative efficiency of taxation and legal sanctions as means for enforcing environmental standards. Consideration is also given to location of polluting activities as a control variable and to some aspects of the law and property rights.

TAXATION OF PRODUCTION: PIGOU'S APPROACH

Pigou observed that the marginal private cost to firms of producing products may diverge from the marginal costs to society of such production (Pigou, 1932). Producers of a particular product, for instance steel, may emit pollutants into the atmosphere which result in uncompensated damage to health and property of others. Consequently, the marginal private costs of production (the costs borne by producers) of the commodity (steel) fail to reflect the marginal costs to society of its production and in a free enterprise competitive economy in which companies seek to maximize their profit, production of the commodity and associated pollution will be socially excessive. The marginal private costs of production by companies can be brought into line with social costs by imposing a suitable tax on the output of the product which is a source of pollution. In the absence of regulation of this type, firms treat the environment as a free resource for waste disposal and pollute excessively.

Pigou's argument is readily illustrated by means of Figure 4.1. Let X represent the quantity of production of an industry causing uncompensated pollution and let BT represent the combined marginal private production costs of all firms in the industry. Because of pollution spillovers the marginal social costs of the combined production of firms, indicated by BS in Figure 4.1, exceed their marginal private costs of production. If AD represents the demand curve for product X (the price which purchasers are prepared to pay for the various quantities of X stated on the X–axis) and if AD also indicates the marginal value to society of extra production of X, it is socially optimal to produce and consume X_1 of X. When X_1 of X is produced, the product's marginal value in consumption is just equal to its marginal social cost of production. But in the absence of charges for the use of the environment, firms will produce a larger and socially excessive quantity of output X_2, the level of output for which the demand price offered by purchasers just equals the marginal (private) costs of production incurred by firms.

Pigou suggests that this level of socially excessive production arising from pollution spillovers might be remedied by imposing a suitable uniform tax on the production of the commodity. For instance, in the case illustrated, the imposition of a tax of $MN on each unit of X produced ensures that the socially optimal quantity of X is produced. After the imposition of the tax the firms' combined marginal costs of production are as indicated by the dotted lines in Figure 4.1. Hence, the tax helps to 'internalize' the pollution externality and the profit–maximizing behaviour of firms leads them to produce X_1 of X.

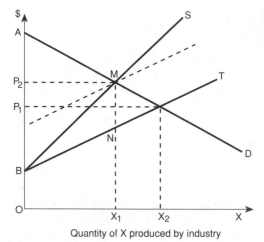

Figure 4.1   Pigovian pollution tax.

However, Pigou's approach has some shortcomings. The main shortcoming is that it can be inefficient to attempt to control the level of pollution by regulating only the quantity of production. If can be more efficient to tax the offending emission directly. For instance, pollution in a particular instance may arise from the use of a particular input in the production process and this input may have a perfect but slightly more expensive substitute. For example, the use of coal with a high sulphur content may be the main source of the pollutant and it may be possible at little extra cost to switch to coal with a low sulphur content. The Pigovian approach will not encourage such a switch but will merely result in a much reduced level of production based on the use of coal with a high sulphur content. On the other hand, a suitable tax on the offending emissions will encourage substitution of inputs. The taxation or regulation of output rather than the taxation of offending emissions is relatively inefficient if the costs of policing, monitoring and enforcing the regulations are similar in both cases. Nevertheless the crude Pigovian approach continues to have supporters. For instance Victor argues (1972, pp. 42–3):

> Although this form of pollution control is more crude than direct effluent charges it is appealing for several reasons. It could be implemented relatively quickly since only rough measures of effluents are required given that in this system of control, effluent discharge is not the tax base and therefore does not need to be measured precisely. This does not mean that precise measures of effluents are not better than imprecise measures...

Another limitation of Pigou's model is its assumption that competition in markets is pure or perfect. While it may be socially justifiable to restrict polluting production in a perfectly competitive environment, this need not be so under monopolistic conditions. A monopolist has an opportunity to create an artificial scarcity of his/her product, to restrict its supply, in order to raise his/her profit and may pursue this anti–social action. Even taking account of the fact that his production gives rise to environmental spillovers of pollutants, restrictions on output by the monopolist may mean that the production level determined by him/her is below a socially optimal one. Any further restriction of the monopolist's output would only worsen the social position, even though a tax on his/her emission of pollutants might improve it.

CONTROLS ON EMISSIONS OF POLLUTANTS THEMSELVES

The simplest model used by economists for discussing the control of emission of pollutants is the one illustrated by Figure 4.2 (Pearce, 1976). The model takes account of the costs of abating the emission of pollutants as well as the external benefits from reducing such emissions. It is recognized that while the costs of pollution abatement and the benefits of such abatement may be difficult to specify in practice, in principle these factors need to be taken into account in determining the optimal level of pollution abatement. Given an existing level of emission of pollutants, it is socially optimal to reduce this level of emission until the marginal external benefits from doing so are equal to the marginal cost of achieving this reduction.

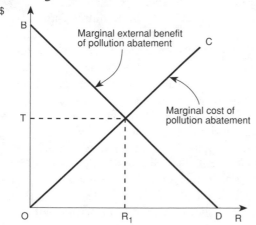

Figure 4.2 Reduction in emission of pollutant.

The socially optimal amount of emission of pollutants could be achieved by imposing a tax of $T on each unit of pollutant emitted. As long as the marginal cost of abating pollution is less than the marginal tax on the emission of pollutants it pays polluters to reduce their emissions. When the pollution tax per unit of emissions is set at T it pays polluters to reduce their level of pollution by OR_1.

Coase argues that the same reduction in pollution can be achieved if parties damaged by pollution pay (bribe) polluters to reduce their level of pollution (Coase, 1960). Line BD in Figure 4.2 represents the marginal amounts which damaged parties would be prepared to pay polluters to reduce their emission of a pollutant and OC represents the marginal amounts which polluters would require to compensate them for their cost of abating pollution. In the absence of significant barriers to negotiations, damaged parties could conceivably pay acceptable bribes to polluters which lead to a reduction in emissions by OR_1. The bribe which damaged parties would be willing to pay for any further reduction beyond OR_1 would not be sufficient to cover the cost of pollution abatement.

The difficulty with Coase's approach is that negotiations are not costless. When large numbers of people are damaged it may be costly for damaged parties to organize collective action and action to stem the damage may be on a smaller scale than warranted because of the presence of free–rider problems (Olson, 1965). Some damaged parties may not participate in collective action to limit pollution because they expect others to act and thus they will obtain benefits at no cost to themselves. Another problem is that this approach can encourage blackmail. Companies may deliberately increase their level of pollution emission in order to obtain extra compensation or larger bribes. As a result they would be rewarded for adding to social cost.

Dales argues strongly in favour of the sale of pollution rights as a means for controlling the level of emission of pollutants (Dales, 1968). In certain circumstances, this method results in a socially optimal level of emission of pollutants. If, as in Figure 4.3, E represents the existing level of emission of pollutants and R_1 indicates the optimal level of reduction in emissions, $E-R_1$ is the optimal level of emissions. Certificates for the right to pollute, to emit $E-R_1$ of pollutants, could be auctioned or sold by the government. The market equilibrium price of these certificates ensures efficiency in the emission of pollutants. Firms which find it more costly to abate pollution will purchase certificates and those that find it least costly will abate pollution rather than buy pollution certificates or rights. Thus any level of pollution reduction is achieved at least cost to the community and in addition, firms have an incentive to invent and adopt pollution reducing technology.

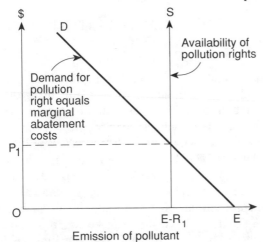

Figure 4.3   Dales's sale of pollution rights.

Even when the level of emission of pollutants is set in accordance with 'community' or other standards, and is not necessarily optimal in the sense discussed above, Dales's method can be used to obtain efficiency in reducing pollution to meet these standards.

Rights to emit pollutants equal to the quantity consistent with the environmental standard could be auctioned or sold at a price which just equates the demand for these rights with their supply. This should ensure that the environmental standard is achieved at minimum cost.

Dales's method of controlling pollution can be illustrated by means of Figure 4.3. Suppose that community standards require the emission of a pollutant to be limited to $E-R_1$. Rights to emit the pollutant can be sold or auctioned and the supply of rights can be restricted to ensure rights to a total emission of $E-R_1$. The availability of pollution rights can be limited to the supply indicated by the vertical line at $E-R_1$ in Figure 4.3. In Figure 4.3, polluters' demand for pollution rights is represented by line DE and corresponds to polluters' cost of reducing emissions from level E. Given the demand curve DE and the supply line marked S, the market equilibrium for pollution rights is established when the price per unit of pollutant emitted is P_1. Under the same cost–benefit conditions, the price of emission rights P_1 equals the optimal pollution tax rate T discussed in connection with Figure 4.2.

The models in Figure 4.3 suggest that efficiency of Dales's method of pollution control and the optimal taxation approach are clear cut. But these models rely on abstractions which are sometimes not warranted. Circumstances discussed in the next section can arise which make these control measures inefficient.

STANDARDS AND CONTROL OF POLLUTION BY FIAT VERSUS CONTROL BY TAXATION

Baumol and Oates argue that a suitable tax on pollution emissions is a more efficient means to reach an environmental standard than the imposition of quantitative pollution restrictions or pollution quotas on polluters, for instance, the use of laws which specify the maximum permissible amount of pollutant which can be emitted by a polluter (Baumol, 1972; Baumol and Oates, 1971). The fiat approach, if it is to be efficient, requires the regulating authorities to have a great deal of information about the pollution control costs experienced by individual polluters whereas the taxation approach does not and the optimal tax rate, the one which ensures that the standard is just met, can be found by trial and error. Their basic argument can be seen from the example illustrated in Figure 4.4. Assume that there are two polluters, firm one and firm two, and measure the emission of the pollutant by firm one, to the right of O and that by firm two to the left of O. Let $\hat{e}_1$ and $\hat{e}_2$ represent the existing levels of emission by the two firms and let line $m\hat{e}_1$ indicate the marginal cost to firm one of reducing its emission from $\hat{e}_1$ and let line $n\hat{e}_2$ specify the marginal cost to firm two of reducing its emission from $\hat{e}_2$. Firm one experiences greater costs in abating pollution than firm two. Imagine that the attainment of an environmental standard requires that the total level of emissions be reduced from $E=\hat{e}_1+\hat{e}_2$ to $\bar{E}=\bar{e}_1+\bar{e}_2$.

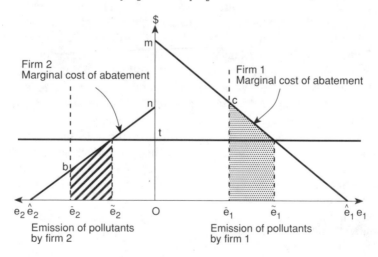

Figure 4.4   Alternative methods of achieving pollution standards.

One fiat or legal solution is to divide the permissible global level of emissions equally between polluters. In the case illustrated this results in each polluter being allowed a maximum level of emission of $\bar{e}_1 = \bar{e}_2$. The total cost of this method of achieving reduction in emissions to $\bar{E}$ is equivalent to the area of triangle $\tilde{e}_1 \, \hat{e}_2 \, c$ plus the area of triangle $\hat{e}_2 \, \tilde{e}_2 \, b$. Hence the global reduction in emissions is not achieved at minimum cost. The differential calculus indicates that the cost of abating emissions for any level of abatement is not a minimum unless the marginal cost of abatement (rate of change of abatement cost) is equal for all polluters. In the case illustrated and assuming that global emissions are restricted to $\bar{E}$, this condition is satisfied when emissions by firm one and firm two are $\tilde{e}_1$ and $\tilde{e}_2$ respectively. Costs to the community of abatement in the optimal case are less than those in the above fiat case by the equivalent of the difference between the area of the dotted quadrilateral in Figure 4.4 and the cross–hatched quadrilateral.

The optimal allocation of emissions to achieve the standard can be achieved by imposing a uniform tax of t on each unit of pollutant emitted. The common rate of tax ensures, if firms are profit maximizers, that the marginal costs of abatement are equalized for all polluters. This method ensures that the necessary condition for minimizing the overall costs of abatement is satisfied. The uniform tax rate can be varied until the proposed environmental standard is observed to be satisfied. The uniform tax solution ensures that the cost minimization is satisfied whereas the fiat solution does not.

But the demonstration by Baumol (1972) and Baumol and Oates (1971) of the superiority of uniform pollution tax compared to fiat regulation and the similar one by Dales (1968) of a uniform market price for the sale of pollution rights assumes that collectively damages from emission depend only on the total global level of emissions. In other words, the place at which the emission occurs makes no difference to the damage which it causes. In many instances this is an inappropriate assumption and when it is violated the optimal abatement of pollution cannot be achieved by the imposition of a uniform emission tax (Tietenberg, 1974). The optimal taxation level or price for emission rights may need to vary from place to place. This is easily demonstrated when the parties damaged by and the spread of pollution from two sources of pollution is disjoint.

Consider the case shown in Figure 4.5 as an illustration. This figure has the same interpretation as Figure 4.4 except that it is now assumed that firm one produces in area one and its emissions have no effect outside this area and that likewise firm two's emissions have no effect outside area two. The marginal external benefit from reducing firm one's emissions from $\hat{e}_1$ (or the marginal damages from e_1) are shown by the broken line CD. Similarly, the marginal external benefits from firm two reducing its emissions below $\hat{e}_2$ is shown by AB. Hence the socially optimal level of emissions for firm one is e_1^* and for firm two is e_2^*. These levels of emission could be achieved by imposing a per–unit pollution of tax t_1 on firm one's emissions and a pollution tax of t_2 on firm two's. Note that the rate of these taxes differ. Because of disjointness the imposition of a uniform tax to achieve a global rate of emission of e_1^* + e_2^* would not be socially optimal. Such a measure would result in socially excessive emission in area 1 and socially excessive abatement in area 2.

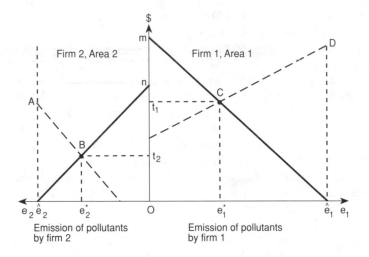

Figure 4.5   Differential pollution taxes.

While the case of disjointness may not be common, it is not unusual for the damages stemming from each unit of emission of a pollutant to vary from place to place. Whenever such variation occurs a uniform emission tax is likely to be a socially inefficient means for regulating pollution. While zoning of the taxation structure can be used to overcome Tietenberg's objection, tax rates have to be tailored for each zone. If the required number of zones is large, a large number of tax rates have to be tailored and the simplicity and low cost of the taxation approach may be lost.

NON-CONVEXITIES

Convexity of relevant production functions has been assumed so far. It should be observed that non-convexity of production possibility sets or preference relations can rule out the possibility of using a simple tax-subsidy method to achieve a socially optimal configuration of production or consumption when externalities occur. Non-convexities can occur for example when increasing returns to production are important.

This can be illustrated by the simple case in which perfectly competitive firms produce one product using one variable input. If the production possibility set of the firms is like that shown in Figure 4.6 (strictly convex in the boundary formed by the production function) any desired level of output or any desired level of use of the variable resource (along the production function) can be achieved by taxes or subsidies on output or on the use of the input. The iso-profit line tangential to the production possibility set can be altered by taxation and subsidies so as to be tangential to it at any desired point. Thus suppose that market prices are such that BC is the iso-profit line tangential to the production function. This results in an output of x^* and employment of Z^*. Assume that (taking account of pollution) an output of $\bar{x}$ is socially optimal. Then a tax can be imposed on the production of X which swings the tangential iso-profit line around to DF and results in the production of $\bar{Z}$ by profit making firms. A possible supporting hyperplane corresponds to each point on the production function (Tisdell, 1972, p.163). But if the production possibility set of the firm is re-entrant as shown in Figure 4.7 and therefore non-convex, the production function boundary of the set cannot have a supporting hyperplane corresponding to each point (Tisdell, 1972, p.163). It is impossible for the production possibility set to have a supporting hyperplane in its re-entrant portion.

Thus suppose that taking account of pollution externalities, an output of $\bar{x}$ is socially optimal and that the firm's production function is as in Figure 4.7. Constant per unit taxes on the output of x are incapable of enticing a firm to produce $\bar{x}$. Thus if market prices are such that the iso-profit line tangential to the production function is BC, it is impossible by imposing a constant per unit tax on the production of X to reduce production to $\bar{x}$. In such a circumstance, it may be necessary to impose a quota on the production of X of $\bar{x}$ or to vary the rate of tax with output (so that the iso-profit lines become curved) in order to achieve the socially desired level of output. But the variable tax rate approach means that the simplicity and the main advantages claimed for the tax-subsidy solution are lost.

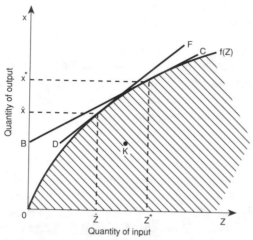

Figure 4.6   Convex case – strictly convex in production function boundary.

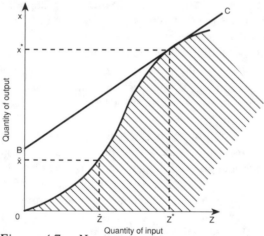

Figure 4.7   Non−convex case.

Also observe that a constant tax–subsidy rate approach is ineffective in achieving a social optimum when the social optimum occurs for a production–combination in the interior of the production possibility set. A firm cannot maximize profit by producing at an interior production combination if prices after tax or subsidy are constant. However, a quota may be used to achieve a desired interior configuration of production.

Again if the production possibility set is convex but not strictly so in its production function boundary, constant per unit tax or subsidy rates may be incapable of steering production to a social optimum different from the private productive optimum for firms. The production function contains linear segments in this case and changes in relative prices cannot be used to direct production with certainty to a point within a linear segment of the production function. For instance the production function shown in Figure 4.8 contains a linear segment between D and F. Suppose that the firm's profit–maximizing level of production is F but that E corresponds to its socially optimal level. Constant per unit rates of taxes cannot be used to swing production to E with certainty. They can only be used to make the after–tax iso–profit lines parallel to DF but in this case any level of production in the range $D \leq x \leq F$ may minimize profit. Perfect control is impossible by constant per unit tax rates or production in this case.

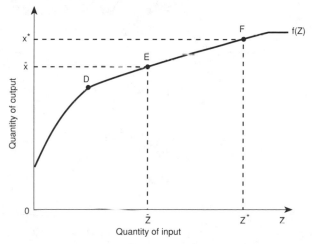

Figure 4.8   Convex but not strictly convex case.

In several production and consumption situations, non–convexities may rule out the use of constant tax–subsidy rates to achieve a social optimum which takes pollution into account. The circumstances mentioned above generalize to n–commodities. Figures 4.9 and 4.10 indicate two additional examples in which taxes and subsidies at a constant rate are not effective in achieving a desired social optimum. Figure 4.9 indicates the production possibility relationship between two products. Due to a non–convexity in the production possibility set, it is impossible to steer the economy to a point such as A by taxes or subsidies at a constant rate per unit on the products produced. In Figure 4.10, combinations of products equally sought after or preferred to any combination form a non–convex set. The indifference curve I_lI_l bounds one such set. Given this relationship, consumption consists either of all one product or the other, and not of some of each. Because of the non–convexity shown it is impossible by changing relative prices by (uniform) taxes or subsidies to steer consumption to a position such as A in which some of both products is consumed. A movement to a position such as A may be desired to reduce unfavourable externalities.

Figure 4.9   Non–convex production possibility set.

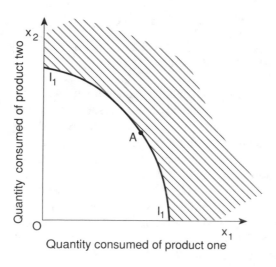

Figure 4.10 Non–convex preference relationship.

MISCELLANEOUS ASPECTS OF POLLUTION CONTROL

The above discussion has concentrated on the abatement costs proper of reductions in the level of pollution and has paid little attention to the agency costs of regulating pollution, that is the costs incurred by a government agency itself in administering pollution control measures. These costs include the cost of collecting information and enforcing regulation. In assessing the social desirability of any government measures to control pollution, account must be taken of abatement costs as well as agency costs. Control measures which are socially desirable when abatement costs alone are considered need not be so when agency costs are taken into account.

Taking account of agency costs Victor (1972, p. 42) says:

> Perhaps the main point in favour of effluent standards and against effluent charges is that standards are easier and therefore cheaper to administer. It is a simpler task to check that the outflow of a particular effluent does not exceed a specified limit than to measure continually the amount of effluent discharge.

Difficulties too arise if the ambient environmental conditions for the release of pollutants vary, possibly in uncertain ways. Emission charges or standards may need to be altered as ambient conditions vary but it may not pay to 'fine-tune' these measures. The question then needs to be considered of determining the optimal rigidity or inflexibility of pollution controls in view of uncertainty, the costs of change and the costs of obtaining accurate information about prevailing conditions and behaviour.

However, even when controls are not continually adjusted to changing ambient conditions, the variability of ambient conditions can have implications for optimal policy. If variability of ambient conditions is ignored in setting emission controls, the optimal level of emission sought may differ from the truly optimal value. Certainty bias may arise (Tisdell, 1973). For example, suppose that the external damages resulting from the emission of a pollutant are simply specified by

$$D = qm^2 \tag{4.1}$$

where D represents the damages in dollars, q is the quantity emitted of the pollutant and m measures the ambient conditions (e.g. reduced flow of water, air, temperature, and so on). For any given q, damages rise at an increasing rate with increases in m, the measure of the ambient condition.

If the ambient condition varies, then for any given q, quantity of emission of the pollutant, damages on average are

$$E[D] = q(E[m]^2 + var\ m) \qquad (4.2)$$

and changes in the average damages per unit of time with respect to q are

$$\frac{dE[D]}{dq} = E[m]^2 + var\ m. \qquad (4.3)$$

Assume that the total cost of keeping emissions at level q (rather than $\hat{q}$ in the absence of control) is

$$C = C(q) \text{ where } C''<0 \qquad (4.4)$$

Then net social damages on average per period or damages for an interval of time are minimized when

$$C'(q) = E[m]^2 + var\ m. \qquad (4.5)$$

In the case shown in Figure 4.11 this social optimum occurs when $q=\bar{q}$.

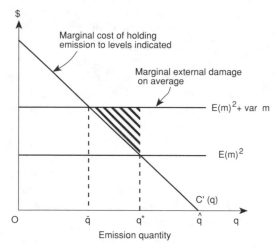

Figure 4.11   Even when production cannot be varied with ambient conditions, variability of or uncertainty of ambient conditions influences the socially optimal level of emission as a rule.

If in contrast the value of q, quantity of pollution emission, is selected so as to be optimal when average ambient conditions prevail, a socially excessive amount of pollution is permitted. In this case

$$D - C = qE[m]^2 - C(q) \qquad (4.6)$$

is maximized and the maximum occurs when

$$C'(q) = E[m]^2 \qquad (4.7)$$

In the example shown in Figure 4.11, this approach results in q^* of emission of the pollutant being allowed per period, a socially excessive amount even taking account of the fact that it is not feasible to alter the amount of emission according to prevailing ambient conditions. The loss in attainable 'social welfare' on average is equivalent to that indicated by the hatched triangle.

While in the above case altering the amount of emissions to accord with average conditions results in excessive emissions being allowed, in other cases the functional relationships may be such that this approach leads to excessive limitation on emissions. This would occur for instance if in the above example

$$D = f(q) - qm^2. \qquad (4.8)$$

The examples illustrate the point that even when quantities of emissions of pollutants cannot be varied with ambient conditions, variability or uncertainty of ambient conditions influence the socially optimal level of emissions as a rule. Considerations involving certainty bias and certainty equivalence are involved (Tisdell, 1973; Theil 1961).

However, pollution charges or adjustments at the margin of pollution activity, like those discussed above, may fail to control pollution in a globally optimal way. For instance, the infra–marginal damages caused by pollution from the use of an existing technique may be much greater than for an alternative technique and the socially optimal action may be for producers to switch to the latter technique. A pollution tax or charge designed to promote optimality at the margin may not induce this switch (Chapter 2; Tisdell, 1970), but merely ensure that pollution with the existing technique is abated in an optimal manner. Problems of this nature and non–convexities in pollution control relationship (Chapter 2 or Tisdell, 1970; Baumol and Bradford, 1972; Chapter 3 or Walsh and Tisdell, 1973) may make 'easy' economic methods for optimally rectifying pollution emissions impossible to apply. Moreover, the above models might be usefully extended to take account of learning.

VARIATIONS IN LOCATION OF POLLUTING ACTIVITIES AS A CONTROL

One method of controlling the damages done by polluting activities is to alter their location. This possibility does not appear to have been studied by economists in depth. While it is not possible to consider the optimality of different patterns of location of polluting activities here in detail, a few observations can be made.

Suppose for example that n sites are available on which a polluting activity can be conducted. How should the pollution generation be distributed between the available sites? Let $D_i(q_i)$ represent the amount of damage (valued in dollars) caused at site in i when the quantity q_i of the pollutant is emitted there or a polluting activity is conducted at level q_i there. Suppose further that the level of pollution to be tolerated is $\bar{Q} = \Sigma q_i$ and pollution is to be distributed to locations so that aggregate damage is minimized.

If the damage functions for each of the sites increases at an increasing rate and pollution occurs for $q_i > 0$, pollution emissions should be allocated such that

$$D_1{}'(q_1) = D_2{}'(q_2) = \ldots = D_n{}'(q_n) \tag{4.9}$$

that is so that marginal damages, are equal at all sites. In this case, all sites will be used as sinks for pollutants. It tends to be optimal to spread out pollution spatially. If the damage functions are the same for all sites damage should be equally distributed between sites.

On the other hand, if damage at each site increases at a decreasing rate, aggregate damage costs will be minimized if polluting activities are concentrated at one site. This may also be so if damages, after rising, reach a plateau at each site. Once the plateau is reached at any site, the marginal damages caused by further emissions at that site are zero.

In some cases, it may be that no economic damage occurs at a site until pollution emissions at the site exceed a threshold level. Let $q_1 = a_1$ represent this level for site i. Then if $\bar{Q} \leq \Sigma a_1$, total emissions can be distributed between sites so that no economic damage from pollution occurs. One solution, for example, is to select sites in any order, allocating a quantity of pollutant equal to the threshold emission to each selected site until sufficient sites have been selected and threshold quantities distributed to fill quota $\bar{Q}$.

In reality, of course, optimal location of pollution is much more complicated than the above simple example indicates. For instance, the goal for locating activities is unlikely to be just one of minimizing pollution damages. For example, the appropriate goal may be one of maximizing economic net benefit taking into account damage from pollution. Again, the extent of damages caused by pollution may vary with the level of pollution at a number of sites; interdependence may exist.

THE LAW, PROPERTY RIGHTS AND POLLUTION

Another means that governments may use to control pollution or environmental degradation is the creation of legal property rights in relation to pollution or the environment. These rights may facilitate the bargaining solution mentioned earlier in this chapter, or facilitate action under tort law as discussed in a later chapter.

For instance, certain persons or productive units may be given a legal right to emit pollutants into a water body. If these rights exist, those adversely affected by the pollution will, if they wish to reduce it or stop it, have to pay polluters to reduce or forgo their pollution of the water body. Conversely, if some group of individuals is given a legal right to a pollution free water body, those wishing to pollute it will need to compensate this group. In the absence of transaction costs, either allocation of legal rights should result in the same socially optimal (efficient) level of pollution, namely that for which the economic value to polluters of pollution emissions equals the marginal cost or damage to those adversely affected by the pollution. Although the pattern of legal assignment of environmental rights does not affect the economic efficiency of the control, it makes a substantial difference to the distribution of income. This can be seen from Figure 4.12.

In Figure 4.12, line OAB represents the marginal cost or damage to non–polluters of pollution emissions and the line CAD represents the marginal benefits to polluters of being able to pollute. The quantity of emissions of pollutant q, maximizing net benefit is q_1. At that level the marginal benefit to polluters of emissions equals the marginal damage to non–polluters. In theory and in the absence of transaction costs, this potential Pareto position could be achieved by assigning the legal rights to pollute to the polluters or giving non–polluters a right to a pollution free environment. If the former is the case, non–polluters would need to pay polluters a minimum amount equivalent to the dotted area in Figure 4.12 if bargaining is to achieve q_1. On the other hand, if legal rights run in the opposite direction, polluters will need to pay non–polluters a minimum amount equivalent to the hatched area if q_1 is to be achieved through negotiation. Thus q_1 can be achieved by either distribution of legal rights. However in one case polluters pay whereas in the other case non–polluters pay. Consequently the income distribution consequences are quite different depending upon the assignment of rights.

Since in the above case either distribution of rights is equally acceptable on efficiency grounds, economic efficiency considerations cannot be used in this case to determine the appropriate distribution of rights. Ethical or moral considerations are needed to choose between the alternatives.

However, transaction costs (likely to be involved in a negotiated or judicial solution) may vary with the assignment of rights. The assignment of rights which minimizes transaction costs may be favoured on efficiency grounds. Nevertheless it may still not be chosen for moral or ethical reasons.

Transaction costs are likely to be important in practice. But when the law is silent or uncertain about assignment of environmental rights, transaction costs are likely to be higher than necessary for negotiations or judicial decisions.

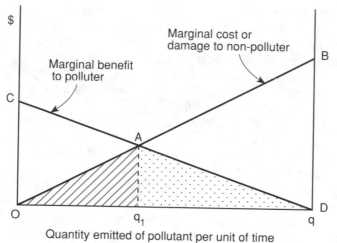

Figure 4.12 Different legal assignments of pollution rights may result in the efficient economic control of pollution but ethically not all these assignments may be equally acceptable.

POLICIES FOR CONTROL OF GLOBAL POLLUTION

Today some forms of pollution have global or geographically very widespread environmental effects. For example, emissions of 'greenhouse gases', for instance carbon dioxide, have been identified as possible agents of global warming. Emissions of CFCs are claimed to cause 'holes' in the ozone layer.

Global concerns about emissions of carbon gases have resulted in demands for the control of such emissions. Measures suggested include a carbon tax (which might be used for funding of the United Nations or for a fund for assistance to less developed countries), or a quota on emissions which may involve the distribution of tradeable permits. In the case of the carbon tax, less developed countries such as China complain that it is likely to be unfair on income distribution grounds. The real cost to China of paying such a tax is for example likely to be much greater than for the United States. If a quota system is used the question arises of how quotas should be initially distributed between nations. Distribution based on recent use of carbon fuels will tend to favour the more developed nations. Thus it can be seen that even though economic efficiency considerations may favour control of emissions of global pollutants, income distribution issues raised by nation states can be significant stumbling blocks to the introduction of such controls, as will be discussed later in this book.

CONCLUDING COMMENTS

It is sometimes claimed that increasing levels of pollution and environmental degradation are a consequence of economic growth and it is suggested rather crudely that the optimal way to control these is by restricting economic growth. While a case may exist for limiting economic growth, the relationship between economic growth and pollution and environmental degradation is complex and multi-dimensional. In some circumstances, economic growth can even lead to reduced pollution, e.g. when it is based on the introduction of less polluting technologies, or on the expansion of less polluting industries, e.g. service industries at the expense of more polluting ones. Nevertheless, both micro- and macro-aspects of environmental change need to be considered simultaneously for effective environmental management (Tisdell, 1991). This will become clearer as this book unfolds, and especially once issues involving sustainability are raised.

REFERENCES

Baumol, W. (1972) 'On Taxation and the Control of Externalities' *American Economic Review*, 62, pp. 307–22.

Baumol, W. and Bradford, D.F. (1972) 'Detrimental Externalities and Non–Convexity of the Production Set', *Economics*, 39, pp. 160–76.

Baumol, W. and Oates, W. (1971) 'The Use of Standards and Prices for the Protection of the Environment', *Swedish Journal of Economics*, 73, pp. 42–54.

Coase, R. (1960) 'The Problem of Social Waste' *The Journal of Law and Economics*, 3, pp. 1–44.

Dales, J.H. (1968) *Pollution, Property and Prices*, University of Toronto Press, Toronto.

Engels, F. (1845) *The Conditions of the Working–Class in England*, German edition, Otto Wigand, Leipzig, Germany.

Olson, M. (1965) *The Logic of Collective Action: Public Goods and the Theory of Groups*, Harvard University Press, Cambridge.

Pearce, D.W. (1976) *Environmental Economics*, Longman, London.

Pigou, A.C. (1932) *The Economics of Welfare*, Macmillan, London.

Theil, H. (1961) *Economic Forecasts and Policy*, 2nd revised ed., North–Holland, Amsterdam.

Tietenberg, T.H. (1974) 'On Taxation and the Control of Externalities: A Comment, *American Economic Review*, 64, pp. 462–6.

Tisdell, C.A. (1970) 'On the Theory of Externalities', *The Economic Record*, 46, pp. 14–25.

Tisdell, C.A. (1972) *Microeconomics: The Theory of Economic Allocation*, Wiley, Sydney.

Tisdell, C.A. (1973) 'Certainty Equivalence and Bias in the Management of Production', *Review of Marketing and Agricultural Economics*, 41, pp. 166–78.

Tisdell, C.A. (1991) *Economics of Environmental Conservation*, Elsevier Science Publishers, Amsterdam.

Victor, P.A. (1972) *Economics of Pollution*, Macmillan, London.

Walsh C. and Tisdell, C.A. (1973) 'Non–Marginal Externalities: As Relevant and As Not', *The Economic Record*, 49, pp. 447–55.

PART III

Project Evaluation, Cost–Benefit Analysis and the Environment

5. The Law, Risk Taking and Environmental Spillovers

The significance of the law for the solution of environmental problems was noted in the previous chapter, especially the importance of clear legal rights either to use an environmental amenity for waste–disposal or material purposes or to be able to enjoy it free of such interference. It was observed that the way legal rights to environmental use are allocated can affect the likelihood of achievement of the socially efficient use of the environment and the distribution of income. But the impact of the law on economic risk taking and its consequences for environmental risks and uncertainties was not discussed. The purpose of this chapter is to address these issues.

The law by shifting the burden of the bearing of risk or of uncertainty between parties in society influences the allocation of resources, income distribution, economic growth and the state of the environment. This can be seen, for example, in relation to the law of torts, laws for the sale of goods and the law of contracts.

Consider for instance the current position concerning the law of torts, the law relating to any wrong other than a criminal wrong. In the UK and Australia there is no liability for damages caused to others without fault on the part of the party responsible for the damage. In assessing fault account is taken of whether there is conspiracy or negligence on the part of parties causing damage, their intent and whether or not the damage is a result of overt acts. In specific cases, little attention is paid to the general resource allocation and economic effects of judgements. Nevertheless the present leaning of the law towards no liability for damages to others without fault grew up in the nineteenth century and Fleming (1977, p.8) suggests was a response to economic circumstances. He says:

> In response to the doctrines of natural law and *laissez–faire*, the courts attached increasing important to freedom of action and ultimately yielded to the general dogma of 'no liability without fault'. The movement coincided with, and was undoubtedly influenced by the demands of the Industrial Revolution.

Fleming goes on to claim that this pattern of liability was accepted by society in order to foster economic change and progress. In order to promote economic growth, it was believed to be better to subordinate the

69

security of individuals to that of enterprises by limiting the liability of enterprises for any accidents, environmental or otherwise, resulting from their enterprise or new projects. By contrast, strict liability or liability for faultless causation was seen as a deterrent to economic progress because the entrepreneur would have to shoulder all the cost of an accident resulting from his or her activity or project, irrespective of whether care had been taken. Thus projects or new economic activities might not be undertaken. Clearly the economic importance of the distribution of environmental and related legal rights was recognized in much earlier times, and since the 1950s economists have also become increasingly aware of the importance of the law in relation to environmental spillovers.

Several economists have pointed out that the law of torts can be an effective means for correcting externalities or spillovers. For instance, J.M. Oliver in his book *Law and Economics* (Oliver, 1979) approvingly cites a case in which a North Carolina poultry farmer successfully sued an airport because the noise of aircraft landings reduced the egg–laying of his birds. The US Supreme Court held that the poultry farmer's 'property' (or a characteristic of it) had been taken contrary to the Fifth Amendment of the US Constitution and that he was therefore entitled to compensation. However, it is also known that where property rights are ill–defined or not defined at all, where many are affected to some small extent individually but by a large amount collectively by an unfavourable externality and where, because of uncertainty about the source and extent of environmental damages legal costs are likely to be high, the scope for tort actions to correct efficiently for spillovers is limited.

While economists have given a great deal of attention to actual spillovers, they have given little attention to the risk of spillovers and the role of the law in protecting individuals from such risk. For instance, the role of the law in protecting outside individuals from the risks of a major accident in a nuclear electricity generating plant or from accidents in factories which may have released a dangerous gas in a neighbourhood, appears to have been inadequately discussed. Does the law result in excessive risks being taken from a social point of view or is it too restrictive of commercial risk taking?

Some criterion or criteria of the socially optimal level of risk taking is needed if progress is to be made in answering this question. The Kaldor–Hicks criterion would seem to favour maximization of expected gain as a socially optimal policy. Arrow (1962, 1966), for instance, has favoured this approach. The rationale for ignoring risk or variance from a collective point of view is that the many risky situations in society are not perfectly correlated so that overall average gains tend towards their mean and so those who gain by chance could compensate those who lose by chance when large numbers are involved.

An objection to this rule from a Paretian point of view is that compensation is not in fact paid in many instances and gains and losses to individuals do not in fact always balance out by chance. There may also be undertakings which involve collective risk taking and so risk cannot be balanced out, for example a decision to join the EEC or a free trade area or to have nuclear weapons based on one's home soil.

THE LAW, SPILLOVERS AND RISK TAKING

Consider the proposition that the operation of the law on the whole is such that those creating risks do not shoulder all the risks or costs associated with these but are permitted to allow some of these risks to spill over to others. Furthermore if this is so, does this encourage a socially excessive amount of risk taking in society?

Spillovers of Risk 'Sanctioned' by Law

A company or individual may fail to bear the overall cost of the damages imposed by his/her risky activities and thus obtain a higher expected gain and have a lower variance in returns than otherwise because:

(i)   There is no general liability under tort law without fault.

(ii) Even if the activity is a particularly hazardous one and (in the light of *Rylands vs. Fletcher*, strict liability applies) compensation paid for damages is likely to fall short of the full damage imposed. This is because compensation for tort (a) tends to be restricted to physical injury, that is to actual property loss (it does not as a rule include loss of amenity or psychological distress), and (b) excludes claims arising from 'remote' causes.

For instance in the case of *Weller and Co. vs. National Foot and Mouth Disease Research Institute* (quoted in Oliver, 1979) it was held that Weller and Co. auctioneers were not entitled to damages for loss of sale of cattle destroyed by the Institute although the owners of the cattle were because the auctioneers did not own the property concerned and were therefore 'remote'. *A fortiori*, any person who might have benefited if the proposed auction had gone ahead as planned, e.g. a casual barmaid by obtaining a day's work would not be entitled to compensation.

(iii) Statute law may restrict liability even though the common law position might favour strict liability. Limits are set to the liability of companies or authorities for nuclear accidents, for instance, in the UK and the USA (See Shrader–Frechette, 1980, Ch. 5).

(iv) Statute may prescribe behaviour which would be regarded as faultless behaviour. In the case of oil drilling on the Barrier Reef, it was proposed that companies should be expected to take specific precautions. If such precautions are taken either no claims may be payable for damages in the event of accident or there may be an upper limit to these payments (see Australian Government and Queensland Government, 1974).

(v) The limited liability form of company may provide a means for not bearing all risks. Subsidiary limited liability companies may be formed for this reason for carrying on risky activities. (Governments recognize this and sometimes require companies to insure or deposit bonds with the government.)

(vi) Compensation is not payable on the mere basis that one's property or person is put at risk. Actual damage must occur. But since transaction costs are involved in claiming for damages, property values may fall if subjected to risk.

(vii) There is the difficult question of what allowance should be made for loss of life and personal injury. In some countries there are limits on damages for loss of faculty (death or permanent unconsciousness). In Australia this is $1,000 for death or $3,000 for permanent unconsciousness.

In all the above cases, the law sanctions risk taking to some extent.

Some Possible Consequences of Risk Spillovers

While, as mentioned earlier, it is sometimes suggested that the shifting of risk burdens (specifically by externalities) is economically advantageous to society on the whole, there are clearcut cases where this is not so and a law that permits it results in an inferior social and economic outcome. This can be seen from a prisoner's dilemma type model (Luce and Raiffa, 1957). In this game–theory model, two participants or players are assumed and each by following his/her own narrow self–interest is worse off than by acting in the collective interest. But optimal collective behaviour is very unstable, because irrespective of the behaviour of others, each individual has an incentive to adopt selfish and anti–social behaviour. This can be illustrated by the matrix shown in Table 5.1.

In that table, two players are assumed, each of whom has a choice of two strategies: a low environmental risk strategy and a high environmental risk strategy. The entries in the cells of the matrix indicate the payoffs to player one and two respectively. If both players adopt a low risk strategy, they achieve a Pareto optimum and maximize the sum of their gains. But suppose spillovers of risk are legally permitted. Each individual acting in his/her own self–interest is likely to adopt a high risk strategy. Consequently the payoffs of participants, instead of being (5,5) are (3,3) and this is clearly an inferior situation.

Table 5.1 In a case such as this the law, by shifting risk, results in an inferior social outcome.

Player 1's strategies ↓	Player 2's strategies →	
	Low risk	High risk
Low risk	$\begin{bmatrix} (5,5) \\ (2,6) \end{bmatrix}$	$\begin{matrix} (6,2) \\ (4,4) \end{matrix}$
High risk		

Even when the law does not fully sanction spillovers of risk, spillovers often continue to some extent after application of the law, as observed above. Consequently, a risk taker's expected returns are higher and his/her variance of returns lower than if he/she had to bear all the losses associated with his/her decisions. Thus risk taking is encouraged. This encouragement, despite the example in Table 5.1, may but need not result in excessive risk taking from a Kaldor–Hicks standpoint. This can be seen from Figure 5.1.

For simplicity assume that each project involves a unique level of investment and that expected gains to society are maximized when all projects with an expected social return of R or more are undertaken. The social indifference curve marked RW_2 is a decision boundary. If the Kaldor–Hicks assumption is adopted, the social indifference curves are horizontal straight lines.

Suppose that the rate of interest is R, and let the indifference curves marked I_1, I_2, I_3 represent the risk–return trade-off of a typical investor. The indifference curves indicate that the investor is risk–averse. Now consider a Project P_1 for which the (mean, variance) return is A when investors meet all social losses involved in the activity. If investors have to meet all spillovers, however, they will not undertake the activity because its certainty equivalent rate of return M is less than the rate of interest R. Even some spillovers are legally allowed and the mean return raised and the variance lowered so that private returns move to position B the project will not be undertaken. Project P_1 will only be undertaken if after spillovers, its private mean–variance combination is on I_3 or above it as at C. Thus despite legalized spillovers, there may be insufficient risk taking from a social point of view.

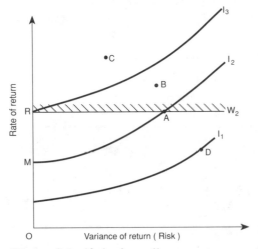

Figure 5.1   If the law allows environmental or similar risks to spill over to persons other than the investor, a Kaldor–Hicks improvement may occur but need not do so.

On the other hand, legalized spillovers can be such that excessive risk taking is encouraged from a Kaldor–Hicks viewpoint. For instance, consider a project P_2 for which the mean–variance combination is D when investors meet all the social losses connected with the project. The expected return of this project is less that R so it is not socially optimal to launch it. But if spillovers are legally allowed, the private mean–variance of returns associated with the project might be as at C. Therefore the project may go ahead even though it is undesirable from a social point of view. Legally allowed spillovers (reductions in private risks) result in a socially inferior choice in this case.

Because of legalized spillovers, risky activities may not be optimally located from a Kaldor–Hicks viewpoint, the best choice of techniques may not be made, and the composition of production may not be optimal.

A Case in which the Law can Lead to a Socially Excessive Reduction in the Risk of Spillovers

Economic considerations seem to play a larger role in the formulation of the law in the USA than in the UK or Australia. Nevertheless, carefully considered legal judgements or practices in the US can lead to decisions about risk which are not optimal from a Kaldor–Hicks standpoint. The following US legal practice illustrates this point: 'The US specification of negligence in unintentional tort cases is that the behaviour is negligent if the loss caused by the accident multiplied by the probability of the accident occurring exceeds the cost of the precautions that the defendant might have taken to prevent it (*United States vs. Caroll Towing Co.* [1974] 159 R2d 169 2nd Cir)' (Oliver 1979). This rule should encourage private expenditure on precautions up to the level where this total expenditure equals the expected damages. In Figure 5.2, for example, where *BD* represents total expected damage and the curve marked *TC* is the total cost of precautions, the risk of accident would be reduced to ρ_2 by following this rule. In this case, there is a greater reduction in risk than is optimal from a Kaldor–Hicks viewpoint. The optimal level of risk of accident from a Kaldor–Hicks viewpoint is ρ_0, the level at which the marginal costs of reducing the risk of accident equals the marginal expected benefit of doing so; that is the level at which the slope of *OE* equals the slope of *TC*.

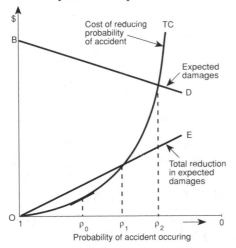

Figure 5.2 United States practice for determining negligence leads to an excessive reduction in risks in this case.

But the US ruling can also result in encouragement of excessive risk taking from a Kaldor–Hicks point of view. The rate of change of the cost curve showing the cost of reducing the risk can be equal to the rate of change of the expected reduction in damage at a point beyond the intersection of the former curve with the expected damages curve. An example is shown in Figure 5.3. Here BG represents expected damages and OH the expected reduction in damages. If the total cost of precautions is as represented by curve OK, the US rule results in risks being reduced to ρ_3 whereas ρ_4 is optimal from a Kaldor–Hicks viewpoint.

It can be shown that where the total cost curve of reducing risk is smoothly increasing and cuts BG to the left of intersection point F in Figure 5.3, the US ruling encourages an excessive reduction in risk. If the curve cuts BG to the right of F it may either encourage insufficient reduction in risk as in the case shown in Figure 5.3 or an excess reduction. The latter occurs if the rate of change of OK should equal that for OH before it crosses BG.

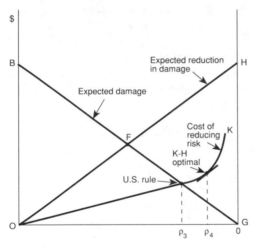

Figure 5.3   The US ruling on negligence can result in excessive risk taking from a Kaldor–Hicks point of view.

AN OBSERVATION ON THE LEGAL PRACTICE OF COMPENSATING FOR DAMAGES SUSTAINED RATHER THAN FOR THE RISKS OF DAMAGE

As a rule compensation is payable under tort action only for damages sustained and not to an individual for merely being subjected to the risk of such damages. This practice tends to reduce the expected payout of those creating risky spillovers as can be illustrated by Figure 5.4.

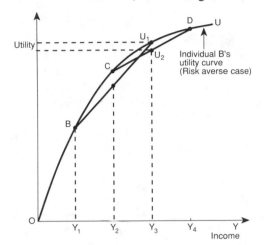

Figure 5.4 It is usually less costly to compensate a victim for damages actually sustained than to compensate him/her for the risk of such damage.

Assume that the risk of an accident caused by individual A and reducing individual B's income from Y_3 to Y_1 is 0.5. The expected damages payable by A to B are 0.5 $(Y_3 - Y_1) = Y_3 - Y_2$. However, a payment from A to individual B of $Y_4 - Y_3 = 0.5$ $(Y_3 - Y_1)$ would be inadequate for B to accept the risk willingly given that individual B is risk–averse as indicated by the strict concavity of his/her utility curve indicated by $OBCD$. If B were paid this sum and had to bear the risk his/her expected utility would be U_2 compared to U_1 in the original situation. A larger payment than the expected loss would be necessary to compensate individual B for bearing the risks of damage. Thus it is more economical to compensate for damages sustained rather than for the risk of damages.

THE LAW AND RISK BEARING IN THE SALE OF GOODS

Market exchange and transactions are a dominant part of the modern socio–economic environment. In relation to this environment the law applying to risk bearing and consumer protection is important. Community attitudes towards consumer protection are changing as Oliver (1979) points out. In earlier times, risk principally fell on the purchasers as summarized in the adage 'let the buyer beware'. It was believed that if customers were innocently supplied with a defective good that this was a risk they might be reasonably expected to take in purchasing in the market place. But this doctrine is being increasingly replaced in practice by the strict liability point of view. According to Oliver (1979), the strict liability doctrine implies that when economic or other forms of interdependence between any two parties involve risks, the risk burden 'should fall on those best able to bear it even though they were not at fault in any normal sense of the word' (Oliver, 1979).

This swing in legal practice increases the likelihood of the risk associated with a product being borne by the supplier or manufacturer. Two British cases of interest involving the sale of goods are *H. Kendall & Sons vs Wm Lillicoe & Sons Ltd* and *Ashington Piggeries Ltd vs. Christopher Hill Ltd*. The plaintiff had in the former case brought poultry feed from the defendant and in the latter case the plaintiff had bought herring meal from the defendant. In both cases the supplier, who it was agreed had not been negligent, lost the case.

Arguments for and against Strict Liability in the Sale of Goods

Economists have occasionally pointed out that the effect of placing strict liability on sellers is usually to raise the price of products to buyers. This can be illustrated in terms of Figure 5.5 which assumes pure competition. Assume that DD is the demand for the product when sellers are strictly liable. The supply curve might then be $S'S'$. If sellers are not strictly

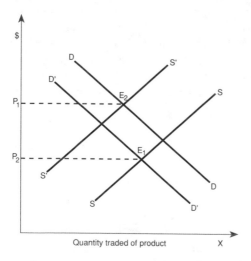

Figure 5.5   One effect of imposing strict liability on sellers is to raise the price of a product subject to strict liability in its supply. In the above case strict liability raises the price of the product from P_2 to P_1.

liable on the other hand the demand curve might be $D'D'$ and the supply curve SS. Hence when sellers are not strictly liable market equilibrium is established at E_1 and when they are liable at E_2. Price is higher in the latter case. However, one cannot conclude from this that strict liability is undesirable from the point of view of consumers. Consumers may well be prepared to pay a higher price for the security of having sellers strictly liable.

The question of whether there is a case for sellers to be strictly liable on efficiency grounds is difficult to decide. In at least one case no efficiency gain comes from interference. If (a) the risk to each consumer is proportional to the amount of a commodity purchased, (b) money compensation is an adequate recompense for damages, (c) no transaction costs or economies are involved in insuring and (d) if all buyers demand insurance against the possibility of defective products, the equilibrium price (after allowing for insurance) and quantity traded of a product are the same whether sellers are strictly liable or not (see Figure 5.6). If insurance is not taken out by sellers it will be taken out by buyers at the same cost. It makes no difference whether sellers are liable or not. However, both sellers and buyers will regret the need for insurance assuming that the supply and demand curves for the product under consideration are normal. The existence of the risk reduces both consumers' surplus and producers' surplus as can be seen from Figure 5.6.

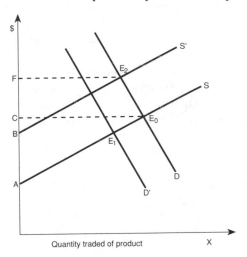

Figure 5.6   Illustration of case outlined in text where the costs of insurance against damages from a product are the same for the seller as the buyer. If the seller is liable, market equilibrium is established at E_2. If buyer accepts liability, market equilibrium is established at E_1.

In the absence of risk, equilibrium is established at E_0 but with expected damage per unit sold of the commodity equal to the difference between curve SS and $S'S'$, the market equilibrium shifts to E_2. Producers' surplus falls by the area of triangle ACE_0 less triangle BFE_2 and consumers' surplus falls by the area of quadrilateral CFE_2E_0. The more elastic the demand curve and the greater the expected damage from use of the product, the greater is the reduction in these surpluses. In the normal case the risk has an adverse incidence both on buyers and sellers.

In the above circumstances, whether or not sellers are strictly liable is of no consequence. On the other hand if there are some buyers who would prefer not to insure but to carry their own risks then it could be inefficient for sellers to be made strictly liable. Under strict liability of sellers, no buyer can opt out of insurance, the cost of which is passed on to him/her through a higher price for the product.

However, the transaction cost of obtaining insurance may well be lower for sellers than buyers. In that case, sellers may find it optimal from their point of view to accept product liability voluntarily. This suggests that a free market may of its own accord strike on the most efficient arrangement for sharing liability. We would expect sellers to accept risks associated with their products when this involves lower insurance costs and when protection is demanded by buyers. From an efficiency point of view it may:

(a) be less costly for sellers to check and monitor the characteristics of their products than for buyers to do this and/or

(b) less costly for sellers to insure against risks from the use and purchase of their products.

Consumers are likely to be much more numerous than sellers and their transaction costs of insurance higher and their costs of checking higher because selling companies can achieve economies of scale in monitoring and spread the use of skilled and specialized resources already likely to be employed by them. But how can consumers be certain that they will be protected by sellers in a situation where insurance or risk coverage by sellers is efficient in the Kaldor–Hicks sense? Dishonesty and deception on the part of some sellers is possible, the extent of insurance cover is not always clear and insurance companies may contest the claims of buyers suffering damage, so adding to costs. Strict liability of sellers in cases where it is most efficient for them to be liable could reduce uncertainty as to liability and lower the costs of claims. The distributional arguments for strict liability may be stronger than the efficiency ones. Let us consider some of these arguments.

Strict liability of sellers may tend to minimize the social burden of risk if (a) sellers tend as a rule to be wealthier than consumers or (b) sellers are in fact companies whereas consumers are not. The first proposition holds if utility functions happen to be similar, comparable and increasing at a diminishing rate. In these circumstances expected utility in society is increased by transferring a risk from a less wealthy member to a wealthier one by, for example, making the wealthier member liable to compensate the poorer one in an event disadvantageous to the poorer one.

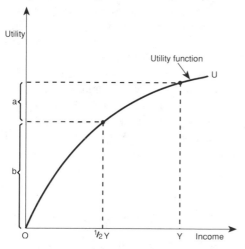

Figure 5.7   The same loss shared amongst a greater number of people (company) causes a smaller loss than when it is shared by a smaller group, it being supposed that incomes and utility functions are similar for individuals and marginal utility diminishes.

The second situation follows from the fact that even if incomes are equal, the aggregate expected loss in utility from a given loss is smaller the more widely the loss is shared. The loss can be widely shared for example by a company. This is illustrated in Figure 5.7. An individual has an income Y but there is a risk that this could be reduced to zero if an event K occurs. His/her loss in utility would then be $a + b$. But if two individuals (a company) share this loss, each suffers a fall in income of only $\frac{1}{2}Y$ and a reduction in utility of a. Given the strict concavity of the utility function $a<b$ and therefore $2a<a + b$. By a company sharing a loss the fall in aggregate utility is smaller than when the loss falls on one individual or comparatively small number of individuals. Note that this effect is independent of any pooling of risks which a company (or seller) may be able to take advantage of.

As mentioned above, the information possessed by one party to a transaction may differ from that of the other (information is asymmetric) or the cost to one party of obtaining information may differ. In such cases efficiency considerations seem to suggest that greater liability should fall on the party having more information or finding it least costly to generate information. Usually, this will be the seller. Inadequate product information (which may be associated with insufficient legal liability) may result in markets failing or operating less efficiently than they could (Akerlof, 1970; Varian, 1990, Ch. 32). There is, however, the difficult case of newer products about whose characteristics no one has complete knowledge e.g. a new drug for the possible treatment of AIDS. At what point is it reasonable to use the drug on humans in an attempt to control the disease? To what extent must one test products which could have adverse environmental consequences, e.g. new pesticides, before their release? Strict liability on the seller may in such circumstances be an unreasonable condition as would no liability. The former is likely to hold back beneficial economic change and the latter is likely to subject the community to unacceptable risk. More research is needed to suggest appropriate policies for such circumstances.

CONCLUSION

On the whole the law appears to favour or encourage risk taking by business enterprises. In the past when incomes were much lower this policy was favoured to encourage economic development. But today with higher incomes there is less need to place so much weight on the development objective and so the law has tended to place increasing liability on business enterprises for the risks, including environmental risks, associated with their economic activities. It can be argued that the law should take a more inclusive view of damages and that in particular more consideration should be given to allowing compensation for the risk of damages. There would also seem to be a case for more widespread adoption of strict liability in the sale of goods. However, this may need to be tempered in its application because sellers are not always richer than buyers and sometimes buyers are companies and sellers individuals even though the opposite appears as a rule to be the case.

   The law plays an important role in environmental management. It can influence not only whether environmental spillovers or externalities will be socially accommodated in an efficient economic manner, e.g. by negotiation (see previous chapter) but also whether economic activities having possible spillover or external effects on others proceed at all. In the latter respect the law is important in shifting the burden of risk or uncertainty and consequently influences economic growth and change as well as the distribution of income.

REFERENCES

Akerlof, G. (1970) 'The Market for Lemons: Quality, Uncertainty and the Market Mechanism', *The Quarterly Journal of Economics*, 84, pp. 486–500.

Arrow, K.J. (1962) 'Economic Welfare and the Allocation of Resources for Invention', in N.B.E.R. *The Rate and Direction of Inventive Activity: Economic and Social Factors*, Princeton University Press, Princeton.

Arrow, K.J. (1966) 'Discounting and Public Investment Criteria', in A.V. Kneese and S.C. Smith (eds), *Water Research*, Johns Hopkins University, Baltimore.

Australian Government and Queensland Government (1974), *Report of the Royal Commission into exploratory and production drilling for petroleum in the area of the Great Barrier Reef*, A.G.P.S., Canberra.

Fleming, J.C. (1977) *The Law of Torts*, 5th ed., Law Book Company, Sydney.

Luce, R.D. and Raiffa, H. (1957) *Games and Decisions*, John Wiley, New York.

Oliver, J.M. (1979) *Law and Economics*, Allen and Unwin, London.

Shrader–Frechette, K.S. (1980) *Nuclear Power and Public Policy*, Reidel, Dordrecht, Holland.

Varian, H.R. (1990) *Intermediate Microeconomics*, 2nd ed., Norton, New York.

6. Externalities and Coasian Considerations in Project Evaluation

Project evaluation or appraisal is important in all economies. This is not only because limited availability of resources means that as a rule every project has an opportunity cost in terms of other projects foregone but also because in some circumstances, optimal policy is not to undertake any investment project at all. In this part of this book, particular attention will be given to three factors in project evaluation – how to take account of externalities from projects, how to deal with lack of information about relevant environmental and other matters and how to allow for sustainability considerations. While particular mention will be made of the relevance of the discussion to less developed countries (LDCs), the discussion is relevant to all economies.

Until comparatively recently, mainstream economists saw little or no need to take externalities or spillovers into account in project evaluation in LDCs. As late at 1974, Little and Mirrlees, who might be regarded as orthodox in their position, claimed that:

> Some economists tend to believe that external economies are of special importance in developing countries; that some industries have important beneficial effects on others in ways which cannot be, or anyway are not, reflected in the price obtainable for the output of the industry, or in the price it pays for its inputs. There has been much speculation and debate on this subject. But there is very little positive evidence (Little and Mirrlees, 1974, pp. 35, 36).

They also warn that wild exaggeration about externalities from projects is all too easy (Little and Mirrlees, 1974, pp. 348, 349). This 'orthodox' position is maintained in Squire and Van der Tak (1975) and in Irvin (1978).

Fortunately, a more accommodating view of the place of externalities in project evaluation in LDCs has developed partially as a result of increased interest in the community about environmental factors and in particular concern about natural resources as factors in economic development (IUCN, 1980; WCED, 1987; IUCN–UNEP–WWF, 1991). Texts and guides for cost–benefit analysis (CBA) for project evaluation in LDCs now exist in which externalities are given serious consideration (Hufschmidt et al., 1983). This is not to say that externalities are an important consideration for every project, but overall they are too pervasive to ignore.

Also it does not seem reasonable to ignore externalities or spillovers in undertaking social evaluation of investment projects in more developed countries. However, the 'Chicago School' has sometimes been caricatured as arguing that externalities are a very minor source of market failure in more developed countries, and further that the cost of taking these into account in social evaluation of projects or of the government interfering to correct for these exceeds the benefits. Where such externalities exist this school generally favours the creation of markets in the amenity involved or the provision of a basis for negotiation between the parties by the appropriate assignment of private property rights. However in some cases, it is recognized that the costs of creating markets or effective private property rights may exceed the social benefit involved and so government intervention to do this is not justified (Demsetz, 1968; Tietenberg, 1992, Ch. 3). In the end, of course, the question of just how important economic spillovers or externalities are in practice can only be resolved by empirical evidence. However, as pointed out in Part II, there are theoretical situations in which externalities are irrelevant from a Paretian efficiency viewpoint. Even though this is the case, there is general consensus in the community that the importance of environmental spillovers is increasing because of new technologies and production methods and the growth of a globally interdependent economy, increasingly organized by the use of market mechanisms. I accept this point of view and believe that it is appropriate to give increased attention to externalities from projects when appraising them from a social viewpoint.

This chapter concentrates on allowances to be made of production or technological externalities in social evaluation of projects. First the general determinants of the relevance and irrelevance of externalities in project evaluation are discussed before concentrating on Coasian considerations in the evaluation of projects.

GENERAL ASPECTS OF THE RELEVANCE AND IRRELEVANCE OF EXTERNALITIES IN PROJECT EVALUATION

Not only those externalities generated by public enterprise but those arising from projects undertaken by private enterprise may be matters for public policy. Even though a private enterprise might not want to take externalities into account privately in assessing a project, the project (especially if it is large) may require an environmental impact statement.

Furthermore any required government approvals, including any approval for the use of foreign exchange, provide governmental authorities with the opportunity of taking externalities into account in determining whether to approve a project or not.

This raises the question of what is an externality. In the case of a private enterprise this is relatively straightforward – it is a beneficial or damaging effect from the operation of the enterprise for which respectively no payment is received or payment is made. Even here there are qualifications as Mishan, (1981, pp. 391–5) points out. However, in the case of public undertakings the assessment of externalities is more complex since government cannot normally be treated as a monolithic organization intent on maximizing social welfare, however defined (Rowley and Peacock, 1975; Niskanen, 1971). Different government organizations may have different charters or aims and externalities or spillovers may only be taken into account by a public organization when they seem to fall within its charter or perceived (limited) purpose. Thus some externalities or spillovers may be ignored by public enterprises even though it is desirable from a collective point of view to take them into account. One of the challenges facing society is to ensure that public organizations take adequate account of externalities in undertaking projects.

While this is needed, at the same time one has to guard against inflated claims for the value of publicly provided goods on the grounds of the supposed generation of favourable externalities. Public bodies in order to obtain greater funds from central budgets sometimes exaggerate the demand for their non–marketed services or the value of these, and there may be scope for doing this in relation to favourable externalities. This may be why orthodox economists such as Little and Mirrlees (1974) are suspicious about allowance for externalities in project evaluation.

Political self–interest to one side, there is sometimes, on the grounds of economic efficiency, a case for ignoring externalities in social CBA or only making a rough allowance for them. As Baumol and Quandt (1964) have pointed out, it is only rational to expand one's information and improve decisions up to the point where the additional cost of doing this is equal to the marginal expected gain. Using this rule as a rough guide, one might expect less assessment of the externalities generated by smaller projects than by larger ones (Chapter 7 or Tisdell, 1983). However, many small but similar projects taken together may give rise to substantial externalities and may justify much greater assessment collectively than individually. Public policy makers need to keep this in mind as well as the general possibility of interaction between externalities from different projects undertaken simultaneously. Where interaction between spillovers from projects is important, more than a partial analysis of projects is called for – the overall spillovers from the sum total of projects planned for a region must be taken into account.

Even ignoring calculation costs, not all externalities are relevant for the optimal allocation of resources. For example, externalities that are infra–marginal (see Chapter 2) to a project may be irrelevant as far as the optimal allocation of funds or resources to the project is concerned. This can be illustrated for a hypothetical project by Figure 6.1. The private marginal net present value (NPV) of the hypothetical project is shown by curve ABC. Thus it is privately optimal to allocate x_2 of funds to the project, if funds are available in unlimited supply at the going rate of interest. The assumed social marginal NPV of the project is shown by curve $DFBC$. A marginal favourable spillover exists up to the investment of x_1 in the project but beyond this level of investment no marginal externality is present. Clearly, the presence of the externality is irrelevant from the viewpoint of determining the socially optimal level of allocation of funds to the project. However, should the social NPV curve be DFG rather than $DFBC$ (in which case a marginal externality would exist for the private allocation of funds, namely x_2), the externality is relevant. From a social viewpoint, x_3 of funds should be allocated to the project rather than x_2.

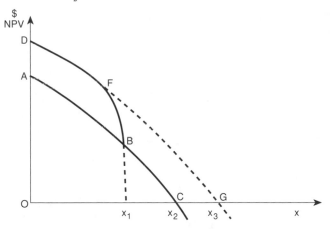

Figure 6.1   Illustration of the irrelevance for project evaluation of favourable infra–marginal externalities from a project.

Although marginal externalities are usually relevant to the socially optimal allocation of resources and for social CBA, this is not always so. If funds are limited and similar marginal externalities exist for the alternative projects under consideration, the externalities may well be irrelevant for the socially optimal allocation of funds or resources. This can be illustrated by Figure 6.2. In this case, it is assumed that two investment projects are available and that available funds are limited to $X = \bar{x}_1 + \bar{x}_2$.   The assumed private marginal efficiency of capital, M.E.C., (or internal rate of return, I.R.R.) for funds invested in project I is shown by line AB and that for project II is indicated by line AC. Private returns are maximized when $\bar{x}_1$ of the available funds are allocated to project I and $\bar{x}_2$ of these funds are allocated to project II. For this allocation the private internal rate of return from project I, MV, equals that from project II, KU. The marginal efficiency of capital when favourable externalities are taken into account are shown by line DF for project I and line DG for project II. These lines differ by a constant from the private marginal internal rate of return lines. Consequently the social internal rate of return from the available funds is maximized when $\bar{x}_1$ of the available funds is allocated to project I and $\bar{x}_2$ is allocated to project II because for this allocation $LU = NV$. In this case, even if externalities are ignored, the socially optimal allocation of funds can be achieved by merely concentrating on the maximization of private returns. However, differences in marginal externalities may arise and call for a social allocation of funds that differs from the optimal private allocation.

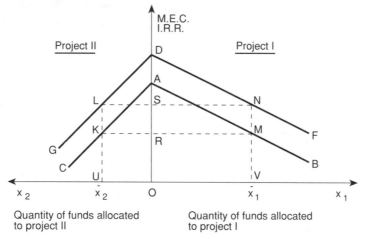

Figure 6.2   A case in which marginal externalities are irrelevant for project evaluation, given capital rationing.

Taking into account the costs and benefits of refining calculations, externalities may be irrelevant (for practical purposes) under a range of conditions. Nevertheless, irrelevant externalities may be more the exception than the rule. Sometimes externalities which at first glance appear to be irrelevant on closer examination turn out to be relevant. Although externalities may, for example, appear irrelevant for the chosen technique, an alternative technique may be available with more favourable externalities. This may yield higher social returns and be the most desirable technique from a social viewpoint (Chapters 2 and 3 or Tisdell, 1970; Walsh and Tisdell, 1973).

In some cases too, extra–marginal favourable externalities may be relevant (Chapter 3 or Walsh and Tisdell, 1973). Thus the question of the relevance and irrelevance of externalities is less straightforward than might be imagined, as is confirmed by the relevant literature (for example, Buchanan and Stubblebine, 1962; Davis and Whinston, 1962).

COASIAN CONSIDERATIONS IN PROJECT EVALUATION

Coase's article of 1960, 'The Problem of Social Cost', raised new issues for the evaluation of externalities. He pointed out that individuals subject to externalities are very often able to adjust to these by altering their techniques or by changing the nature of their economic activity, and he also throws doubt in this article on the Pigovian view that those generating unfavourable externalities should be taxed (by an amount corresponding to the marginal externality) in order to increase economic efficiency (Coase, 1960, esp. pp. 41,42). The main concern here is with consequences of the Coasian outlook for project evaluation from a social viewpoint.

In socially evaluating a project with a spillover, account must be taken of the adjustments of recipients of the spillover to the presence of the externality. If recipients of an externality from a proposed project have some choice of techniques, then usually the social benefit of a project will tend to be underestimated if it is assumed in the evaluation that recipients will continue with the same techniques and economic activities as prior to the project. In this case, the costs of unfavourable spillovers are over–estimated and the benefits of favourable externalities are underestimated. (For practical examples of this in relation to pest control see Tisdell, 1982, esp. pp. 32, 53, 54, 358.)

This proposition can be illustrated by supposing that just one technique is available for the project to be evaluated and assuming that the recipients of the spillover from the project have two alternative techniques, I and II, to choose from. In Figure 6.3, *EF* represents the marginal net benefits directly 'appropriated' from the project by those undertaking it and line *OAB* indicates the marginal damages to those subject to unfavourable externalities from the project if they use technique I, the technique adopted in the absence of the project. At the scale of x_1 for the project (the socially optimal scale if technique I is used by recipients or victims of the spillover) the net social benefits generated by the project are indicated by the area of triangle *OAE*. However, it is optimal for the recipients of the spillover to change their 'technique' (for instance, their land use, type of crop grown, for example) to technique II. This makes the marginal (net) damage function *ODC* relevant and the socially optimal scale of the project becomes x_2. At this scale, the net social benefits of the project are equivalent to the area of triangle *ODE*. Hence, because recipients have a choice of technique in response to the spillover, social benefits are greater by the area of triangle *ODA*. Even if the scale of the project is not adjusted to a socially optimal level, for example, if scale x_3 prevails, it is still important to take the adjustment of recipients to the externality into account. Indeed, if a scale of x_3 prevails social benefits of the project will be underestimated by the equivalent of the area of triangle *OCB* if adjustment of techniques by those damaged is ignored.

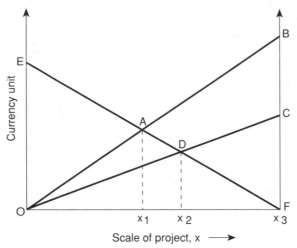

Figure 6.3   Illustration of the importance for social CBA of taking account of the ability of recipients of unfavourable externalities from a project to adopt techniques to reduce the impact on them of these externalities.

A similar situation prevails for a favourable externality. This can be illustrated by Figure 6.4. Here *ABC* represents the private marginal benefits appropriated from the proposed project and *DFG* is its social marginal benefit given that recipients of the favourable externality continue using their existing technique, technique I. Curve *DHJ* represents marginal social benefits if recipients of the externality adopt technique II. If the privately optimal scale of the project adopted is x_1 social benefits are equal to the area of 'quadrilateral' *OBFD* if technique I is adopted by those enjoying the favourable spillover. However, if technique II is adopted, social benefits are equivalent to the area of 'quadrilateral' *OBHD*. In the latter case, social net benefits are greater by the equivalent of the triangular area *DFH*. Similarly, when technique II rather than technique I is adopted by recipients of the spillover, greater social net benefits exist for the scale of investment x_2, and also for the socially optimal scale, x_3.

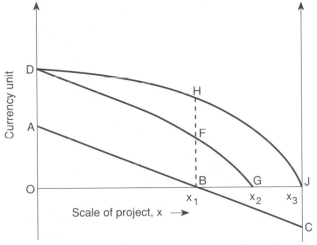

Figure 6.4   Illustration of the importance for social CBA of taking account of the ability of recipients of favourable externalities to adopt techniques to take advantage of these spillovers

There may be a number of alternative techniques or methods available for completing a project and this may need to be specifically taken into account in social CBA. For example, suppose that two alternative techniques α and ß are available for completion of the project, and imagine that both give rise to favourable spillovers. Privately optimal techniques for the project may not be socially optimal when account is taken of spillovers. In addition, in some instances account needs to be taken of the fact that alternative techniques are not only available for completion of the project but alternative techniques may be available as well as for recipients of any spillovers. In the simplest case where two alternative techniques are available to those undertaking the project and two are available to the recipients of spillovers from the project, the possibilities can be represented by the matrix in Table 6.1. The a_{ij} entries in the body of the table represent (evaluated) social net benefits corresponding to the possible combinations of chosen 'techniques' assuming a given level of activity.

Table 6.1 Simple social payoff matrix taking account of possible simultaneous choice of techniques for a project as well as by recipients of externalities from the project.

		Alternative techniques available to recipients of an externality	
		I	II
Alternative techniques for project available to investors	α β	$\begin{matrix} a_{11} \\ a_{21} \end{matrix}$	$\begin{matrix} a_{12} \\ a_{22} \end{matrix}$

The reactions of recipients of spillovers in choosing techniques in response to techniques chosen by investors in a project may need to be taken into account specifically in project evaluation. For example, in the above case, and taking into account relevant reactions, technique ß rather than α may provide the greatest social net benefits. For instance, recipients of the spillover may choose technique I when α is adopted and II when ß is adopted. If a_{22} is in fact the largest net social benefit, technique ß is then socially optimal for the project given the reaction relationship.

However, the reactions of recipients of externalities may not always be such as to ensure social optimality. For example, suppose that the above reaction function applies but the a_{21} corresponds to the highest level of net social benefit. To achieve this level, it would be necessary for investors to adopt technique ß and for the government to restrain recipients of spillovers in their choice of techniques – in fact, to require them to use technique I.

The evaluation of the net social benefits from a project therefore depends upon the range of techniques available for its completion, the predicted responses of recipients of spillovers in altering their behaviour and techniques, and any actions that the government may take to influence the reactions of the recipients of spillovers. Thus a range of possibilities may need to be considered even in simple cases of project evaluation.

Most projects have influences extending over several years and this can influence valuations using social CBA. For example, the presence of a spillover may induce technological progress as recipients of the externality endeavour to take greater advantage of favourable spillover or to minimize the cost to them of an unfavourable spillover. Induced technological progress is likely to increase the social NPV (net present value) of a project in the long term compared to circumstances in which no such progress is induced. However, it is difficult to predict technological change. Furthermore, in the long term independent economic changes can be expected to occur. New technologies and new economic possibilities may become available to those affected by an externality. Once again, these possibilities should theoretically be taken into account when evaluating the social NPV of a project, even though it may be difficult to do this adequately because of the uncertainty of future possibilities.

CONCLUSION

It is not always easy to determine whether externalities are relevant or irrelevant for the evaluation of social net benefits of a particular project, but there is little ground for supposing that as a rule externalities are irrelevant for project evaluation (social CBA). The importance of spillovers, especially for natural resources in LDCs and development planning, is now more widely appreciated by economists than in the past. *The World Conservation Strategy* (IUCN, 1980) and its successor (IUCN–UNEP–WWF, 1991) reinforces this trend by placing emphasis on spillovers and conservation considerations as elements in sustainable economic development and in development planning.

This chapter also emphasizes the desirability of taking account of Coasian considerations in CBA. It can be important to evaluate social returns for the alternative techniques available for undertaking a project, taking account of the possible alternative techniques of any recipients of externalities from the project. Such considerations seem to be important in most countries, whether less developed or not.

REFERENCES

Buchanan, J. and Stubblebine, W.M. (1962) 'Externality', *Economica*, 29, pp. 371–84.
Baumol, W. and Quandt, R. (1964) 'Rules of Thumb and Optimally Imperfect Decisions', *American Economic Review*, 54, pp. 23–46.

Coase, R.H. (1960) 'The Problem of Social Cost', *Journal of Law and Economics*, 3, pp. 1–44.

Davis, O. and Whinston, A. (1962) 'Externalities, Welfare and the Theory of Games', *Journal of Political Economy*, 70, pp. 241–62.

Demsetz, H. (1968) 'The Cost of Transacting', *The Quarterley Journal of Economics*, 1968, 82, pp. 33–53.

Hufschmidt, M.M., James, D.E., Meister, A.D., Bower, B.T. and Dixon, J. A. (1983) *Environment, Natural Systems and Development: An Economic Valuation Guide*, Johns Hopkins University, Baltimore.

Irvin, G. (1978) *Modern Cost Benefit Analysis*, Macmillan, London.

IUCN (1980) *The World Conservation Strategy: Living Resource Conservation for Sustainable Development*, International Union for the Conservation of Nature and Natural Resources (IUCN), Gland, Switzerland.

IUCN–UNEP–WWF (1991), *Caring for the Earth: A Strategy for Sustainable Living*, World Conservation Union, Gland, Switzerland.

Little, I.M.D. and Mirrlees, J.A. (1974) *Project Appraisal and Planning for Developing Countries*, Heinemann, London.

Mishan, E.J. (1981) *Introduction to Normative Economics*, Oxford University Press, New York.

Niskanen, W.A. (1971) *Bureaucracy and Representative Government*, Aldine Atherton, Chicago.

Rowley, C.K. and Peacock, A.T. (1975) *Welfare Economics: A Liberal Restatement*, Martin Robertson, London.

Squire, L. and Van der Tak, H. (1975) *Economic Analysis of Projects*, Johns Hopkins University Press, Baltimore.

Tietenberg, T. (1992) *Environmental and Resource Economics*, Harper Collins, New York.

Tisdell, C.A. (1970) 'On the Theory of Externalities', *The Economic Record*, 46, pp. 14–25.

Tisdell, C.A. (1982) *Wild Pigs: Environmental Pest or Economic Resource?*, Pergamon Press, Sydney, Oxford.

Tisdell, C.A. (1983) 'Cost–Benefit Analysis, the Environment and Informational Constraints in LDCs', *Research Report or Occasional Paper No. 91*, University of Newcastle, NSW 2308.

Walsh, C. and Tisdell, C.A. (1973) 'Non–Marginal Externalities: As Relevant and as Not', *The Economic Record*, 49, pp. 447–55.

WCED (World Commission on Environment and Development) (1987), *Our Common Future*, Oxford University Press, New York.

7. Cost–Benefit Analysis, the Environment and Informational Constraints

No matter what views one holds about the desirability of cost–benefit analysis, the extent to which it is used both in developed and less developed countries (LDCs) has increased and many economists advocate its more widespread use (or that of closely related techniques) as a means to decide whether to commit resources to particular projects or to choose between competing projects when resources are scarce. The technique, which adopts a rational approach to resource use, attempts to convert the advantages (benefits) and disadvantages (costs) of projects into monetary sums. It follows A.C. Pigou's advice (Pigou, 1932) of trying to use the measuring rod of money as an indicator of economic welfare, and in most formulations relies heavily on the Kaldor–Hicks principle (Little, 1957; Dasgupta and Pearce, 1972).

The method appears to have been first used in the USA to evaluate water–resource projects and interest in the method grew in developed countries from the 1950s onwards (Hufschmidt, James et al., 1983, Ch. 1). However, it was not until the 1970s that considerable efforts were made to extend its use to project evaluation in less developed countries. Publications such as UNIDO, *Guidelines for Project Evaluation* (1972), Little and Mirrlees, *Project Appraisal and Planning for Developing Countries* (1974) and Squire and van der Tak, *Economic Analysis of Projects* (1945) provided stimulus for this extension of its application. International aid and loan bodies such as the World Bank, the International Monetary Fund (IMF) and the Food and Agricultural Organization (FAO) have become increasingly committed to this technique. Furthermore, coverage of cost–benefit techniques is included in the economics curriculum at most universities, a number of texts exist on the subject and several developed countries run extension courses to teach CBA techniques to appropriate decision makers from LDCs.

Unpriced goods and services and 'inadequately' priced commodities provide one of the greatest challenges to policy makers trying to apply CBA. Many unpriced or inadequately priced commodities involve environmental factors. As Hufschmidt and co–authors point out in

Environment, Natural Systems and Development, there was a lag in allowing for environmental factors in CBA in developed countries and a longer lag has occurred in taking environmental factors into account in project evaluation in LDCs (Hufschmidt, James et al., 1983). Indeed, techniques for taking account of environmental factors continue to evolve and the application in LDCs of CBA taking account of environmental factors is still in its infancy.

CONSIDERATION OF ENVIRONMENTAL FACTORS IN PROJECT EVALUATION FOR LDCS – THE RECORD AND NEED

Only in the last few years have environmental effects of projects become important considerations in distributing foreign aid and making loans to LDCs. For example, the World Bank and USAID now undertake environmental assessments in deciding whether to support Third World projects. This has helped to stimulate interest in the art of environmental assessment of projects in LDCs. Nevertheless, some international aid and lending institutions may still pay little or no regard to the environmental consequences of projects supported in LDCs (Myers, 1979), but this has become the exception.

Until recently, mainstream economic literature about CBA for project evaluation in LDCs paid little attention to external or collective effects and intangible consequences of projects. Environmental effects have been largely ignored. This is true, for example, of work by Little and Mirrlees (1974) as well as a text by Irvin (1978). While Little and Mirrlees include a chapter on externalities they nevertheless have misgivings about paying attention to unpriced aspects of projects. They comment, for example, that there is much naive wishful thinking about the existence of externalities but very little positive evidence about their importance (Little and Mirrlees, 1974, pp. 35–6). They suggest however:

> If it is thought that the presence of external effects will be strongly claimed by opponents or proponents of a project, every effort to achieve a sensible, albeit rough, quantification should be made. Otherwise, wild exaggeration is all too easy (Little and Mirrlees, p. 349).

Thus there is only a begrudging recognition of the possible importance of external effects of projects and then only in reaction to the possible need for political action. As for Irvin, he mentions externalities only briefly and makes no reference to public good characteristics of projects so one can only assume that he believes these to be of practically no importance for the economic and social appraisal of development projects (Irvin, 1978).

The past comparative neglect of environmental factors in project assessment in LDCs could have its origins in one or more of the following views:

(1) Environmental spillovers are quantitatively smaller in LDCs than in industrialized countries – pollution is essentially a phenomenon of industrialization (Little and Mirrlees, 1974, p. 337). But particularly when damage to national resources is taken into account, it is far from clear that environmental spillovers are of much less importance in LDCs than in industrialized countries.

(2) Demand for improved environmental quality is an income elastic good and countries with low per capita incomes will therefore give greater weight to raising material incomes than to any consequent deterioration in environmental quality (Victor, 1972).

(3) High rates of discount in LDCs mean that future impacts of projects including environmental ones are to be given little weight in decision making (Tisdell, 1991, Ch. 4).

(4) Where projects are implemented by foreign companies or countries, they may be insensitive to environmental factors given the distance of the principals from the areas involved (Tisdell, 1990, Ch. 2). Furthermore private profit–making companies will give the greatest weight in decision making to their own profits. CBA designed principally to influence the decisions of this group could be expected to give trivial weighting to environmental factors.

(5) Political resistance to (diffused) environmental spillovers in LDCs may be weaker than in developed countries because of traditional power structures. Even where democratic resistance is possible, it may be relatively more costly in real terms for those affected by environmental spillovers to press their case.

(6) The degree of uncertainty about environmental effects is so great and the chances of reducing this uncertainty in the near future is so small that it is advisable to ignore these effects. Favourable and unfavourable spillovers are 'equally plausible' and therefore on the basis of the 'principle of insufficient reason' both effects should be treated as equally likely and of similar magnitude which means that they should be ignored in decision making. But this is a naive view for it implies that uncertainty or the range of possibilities has no consequences for rational decision making.

(7) Additionally it may be argued that the environments of LDCs are not overloaded and they have considerable capacity for assimilating

unfavourable environmental spillovers.

(8) It may also be felt that to allow for environmental spillovers will hamper enterprise and risk taking and as a result economic growth which is a high priority for most LDCs (Fleming 1977, Chapter 6 or Tisdell, 1983).

Some of these views are, of course, over–generalizations and several may be in error. For example, framers of the World Conservation Strategy and its update maintain that conservational and environmental considerations, far from being unimportant for planning development in LDCs, are of vital importance for sustaining development (IUCN, 1980; Tisdell, 1983; IUCN–UNEP–WWF, 1991). Additional reasons as to why it is important to incorporate environmental considerations in development planning in LCDs have for example been pointed out by WCED (1987). In fact, many situations can be identified in which it is important to take account of environmental factors in LDCs even on such limited grounds that failure to do so will reduce material incomes of the indigenous people. However, the compilation of cost–benefit analyses and the collection of information is not costless and this needs to be specifically taken into account.

The remainder of this chapter pays special attention to methods that have been suggested, or might be used, to deal with informational constraints on the use of CBA in LDCs, particularly when CBA requires consideration of environmental factors. Informational constraints on project evaluation in developing countries are especially important because of the following factors:

(1) Inadequacies in the technical economic and administrative expertise available for the planning and implementation of environmental management programmes;

(2) Widespread market failures which require extensive use of shadow prices to replace market prices;

(3) Minimal participation in environmental quality planning, either by the general public or by many affected governmental agencies;

(4) Inadequacies in environmental, economic and social data, including difficulties in data collection and processing and lack of knowledge of past trends and baselines, which limit the quality of the analysis;

(5) Wide diversity of cultural values, which increases the difficulty of social evaluation of environmental quality effects (Hufschmidt, James, et al, 1983).

Hanson (1981) points out that 'a general complaint in developing countries, including Indonesia, concerns the lack of basic information needed for adequate resource and environmental planning'.

SURROGATE PRICES AND SHADOW PRICES

Where markets do not price commodities within a country or are believed to do so inadequately, a number of ways of estimating appropriate shadow or surrogate prices have been suggested. One suggestion is that in many circumstances international prices for commodities can be used as suitable surrogates. Little and Mirrlees (1974) subscribe to this view whereas Mishan (1972) argues that even imperfect domestic prices may be a more reasonable approximation to opportunity costs than world prices. However, neither set of prices may be satisfactory when account is taken of transaction costs (such as transport costs) involved in marketing the commodities and of the fact that because these costs are high in LDCs, a considerable amount of production is not marketed.

To illustrate this problem, assume that peasants in a region of an LDC are producing a commodity, e.g. rice, which they do not trade but consume within their own families. How should one value the benefits from any scheme to increase rice production in the region? Should it be valued at the international price of rice? If not, should the price be lower or higher than this?

Let curve DD in Figure 7.1 represent the demand for rice within the region and SS indicate its supply and assume that the economic conditions facing all the members of the community are the same. Furthermore, suppose that the international price for rice is $\bar{P}$ per unit. However, if farmers in the region are to sell on the international market this involves a cost of $\bar{P} - P_S$ per unit (e.g. a transport cost). If they wish to buy rice on the international market there are also transaction costs so the landed price is P_B. At the farm gate, there is a difference between the selling and buying price of rice.

If the supply curve of rice in the region should cut the demand curve between A and C, no trade occurs in rice, and the appropriate shadow price would seem to be the value for which this supply curve intersects the demand curve. For example, for the case shown, this is $\hat{P}$. Should the supply curve cut the demand curve above A, rice is imported and the appropriate shadow price would appear to be P_B. If, on the other hand, the supply curve cuts the demand curve below C, the price P_S would appear to be the appropriate surrogate price. The problem is similar to that for shadow pricing within a firm when there are costs involved in using outside markets (Gould, 1964; Tisdell, 1990).

Even ignoring questions of exchange rate distortion, international prices can be poor surrogate prices for valuing changes in production in remote areas or regions of LDCs if substantial transaction costs must be incurred to participate in international or distant markets. The appropriate shadow price in such circumstances may well be considerably above the international price (above B in Figure 7.1) but can also be below it. However, the appropriate shadow price in the case formulated always falls in the range $P_S \leq P \leq P_B$, that is equal to or between the price received in the region for exports and the price to be paid in the region for imports.

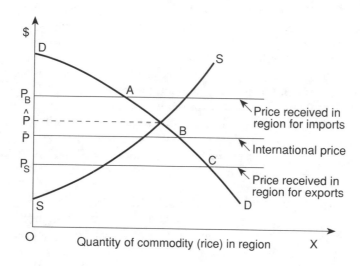

Figure 7.1   Appropriate surrogate prices for CBA in relation to international prices.

Of course one must be careful not to become preoccupied with the calculation of appropriate shadow prices to the neglect of other considerations. One of the dangers of the Central Office of Project Evaluation (COPE) suggested by Little and Mirrlees (1974) is that it may become overly concerned with academic matters to the neglect of in–field considerations especially as far as rural projects are concerned. Project officers may tend to remain in the cities and not become familiar with local conditions. Theoretical rules and economic calculation may be substituted for observation and empirical assessment. This 'top–down' approach to project evaluation may result in exercises out of contact with reality, especially as far as natural and social relationships in the field are concerned.

MARKET VALUE OR PRODUCTIVITY APPROACHES AND SURVEY–BASED VALUATION TECHNIQUES

Dixon and Meister (1983) outline a number of methods by which environmental spillovers from projects in LDCs can in principle be allowed for in project evaluation (see Hufschmidt, James, et al., 1983, Ch. 6 and Hyman, 1982; and Hyman, 1982). Many projects, especially rural projects, have direct spillover effects on the level of production within a regional context and resulting changes in production can frequently be valued using market prices or surrogate prices. Changes to be expected in production within a region taking account of spillovers from a project may be predicted by using scientific and technical information and valued by using market or surrogate prices. However, some goods, namely pure public goods, cannot be valued by means of market prices because they cannot be marketed or easily marketed. These goods can include those relating to environmental quality, for example clean air, scenic beauty or abundance of wildlife. Survey–based valuation techniques have been suggested or tried as a means of valuing effects on the supply of such goods. They have also been applied to other goods, which could be marketed but for one reason or another are not. Dixon and Meister (1983) summarize the main survey methods – the bidding–game approach, trade–off games, costless choice and the priority evaluator technique (in Hufschmidt, James et al., 1983). All involve the interview of at least a sample of individuals affected or likely to be affected by a change in the supply of the good under consideration. They are frequently described as contingent valuation methods.

The development of these techniques may still be in its infancy and the scope for applying them in developing countries at present seems relatively limited. Valuation of recreational, scenic and general environmental quality benefits in developing countries may be low in comparison to the weight placed on increased material output. Furthermore, as Dixon and Meister point out, the methods are costly to apply (direct interviewing is costly) and subject to a number of biases which may be greater in developing countries than in developed ones. Dixon and Meister (1983, p. 254) come to the conclusion that,

> Applying these techniques in many developing countries will be challenging. Greater suspicion towards interviewers may exist, as well as greater difficulty in understanding hypothetical alternatives. Making clear presentations of the problem, the choices, and the method of payment of compensation will be essential. Different techniques can be applied in the same setting to see if the results are similar.

Contingent valuation methods involve many problems whether or not they are applied in less or more developed countries. These include the possibility of (1) hypothetical bias, (2) information bias, (3) strategic bias, (4) sampling bias, (5) bias due to partialism, (6) circumstantial bias, (7) present generation bias, (8) instrument bias and (9) bias to please or satisfy interviewers.

Hypothetical bias may arise because respondents are unable to envisage correctly an environmental or similar change which is the subject of evaluation. It may be too hypothetical from the point of view of respondents. Apart from this it is not always easy to portray options accurately to the respondents even when it is intended to do so. Further the responses of respondents may exhibit information biases – their information may be inaccurate, for example, about the environmental effects of a particular change, or even though their information is not inaccurate, it is incomplete and the set of information available to them gives rise to inferences that are biased and inaccurate. Strategic bias occurs if respondents select their answers in an attempt to influence any policies which they perceive are dependent on the responses to the interviews.

Sampling bias may occur when all persons valuing the change or commodity being evaluated cannot be interviewed. The usual problems of obtaining a representative sample arise in such a case. Bias due to partialism arises because usually only part of the options or possibilities are presented to the respondent. The respondent therefore, as a rule, assumes that everything else is constant whether this is true or not. Moreover, incorrect valuations may result if a number of alternatives are independently evaluated but their values are interdependent. For example, suppose three natural areas, A, B and C exist. Suppose further that a contingent valuation is carried out to decide whether to conserve area A or B. The valuation may depend on whether C continues to exist. Furthermore, the valuation for A and B together may differ from that for A and B conserved independently. Partial specification of the options may lead to misleading results from contingent valuation (Tisdell, 1991, sec. 7.4).

Circumstantial bias refers to the tendency of respondents to be heavily influenced by current circumstances, prevailing popular opinions, interests and prejudices. Also there is clearly present generation bias because, of necessity, this is the only group that can be interviewed. Instrument bias may exist if respondents do not fully appreciate that the means necessary to achieve their preferred alternatives will impose a cost on them. Finally in some cultures, respondents are liable to give the answers which they believe the interviewer would like to hear rather than reveal their true valuation. Factors such as these, and others, should make us wary about placing too much faith in contingent valuation methods as a means of measuring benefits from projects.

THE BALANCE OF INFORMATION

In undertaking cost–benefit analysis for most projects economists need to cooperate with others outside their discipline or operate as part of an interdisciplinary team. Economic data are only part of the data used in CBA. Depending on the problem, apart from economic information, there is usually a need for biological, technical and other natural science data as well as additional social science material. It needs to be realized that we rarely have perfect knowledge in any of these areas. Therefore, in using our limited resources for CBA, decisions have to be made about the development of an appropriate data base. What balance should be aimed for between adequacy of economic data and other data when it is necessary to make a trade–off between the two? CBA based upon perfect economic data but dubious non–economic data may be useless, and vice versa. The project evaluation leader needs to see that an appropriate balance is achieved in the data base.

Conceptually, the problem can be considered by means of Figure 7.2. Suppose that a given budget has been allocated to evaluate a particular project. Assume that this sum amounts to OA. Then line AE in Figure 7.2 is the budget line indicating the possible trade–off in expenditure in gathering economic data and in obtaining non–economic data, for example, hydrological or other natural science data. The line KCL is an iso-expected value curve of information from a set of such curves which, for the time being, we assume to have similar properties to sets of isoquants or indifference curves. If the aim is to maximize expected gain then the combination at C is optimal. This involves the expenditure of x'_1 to collect non–economic information and x'_2 to collect economic data. At the optimum, the expected value of benefit from spending the last dollar on gathering non–economic data is equal to that for the last dollar spent on the collection of economic data.

The above is the necessary condition for an internal optimum. However, corner–point solutions are also possible, for example, if the iso–expected value curves have sufficient tilt. In that case, the optimal strategy would be to gather only economic information if the maximum occurs for a point A on the x_2–axis, or to concentrate purely on the gathering of non–economic information if the maximum corresponds to E.

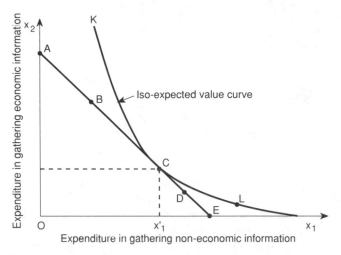

Figure 7.2   Optimal balance between expenditure on gathering economic information and non–economic information.

While it is easy to see this optimization problem conceptually and its general solution, to make the solution operationally useful is another matter. It remains to be seen whether useful rules of thumb can be devised for dealing with the balance of information problem. Furthermore, consideration should be given to the optimal sequence in which to collect different types of information. In some instances, there may be little point in collecting economic information until sufficient non–economic data are to hand. In addition, the quality of the non–economic data obtained can be expected to influence the appropriate pattern of collection of economic data.

THE OPTIMUM AMOUNT OF INFORMATION, CALCULATION AND ACCURACY IN PROJECT EVALUATION

Not only is there a problem of obtaining the best balance of information but also of deciding how much information to collect and the extent to which to process it.

As is well known it is usually not optimal (rational) to seek perfect information if the gathering or processing of information involves a cost. Baumol and Quandt (1964), for example, have pointed out that it is only rational to collect and process information up to the point where the marginal cost of doing so is equal to the marginal expected benefit from the extra information, assuming that the decision maker aims to maximize expected net gain. If the marginal costs of evaluating projects are higher in LDCs than in developed countries, this tends, other things equal, to make less evaluation optimal in developing countries. This is also the case if the marginal benefits from evaluation tend to be lower in LDCs, for instance, because CBA recommendations may be more commonly ignored in the political process.

It is pertinent to note that the scope for bounded rationality in project evaluation is much greater than is commonly supposed (cf. Tisdell, 1975, 1976). For example, it may be known that available resources are such that it will definitely be optimal to undertake all projects with an anticipated return of x per cent or more. This being so, as soon as it is established that a project has a return of x per cent or more it is irrational (in terms of the costs of extra calculation and the fact tha extra precision is of zero extra value) to try to calculate the return any more precisely. Similarly, it may be known that resource constraints are such (and reasonable expectations about availability of other projects are such) that no project with a return of y per cent or less will be adopted using CBA. Hence, as soon as it is clear that a project has a return of y per cent or less it should be dropped from consideration. To calculate the exact return in such a case is pointless.

This suggests that a procedure not unlike Simon's satisfying approach is optimal (Simon, 1957a, 1957b). As soon as it is established that certain projects have a return above a particular level they should be accepted as 'satisfactory' and those below a particular level should be rejected as unsatisfactory. This leaves a group of projects warranting further research or consideration. However, unlimited persistence in considering these also is unlikely to be rational.

In fact, filtering processes along the above lines may be developing. Hanson (1981) describes the way in which projects likely to involve foreign aid agencies are selected in Indonesia. Project concepts are first forwarded by originating government departments to BAPPENAS (National Planning Bureau) which selects a list from these. Donor countries can then select projects from this list for further investigation. Once a project is selected then it is further evaluated and a choice made. This, of course, is not to suggest that projects are filtered purely on cost–benefit consideration – political factors and window dressing may play a role.

RULES OF THUMB AND SURROGATE 'OPTIMIZATION' PROCEDURES IN CBA

Baumol and Quandt (1964) have observed that when imperfect decision making is optimal, as it usually is, rules of thumb and surrogate procedures for optimization may be optimal. When information is imperfect and costly to collect, an attempt to satisfy the first order conditions necessary for a maximum which would require perfect knowledge of appropriate marginal relationships may be irrational. As Baumol and Quandt suggest, it may be more sensible to follow rules of thumb or approximation procedures when account is taken of the fact that increased accuracy of optimization involves extra cost – for example, in the case of a firm, cost plus pricing may be more rational than pricing based on equating marginal cost and marginal revenue.

There is a need to devise and explore appropriate rules of thumb and surrogate optimizing procedures for CBA given the extra costs entailed in more sophisticated approaches to CBA. Appropriate short–cut procedures may be of particular value to Third World countries.

Here the possibilities for two such surrogate procedures are discussed assuming that the net social returns (expressed in terms of net present value) from projects depend upon their size or scale. These alternative possibilities are:
(1) Each project selected is on a scale that maximizes the net social return per dollar of funds allocated to it.
(2) The size of all projects undertaken is adjusted so as to equalize the return per dollar allocated to each.

The first procedure involves maximizing average returns per dollar for each project undertaken. The second procedure involves equalizing average returns per dollar for all projects selected.

The ideal maximizing procedure, if returns from projects are independent, is to allocate funds only to those projects for which the net social return is positive; secondly, to ensure that for all projects in which investment occurs the level of investment is such as to equate their net marginal social returns, and thirdly to ensure that net marginal social returns are declining. Priority in allocating funds should be given to those projects with the highest maximum return per dollar. What benefits are likely to be forgone by not applying this method but by adopting one of the alternative procedures mentioned above and which of these alternative procedures might be favoured on information grounds?

Maximizing Net Social Return per Dollar for Each Project Undertaken as a Procedure

Consider the procedure of adopting the scale for each project that maximizes its net social return per dollar invested and of selecting projects by giving priority to those with highest returns. All funds will be allocated if the last project selected, the one with the smallest maximum return per dollar amongst those selected, gives a positive discounted net return when all funds are allocated. Only those projects should be undertaken which have a positive discounted return.

This procedure, compared to the ideal maximizing one, results in a small loss (small reduction in benefits forgone):

(1) if marginal returns for each project as a function of the level of investment in it decline sharply after maximum return per dollar is achieved, or

(2) if maximum returns per dollar for projects brought on stream as a result of funds saved from projects with high returns are only slightly less than those returns for projects with superior returns. This can be illustrated by means of Figure 7.3. Assume that three projects I, II and III (of declining net benefit) are available. The curve marked $A_1(x_1)$ indicates the net social return per dollar (the average social return) of investment in project I and the curve marked $M_1(x_1)$ is its corresponding marginal curve. These curves are indicated in a similar way for the other projects. For simplicity, scale has been assumed to be unimportant for project III.

If the fixed sum of funds $X = \bar{x}_1 + \bar{x}_2$ is to be allocated, the ideal allocation for maximizing social returns is to distribute $\bar{x}_1$ to project I and $\bar{x}_2$ to project II. This allocation equalizes marginal social returns. Now suppose that the alternative procedure first mentioned is adopted.

This procedure results in only $\hat{x}_1$ of funds being allocated to project I and $\hat{x}_2$ being distributed to project II. Consequently, the aggregate net benefit derived from each project falls by the area of the hatched areas plus the dotted ones in Figure 7.3. Other things equal, the steeper the marginal return functions the closer are the $\hat{x}$ values to the $\bar{x}$ values and the smaller is this area of loss. Furthermore, the less divergent these values, the smaller is the amount of funds left over for investment in other projects that would not be undertaken in the ideal maximization case, because they give an inferior return.

In the case illustrated, the returns lost (forgone) on projects I and II are offset to some extent by returns from investment of $x = (\bar{x}_1 - \hat{x}_1) + (\bar{x}_2 - \hat{x}_2)$ in project III. This adds an amount equal to the rectangle indicated by crosses. Consequently, allowing for this offset, the net reduction in aggregate net benefits from using the optimum individual scale procedure is equal to the sum of the dotted areas in Figure 7.3. If the return of project III is lower than $A_3(x_3)$, the reduction is aggregate net benefits will be greater. For example, if it is $A'_3(x)$, the extra 'loss' is equivalent to that part of the area of the rectangle shown by crosses above the broken line. The 'loss' will be greater the further returns from project III (other projects) fall below the return from ideal projects.

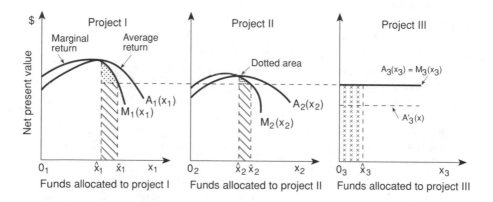

Figure 7.3   Net returns forgone by adopting a scale for each project undertaken which maximizes its net returns.

Equating Average Returns (Returns per Dollar) rather than Marginal Returns from Chosen Projects

In some circumstances, information may be such that it is more convenient to equate returns per dollar (average returns) for each project undertaken rather than equate marginal returns. If so, when will this procedure give a close approximation to the ideal maximizing result?

If, for all projects that would be undertaken using the ideal allocative approach, average returns from each project exceeds marginal returns by the same constant as the ideal allocation of funds for each project, this surrogate procedure results in an ideal allocation of funds. The surrogate procedure maximizes aggregate net benefit subject to the constraint imposed by available funds.

This can be illustrated by Figure 7.4. Suppose that a fixed quantity of funds $X = \bar{x}_1 + \bar{x}_2$ are available for allocation between two projects I and II. Interpreting the curves shown in Figure 7.4 in a similar way to those for Figure 7.3, it is ideal to allocate $\bar{x}_1$ to project I and $\bar{x}_2$ to project II.

This allocation of funds ensures that marginal returns are equalized and declining.

Suppose that average returns at $\bar{x}_1$ exceed marginal returns by the same amount as at $\bar{x}_2$. Let the difference between marginal and average returns at these points be k. In these circumstances, equating average returns from the projects incidentally equates their marginal returns and so ensures the ideal allocation of funds. In this case no benefits are lost by using this surrogate procedure.

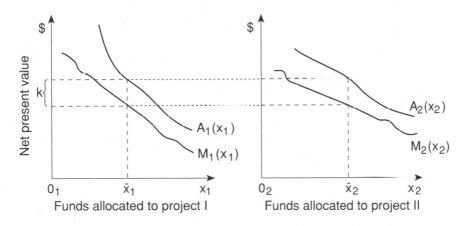

Figure 7.4   Equalising average return from projects maximizes social returns in some cases.

The above result can be seen in simple mathematical terms. Let the marginal net social return functions for Project I and II be represented respectively by $f_1'(x_1)$ and $f_2'(x_2)$. If $f_1'(x_1)=f_2'(x_2)$ for $x_1=\hat{x}_1$ and $x_2=\hat{x}_2$ (and the second order conditions are satisfied), $f_1'(x_1)+k = f_2'(x_2)+k$ where k is a constant, for $x_1=\hat{x}_1$ and $x_2=\hat{x}_2$. If the average functions equal marginal return functions plus the same constant, equalizing average returns between projects will clearly result in an optimal allocation of funds. However, the constant difference need not be maintained throughout the range of functions. It is only necessary for it to be maintained in the neighbourhood of the optimal location.

Circumstances could also be investigated in which this surrogate procedure yields a useful approximation to the ideal allocation rather than the ideal allocation itself.

One may wonder whether the above procedures require less information than marginal analysis. The optimum scale procedure (the first one considered) definitely economizes on information and calculation. The optimum scale of each project is independently determined and only a limited amount of information is needed to do this. Application of the second procedure requires more information and calculation than the first procedure, but the required information may still be easier to obtain than that needed for marginal analysis.

In practice, we should also be investigating actual rules of thumb for CBA that have evolved and be considering whether or not they can be justified on rational grounds. For instance, it seems often to be the case that projects involving small outlays are not investigated or only cursorily evaluated. If there are economies of scale in evaluation and some fixed cost in doing any investigation, this may be justified on economic grounds. However, where many similar small projects are being undertaken, albeit independently, there is likely to be a case for at least a general economic and environmental evaluation of these. This may provide rules that can be applied quickly and easily to the evaluation of individual projects. Even if individual projects are small, collectively and even individually, they may have a substantial environmental impact. This seems so in practice despite Schumacher's (1973) contention that small projects are usually environmentally benign.

UNCERTAINTY AND PARTICIPATION IN PROJECT EVALUATION AND IMPLEMENTATION

It might be argued that the above coverage fails to address some vital features of uncertainty and of processes of information gathering in project evaluation. For instance, this coverage may appear to involve essentially top–down approaches and to assume that the world is more structured or predictable than it really is. For example, even in the case of contingent valuation or interview method of assessment, there may be minimal involvement or participation by those interviewed. The questions to be asked, the options to be considered and the items to be taken into account are likely to be decided at the top. So passive rather than active participation by those interviewed occurs. Biases may be introduced consciously or unconsciously from the top down, especially if the projects involve aid from one country to another with differing cultural values. It is, therefore, argued by those advocating participatory planning and project evaluation that active rather than nominal participation is needed by those affected by the plan or project under consideration.

Possible advantages of such participation are an improved flow of information from those affected by projects to those initiating these, and vice versa. This helps to reduce uncertainty. It is sometimes claimed that local people have superior knowledge about local environmental conditions compared to those at the top who usually are remote from the local area (Cf. Tacconi and Tisdell, 1992; Lélé, 1991, pp. 615–6). Furthermore it is often believed that their predictions about the effects of projects resulting in local environmental changes are likely to be more accurate than those made by outsiders. However, while this may be so, in reality it is impossible to generalize about this. Local communities sometimes make less reliable predictions, especially when new technologies or methods are introduced with which they have had no previous experience. They may not have as wide a comparative knowledge as some outsiders nor have an adequate grasp of relevant general principles. This is not to suggest that local knowledge should be ignored (it would be arrogant to do so), but rather that knowledge or views from all sources should be considered and evaluated if one is to seek the truth.

After all knowledge that can be reasonably collected has been collected and evaluated, a great deal of uncertainty is likely to remain. Thus it becomes necessary to decide how to choose projects given that net benefits are uncertain. The Kaldor–Hicks criterion might suggest that project choices should be made so as to maximize expected net social benefit. But this assumes that the probabilities for the possible states of nature can be estimated (and/or agreed on by all) and that it is appropriate to ignore differences in aversion to risk or uncertainty of those affected by the project. If risk aversion is important it may be more appropriate to adopt a security–maximizing criterion (minimax loss criterion) rather than the criterion of maximizing expected net benefit, or at least, an 'intermediate' criterion giving some weight to security. Even if a security–maximizing criterion is adopted, it is necessary to decide which set of perceived possible states of nature to suppose, if there is disagreement about what is possible.

Some may argue that even this approach to project evaluation is still too prescriptive because it is concerned with finding an optimum in advance. Given uncertainty, this may not be really possible. In these circumstances, rational choice involves providing a favourable setting for adaptation of behaviour with learning and to adjust to independent environmental changes. Projects which help retain scope for adaptation and learning and provide flexibility may be preferred. In some circumstances, these will be projects which preserve diversity in the social and natural world. Project selection is signficantly influenced by whether or not the selection preserves options for future choices, that is by its role in the possible evolution of sets of choices given the changing state of the natural environment and the continual change of society itself.

Some of these issues will be addressed in the next chapter. But it is clear that the organic nature of the world may limit the value of formal optimizing models of the type commonly used in economics.

It should also be observed that traditional CBA tends to concentrate on evaluating a set of given projects. While choosing the best projects from a set is not unimportant, it may be much more important to ensure that all socially promising possible projects are included in the set to be evaluated. Whereas the former matter can be addressed by the use of scholastic techniques, the latter is not amenable to such an approach. It requires originality, persistence, entrepreneurship, good judgement and possibly good luck to ensure that the best available set of possible projects are included in the set for evaluation. This process of obtaining that set may be assisted by the participation of local people. This problem of discovering what projects are possible and making sure that the most promising ones are included in the set to be evaluated would seem to be worthy of greater attention than has been traditionally given to it in economics.

CONCLUDING COMMENTS

Environmental considerations in project evaluation in LDCs are more important than has been recognized in the past. Environmental spillovers from projects can have significant effects on the level of material production and appropriated economic gains so that even from a narrow point of view there is a case for not neglecting them. However, the collection and evaluation of environmental information in LDCs is costly and the assessment of economic benefits involving environmental effects frequently entails the calculation of shadow or surrogate prices or occasionally the use of direct surveys. Such methods leave room for inaccuracy, and in common with much cost–benefit analysis, require creative thought for most individual projects evaluated. Even if precise CBA could be justified on economic grounds (which it cannot be) in many LDCs there is insufficient expertise to use such refined methods, especially in micro–states, some of which have populations of less than 10,000 (Tisdell and Fairbairn, 1983). There is therefore a case for investigating whether a useful role can be played by short–cut methods, rules of thumb and approximations in undertaking CBA. In this chapter some of the possibilities for two methods based on average rather than marginal concepts have been noted. These are indicative of possible areas for investigation rather than prescriptive.

It seems wise to heed Hufschmidt's judgement that while economic analysis holds great promise for improving environmental quality management, one should have modest expectations about it (Hufschmidt, James et al., p.5). It cannot be applied in a vacuum. It requires supporting non–economic data and sometimes this information is so poor that economic input into the evaluation process may be of limited extra value – thus the importance of the balance problem mentioned earlier. Furthermore, we need to be cautious because values and benefits change with time and the future is extremely difficult to predict. This may necessitate an evolutionary approach to economic development and project selection which in turn raises questions about sustainability, some of which are addressed in the next chapter.

REFERENCES

Baumol, W.J. and Quandt, R.E. (1964) 'Rules of Thumb and Optimally Imperfect Decisions', *American Economic Review*, 54, pp. 23–46.

Dasgupta, A.K. and Pearce, D.W. (1972) *Cost–Benefit Analysis: Theory and Practice*, Macmillan, London.

Dixon, J.A. and Meister, A.D. (1983) 'Environmental Quality Valuation from the Benefit Side', pp. 170–260 in M.H. Hufschmidt, D.E. James, A.D. Miester, B.J. Bower and J.A. Dixon (1983) *Environment, Natural Systems, and Development: An Economic Valuation Guide*, The Johns Hopkins University Press, Baltimore.

Dixon, J.A. and Hufschmidt, M.M. (eds)(1986) *Economic Valuation Techniques for the Environment – A Case Study Workbook*, Johns Hopkins University Press, Baltimore.

Fleming J.C. (1977) *The Law of Torts*, 5th ed., Law Book Company, Sydney.

Gould, J.R. (1964) 'Internal Pricing in Firms Where There are Costs of Using Outside Market', *Journal of Business*, 37, pp. 61–7.

Hanson, A.J. (1981) *Environmental Considerations in Foreign–Donor–Supported Projects: Some Experiences in Indonesia*, Research Report No. 1, East–West Environment and Policy Institute, East West Center, Honolulu.

Hufschmidt, M.M., James, D., Meister, A.D., Bower, B.,T. and Dixon, J.A. (1983) *Environment, Natural Systems and Development: An Economic Valuation Guide*, Johns Hopkins University Press, Baltimore.

Hufschmidt, M.M. and Hyman, E.L. (1982) *Economic Approaches to Natural Resources and Environmental Quality Analysis*, Tycooly, Dublin.

Hyman, E.L. (1982) 'The Valuation of Extramarket Benefits and Costs in Environmental Impact Assessment', *Environmental Impact Assessment Review*, 2 (3), pp. 227–58.

Irvin, G. (1978) *Modern Cost–Benefit Methods*, Macmillan, London.

IUCN (1980) *World Conservation Strategy*, International Union for the Conservation of Nature and Natural Resources, Gland, Switzerland.

IUCN–UNEP–WWF (1991) *Caring for the Earth: A Strategy for Sustainable Living*, World Conservation Union, Gland, Switzerland.

Lélé, S. (1991) 'Sustainable Development: A Critical Review', *World Development*, 19, pp. 607–21.

Little, I.M.D. (1957) *A Critique of Welfare Economics*, 2nd ed., Oxford University Press, London.

Little, I.M.D. and Mirrlees, J.A. (1974) *Project Appraisal and Planning for Developing Countries*, Heinemann Educational Books, London.

Mishan, E.J. (1972) *Elements of Cost–Benefit Analysis*, George Allen and Unwin, London.

Myers, M. (1979) *The Sinking Ark: A New Look at the Problem of Disappearing Species*, Pergamon Press, Oxford.

Pigou, A.C. (1932) *The Economics of Welfare*, 4th ed., Macmillan, London.

Schumacher, E.F. (1973) *Small is Beautiful: A Study of Economics as if People Mattered*, Blond and Briggs, London.

Simon, H.A. (1957a) *Administrative Man*, 2nd ed., Macmillan Company, New York.

Simon, H.A. (1957b) *Models of Man*, Wiley, New York.

Squire, L. and van der Tak, H. (1945) *Economic Analysis of Projects*, Johns Hopkins, Baltimore.

Tacconi, L. and Tisdell, C. A. (1992) 'Rural Development Projects in LDCs: Appraisal, Participation and Sustainability: *Public Administration and Development* (in press).

Tisdell, C.A. (1975) 'Concepts of Rationality in Economics', *Philosophy of the Social Sciences*, 5, pp. 259–72.

Tisdell, C.A. (1976) 'Rational Behaviour as a Basis for Economic Theories', pp. 196–222 in S.I. Benn and G.W. Mortimore (eds) *Rationality and the Social Sciences*, Routledge and Kegan Paul, London, 1976.

Tisdell, C.A. (1983) 'Law, Economics and Risk–Taking', *Kyklos*, 36, pp. 3–20.

Tisdell, C. A. (1990) 'Market Transaction Costs and Transfer Pricing: Consequences for the Firm and for Technological Change', *Revista Internazionale di Scienze Economiche e Commerciali*, 37, pp. 203–18.

Tisdell, C. A. (1991) *Economics of Environmental Conservation*, Elsevier Science Publishers, Amsterdam and New York.

Tisdell, C.A. and Fairbairn, I.J. (1983) 'Development and Problems and Planning in a Resource–Poor Pacific Country: The Case of Tuvalu', *Public Administration and Development*, 3, pp. 341–59.

United Nations Development Organization (UNIDO) (1972) *Guidelines for Project Evaluations*, United Nations, New York.

Victor, P.A. (1972) *Economics of Pollution*, Macmillan, London.

WCED (World Commission on Environment and Development) (1987) *Our Common Future*, Oxford University Press, New York.

8. Project Appraisal and Sustainability

In discussing aspects of project appraisal in this book, most attention so far has been given to externalities and to informational constraints. There has been no specific discussion of ways to allow for differences in the time–patterns of net benefits from alternative projects and for differences in the sustainability of their net benefits. Traditionally differences in the timing of net benefits have been allowed for in economic evaluation of projects by discounting future net benefits by an 'appropriate' discount rate based usually on a prevailing interest rate. But recently sustainability of returns has also been accepted by many as an important characteristic to take into account when evaluating projects from a social point of view. This is partially, but not completely, a response to interest in the possibility of attaining sustainable development, a concept (or set of concepts) which will be discussed in some detail in Part IV.

'Sustainable' will be used here in its common or everyday sense of implying something that can be maintained as time passes. Sustainable net returns for example are returns which can be maintained with the elapse of time. But we do not live in a mechanical and simply ordered world. There are for example possibilities for discovering and learning and for human reaction to discovery and learning. Appropriate human reactions can help to maintain economic returns but the scope for such variations will depend upon the options that remain available to decision makers. Thus questions involving sustainability require attention to be given to the keeping open of options and to the retention of flexibility, and consideration of the presence of uncertainty and possibilities for learning. The presence of externalities may also have consequences for sustainability of economic processes considered from a regional perspective or at least from the point of view of production or economic activity involving a number of economic units. Let us consider sustainability of economic returns or economic activity, taking into account externalities, learning, uncertainty and flexibility, measurement of sustained or maintained returns, the proposal of Pearce and co–authors (1989) for allowing for sustainability in project evaluation, systems analysis such as that proposed by Conway (1985, 1987) and evolutionary models of decision making.

EXTERNALITIES AND SUSTAINABILITY

Not surprisingly policy discussions about economic sustainability and sustainable development give a great deal consideration to externalities particularly in relation to economic production. Unfavourable externalities in production can result in the level of economic production not being maintained. Take externalities from the use of water for agricultural production, for example.

Use of water from a common pool, e.g. underground aquifer, by a farmer may reduce the supply of water available to other farmers. Common water use involves externalities, and may result in all water users needing to sink deeper tube wells so adding to their capital costs and water pumping costs. Furthermore water stocks may be depleted after a time and offtake of water for irrigation may be limited to replenishment flows. Thus agricultural production based on water use drawing on existing stocks becomes impossible to maintain and production in the end is limited to that made possible by use of replenishment flows only. For further discussion of this case and related cases see Tisdell (1991, Ch. 9).

To take another case, felling of rainforest in tropical areas can result in unsustainable production levels. Apart from the problem of maintaining the productivity of the cleared land for agriculture, such felling can result in unfavourable production externalities. For example, felling of rainforests in Palawan in the Philippines was found to give rise to this problem (Dixon and Hufschmidt, 1986). The forest felling increased soil erosion, added to the sediment load of rivers and during the wet season, to freshwater flows in rivers. Freshwater combined with sediments kill corals when these are discharged into the ocean from rivers. Consequently fishing and tourism can be adversely affected, and the total value of economic production can fall.

In Bangladesh, increased use of water for agriculture has led to a number of unfavourable externalities which undoubtedly make it more difficult to sustain economic production. Offtake of water from rivers and other surface waters for irrigation is reducing the rate at which underground water supplies are being recharged, reduction in water bodies and water quality has reduced fish stocks and fish supplies from inland waters, the navigability of rivers has been reduced (a serious problem in Bangladesh which makes considerable use of rivers for transport) and saltwater has moved upstream along the estuaries of its rivers such as the Ganges because of reduced freshwater flows in the dry season, so denying freshwater supplies to an increased number of farmers. All these factors make it more difficult to sustain agricultural and economic production overall.

Many other examples can be cited. For example in fishing, common or open access to stocks of fish may result in unsustainable levels of production. Each fisherman ignores the impact of his fishing behaviour on the fishing prospects of other fishermen and can gain virtually nothing from conserving fishing stocks. Thus there are strong incentives to overharvest commercial fish stocks, and some varieties of fish may be driven to extinction.

Genetic loss is to some extent a result of externalities. Suppose that a variety of cultivated species occurs wild in a particular area, and further that this variety could have future value for maintaining the productivity of the cultivated species (e.g. to develop a disease–resistant variety). The expected value of this area might greatly exceed the value of utilizing the area in question for an economic   purpose which would lead to cradication of the wild variety. But owners of the area may be able to appropriate little or none of the benefits from conserving the wild variety, and thus they have no economic incentive to conserve it. They will prefer to utilize the area for other purposes.

Of course, traditional cost–benefit analysis has been extended to take account of externalities. But it is also useful to look upon externalities as factors likely to influence the sustainability of production and economic activity. This needs to be emphasized in the current debate about sustainability.

UNCERTAINTY, LEARNING, FLEXIBILITY AND IRREVERSIBILITY

Uncertainty is a normal aspect of economic life but is especially important in relation to environmental and ecological change because prior knowledge is likely to be limited, especially if new technologies are being introduced. The scope for experimenting and small scale tests may be limited, particularly where environmental change is occurring on a global scale such as is occurring with the release of greenhouse gases.

Not only are many environmental changes and their consequences uncertain but they are also irreversible. For example the extinction of a particular species of life is irreversible once it occurs. Once the global warming process has reached a particular stage, its lagged effects such as melting of the polar ice caps may continue to occur irreversibly.

Sometimes the only way of learning about or obtaining substantial knowledge about an environmental change is by 'doing', that is, by causing or allowing the environmental change and observing its consequences. But this can be extremely risky, if its effects are irreversible and particularly so if at the same time as the knowledge becomes available the irreversibility occurs. The knowledge obtained then is useless from the point of view of guiding action since no options remain for altering actions in the light of the knowledge obtained. In some cases too, current results from the environmental change cannot be simply extrapolated forward because a jump or discontinuity in the relationship (as well as irreversibility) may occur once particular environmental thresholds or barriers are passed. Environmental disasters may cast little or no shadow (provide little or no forewarning) and even if they do, by the time the shadow is observed it may be impossible to avert the disaster. This is not to say that all environmental problems are of this nature, but we cannot ignore the possibility that some important ones are.

Sometimes one may learn by waiting for knowledge to accumulate. But waiting means doing nothing except observing the outside world. Moran et al. (1991) suggested that, as far as government action to control greenhouse gas emissions is concerned, this is the correct policy. They suggest waiting for another decade before taking action, if required, since by then there will be less uncertainty about whether the greenhouse effect is really occurring and to what extent environmental changes can be expected. But is this rational if by then the irreversible environmental effects have already been put in train?

Usually when there is uncertainty and possibilities for learning, it is worthwhile keeping options open or retaining flexibility in decision making so as to adjust to what is learnt. However, the extent to which it is worthwhile keeping options open depends upon the cost of doing this as well as perceived benefits. Irreversible environmental change may well reduce economic options and so reduce flexibility. It has long been recognized in cost–benefit analysis that irreversibility may weigh in favour of conservation of natural resources (Arrow and Fisher, 1974).

However, when loss of natural resources provides resources to fund scientific or technological advances, this may contribute a new set of options, even though one set is lost. This adds even more to the uncertainty about the consequences of natural resource loss.

Some uncertainty and irreversibility issues involved in environmental conservation decisions can be appreciated by considering a simple example. Suppose that three alternative projects (a_1, a_2, a_3) are under consideration. Project a_1 involves the conservation of environment A (e.g. species A) but not environment B (e.g. species B), project a_2 involves the opposite situation and project a_3 involves conservation of both environments A and B. The net benefits of conserving the environments in question will only be revealed with certainty in the future but are known to depend on whether circumstance s_1 or s_2 prevails.

Imagine that the net benefits from the projects are as indicated in the matrix shown as Table 8.1. As can be seen, the cost of conserving both environments A and B, that is of adopting α_3 and keeping both options open, is 10 units. But this may be a small cost to pay in relation to the benefits of keeping both options open.

Table 8.1 Net benefits available from alternative projects and the value of keeping options open.

Project	Event		
	s_1	s_2	
A – conserves environment A α_1	100	0	0
B – conserves environment B α_2	0	50	0
C – conserves both environments α_3	90	40	40 Maximin

The optimal choice of a project will depend upon attitudes to the bearing of risk or uncertainty. However even if a neutral attitude to risk bearing is taken, it may pay to keep options open. In the case indicated in Table 8.1, if the probability of s_1 is between 0.1 and 0.8, expected benefits are maximized by adopting strategy α_3. For example if the probability of s_1 is 0.5, the expected net value of project α_1 is 50, of α_2 is 25 and of α_3 is 65.

The relationship between the expected net return from projects and the probability of s_1, say P_1 is shown in Figure 8.1. Line *ON* is that for project α_1, *KR* is that for project α_2 and *ST* is that for project α_3. The upper boundary *KLMN* represents expected net returns achievable by varying project choice as the probability of event s_1 varies.

From Figure 8.1, it can be observed that the higher the cost involved in adopting the project which keeps options open, α_3, the narrower becomes the range of probabilities for which it pays to keep options open. A higher cost of keeping options open results in line ST being displaced downwards. Conversely the smaller the cost of keeping options open, the greater the range of probabilities for which it pays to keep options open. Thus even on the basis of maximizing expected benefits, it may pay to keep options open at a cost, given the existence of uncertainty.

However, individuals who are adverse to risk taking are likely to reject the expected gain criterion and may adopt a security maximizing criterion, such as that implicit in the safe minimum standard approach to decision making about conservation (Bishop, 1978, 1979; Ciriacy–Wantrup, 1978). In these circumstances, retention of options is strongly favoured.

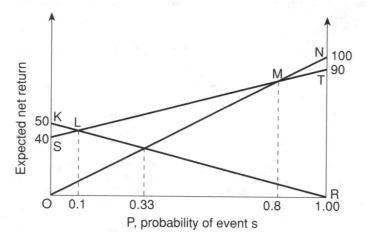

Figure 8.1 Expected net benefits from the alternative available projects.

Decision making for maximizing security can be modelled by the maximin gain (or minimax loss) criterion. In the case shown in Table 8.1, the maximin gain project is α_3 if s_1 or s_2 are possible. Even if s_1 is highly likely e.g. P = 0.95, this criterion still opts for α_3. Furthermore, it will choose the strategy of keeping options open even when the costs of this are quite high, and higher than would result in this choice if expected net benefit maximization is adopted. For example, if in the case shown in Table 8.1 the cost of adopting α_3 happened to be almost 50 units, this would still result in α_3 being adopted. If, for example, this cost was 49 units, the maximin value would be 1.

A serious problem in practice is that those subject to environmental risks may differ in their attitude to risk taking and also disagree about the likelihood of possible future events. It is not yet clear how these differences of values and opinions should be resolved in relation to collective decision making. But up to a point both risk avoiders and those who are risk neutral may have common ground in keeping particular environmental options open. Nevertheless they may disagree about the desirability of keeping some options open. In general risk avoiders will wish to keep open a wider set of options than those who are risk neutral.

The keeping open of options can be regarded as contributing to sustainability of net returns. In the case illustrated by Table 8.1, project α_3 prevents net returns from falling to a zero level.

SUSTAINED OR MAINTAINED RETURNS

It is sometimes suggested that projects for which net benefits are sustained or maintained with the passage of time are to be preferred to those for which this is not so, other things equal. In Figure 8.2, for example, project 1 may give a flow of net returns during the planning period, $o \leq l \leq n$, indicated by line *DBF* and alternative project 2, that indicated by line *ABC*. Cumulative returns from each of the projects for the planning period is the same ($OD = 2OA$). The sustainability criterion will tend to favour project 2 but traditional cost–benefit analysis based on net present value or internal rate of return analysis will favour project 1 because given a positive rate of interest it will yield the largest net present value or the highest internal rate of return.

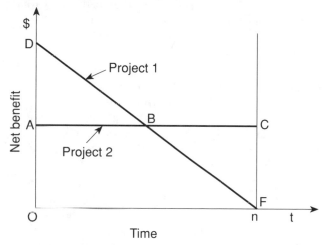

Figure 8.2 Differences in extent to which net returns are sustained from two different projects.

It is sometimes suggested that sustainability might be allowed for by applying a zero discount rate. But this is not satisfactory. It would for example result in both the projects illustrated by Figure 8.2 being equally desirable, whereas this is clearly not so from a sustainability point of view.

If many projects are being undertaken, it is unnecessary for returns from all projects to be sustained in order to maintain overall returns. For example, returns which increase for one set of projects as time passes may offset declining returns from other projects.

PROPOSALS OF PEARCE AND CO–AUTHORS TO EXTEND COST–BENEFIT ANALYSIS TO INCORPORATE SUSTAINABILITY CONSIDERATIONS

Intergenerational Equity

The proposal of Pearce and co–authors (1989) for extending cost–benefit analysis to take account of sustainability considerations is related to their view of sustainable development. Their basic view is that sustainable development requires the standard of living or welfare of future generations to be no smaller than that of present generations. They believe that this is most likely to be achieved when future generations inherit a stock of environmental or natural resource capital no less than the current stock. This matter will be discussed in some depth in Part IV and is merely mentioned here by way of background.

The Suggested Operational Model

Pearce and co–authors (1989) suggest that traditional cost–benefit analysis (CBA) be modified to allow for sustainability by introducing the constraint that projects be selected so that the depletion or degradation of the stock of natural capital is non–positive overall. Yields from investment in projects should be maximized or 'all projects yielding net benefits should be undertaken subject to the requirement that environmental damage (i.e. natural capital depreciation) should be zero or negative' (Pearce et al., 1989, p. 127). They suggest that this requirement be applied across the set of projects or programmes undertaken by economic entities. If $i = 1,...n$ projects are being undertaken at the programme level and if E_i is the environmental damage caused by the i–th project, they require that

$$\sum_i E_i \leq 0 \tag{8.1}$$

Let us consider how their method of evaluation differs from standard CBA and extended CBA which takes account of externalities. Standard CBA aimed at maximizing the present value of net benefits obtained by an economic entity requires that

$$\sum_t d^t (B_{it} - C_{it}) > 0 \tag{8.2}$$

where t represents time, d_t represents the discount factor, B the benefits received and C the costs incurred by the economic entity, for all projects undertaken. If unlimited funds are available at the going interest rate, then all projects should be undertaken which have a positive net present value.

In the extended CBA model, externalities including environmental damage are taken into account in the evaluation. Where E_{it} represents the environmental damage caused by project i in the $t-th$ period each project should be undertaken for which the net present value is positive after including the environmental term, that is all projects for which

$$\Sigma_t d^t (B_{it} - C_{it} - E_{it}) > 0 \qquad (8.3)$$

It is however quite possible that for the set of projects satisfying the above that

$$\Sigma_t d^t \Sigma_i E_{it} > 0 \qquad (8.4)$$

namely positive environmental damage or depletion of natural capital occurs overall. Thus the sustainability criterion or constraint would not be satisfied. If this constraint is to be satisfied, the set of projects selected in the programme should also satisfy the constraint

$$\Sigma_t d^t \Sigma_i (E_{it}) \leq 0 \qquad (8.5)$$

that is, according to Pearce et al., (1989), they should satisfy the condition that the present value of environmental damages caused by the projects be non-positive.

As can be seen this would require environmentally enhancing projects to compensate for those which are environmentally damaging. In the above case the normal rules for extended CBA would be satisfied subject to the constraint. From the set of projects satisfying the constraint (8.5) those projects would be undertaken which satisfy condition (8.3). It is hoped that there will be a set of projects available that will satisfy all the conditions, but there is no guarantee of this.

But the above is not the exact rule which Pearce and co-authors (1989) suggest, even though the above seems a logical extension of extended CBA to allow for sustainability. Rather they suggest a dichotomous procedure, namely that conventional extended CBA be applied to selection of projects involving environmental depletion, and that projects involving environmental enhancement be treated differently. These should be selected, it is said, to compensate for environmental damages done by the first mentioned set of projects, but so as to minimize the cost of achieving the sustainability criterion.

Thus if n environmentally damaging projects are being undertaken with environmental damages amounting to a present value of $\Sigma_i PV(E_i)$, m environmentally enhancing projects adding A_j to natural capital stock need to be undertaken so that

$$\Sigma_j \ PV(A_j) = \Sigma_i \ PV(E_i) \tag{8.6}$$

Pearce and co–authors (1989) claim that the normal decision rules of CBA need not apply to selection of the environmentally enhancing projects. While this seems true in relation to non–extended CBA, it is difficult to see in the case of extended CBA that it would be acceptable for the rule mentioned in relation to (8.3) to be violated. The dichotomous optmizing procedure suggested by Pearce and co–authors therefore seems to involve a deficiency. It seems preferable to integrate sustainability into CBA using the standard rules for extended CBA. But this is not to suggest that it is operationally easy to allow for sustainability of natural capital or the natural environment.

Limitations of the Model for Incorporating Sustainability

Apart from the difficulty just noted, some limitations of the method suggested by Pearce et al., (1989) for integrating sustainability into CBA can be mentioned. The first problem relates to the measurability of environmental damages and depreciation or appreciation of natural capital stock. The measurement of such factors is not straightforward, is subject to uncertainty and is influenced by value judgements. Furthermore, Pearce and co–authors do not distinguish clearly between environment and natural capital stock. In fact, the impression is given that these are the same. But it seems possible for environmental change to occur that does not influence the natural capital stock. For example, the emission of noise can detract from an environment but it may not reduce the natural capital stock. Once the noise is stopped the natural capital stock may remain intact.

Another problem is their suggestion, possibly for practical purposes, that the requirement of non–positive depreciation of natural resource stock be limited to the programme (set of projects adopted) of each economic entity. But if trade is possible between entities in environmental surpluses and deficits arising from their programmes, this would seem to be advantageous. It seems more appropriate for the constraint of non–depreciation of natural capital stock to apply to the set U of all projects undertaken rather than to the programme of each economic entity. In any case, the actual way in which projects are divided between economic entities is one of the many possible divisions and the actual division does not have any special virtue in itself.

The question should also be addressed of who is going to measure the environmental damages and benefits arising from projects. It each economic entity is to satisfy the Pearce rule, then some authority needs to see that it is in fact being observed. This will involve agency and transaction costs. Disagreement about how to measure environmental effects or natural resource changes appropriately is likely to be a stumbling block. This is not to suggest that a system of environmental offsets to environmentally damaging projects is not worth exploring but to suggest that it is not a straightforward exercise.

SYSTEMS ANALYSIS OF CONWAY

A number of characteristics of projects which may be relevant to their assessment have not been discussed above. Conway (1985, 1987), referring particularly to agricultural projects and systems, suggests that four characteristics may be of particular interest, namely (1) level of returns (2) stability of returns (3) sustainability of returns and (4) their impact on the distribution of income. Conway suggests that projects or techniques are to be preferred, other things equal, the higher their level of returns, the less variable their returns, the greater the sustainability of their returns and the greater the equality which they induce in the distribution of income. But the precise way in which these characteristics are to be measured is not stated. Furthermore, the appropriate trade-off to make when no single project dominates all other projects in terms of the above properties is not mentioned.

Conway considers sustainability of agroecosystems in terms of their ability to recover from environmental stress after removal of this stress. Thus sustainability as used by Conway refers to the resilience of a system, a concept which may be related to stability of the equilibria of systems. In addition however the robustness of systems needs to be considered, that is how prone systems are to being deflected from their stationary or regular paths as well as their ability to return to those paths, that is, their resilience.

In Conway's view, modern agricultural systems promise high returns but not very sustainable returns compared to many traditional agricultural systems (Conway, 1987). Modern agricultural systems may be less resilient and less robust than traditional systems. If there are irreversible losses, e.g. of traditional varieties of crops, when modern agricultural techniques replace traditional ones, this clearly poses dangers. If the use of modern techniques proves to be unsustainable, it will not be possible in this circumstance to fall back to using traditional techniques. Thus aspects both of sustainability and irreversibility arise. The latter involves a reduction in available options. This may be undesirable if there is uncertainty about the sustainability of modern techniques. However, it should be noted that not all agricultural scientists believe that modern agricultural techniques are less sustainable environmentally than traditional techniques.

It was mentioned above that Conway gives no definite guide to policy makers about trade–offs which should be made between the characteristics of projects. Nevertheless, he suggests that those trade–offs be decided by participation of those involved in carrying out the projects e.g. at the village level in less developed countries. He strongly favours grass–roots participation as a method of providing information and assessing the characteristics of alternative projects.

PROJECT CHOICE AND EVOLUTIONARY PROCESSES

In practice, decision making and project choice are not static maximization problems but dynamic ones in which learning and exploration play a large role. Choice mostly involves evolutionary–type processes and these occur in a world which is characterized by uncertainty, that is, a world in which lack of perfect knowledge is the norm. In this type of world, it is important to keep options open, that is to maintain a diversity of possible choices or to sustain the range of possibilities for choice.

However, it may be valuable not only to sustain the range of existing choices but to extend these. Usually this can only be done by exploration and experimentation, that is, by trial–and–error processes. Error is just as much a part of the learning process as success.

In extending choices through the process of exploration and experimentation, one should consider whether this will result in any existing choice possibilities being lost. Trial of new methods may lead to the loss of some pre–existing choices or of essential components for such choices. Nevertheless it may be worthwhile to forgo irreversibility for some pre–existing possibilities for choice. New possibilities may be superior to the pre–existing ones and sustainable for as long as wished. Still the problem of forgone choices must be recognized.

In an evolutionary world, one of the most important matters is to consider how best to design experiments or trials to yield information and extend possibilities for choice. For example this may require trials to be made of a range of projects. Up to a point diversity may be beneficial so as to learn which projects are likely to be successful and which not. Such trials allow selection to take place and it is the overall results which count. Without such trials, a static non–improving situation is likely to prevail.

CONCLUDING COMMENT

Project evaluation from a social viewpoint involves greater complexities than have usually been recognized in traditional methods of project assessment. As should be clear from the above discussion involving sustainability issues, project selection rarely involves simple static optimization problems in the way often portrayed in introductory texts. Search and experimentation are essential features of the selection process. The question of how best to take account of sustainability of returns has not yet been fully resolved, although a number of useful suggestions have been made in the literature about how this might be done. Possibly one way to make progress with this issue is to define more carefully the various concepts of sustainability which are being used and to provide measures for those which are capable of measurement. Some concepts of sustainability which are being applied to project assessment e.g. by Pearce and co–authors (1989) are clearly related to concepts of sustainable development. These concepts will be discussed extensively in the next part of this book.

REFERENCES

Arrow, K.J. and Fisher, A.C. (1974) 'Environmental Preservation, Uncertainty and Irreversibility', *Quarterly Journal of Economics*, 88, pp 313–9.

Bishop, R.C. (1978) 'Endangered Species and Uncertainty: The Economics of a Safe Minimum Standard', *American Journal of Agricultural Economics*, 60, pp 10–18.

Bishop, R.C. (1979) 'Endangered Species and Uncertainty: A Reply', *American Journal of Agricultural Economics*, 61, pp. 376–9.

Ciriacy–Wantrup, B.V. (1978) *Resource Conservation: Economics and Policies*, 322rd ed., Division of Agricultural Science, University of California, Berkeley, CA.

Conway, G. (1985) 'Agricultural Ecology and Farming Systems Research' in J.V. Remenyi (ed.), *Agricultural Systems Research for Developing Countries*, ACIAR Proceedings No. 11, Canberra, Australian Centre for International Agricultural Research, pp. 43–9.

Conway, G.R. (1987) 'The Properties of Agroecosystems', *Agricultural Ecosystems*, 24, pp. 95–117.

Dixon, J.A. and Hufschmidt, M.M. (eds) (1986) *Economic Evaluation Techniques for* the Environment – A Case Study, Workbook, Johns Hopkins University Press, Baltimore.

Moran, A., Chisholm, A. and Porter, M. (1991) Markets, Resources and the Environment, Allen and Unwin, North Sydney.

Pearce, D., Markandya A. and Barbier, E.B. (1989) Blueprint for a Green Economy, Earthscan Publications, London.

Tisdell, C.A. (1991) Economic Environmental Conservation, Elsevier Science Publishers, Amsterdam.

PART IV

Sustainable Development and Economic Activity

9. The Nature of Sustainability and of Sustainable Development

Sustainability and sustainable development have already been introduced in this book but have not been discussed in as much depth as desirable. This part should remedy this. It concentrates on concepts of sustainable development, particularly as they relate to economic activity. It draws out a number of implications and limitations of these concepts in this chapter 10 and Chapter 10. Applications of these concepts to agriculture (Chapter 11) and to situations involving the use of biological techniques are given (Chapter 12).

Popular use of the terms sustainability and sustainable development is widespread, and for some users they have almost become synonymous with that which is good or desired. This is unfortunate because not all things are worth sustaining, e.g. gross inequality of income, poverty or injustice. There is no virtue in sustaining some particular types of societies. Much loose use and misuse of these terms is occurring and as Lélé (1991) points out there is so much fuzziness about the concept of sustainable development that it is in danger of becoming as ill–defined as the concept of appropriate technology.

The rational pursuit of sustainability, global or otherwise, is only possible if we know what sustainability is or, more exactly, if we know what we want to sustain and in what respect. Many individuals now claim that they favour sustainability, the attainment of a sustainable society or the achievement of sustainable development. On closer examination, however, it is often found that they want to sustain different things. Some wish to promote and sustain close–knit caring (local) communities, some want to sustain the economic welfare of future generations, some want to ensure that the human species is sustained for the longest span of time possible and others wish primarily to sustain biodiversity. These are not exactly the same goals even though the means to achieve them may well run parallel up to a point. Originally the concept of sustainable development was introduced by those supporting the view that environmental conservation and economic development or economic growth could be made compatible. Very often, it is useful to refer back to this original intent. A hallmark of most contemporary proponents of sustainable development is their emphasis on the need to conserve natural resources and natural environments as a means towards achieving their goals. Many take the view that existing institutions, including market mechanisms, are likely in the absence of pro–conservation directives to conserve natural resources and environments inadequately, thereby making for non–sustainable development.

Let us consider some of the main concepts of sustainable development which have been raised in the economic literature or closely associated literature.

SUSTAINING   INTERGENERATIONAL   ECONOMIC WELFARE

Tietenberg (1988, p. 33) claims that 'the sustainability criterion suggests, that at a minimum, future generations should be left no worse off than current generations'. In broad terms, this amounts to saying that the actions of present 1generations in using resources should not reduce the standard of living of future generations below that of present generations. The ethical basis of this is often taken to be John Rawls's (1971) principle of justice. Given that every individual could have been born into the situation of any other, and that everyone in a hypothetical original position involving 'a veil of ignorance' would be uncertain of when and in what situation they would be born, they would it is argued opt for equality of 'income' unless inequality was to the advantage of all. Thus it would be fair or just to honour this hypothetical original contract.

However, once one adopts Rawls's principle one must not only apply it between generations but also within them for it also implies that a similar degree of equality is just between existing individuals. In particular, it would seem to imply on a global scale that much larger income transfers should be made from developed to less developed nations than those taking place now or likely to take place in the foreseeable future. Indeed, we appear to have the irony that resource transfers from less developed nations exceed those in the opposite direction, and the developed nations are reducing their aid to the Third World.

Somewhat weaker equity rules between individuals now and in the future are also espoused. They are that the basic needs of all should be met because of the chance circumstances we all face or may face. In essence all should be assured a minimum standard of living, without standards of living being necessarily made equal. The World Commission on Environment and Development (1987,

p. 43) states that 'sustainable development is development that meets the needs of the present without compromising the ability of future generations to meet their own needs'. The interpretation, of course, all depends upon how one interprets the term 'needs' but if it implies basic needs then this is similar to the view just outlined. The Commission goes on to say that overriding priority should be given to the concept of 'needs', in particular the essential needs of the world's poor and that full account should be taken of the influence of the state of the environment on the ability to meet present and future needs.

Pearce, Markandya and Barbier (1989, p. 2) express a similar point of view stating that 'sustainable development places emphasis on providing for the needs of the least advantaged in society 'intragenerational equity', and a fair treatment of future generations 'intergenerational equity". They suggest as a general principle that 'future generations should be compensated for reductions in the endowments of resources brought about by the actions of present generations' (Pearce, Markandya and Barbier, 1989, p. 3). Capital endowments by present generations are seen as one possible means of compensation and human capital endowment such as increases in scientific and technological knowledge are seen as possibly attractive bequests. However, basically Pearce et al., (1989) do not regard man–made capital a very suitable substitute for natural resouce capital from the point of view of attaining sustainable development. This should be clear from the discussion in the previous chapter outlining their proposal for project selection subject to the constraint that there be no reduction in the stock of natural resource capital.

A number of critical observations can be made about the application of Rawls's theory of justice in this context. These include the following:

(1) Should only human beings count (as is the case in Rawlsian applications) in determining what is just? If we could have been born as any other individual could we not have been born as any other living thing, say an animal of some type? In other words, what is the appropriate universe of possibilities to consider? Could also, for example, a European have been born an Indian? What difference does it make to the application of Rawls's theory if one believes in reincarnation as do many Buddhists and Hindus? Given these points, the Rawlsian principle of justice is not unassailable in its strict form (Tisdell, 1990b or Chapter 10). If the possibility is accepted that a human being might have been born as any living thing, this would seem to establish on the Rawlsian approach some ethical responsibility for caring for other living things.

(2) The number of individuals who will be born in the future is uncertain but it is partially under the control of present generations. This of course raises

a practical difficulty for determining the size of the appropriate bequest for future generations. It also means that we face the difficulty that future population sizes are not uncontrolled variables. If we are scrupulous about observing the logic of Rawls, we should ask what are the wishes or desires of those who could have been born but were not. If any of us could have also been in that position what would we have opted for? Would we have chosen to live if we were provided with at least bare subsistence? Optimal human population policy is not effectively addressed by the approach of Rawls and of those environmental economists following his line.

(3) Rawls may overemphasize the role of chance rather than choice in our lives. Chance appears to be made dominant in his theory but arguably in our life we also have some choice, including the amount of effort to expend on various goals. Thus his principle tends to de–emphasize reward for effort (Cf. Tisdell, 1982, pp. 416, 417).

On a somewhat different point, the idea that man–made capital can be a suitable compensatory bequest for future generations is appealing to proponents of economic growth. But such capital formation may hasten environmental deterioration and may disappear itself long before the natural resources which produced it would have. Man–made physical capital is relatively impermanent whereas natural living resources such as forests and species have in normal circumstances much longer periods of longevity.

MAXIMIZING THE SPAN OF EXISTENCE OF THE HUMAN SPECIES

A rather different point of view of sustainability is that embraced by economists such as Hermann Daly (1980) and Georgescu–Roegen (1971, 1976). They suggest that our basic goal should be to ensure the survival of the human species for as long as is possible – in Daly's words, as long as is compatible with God's will. These are essentially man–centred approaches but differ from the above cases in relation to objectives. I have discussed these to some extent critically elsewhere (Tisdell, 1988 or Chapter 10). Daly suggests that our basic aim should be to ensure that the maximum number of people live in the maximum time span for which it is possible for the human species to survive. He suggests in practice that this involves zero population growth, restrictions on the rate of use of non–renewable resources and limiting consumption per head to a minimum acceptable level. In his view, this will result in a sustainable society.

Georgescu–Roegen (1976), on the other hand, while favouring restricted per capita consumption, argues that human population should be reduced to that level which can be supported by the use of renewable resources alone. This, in his view, provides the best chance for the human species to survive for as long as is possible given the inexorable working of the Law of Entropy. This, I suppose, raises the question of whether Georgescu–Roegen has taken the concept of sustainability to extremes. In my view this is so and this is discussed in the next chapter.

It might be noted that neither of the above approaches make particular allowance for the 'rights' of other species and in that respect they are similar to the previously mentioned economic approach. It is, however, true that Hermann Daly (1980) suggests that Christians have some duty of care for other living things, even if this is not a major duty. But these approaches, on the whole, avoid the open–endedness or fundamental indeterminacy of Rawlsian–based approaches. For example, Daly's approach is relatively clear on its population objective. Nevertheless, Daly's objective may not appeal to everyone.

RESILIENCE OF PRODUCTION AND ECONOMIC SYSTEMS

Some thinkers such as Conway (1987) and Barbier (1987) have looked upon the sustainability of systems as their resilience, that is, their ability to recover when subjected to shocks. This is an interesting and useful concept which may have parallels with the concept of stability of equilibria (Tisdell, 1988). It is also discussed by Redclift (1987). As the amount of biodiversity is reduced, as variety of all types is reduced in the world and as the environment is degraded by economic processes, economic activity may become less resilient when subjected to environmental and other shocks. Thus desirable production and economic states may no longer be sustainable in the long term given the possibilities of stresses on the system or shocks to it. Systems may become subject to jumps and irreversibilities (Tisdell, 1990a). The issues involved are worthy of continuing study and are of considerable relevance in modern times.

NON–ECONOMIC CONCEPTS OF SUSTAINABILITY

There appear also to be a number of concepts of sustainability which are not dominantly economic. Douglass (1984) suggests that sustainability of community is an important concept. It is a complex concept but it appears to be favoured in particular by some 'alternative life–style' groups. It is a complex concept but it implies amongst other things full participation of community members in the social–political systems of the community, a fair distribution of income and co–operation with nature rather than domination of it (cf. Alauddin and Tisdell, 1988). Social structures which take power away from local communities, such as multinational corporations or large corporations with headquarters in distant places, are seen as being a threat to a sustainable economic order in harmony with nature (Cf. Tisdell, 1983, 1989, 1990b).

A number of concepts of sustainability have also been established by a group of ecologists and conservationists who believe that Nature has a right to exist independently of the wishes of mankind. Possibly Aldo Leopold is representative of this group which desire basically to sustain nature in its diversity. Aldo Leopold (1933, 1966) sees humans as a part of a holistic organic community in which humans have no right to exterminate a part of it. His 'land ethic' was developed in opposition to the view that nature should be manipulated or exterminated to satisfy the narrow economic interests of man. It might be noted that prior to adopting this philosophy, Leopold was involved in USDA campaigns to control mammalian pests. Possibly this ethic will gain ground, at least in modified form. It is possible that humanity will come to accept increasing responsibility for nature, and do so not merely for man centred ends or purposes. Even within this framework, there would be a role for economics (Tisdell, 1991).

This by no means exhausts the lists of possible non–economic concepts of sustainability. They are merely put forward to indicate that economists are not alone in the field in providing prescriptions for a 'good society or for a good world'.

CONCLUDING COMMENTS

Some of the early proponents of sustainability and of sustainable development have now become wary of these concepts because they feel that these concepts have become vague and debased in popular use, or because confusion has resulted from the multiplicity of concepts which have emerged. But to dismiss these concepts for these reasons would be premature. A multiplicity of concepts might even be regarded as a bonus provided they are defined and appropriately identified. Multiplicity of concepts provides scope for expanding knowledge in a number of different directions.

Already discussions of sustainability by economists have advanced our understanding of the world in several respects. Existing institutional mechanisms, including market mechanisms, for resource allocation have been found to be wanting from the point of view of economic sustainability (in one or more of its forms). The adequacy of traditional cost–benefit analysis has been questioned and modifications or alternatives to it have been suggested. Most recently Pearce, Markandya and Barbier (1989, pp. 127–9) suggested that 'sustainability be integrated' into cost–benefit analysis by imposing a constraint (requirement) that for a group of projects 'environmental damage (i.e. natural capital depreciation) should be zero or negative' (see Chapter 8). One wonders how this damage will be measured but at least it is a positive suggestion for consideration.

It might also be claimed that those who have argued for the application of a safe minimum standard in the preservation of species (Ciriacy–Wantrup, 1968; Bishop, 1978, 1979) belong to the sustainability stream of thought. They reject conventional approaches adopted in cost–benefit analysis for taking account of risk and uncertainty (Chisholm, 1988; Tisdell, 1990c). They argue that uncertainty rather than risk characterizes environmental decision making. Proponents of sustainability concepts appear to believe that because of uncertainty less structured and mechanical approaches to choice than those traditionally employed in economics, especially neo–classical economics, are appropriate.

Another advance which is closely connected with the sustainability mode of thought is the development of environmental or natural resource accounting. This accounting involves the modification of national income accounts (which were developed principally with the needs of Keynesian economics in mind) so as to provide a measure of sustainable income (See for example Pearce, Markandya and Barbier, 1989, Ch. 4), and/or to measure national welfare more accurately, even if still crudely.

Thus there have been a number of significant advances in economic thought which have been stimulated by sustainability concepts and debate. This stimulation is continuing and we can expect new worthwhile contributions in the years ahead.

REFERENCES

Alauddin, M. and Tisdell, C. (1988) 'New Agricultural Technology and Sustainable Food Production: Bangladesh's Achievements, Predicaments and Prospects', pp. 35–62 in C.A. Tisdell and P. Maitra (eds), *Technological Change, Development and the Environment: Socio–Economic Perspectives*, Routledge, London.

Barbier, E.B. (1987) 'The Concept of Sustainable Economic Development', *Environmental Conservation*, 14(2), pp. 101–10.

Bishop, R.C. (1978) 'Endangered Species and Uncertainty: The Economics of a Safe Minimum Standard', *American Journal of Agricultural Economics*, 60, pp. 10–18.

Bishop, R.C. (1979) 'Endangered Species and Uncertainty: A Reply', *American Journal of Agricultural Economics*, 61, pp. 376–9.

Chisholm, A.H. (1988) 'Sustainable Resource Use and Development: Uncertainty, Irreversibility and Rational Choice', pp. 188–216 in C. Tisdell and P. Maitra (eds), *Technological Change, Development and the Environment: Socio–Economic Perspectives*, Routledge, London.

Ciriacy–Wantrup, S.V. (1968) *Resource Conservation: Economics and Policies*, 3rd ed, University of California Division of Agriculture Science, Berkeley.

Conway, G.R. (1987) 'The Properties of Agroecosystems', *Agricultural Systems*, 24, pp. 95–117.

Daly, H. (1980) *Economics, Ecology and Ethics: Essays Towards a Steady–state Economy*, Freeman, San Francisco.

Douglass, G.K. (1984) 'The Meanings of Agricultural Sustainability', pp. 3–99 in G.K. Douglass (ed.) *Agricultural Sustainability in a Changing World Order*, Westview Press, Boulder, Colorado.

Georgescu–Roegen, N. (1971) *The Entropy Law and the Economic Process*, Harvard University Press, Cambridge, Mass.

Georgescu–Roegen, N. (1976) *Energy and Economic Myths: Institutional and Analytical Economic Essays*, Pergamon Press, New York.

Lélé, S.M. (1991) 'Sustainable Development: a Critical Review', *World Development*, 19 (6), pp. 607–21.

Leopold, A. (1933) *Game Management*, Scribner, New York.

Leopold, A. (1966) *A Sand Country Almanac: with Other Essays on Conservation from Round River*, Oxford University Press, New York.

Pearce, D., Markandya, A., and Barbier, E.B. (1989) *Blueprint for a Green Economy*, Earthscan Publications, London.

Rawls, J.R. (1971) *A Theory of Justice*, Harvard University Press, Cambridge, Mass.

Redclift, M. (1987) *Sustainable Development: Exploring the Contradictions*, Methuen, London.

Tietenberg, T. (1980) *Environmental and Natural Resource Economics*, 2nd ed., Scott, Foresman and Company, Glenview, Illinois.

Tisdell, C.A. (1982) *Microeconomics of Markets*, Wiley, Brisbane.

Tisdell, C.A. (1983) 'Conserving Living Resources in Third World Countries', *International*

Journal of Environmental Studies, 22, pp. 11–24.

Tisdell, C.A. (1988) 'Sustainable Development: Differing Perspectives of Ecologists and Economists, and their Relevance to LDCs', *World Development*, 16 (3), pp. 373–84.

Tisdell, C.A. (1989) 'Environmental Conservation: Economics, Ecology and Ethics', *Environmental Conservation*, 16 (2), pp. 107–12, 162.

Tisdell, C.A. (1990a) 'Ecological Economics and the Environmental Future', *Discussion Paper in Economics No. 28*, Department of Economics, University of Queensland, Queensland 4072, April 1990. Revised version to be in J. Burnett and N. Polunin (eds), *Surviving with the Biosphere*, Edinburgh University Press, forthcoming.

Tisdell, C.A. (1990b) *Natural Resources, Growth and Development: Economics, Ecology, and Resource–Scarcity*, Praeger, New York.

Tisdell, C.A. (1990c) 'Economics and the Debate about Preservation of Species, Crop Varieties and Genetic Diversity', *Ecological Economics*, 2, pp. 77–90.

Tisdell, C.A. (1991) *Economics of Environmental Conservation*, Elsevier Science Publishers, Amsterdam.

WCED (World Commission on Environment and Development) (1987) *Our Common Future*, Oxford University Press, Oxford.

10. Sustainable Development–Differing Perspectives of Ecologists and Economists

The *World Conservation Strategy* (IUCN, 1980) suggested that humankind should aim for sustainable development, and many ecologists see the sustainability of productive systems, including agricultural systems, as an important goal. While ecologists place considerable stress on the desirability of economic sustainability, economists have given much less attention and emphasis to this characteristic. Until recently, it has mainly been economists outside the mainstream of economics who have concerned themselves with the sustainability of productive systems.

Given the emphasis placed by ecologists on the sustainability of productive systems and the growing interest of economists in the subject, it is important, as pointed out in the previous chapter, to have a clear idea of what is meant by sustainability or the lack thereof. Examination of the work of ecologists indicates that their conception of sustainability is unclear.[1] For example, the *World Conservation Strategy* (IUCN, 1980) defines development as 'the modification of the biosphere and the application of human, financial, living and non–living resources to satisfy human needs and improve the quality of life' and conservation as 'the management of the human use of the biosphere so that it may yield the greatest sustainable development to present generations while maintaining its potential to meet the needs and aspirations of future generations'. Conservation of this type is intended to promote sustainable development.

These definitions raise some queries. Do they imply that no development is desirable which temporarily raises the income of existing generations? Is it, for example, ever acceptable to engage in current developments that reduce the potential of future generations to meet their needs? What trade–offs, if any, are acceptable between present generations and future ones?

The *World Conservation Strategy* claims that sustainable economic development requires:
(1) the maintenance of essential ecological processes and life–support systems;
(2) the preservation of genetic diversity; and
(3) sustainable utilization of species and eco–systems.

Agricultural systems, forests, and coastal and freshwater systems are claimed to be the most important life–support systems for humans and to be under the greatest threat. To what extent, however, must each of these matters be attended to ensure sustainability of development? To what extent is it acceptable to extend agricultural systems at the expense of other life–support systems? To what extent can we expect extensions of agriculture and the use of more intensive agricultural systems to be unsustainable?[2] While some of these issues were recognized in the *World Conservation Strategy* little progress was made in debating trade–offs and considering opportunity costs. These are discussed to some extent in Chapter 14 of this book.

Conservational pressure groups strongly advocate a sustainable society. For example, Lester Brown and Pamela Shaw of the Worldwatch Institute promote policies to this end (Brown, 1981; Brown and Shaw, 1982). They suggest that six steps need to be taken: (1) stabilize world population; (2) protect cropland against soil crosion; (3) reforest the Earth; (4) recycle more resources; (5) conserve energy; (6) rely more on renewable energy. I do not intend to debate these specific policy recommendations here but wish to underline the significance of the concept of sustainability in current debates. Furthermore, it should be pointed out that many advocates of a sustainable society are highly critical of the prescriptions of traditional economics and believe that a market economy in itself will not promote a sustainable society (Brown and Shaw, 1982, pp. 6, 12–13). For instance, Brown and Shaw (1982, p. 12) say 'In a world where the economy's environment support systems are deteriorating, supply–side economics – with its overriding emphasis on production and near blind faith in market forces – will lead to serious problems'.

Thus, the view is now being widely propagated that if economic development is to be sustainable, the ecological systems on which economic production ultimately relies also need to be sustainable (see Thibodeau and Field, 1984). In addition, sustainable development may require sustainable patterns of economic exchange (see Tisdell and Fairbairn, 1984; Bertram, 1986) as well as sustainability of political and social structures or sustainability of community, as for example outlined by Douglass (1984, pp. 19–20). Thus the concept of sustainability now arises in many contexts involving development.

ECONOMISTS AND SUSTAINABILITY

Economists such as Hermann Daly (1980), expressing views similar to that of Brown and Shaw (1982), have argued in favour of a steady state economy in which there is zero population growth and in which per capita consumption is restrained. They argue this principally on the grounds that it will preserve the earth's capacity to sustain life and promote the longevity of the human species. Daly believes that such an approach will promote an objective which he sees as important: maximizing the greatest number of people who will ever live subject to maintaining a sufficient or satisfactory per capita level of income or product (Daly, 1980, pp. 353–4). He states that 'It is hard to find any objections to maximizing the number of people who will ever live at a material level sufficient for a good life[13] (Daly, 1980, p. 353). Nevertheless, Daly accepts Georgescu–Roegen's view about entropy (Georgescu–Roegen, 1975) and points out that a steady state economy does not guarantee ecological salvation and eternal life for the species (Daly, 1980, p. 370).

However, is a stationary state necessary to ensure that humankind survives for as long as is possible? This may not be so. It is uncertain whether the economic activity of man will seal his fate. If humankind is highly likely to extinguish itself through nuclear or similar misadventure in the next 100 years (or so) a steady state economy would hardly seem relevant. Again, some may argue that maintaining the existence of human beings on earth for as long as possible is not a worthwhile goal.[4] Rather, one should concentrate on ensuring that the maximum number of souls get to Heaven or Paradise or some equivalent.[5] Furthermore, would it be unsatisfactory to allow population to increase now if this would force future generations to have smaller families than current generations? This adds a new dimension to the intergenerational conflict, namely possible intergenerational conflict about family size.

Many economists have argued that individual development plans should be assessed in terms of their net present value. In terms of this approach, there is no reason to favour per se a project that provides a sustained income over one which gives a high income now followed by a much lower level of income later. In fact, if the stream of income associated with the latter project has a higher net present value than the former stream, the latter project is to be preferred.

As Clark (1976) points out, the net present value criterion may justify the extinguishing of a species. If the rate of increase in the value of the stock of a species is less than the rate of interest, and if harvesting costs are zero, the owner of the stock can make an economic gain by harvesting the whole stock. However, from a social point of view, the social value of a species ought to be assessed. For example, account should be taken of the existence value of the species. Even after this has been done, there may well be some species that it would pay to extinguish. Nevertheless, especially when uncertainty about the future value of a species is important the above may be too simplistic an answer. This is, for example, suggested by the theory of a safe minimum standard designed to allow for uncertainty about the future repercussions from extinction of species (Ciriacy–Wantrup, 1968; Bishop, 1978; Page and MacLean, 1983). This theory is discussed later in this chapter.

SUSTAINABILITY, AGRICULTURAL SYSTEMS AND DEVELOPMENT – AN ECOLOGIST'S APPROACH

One ecologist who has devoted much attention to the principles of agricultural development is Gordon Conway (1983a, 1983b, 1985b) and he has given particular attention to the development of agroecosystem technology in LDCs (Conway, 1985a). He suggests that agricultural systems should be assessed on the basis of four properties:
(1) productivity (measured in terms of yield or net income);
(2) stability of yield or net income;
(3) sustainability of yield or net income;
(4) equitability in terms of income distribution.

Economists have given attention to all these properties but have not given very much attention to the concept of sustainability and its economic significance. These properties of a productive system are illustrated in Figure 10.1.

Conway's concept of sustainability deals with the propensity of a system to withstand collapse under stress and recover once the stress is removed. It has to do with the robustness and resilience of productive systems. Some agricultural systems may be highly productive but subject to substantial risk as far as their sustainability is concerned. Indeed, ecologists are worried that advanced agriculture is becoming subject to greater risk as far as sustainability is concerned because of its growing dependence on a narrower genetic base than ever before (Harlan, 1977; *IUCN*, 1980).

In this respect Harlan (1977, p. 57) observes

> The trends for more and more people to be nourished by fewer and fewer plant and animal food sources has reached the point today where most of the world's population is dependent on a handful of species...This is a relatively recent phenomenon and was not characteristic of the traditional subsistence agriculture abandoned over the past few centuries. As the trend intensifies, man becomes even more vulnerable.His food supply now depends on the success

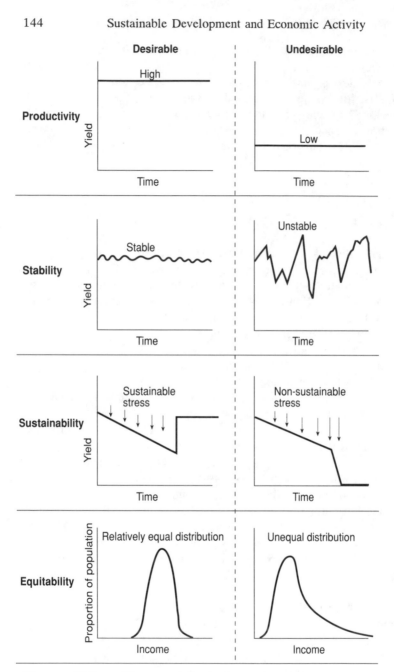

Figure 10.1   Characteristics of a desirable and an undesirable agricultural system according to Conway's criteria.

of a small number of species, and the failure of one of them may mean starvation for millions of people.

For this reason, many ecologists urge us to maintain genetic diversity in the world either by preserving natural areas containing potential cultivars or by maintaining artificial banks of reproductive material.

Conway argues that traditional agriculture systems have high sustainability whereas improved or modern systems have low sustainability. On the other hand, modern systems have high productivity compared to traditional systems. Yet, one should not be categorical about the notion that modern agricultural systems are less sustainable than traditional ones and more damaging to the natural environment. This may not be true of all modern agricultural systems. Schultz (1974, p. 74) argues the opposite to Conway's view. He claims that 'modern agriculture enlarges the environmental possibilities, improves and makes Nature somewhat less unstable' and he points out that the modernization of agriculture in the plains states of the United States has made this area less vulnerable to dust storms. If minimum and low tillage practices are also regarded as a part of modern agriculture, it could be that some of these will add to sustainability. It seems inappropriate to generalize about this matter. Some modern techniques would make for less sustainability than particular traditional ones but the opposite is the case for others, and therefore the position needs to be assessed for individual techniques.

In amplifying the concept of sustainability, Conway says:

> Sustainability can be defined as the ability of a system to maintain productivity in spite of a major disturbance such as that caused by intensive (maintained) stresses or a large perturbation ... Satisfactory methods of measuring sustainability have still to be found, however. Lack of sustainability may be indicated by declining productivity but, equally, collapse may come suddenly and without warning. (Conway, 1983a, p. 12)

The following observations about Conway's approach to assessing agricultural systems and development seem pertinent:

(1) It is qualitative rather than quantitative.

(2) A method of comparing the desirability of different income flows in time, such as a net present value measure, is not given.

(3) No clear indication is given as to what types of trade-offs should be made between characteristics when a choice is available or who should make trade-off judgements. Of course, this problem will not arise if one agricultural system dominates another in terms of desirable qualities but this situation may not be common. Nevertheless, Conway's own work suggests that he sees sustainability as the prime objective. He has devoted considerable research to

devising sustainable agricultural systems for the tropics.

(4) He sees sustainability in terms of the ability of an agricultural system to withstand (environment) stress, and recover from it. The factor affecting sustainability is exogenous to the agricultural system itself. However, there may be some agricultural systems that are unsustainable because they themselves generate unfavourable environmental changes, for example, soil depletion. The factor leading to lack of sustainability is endogenous to the system rather than exogenous to it in this case. The growing of particular crops for example may deplete soil nutrients and lead to a deterioration in its structure so that a 'pure mining effect' is present in this case. Clearly also on Conway's conception, the risk and uncertainty characteristics associated with the occurrence of the stress factor would be important in deciding on the suitability of an agricultural system. If, for example, the stress factor is certain to occur and can be well predicted, then it can be argued that the system is akin to a pure mining one. If its occurrence is uncertain then some rules for decision making under risk or uncertainty are required.

(5) What relationship does the concept of sustainability have to that of equilibrium and to catastrophe theory (Jones, 1977; Zeeman, 1976)? Is a sustainable agricultural system to be identified as one which has a unique equilibrium value that is stable? If so, then the impact of any shock and the dynamic path of return to equilibrium will be important characteristics for the purposes of evaluation. Do some agricultural systems have more than one equilibrium and are some of these inherently unstable? However, the situation may be more complicated than this because certain changes may be irreversible. For example, while it may be possible to maintain one equilibrium in the system in the absence of a significant shock, the occurrence of a major shock may drive the system towards another equilibrium. It may be impossible to return from the new equilibrium to the previous one. Something even more limiting than mere hysteresis[6] may occur, namely 'blocking' of return to an earlier equilibrium once particular values of the system are experienced, no matter what 'available' shocks are applied in an attempt to return to the earlier equilibrium.

More thought needs to be given to clarifying the concept of sustainability, measuring it and deciding how individuals and society might judge the desirability or otherwise of different types of sustainability. It ought to be noted that an equilibrium state or a strongly stable equilibrium state is not necessarily ideal. In this respect Mentis (1984, p. 538) has observed:

Agriculturally the most desirable conditions are unlikely to be equilibrated states. There is a need to manage to keep disequilibrium – this is why management is tricky! The ideal state in one case need not be so in another. Thus the central eco-agricultural paradigm based on the delightfully simple and superficially plausible neo–Clementsian doctrine is mistaken. Mother nature cannot be divided into natural and unnatural, harmonious and disharmonious. We have to return to our frame of reference to distinguish right from wrong.

As noted earlier, many economists assess activities in terms of discounted net income flows, adjusted where necessary to allow for social factors. This, for example, has tended to be the approach adopted in cost-benefit analysis as discussed in Chapter 8. It leads to the view that sustainability is not a virtue in itself and that it may be optimal from the point of view of maximizing discounted net benefits to drive or exploit a system so that it is no longer sustainable. For example, it can be quite rational from this point of view to harvest slowly reproducing species or slowly growing populations of species to the extent that they are exterminated (Clark, 1976). Even some salting, erosion or degradation of soils can be justified on the basis of discounted net income flow provided, of course, that all externalities and similar considerations are taken into account (Dumsday et al., 1983).

This is not to deny that there are economic arguments for sustainability. For example, by sustaining species one keeps options open and this can have an economic value. Furthermore, with the collapse of a productive system, for example an agricultural system, unwelcome income distributional and social consequences could follow. Again, as will be discussed in the next section, rational doubts have been expressed about the universal applicability of the expected utility hypothesis as widely employed by economists. The arguments involved tend to support more risk conservatism than implied by the expected utility approach.

More discussion is needed by economists of the concept of sustainability. Both economists and ecologists need to give more consideration to the types of trade–offs that should be made between the type of objectives specified by Conway. So far ecologists have given us little guidance about the desirability of trade–offs. Since not all objectives can be simultaneously achieved as a rule, trade–offs are inescapable.

THE ECONOMICS OF A SAFE MINIMUM STANDARD: A BRIDGE BETWEEN ECONOMISTS AND ECOLOGISTS?

The preservation of species and thereby genetic diversity has been seen as an important requirement for sustaining economic development (IUCN, 1980; McNeely, 1988; McNeely et al., 1990).[7] The desirability of preserving species has been approached in two ways by economists. The approach at Resources for the Future (RFF) has been to extend 'conventional criteria for optimal public investment to take account of the irreversibilities associated with actions involving natural environments' (Smith and Krutilla, 1979). In this approach to evaluating the desirability of preserving endangered species, uncertainty is characterized by a probability distribution of possible states of nature each of which has a known payoff, and the objective may be (usually is) the maximization of expected utility. Economists such as Ciriacy–Wantrup (1968) and Bishop (1978) are critical of this approach and argue in favour of an approach based on the minimax loss principle.[8] Bishop is critical of the RFF approach because he believes that it does not adequately take account of the degree of uncertainty about the likely value of species in the future.

Species form a genetic reservoir and in his view any reduction in the reservoir is shrouded both in social and natural uncertainty.

> By social uncertainty is meant the lack of knowledge about future time paths for the income levels, technologies, and other variables that will determine which life–forms eventually become resources and which will not. History is replete with examples where unanticipated events caused natural phenomena to become resources. Our future must certainly be equally unpredictable. Natural uncertainty refers to large gaps in knowledge about the characteristics of flora and fauna that may eventually prove useful to humans. Though less well–known to economists, natural uncertainty is as impressive as social uncertainty. It is an understatement to say that there is still a great deal to be learned about nature. (Bishop, 1978, p. 12)

Given the degree of ignorance and uncertainty about possible losses from the extinction of a species, the choice about whether or not to save a species is best considered in terms of game theory. Ciriacy–Wantrup and Bishop suggest that it might be appropriate to apply the minimax loss principle for making this choice. The nature of the game can be illustrated by the matrix set out in Table 10.1.

Table 10.1 Matrix of possible losses from extinction and conservation of a species.

	States of nature		Max. losses
	1*	2†	
Extinction	0	Y	Y
Safe minimum	X	X−Y	X

* State of nature such that there is no loss from extinction.
† State of nature involving a loss from extinction.

If the size of the possible loss, Y, from extinction of the species exceeds the cost, X, of maintaining the species at a safe minimum population level (that is, one that avoids the extinction of the species), the minimax strategy is to opt for preservation of the species at the safe minimum level. Otherwise, extinction is the minimax strategy. The matrix indicates that, other things held equal, the preservation strategy is more likely to be an optimal minimax one, the lower the cost of ensuring a safe minimum level of the population of the species. Bishop (1978) argues that the cost of preserving many species is extremely low in relation to the potential gain forgone by not saving them. Furthermore, the minimax principle should not be followed blindly. If the difference between X and Y is very small and X is very high, it may not be desirable to adopt the minimax strategy. However, Bishop does not provide us with a specific rule in this case.

Bishop (1978, p. 13) suggests that 'not only are the probabilities poorly understood but also the outcomes themselves and the associated losses' so that the payoff values attaching to alternative strategies can be quite uncertain. Furthermore, what do the payoffs measure? The cost of saving a species from extinction is likely to fall principally on current generations whereas future generations are likely to be the main beneficiaries. How are intergeneration income distribution questions to be settled? Despite such differences Bishop believes that the safe minimum standard/game theory approach is useful in conceptualizing the choices facing society and of greater operational value than the Resources for the Future approach (Bishop, 1979).

Without necessarily embracing the minimax approach, Talbot Page and Douglas MacLean (1983) argue convincingly that expected utility theory has defects under particular circumstances both as a description of actual behaviour and as a normative doctrine. When these circumstances prevail 'a policy maker might reasonably adopt a strategy more risk conservative than the usual risk–benefit analysis' (Page and MacLean, 1983, p. 1,025). Risk conservatism involves more than mere risk aversion as would be implied by strictly concave utility functions. For example, where one is uncertain of the probabilities of payoffs associated with a particular event such as the extinction of a species or of a productive system, this may result in at least temporary uncertainty avoidance. This may take the form of further information gathering and delay during which time it can be important to keep the existing system functioning, that is in a sustained state. Page and MacLean believe that the expected utility theory is appropriate under some circumstances but not others. As summarized by Chisholm (1988) several other economists have also recently criticized expected utility maximization as a relevant objective for individual decision making in many circumstances. These critiques raise the question, taken up later, of whether risk conservatism is likely to be more appropriate for less developed countries (LDCs) than for developed countries (DCs).

The expected utility criterion seems even more vulnerable to criticism when it is applied to social rather than individual decision making. Most development issues involve a social dimension. The disappearance of species and varieties of living organisms, for instance, affects the whole of society and all future generations. Many of the global environmental risks which we face do not have potential effects that would average out over the whole population. The statistical law of large numbers does not apply to these events or risks as it does to various risks for which insurance exists. They remain risks for us all *in toto*.

How we should decide in relation to such global or pervasive risks is complicated in a social context because
(1) different individuals may have markedly different attitudes to uncertainty and risk bearing;
(2) different individuals may have diverse perceptions and estimates of the actual risks and dangers involved; and
(3) individuals may obtain or suffer unequal amounts of expected gain or loss in relation to the risk borne (which itself may but need not be equally borne).

Differences in estimates of risk may be held rationally and it may not be possible to obtain consensus about estimates on the basis of available knowledge even with goodwill.

In most cases, the event giving rise to the risk does not satisfy the Paretian gain test – some of those affected feel better off while others are worse off. Kneese and Sweeney (1985) discuss this ethic and others specifically in relation to an environmental risk involving several generations such as nuclear waste storage. Even if an environmental risk passes the Kaldor–Hicks test, that is involves a potential Pareto improvement in that the gainers could compensate the losers, there are still, as is well known, many limitations to such a test for determining increases in social welfare (Ng, 1979, Ch. 3) such as its lack of resolution in relation to income distribution changes. But in the present context, there are additional problems. Those that expect to gain from a risky event which may result in non–sustainability may have an inflated idea of gains to be achieved and may underestimate risks. If this is true, they may not be in a position to compensate losers even in a probability or expected sense. However, let us suppose that the expected gainers are right in their 'probability' estimates. They may only be able to pay compensation if a favourable outcome occurs. The payment of the compensation (or the possibility of its payment) is conditional upon a favourable outcome to the 'lottery' in which all are required to participate (no free choice). Both on these two grounds and on the ground that the risks being faced are uncertain and the probabilities could be to some extent 'fictional', some risk conservatism would not be misplaced. This seems especially so for events which involve a low risk of high damage to individuals since in such circumstances individuals appear typically not to follow expected utility rules (Chisholm, 1988; Page and MacLean, 1983; Loomes and Sugden, 1982).

Table 10.2 Matrix of possible losses from sustainable and unsustainable production strategies.

	States of nature		
	No stress	Stress occurs	Max loss
Not sustainable	0	−10	−10
Sustainable	−3	−4	−4∗

∗ Minimax value

Returning to the minimax principle of Bishop – what is its relationship to the desirability of sustainable development or sustainable productive systems?   In certain cases, sustainable systems may be those that minimize the maximum possible loss. In that case, a 'sustainable' development or productive strategy would correspond to extreme risk avoidance. This is so for the loss matrix shown in Table 10.2.

PREFERENCE OF LDCs FOR SUSTAINABLE PRODUCTIVE SYSTEMS

Would LDCs be more likely than DCs to favour a minimax approach to determining economic development programmes and the desirability of alternative production systems?   This is a difficult question to answer *a priori*. On the one hand because of low incomes the inhabitants of LDCs might be expected to have a high time–preference for consumption now rather than conservation for future generations. High interest rates in LDCs may also militate against conservation. Some writers argue that in the stage of backward economic development, societies prefer to take environmental risk for the sake of economic growth (Fleming, 1977, p.8; Tisdell, 1983b or Chapter 5). On the other hand, forces are present in LDCs which might make sustainable productive systems more appropriate for them than for DCs (see Tisdell, 1985 or Chapter 15) and more suitable than less sustainable ones or ones subject to a high risk of non–sustainability.

In the above respect, the following factors need to be taken into account:

(1) Population rises in response to increased income may be greater in LDCs than in DCs. If income cannot be maintained, there are considerable welfare problems involved in the long term given that population levels cannot be easily reduced (see Tisdell and Fairbairn, 1984).

(2) Capital and labour mobility in LDCs is less than in DCs and the societies of LDCs are more heterogeneous. If environmental deterioration or collapse of productive systems occurs in a local area or region of an LDC those individuals affected are not easily able to find alternative employment in the economy and may find considerable difficulty in adjusting to a different social situation in another part of the country. Furthermore, because incomes are already low in LDCs, individuals have little or no reserves to search for employment or alternative living conditions elsewhere in the economy. In addition, the costs of search are likely to be high in LDCs compared to DCs because communication systems are poor.

(3) Since incomes in some areas in many LDCs are barely above

subsistence levels, there are few reserves for taking a risk on non–sustainability. The consequence of failure may be death. The option exists of avoiding this risk and as Page and MacLean (1983, p. 1,024) indicate it may be rational to do so.

(4) Dire consequences for the individual of failure of productive systems in an area are also more likely in LDCs because social insurance or security systems (e.g. public unemployment benefits) are poorly developed and there are few national reserves for subsidizing regions or industries in economic difficulties. Inhabitants in LDCs are more likely to 'have to' stay put in the face of adverse economic difficulties and less likely to get aid from outside communities than in DCs.

(5) LDCs are comparatively more dependent on environmentally based living–resource production than are DCs, e.g., on agriculture and fisheries. The structure of societies in LDCs is likely to be severely disrupted if any of these major industries becomes non–sustainable.

(6) There may be greater uncertainty about the probable effects of new technology or developments in LDCs than in DCs. Knowledge about the value in the tropics of various agricultural systems developed in temperate areas may be limited. There is a lack of knowledge about the value of various species and practices indigenous to LDCs. Possibly 'asymmetric uncertainties as to probabilities' (Page and MacLean, 1983, p. 1,024) are greater in LDCs than in DCs. This would suggest that greater risk conservatism would be rational in LDCs. This may imply that species and existing systems should be preserved (or preserved up to a reversible level) until more knowledge is gathered.

(7) In certain circumstances, a government may desire to sustain or to see sustained particular productive systems because political support for it comes from those involved in these systems. This, however, is not peculiar to LDCs.

Thus it can be seen that LDCs may have a greater preference for sustainable productive systems than DCs. This does not imply the non–introduction of new productive systems but that these need to be considered more carefully before being adopted in LDCs. One upshot of this discussion is that expected utility analysis or traditional risk–benefit analysis may, using the criteria suggested by Page and MacLean (1983), be more appropriate for DCs than for LDCs. This is somewhat at variance with the view also expressed in the literature that economically 'backward' countries should be (or are) less averse to environmental risk taking (Fleming, 1977, p.8) than are DCs. Certainly this matter is by no means settled. In DCs some conservation groups have expressed strong opposition to traditional risk–benefit analysis and associated values and prefer a minimax regret approach to an expected value one (Bergstrom, 1984, p. 12).

MORE ON ECOLOGISTS AND SUSTAINABILITY OF PRODUCTION

As further evidence of the importance that ecologists place on sustainable production, consider the following three recommendations from a report from Dasmann and Poore (1979):

- The stocking of rangelands in high mountain areas with domestic animals must be planned so that the grazing lands can support the numbers proposed without the long–term loss of productivity of either plants or animals (p. 25).
- Where grasslands have been so overgrazed that their productivity and stability have been impaired, the pressure on them should be reduced to restore their productivity (p. 27).
- Especially in arid and semi–arid regions, nomadic grazing and transhumance often makes the best sustained use of grazing lands; these traditional practices should not be changed without very good reason (p. 27).

The precise meaning of these recommendations is unclear. Are the authors concerned with maximum sustainable yield or maximum economic yield? Why is sustainability so desirable? Nevertheless, it is clear that nomadic grazing and transhumance[9] often make the best economic use of grazing lands and that the establishment of individual plots of private land in some areas interferes with or supplants nomadic activity and may reduce economic productivity. (Has this, for example, occurred in parts of Kenya?) The establishment of private ownership in land subject to nomadic activity could impose a high transaction cost on nomads wanting to use it and render nomadism uneconomic even when it represents the best form of land use.

There is also evidence that some common–property resources (shared land resources) can provide a highly productive and equitable use of land even in settled agricultural communities if they are collectively managed. Jodha (1985) points out the substantial economic advantages of such areas (compared to completely private land ownership) in farming in arid and semi–arid tropical India. His conclusions are based on detailed studies in villages in Rajasthan and Madhya Pradesh. It is most important, however, that there be an appropriate social or political framework for the management of such areas otherwise erosion and degradation are liable to occur with rising economic demands on scarce land resources. In the absence of this framework, use of the resource becomes unsustainable. This underlines the point that resources and productive systems may become unsustainable not just on account of new technology but also on account of new political and social systems (see Jodha, 1985; Tisdell, 1983b or Chapter 14).

CONCLUDING COMMENTS

The sustainability criterion has played a much greater role in the type of policy advice given by ecologists than that given by economists. Why is it that ecologists focus so much on this characteristic and economists give it so little attention? Since ecologists and biologists put so much store on sustainability why is this concept not more carefully defined and measured by them? Are sustainable agricultural systems more appropriate for LDCs than less sustainable systems such as those reputed to be widely used in developed countries? I have no definite answers to these questions.

On the other hand, it is not clear where economics and economists stand on the desirability of sustainability. Most economists have not seen sustainability as a desirable goal in itself but more are coming to accept sustainable development as a desirable goal, e.g. Pearce, Markandya and Barbier (1989) and other authors as mentioned in Chapters 8 and 9. Traditional economic principles suggest that the 'mining' depletion or elimination of living resources is justifiable from an economic point of view and that unsustainable productive activities may be economically rational. This being so, what scope is there for economists and ecologists to agree on this matter? To what extent do the theories of Ciriacy–Wantrup, Bishop, Page and MacLean provide a bridge between economists and ecologists?

Despite continuing differences between some economists and ecologists on the desirability of sustainable productive systems and the desirability of sustainable development, it would seem unwise for economists and others undertaking social cost–benefit analysis of projects for LDCs to ignore ecological considerations and spillovers. Indeed, the claims in the traditional economic manuals for project evaluation in LDCs that such matters are likely to be unimportant is a serious shortcoming (Little and Mirrlees, 1974; Dasgupta et al., 1972; Tisdell, 1986 or Chapter 8). The ecological consequences of many projects and developments in LDCs have been far from minor as evidenced by James (1978).

NOTES

1. However, a vague definition is better than spurious precision and much better than ignoring the issue, especially if it subsequently stimulates further development of new concepts, as discussions of sustainability should.
2. For discussion of these matters in relations to Bangladesh and the 'green revolution', see Alauddin and Tisdell (1986, 1991).
3. While this objective appears quite anthropocentric, it is likely to be much more favourable to the survival of other species than the objective of myopic, all-out economic growth. It also is apparent that Daly's personal values do include a naturalistic element not captured in the above objective for he has also stated that 'the SSE (steady state economy) is simply a strategy of good stewardship for taking care of God's creation for however long he wills it to last. In taking care of that creation, special, but not exclusive, attention must be given to humanity, including not only the present but also future generations ...' (Daly, 1980, pp. 370–1).
4. It was suggested by a reviewer for *World Development* that this may not in fact be Hermann Daly's goal, but rather that his goal is to maximize the longevity of existence of the human species. This raises the question of whether one might have to forgo some longevity of the species in order to increase the cumulative number of lives ever lived over time at a per capita consumption level that is sufficient for a good life.
5. This need not be inconsistent with Daly's objective. However, if the same proportion of individuals who ever live are 'saved' irrespective of their per capita income, this would suggest that the objective ought to be to maximize the number of individuals who ever live (long enough to be 'saved'). This suggests an optimal income per capita somewhat lower than Daly's level sufficient for a good life. But of course, the proportion of individuals 'saved' may not be independent of per capita income levels. For some individuals, the objective of maximizing the number of souls that get to Heaven could be a serious objective. This objective can conflict with Daly's objective and is likely to be at serious odds with myopic maximum economic growth objectives which may seriously limit the maximum number of individuals who ever live.
6. Hysteresis occurs when the extent of control over a system depends on the sequence and values of past events which have affected the system. Some past events may make it more difficult but not impossible to return to a previous equilibrium.
7. Incidentally the set of priorities put forward in the *World Conservation Strategy* (IUCN, 1980) for saving species from extinction is of dubious value. For example, it is suggested that priority should be given to saving endangered families rather than say an endangered species within a family. But why should a family (which may contain one species) necessarily be of greater value than a species within a family that itself is not endangered? There is no *a priori* reason why one should adopt the WCS priorities. However, it could be argued, even though this point is not made in WCS, that by saving a family, one leaves possibilities for genetic manipulation and change more open. Nevertheless, the approach to species preservation of ecological policy advisers involved in the *World Conservation Strategy* is somewhat disappointing (see IUCN, 1980;

Tisdell, 1983a). Some ecologists, in particular Myers (1979), are however taking an approach which is helping to bridge the gap between ecologists and economists in the discussion of the issue of species preservation.

8. This principle requires the decision maker to adopt the strategy which maximizes the minimum possible gain, or which minimizes the maximum possible loss. It entails the highest possible avoidance of risk. See for example, Luce and Raiffa (1966).

9. Transhumance is the seasonal movement of stock from one region to another, e.g. from lowland areas to mountainous areas during the summer.

REFERENCES

Alauddin, M. and Tisdell, C., (1988) 'New Agricultural Technology and Sustainable Food Production: Bangladesh's Achievements, Predicament and Prospects,' Ch. 3 in C.A. Tisdell and P. Maitra (eds), *Technological Change, Development and the Environment: Socio–Economic Perspectives*, Croom Helm, London.

Alauddin, M. and Tisdell, C. (1991) *The 'Green Revolution' and Economic Development: The Process and its Impact in Bangladesh*, Macmillan, London.

Bergstrom, S. (1984) *Economic Growth and the Role of Science*, Department of Business Administration, Stockholm University.

Bertram, G. (1986) '"Sustainable Development" in Pacific Micro–Economies', *World Development*, 14(7) pp. 809–22.

Bishop, R.C. (1978) 'Endangered Species and Uncertainty. The Economics of a Safe Minimum Standard', *American Journal of Agricultural Economics*, 60(1), pp. 10–18.

Bishop, R.C. (1979) 'Endangered Species, Irreversibility and Uncertainty: A Reply', *American Journal of Agricultural Economics*, 61(2), pp. 376–9.

Brown, L.R. (1981) *Building a Sustainable Society*, W.W. Norton, New York.

Brown, L.R. and Shaw, P. (1982) *Six Steps to Sustainable Society*, Worldwatch Institute, Washington, DC.

Chisholm, A. (1988) 'Sustainable Resource Use and Development: Uncertainty, Irreversibility and Rational Choice', Chap. 9 in C.A. Tisdell and P. Maitra (eds), *Technological Change, Development and the Environment: Socio–Economic Perspectives*, Croom Helm, London.

Ciriacy–Wantrup, S.V. (1968) *Resource Conservation: Economics and Policies*, 3rd ed., University of California Division of Agriculture Science, Berkeley.

Clark, C.W. (1976) *Mathematical Bioeconomics*, John Wiley, New York.

Conway, G.R. (1983a) 'Agroecosystem Analysis', ICCET Series E, No. 1, Imperial College, London.

Conway, G.R. (1983b) *Applying Ecology*, Centre for Environmental Technology, Imperial College, London.

Conway, G.R. (1985a) 'Agricultural Ecology and Farming Systems Research', in J.V. Remenyi (ed.), *Agricultural Systems Research for Developing Countries*, Australian Centre for International Agricultural Research, Canberra.

Conway, G.R. (1985b), 'Agroecosystems Analysis', *Agricultural Administration*, 20, pp. 31–5.

Daly, H. (1980) *Economics, Ecology and Ethics*, Freeman, San Francisco.

Dasgupta, P.A., Sen, A. and Marglin, S. (1972) *Guidelines for Project Evaluation*,

United Nations Industrial Development Organization, New York.

Dasmann, R.F. and Poore, D. (1979) *Ecological Guidelines for Balanced Land Use, Conservation and Development in High Mountains*, IUCN, Gland, Switzerland.

Douglass, G.K. (1984) 'The meanings of agricultural sustainability', pp. 3–29 in G.K. Douglass (ed.) *Agricultural Sustainability in a Changing World Order*, Westview Press, Boulder, Colorado.

Dumsday, R.G., Oram, D.A. and Lumley, S.E. (1983) 'Economic Aspects of the Control of Dryland Salinity', *Proceedings of the Royal Society of Victoria*, 95(3), pp. 139–45.

Fleming, J.C. (1977) *The Law of Torts*, 5th ed., Law Book Company, Sydney.

Georgescu–Roegen, N. (1975) 'Selections from "Energy and Economic Myths"', *Southern Economic Journal*, 41(3), (Reprinted in Daly 1980.)

Harlan, J.R. (1977) 'The Plants and Animals that Nourish Man', in *Scientific American Book, Food and Agriculture*, Freeman, San Francisco.

IUCN (1980) *World Conservation Strategy*, IUCN, Gland, Switzerland.

IUCN–UNEP–WWF (1991) *Caring for the Earth: A Strategy for Sustainable Living*, IUCN, Gland, Switzerland.

James, J. (1978) 'Growth, Technology and the Environment in Less Developed Countries: A Survey', *World Development*, 6, pp. 937–65.

Jodha, N.S. (1985) 'Common Property Resource in Farming in Arid and Semi–arid Tropical India', ICRISAT, Pantancheru, PO 502 324, AP India.

Jones, D.A. (1977) 'The Application of Catastrophe Theory to Ecological Systems', *Simulation*, 29(1), pp. 1–15.

Kneese, A.V. and Sweeney, J.W. (1985) 'Ethics and Environmental Economics' in A.V. Kneese and J.L. Sweeney (eds) *Handbook of Natural Resource and Energy Economics*, Elsevier Science, Amsterdam.

Little, I.M.D. and Mirrlees, J.A. (1974) *Project Appraisal and Planning for Developing Countries*, Heinemann Educational Books, London.

Loomes, G. and Sugden, R., (1982) 'Regret Theory: An Alternative Theory of Rational Choice under Uncertainty', *The Economic Journal*, 92, pp. 805–24.

Luce, R.D. and Raiffa, H. (1966) *Games and Decisions*, Wiley, New York.

McNeely, J.A. (1988) *Economics and Biological Diversity: Developing and Using Economic Incentives to Conserve Biological Resources*, IUCN, Gland, Switzerland.

McNeely, J.A., Miller, K.R., Reid, W.N., Mittermeier, R.A. and Werner, T.B. (1990) *Conserving the World's Biological Diversity*, IUCN, Gland, Switzerland.

Mentis, G. (1984) 'White Paper on Agricultural Policy', *South African Journal of Science*, 80, pp. 538–9.

Myers, N. (1979) *The Sinking Ark*, Pergamon Press, Oxford.

Ng, Y. (1979) *Welfare Economics*, Macmillan, London.

Page, T. and MacLean, D. (1983) 'Risk Conservatism and the Circumstances of Utility Theory', *American Journal of Agricultural Economics*, 65, pp. 1021–6.

Pearce, D., Markandya, A., and Barbier, E.B. (1989) *Blueprint for a Green Economy*, Earthscan Publications, London.

Schultz, T.W. (1974) 'Is Modern Agriculture Consistent with a Stable Environment?', in *The Future of Agriculture: Technology, Policies and Adjustment*. Papers and Reports, 15th International Conference of Agricultural Economists, Oxford Agricultural Economics Institute, Oxford.

Smith, V.K. and Krutilla, V. (1979) 'Endangered Species, Irreversibilities, and Uncertainty: A Comment', *American Journal of Agricultural Economics*, 61, pp.

371–5.

Thibodeau, R. and Field, H. (1984) *Sustaining Tomorrow: A Strategy for World Conservation and Development*, University Press of New England, Hanover.

Tisdell, C.A. (1983a) 'An Economist's Critique of the World Conservation Strategy with some examples from Australian experience', *Environmental Conservation*, 10, pp. 43–52.

Tisdell C.A. (1983b) 'Conserving Living Resources in Third World Countries: Economic and Social Issues', *International Journal of Environmental Studies*, 22, pp. 11–24.

Tisdell, C.A. (1986) 'Cost–benefit Analysis, the Environment and Informational Constraints in LDCs', *Journal of Economic Development*, 11, pp. 63–81.

Tisdell, C.A. and Fairbairn, T.I. (1984) 'Subsistence Economies and Unsustainable Development and Trade: Some Simple Theory', *The Journal of Development Studies*, 20, pp. 227–41.

Zeeman, E.C. (1976) 'Catastrophe Theory', *Scientific American*, 234, pp. 65–73.

11. Economics, Ecology and Sustainable Agricultural Systems

International emphasis on the importance of promoting ecologically sustainable development has increased. The *World Conservation Strategy* (IUCN, 1980) took the view that the conservation of living resources and their life–support systems is necessary if economic development is to be sustained. This view was also taken by the World Commission on Environment and Development (1987) and in the follow–up to the *World Conservation Strategy* (IUCN–UNEP–WWF, 1991). Consequently, it is argued that economic development and conservation should be approached as complementary activities rather than competing ones. International bodies were already becoming concerned about sustainable development in the mid–1980s. Caldwell (1984, p. 307) pointed out in the mid–1980s 'that in the last two decades, the concepts of limits to growth and of the necessity of an ecologically sustainable economic order have gained international recognition. These concepts are not yet understood by most people or most governments, but belief in the necessity for planning for a sustainable future is growing'.

A number of countries, including Australia, were motivated by this concern to formulate national conservation strategies. Concern for sustainable development was also expressed in the South African *White Paper on Agriculture* issued by the Ministry of Agriculture in 1984. Mentis (1984, p 538) stated that the 'white paper marks the start of a new initiative in planning for sustainable use of agricultural resources in South Africa. If the initiative fails it may not be entirely the fault of the Minister and his Department of Agriculture'. Resource scientists in his view need to build on this initiative and give greater attention to the formulation of relevant priorities and values. The quest for sustainable development clearly calls for greater co–operation between economists, ecologists and other resource scientists. This chapter highlights the need for their co–operation, particularly in relation to the choice of alternative agricultural systems and different patterns of rural land use. With the widespread acceptance of the desirability (in principle) of sustainable development the need for such co–operation is greater than ever.

ECONOMICS AND ECOLOGY

Alfred Marshall observed in his *Principles of Economics* (1930) that economists should seek inspiration for their models in biology rather than from physics and he draws a number of analogies in his work from biology. In fact, Marshall (1930, p. 772) says 'economics has no kinship with any physical science. It is a branch of biology broadly interpreted'. Be that as it may, economists have been surprisingly little influenced by biological and ecological modelling, and until comparatively recently ignored the inter dependence between economic activity and ecological processes. There are at least two major reasons why economists might take an interest in biological and ecological models: first, such models can be a source of inspiration for economic modelling (and vice versa) (cf. Hirshleifer, 1977; Worster, 1985); and second, human beings are an organism and their activities (including their economic activities) depend upon and influence the environment, especially the biosphere. The World Commission on the Environment and Development (1987) emphasized the importance of the latter relationship in the modern world, especially in the light of the increasing importance of environmental externalities or spillovers from economic activity.

Ecology is described in *The Macquarie Dictionary* (1981) as 'the branch of biology which treats the relations between organisms and their environment; bionomics'. Ecology is, according to the *Concise Oxford Dictionary* (1951), the 'branch of biology dealing with living organisms' habits, modes of life, and relations to their surroundings'. Given these definitions, there is clearly an overlap between economic activity and the area of ecology. It is also interesting to note that both the words 'economics' and 'ecology' have a common Greek root, namely *oikos* meaning house, so one would expect these subjects to be closely connected.

Despite Alfred Marshall's view, serious discussions by economists of biological work and incorporation in their work of *models inspired* by biology have been rare. However, Kenneth Boulding made some progress in this regard with his publication in 1950 of *A Reconstruction of Economics*, and in 1977 in a long article Jack Hirshleifer examined economics from a biological point of view. Both publications were concerned with biology and economics as sources of mutual inspiration for model building.

Economics, biology and ecology need to be linked in assessing the relationship between economic activity and the environment. While it can be argued that classical economists such as T.R. Malthus (1798) and D. Ricardo (1817) paid particular attention to some types of environmental constraints on economic development, neo–classical economists beginning from Marshall onward tended to ignore these. For 100 years or more, economists mostly, but with the exception of Pigou (1932), ignored the impact of economic activity on the environment and various environmental constraints on economic growth and development. Only in the last few decades have economists shown renewed interest in the relationships between economic activity, economic development and the environment. Topics such as the economics of pollution, the economic management of natural resources, resource depletion and species extinction have been increasingly discussed by economists. In line with this new concern, undergraduate or graduate courses in environmental economics have been introduced into many (possibly most) universities.

Boulding (1980), with his concept of spaceship earth, was one of the first economists to make others aware of the interdependence of economic man with his environment. The spaceship earth concept emphasized that man lives in a closed system, the earth. He is dependent on earth for his sustenance and it also receives all of his wastes. Production and consumption by humans are only a part of the system of material balances on earth. For example, consumption is not the end of a process but gives rise to wastes or by–products which in turn may be recycled through the system to provide more production for humans. The materials balance approach, as, for example, outlined by Pearce (1976), Kneese, Ayres and D'Arge (1970), and others, emphasizes the importance of looking beyond immediate economic production and consumption in considering the influences of economic activity and its sustainability. Nevertheless, it is probably true to say that the main focus of these studies is on physical interdependencies rather than biological ones (that is, the range of living things) as important elements in human existence and economic welfare.

Hermann Daly (1980), in his book *Economics, Ecology, Ethics,* brings together the views of a number of economists who are trying to apply economics to the biophysical world. They are all sympathetic to Boulding's view (1980, p 258) that

> The closed earth of the future requires economic principles which are somewhat different from those of the open earth of the past. For the sake of picturesqueness, I am tempted to call the open economy the 'cowboy economy', the cowboy being symbolic of the illimitable plains and also associated with reckless, exploitative, romantic, and violent behaviour, which is characteristic of open societies. The closed economy of the future might similarly be called the 'spaceman economy', in which the earth has become a single spaceship, without limited reservoirs of anything, either for

extraction or for pollution, and in which, therefore, man must find his place in a cyclical ecological system which is capable of continuous reproduction of material form even though it cannot escape having inputs of energy!

Many of those individuals, such as Daly, who are convinced of the environmental dangers of continuing population growth and rising levels of consumption, favour a steady state economy, that is, one in which population levels and consumption levels are constant or stationary. Furthermore, they favour a reduction in per capita consumption levels in developed countries and among people who already have high consumption levels. The aim of Daly in advocating such a position is to ensure the continuing existence of *homo sapiens* (the human race) for as long as possible or as long as is compatible with God's wishes. In his view, the continuing existence of the species has to take precedence over the wants of individual members. Even if one accepts this proposition, one can argue about whether or not a steady state economy is most likely to maximize the length of existence of the human race. Furthermore, some may not accept the over–riding desirability of the aim of maximizing the length of existence of the human species on earth. They may on religious grounds, for example, be more interested in saving the maximum number of souls, and/or if they believe in the resurrection of the body, the length of temporal existence of the human species may not be viewed as a real problem (Tisdell, 1983). However, one need not be concerned with such metaphysical or long–term matters to see that deterioration in the resource base of an economy can threaten living standards, bring economic growth to an end and even lead to a collapse in economic fortunes in a relatively short period of time.

It is easy for governments to become engrossed in short–term economic management and to put off policy issues involving long–term development. This has led some environmental advocates to castigate traditional economic approaches as failing to ensure security of the global resource base (Brown and Shaw, 1982). These authors (1982, p. 6) argue that 'new sources of economic stress require public policy initiatives that go far beyond mere adjustments in fiscal and monetary policy. Our prospects hinge ultimately not on our ability to fine tune economic policies, but on our success in stabilizing our numbers and protecting our environment.'

THE WORLD CONSERVATION STRATEGY AND SUSTAINABLE DEVELOPMENT

The *World Conservation Strategy* (IUCN, 1980) also stressed the importance of sustainability of economic activity and pointed out that if economic development is to be sustainable, continuing and proper attention must be paid to the biosphere and natural ecosystems within it. Historically, it was an important document in the development of global recognition of the desirability and possibility of sustainable development. The *World Conservation Strategy* (WCS) was drawn up by IUCN (International Union for the Conservation of Nature and Natural Resources) in consultation with UNEP, FAO, UNESCO, and many other bodies and individuals throughout the world and was jointly financed by UNEP and WWF. One of its aims was to encourage most countries to formulate national conservation strategies and it was hoped that the 1980s, the Third Development Decade, would become a decade of sustainable development. The document focuses attention on living resources as essential requirements for continuing human existence. This emphasis is continued in *Caring for the Earth: A Strategy for Sustainable Living* (IUCN–UNEP–WWF, 1991). As time passes and non–renewable resources become increasingly depleted, humankind will become more dependent on living resources for its economic welfare. Living resources are important now for human existence but they are likely to be more so in the future.

The main inspiration of the document came from ecologists and biologists. It argued in favour of sustainable economic development and suggested that this requires:
- the maintenance of essential ecological processes and life–support systems
- the presentation of genetic diversity
- measures to ensure the sustainable utilization of species and ecosystems.

Each one of these requirements is considered in detail. Agricultural systems, forests, and coastal and freshwater systems are claimed to be the most important life–support systems for mankind and to be under the greatest threat.

While the *World Conservation Strategy* (IUCN, 1980) provided several guidelines and priorities, it gave little guide to how conflicts between priorities are to be resolved when they do occur. Furthermore, when methods for resolving conflicts are stated, they are often of limited operational value. For example, WCS suggests that priority should be given to conserving an endangered family of living organisms rather than an endangered species within a family. However, what is to be done if the endangered family is considered to be of little relative value by humans or is in fact a nuisance?

Nevertheless choices about the saving of species or their extinction are important if mankind is not to ignore a major problem. Projected growth in human populations and economic activity is likely to generate considerable economic and political pressure to convert wild lands and lands used with low economic intensity to more intense use. In 1980, it was estimated that, as a result of loss of habitat, 15 to 20 per cent of species on earth might be lost by the end of the twentieth century (Barney, 1980). While natural extinction of species is an ongoing process, extinction on this scale is primarily a result of human activities and is continuing. A large proportion of such extinctions is expected to come about as a result of the clearing of tropical forests. Species threatened with extinction could be a sustainable source of new foods, building products, pharmaceuticals and so on and considerable loss in economic value may occur (Oldfield, 1989). In the past, most countries, including UK, USA, Australia and South Africa (Cubitt and Steele, 1980), have witnessed species extinction due to human activity but the problem has now become more pressing on a world scale.

Human beings have some choice about which species are to disappear. How should they choose in their life–and–death role? Certainly from an economic viewpoint, there is no categorical reason for preferring the preservation of a family over a genus or over a species, unless, of course, it is held that as a result of genetic engineering and other developments, the preservation of a family rather than a species will allow greater scope for mankind in manipulating biological diversity. However, the case has to be argued and choices still need to be made. Economists and social scientists with their interest in values can help identify factors that need to be taken into account in making a choice. These include a consideration of likely economic options that may be closed off by the disappearance of a species, the loss of its existence value and the disappearance of any existing economic activity that depends upon the presence of the species. Existing economic activities based upon the presence of species may include amongst other things their utilization for food and for recreation. A number of these issues are discussed further in Tisdell (1991, Ch. 5).

Other policies proposed in the WCS require further consideration, especially its recommendations in relation to agriculture. Trade–offs are not always correctly assessed and this leads to the recommendation of policies that do not efficiently achieve intended aims. I shall elaborate on this matter later but note that it has been common for ecologists writing on development to provide a catalogue of priorities without giving us firm guidance as to how conflicts between priorities are to be resolved and without looking fully at the interdependence of different systems (consider Dasmann and Poore, 1979; Dasmann, Milton and Freeman, 1973). In such cases, stated priorities may become an amalgam of prejudice and self–interest. Nevertheless, it is better to address a relevant problem improperly than to ignore it. Most economists became interested in the concept of sustainable development later than ecologists, and in the early stages of the development of the concept interaction between economists and ecologists was limited. Nevertheless some interaction between economists and biologists was present because of the dependence of certain areas of economics on biological information.

Agricultural economists interested in production must, as a rule, pay some attention to ecological and biological relationships. Fisheries and forestry economists and those interested in the utilization of living natural resources must consider ecological and biological constraints and relationships. An economist interested in the economics of pest control can hardly ignore ecological relationships (cf. Tisdell, 1982; Tisdell, Auld and Menz, 1984; Auld, Menz and Tisdell, 1987). This is also true of an economist interested in the economics of high–yielding varieties of crops. In such areas, the distinction between ecology and economics becomes rather artificial since many problems requiring solutions have to be considered from an overall perspective and may best be solved by a team, the members of which are trained in different disciplines.

ECONOMICS AND SUSTAINABILITY OF AGROECOSYSTEMS

Several ecologists have placed emphasis on the socio–economic importance of ensuring sustainable ecosystems. The work of Gordon Conway (1983a, 1983b) is interesting in this respect. Conway suggests, as pointed out in the previous chapter, that agricultural systems should be assessed on the basis of four properties:
– Productivity (measured in terms of yield or net income).
– Stability of yield or net income.
– Sustainability of yield or net income.
– Equitability in terms of income distribution.

If two alternative agricultural systems are being evaluated, Conway suggests that the one showing greater productivity, less instability of yield or net income, greater sustainability of yield or net income, and a more equitable distribution of income is to be preferred. However, it may be rare for the desirable attributes of one agricultural system to dominate another in this way. Often some attributes of one system are better than those of another and others are less desirable. For example, the yields on average of high–yielding varieties of crops may be greater than from traditional varieties but their yields or net incomes may be subject to greater instability, at risk of not being sustainable, and may lead to a more uneven distribution of income (Harrison, 1981; Harlan, 1977). Usually, we need guidelines about acceptable trade–offs of these characteristics.

As mentioned in the previous chapter, the sustainability of productive systems is for Conway about their resilience. In the case of agroecosystems it is about their ability to recover (in terms of levels of production or returns) from stress once the stress is removed. In addition in measuring productive systems we should also consider their ability to withstand or not to succumb to environmental stress or to do so only to a moderate degree. This might indicate the robustness of the system. In the illustration shown in Figure 10.1, the more sustainable system is both more resilient and more robust.

Since a number of general aspects of the sustainability of agroecosystems have already been discussed in Chapter 10, it may be useful here to consider some examples, relate these to the stability of equilibrium and to indicate why non–sustainable techniques may be adopted in a market system even when their discounted net present value is lower than for sustainable techniques of production.

Consider first the control of an agricultural pest, e.g. insect or weed, by the use of a chemical pesticide. The initial use of this pesticide may be very effective in reducing the pest population and could add significantly to agricultural production and returns. But after a time the targeted pest may develop increasing resistance to the pesticide necessitating increasing applications of the pesticide or resulting in rising populations of the pest or both. After a point, resistance of the pest to the pesticide may grow to such an extent that application of the pesticide is no longer economic. Once application stops, the population of the pest may climb to levels in excess of levels predating use of the pesticide and may remain permanently above levels prior to use of the pesticide e.g. because the pesticide has eliminated (as a by–product) a predator of the pest. The type of scenario shown in Figure 11.1 is possible.

In the absence of use of the pesticide the population of the pest might remain stationary at OA or follow the stationary or equilibrium path AH. Now suppose that the chemical pesticide is used at t_1 and that applications of it increase. The population of the pest may now follow the path BCD. The population at first declines but begins to rise again later as resistance to the chemical develops. The use of the chemical control creates disequilibrium in the system. At point t_2, use of the chemical control is no longer economic and is discontinued. The population size of the pest suddenly explodes, and may then decline, moving along path *EFG*. A new stationary equilibrium is established along *FG* and the stationary population level is now higher than before use of the chemical. Not only has the control been unsustainable but it has exacted an environmental penalty.

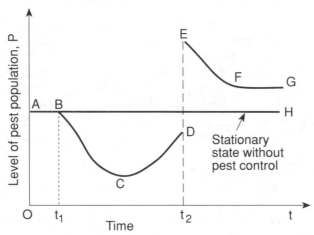

Figure 11.1   Use of a chemical pesticide to control the population of an agricultural pest may prove to be unsustainable.

It should be observed that even if the net present value from use of the pesticide to control the pest is less than relying on natural controls for each farmer privately, the pesticide may be used. Once it begins to be used by others, remaining farmers may need to use it for defensive economic reasons. For example, the price of the agricultural product may initially fall with use of the pesticide by some farmers. Farmers not using the pesticide may be forced to use it to avoid an economic loss. A type of prisoner's dilemma exists due to external effects. Defensive use of the pesticide becomes necessary by non–users so as to ensure their economic survival.

Of course, the chemical technique may be adopted for reasons other than the above. These may be ignorance about its long–term sustainability – it may be believed to be more sustainable than is in fact the case. Furthermore, chemical companies selling the pesticide have an incentive to push its use by advertising and promotion and this may create bias in favour of its use (Tisdell et al., 1984).

It is worth noting that farmers may become locked into 'unsustainable' agricultural systems once they are adopted because of the heavy initial costs of switching to more sustainable systems and the need for all to act simultaneously in the switching process if economic losses are to be avoided. This can be illustrated by Figure 11.2. There line *ABC* represents economic returns with a traditional organic agricultural technique. This shows, say, sustainability. As an alternative suppose that a modern non-organic technique can be adopted. If this is adopted at time t_1, returns might follow the path *ABDEF*. Initially they are well above that for the traditional technique but fall and eventually become smaller than with the traditional technique. However, return to the traditional technique may not be economically possible for an individual farmer (unless produce from the use of this technique sells with a high price premium) because there can be high withdrawal costs. For example, if a switch is attempted at t_2, the path *FGH* may be followed. If however, all farmers were to switch at t_2, the price of the product would rise normally and this would make switching easier from an economic viewpoint. The possibility of economic 'locking–in' occurring as a result of the adoption of unsustainable economic techniques should not be ignored (Tisdell, 1991, Ch. 9).

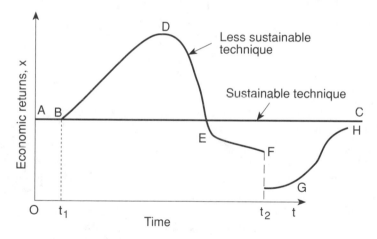

Figure 11.2 Producers may become locked into the use of a relatively unsustainable technique such as the less sustainable one indicated here.

Consider another example, namely land clearing for agricultural development in a tropical area to replace traditional land use. The effect of this may be to raise the value of production from the land initially. But the area may be subject to intermittent tropical downpours of heavy rain concentrated for example with the occurrence of cyclones or monsoons. The value of output from the land use may then follow patterns similar to those shown in Figure 11.3. With traditional land use, pattern *AJ* may prevail. The value of production falls as a result of the occurrence of tropical downpours but recovers. The modern system involving land clearing might result in pattern *ABCDEFGH*. Initially the value of production is high, but a tropical downpour seriously affects the value of production. While there is some recovery, the extent of recovery becomes smaller as further downpours are experienced and eventually the value of production falls   below that which is sustainable using traditional methods.

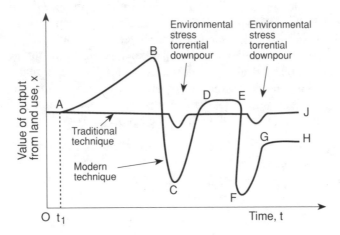

Figure 11.3   Environmental stress, e.g. caused by tropical downpours as a source of unsustainability of modern systems of land use.

To take one more possible case, consider the possible impact of grazing stock on the composition of plant species in an area. For simplicity assume that two species of plants exist in the area – one a species suitable for grazing and the other a weed species. The populations of these two species are interdependent. The population of the species for grazing as a function of the population of the weed species might be as indicated in Figure 11.4 by line *ABC*. The population of the weed species as a function of the species for grazing might be as indicated by curve *DFG*. Thus two equilibrium points exist in this model; one at E_1 and the other at E_2. Let $f_2(x)$ represent *ABC* and $f_2(x)$ represent curve *DFG*. Then if the weed population increases for $f_2(x)-f_1(x)>0$ and if the population of the fodder species increases for $f_1(x)-f_2(x)>0$ equilibrium E_1 is unstable and E_2 is stable.

In a virgin state, equilibrium E_1 may prevail. But the introduction of domestic grazing stock will reduce the population of the species used for grazing below its initial equilibrium value. Hence the population of the weed will increase and the system will gravitate to E_2 which is a stable equilibrium. In this model, any level of grazing means that the original equilibrium cannot be sustained.

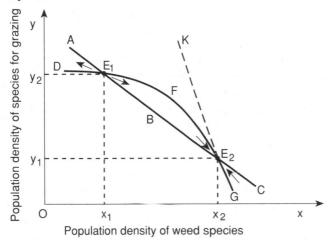

Figure 11.4   Grazing by domestic stock may result in unsustainable availability of species and plants used for grazing.

If after some time grazing is discontinued the system does not return to E_1. This would only be possible if active intervention were undertaken to reduce the population of the weed to x_1. However, it is also possible that grazing introduces a change in the interdependence of the species. For example, after a time curve *DFG* may be replaced by KE_2G. In that case complete irreversibility in species composition has been established.

Other examples could also be given. But this should be sufficient to indicate that a wider set of possibilities exists. In addition, the matter will be discussed further in the next section where more attention is given to market failure in relation to choice of sustainable techniques.

DIGRESSION ON THE RECOMMENDATIONS OF WCS CONCERNING AGRICULTURAL SYSTEMS

The *World Conservation Strategy* stated that agricultural systems are under particular threat from the economic activities of mankind. Serious losses of agriculturally productive land are claimed to occur because:

- man–made facilities, such as buildings, roads and airports are encroaching on agricultural land as urban growth proceeds;
- soil erosion is accelerating as a result of human activities and unwise farming practices;
- soil degradation is becoming more widespread, because human activities result in a spread of soil salinity, increased severity and frequency of flooding and loss of soil nutrients and suitable soil structure.

The WCS urged the governments and other bodies to encourage farmers to manage agricultural land on the basis of ecologically sound principles. In LDCs (less developed countries), the preference of WCS (IUCN, 1980) seemed to be for self–sufficient sustainable systems rather than those which rely on considerable energy and resource inputs from outside the farm or the country in question.

WCS recommended that governments should reserve good cropland for farming. This involves some system of zoning. However, zoning of this type could actually decrease food production because food is not produced by good cropland alone (Tisdell, 1983 or Chapter 14). Furthermore, such zoning may hamper the distribution of food and lower the total amount of food available for human consumption. For example, roads or other communication routes may have to go by circuitous routes to avoid good cropland. The extra resources that have to be withdrawn from food production to handle the extra transport might result in a greater reduction in food production than if transport were by a more direct route and at the expense of some good cropland. One should be wary of simplistic notions of economic production and not rush into zoning based on the WCS principles.

This is not to suggest that optimal decisions are already being made about the siting of human facilities and that land use is always socially optimal. Externalities are involved in many economic activities and government departments responsible for developing infrastructure do not always give adequate consideration to the social costs to the community of their proposals. There is a case for zoning and restrictions on land use in some cases, such as the removal of natural vegetation in areas subject to high erosion risks. However, caution is needed, for extensive zoning may become an impediment to economic progress and, unless carefully devised, can interfere with the fulfilment of its objectives.

SOME FURTHER AGRICULTURAL DEVELOPMENT CONSIDERATIONS

In the past, many economists have taken a mechanical approach in recommending means for the development of less developed areas. The provision of capital and industrially produced inputs such as fertilizer have been seen as extremely important as a means for raising agricultural productivity. Less attention has been given to the sustainability of such developments. Even on the question of reforms in land ownership, the security or sustainability characteristics of alternative forms have not always been juxtaposed with their alternative productivity characteristics. Ecologists are playing a useful role in suggesting that matters of this type need more consideration.

Erskine (1985) has pointed out the importance of combining socio-economic and ecological factors in considering the development of rural areas in South Africa. Whether or not one agrees with his basic thesis, his article makes it clear that the protection of agricultural resources in many areas is dependent on socio-economic developments. He argues that modernization of agriculture and the conversion of the subsistence economy in areas where it exists to a market-oriented economy would help in reducing soil erosion. He suggests that, if this is combined with rapid urbanization, it might act as a brake on rates of population increase and reduce the crowding of population cultivating the land. On the other hand, of course, it would make the population concerned subject to vagaries in the fluctuation of the market system.

Unlike Erskine (1985) not all ecologists see modern agricultural systems as more sustainable than traditional ones. Conway (1983a, 1983b) argues that traditional agricultural systems have a high sustainability whereas modern systems have low sustainability but higher productivity compared with traditional systems. However, it is doubtful whether one can generalize in this way. For instance, systems of shifting agriculture may be quite sustainable when human populations are low but can become unsustainable when population densities rise. As a result of rising population levels, the period may become shortened in which land is allowed to reafforest and rejuvenate, and serious erosion and soil-nutrient loss may occur. Some modern agricultural techniques would appear to have favourable environmental impacts and to make for sustainability. For instance, some low tillage or minimum tillage agricultural system can have this effect. Other systems involving intensive cultivation and tree removal may accelerate the rate of soil erosion or environmental degradation.

Like Erskine, Schultz (1974) argues that modern agriculture makes for a more stable environment and suggests that the vulnerability of the plains states of the United States to dust storms has been substantially reduced by modernization of agriculture there. Nevertheless all modern agriculture techniques do not make for a more stable environment and greater sustainability of agricultural production. There is a wide range of modern agricultural techniques and systems as well as a variety of traditional ones. While some modern agricultural techniques and systems result in greater sustainability of production than traditional ones, the reverse is so for others. Furthermore, the sustainability of production and the desirability of an agricultural system can vary with surrounding conditions, such as variations in population levels. There is one sense in which most modern agricultural systems are less sustainable than most traditional ones; they are much more dependent on the use of non–renewable resources for their maintenance. This includes fossil fuels such as oil, chemical fertilizers and chemical pesticides. Modern agricultural techniques essentially create and maintain artificial environments for cultivated plants and domestic stock (Oldfield, 1989) and usually these environments require large inputs of energy for their maintenance. They can only be sustained wherever supplies of non–renewable resources can be maintained. Furthermore, modern agricultural systems generally rely on a long chain of dependence for supply of a number of their essential inputs. Thus farmers lack self–sufficiency or near self–sufficiency and are vulnerable to any problems that arise in the chain of economic dependence.

Sustainability of production systems is of great importance in less developed areas where populations are relatively immobile and limited or little or no aid is available for the relief of individual economic misfortunes (Tisdell, 1985 or Chapter 15). This is likely to be the case in much of rural Africa and Asia.

In conclusion, it can be seen that economics and ecology are related and complex sciences. Both subjects need to be combined in dealing with the use of agricultural resources, the conservation and utilization of living resources and the development of rural communities. The difficult concept of sustainable economic development may prove to be a common rallying point for these subjects (Tisdell, 1985 or Chapter 15).

The usefulness of sustainability characteristics has already been demonstrated in assessing agricultural techniques. The next chapter will discuss the concept further looking at its wider ramifications, e.g. for medicine and further developing this economic theory about optimal use of techniques, the effectiveness of which cannot be sustained.

REFERENCES

Auld, B.A., Menz, K. and Tisdell, C.A. (1987) *Weed Control Economics*, Academic Press, London.

Barney, G.O. (1980) *The Global 2000 Report to the President of the U.S. Entering the 21st Century,* Pergamon, New York.

Boulding, K. (1950) *A Reconstruction of Economics*, Wiley, New York.

Boulding, K. (1980) 'The Economics of the Coming Spaceship Earth', Daly, H. (ed.), *Economics, Ecology and Ethics*, Freeman, San Francisco.

Brown, L.R. and Shaw, P. (1982) *Six Steps to a Sustainable Society*, Worldwatch Institute, Washington.

Caldwell, L.K. (1984) 'Political Aspects of Ecologically Sustainable Development', *Environmental Conservation*, 11(4).

Ciriacy–Wantrup, S.V. (1968) *Resource Conservation: Economics and Policies*. Division of Agricultural Science, University of California, Berkeley.

Conway, G.R. (1983a) *Applying Ecology*, Centre for Environmental Technology, Imperial College, London.

Conway G.R. (1983b) *Agroecosystems Analysis*, ICCET, Series E(1), Imperial College, London.

Cubitt, G. and Steele, D. (1980) *South African Wildlife and Wilderness*, Don Nelson, Cape Town.

Daly, H.E. (1980) *Economics, Ecology, Ethics*, Freeman, San Francisco.

Dasmann, R.F. Milton, J.P. and Freeman, P.H., (1973) *Ecological Principles for Economic Development*, John Wiley, New York.

Dasmann, R.F. and Poore, R. (1979) *Ecological Guidelines for Balanced Land Use, Conservation and Development in High Mountains*, IUCN, Gland, Switzerland.

Erskine, J.M. (1985) 'Ecology and Development', *Development Southern Africa*, 2(1).

Harlan, J.R. (1977) 'The Plants and Animals that Nourish Man', *Scientific American* book, *Food and Agriculture*, Freeman, San Francisco.

Harrison, P. (1981) *Inside the Third World*, Penguin, Harmondsworth.

Hirshleifer, J. (1977) 'Economics from a Biological Viewpoint', *The Journal of Law and Economics*, 30.

IUCN (1980) *World Conservation Strategy*, IUCN, Gland, Switzerland.

IUCN–UNEP–WWF (1991) *Caring for the Earth: a Strategy for Sustainable Living*, IUCN, Gland, Switzerland.

Kneese, A. Ayres, R.V. and D'Arge, R. (1970) *Economics and the Environment*, Johns Hopkins, Baltimore.

Malthus, T.R. (1798) *An Essay on the Principle of Population as it Affects the Future Improvement of Mankind*, J. Johnson, London.

Marshall, A. (1930) *Principles of Economics*, 8th ed., Macmillan, London.

Mentis, M.T. (1984) 'White Paper on Agricultural Policy', *South African Journal of Science*, 80.

Oldfield, M.I. (1989) *The Value of Conserving Genetic Resources*, Sinauer Associates, Sunderland, Mass.

Pearce, D.W. (1976) *Environmental Economics*, Longman, London.

Pigou, A.C. (1932) *Economics of Welfare*, 3rd ed., Macmillan, London.

Poore, D.W. (1976) *Ecological Guidelines for Development in Tropical Rain Forests*, IUCN, Morges.

Ricardo, D. (1817) *The Principles of Political Economy and Taxation*, London.

Schultz, T.W. (1974) 'Is Modern Agriculture Consistent with a Stable Environment?' International Association of Agricultural Economics, *The Future of Agriculture: Technology, Policies and Adjustment*, Agricultural Economics Institute, Oxford.

Tisdell, C.A. (1982) *Wild Pigs: Economic Resource or Environmental Pest?*, Pergamon Press, Sydney.

Tisdell, C.A. (1983) 'An Economist's Critique of the World Conservation Strategy, with Examples from Australian Experience', *Environmental Conservation*, 10(1), pp. 43–52.

Tisdell, C.A., Auld, B. and Menz, K.M. (1984) 'On Assessing the Biological Control of Weeds', *Protection Ecology*, 6, pp. 169–79.

Tisdell, C.A. (1985) 'World Conservation Strategy, Economic Policies and Sustainable Resource–use in Developing Countries', *Environmental Professional*, 7, pp. 102–7.

Tisdell, C.A. (1991) *Economics of Environmental Conservation*, Elsevier Science Publishers, Amsterdam.

WCED (World Commission on Environment and Development) (1987) *Our Common Future*, Oxford University Press, New York.

Worster, D. (1985) *Nature's Economy: A History of Ecological Ideas*, Cambridge University Press, Cambridge, UK.

12. Exploitation of Techniques that Decline in Effectiveness with Use

Many techniques decline in overall or global effectiveness with their increased use. This is especially evident for various techniques to control living things, for instance, the use of penicillin or drugs to control certain diseases. In time, pathogens may, by natural selection and other means, build up resistance to strains of penicillin and to drugs employed to treat or prevent disease. Furthermore, biological control of pests may encounter similar resistance problems. For example, with the continued use of myxomatosis virus to control rabbits in Australia, rabbits have developed resistance to the earlier strains and the continuing effectiveness of the virus has become increasingly dependent on the development of new strains.

However, it should not be thought that species only develop resistance to biological controls. Natural selection can also result in a species developing resistance to chemical, physical, or other types of control. The more resistant members of a species to chemical controls (for instance flies more resistant to fly poisons) may increase in proportion to the total population with the use of the chemical controls.

In the treatment or prevention of diseases and in the control of pests of various kinds, a decline in the effectiveness of techniques with their increased use is common. This raises an important social problem.

Individuals are inclined to use such techniques more quickly or frequently than is socially optimal. This is because from the individual's point of view there is negligible decline in the effectiveness of the technique with his/her use of it. The effectiveness impact is mostly external to the individual. For example, if there are a million users of the technique, the decline in effectiveness of the technique is shared with 999,999 other individuals. Even though the effect on each may be almost negligible, it may be significant overall. The small individual effects (possibly below the thresholds of perception of many individuals) plus the unfavourable externality may result in greater and earlier use of the technique than is socially optimal. But even if users are aware of the unfavourable externality, acting individually they are unlikely to restrict the use of the technique for the collective good. This is because the problem is akin to the prisoner's dilemma problem (Luce and Raiffa 1957, pp. 94–101).

From a self–interest point of view, each individual has an incentive to use the technique to the optimal extent from his/her own selfish point of view. His/her actions are not materially affected by whether others moderate their use or not. Consequently no individual is likely to moderate his or her use of the technique even though it may be in the collective interest for all to moderate their use of the technique.

The use of antibiotics in stock foods provides another illustration of the problem. As a result of the use of antibiotics in such food, animals make greater weight gains in relation to food consumed. However, as the exposure of pathogens to antibiotics increases, the resistance of pathogens rises, and in the end some of the antibiotics may become useless for treating particular diseases of livestock or humans. But no individual farmer has an incentive if the antibiotic is cheap enough to omit it from the food for his/her livestock. His/her decision is not affected, if he/she acts in his/her own selfish interest, by whether other farmers add the antibiotic or not to their stock food. In the absence of government regulation, the antibiotic is liable to be overused from a collective point of view.

The purpose of this chapter is to examine some simple models that illustrate the phenomenon of decreasing effectiveness of a technique and the social optimality of its use. Models are considered in which the effectiveness of the technique declines with the number of exposures or 'doses', and with the duration of use. Thus it provides specific models for analysing sustainability issues.

The models provide an illustrative introduction to the role of the government in the regulation of drug use and indeed in controlling the application of remedies of all kinds where the effectiveness of the remedies falls collectively with their use. This chapter is concerned with collective protection rather than with the safeguarding of (individual) consumers from unwanted and unknown (self–centred) side–effects of drugs or other techniques.

The models considered are polar extremes. In the case of the quantity–dependent model of effectiveness (discussed in the next section), the technique goes from being fully effective as a remedy for those cases treated to being completely ineffective once the quantity of collective doses exceeds a specified amount. In practice one might expect the degree of effectiveness to decline gradually as the number of doses is increased. In some cases, the treatment may not be completely effective initially and as the quantity of use increases may fall but not necessarily to zero, if effectiveness is measured by say the percentage of cases cured after treatment to total number of cases treated. In more realistic models, greater attention would need to be paid to what constitutes effectiveness, e.g., what account should be taken of possible variations in time required for a cure as a technique becomes less effective. Other relevant definitions of effectiveness are also possible.

In the time dependent model (discussed in the section following the next one) effectiveness is assumed to alter from fully effective to zero after a specified period of use. Once again, this is an extreme assumption.

It is difficult to imagine relevant processes that are solely quantity–dependent or solely time dependent for their collective effectiveness. However, some cases of biological pest control may be heavily time–dependent for their effectiveness. For example, once the nucleus population of a predator of a pest is established in a country, the predator may be left to expand its population by natural means. Its effectiveness in altering the population of the pest then tends to be time–dependent.

In practice, the quantity of exposures to a new control technique and their time–pattern need to be simultaneously considered, as for example is apparent from the following hypothetical case: Suppose that in a population of a pathogen or pest y per cent of the initial population is completely resistant to a new treatment or control and that the remainder shows no resistance. If the number of doses is such that the whole population of pathogens or pests is exposed initially, $1-y$ per cent of the initial population is destroyed. The future then of the pathogens or pests depends on the dynamics of population change of the resistant group in the initial population. Is this reservoir sufficient to enable the population of the species to recover? If so, how long will recovery take and will the resistant group become as common as the earlier population consisting of resistant and non–resistant varieties? Where the resistant group eventually replaces the non–resistant one, the effectiveness of the treatment might be judged in relation to the reduction in the pathogen or pest population in the interval that elapses before replacement is completed. What is the likely impact on the pathogen or pest population when the scale of treatment is such that the whole population is not exposed initially? Indeed, what are the effects on pathogen and pest populations of different rates of exposure to a treatment or control over time? The answers to such questions depend on biological data, experimentation, and enquiry. The problems to be modelled are likely to be more complex than those considered in the next two sections. However, it is useful as a basis for further enquiry to consider problems of regulation that arise even in simplified cases.

DECLINE OF EFFECTIVENESS OF TECHNIQUE WITH NUMBER OF EXPOSURES

One of the simplest models is that in which the effectiveness of a new technique only lasts for a given number of exposures or doses. The 'resource', the potential effectiveness of the technique, is therefore of a finite quantity like a given mineral reserve. There is some finite quantity or 'stock' of doses available before the technique becomes entirely ineffective. But this stock is common property.

Given the externality, the technique in any period can be expected to be used in a competitive market or when it is known freely to all and can be applied at constant cost, up to the level where demand for it in the period equals the marginal direct cost of applying it. In this case, there is common or open access to the technique as such.

Thus in a single period case, where in Figure 12.1, D_1D_1 represents the demand for doses and S_1S_1 is the per unit cost of supplying the doses, $\bar{x}_1$ is the number of exposures likely to be made to the technique. In appropriate cases (such as pest control) the D_1D_1 can be interpreted as the value of the marginal product of doses of the technique, assuming that the technique remains effective.

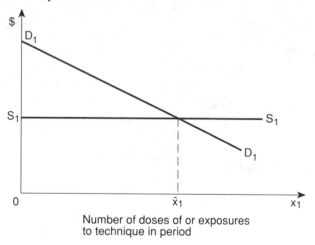

Number of doses of or exposures
to technique in period

Figure 12.1   Use of a technique in an industry where there is common access to it but it remains effective despite the extent of its use.

Suppose that the technique is only effective for $\bar{x}_1$ exposures and that the relevant planning interval consists of two periods, namely, period one and period two. If $\bar{x}_1$ exposures of the technique occur in period one, the

technique is ineffective in period two. The problem is to regulate the
number of exposures in period one so that the social gain from the use of
the technique is maximized for the whole planning period.

If the discounted demand curve and discounted per unit cost curves in
period two turn out to be the same as those in period one, then in order
to maximize the discounted surplus (consumers' or producers' surpluses as
the case may be) the number of exposures to the technique should be the
same in period two as in period one, namely $0.5 \ \bar{x}_1$ exposures. This
ensures that the demand for using the technique in period one, D_1D_1, less
the marginal cost of using it, S_1S_1, is equal to the discounted demand for
use of the technique in period two less the marginal discounted cost of
applying it, S_2S_2. This is the necessary condition for maximizing the
discounted surplus.

The optimal number of exposures per period is illustrated in Figure
12.2. This optimality could be achieved by the government imposing a
tax of AB on each application of the technique in period one and a tax
having a present value of JH on each application in period two.

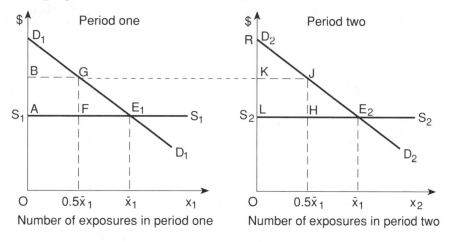

*Figure 12.2   Common or open access to a technique which declines in
effectiveness with the number of times it is used results under perfect
competition in its excessive use at an early stage in its adoption.*

The social gain from optimal government interference in the application
of the technique can be expected to be greater the more inelastic is
demand for exposures to the technique or the faster is the decline in its
value of marginal product, other things equal, relative to say the fixed
points E_1 and E_2. In other words, the steeper are the curves D_1D_1 and
D_2D_2 in Figure 12.2, assuming E_1 and E_2 are fixed points, the greater is

the deadweight social loss or Kaldor–Hicks loss in the absence of government restriction of the use of the technique. In the case illustrated in Figure 12.2, the deadweight loss in the absence of regulation is equal to the area of quadrilateral *LHJR* minus the area of triangle FE_1G. Because in this case, the area of triangle FE_1G equals that of triangle *KJR*, the deadweight loss is equal to the area of rectangle *LHJK*. Because *JH* increases in length and *LH* remains unchanged in length as the demand curves become steeper, the area of *LHJK*, the amount of deadweight loss, rises.

Other things equal, the lower the per unit costs of applying the technique, the more likely is it that a greater than socially optimal number of exposures will be made at an early stage. Thus the more likely is it that optimal government regulation will be a social advantage. For example, in the case shown in Figure 12.2, if S_1S_1 happened to pass through *BG* and S_2S_2 through *KJ*, a socially optimal number of applications of the technique are made in each period.

Therefore it appears that the greatest potential social gain can be expected from government regulation in the use of techniques that decline in collective effectiveness with use, (a) when the technique is of very great value in each period for a limited number of cases or a small group but is of much less value for other cases or groups and/or (b) when the per unit cost of each application of the technique is low.

In the particular case illustrated in Figure 12.2, if monopoly rights exist in the application of the technique, a socially optimal pattern of exposure from a Kaldor–Hicks viewpoint occurs. The monopolist maximizes his/her profit by permitting 0.5 $\bar{x}_1$ exposures to the technique in each period. Thus he/she charges *AB* for each use of the technique in period one, making the total cost to the user *OB*.

However, monopoly does not necessarily result in a socially optimal amount of exposure. A monopolist may restrict the use of a technique unduly from a social point of view. If the above technique is effective for 1.9 $\bar{x}_1$ exposures rather than $\bar{x}_1$ in the whole of the planning period, the monopolist in order to maximize his/her profit will restrict the exposures to 0.5 $\bar{x}_1$ in each period whereas the discounted surplus is maximized by 0.95 $\bar{x}_1$ exposures in each period.

The above ignores the possibility that new effective techniques will be discovered during the planning period. The greater this possibility, the more desirable is exposure of the known technique during its early life. Conversely, the less the likelihood of the continuing discovery of effective techniques, the greater is the social desirability of conserving the effectiveness of existing techniques, and the greater the need for public regulation to limit the application of a technique that declines in effectiveness with use.

While the above is clearly a very simplified model, it has served its main purpose of illustrating the nature of the problem. A more complicated model could, for example, be built by allowing the parameters of the demand function or the value of marginal product function for period two to vary with the size of x_1.

TECHNIQUES DECLINING IN EFFECTIVENESS WITH DURATION OF USE

Another interesting limiting case is that in which the effectiveness of a technique declines solely with the duration of its use. A number of patterns of decline in effectiveness are conceivable. For example if unity represents complete effectiveness, the index of effectiveness of a technique might take the form e^{-rt}, where r is a constant and t is the duration of exposure.

Given common or open access to a technique, it is likely to be adopted prematurely from a collective point of view when its effectiveness declines with its duration of use. The technique is likely to be applied (once it is known) as soon as the gain from using it in any period exceeds the cost of doing so, even though greater collective gains can be made by delaying its use. This can be seen from a simple case.

Suppose the discovery of a technique with the discounted per unit costs of use in both period one and period two as indicated in Figure 12.3 by curve SS. Assume that the technique is effective only for one period. In period one the demand for application of the technique (or the value of its marginal product in some cases) is as indicated by D_1D_1 and in period two the discounted demand curve for it is D_2D_2. If the planning interval consists of two periods, surplus is maximized by confining the use of the technique to period two. However, under competitive conditions or open access to the technique, it will be used in period one to the extent x_1, and will yield a surplus equivalent to the dotted area. If on the other hand, it is delayed in use until period two, the surplus will be equal to the dotted plus the hatched area. Hence, it is socially optimal to delay application of the technique until period two.

Although optimal delay in the application of the technique does not occur under perfect competition or open access to the technique, monopoly results in optimal delay in this particular case. A firm with a monopoly of the application of the technique maximizes its gains from sale of rights to use the technique by delaying application of the technique until period two.

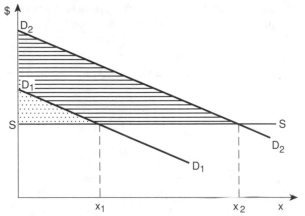

Number of exposures to or doses of the technique

Figure 12.3   Given open access to a technique it is likely to be used prematurely under perfect competition when its effectiveness falls with the duration of its application.

Even so the monopolist restricts application of the technique. In order to maximize his/her profit, the monopolist allows only $1/2x_2$ applications of the technique in period two, and a deadweight loss occurs. Consumers' plus producers' surplus would be maximized by x_2 applications of the technique in period two, and this comes about if there is open access to the technique in period two. Despite the better timing by the monopolist, it is possible (because of the restrictive action of the monopolist) for consumers' surplus plus producers' surplus to be less under monopoly than under open access to technology with poor timing in its application. The total surplus under monopoly is more likely to be lower than under open access, the closer curve D_1D_1 is to D_2D_2 in the above case. Monopoly is not necessarily a superior social solution to open access to new technology that declines in effectiveness with use.

This, however, brings us back to a central issue in economics. The invention of new techniques may not be independent of the right to exploit them. One justification sometimes put forward for the patent system is that it speeds up invention. Thus policies need to be devised taking into account both issues.

In theory, the government should be able to obtain the socially optimal use of the technique. This could be done by prohibiting its use in period one and allowing open access to it in period two. The greater the value placed upon the application of the technique in a later period rather than earlier (as indicated by the hatched area in Figure 12.3) or the larger the difference in consumers' surplus between that attainable by application of the technique in a later period rather than an earlier one, the greater the scope for a social gain from the government delaying the use of a technique the collective effectiveness of which declines with use. The difference in consumers' surplus tends to be larger the greater is demand and the more inelastic is demand in the later period compared to the earlier one.

In the examples discussed so far, the collective effects have provided a possible reason for governments to restrain the use of techniques or remedies. However, collective effects can give rise to special circumstances in which it may be optimal for the government to speed up the rate of application of a technique or remedy, and this might be achieved by a subsidy on its application. For example, in the case considered at the end of the introductory section, if the technique is capable of reducing the population of the pathogen or pest to a level where it does not recover, a social gain may be made by ensuring that aggregate application of the technique is on such a scale and made with a timing that ensures that the population is reduced to the critical level. It might be noted that in circumstances such as this, monopoly would reduce the chances of an optimal solution being achieved in the absence of public interference.

The discussion makes it clear that the collective or public good aspects of the application of certain techniques or control remedies can leave scope for the government to increase social welfare by regulating the timing and rate of application of such techniques. This is so even though the actual relationships involved may sometimes be complex and uncertain.

CONCLUSION

When there is open or common access to a technique that declines in effectiveness with use, it is likely to be exploited more quickly than is socially optimal. The first application of it may occur at an earlier date than socially optimal and it is liable early in its use to be employed on a greater scale than is socially optimal. If monopoly rights are established in the technique this may improve the timing of its use from a social point of view. But a deadweight loss will occur and when this is taken into account the monopoly may not constitute a social improvement from the Kaldor–Hicks point of view. On the other hand, the possibility of obtaining a monopoly may speed up the rate of invention and this tends to make the monopoly solution to the problem more attractive, even though it is not a perfect solution.

In principle, the government could obtain the perfect solution by regulating the use of known techniques and providing inducements for the discovery of new ones. But the knowledge of government officials is not perfect and government is subject to political pressures. Indeed, the myopia of democratic governments may tend if timing of the use of techniques is under their control to speed up the application of techniques of declining effectiveness in use rather than delay their use in an optimal way. At least, we cannot assume perfect government is the way out of the problem.

Nevertheless governments have at least begun to attack the problem at the margin. In some countries, for example, the use of particular antibiotics in stock food is prohibited. But governments have been reluctant to regulate use of drugs or treatments in the medical and veterinary field where their excessive use reduces the collective effectiveness of the techniques. This raises the question of the extent to which individual doctors and veterinarians are likely to consider collective welfare in prescribing treatments. It is not unlikely that each operates on an individualistic self–interest basis and that some drugs, antibiotics, and treatments are overprescribed when account is taken of the induced reduction in their collective effectiveness. The problem, therefore, is one worthy of continuing consideration. The general issues discussed here apply not only to medical technologies, but to agriculture, silviculture and other industries.

By identifying additional mechanisms that make for lack of sustainability in the effectiveness of economic activities, this chapter adds to the debate about sustainability. It also does this by directly identifying market failures, such as externalities due to the existence of common–property characteristics, which make for lack of sustainability. It is apparent from this chapter and from this part of this book that the concept of sustainability of economic activity is multi–dimensional and that in specific contexts it is not an amorphous concept. The need now is to define and measure its different dimensions more precisely. When this is done, the concept will prove not to be a 'flash–in–the–pan' and to have policy implications both at microeconomic and macroeconomic levels.

REFERENCE

Luce, R.D. and Raiffa, H. (1957) *Games and Decisions: Introduction and Critical Survey*, John Wiley, New York.

PART V

Environmental Policies and Global Conservation

13. Ecological Economics and Major Policy Issues

Economics studies the relationship between the social administration or management of resources and scarcity. Scarcity arises because available resources are insufficient to satisfy human wants. Consequently one of the main contributions of economics is to suggest institutional and other changes (such as variations in market or political mechanisms, or in some cases the introduction or withdrawal of social mechanisms) to improve the management of resources in order to reduce scarcity.

Economists have claimed that there are four main ways to reduce economic scarcity (see for example, Kohler, 1977; Tisdell, 1982). These are:

(1) by improving the allocation of resources between alternative uses so that the efficiency of the economic system in satisfying human wants is increased,

(2) by ensuring full employment of all persons wanting to work for the value of their addition to production (that is, by eliminating involuntary unemployment of labour),

(3) by promoting economic growth, and

(4) as far as relative scarcity is concerned, by improving the distribution of income.

Basically, pursuit of the first three goals increases the size of the economic cake, whereas the pursuit of the last goal leads to a more equitable sharing of the economic cake.

Now, however, it is realized that at least one of the suggested means for reducing scarcity may add to the problem. Economic growth may add to the problem of scarcity because it may not be sustainable. While economic growth may reduce scarcity in the short or medium term, it could result in much greater economic scarcity in the long term due to depletion of non-renewable resources and to the irreversible environmental deterioration caused by it. Thus economic growth of the past, which has been seen by many as the surest way to economic salvation for mankind, is being questioned. Economic growth may result in increased scarcity in the long term. It may not lead to a socially

189

satisfying society in terms of interpersonal relationships and self–development. It may have unacceptable environmental consequences, for example, it may result in the extinction of an unacceptably large number of species of other living things. Such issues have been debated by those interested in ecological or green economics since at least the early 1970s, but it is only in the 1990s that there has been widespread interest in such issues.

WHAT IS ECOLOGICAL OR GREEN ECONOMICS?

Different individuals have different ideas about what ecological or green economics is or should be. For some ecological economics is no more than an alternative name for environmental economics or even natural resource economics. In practice, studies in all of these areas overlap considerably in subject matter. But basically ecological economics places much more emphasis than these other subjects on the importance of living things as a means for sustaining economic activity, on the need to protect the biosphere and on the importance of conserving living things in order to achieve or retain a desirable world.

The conservation of living things, even those not presently utilized by mankind, is central to ecological or green economics. While ecological economics can be regarded as a part of environmental economics, it differs from environmental economics because of its greater emphasis on living things as being important for future economic development, for sustaining economic production, and/or for the creation or maintenance of a 'good society'. Since living things, especially humans, rely on the use of non–renewable resources to maintain their current state of existence, the depletion of non–renewable resources (such as fossil fuels) is also of concern to ecological economists. Indeed, some ecological economists see the conservation of energy as being the prime issue requiring attention. While the rate of use of energy resources is an important issue, I do not see it as the prime issue. The problem of maintaining biological diversity is a more important issue.

Since the United Nations Conference on the Human Environment was held in Helsinki in 1972, interest in the relationship between economic development and the environment has passed through two phases. The first in the 1970s was concerned principally with the imminent prospect of exhaustion of non–renewable resources, such as fossil fuels, and with increasing levels of pollution arising from economic activity. These fears were fanned by the oil crises of the period and the pessimistic global predictions of the Club of Rome (cf. Forrester, 1971; Meadows, et al., 1972) of exhaustion of many non–renewable resources in as little as 50 years. The second phase of interest in conservation and economic development began in the 1980s and is continuing. It is characterized by much greater interest in the conservation of the living environment, in the protection of the biosphere and in the maintenance of biodiversity. The publication of the *World Conservation Strategy* document by the World Conservation Union (IUCN) in 1980 marks the beginning of this new phase. In this new phase, ecological economics has become central.

Some ecological economists claim that ecological economics should be distinguished from other branches of economics because of its methodology. It is not committed to traditional economic paradigms or existing economic methods. Most ecological economists accept that the world is complex and that the same problem often needs to be studied from several different points of view to obtain an adequate appreciation of it. In this respect Costanza (1989) has said: 'there is probably not one right approach or paradigm, because like the blind man and the elephant, the subject is too big and complex to touch it all with one limited set of perception tools'. Norgaard (1989, p. 37) claims that 'all aspects of complex systems can only be understood through multiple methodologies. Since ecological economics seeks to understand a larger system than either economics or ecology seeks to understand, a diversity of methodologies is appropriate and pressure to eliminate methodologies for the sake of conformity should be avoided'. A similar view has also been recently expressed by Soderbaum (1990) in contrasting neo–classical and institutional approaches to environmental economics.

Most ecological economists believe that dominant existing paradigms with their roots in neoclassical, Keynesian or Marxian economics are inadequate for dealing with the environmental and economic development problems facing the world today. Keynesian economists did not raise environmental issues. They did not feature in Marxian economics even though Marx himself did point to the human trauma that can arise if industrialization and urbanization alienate man from nature. But in practice Marx and his followers such as Engels were anti–Malthusian and pro–economic growth. They rejected the views of Thomas Robert Malthus (1798) that human population is liable to outstrip the means of subsistence. They argued that while the level of human population may increase in geometrical progression, as suggested by Malthus, scientific knowledge increases in faster geometric progression and nothing is impossible to science (Engels, 1959, p. 204). In their view, scientific advance and capital accumulation can be relied on to overcome any resource constraints that might be encountered as human populations increase. They were technological optimists. Indeed, commencing in the last half of the nineteenth century, the bulk of economists, no matter what their persuasion (neoclassical, Keynesian, Marxian or otherwise), have been technological optimists.

In the case of neoclassical economic thought (the predominant current school of economic thought in the West which usually extols the economic virtues of the market system), environmental impacts of economic activity were mainly treated as minor until at least the 1960s. Environmental spillovers from economic activity were seen as examples of economic externalities. Followers of the English economist Pigou (1932) suggested that the presence of externalities in a market economy calls for a limited degree of government intervention involving, for example, taxes on unfavourable externalities such as pollution. On the other hand, members of the Chicago School of economics, opposed in general to government intervention, argued that the frequency and size of external effects from economic activity are often exaggerated and that in any case, they usually disappear if private property rights are clearly defined and extended to cover environmental resources (cf. Coase, 1960). However, the Chicago School recognized that in some cases, the costs of establishing private property rights or of the government intervening might exceed the benefits of doing so. In such cases, Chicago economists suggested that it would be best from an economic view to manage with an existing imperfect economic system and without government intervention. Hence, from both points of view, the Chicago School sees little need for direct government intervention in the economy.

As for the use of non-renewable resources, neoclassical economists claim that, on the whole, the market mechanism leads to the optimal conservation of such resources, provided that property rights are 'correctly' established. Thus, the general thrust of recent neoclassical economic thought is that if market forces are allowed to operate and the market system is extended as widely as possible, few serious environmental and resource problems will occur and little direct government intervention will be needed.

This basically *laissez-faire* point of view is questioned by the neo-Malthusians, those who believe that unless positive action is taken by governments and other economic agents, considerable economic scarcity will occur in the future due to resource depletion or to pollution brought about by overconsumption and overpopulation of the globe by humans. Neo-Malthusians include Paul and Ann Ehrlich (1977), Hermann Daly (1968), Georgescu-Roegen (1971), Mishan (1967) and Perrings (1987).

Neo–Malthusians focus attention on resource and environmental problems which were largely ignored or dismissed by neoclassical economists and by most economists prior to the great environmental debate which began in the 1970s. Most economists did not see overconsumption as a problem from the point of view of scarcity. Indeed, it was considered desirable for the economic system to be geared towards greater consumption because individuals (humans) could then have more of what they wanted to satisfy their needs. Greater consumption by humans was seen as the sole end of economic activity, if not of all activity. This view can be traced back to Adam Smith (1910) who, in arguing against the mercantilist system of economics, emphasized that consumption is the sole end of economic activity, that is, consumption by the whole population of the nation. Basically, the aim of mercantilists was to suggest economic measures to enhance or maintain the power (and wealth) of the prince or the king rather than that of the whole community.

THE NEED FOR A NEW PERSPECTIVE

At the time when Adam Smith wrote, life was short and probably brutish for most people. There was a constant struggle to satisfy even basic economic needs. Mankind was at Nature's mercy then. Today the position seems broadly to be the other way around. At the time, it seemed appropriate to emphasize the importance of increasing the material economic welfare of all by increasing their consumption of desired commodities. But per capita consumption levels in developed countries today greatly exceed those of these earlier times. Consumption levels are much greater than is needed to satisfy basic needs and for most permit a measure of luxury. Indeed, the health and welfare of some individuals in developed countries suffers as a result of their 'excessive' consumption of commodities and as a result of their restless and never–ending desire for greater income and levels of material consumption. Therefore, it is legitimate to question in the case of the more developed countries whether an even higher level of material consumption per head is an appropriate goal.

Furthermore economists know, for example, from empirical studies estimating Engel curves, that as the incomes of individuals rise, the type of commodities demanded by them alters. We know that as the incomes (and educational attainment) of individuals rise, they demand proportionately more environmentally provided commodities. As incomes rise, we expect individuals to demand a lower proportion of material goods and a higher proportion of services including non–consumptive goods such as those provided by natural environments. Often the services provided by natural environments can only be retained through government intervention.

There are also other reasons why we need a new perspective. Today we face the prospects on a global scale of irreversible environmental impacts from economic activity of which the greenhouse phenomenon is just one example. Not only this, we are uncertain about the occurrence of such impacts, their rate of onset and their likely consequences. We face the possibility of sudden and irreversible jumps in environmental conditions. Past trends and signs may provide little forewarning of approaching economic and environmental collapse due to resource depletion and environmental degradation. By the time signs of future collapse become apparent, it may already be too late to reverse the deteriorating situation and avoid catastrophe.

The great English economist Alfred Marshall (1890) was able to declare in the last century that 'Nature does not proceed by leaps and bounds'. In his framework of thought, marginal certain change is almost assured. But now we fear that nature may sometimes proceed by leaps and bounds and can do so in unpredictable ways and irreversibly.

Since the effects of environmental change can be widespread, even global, we all can be affected. Thus, we all have a stake in what is happening to the environment. Essentially the global environment is a shared resource so the use of it can never be an entirely individualistic matter. Resolving our conflicts about the use of our shared environment is no easy matter since many of us have different attitudes to risk taking and uncertainty and we differ in the relative gains and losses that we individually are likely to make in taking risks with this environment. This has to be recognized in our decisions about resource use.

Humans have come to dominate nature but are still subject to its basic laws. There is no guarantee that mankind will be able to sustain and expand economic activity in the same way as in the past, despite all technological change and optimism. There is a possibility of unwanted economic and ecological impacts or possible disasters from economic growth. In such circumstances, it is rational to retain flexibility in resource and response systems. For example, options can be kept open through conservation, for instance, by maintaining biodiversity. Thus for this reason and the others given above, there is currently considerable emphasis on the desirability of attaining sustainable development (cf. Pearce, et al., 1989).

SOCIAL RECOGNITION OF THE NEED FOR A CHANGED ATTITUDE

Social recognition of the need for a changed attitude towards the environment and the relationship between economic growth and the environment has come from several quarters in recent decades. It has occurred at the local, regional, national and international level.

The World Commission on Environment and Development (1987), which was established by the United Nations under the chairmanship of Gro Brundtland, former Prime Minister of Norway, points out in its Report, *Our Common Future*, that the world does not face a separate environmental crisis, separate energy crisis or a separate development crisis. They are all one. Broad areas of concern (environmental, economic and social) cannot be compartmentalized or confined to local areas. The Earth has become a global village in which economic, ecological and social problems are interlocked and this calls for a holistic approach by governments to policy making. The Commission points out that 'Ecology and economy are becoming ever more interwoven – locally, regionally, nationally, and globally – into a seamless net of causes and effects' (World Commission on Environment and Development, 1987, p. 5).

The Brundtland Report was amongst a number of official reports and documents of international bodies in the 1980s championing the objective of sustainable development. Possibly the *World Conservation Strategy* document, (IUCN, 1980) published by the World Conservation Union (but a joint effort of several international agencies) was the first official international document to promote sustainable development as an important objective and to stress the importance of biological conservation for sustainable development. The interdependent nature of biological conservation and socio–economic conditions were explicitly emphasized in the document. It was pointed out, for example, that individuals in poverty in less developed countries are unlikely to be interested in biological conservation unless it results in rather immediate and tangible material benefits to them.

At the national level, political gains by 'green' parties and by parties incorporating ecological concerns in their agenda are signs of increased public concerns about these matters (cf. O'Riordan, 1988). Established parties which previously had not incorporated ecological or green issues in their agenda have been forced to do this in order to retain their electoral support. Despite this, representatives of 'green' parties are being elected to parliaments and in some cases, hold the balance of power.

Conflicts between environmentalists and developers are by no means new. Past conflicts in Australia include mining on the Great Barrier Reef (particularly the possibility of oil mining); mineral sands development versus conservation, for instance, on Fraser Island and in the Cooloola sands; the Franklin River proposed hydro–electricity works, and so on. But there were no settled institutional mechanisms to deal with such conflicts, nor were ecological concerns well integrated with economic considerations.

Some institutional developments have recently occurred at the Australian Federal Government level designed, at least partially, to remedy this situation. Recently there has been the appointment of an Environmental (Economics) Commissioner to the Industries Commission, a body which makes recommendations to the Australian Government about assistance for industry, and the establishment of the Resources Assessment Commission as a result of The Resources Assessment Commission Act, 1989. This Commission investigates matters referred to it by the Prime Minister and reports its findings directly to him.

The Resources Assessment Commission has inquired into the options for Australia's forest and timber resources and into the future use of the Kakadu Exploration Zone. The Australian Government has requested it to examine major coastal zone development issues. In its assessments, the Commission has been asked to take account of the environmental, cultural, social, industry, economic and other values involved in the use of resources. Section 7 of the Act sets out the principles that the Commission should take into account in resolving competing claims for the use of resources. One of these principles is that 'resource use decisions should seek to optimise the net benefits to the community from the nation's resources, having regard to efficiency of resource use, environmental considerations, ecological integrity and sustainability, the sustainability of any development, and an equitable distribution of the return on resources'. The influence of the Commission will depend upon the extent to which matters are referred to it by the Prime Minister for inquiry and the willingness of the Government to act on its recommendations. Currently each inquiry of the Commission is being undertaken by two Commissioners, one of whom is an economist and the other an ecologist.

MAJOR ISSUES FOR ECOLOGICAL OR GREEN ECONOMICS

Sustainability, whether of economic systems, or of development, or of ecosystems, or of human society, is currently a focal point for much debate about issues in ecological or green economics. The presumption is that sustainability in some sense is desirable. But whether or not that is so depends upon what we desire to sustain and why we want to do it. Sometimes these objectives are unclear in the debate. Little progress can be made until they are clarified (see for example Chapter 9).

Some writers have suggested that our aim should be to sustain biodiversity, that is, as wide a range of species and variety of species as possible.

Loss of genetic diversity is occurring on a massive scale. While extinction is the normal fate of virtually all species, processes of gradual natural extinction are now being dwarfed by the rate of human–generated extinctions of species and their varieties. It was estimated in 1980 that possibly 15–20 per cent of existing species, that is a half to two million species could disappear over the next two decades or so, primarily as a result of human activity (Barney, 1980, pp. 37–8). While these estimates cover all biota, they include about 1,000 animals and birds as likely candidates for man–induced extinction.

Some of the most important genetic losses may not be of species but of subspecies and varieties of biota used commercially or directly by humankind, such as foodgrains. It has been estimated that four–fifths of the world's food supplies are derived from less than two dozen plants and animal species. 'Wild and local domestic strains are needed for breeding resistance to pests and pathogens into the high–yield varieties now widely used. These varietal stocks are rapidly diminishing as marginal wild lands are brought into cultivation. Local domesticated varieties, often uniquely suited to local conditions, are also being lost as higher–yield varieties displace them' (Barney, 1980). Thus modern agriculture becomes more vulnerable as its genetic base is constantly and surreptitiously eroded.

The importance of maintaining biodiversity has been argued from two points of view, (1) an anthropocentric or man–centred point of view, and (2) a non–anthropocentric viewpoint.

The anthropocentric point of view is that genetic diversity is of considerable economic value to mankind and may be essential in the long term for maintaining the level and desired variety of economic production. Several arguments have been put forward for maintaining biological diversity on economic grounds, not all of which can be noted here. However, some are:

(1) Strains and varieties of living things used in commercial production usually have a limited life of about five years and depend upon three or four varieties for the bulk of production of major crops (cf. IUCN, 1980). For example, major crop varieties fail periodically due to lack of resistance to new diseases and scientists can usually only breed new varieties with resistance if they have access to the wild relatives or primitive cultivars of the domesticated varieties. If this wild, diverse gene pool or bank is no longer available, commercial production may become unsustainable.

(2) Non–renewable resources such as minerals are being depleted by economic activity. Once these are depleted mankind will be entirely dependent on biological resources and the energy from the sun. Thus, in the very long term, the stock of biological resources will be essential resources for the survival of future generations. Even before non–renewable resource depletion (or entropy) occurs eventually, if it does occur, the degree of dependence of human beings on biological resources will increase dramatically, so the stock will be a valuable asset even in the shorter run.

(3) The depletion of non–renewable resources can be expected to be uneven. Biological resources may be important substitutable backstop resources for non–renewable resources depleted early. Biological resources, for instance, are potential sources of liquid or gaseous fuels. Thus back–up or backstop biological resources may be needed earlier than had previously been realized.

(4) Biological diversity helps to keep economic options open for the future. This is valuable given uncertainty about the exact future economic use and worth of many biological resources, e.g. particular species or varieties of species.

(5) Individuals place an economic value on biological diversity for recreation and enjoyment as evidenced by their willingness to pay, for example, for tourism based on such diversity, e.g. in the case of visitors and tourists to national parks.

Non–anthropocentric reasons have also been put forward for preserving genetic diversity. These include the 'land ethic' of Aldo Leopold (1933, 1966). His land ethic was developed in opposition to the view that nature should be manipulated or species exterminated purely to satisfy the narrow economic interests of humanbeings. To him, mankind is part of a holistic organic community. Humanbeings have no right to exterminate parts of that community but should live in harmony with it. This suggests that species other than homo sapiens have an independent right to existence. It is possible that this ethic, at least in modified form, will gain increasing community support. Even if it does, there would still be a role for economics.

The survival or extent of survival of other species is likely to depend on control of levels of human population, regulation of per capita levels of material consumption by humans, more control of discharges of pollutants and wastes from economic activity and greater recycling as well as better planning of the nature of resource use at local level. For example, at local level, land use planning might incorporate biosphere reserves along the lines suggested by UNESCO in its Man and the Biosphere (MAB) Programme, even though this is not the only model worth considering (see, for example, McNeely, et al., 1990). These are all matters about which we have a choice.

But if global economic growth is to be limited to attain ecological sustainability, this raises several issues. How will the poorest, less developed countries increase the incomes of their residents? Will less developed countries also be expected to forgo economic growth? To what extent are the developed countries prepared to redistribute income to the less developed countries if they forgo economic growth, especially bearing in mind that a redistribution of income is likely to mean a redistribution of economic and military power? If the less developed countries commence economic growth or continue to have economic growth, this could be damaging economically, environmentally and ecologically to developed nations because of the global environmental impacts of the developing countries. This has, for example, been pointed out strikingly in relation to the greenhouse effect, given the capacity of China, India and Brazil to add to it by their burning of fossil fuels (see, for example, Burnett and Polunin, forthcoming). If we ignore such issues, they certainly will not disappear.

Given the strong desire for economic growth, especially in less developed countries, man–induced extinction of species is likely to continue even though the consequences of this for the long term economic well–being of Mankind are uncertain and could be quite disastrous. In these circumstances, we may however have a choice of which species to save and which to extinguish. How should we choose which species to save? This is a question for ecological economics and one which we all have a responsibility to consider. We are being forced to be latter–day Noahs.

CONCLUSION

Economic systems are not ends in themselves but means to ultimate ends. Primarily we need to decide on the type of society that we want and then consider economic systems that will help to bring about that type of society. It is illogical and involves putting the cart before the horse to decide on the economic system that we want and then merely accept the type of society that results. Economic systems help to determine the nature and structure of society and sociological and interpersonal relationships within them. For example, an efficient society in providing material goods and services may be a non–caring society in which individuals are subjected to considerable emotional stress and alienation. It may also be that such a society pays insufficient attention to the preservation of nature.

There is associated with the conservation movement a school of thought which argues in favour of sustainable communities. It appears to favour small sustainable communities in charge of their own affairs and is favoured by some 'alternative life–style' groups. Proponents argue that there should be full participation by all in the social–political systems of the community, a fair distribution of income and co–operation with nature rather than domination of it. According to this view, individuals should not be subject to the tyranny of technologies such as those involving large economies of scale. Technologies should be appropriate to the community and to the demands of nature. Social structures which take decisions away from local communities, such as those involving large companies or 'big' centralized governments, are seen as a threat to a sustainable and satisfactory social and economic order in harmony with nature. Such views have, for example, been expressed by Schumacher (1978) and by others (Douglass, 1984).

If these principles were put into effect they would alter the social and economic fabric of existing developed economies fundamentally. They would have a cost in terms of forgone levels of material production, at least in the short term. Whether the social and ecological benefits from the system would outweigh the material costs is partially a value judgement. But it might be noted that a country putting these principles wholeheartedly into effect might be unable to defend itself against external aggression because the type of industries vital to an effective war effort would suffer. Thus, this way of life may only be a secure way of life in a world which has effective global government. From this point of view, as well as from many other points of view, it can be seen that social, economic and ecological considerations are all intertwined.

In studying ecological economics, one cannot avoid considering the ultimate purpose or values of economic activity and human existence, the 'rights' of future generations and of living things apart from man. Is it desirable to continue maximizing current consumption per head and economic growth? Do growing human populations pose a threat to economic and ecological sustainability? If economic growth is no longer to be the norm, how will less developed countries overcome poverty? What economic sacrifices should be made to save other species from extinction and, if we must choose, which species ought to be saved? How do economic, social and ecological systems influence one another? Should economic systems be modified to obtain more acceptable 'social structures' and ecological effects? These partly philosophical and ethical issues are central to ecological economics and affect us all. (They are discussed to some extent in Tisdell, 1990.)

We can conclude that ecological or green economics is unlikely to be a passing fad. Rather, it will continue developing and making a genuine contribution to economic thought. The issues involved in ecological economics are fundamental consequences of our current predicament and there is no retreating from the difficulties which we face. Everything cannot be turned backwards. At the same time, the degree of interest in this subject is likely to vary over the years and it may not always be as fashionable as it appears to be in the 1990s.

REFERENCES

Barney, G.O. (1980) *The Global 2000 Report to the President of the U.S. Entering the 21st Century*, Pergamon, New York.

Burnett, J. and Polunin, N. (eds) (forthcoming) *Surviving with the Biosphere*, Edinburgh University Press, Edinburgh.

Coase, R.H. (1960) 'The Problems of Social Cost', *The Journal of Law and Economics*, 3.

Costanza, R. (1989) 'What is Ecological Economics?', *Ecological Economics*, 1, pp. 1–7.

Daly, H.E. (1968) 'On Economics as a Life Science', *Journal of Political Economy*, 76, pp. 392–406.

Douglass, G.K. (1984) 'The Meanings of Agricultural Sustainability', pp. 3–99 in G.K. Douglass (ed.) *Agricultural Sustainability in a Changing World Order*, Westview Press, Boulder, Colorado.

Ehlrich, P.R., Ehlrich, A. and Holdren, J.P. (1977) *Ecoscience: Population, Resources and Development*, 3rd ed. Freeman, San Francisco, Cal.

Engels, F. (1959) ' Outlines of a Critique of Political Economy'. In K. Marx, *Economic and Philosophic Manuscripts of 1844*, Foreign Languages Publishing House, Moscow.

Forrester, J.W. (1971) *World Dynamics*, Wright Allen Press, Cambridge, Mass.

Georgescu–Roegen, N. (1971) *The Entropy Law and the Economic Process*, Harvard University Press, Cambridge, Mass.

IUCN (1980) *World Conservation Strategy: Living Resource Conservation for Sustainable Development*, International Union for the Conservation of Nature and Natural Resources (World Conservation Union), Gland, Switzerland.

Kohler, H. (1977) *Scarcity and Freedom: An Introduction to Economics*, Heath, Lexington, Mass.

Leopold, A. (1933) *Game Management*, Scribner, New York.

Leopold, A. (1966) *A Sand Country Almanac: with Other Essays from Round River*, Oxford University Press, New York.

Marshall, A. (1890) *Principles of Economics*, 1st ed., Macmillan, London.

Malthus, T.R. (1798) *An Essay on the Principle of Population as it Affects the Future Improvement of Mankind*, J. Johnson, London.

McNeely, J.A., Miller, K.R., Reid, W.V., Mittermeier, R.A., and Werner, T.B. (1990) *Conserving the World's Biological Diversity*. IUCN, Gland, Switzerland; WRI, CI, WWF–US, and the World Bank, Washington, D.C.

Meadows, D.H., Meadows, D.L., Randers, J. and Behrens, W. (1972) *The Limits to Growth: A Report for the Club of Rome's Project on the Predicament of Mankind*, Universe Books, New York.

Mishan, E.J. (1967) *The Costs of Economic Growth*, Staples Press, London.

Norgaard, R.B. (1989) 'The Case for Methodological Pluralism', *Ecological Economics*, 1, pp. 37–57.

O'Riordan, T. (1988) 'The Politics of Sustainability', pp. 29–50 in *Sustainable Environmental Management* (ed. R.K.Turner), Belhaven Press, London.

Pearce, D., Markandya, A. and Barbier, E.B. (1989) *Blueprint for a Green Economy*, Earthscan Publications, London.

Perrings, C. (1987) *Economy and Environment: A Theoretical Essay on the Interdependence of Economic and Environmental Systems*, Cambridge University Press, Cambridge, U.K.

Pigou, A.C. (1932) *The Economics of Welfare*, 4th ed., Macmillan, London.

Schumacher, E.F. (1978) *Small is Beautiful: A Study in Economics as if People Mattered*, Abacus, London.

Smith, A. (1910) *Wealth of Nations*, Dent, London. First edition 1776.

Soderbaum, P. (1990) 'Neoclassical and Institutional Approaches to Environmental Economics', *Journal of Economic Issues*, 24, pp. 481–92.

Tisdell, C.A. (1982) *Microeconomics of Markets*, Wiley, Brisbane.

Tisdell, C.A. (1990) *Natural Resources, Growth and Development: Economics, Ecology and Resource–Scarcity*, Praeger, New York.

WCED (World Commission on Environment and Development) (1987) *Our Common Future*, Oxford University Press, Oxford.

14. The World Conservation Strategy: An Economic Critique

The *World Conservation Strategy* (IUCN, 1980) has played a significant role in fostering global interest in policies for sustainable development and proved to be an effective follow–up to the United Nations Stockholm Conference in 1972 which first developed the concept of ecologically sustainable development within an international framework. The United Nations Conference on Environment and Development held in Brasilia in 1992 was intended to strengthen this interest and initiate appropriate global policies.

The main theme of the World Conservation Strategy was the need for ecological conservation in order to attain sustainable development. This relationship was also emphasized by the World Commission on Environment and Development (1987) in *Our Common Future.* In the follow–up to the World Conservation Strategy (IUCN–UNEP–WWF, 1991) the theme is broadened to become a strategy for sustainable living or for a sustainable society. This extended strategy will be discussed in Chapter 16 – it is less anthropocentric than the original strategy and pays greater attention to economic instruments as a means for attaining ends. However, historically the original strategy has been influential and it raises a number of policy issues which are still relevant. Therefore let us consider it in some detail. Although this is done critically, this is not done to belittle the importance of the World Conservation Strategy but to raise practical issues and problems in implementing its policy proposals.

ORIGINS OF THE WORLD CONSERVATION STRATEGY

The *World Conservation Strategy* (WCS) expressed concern about the irreversible damage that man is doing to the biosphere. As a result of human activity (mostly economic activity), species are disappearing at a frightening rate, forests are being rapidly cut out as well as down, soils are being denuded and terrain made useless, and many natural ecosystems are being lost. Trends in the deterioration of the biosphere are documented in Myers (1979) and Allen (1980), and the *Global 2000 Report* (1980) predicted extinction of species on a massive scale. If such deterioration continues, the economic welfare of mankind is likely to be undermined; not only may current standards of living in developed countries be no longer sustainable, but development in more impoverished countries may be short–lived. Moreover, grave concern for the biosphere as a whole has been expressed for example in an 'Open Letter' from leaders in all the world's inhabited continents (Pauling et al., 1982), and a world campaign for the biosphere has been declared (Anon., 1982; Polunin, 1982; Worthington, 1982).

In bald terms, the message of the WCS is that we are ruining sustainable natural systems that form the basis of our own life support now, and that could support mankind once all non–renewable non–living resources of significance are used up or dispersed by mankind. Concern about the depletion of non–renewable resourccs such as oil and coal does not appear to have been matched by as much concern for living resources that are the basis of much economic activity. Although living resources are renewable, they can also be (irreversibly) destroyed by human activities, and indeed are being destroyed to the long–term detriment of mankind.

To address this problem, the drawing up of the World Conservation Strategy was commissioned by the United Nations Environment Programme (UNEP) and jointly financed by it and the World Wildlife Fund (WWF). The actual document was executed by the International Union for Conservation of Nature and Natural Resources (IUCN) in consultation with UNEP, WWF, the United Nations Food and Agriculture Organization (FAO), and the United Nations Educational Scientific and Cultural Organization (UNESCO). Widespread consultation with government agencies and conservation organizations as well as individuals in over 100 countries was involved. The resulting 'compromise' document was endorsed by the Ecosystem Conservation Group (UNEP, FAO, UNESCO and IUCN), and launched in March 1980 with a view to making the Third Development Decade, the decade of sustainable development. The document therefore had the support of the 'international public service', and the prospects of governmental follow-up by several nations in view of the consultative processes used.

The WCS document was intended as a framework to nudge each nation into preparing a conservation strategy of its own that should take account of the principles outlined in the WCS document, to influence countries giving aid to developing countries to take account of environmental issues in providing such aid, and to persuade nations to support various international conservation efforts – for example by bilateral and multilateral assistance.

In 1984 Australia, for instance, developed a National Conservation Strategy using the framework provided by the World Conservation Strategy. In 1990, the Prime Minister of Australia set up a number of working groups to recommend specific policies for attaining ecological sustainability in relation to specific sectors of the economy, but also, with a mandate to examine intersectoral issues with a view to integrating economic and economic goals. Draft reports were produced in August 1991 on agriculture, fisheries, forest use, energy production, manufacturing, mining, energy use, tourism and transport (Commonwealth of Australia, 1991). The extent to which recommendations of the working groups will be accepted for policy purposes remains to be seen. However, the Australian example indicates the impact which the World Conservation Strategy has had directly or indirectly on considerations of economic policy.

AIMS AND PRINCIPLES UNDERLYING THE WORLD CONSERVATION STRATEGY

The main aim of the World Conservation Strategy was to foster 'sustainable development through the conservation of living resources' (IUCN, 1980; cf. Talbot, 1980). It attempted to involve major pressure groups in support of nature conservation. Sir Peter Scott, when Chairman of the World Wildlife Fund, claimed that the WCS shows clearly 'how conservation can contribute to the development objectives of governments, industry, commerce, organized labour, and the professions', and suggests that it envisages development as a major means of achieving conservation rather than obstructing it. While evidence in the WCS document for Sir Peter Scott's last assertion is not overwhelming, undoubtedly the real politik behind the document is to get developers and influential economic pressure groups on its side.

It has been contended that,

> To be more effective, conservationists need radically to change the public perception of their attitude to development. Too often conservationists have allowed themselves to be seen as resisting all development, although often they have been forced into that posture because they have not been invited to participate in the development process early enough. The result has been not to stop development, but to persuade many development practitioners, especially in developing countries, that conservation is not merely irrelevant but harmful and anti-social. Consequently, development

has continued unimpeded by conservationists yet with the seeds of its eventual failure lying in the ecological damage that conservation could help to prevent, (Allen, 1980, p. 148).

Allen goes on to say that conservationists need to be willing to compromise, that they: 'must come to distinguish more clearly and carefully between environmental alteration that is worth the biological cost and that which is not... They should work with development practitioners to ensure that development is indeed environmentally sound'.

Nevertheless, putting the rhetoric aside, the main aim stated in the WCS is to foster 'sustainable development through the conservation of living resources'. Thus conservation of living resources is seen as a prerequisite for sustainable development, and sustainable development is seen as eminently desirable. This aim is, however, far from clear, as can be seen when we examine the following amplifying statement in the WCS document:

> Conservation is defined here as: the management of human use of [the biosphere,] so that is may yield the greatest sustainable benefit to present generations while maintaining its potential to meet the needs and aspirations of future generations (IUCN, 1980, sec. 1.4).

This statement raises the following questions: Is the greatest sustainable benefit to those alive now ('present generations') to be taken as the greatest stationary benefit to present generations? Furthermore, how is benefit to be determined? (Certainly, welfare economists have encountered a myriad of problems in trying to throw light on the subject.) There is likely to be conflict in some cases between conserving resources 'to meet needs and aspirations of future generations', and maximizing sustainable benefits to present generations. How is the trade−off to be resolved? No hint is given of how to resolve this economic problem. But as mentioned in Chapters 8 and 9, economists such as Pearce et al. (1989) have given considerable attention to this issue in recent years and have suggested ways to deal with trade−off problems.

Problems are left unresolved about the optimal path for those who are alive now and may be expected to live in the future. There is no indication, for example, as to whether a path that involves considerable benefits now (but at the expense of small forgone benefits in the future) is to be preferred. For example in Figure 14.1, is path (1) to be preferred to path (2), or is path (3) to be preferred to (1)? Economists in the past have attempted to resolve these problems (though not with complete success) by using discount rates. It should be noted that the approach in the WCS is man−centred, benefits from conservation being judged by 'what man wants'. It is even stated that 'conservation, like development, is for people' (IUCN, 1980, sec. 1.5).

Some environmental economists, such as Daly (1980), would contend that there is no way that a world conservation strategy can be sensibly settled until we agree on ultimate ends. He believes that we should aim principally to ensure economic and environmental conditions that maximize the possibility of the human race existing for the longest possible time – that the survival of the human species ought to be our basic goal even though other aspects are not to be ignored. He sees a steady–state economy as a way of contributing to this goal.

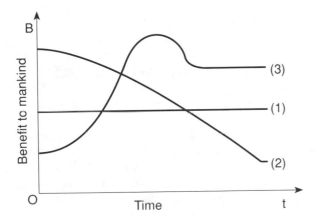

Figure 14.1   The conservational goal of the World Conservation Strategy is ambiguous. For example, it is not clear which of these alternative paths would be favoured by it.

Daly raises many issues, several of which are not resolved either by the World Conservation Strategy or by Daly, but which point to our inability to make much progress in this area without moral wisdom. In his penultimate paragraph of *Economics, Ecology and Ethics* (1980) he says:

> ...The SSE [steady–state economy] is simply a strategy of good stewardship for taking care of God's creation for however long his will is to last. In taking care of that creation special, but not exclusive, attention must be given to humanity, including not only the present but future generations... Nor should our concern be exclusively with human beings, past, present, and future. If a man is worth many sparrows, then a sparrow cannot be worthless. Stewardship requires an extension of brotherhood, first to all presently existing people but also to all future and past people, and to subhuman life, all in some appropriate degree.

Even if we could agree that all of these elements should be variables in our objective function, resolving the appropriate trade-offs will be no easy matter. To what extent should other species be respected, even when they are of no value to man or may even be a nuisance? (Tisdell, 1979, 1990, 1991).

Most of the world's current conservation problems arise from increasing human populations and attempts to maintain or increase per capita material consumption. Difficult new welfare and population questions arise, because human population levels are to a large extent a matter of choice. Daly (1980) suggests that the Benthamite principle of the 'greatest good for the greatest number' should be replaced by the principle of 'sufficient per caput product for the greatest number over time'.

On one interpretation of Daly's writing, his view is that policies should be so devised that (1) the human species survives (on Earth?) for as long as is possible; (2) the greatest number of people live during that interval of time, with each being ensured a 'satisfactory' level of income, but that this should be (3) subject to other constraints such as some concern for sub-human species.

At the risk of being too metaphysical and diverging somewhat from the substance of the World Conservation Strategy, let us consider three hypothetical sets of policies that lie open to mankind as indicated in Figure 14.2. Policy set (1) enables a large population to live now and in the near future at a satisfactory per capita level of income but leads to the end of the human species before its maximum allotted time, n. Policy set (2) enables the human species to survive for its maximum allotted time but only at much-reduced levels of population in the future. Policy set (3) represents a possible steady-state solution, with population levels remaining stationary throughout the period in which the human species can survive.

The values of Daly (1980) would lead him to reject policy set (1), and he does in fact believe that a policy set indicated by (3) is likely to be optimal. He suggests that a steady-state economy is the only type which will enable the human species to reach end-point, n, and that it is the only one that meets his second principle mentioned above, being the only one that enables the maximum number of people to live at a satisfactory level of income during the allotted time-interval for the human race.

For each of the policies under consideration, let $f_1(t)$, $f_2(t)$, and $f_3(t)$, represent the alternative paths of population associated with these policies. Daly (1980) appears to contend that $_0\int^n f_3(t)dt$ is greater than $_0\int^n f_1(t)dt$, and also greater than $_0\int^n f_2(t)dt$ (if such a path exists). In his view, the steady-state economy enables the maximum number of satisfactorily well-off individuals to live during the possible life-span of the human race. But can we be sure that this is so? Could not a path such as (2) or even (1) give such a maximum? If a path such as (1) would give this maximum, why should it not be adopted? If a path such as (2) would give the type of maximum under consideration, would there be any reason to favour the steady–state economy?

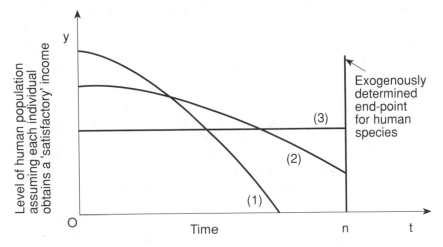

Figure 14.2 Daly's (1980) conservational goal relates to the survival of the human species and to its potential population. He suggests that a steady path such as (3) will ensure that the species exists as long as possible, and will maximize (subject to satisfactory levels of income) the number of individuals who will live during the span of the human race.

Possibly the time–scale involved is so long, and uncertainties are so great, that it is senseless to concern ourselves with the above problem. Whether or not this is so, many of us do not wish to dwell on the above issues. However, even if we do not look beyond the interests – even the materialistic interests – of those alive now, conservation policies need to be considered in order to maximize short–run gains from resource utilization.

Three specific objectives for living–resource conservation were put forward in the *World Conservation Strategy*.
These were:
    (1) to maintain essential ecological processes and life–support systems;
    (2) to preserve genetic diversity; and
    (3) to ensure the sustainable utilization of species and ecosystems.
Let us consider each of these objectives in turn.

Maintaining Essential Ecological Processes and Life-support Systems

The *World Conservation Strategy* states that special attention should be given to maintaining systems that are essential for human survival and sustainable development – the so-called life-support systems. The most important and threatened life-support systems according to the WCS document are:

(1) agricultural systems;
(2) forests; and
(3) coastal and freshwater systems.

Agricultural systems are said to be under special threat because of the loss of agriculturally productive land due to

(a) encroachment of man-made facilities onto such land, for example the extension of cities and other human settlements and the construction of roads and runways;

(b) accelerated soil erosion as a result of human activities, for example unwise farming practices; and

(c) soil degradation due to salinity, leaching of nutrients, flooding, and so on, due to human activities.

The world's forests are disappearing at a fast rate because they are being logged for timber (mostly exported from developing countries to developed countries), are being cleared for agriculture, are being cut for fuel, and are not in many cases regenerating because of subsequent overgrazing etc. About 110,000 square kilometres of tropical forests are estimated to be logged, felled or burnt each year, and it is expected that at current rates of exploitation practically all such forest will be depleted within the 21st century (Allen, 1980; Myers, 1980).

Almost one-half of Australia's forest cover has disappeared since European settlement commenced in 1788, having been cleared in the main for agriculture. The remaining forest covers only 6 per cent of the land-mass of Australia – a proportion smaller than in India. Nearly all of the remaining forest is native, but plantations of introduced coniferous species (unsuitable as habitat for native birds and some mammals) have increased in numbers. The remaining Australian native forests are important for maintaining Australian species of both these groups. McIlroy (1978) points out that more than one-third of Australia's species of birds, and more than 50 per cent of its species of mammals, are found only in its native forests. The logging of the remnant rainforests in Australia, and the clear-felling of some forests for the supply of chips (mostly to Japan), have been amongst the main concerns of Australian conservationists. Political action and demonstrations by conservationists have resulted in some rainforest areas being withdrawn from logging, despite the protests of timber interests stressing the loss of jobs and the foregoing of commercial gains.

Loss of forests can have many environmental ill–effects. As a result of the loss of forest cover, soil erosion can accelerate, flooding and siltation problems in river basins can magnify, water supplies in streams may become more variable than formerly, ground–water supplies can be lowered, and water quality may be reduced. Moreover, it is even possible for wider–than–local climatic conditions to be altered.

As illustrated in the Australian case, forest removal also threatens the existence of many animal species that depend upon the forest as a habitat and food source, and of many plants that depend on the environmental conditions which forests alone offer.

The WCS document also expresses concern about the loss of coastal and freshwater systems which are important breeding grounds for commercial fish. These systems (for example areas of mangroves) are being lost owing to such factors as the release of water–borne pollutants by human reclamation works for industry (for instance, the use of 'filling' for waterfront industries), and through housing development – for instance of 'canal estates'.

The WCS document recommends a number of policies for adoption (presumably by governments) to deal with these perceived problems. These prescriptions seem to have been dominated by the ecological background of the framers of WCS, and do not pay very much attention to economic trade–off problems.

The main recommendation as far as the disappearance of agricultural land is concerned, is for the government to reserve good cropland for crops, and to encourage management of agricultural land based on ecologically sound principles. Presumably this means that governments should discourage the establishment of cities in areas of good cropland, and that urban activities in established cities should be directed away from locations on good cropland. While not doubting that natural market, social and political mechanisms will fail to promote the optimal pattern of growth of cities and urban areas and the 'best' location of urban settlements (Tisdell, 1975, 1982a, Ch. 15), and while believing that planning could potentially improve the situation, the priority stated in WCS seems to be based on oversimplified assumptions. Inadequate account is taken of economic interdependencies, and the fact is ignored that good production depends upon 'inputs' that are additional to good cropland.

To see at least the nature of some of the difficulties involved, consider a simple hypothetical example. Suppose, as illustrated in Figure 14.3, that there is a circular territory of good cropland surrounded by a band of land that is useless for crops but entirely adequate for housing or urban development. The location of all dwellings on the useless land for crops may add greatly to transport costs, and net food production could be lower than if dwellings were located on good cropland. Those cultivating the land may lose valuable time in travelling if they are located on the periphery, while increasing costs may be involved in transporting inputs and in distributing the harvest. In the absence of dwelling constraints, ignoring transport costs and given a fixed quantity of other resources, the good cropland could produce 100 units of food p.a. If dwellings are located on the good cropland, 10 per cent of the potential crop might be lost. But if dwellings are located on the land useless for crops, 20 per cent of the potential output of the crop may be forgone because of transport costs and transport difficulties. One can also think of other reasons (such as economies of scale) why it may be economical to forgo good agricultural land for dwellings and urban settlements. Nevertheless the loss of good cropland is a matter for concern, as our 'system' directs it in a rather haphazard way.

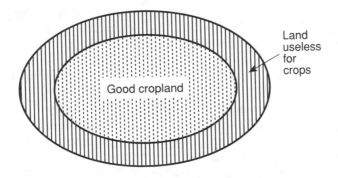

Land useless for crops

Good cropland

Figure 14.3   The dictum in the World Conservation Strategy, that agriculture should generally be given precedence on high-quality cropland, ignores the fact that crops are not produced by land alone. To site buildings and other man-made structures only on land that is unsuitable for crops can reduce total crop production as explained in the text.

Not only is it said in the WCS that 'Since it is not possible to resite high-quality cropland but it is possible to be flexible about the siting of buildings, roads, and other structures, agriculture as a general rule should have precedence', but also that agriculture should usually have precedence over unmodified ecosystems provided the land concerned has no serious limitations for agriculture (IUCN, 1980, secs 5.1-2). This is heralded as important on the basis that conservation in itself is not an absolute good but is only desirable to the extent that it meets the needs of mankind. But as pointed out in Tisdell (1991, Ch. 2) the dictum that good cropland should be reserved for crops overlooks the principle of comparative costs.

The WCS maintains that the overriding consideration in forest management should be to protect and preserve watersheds. But to what extent should watersheds be protected? There will be circumstances in which the benefits from some forest clearing will more than offset the costs of watershed deterioration. This is not to deny that 'spillovers' in watershed management have been greatly neglected.

Again a single priority is stated (and then modified to some extent) for coastal ecosystems, namely to 'ensure that the principal management goal for estuaries, mangrove swamps, and other coastal wetlands and shallows [that are] critical for fisheries, is the maintenance fo the processes on which the fisheries depend' (IUCN, 1980, sec. 5.7). But should not the costs and benefits be weighed up in each particular instance and trade-offs specifically considered, or have economists been taking the wrong approach? This raises the possibility in my mind that the WCS priorities are intended as a way of focusing attention on issues, rather than as a practical guide to policy. But then I might be wrong about the intentions of those involved in drawing up the WCS document.

Preserving Genetic Diversity

Another important aim of the WCS is to prevent the extinction of species and 'preserve as many varieties as possible of crop plants, forage plants, timber trees, live-stock, animals for aquaculture, microbes, and other domesticated organisms and their wild relatives' (IUCN, 1980, sec. 6.4). This is important both to promote diversity for biological stability and in order not to close off useful options for man in the use of species and varieties. We do not know what species and varieties will be of value to man in the future (for surely we have not discovered all of them yet), but it seems certain that man will in time make use of some that are not used now. Because of uncertainty, there is a rational argument for keeping flexibility even at some cost (Hart, 1942; Tisdell, 1970, 1972; Cicchetti and Freeman, 1971). However, species and varieties will continue to be lost, and therefore the WCS realistically recognizes that priorities need to be drawn up in choosing what species etc. to preserve.

Basically, WCS suggests that priority should be given to saving species where the size of the loss is large and also imminent. The exact priority rating suggested in the WCS document is indicated in Table 14.1 (IUCN, 1980, sec. 6.2).

Table 14.1   *Priorities suggested in the IUCN document for conserving species.*

		Imminence of loss		
		Rare	Vulnerable	Endangered
Size of loss	Family	4**	2***	1***
	Genus	7*	5**	3***
	Species	9*	8*	6**

Notes: 1–9   Suggested order of priority
        ***   Top priority
        **   Intermediate priority
        *   Lower priority

However, this system of priorities seems to be rather coarse. No specific account is taken of the benefits and costs of preservation. Presumably, if the costs of saving a whole plant or animal family are very high in relation to the benefits, and the benefits of saving a separate species at the same cost are high and resources are insufficient to meet both objectives, it would be sensible to save the species rather than the family.

Great problems and uncertainties are involved in trying to estimate what the potential value of a species might be in the future. In drawing up our priorities, attention needs to be paid not only to the expected value but also to the degree of uncertainty of our estimates. The greater the uncertainty may be in some cases, the more rational it is for us to err on the side of preservation. However, this raises the issue, not discussed in the WCS, of what attitude the community should take to collective decision making under uncertainty. For example, should a minimax loss approach, expected gain maximization, expected utility maximization, or yet some other criterion, be used in conservation decisions?

In the WCS document, various ways are suggested of preserving genetic diversity. These include on–site protection (e.g. national parks), off–site protection of the whole organism (e.g. in zoos, botanical gardens, etc.), and off–site preservation of reproductive portions of organisms (e.g. seed–banks). None of these are costless and, of course, there are social choices to be made as to how much in the way of resources should be allocated to each.

I shall not go into the complex issues involved here. However, I do have some queries about the WCS–suggested geometric principles for the design of nature reserves. For example given homogeneity, one large reserve is considered to give a higher probability of survival of species than several separated reserves of the same aggregate size (IUCN, 1980, sec. 6.10). While there are no doubt circumstances in which this is so, there may be cases in which separation increases the probability of survival of species. Provided each separated reserve is above some critical level in size (whatever that may be), the risk of a particular species being wiped out by occurrences such as a new predator or disease, drought, etc., could be lower than for one large reserve.

The random occurrence, e.g. of a new disease, might arise only in one reserve and not be able to spread to the separated reserves, and/or time may be given to officers of reserves to adopt counter–measures before the disease can reach the other reserves. It might be relevant to note here that Australia's relative isolation from the other continents was probably a factor ensuring the survival of its unique species and many higher taxa, and that this isolation probably increased the number of species in existence in the world. Of course, the design and positioning of reserves is not likely to be decided just as a means of species preservation – multiple uses and economic trade–offs also need to be taken into account.

Although no very large range of native Australian biota are used overseas, some significant species are. These include rather many eucalypts, which are grown for timber in several less – as well as more – developed countries, and Macadamia nuts, derived from members of the Proteaceae which are natives of the Australian rainforest, and are grown commercially for example in Hawaii. It is likely that commercial use will be found for some Australian native species that are as yet unexploited. Indeed it could be argued from an economic standpoint that Australia, because of its high income status, has a particular responsibility to help to preserve a genetic reserve of those of its species which have commercial use or potential.

Towards Sustainable Utilization of Species and Ecosystems

The WCS recommends that commercially exploited species and ecosystems should not be utilized to such an extent that they are driven to extinction or collapse. However, it should be pointed out that there are economic circumstances in which it pays, even in the absence of a common–property problem, to use up the stock of a species completely.

For example, if the biomass of the species grows at a slow rate, and so does its value in relation to the rate of interest, and moreover the cost of harvesting it is low, extinction may be a profitable course of action (Clark, 1976; Tisdell, 1979). If one has a tree variety that increases in value (partially because of slow growth) at only 2 per cent per year and the rate of interest is 10 per cent, then it will pay to liquidate these trees if the cost of doing so is low. Furthermore, if they can be replaced by a variety that increases in value at 12 per cent per year, there is a further economic incentive to eradicate the slow–growing variety (e.g. of cedar, jarrah, or teak).

The slow–growing Australian red cedar tree (*Cedrela toona* var. australia) has virtually disappeared from Australia because of its beautiful wood for furniture making, its specificity to good land for agriculture, and the fact that it grows so slowly that it is unprofitable to undertake commercial planting of it. The Huon pine (*Dacrydium franklinii*) of Tasmania is in a similar position, and it is being argued that the jarrah (*Eucalyptus marginata*) forests of Western Australia are so slow–growing that it would be commercially desirable to replace Jarrah by faster-growing species – a possibility which appalled the late E.F. Schumacher.

Biological 'optima' are suggested as desirable aims in managing the utilization of species. For example, the WCS recommends that 'when a single species (rather than a group of species or an ecosystem) is exploited and that species is at the top of the food chain, stocks should be kept at or above the level at which they provide the greatest annual increment'. This, of course, assumes that the exploited species is not to some extent a pest, and ignores the question of competing species at the top of the food chain.

Where there are two or more competing animal species at the top of the food chain, the optimum stock of one species is not independent of the stock of the other(s). Take the case of the two competing species illustrated in Figure 14.4. The population level of species 2 depends on that of species 1, and vice versa. The maximum annual increment for species 2 may occur for a population of $\bar{x}_1$ of species 1, and the maximum annual increment of yield for species 1 may occur for a population of $\bar{x}_2$ of species 2. It is impossible to achieve these yields simultaneously. The sustainable yield of one species may have to be traded off against the sustainable yield of the other. In some areas of Australia, the commercially harvested grey kangaroo (*Macropus giganteus* and others) and the red kangaroo (*Megaleia rufa*) overlap in their range, their populations compete, and the sustainable yield of one species needs to be traded off against that of the other.

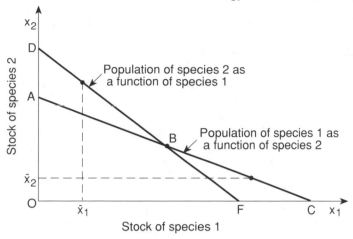

Figure 14.4   The World Conservation Strategy recommends that the harvesting of an animal species existing at the top of the food chain should be regulated to keep its population at or above its maximum sustainable yield. However, as explained in the text, this ignores competition between harvested species at the top of the food chain.

The difficulties stemming from the commercial exploitation of species that are not at the top of the food chain are mentioned in the WCS, but the interdependence problems involved are not fully explored and the policy recommendations are vague. For instance, it is recommended that 'if the species is not at the top of the food–chain, stocks should not be depleted to a level such that the population's productivity, or that of populations of other species dependent on it, is significantly reduced' (IUCN, 1980, sec. 7.12).

Other recommendations for sustainable utilization include: attempting to reduce any incidental take of non–commercial species while harvesting (for example turtles); helping subsistence communities to utilize resources sustainably; adopting the land–use that can supply most food, most economically, on a sustainable basis; limiting international trade in wild plants and animals that are threatened with overexploitation; managing timber concessions so that watersheds are protected, trees replanted, and other conservation programmes encouraged; taking measures to prevent unsustainable use of timber for firewood (a particular problem in many Third World countries); ensuring that grazing lands are not overstocked; and utilizing indigenous wild herbivores, alone or in combination with livestock, where the use of domestic stock alone will degrade the land (IUCN, 1980, sec. 7.12). This could mean, for example in Australia, that greater economic use should be made of kangaroos on arid land rather than cattle. Particular 'economic' measures that might be taken to encourage the fulfilment of these objectives are not outlined.

Approximately 70 per cent of the land mass of Australia is subject to agricultural use, and much of this land is located in the arid or semi–arid zone. Only one–sixth of Australian agricultural land is privately owned, the remainder being leased or licensed from the State (the Crown). Most of the land is used for livestock grazing. Grazing by sheep and cattle in arid and semi–arid areas has hastened erosion and, through habitat destruction, has contributed to the extinction of some of the smaller Australian mammals and seriously reduced the population of others (Frith, 1973). As yet graziers have not turned to the grazing of kangaroos, even though kangaroos are harvested by hunters for hides and meat processing.

Feral animals such as feral pigs, goats, donkeys, horses, cattle, camels, cats and dogs, as well as introduced wild species such as the rabbit (*Oryctolagus cuniculus*), red fox (*Vulpes vulpes*), brown hare (*Lepus europaeus*), and various types of deer (*Cervidae*), have added to the difficulties of conserving Australian native species which have evolved in the absence of such animals. The problem of conserving native animals is made the more acute because feral animals do not respect nature reserve or national park boundaries. In fact, these feral animals are well established in most nature reserves and national parks in Australia (Tisdell, 1982b), threaten some native species, and are disrupting natural ecosystems.

A NATIONAL CONSERVATION STRATEGY FOR AUSTRALIA

Australia, as a follow–on from the World Conservation Strategy, drew up a national conservation strategy in 1984. The Department of Home Affairs and Environment has issued a discussion paper to help the process (Department of Home Affairs and Environment, 1982). In this paper, forty–eight policy options are set out for living resource conservation for sustainable development in Australia.

The objective of the National Conservation Strategy for Australia was said to be 'to enable development to satisfy the present needs and aspirations of society while ensuring that the use of living resources, upon which development is based, can be sustained in perpetuity' (Department of Home Affairs and Environment, 1982, p. 68). Immediately, of course, the query springs to mind as to what are the objectives and aspirations of Australian society. Furthermore, if we can identify these within reason, are they compatible with the conservation of living resources in perpetuity? The view expressed in the discussion paper seems to be that Australia is a lucky country compared with the rest of the world, and that its population and standard of living pose no real problem for conservation. It is concluded that 'in a global sense Australia is in the fortunate position of having a low population compared to the size of its resources. Thus there is scope for further development in Australia' (Department of Home Affairs and Environment, 1982, p.5).

The options for the National Conservation Strategy for Australia (NCSA) involve recommendations about the integration of conservation and development, environmental assessment, more effort in education towards emphasizing the importance of living resources, better management of living resources, financial incentives and disincentives to encourage behaviour in accordance with NCSA, and further research on these subjects. An expanded role is envisaged in the future for government (bureaucracy?) towards these ends.

It is said to be necessary for the future of the strategy to provide resources to conservation and development organizations that adopt its principles, to evaluate its impact, to provide assistance to developing countries adopting programmes related to the WCS, and to follow through by promoting 'the development and implementation of conservation strategies and plans at both the State and regional levels, and for specific sectors such as the manufacturing and mining industries, forestry, agriculture, and fisheries' (Department of Home Affairs and Environment, 1982, p. 67). Cynics might see here some evidence to support the self–interest theory of bureaucracy, but many of the theories propounded are compatible with the given facts of the situation, and the general thrust of WCS is to encourage an increased involvement of government in conservation planning and implementation.

The National Conservation Strategy for Australia will have little effect until it concentrates on concrete conservation problems either at the regional level or on those caused by (or of most concern to) specific sectors. An attempt to overcome this was made by the Australian Prime Minister by setting up working groups for specific sectors to recommend policies for their ecologically sustainable development (Commonwealth of Australia, 1991). Implementation of Australia's National Conservation Strategy is, however, likely to be hampered by the virtual absence of bodies at the regional level (for example, watersheds) facilitating the overseeing of conservation. It also seems to me that other sectors, besides those mentioned above, should be taken into account in framing and implementing the strategy. Thus account should be taken of the urban construction and development sector – indeed of the whole 'tertiary' sector, including the tourist industry. Urban development, especially of coastal resorts, has been responsible for considerable loss of natural areas in Australia – as elsewhere widely in the world. Coastal resort development, for example, has destroyed a considerable amount of coastal heathland and various natural ecosystems – to the extent that coastal natural ecosystems on the eastern Australian coast are becoming rare. The tourist industry is an important sector to consider, as it can benefit by Nature conservation but, if uncontrolled, can destroy the environment on which both depend.

Economists seem to have had 'some' influence on the options that have been drawn up for NCSA. Thus there is considerable emphasis on the use of financial incentives to promote activities and land use that would be consistent with NCSA objectives, as well as on the use of disincentives for inconsistent use. Policy options are mentioned – such as reviewing taxation and financial policy to promote consistency with NCSA objectives, and promoting the polluter/user pays principle.

In relation to the specific objectives of WCS, the following ideas on fiscal and economic incentives were canvassed in the NCSA discussion paper:

(1) 'Maintaining essential ecological processes and life–support systems in Australia': In relation to 'soil', consideration should be given to fiscal incentives to establish trees or retain trees and other cover, and to removing taxation incentives for land clearing. In the case of 'water' and 'the polluter pays principle', more realistic water pricing and a better assessment of all costs and benefits of water projects are suggested.

(2) 'Preserving genetic diversity': It is suggested that fiscal incentives should be looked at as a means of preserving threatened species on non–nature reserve land, as for instance privately owned land.

(3) 'Sustainable use of living resources': In relation to forestry, it is suggested that timber royalties and other charges should cover the full cost of environmental protection: thus 'the user pays principle' should be adopted.

Doubts are also raised in the discussion paper about the sustainability of agriculture on marginal land and the sustainability of some forest practices (such as those involved in the harvesting of forests for chips) that are shortening the harvest cycle. Agriculture is marginal on much of the inland arid lands of Australia, and has adverse environmental effects as mentioned earlier. As much of the land is Crown (State) land that is leased to graziers, governments would be in a position, when leases came up for renewal, to phase out agricultural use of such land. Clear–felling of forests, and a shortening of the harvest cycle, appear to be reducing the nutrient levels of forest soils, with the effect of slowing down forest regrowth progressively with repeated harvests. Apart from this, as mentioned earlier, such harvest practices can have a serious impact on native wildlife that is specific to forests.

In relation to agriculture, a priority that as suggested in the WCS and discussed earlier has been followed up, namely to identify highly productive agricultural land and preserve its potential availability for agricultural use. The NCSA discussion paper indicates that it might be desirable to limit the encroachment of non-agricultural uses on prime agricultural land. Just how this is to be achieved, and what priorities are to apply, was not covered in the discussion paper.

The discussion paper also embraces the WCS suggestion, discussed earlier in this chapter, that measures should be taken to ensure that the harvesting of living resources does not exceed sustainable levels; but it does not come to grips with the difficulties, also discussed earlier, in applying such a criterion.

Many other options are discussed in the NCSA discussion paper, but no consideration is given either to the trade-offs that would have to be made in implementation or to how worthwhile it would be to make these. For example, it is said that Australia might 'ensure that parks and reserves are large enough to conserve species even under adverse conditions such as drought' (Department of Home Affairs and the Environment, 1982, p. 70). But to what extent should we be prepared to sacrifice alternative possible uses of the land for this goal?

It may of course be unrealistic to expect attention to much detail in a document which is intended to encourage a wide range of public participation in drawing up the National Conservation Strategy for Australia. Nevertheless, it needs to be realized that considerable complexities are involved and that it will require more than goodwill or wide public participation to resolve them, if indeed they can be resolved.

There is a need to be more specific than at present about priorities for conservation in Australia, and to draw out the implications of these priorities for actual species and, particularly, ecosystems. In principle, it should be possible to answer questions such as the following: To what extent should the Great Barrier Reef complex be preserved as a natural system? How can fishing, tourism and other activities be harmonized with such preservation? To what extent should the remaining rainforests in Australia be conserved, and in what areas should they be strictly preserved? To what extent should agriculture be excluded from arid or semi-arid lands, and what measures should be taken to control the populations of feral animals or eliminate them in Australia? Which Australian species should be given a high priority for preservation? Ought it to be ones for which the population is low and a family or genus is at stake, or ought it to be the cultivars or stocks of taxa that are used commercially, such as many *Eucalyptus* trees or Macadamia nut trees; and moreover, what account should be taken of costs? What measures should be adopted to limit urban encroachment on agricultural land, and where?

CONCLUSION

The issues raised in the World Conservation Strategy and in the NCSA discussion paper are important, and my critical assessment is not intended to detract from that importance. The World Conservation Strategy appears to have been formulated basically by some ecologists, with economists making little input. This helps to explain why a number of trade-off and valuation issues are not discussed to any extent. Ecologists are trying to give policy advice to governments on how to use resources for development, and indeed if we look at the contributions of such writers as Dasmann et al. (1973) they have been doing so for some considerable time. Ecologists provide an additional or alternative source to economists for policy advice to governments on 'resource use', and the mechanisms for determining resource use. A large number of these would be explained by economists as arising from externalities or spillovers, whereas lack of knowledge is also regarded in the WCS as a particular problem to be overcome – especially in subsistence economies.

The intention of the World Conservation Strategy is to encourage greater social responsibility in natural resource use, but the extent to which it succeeds will depend upon the realities of politics. In the United States there has been a strong lobby in favour of 'privatizing' public lands (Manhattan Institute for Economic Policy, 1982). A few leading American economists support privatization and see it as a way of reducing the US National Debt by using the revenue obtained from sales of public land. The ability of governments to direct conservation in a socially responsible manner is uncertain in a number of countries. In general, doubts have been raised about how well governments direct policy matters. Therefore, liberal economists are likely to have little sympathy for the WCS, given their distrust of government. However, as will be discussed in Chapter 16, and has been discussed in IUCN–UNEP–WWF (1991), the follow-up to WCS gives much more attention to economic instruments to encourage conservation and is less reliant on direct controls than WCS.

REFERENCES

Allen, R. (1980) *How to Save the World: Strategy for World Conservation*, Kogan Page, London.

Anon (1982) 'Declaration: The World Campaign for The Biosphere', *Environmental Conservation*, 9(2), pp. 91–2.

Cicchetti, C.J. and Freeman, A.M. (1971) 'Option Demand and Consumer Surplus'. *Quarterly Journal of Economics*, 85, pp. 528–39.

Clark, C.W. (1976) *Mathematical Bioeconomics: The Optimal Management of Renewable Resources*, John Wiley, New York.

Commonwealth of Australia (1991) *Draft Reports – Ecologically Sustainable Development Working Groups*, Australian Government Publishing Service, Canberra.

Daly, H.E. (1980) *Economics, Ecology and Ethics: Essays Toward Steady-state Economy*, Freeman, San Francisco.

Dasmann, R.F., Milton, J.P. and Freeman, P.H. (1973) *Ecological Principles for Economic Development*, John Wiley, London.

Department of Home Affairs and Environment (1982) *Towards a National Conservation Strategy: A Discussion Paper*, Australian Government Publishing Service, Canberra.

Frith, H.J. (1973) *Wildlife Conservation*, Angus & Robertson, Sydney.

Global 2000 Report (1980) *The Global 2000 Report to the President of the U.S.: Entering the 21st Century*, Council on Environmental Quality and US State Department, US Government Printing Office, Washington, DC.

Hart, A.G. (1942) 'Risk, Uncertainty and the Unprofitability of Compounding Probabilities', pp. 111–8 in *Studies in Mathematical Economics and Econometrics* (ed. O. Lange, F. McIntyre and F. Yntema) University of Chicago Press, Chicago, Illinois.

IUCN (1980) *The World Conservation Strategy: Living Resource Conservation for Sustainable Development*, IUCN, Gland, Switzerland.

IUCN–UNEP–WWF (1991) *Caring for the Earth: A Strategy for Sustainable Living*, IUCN, Gland, Switzerland.

McIlroy, J.C. (1978) 'The Effects of Forestry Practices on Wildlife in Australia: A Review', *Australian Forestry*, 41(2), pp. 78–94.

Manhattan Institute for Economic Policy (1982) *Manhattan Report on Economic Policy*, 11(3), 12 pp.

Myers, N. (1979) *The Sinking Ark: A New Look at the Problem of Disappearing Species*, Pergamon, Oxford.

Myers, N. (1980) 'The Present Status and Future Prospects of Tropical Moist Forests', *Environmental Conservation*, 7(2), pp. 101–14.

Pauling, L., Benavides, F., Wahlen, F.T., Kassas, M., Vohra, B.B. and Knox, G.A. (1982) 'Open Letter: To All Who Should Be Concerned, *Environmental Conservation*, 9(2), pp. 89–90.

Pearce, D., Markandya, A. and Barbier, E.B. (1989) *Blueprint for a Green Economy*, Earthscan Publications, London.

Polunin, N. (1982) 'Our Global Environment and the World Campaign for The Biosphere', *Environmental Conservation*, 9(2), pp. 115–21.

Talbot, L.M. (1980) 'The World's Conservation Strategy', *Environmental Conservation*, 7(4), pp. 259–68.

Tisdell, C.A. (1970) 'Implications of Learning for Economic Planning', *Economics of Planning*, 10(3), pp. 177–92.

Tisdell, C.A. (1972) 'Provision of Parks and the Preservation of Nature – Some Economic Factors', *Australian Economic Papers*, 11, pp. 154–62.

Tisdell, C.A. (1975) 'The Theory of Optimal City–sizes: Some Elementary Considerations', *Urban Studies*, 12, pp. 61–70.

Tisdell, C.A. (1979) *On the Economics of Saving Wildlife from Extinction*, Department of Economics, University of Newcastle, New South Wales 2308, Australia, Research Report or Occasional Paper No. 48.

Tisdell, C.A. (1982a) *Microeconomics of Markets*, John Wiley, Brisbane.

Tisdell, C.A. (1982b) *Wild Pigs: Environmental Pest or Economic Resource?* Pergamon, Sydney.

Tisdell, C.A. (1990)   *Natural Resources, Growth and Development,* Praeger, New York.

Tisdell, C.A. (1991)   *Economics of Environmental Conservation*, Elsevier Science Publishers, Amsterdam.

WCED (World Commission on Environment and Development) (1987) *Our Common Future*, Oxford University Press, New York.

Worthington, E.B. (1982) 'World Campaign for The Biosphere', *Environmental Conservation*, 9(2), pp. 93–100.

15. Resource Conservation and Sustainability in Developing Countries and Global Concerns

The *World Conservation Strategy* (IUCN, 1980), as discussed in the previous chapter, arose from the fear that world economic activity, growth and development could prove unsustainable because of its damage to the biosphere and failure of decision makers to make adequate allowance for this. The biosphere provides ecosystems supporting all life, including human life, and damage to it, especially if permanent, can at the very least be expected to reduce economic productivity. Population growth, rising consumption levels, inadequate environmental planning and lack of forethought may be so damaging ecologically that economic growth cannot be sustained and, indeed, affluence may give way to poverty.

However, the *World Conservation Strategy* (WCS) proposed that if basic ecological guidelines are followed sustainable economic development is possible and pointed to particular measures that need to be taken in developing countries. The concept of sustainable resource use and development is important but needs to be defined more carefully, as was pointed out in previous chapters. In this chapter, it is argued that policies for sustained resource use may be of more importance to less developed countries (LDCs) than developed countries. Policies for promoting environmentally sound use of resources are discussed together with obstacles to their implementation.

WCS, SUSTAINABLE DEVELOPMENT AND SELF-INTEREST

WCS is based on the view that unless proper attention is paid to conserving the biosphere and natural ecosystems within it, economic development will be unsustainable. Man depends on living resources for his survival and economic wellbeing and it is for this reason that serious attention must be given to the deteriorating state of the biosphere. The biosphere contains ecosystems supporting all life, including human life,

225

and damage to it, especially if permanent, can at the very least be expected to reduce economic productivity. The WCS claims that ecological considerations are not a luxury but a necessity for sound and sustainable economic development.

Basically WCS was anthropocentric in focus. Human beings need to manage, arrest or slow down the deterioration of the biosphere for their own benefit. While the framers of the strategy may have a reverence for all life (for all species) they believe that most human beings are swayed by their own self-interest and therefore conservation proposals need to appeal to self-interest in order to gain widespread support.

There is little point, as recognized by the framers of WCS, in campaigning for the utopian conservation goals which policy makers have no leeway for adopting. A more realistic approach to influencing policy makers is required, namely, one which ensures that conservational aspects are taken into account in relation to the options actually open to the policy maker. For example, it may have to be accepted that various species and certain natural ecosystems will continue to disappear for some time yet. If this is so conservationists should provide guidelines on those species or ecosystems that should be given preference for preservation.

WCS stated that sustainable economic development requires:
- the maintenance of essential ecological processes and life support systems.
- the preservation of genetic diversity
- measures to ensure the sustainable use of species and ecosystems.

Agricultural systems, forests, and coastal and fresh water systems are claimed to be the most important life support systems for human beings and to be under the greatest threat. Economic growth in less developed countries (LDCs) involving the unmitigated exploitation of these systems (such as felling of tropical forests, the removal of mangroves, the felling of forests on steep hill slopes, open-access fishing) may result only in a temporary economic improvement in LDCs. The long-term economic productivity of the land and the sea may be reduced by such exploitation of nature and may result in an eventual economic and ecological crisis especially if the country's population rises in the interim (Tisdell and Fairbairn, 1984).

The *World Conservation Strategy* sees informed self-interest as being a powerful force for conservation in LDCs as well as in more developed countries. One of the ways in which LDCs might benefit from conservation is, for instance, through tourism based on conserved natural resources. But unfortunately such tourism sometimes fails to benefit local people who are forced to make a sacrifice for nature conservation. For example, Mishra (1982) found that local people in some parts of Nepal have been impoverished as a result of the establishment of national parks (Tisdell, 1983).

CONSERVATION IN LDCs, DISTRIBUTION OF GAINS, POVERTY

The way in which the costs and gains to nature conservation are distributed cannot be ignored. WCS points out that 'local commitment to a protected area can only be assured through provision of local advantage such as increased opportunities for employment and commerce'.

Nevertheless, LDCs may not appropriate all the benefits from their conservation efforts – many of the benefits may spill over to inhabitants of more developed countries without payment being made for them. Furthermore, poverty itself in LDCs is a substantial barrier to conservation. WCS states:

> Much habitat destruction and overexploitation of living resources by individuals, communities and nations in the developing world is a response to relative poverty, caused or exacerbated by a combination of human population growth and inequities within and among nations...Every country should have a conscious policy to avoid as far as possible the spread of such situations, and eventually to achieve a balance between numbers and environment. At the same time it is essential that the affluent constrain their demands on resources, and preferably reduce them, shifting some of their wealth to assisting the deprived.

Changes in the world economic order such as the removal of trade barriers to goods from developing countries and great development assistance to LDCs may help to improve their economic lot and scope for conservation. Nevertheless, rapid economic transformation of most LDCs is unlikely in the near future, even assuming widespread change in the world economic order. In fact, the present global economic system and its spread appears to be unfavourable to conservation and the achievement of sustainable development in most LDCs (Tisdell, 1992).

INTERNATIONAL DISTRIBUTION OF BENEFITS FROM CONSERVATION IN LDCs

Most advocates of sustainable development not only advocate measures to ensure that the standard of living of future generations is not less than that of current generations, but also favour greater intragenerational equality of income. The latter on average requires a redistribution of income from the more developed nations to the less developed ones. Such redistribution has been proposed by Daly (1980) and is implied by the ethics of Pearce, Markandya and Barbier (1989) as discussed in Chapter 9. Presumably greater quality of income is also called for in LDCs – in several LDCs gross inequality of income exists and in a country such as India the income levels of the wealthiest 10 per cent of the population would compare more favourably with average income levels in developed countries.

However, there is little sign that more developed countries (DCs) are prepared to redistribute income significantly in favour of LDCs. Although this would alleviate the economic condition of LDCs, it would reduce the economic (and military) power of DCs. In fact DCs have on the whole been reducing their aid to LDCs. Furthermore, in the case of most LDCs there is a net capital outflow as residents attempt to invest in DCs. This capital flight often takes place via the underground or unrecorded economy (cf. Brown, 1992). Apart from the above issue, several LDCs, or significant elements within them, believe the global conservation strategies are either intended to or in practice, benefit DCs at the expense of LDCs. Therefore, serious distribution and equity considerations are being raised by LDCs and some LDCs are demanding more aid from DCs in return for greater conservation and/or less environmental damage. Conservation of natural resources and measures to protect environmental quality by a nation can give rise to a number of favourable spillovers or externalities. Such favourable spillovers include reduction in emission of greenhouse gases and preservation of genetic resources which may be of value to developed countries.

Developed countries may also benefit by the preservation of better environments for their international tourists, retention of existence, option and bequest values of natural resources in LDCs, cheaper supply of products from natural resources in the long run and the need for less aid to LDCs in the long term than otherwise might be the case.

On the other hand, many spokespersons in LDCs charge DCs as being the main culprits responsible for global environmental deterioration. DCs have destroyed many of their own natural living resources as well as those of LDCs, and they have up until now at least mainly been the source of build–up of greenhouse gases. But conservation projects in an LDC can benefit the LDC. At the same time they may benefit DCs or other LDCs.

A range of alternative international distributions of gains from conservation in an LDC is possible. Table 15.1 sets out some possibilities. Leaders in some LDCs are concerned that possibility 4 will prevail. But it is not the only possibility. There may even be cases in which situation 6 prevails, e.g. because the benefits from conservation projects are inaccurately or falsely predicted.

Table 15.1   Some possible international distributions of net gains from conservation in an LDC.

Possibility	Net benefit to LDC	Net benefit to rest of world	Global welfare change
1	+	+	+
2	+	0	+
3	+	−	?
4	−	+	?
5	−	0	−
6	−	−	−
7	0	+	+
8	0	0	0
9	0	−	−

* Assuming the Paretian Test

More complicated patterns of distribution of gains could of course be specified by listing all countries individually. It should also be noted that conservation in a DC can have favourable consequences for LDCs, e.g. conservation of wild varieties of maize or sunflower in the USA might provide genetic resources of assistance to Latin America.

Even when both LDCs and the rest of the world gain by conservation in an LDC difficult income distributional questions can arise. These can be illustrated by the case shown in Figure 15.1. In Figure 15.1, line *DBH* represents the marginal benefit to an LDC of conserving its natural resources, e.g. protecting its natural areas. *FGC* represents the marginal benefits to the whole world of conservation in the LDC. The difference between line *DBH* and *FGC* represents the extent of the favourable marginal externality generated by conservation in the LDC. If the conservation results in the provision of a pure public good, then these curves can also be interpreted as marginal evaluation curves. Line *ABC* represents the marginal cost to the LDC of its conservation activity.

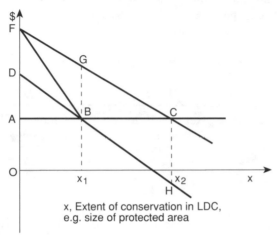

Figure 15.1   Conservation in an LDC may give rise to favourable externalities for the rest of the world. Consequently economic efficiency and equity problems may arise internationally.

In the case shown in Figure 15.1, the LDC would find it optimal acting in its own self–interest to conserve x_1 of its natural resources. From this it would achieve a net benefit equivalent to the area of triangle *ABD*. The rest of the world would make a net gain of an amount equal to the area of quadrilateral *DBGF*. It would thus be free–riding on the LDC. It would seem equitable that the rest of the world contribute to conservation in the LDC.

Apart from the equity question, it can be seen that the non–cooperative solution whereby the LDC conserves x_1 of its natural resources is not globally efficient from a Kaldor–Hicks point of view. Global efficiency requires that natural resources in the LDC be conserved up to the point where the global (collective) marginal evaluation of conserving the natural resource equals the marginal cost of doing so. This occurs in the case illustrated when x_2 of the natural resource is conserved by the LDC. But if this optimality is to be achieved, there must be a transfer from the rest of the world to the LDC to defray the entire cost involved in its extra conservation effort. The amount that needs to be transferred to the LDC if it is not to lose by the extra conservation effort required is an amount equal to the area of triangle *BHC*. This is the minimum amount which might induce the extra effort on the part of the LDC. However, it may demand more, that is in addition, some part of the surplus generated by it for the rest of the world. So a difficult bargaining problem can emerge.

Figure 15.1 can also be modified to illustrate other cases. For example, the case of an infra–marginal externality could arise (see Chapters 2 and 3). For instance, assume that everything else is unchanged in Figure 15.1 but that global marginal benefits instead of being shown by line *FGC* are indicated by curve *FBH*. Conservation levels in the LDC would then achieve a Kaldor–Hicks optimum if the LDC acted in its own self–interest but the equity or distributional question would still remain. Other possibilities can also be explored using the theory outlined in Chapters 2 and 3.

It is also possible that line *DBH* falls below marginal cost curve *ABC* but nevertheless *FGC* is above it. In that case no conservation will occur in the LDC unless it is subsidized by the rest of the world. Global efficiency in satisfying human wants requires in this case that conservation be undertaken in the LDC and thus redistribution becomes necessary to achieve efficiency.

The various cases listed in Table 15.1 can be illustrated by modifying Figure 15.1. In the case of possibility 6 for instance, both lines *DBH* and *FGC* would lie below the per unit cost line *ABC*. Simple economic theory is able to clarify a number of the global issues and concerns involved in policies to encourage conservation in LDCs.

IMPORTANCE OF SUSTAINABILITY OF RESOURCES AND ENVIRONMENT IN LDCs

Views about the importance of sustaining resource use in LDCs and the value of conservation to LDCs differ significantly. One view is that natural resource conservation is of very little value to LDCs and they would possibly be best off by sacrificing their natural resources to attain economic growth, or extend the period of their economic survival. The opposite point of view is that, given the nature of the economies of many LDCs, the slim prospects of most for sustainable economic growth in the foreseeable future and the heavy dependence of their populations on natural resources for their livelihood, conservation of natural resources should be a high priority for LDCs if they act in their own self–interest. The matter cannot be resolved here but some relevant observations can be made.

Adverse environmental impacts of economic activity in LDCs can have more serious consequences for human welfare than in developed countries. When the adverse environmental effects of economic activity in an area reduce future productivity there, affected communities in more developed countries find it relatively easy for their members to move elsewhere to other economic opportunities. Most developed countries are characterized by a high degree of mobility of labour and capital, and considerable social homogeneity.

On the other hand, most LDCs have low mobility of labour and capital (Todaro, 1981; Gunatilleke, 1973) and considerable social heterogeneity. This means that when an environmental disaster or misfortune strikes a particular area and threatens the livelihood of local people in LDCs, they are less able to   move and obtain equal or comparable economic opportunities and social satisfaction elsewhere to those previously enjoyed. Thus their income suffers and they may be thrown into extreme poverty.

A further reason why the assessment of the environmental impacts of projects is likely to be important in LDCs is that when a project has an adverse effect on income or human welfare in a locality, it can be expected that compensating relief from elsewhere in the economy will be limited. Social security systems are poorly developed in LDCs (Nugent and Gillaspy, 1983) and the scope for giving aid from intra–national sources is limited.

The inhabitants of less developed countries are much more dependent for their livelihood on living resources than those of developed countries. The bulk of the population of LDCs is typically employed in agriculture, fishing and forestry and other industries directly dependent on a living resource base (Todaro, 1981). Disturbances to the ecosystems on which these industries depend can have widespread economic consequences. This is an additional reason why any developments in LDCs giving rise to ecological effects need careful assessment.

NATURAL RESOURCE DEPLETION BY LDCs SO AS TO OBTAIN ECONOMIC GROWTH

In order to achieve economic growth and development, today's developed countries drew heavily on the world's natural resources including their own. Natural resource depletion contributed to their economic growth. While today's LDCs may have less scope for drawing on the natural resources of the rest of the world, many still have considerable reserves of natural resources.   The question then arises of whether they can emulate the economic growth achieved by DCs by running down these resources, e.g. mineral deposits and forests to achieve economic growth, for instance by converting their natural capital into man–made capital. In any case, it seems that many LDCs have embarked on or are trying to embark on this possible economic growth path. The extent to which they will be able to succeed is uncertain.

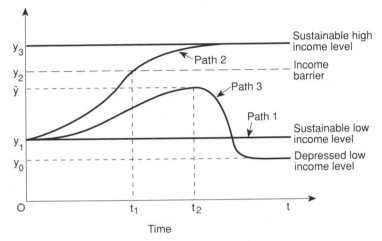

Figure 15.2 Some alternative possible economic development paths for LDCs funding economic growth by natural resource depletion.

If the most favourable scenario prevails, LDCs will be able to raise their per capita incomes sufficiently to cause human population growth to fall to zero or near zero and to engender increased concern for environmental protection and acceptance of moderation in consumption by human beings as a goal. But it is also possible that attempts to achieve such growth could fail, particularly if commenced prematurely, and create greater resource scarcity than prior to the attempt to attain sustainable development by achieving sufficiently high per capita levels of income. For example, suppose that a country is in a low–level equilibrium trap with per capita income of y_1. Path 1 in Figure 15.2 prevails in the absence of special development effort. But if the nation can launch a development effort which enables per capita income to exceed y_2 before 50 per cent of its initial stock of natural resources is exhausted, sustainable economic development might be possible. For instance in this case, a path like path 2 may prevail. However, barriers may prevent path 2 from being achieved. Attempted development might follow path 3. At time t_2 more than half of initial resource stocks might be exhausted and per capita income level $\bar{y}$ may not be sustainable. Income per head falls, population levels may now be much larger initially and eventually income per capita may fall to y_0, a lower level than initially. Attempts at economic growth or development have proven to be counterproductive – they have had miserizing results. Thus there are both optimistic and pessimistic scenarios to choose from concerning the prospects of LDCs achieving sustainable economic development by drawing on their natural resource stocks. It is possible in practice that some could follow a path like path 2 and others one like path 3.

It might be observed that DCs would be damaged as a result of either path 3 or 2 being followed by an LDC. Both involved loss of natural resources globally and path 2 may mean that the LDC is adding continually to global pollution once it attains a high per capita income level, e.g. through emissions of greenhouse gases (Tisdell, 1991; Myers et al., 1990).

POLICY FORMULATION

Given the importance of the environment (especially the biosphere) to economic activity and human welfare in LDCs, what policies can be adopted to ensure wise resource use and development in LDCs? Policies can be improved on in this regard but one must also remember that the putting into effect of government policies is itself not without cost. Policies have to be devised (this may involve costly research and bargaining) and implemented, and implementation can involve communication, regulation and enforcement costs which can weigh heavily on countries that are already poor.

The cost of policies must be weighed against their likely effectiveness and consequent benefits. A policy that cannot be carried out is of no benefit and indeed may involve considerable cost to the community if government and administrators spend their time in devising and debating it. Difficulties, however, are not an adequate excuse for taking no action.

It is important that when public projects are evaluated in LDCs (and the same is also true of private projects that come under public scrutiny) that account is taken of their main environmental impacts. Social cost–benefit analysis should not ignore environmental impacts and ecological spillovers in the assessment of projects in LDCs. In the past, however, major public projects, such as the building of the Kariba Dam, have gone ahead without any prior ecological surveys (James, 1978).

Failure to take account of ecological factors has sometimes occurred for reasons of political expediency, at other times because of failure to realize the potential importance of such variables, and on other occasions because of lack of skilled persons able to carry out evaluation. Lack of skilled evaluators, especially in very small countries (micro–states), can be a significant constraint in project evaluation; this, however, can be overcome to some extent and at a cost by drawing on the worldwide body of professionals in the field.

In foreign aid projects, it is important that environmental dimensions are kept in view. Increasingly, environmental assessments are being made of aid and related projects; for example, United States AID (Agency for International Development) is doing this and so is the World Bank. To the extent that the menu or list of available projects presented to such agencies for possible aid involves presorting by power groups in aid–receiving countries, there may already be some bias against projects that are environmentally sound but less beneficial to those power groups. Yet it is very difficult to think of practical ways of avoiding such potential biases.

IMPORTED TECHNOLOGIES

Technologies introduced to LDCs from abroad need to be assessed carefully. While some may lead to improved socio–economic and environmental conditions, other technologies may have adverse consequences. Some of the technologies in developed countries (DCs) are inappropriate to the factor composition of LDCs and may give only temporary (non–sustainable) benefits.

For example, the use of chemical pesticides in some LDCs has brought a temporary increase in crop yields but has been followed in some cases by increased resistance of pests to the chemicals involved and an increase in the population of the pests. Farmers become 'trapped' into continuing use of the technology even though it would have been best from a collective point of view never to have used it at all. This, however, is not to deny the occurrence of circumstances where enlightened use of pesticide technology is preferable to its non–use.

One can take as another example the mechanization of the traditional fisheries (Yahaya and Wells, 1983). The fishing stock exploited by fishermen in many pars of the world is already overfished both from the point of view of obtaining maximum sustainable yield and from the point of view of obtaining maximum economic yield. The mechanization of fisheries initially increases the catch, and improved economic gains may be noted at first. However, it eventually leads to a reduction in the fishing stock and a decrease in the total catch if common access to the fisheries is the rule and overfishing is already occurring.

It is possible (indeed, certain, under plausible conditions) that the total catch will eventually he lower than prior to the introduction of the new technology and the cost per unit of the catch higher than before its use. Thus, in the common–access case or in cases where it is not really possible for the government to limit access and exploitation rates or resources, the introduction of new technology can, in the end, have adverse economic and environmental consequences.

In certain cases, introduction of new technology will speed up the rate of extinction of species.   Both turtles and dugongs (sea cows), for example, have suffered as a result of the introduction of modern technology (Carr, 1968; Tisdell, 1983): outboard motors make it easier to pursue and capture these animals than was the case with non–mechanized boats.   Also, in the case of turtles, mechanization makes it easier to visit nesting grounds in remote areas and take eggs and adults.

Factors Influencing Introduction of Technologies

Political and economic pressure exists for the introduction of modern technologies into industries harvesting natural resources to which there is common access, despite adverse long–term consequences.   Those who obtain the technology first may gain substantially.   If the technology is widely available, all will gain at first.   Any group which does not have the technology may press to maintain its share in the catch or to restore it.   Thus, politically, a government may support the introduction of the technology even though collectively its introduction is economically and environmentally damaging in the medium to long term.   Furthermore, those firms and countries able to sell their technology or equipment embodying the technology have an interest in promoting its adoption.   In some cases, expressions of individual self–interest may conflict with collective long–term interests in resource use.

The economic and environmental desirability of introducing a new technology to an LDC often depends on whether use of the technology can be or will be regulated by the government of the LDC.   The economic scope for regulating economic activity in LDCs is more limited that in DCs.   Consequently technologies that prove to be desirable in DCs may turn out to be unsatisfactory in LDCs because little control over their use can be exercised in LDCs.   LDCs need to be selective in their import of foreign technologies.

To the extent that regulation of resource use in LDCs is possible and socially desirable, governments in LDCs should adopt appropriate regulatory policies.   An example would be land use zoning.   Furthermore, educational programmes and extension services can be employed to encourage environmentally sound methods of production and make individuals aware of changing environmental conditions. Sometimes individuals are slow to perceive or to foresee fundamental changes in ecological and environmental conditions (Tisdell, 1983). Nevertheless, one cannot rely purely on education and communication as the means of encouraging the most socially beneficial use of resources.

CONCLUSION

LDCs do have an interest in the conservation of living resources, at least from the point of view of maintaining production dependent on these resources. This is not to say that LDCs have an interest in conserving or maintaining all of their living resources. Sometimes they find it worthwhile to sacrifice some of these resources for short–term gains.

Again, the prime beneficiaries of nature conservation in LDCs are not always the local people but individuals in DCs and/or the wealthier members of the LDC. This has sometimes led to the view that conservational causes are those of a 'rich men's club', and that efforts to promote conservation in LDCs are a scheme primarily to benefit DCs. Nevertheless, all types of conservation in LDCs do not favour the rich nor do they benefit primarily DCs, even though some may. One's view about the desirability of any conservation scheme is liable to be influenced by the way in which its costs and benefits are distributed. Therefore, not only total benefits and costs but also distributional factors should form a part of the assessment of conservational strategies in LDCs.

REFERENCES

Brown, R.P.C. (1992) *Public Debt and Private Wealth: Debt, Capital Flight and the IMF in Sudan*, Macmillan Press, London.

Carr, A. (1968) *The Turtle: A National History of Sea Turtles*, Cassell, London.

Daly, H. (1980) *Economics, Ecology and Ethics*, Freeman, San Francisco.

Gunatilleke, G. (1973) 'The Urban–rural Balance and Development: The Experience of Sri Lanka', *Marga Quarterly Journal* 2(1), pp. 35–68.

IUCN (1980) *The World Conservation Strategy: Living Resource Conservation for Sustainable Development*, International Union for the Conservation of Nature, Gland, Switzerland.

James, J. (1978) 'Growth, Technology and the Environment in Less Developed Countries: A Survey', *World Development* 6, pp. 937–65.

Nugent, J.B. and Gillaspy, R.T. (1983) 'Old Age Pensions and Fertility in Rural Areas of Less Developed Countries: Some Evidence from Mexico', *Economic and Cultural Change*, 31(4), pp. 809–29.

Mishra, H.R. (1982) 'Balancing Human Needs and Conservation in Nepal's Royal Chitwan National Park', *Ambio*, 11(5), pp. 246–51.

Myers, N. (1979), *The Sinking Ark: A New Look at the Problem of Disappearing Species*, Pergamon Press, Oxford.

Myers, N., Ehrlich, P. R. and Ehrlich, A.H. (1990) 'The Population Problem: As Explosive as Ever', Paper delivered at Fourth International Congress on Environmental Future, Budapest. To appear in *Surviving With the Biosphere*. J. Burnett and N. Polunin (eds), Edinburgh University Press, Edinburgh.

Pearce, D., Markandya, A. and Barbier, E. G. (1989), *Blueprint for a Green Economy*, Earthscan Publications, London.

Tisdell, C.A. (1983), 'Conserving Living Resources in Third World Countries: Economic and Social Issues', *International Journal of Environmental Studies*, 22, pp. 11–24.

Tisdell, C.A. (1991) 'Population Growth and Environmental Protection: The Situation of Developing Countries in Global Perspective', pp. 224–38 in K.C. Roy, R.K. Sen, C.A. Tisdell and M. Alauddin, *Economic Development of Poor Countries*, World Press Private, Calcutta.

Tisdell, C. A. (1992) 'Conservation, Protected Areas and the Global Economic System: How Debt, Trade, Exchange Rates and Macroeconomic Policy Affect Biological Diversity', *Discussion Papers* No. 80, Department of Economics, The University of Queensland, Australia, 4072. Also in *Parks for Life: Plenary Sessions and Symposium Papers*, IVth World Congress of National Parks and Protected Areas, Caracas, Venezuela 10–21 February 1992. IUCN, Gland, Switzerland.

Tisdell. C. and Fairbairn, T.I. (1984) 'Subsistence Economies and Unsustainable Development and Trade: Some Simple Theory, *The Journal of Development Studies* 20(2), pp. 227–41.

Todaro, M.P.(1981) *Economic Development in the Third World*, 2nd ed., Longman, London.

Yahaya, J. and Wells, R.J.G. (1983) 'A Case Study of Three Gears in the Treggaun Fishery, Malaysia', *The Developing Economies* 20(1), pp. 73–99.

16. Economic Instruments for the Control of Global Environmental Problems – Recent Policy Proposals for Caring for the Earth

Compared to the World Conservation Strategy document (IUCN, 1980) its successor *Caring for the Earth: A Strategy for Sustainable Living* (IUCN–UNEP–WWF, 1991) gives much more attention to the possibility of using economic instruments to deal with environmental problems. The *World Conservation Strategy* placed most of its emphasis on administrative solutions to conservational environmental problems (Tisdell, 1983a).

Caring for the Earth recognizes that many of our environmental and sustainability problems arise in practice because the prices received and the costs paid by individual economic agents to use the environment and natural resources do not fully reflect the social costs involved (cf. NcNeely, 1988; McNeely et al., 1990). Too often environmental goods are treated as free goods, when they are, in fact, relatively scarce and therefore, from an economic point of view, should have a price attached to their use reflecting their social value. 'Clean' air, for instance, is scarce. Therefore, those who use the atmosphere to dispose of pollutants without payment for its use are making choices on a price system which does not incorporate true social economic values or costs. Such a system is bound to lead to unsatisfactory economic and environmental results.

PRICING OF NATURAL RESOURCE USE AND CARING FOR THE EARTH

Mainstream economic thought maintains that if environmental resources and natural resources are correctly priced, so as to reflect the costs of using them in terms of environmental deterioration and in terms of forgone future benefits, i.e. user costs, greater conservation will be encouraged. This view has been reflected in *Caring for the Earth*.

In common with the *World Conservation Strategy* (IUCN, 1980), *Caring for the Earth* (IUCN–UNEP–WWF, 1991) argues that sustainable development needs to be conservation–based. This, it is claimed, requires:

239

(1) conservation of life-support systems, 'the ecological processes that keep the planet fit for life' (2) conservation of biodiversity and (3) the sustainable use of renewable resources. The document recognizes that economic policy can be a powerful force for the maintenance of life support systems and the conservation of natural resources. In fact it goes further and states:

> Economic policy is also an essential instrument for achieving sustainability. Once environmental resources are correctly valued and included in national assessments, and the costs of their depletion becomes evident, the case for conservation is greatly strengthened. Economic instruments are also valuable tools for the establishment of sustainable practices because they provide a strong incentive force, while leaving individuals and industries a freedom of choice as to the precise measures they adopt (IUCN–UNEP–WWF, 1991, p. 69).

Correct valuation is required so that producers and consumers face the full social costs of their decisions and so that public planners make a more realistic evaluation of economic possibilities. Full social costs include environmental costs and user costs (benefits forgone by future users of resources as a result of decisions made by current users).

In market-oriented economic systems this implies improvements (a) in pricing policies, (b) in the allocation of property rights and (c) in the use of economic instruments (such as taxes, subsidies and tradeable permits). In those cases where the economy is of a command-planned type, or in those areas of the economy where directives rather than market signals are used to determine resource use, planning valuations (implicit or shadow prices) should reflect full social costs, that is include environmental plus user costs. All too often this is not done.

On the whole, *Caring for the Earth* favours the approach of making economic agents pay the full social cost associated with their use of resources, e.g. by adopting the Polluter Pays Principle or the User Pays Principle (IUCN–UNEP–WWF, 1991, p.70) but recognizes that a number of alternative economic instruments exist for trying to achieve this aim, each of which has its advantages and its disadvantages. The document suggests that economic measures are often more effective and efficient in terms of resource use than administrative methods in achieving resource conservation. Furthermore, a number of economic measures such as taxes on polluters, appropriate charges for natural resource use and in certain cases tradeable permits for resource or environmental use, generate public revenue. In other cases, such as deposit/refund schemes and performance bonds, the public finance effects may be neutral or almost so. On the other hand, subsidies to reduce environmentally damaging activity are a drain on public revenues, even though these can be justified in some cases, e.g. on income distributional grounds when the polluter cannot afford to adjust if taxed on pollution emissions.

The working document predating *Caring for the Earth* does not, however, suggest that there is no role for regulation. It realistically states:

A combination of incentives and regulations is the best way of protecting the environment ...

Regulations alone provide little incentive to innovate or reduce emissions below the mandatory level. Economic incentives can enable industry and other resource users to meet the standards in the most cost–effective way, and to add their resources to those of government to protect the environment. More fundamentally, they help to correct the bias of the economic system caused by the underpricing of natural assets. (IUCN–UNEP–WWF, 1990, sec. 5.29, p. 42)

Advantages of environmental policies which include economic incentives are seen to be:

(1) the encouragement of the best choice of technology and economic practices to achieve environmental goals,

(2) the harnessing of market forces such as individual self–interest,

(3) no greater cost as a rule to administer than regulation; yield government revenue if taxation, pricing, etc. is involved,

(4) encouragement of the development of pollution–reducing technology, and

(5) provision of incentives for the use and development of alternative environmentally sound products and processes (IUCN–UNEP–WWF, 1990, p. 42).

Economic measures considered in *Caring for the Earth* for correcting economic biases caused by underpricing of natural resource use include resource taxes, appropriate charges for natural resource use, subsidies, tradeable permits, deposit/refund schemes and performance bonds in this context. All, except subsidies, are intended to ensure that the user of natural resources or the environment pays for using these scarce resources, and all except subsidies are capable of providing government revenue. Most of these economic instruments were discussed in Chapter 4 of this book but it may be useful to comment on each of these in a general conservation context.

SPECIFIC ECONOMIC INSTRUMENTS FOR CARING FOR THE EARTH

Most of the economic instruments outlined in *Caring for the Earth* are intended to make the polluter or the resource user pay for environmental damage thereby internalizing the social cost of their economic decisions. But, of course, the actual polluter or resource user may not pay the whole cost because a part of it may be passed onto other economic agents in the chain of economic exchange. For example, if the pollution charge is imposed on the producer of a product this may be passed on in part to consumers or purchasers of the product in the form of a higher price for the product. The incidence of the tax rarely falls completely on the polluter or resource user if it is levied on him or her (Tisdell, 1982, sec. 15.4).

In view of the above, in some cases it makes little difference from the point of control of environmental quality whether the pollution charge is imposed on the actual polluter or the purchaser of a commodity causing pollution or on a commodity produced in a particular way that is causing pollution. To some extent all the parties involved in the exchange and economic processes are morally responsible for environmental damage when it occurs at any level in the economic process. The best point at which to levy the pollution charge in the chain of exchange seems to depend more on economic efficiency in the collection of charges and the directness of economic response to these than on morality. For example, taking into account the costs of collecting tax revenue, it may be better to impose an environmental degradation tax on producers of a product causing environmental degradation than on purchasers of the product.

Resource Taxes

The exact nature of resource taxes proposed in *Caring for the Earth* is unclear but they appear to imply taxes on the use, of natural resources so as to reduce the level of their aggregate use, e.g. to reduce the speed at which non-renewable resources are being utilized. The document (IUCN-UNEP-WWF, 1991, p. 71) suggests that 'they could replace existing taxes, or the money they raise could be returned to the taxpayer as subsidies for more sustainable technologies and practices (for example, investment in better pollution control equipment)'.

It is not suggested that the tax rates on natural resource use be uniform but that rates vary to reflect the size of externalities generated by the use of such resources. One effect of such taxes may be to encourage some restructuring of economies, e.g. in favour of environmentally benign industries, perhaps some services industries. But much will depend upon the elasticity of demand for natural resource use. If it is relatively inelastic demand may be little reduced. Furthermore within a monetary economic system, increases in money wages may be demanded to compensate for increased costs of products using natural resources subject to a resource tax. Such increases if granted will tend to offset the taxes imposed. In any case, widespread application of resource taxes will have economy–wide or macroeconomic ramifications.

Charges for the Use of Natural Resources

This suggestion seems to overlap to some extent with the above one in so far as pollution charges or taxes are concerned. These are taxes to use natural resources such as air or water as disposal sinks for wastes from economic activity and land areas such as garbage or refuse dumps for solid wastes. These charges or taxes should reflect the full social costs in making use of these facilities.

Appropriate charges should also be introduced for use of resources such as water, for example for irrigation and household use. This is likely to lead to the more efficient allocation of water resources (Tisdell, 1991, sec. 9.2) and in addition should have environmentally beneficial results, e.g. reduce offtake of waters and maintain stream flows thereby helping to sustain water quality.

In addition, tourism fees are recommended for tourist visits to protected areas. Undoubtedly there are protected areas for which charges could be introduced or increased to generate greater revenue. But the situation is complicated from an economic point of view (Tisdell, 1972a). For example, to charge a monopoly price for entry to a protected area is usually not socially optimal from a Kaldor–Hicks point of view. Furthermore, the cost of collecting fees and of excluding non–payers of fees is likely to exceed the revenue raised for some protected areas. Nevertheless their protection may still have a net economic value.

Subsidies for Environmental Protection

In some cases it may be appropriate to pay a subsidy to economic agents who adopt measures to protect or improve the environment. For instance, the external benefits obtained from tree planting in the headwaters of a drainage system may justify the payment of a subsidy to landholders in the headwaters who engage in such a programme. Subsidies do have a role when positive environmental action is or can be taken by economic agents to benefit others.

Subsidies may also in some cases have a role in encouraging economic agents not to engage in environmentally destructive behaviour, e.g. not to fell or clear existing tree cover on a property, not to discharge noxious substances from a factory. But it may not always be morally appropriate to use this instrument. One needs to consider morally how rights to degrade or not degrade the environment should be allocated. Views on this would however in most cases be modified by income distribution questions. For example, it may be morally unreasonable to expect a very poor landholder to refrain from forest destruction needed for family survival unless the individual is subsidized or provided with an alternative economic opportunity. On the other hand, if the factory owner in the above example is rich, it may be morally reasonable to apply the polluter pays principle.

As pointed out in *Caring for the Earth*, subsidies on environmental destructive behaviour should be removed. Until recently in many countries (and to some extent, still), subsidies or tax concessions were given to agriculturalists for environmentally damaging actions, e.g. clearing of tree cover, drainage of wetlands, use of chemical pesticides and fertilizers.

Deposit/Refund Schemes and Performance Bonds

Deposit/refund schemes and performance bonds are basically adopted as a measure to insure against non-compliance with an environmental requirement. For example, a mining company may be required to rehabilitate a mining site after completion of mining by contouring it and revegetating it. Once this is done, its deposit may be refunded to it by the public authority concerned. To be fully effective as a guarantee the deposit should equal or exceed the cost of rectifying the environmental damage caused. Otherwise the company or firm involved has an economic incentive not to undertake the rectification and forfeit the deposit or bond. When the bond involves an undertaking to avoid certain types of environmental damage, the bond should exceed or equal the value to the company of causing the environmental damage in question.

Tradeable Pollution or Resource Use Permits

Permits to release pollutants or to use a natural resource up to some overall allowable level may be allocated by auction or on the basis of historical use and may be tradeable, as discussed in Chapter 4. If permits are allocated on historical use, as is quite common, possibly for political reasons, they are likely to provide a windfall economic gain to historical users if the permits can be traded. Whether or not traditional users should be assigned property rights in this way is, however, a moot point. For example, take the case of fish in the coastal waters of a country – should they be regarded as national property or the property of fishing groups? If the former is the case an auctioning of permits would seem more appropriate than historical assignment. Nevertheless, the results of auctioning will depend upon the number of competitors or extent of competition in the industry. However, a tradeable permit system can be an efficient method of controlling use of the environment.

Caring for the Earth (IUCN–UNEP–WWF, 1992, p. 72) gives the impression that in some respects tradeable permits may not be as satisfactory as pollution or environmental degradation charges or taxes. They may be seen as giving pollution rights to permit holders. The document states 'to avoid controversy over this "polluter–buys" mechanism, money raised in this way is best earmarked for compensation for environmental damage, clean up of pollution and restoration of degraded ecosystems' (IUCN–UNEP–WWF, 1992, p. 72). But it is hard to see in this respect how this mechanism differs from charges for pollution, or taxes on pollution for that matter. Having paid the charge or tax, the payee has the right to pollute also.

Comment

It might be noted that the document does not mention environmental offsets as a possible part of economic policy. As discussed for example in Chapter 8 of this book, Pearce, Markandya and Barbier (1989) see environmental offsets as possibly playing an important role in attaining sustainability of development.

While the economic instruments mentioned in *Caring for the Earth* can help, they are by no means a magical solution in themselves to environmental and sustainability problems. The effective use of such instruments requires an adequate legal system, monitoring of performance, and enforcement of charges. Legal, monitoring and enforcement systems are not always well developed. In general, monitoring and enforcement costs tend to be relatively higher and less reliable in developing countries than in developed ones (Tisdell, 1972b, 1983b, 1990, 1991). Thus it may be more difficult, even uneconomic, to apply such economic instruments as widely in less developed countries as in developed ones. They are likely to be easier to apply in market systems than in economies where market systems are not well developed. There are also problems to be overcome, such as their application on a global scale. Many environmental issues such as the greenhouse issue require action on a global scale, that is by all nations (cf. World Commission for Environment and Development, 1987).

INTERNATIONAL ASPECTS OF USING ECONOMIC INSTRUMENTS FOR ENVIRONMENTAL CONTROL

The possibility of a global carbon tax or global tradeable carbon permits highlights many of the difficult issues which we have to face up to in controlling global pollution. While a taxation system might be efficient, residents in less developed countries might be least able to pay taxes on energy use. Tradeable carbon use permits are a possibility. But how will the initial allocation of permits be made? If the allocation is on the basis of current carbon use, the largest initial allocation of rights would go to developed countries. In the absence of world government, how will countries be forced to keep within the carbon use limits set by their holding of carbon use permits? No matter what means we use to control carbon use, we shall have to address such issues.

Note also that another international aspect needs to be considered. This is the comparative speed with which different countries shift to a system of charging for resource depletion and environmental use. This affects the comparative competitiveness of industries in different countries and can alter the international location of industries. In the absence of co-ordination, an optimal range of policies may not occur internationally. There is also the problem that encouraging 'clean' industries at home, such as knowledge–intensive and low energy–using industries, and discouraging polluting industries may result in the growth of 'dirty' industries abroad, the products of which are imported to the home country. Thus pollution is apparently exported. But if the effects of the polluting industries are global, these changes could result in greater pollution globally than if the dirty industries were kept at home. This will be so if there is greater pollution control at home but a lot less control offshore. In any case, global interdependence must be recognized in relation to these issues and the international dimensions need to be addressed.

In general, possibly on income distribution grounds and the basis of practicability, *Caring for the Earth* suggests that high–consumption countries move quickly to ensure that the prices of natural resources used reflects fully their social cost. But in the case of other countries it suggests a softer policy option. It suggests that 'governments in other countries, while seeking the same goal, should introduce such measures more gradually and specifically applying them first to industrial sections and urban areas where energy consumption is high and wasteful' (IUCN–UNEP–WWF, 1992, p. 48). Such a differentiated approach between high and low income countries will clearly add to the distortions mentioned above.

Returning to the question of a global carbon tax or a global tradeable carbon permits system, less developed countries are unlikely to accept a uniform carbon tax on the basis that it is likely to disadvantage them on distributional grounds. Even if the tax were to be used to fund the United Nations or be used in part to provide LDCs with income supplements it still may not be acceptable for political reasons. In relation to tradeable permits the initial allocation is likely to be a stumbling block. A system of auctioning is unlikely to be acceptable to less developed countries on distributional grounds. An allocation based on historical use would most likely be considered unfair by less developed countries since it would result in the lion's share of allocation going to high income countries, and would be perceived as an impediment to the development of LDCs. We are a long way from solving the global prisoner dilemma type problems involved.

CONCLUDING COMMENTS

The use of economic instruments can help ensure a better balance between the conservation of environmental commodities, conservation of natural resource capital and the supply of man–made or non–environmental commodities. Many of our environmental and sustainability problems are a result of deficiencies in economic systems which can be overcome to some extent by the use of appropriate economic instruments. The recognition of this in the document *Caring for the Earth* is an advance in policy perception compared to the *World Conservation Strategy* (IUCN, 1980). But not all of our conservation and environmental problems arise from inadequate pricing of use of the environment and natural resources. For example, attitudes, including moral attitudes, also play a role and population growth may not be an entirely economic matter. At the same time as making more use of the type of economic instruments mentioned above, we need to make renewed efforts on other fronts such as in population control policy and in improving perceptions about environmental and sustainability issues. *Caring for the Earth* recognizes the need to make advances simultaneously on several fronts. Most of the broad policy measures considered in this document (IUCN–UNEP–WWF, 1991) are complements rather than substitutes for one another.

While *Caring for the Earth* does not provide perfect policy measures for dealing with global environmental problems, it highlights the need for action and identifies several worthwhile policy responses. However, the main barrier to implementing global policies may be a political one. The continuing existence of nation states and the interest of most in strengthening or maintaining their international power, which in the long term is related to their comparative economic wealth, makes it difficult to implement many policies worldwide which would ease global environmental problems. There is little evidence that high income nations are willing to share their wealth with poor nations on any significant scale. They are likely to be equally reluctant to forgo their use of energy resources on a major scale in favour say of industrializing low income countries so as to reduce greenhouse emissions. But it should be observed that the wealthy in less developed nations may be no less averse to sharing their wealth with the poor. There is a long way to go in practice before the sharing ethic advocated by a number of proponents of sustainable development is accepted in practice.

There is also the further political problem especially in democracies but not exclusively so, that short–term results may be preferred to long–term sustainable ones. Political parties in power may find it necessary to provide benefits to the electorate within an election period and this may result in myopia in political decision making. Furthermore, votes may depend upon political parties satisfying particular interest groups within the electorate. Persons outside the electorate do not count directly for voting purposes, e.g. persons outside the electorate living in less developed countries.

In view of the above political factors, significant political limitations must be overcome before global environmental policies and measures to attain worldwide sustainable development are likely to be fully implemented. The absence of effective world government and the selfish interest of individual nations wanting to maintain their international power (often not unreasonably in order to preserve their way of life in a world in which values sometimes clash) is a major stumbling block to overcome in implementing policies for global environmental conservation. Even though these difficulties must be recognized, we cannot afford to ignore consideration of what needs to be done internationally to address our global environmental problems effectively.

REFERENCES

IUCN (1980) *World Conservation Strategy*, IUCN, Gland, Switzerland.

IUCN–UNEP–WWF (1990) *Caring for the World: A Strategy for Sustainable Living*, 2nd draft, IUCN, Gland, Switzerland.

IUCN–UNEP–WWF (1991) *Caring for the Earth: A Strategy for Sustainability*, IUCN, Gland, Switzerland.

Pearce, D., Markandya, A. and Barbier, E.B. (1989) *Blueprint for a Green Economy*, Earthscan Publications, London.

McNeely, J.A. (1988) *Economics and Biological Diversity: Developing and Using Economic Incentives to Conserve Biological Resources*, IUCN, Gland, Switzerland.

McNeely, J.A., Miller, K.R., Reid, W.V., Mittermeier, R.A., Werner, T.B. (1990) *Conserving the World's Biological Diversity*, IUCN, Gland, Switzerland.

Tisdell, C.A. (1972a) 'Provision of Parks and Preservation of Nature – Some Economic Factors', *Australian Economic Papers*, 11, pp. 154–62.

Tisdell, C.A. (1972b) 'The Economic Conservation and Utilisation of Wildlife Species', *The South African Journal of Economics*, 40(3) pp. 235–48.

Tisdell, C.A. (1982) *Microeconomics of Markets*, John Wiley, Brisbane.

Tisdell, C.A. (1983a) 'An Economist's Critique of the World Conservation Strategy, with examples from Australian Experience', *Environmental Conservation*, 10(1), pp. 43–52.

Tisdell, C.A. (1983b) 'Conserving Living Resources in Third World Countries: Economic and Social Issues', *The International Journal of Environmental Studies*, 22, pp. 11–24.

Tisdell, C.A. (1990) *Natural Resources, Growth and Development: Economics, Ecology and Resource–Scarcity*, Praeger, New York.

Tisdell, C.A. (1991) *Economics of Environmental Conservation*, Elsevier Science Publishers, Amsterdam.

WCED (World Commission for Environment and Development) (1987) *Our Common Future*, Oxford University Press, New York.

Acknowledgements

All of the chapters of this book (except Chapter 8), are based on a selection of my previously published articles, the originals of which have been modified or extended. These are specified below. I am grateful to the appropriate editors and/or publishers for their permission to me to draw on or to reproduce these works in those cases where permission was required.

Chapter   Article

1.   'Markets and Economic Analysis as Guides to Conservation', pp. 63–73 in J.R.G. Butler (ed.) *Current Economics Issues 1986*, Department of Marketing and Applied Economics, Brisbane College of Advanced Education, Kedron, Queensland 4031, 1986.
2.   'On the Theory of Externalities' *The Economic Record*, 46(113), 1970, pp. 14–25.
3.   'Non–marginal Externalities: As Relevant and as Not', *The Economic Record*, 49(127), 1973, pp. 447–55 (with C. Walsh).
4.   'Pollution Control: Policies Proposed by Economists', *Journal of Environmental Systems*, 12(4), 1983, pp. 363–80.
5.   'The Law, Economics and Risk–Taking', *Kyklos*, 36(1), 1983, pp. 3–20.
6.   'Externalities and Coasian Considerations in Project Evaluation: Aspects of Social CBA and LDCs', *Indian Journal of Quantitative Economics*, 1(1), 1985, pp. 33–43.
7.   'Cost–Benefit Analysis, the Environment and Informational Constraints in LDCs', *Journal of Economic Development*, 11(2), 1986, pp. 63–81.
9.   'The Nature of Sustainability and of Sustainable Development', *Middle East Business and Economic Review*, 4(1), 1992, pp. 21–5.
10.   'Sustainable Development: Differing Perspectives of Ecologists and Economists and Relevance to LDCs', *World Development*, 16, 1988, pp. 373–84.
11.   'Economics, Ecology, Sustainable Agricultural Systems and Development', *Development Southern Africa*, 2, 1985, pp. 512–21.

12.   'The Exploitation of Techniques that Decline in Effectiveness with Use', *Public Finance*, 37(3), 1982, pp. 153–71.
13.   *Ecological or Green Economics: Genuine Contribution or Fashionable Fad?*, The University of Queensland Inaugural Lecture, University of Queensland Press, St. Lucia, 4067, Australia, 1991.
14.   'An Economist's Critique of the World Conservation Strategy with Examples from Australian Experience', *Environmental Conservation*, 10(1), 1983, pp. 43–52.
15.   'World Conservation Strategy, Economic Development and Sustainable Resource–Use in Developing Countries', *Environmental Professional*, 7, 1985, pp. 102–7.
16.   'Application of Economic Instruments to Environmental Problems: Proposals for the updated World Conservation Strategy'. A paper presented to Workshop One of the 18th General Assembly of the IUCN (World Conservation Union), Perth, Western Australia, 1990.

As requested by the Managing Editor of *Public Finance*, I would like to mention specifically that Chapter 12 was originally published in *Public Finance/Finances Publiques*, 37, 1982, pp. 153–71. It is reprinted with the permission of the publisher, Foundation Journal Public Finance.

Index

The Physics of Quantum Information

Springer
Berlin
Heidelberg
New York
Barcelona
Hong Kong
London
Milan
Paris
Singapore
Tokyo

Physics and Astronomy ONLINE LIBRARY

http://www.springer.de/phys/

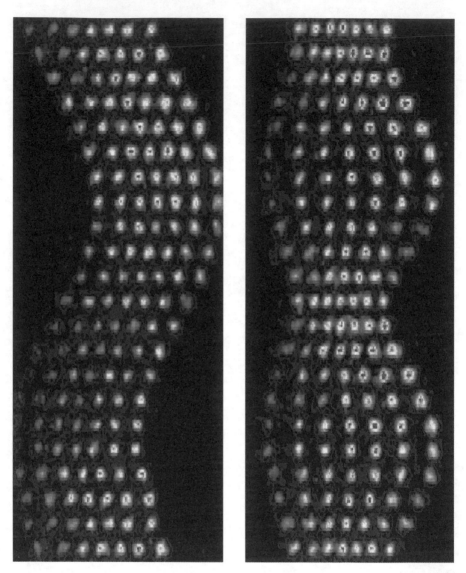

Experimental demonstration of the breathing mode (left) and the centre-of-mass motion (right) of a string of 7 ions which form an array of 7 qubits. The figures are compilations of a sequence of snapshots taken of the string of ions (see Chapter 5). Figures by J. Eschner, F. Schmidt-Kaler, R. Blatt, Institut für Experimentalphysik, Universität Innsbruck.

Dirk Bouwmeester
Artur Ekert
Anton Zeilinger (Eds.)

The Physics
of Quantum Information

Quantum Cryptography
Quantum Teleportation
Quantum Computation

With 125 Figures

 Springer

Dr. Dirk Bouwmeester
Prof. Artur Ekert
Centre for Quantum Computation
Clarendon Laboratory
University of Oxford
Parks Road
Oxford OX1 3PU
United Kingdom

Prof. Anton Zeilinger
Institut für Experimentalphysik
University of Vienna
Boltzmanngasse 5
1090 Vienna
Austria

Cover picture: Photo by P. Kwiat and M. Reck, © Institut für Experimentalphysik, University of Vienna

Library of Congress Cataloging-in-Publication Data applied for.

Die Deutsche Bibliothek - CIP-Einheitsaufnahme

The physics of quantum information : quantum cryptography, quantum teleportation, quantum computation / Dirk Bouwmeester ... (ed.). - Berlin ; Heidelberg ; New York ; Barcelona ; Hong Kong ; London ; Milan ; Paris ; Singapore ; Tokyo : Springer, 2000
ISBN 3-540-66778-4

ISBN 3-540-66778-4 Springer-Verlag Berlin Heidelberg New York

First Edition 2000. Second Printing 2001

Springer-Verlag Berlin Heidelberg New York
a member of BertelsmannSpringer Science+Business Media GmbH
© Springer-Verlag Berlin Heidelberg 2000
Printed in Germany

The use of general descriptive names, registered names, trademarks, etc. in this publication does not imply, even in the absence of a specific statement, that such names are exempt from the relevant protective laws and regulations and therefore free for general use.

Camera-ready by the editors using a Springer TeX macro package.
Cover design: Erich Kirchner, Heidelberg

SPIN: 10793524   56/3111 – 5 4 3 2 1 – Printed on acid-free paper

Preface

Information is stored, transmitted and processed by physical means. Thus, the concept of information and computation can be formulated in the context of a physical theory and the study of information requires ultimately experimentation. This sentence, innocuous at first glance, leads to non-trivial consequences.

Following Moore's law, about every 18 months microprocessors double their speed and, it seems, the only way to make them significantly faster is to make them smaller. In the not too distant future they will reach the point where the logic gates are so small that they consist of only a few atoms each. Then quantum-mechanical effects will become important. Thus, if computers are to continue to become faster (and therefore smaller), new, quantum technology must replace or supplement what we have now. But it turns out that such technology can offer much more than smaller and faster microprocessors. Several recent theoretical results have shown that quantum effects may be harnessed to provide qualitatively new modes of communication and computation, in some cases much more powerful than their classical counterparts.

This new quantum technology is being born in many laboratories. The last two decades have witnessed experiments in which single quantum particles of different kinds were controlled and manipulated with an unprecedented precision. Many "gedanken" experiments, so famous in the early days of quantum mechanics, have been carried out. New experimental techniques now make it possible to store and process information encoded in individual quantum systems. As a result we have a new, fledgling field of quantum information processing that represents a highly fertile synthesis of the principles of quantum physics with those of computer and information science. Its scope ranges from providing a new perspective on fundamental issues about the nature of physical law to investigating the potential commercial exploitation by the computing and communications industries.

As part of the worldwide effort in the field, the European Commission, within the framework of the TMR (Training and Mobility of Researchers) programme, is supporting a network entitled "The Physics of Quantum Information". The chapters in this book are mainly written by various members of the network in different forms of collaboration, and they are all intended to give a didactic introduction to essential, new areas. In addition, several sections present important achievements by researchers outside the TMR network. However, it was not our aim to write a monograph giving a complete overview of the field. Research in this field has become very active, and any comprehensive review of the field would be obsolete in a short time. The topics that are covered by this book include theoretical and experimental aspects of quantum entanglement, quantum cryptography, quantum teleportation, quantum computation, quantum algorithms, quantum-state decoherence, quantum error correction, and quantum communication.

We hope that this book will be a valuable contribution to the literature for all those who have a modest background in quantum mechanics and a genuine interest in the fascinating possibilities that it is offering us.

We are very grateful to Thomas Jennewein for the numerous figures that he drew for this book.

Oxford, Vienna, March 2000

Dirk Bouwmeester
Artur Ekert
Anton Zeilinger

Contents

List of Contributors

H. Baldauf
Sect. 5.3
Max–Planck–Institut
für Quantenoptik
Hans–Kopfermann–Str. 1
85748 Garching, Germany

R. Blatt
Sects. 5.2, 5.3
Institut für Experimentalphysik
Universität Innsbruck
Technikerstrasse 25
6020 Innsbruck, Austria

S. Bose
Sect. 3.11
Centre for Quantum Computation
Clarendon Laboratory
University of Oxford
OX1 3PU Oxford, England

D. Bouwmeester
Chap. 1, Sects. 3.1–3.3, 3.5–3.10, 6.3
Centre for Quantum Computation
Clarendon Laboratory
University of Oxford
OX1 3PU Oxford, England

H.-J. Briegel
Sects. 6.2, 8.2, 8.6, 8.7
Sektion Physik
Ludwig–Maximilians–Universität
Theresienstrasse 37
80333 München, Germany

M. Brune
Sect. 5.2
Laboratoire Kastler Brossel
Département de Physique
de l'Ecole Normale Supérieure
24 rue Lhomond
75231 Paris, Cedex 05, France

J.I. Cirac
Sects. 4.3, 6.2, 8.6, 8.7
Institut für Theoretische Physik
Universität Innsbruck
Technikerstrasse 25
6020 Innsbruck, Austria

M. Daniell
Sect. 6.3
Institut für Experimentalphysik
Universität Wien
Boltzmanngasse 5
1090 Wien, Austria

D. Deutsch
Sect. 4.1
Centre for Quantum Computation
Clarendon Laboratory
University of Oxford
OX1 3PU Oxford, England

W. Dür
Sects. 8.6, 8.7
Institut für Theoretische Physik
Universität Innsbruck
Technikerstrasse 25
6020 Innsbruck, Austria

A. Ekert
Chap. 2, Sects. 4.1, 7.2, 7.6
Centre for Quantum Computation
Clarendon Laboratory
University of Oxford
OX1 3PU Oxford, England

S.J. van Enk
Sects. 6.2, 8.6
Norman Bridge Laboratory of Physics
California Institute
of Technology 12-22
Pasadena, California 91125, USA

J. Eschner
Sects. 5.2, 5.3
Institut für Experimentalphysik
Universität Innsbruck
Technikerstrasse 25
6020 Innsbruck, Austria

N. Gisin
Chap. 2, Sects. 3.4, 8.3
University of Geneva
Group of Applied Physics
20 Rue de l'Ecole de Médecine
1211 Geneva 4, Switzerland

S. Haroche
Sect. 5.2
Laboratoire Kastler Brossel
Département de Physique
de l'Ecole Normale Supérieure
24 rue Lhomond
75231 Paris, Cedex 05, France

S.F. Huelga
Sect. 7.6
Departamento de Fisica
Universidad de Oviedo
Calvo Sotelo s/n.
33007 Oviedo, Spain

B. Huttner
Chap. 2, Sect. 8.3
University of Geneva
Group of Applied Physics
20 Rue de l'Ecole de Médecine
1211 Geneva 4, Switzerland

H. Inamori
Chap. 2
Centre for Quantum Computation
Clarendon Laboratory
University of Oxford
OX1 3PU Oxford, England

J.A. Jones
Sect. 5.4
Centre for Quantum Computation
Clarendon Laboratory
University of Oxford
OX1 3PU Oxford, England

R. Jozsa
Sect. 4.2
Department of Computer Science
University of Bristol
Merchant Venturers Building
Woodland Road
BS8 1UB Bristol, England

P.L. Knight
Sects. 3.11, 6.4, 7.3, 8.5
Optics Section
Blackett Laboratory
Imperial College London
London SW7 2BZ, England

W. Lange
Sect. 5.3
Max–Planck–Institut
für Quantenoptik
Hans–Kopfermann–Str. 1
85748 Garching, Germany

D. Leibfried
Sect. 5.2
Institut für Experimentalphysik
Universität Innsbruck
Technikerstrasse 25
6020 Innsbruck, Austria

C. Macchiavello
Sects. 7.4, 7.6, 8.4
Dipartimento di Fisica "A.Volta"
and INFM-Unité di Pavia
via Bassi 6
27100 Pavia, Italy

M. Murao
Sect. 8.5
Optics Section
Blackett Laboratory
Imperial College London
London SW7 2BZ, England

H.C. Nägerl
Sects. 5.2, 5.3
Institut für Experimentalphysik
Universität Innsbruck
Technikerstrasse 25
6020 Innsbruck, Austria

G.M. Palma
Sects. 7.2, 7.4
Dipartimento di Scienze Fisiche
ed Astronomiche & unita'INFM
via Archirafi 36
90123 Palermo, Italy

J.-W. Pan
Sects. 3.7, 3.10, 6.3
Institut für Experimentalphysik
Universität Wien
Boltzmanngasse 5
1090 Wien, Austria

M.B. Plenio
Sects. 6.4, 7.3, 7.6, 8.5
Optics Section
Blackett Laboratory
Imperial College London
London SW7 2BZ, England

S. Popescu
Sect. 8.5
5BRIMS Hewlett–Packard
Laboratories
Stoke Gifford
Bristol BS12 6QZ, England

J.F. Poyatos
Sect. 4.3
Centre for Quantum Computation
Clarendon Laboratory
University of Oxford
OX1 3PU Oxford, England

J.-M. Raimond
Sect. 5.2
Laboratoire Kastler Brossel
Département de Physique
de l'Ecole Normale Supérieure
24 rue Lhomond
75231 Paris, Cedex 05, France

J.G. Rarity
Sect. 3.4
DERA Malvern
St. Andrews Road, Malvern
Worcester WR14 3PS, England
and
Centre for Quantum Computation
Clarendon Laboratory
University of Oxford
OX1 3PU Oxford, England

F. Schmidt-Kaler
Sects. 5.2, 5.3
Institut für Experimentalphysik
Universität Innsbruck
Technikerstrasse 25
6020 Innsbruck, Austria

A. Steane
Sect. 7.5
Centre for Quantum Computation
Clarendon Laboratory
University of Oxford
OX1 3PU Oxford, England

K.-A. Suominen
Sect. 7.2
Helsinki Institute of Physics
PL 9, FIN-00014 Helsingin
Yliopisto, Finland

V. Vedral
Sects. 3.11, 6.4, 8.5
Centre for Quantum Computation
Clarendon Laboratory
University of Oxford
OX1 3PU Oxford, England

G. Weihs
Sect. 3.4
Institut für Experimentalphysik
Universität Wien
Boltzmanngasse 5
1090 Wien, Austria

H. Weinfurter
*Chap. 2, Sects. 3.1–3.3, 3.5–3.7,
3.10, 6.3*
Sektion Physik
Ludwig–Maximilians–Universität
München
Schellingstr. 4/III
80799 München, Germany

H. Walther
Sect. 5.3
Max–Planck–Institut
für Quantenoptik
Hans–Kopfermann–Str. 1
85748 Garching, Germany

A. Zeilinger
*Chap. 1, Sects. 3.1–3.3, 3.5–3.7,
3.10, 6.3*
Institut für Experimentalphysik
Universität Wien
Boltzmanngasse 5
1090 Wien, Austria

P. Zoller
Sects. 4.3, 6.2, 8.6, 8.7
Institut für Theoretische Physik
Universität Innsbruck
Technikerstrasse 25
6020 Innsbruck, Austria

1. The Physics of Quantum Information: Basic Concepts

D. Bouwmeester, A. Zeilinger

1.1 Quantum Superposition

The superposition principle plays the most central role in all considerations of quantum information, and in most of the "gedanken" experiments and even the paradoxes of quantum mechanics. Instead of studying it theoretically or defining it abstractly, we will discuss here the quintessential experiment on quantum superposition, the double-slit experiment (Fig. 1.1). According to Feynman [1], the double-slit "has in it the heart of quantum mechanics". The essential ingredients of the experiment are a source, a double-slit assembly, and an observation screen on which we observe interference fringes. These interference fringes may easily be understood on the basis of assuming a wave property of the particles emerging from the source. It might be mentioned here that the double-slit experiment has been performed with many different kinds of particles ranging from photons [2], via electrons [3], to neutrons [4] and atoms [5]. Quantum mechanically, the state is the coherent superposition

$$|\Psi\rangle = \frac{1}{\sqrt{2}}(|\Psi_a\rangle + |\Psi_b\rangle)\,, \tag{1.1}$$

where $|\Psi_a\rangle$ and $|\Psi_b\rangle$ describe the quantum state with only slit a or slit b open.

The interesting feature in the quantum double-slit experiment is the observation that, as confirmed by all experiments to date, the interference pattern can be collected one by one, that is, by having such a low intensity that only one particle interferes with itself. If this happens, we might be tempted to ask ourselves which of the two slits a particle "really" takes in the experiment. The answer from standard quantum mechanics is that it is not possible to make any sensible statement about the question "which slit does the particle pass through?" without using the appropriate set-up able to answer that question. In fact, if we were to perform any kind of experiment determining through which of the two slits the particle passes, we would have to somehow interact with the particle and this would lead to decoherence, that is, loss of interference. Only when there is no way of knowing, not even in principle,

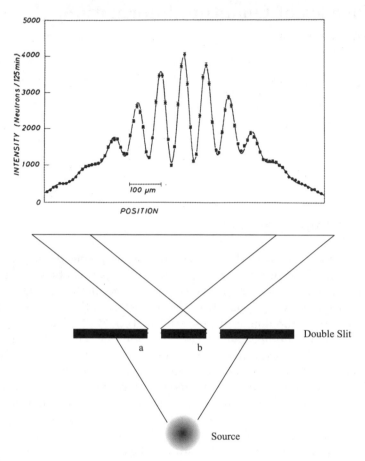

Fig. 1.1. Principle of the double-slit experiment. An interference pattern arises in an observation plane behind a double-slit assembly, even if the intensity of the source is so low that there is only one particle at a time in the apparatus. The actual interference pattern shown here is the experimental data obtained for a double-slit experiments with neutrons [4].

through which slit the particle passes, do we observe interference. As a small warning we might mention that it is not even possible to say that the particle passes through both slits at the same time, although this is a position often held. The problem here is that, on the one hand, this is a contradictory sentence because a particle is a localised entity, and, on the other hand, there is no operational meaning in such a statement. We also note that one can have partial knowledge of the slit the particle passes at the expense of partial decoherence.

1.2 Qubits

The most fundamental entity in information science is the bit. This is a system which carries two possible values, "0" and "1". In its classical realisation the bit, which, for example could be imagined to be just a mechanical switch, is a system which is designed to have two distinguishable states; there should be a sufficiently large energy barrier between them that no spontaneous transition, which would evidently be detrimental, can occur between the two states.

The quantum analog of a bit, the *Qubit* [6], therefore also has to be a two-state system where the two states are simply called $|0\rangle$ and $|1\rangle$. Basically any quantum system which has at least two states can serve as a qubit, and there are a great variety possible, many of which have already been realised experimentally. The most essential property of quantum states when used to encode bits is the possibility of coherence and superposition, the general state being

$$|Q\rangle = \alpha|0\rangle + \beta|1\rangle\,, \tag{1.2}$$

with $|\alpha|^2 + |\beta|^2 = 1$. What this means is not that the value of a qubit is somewhere between "0" and "1", but rather that the qubit is in a superposition of both states and, if we measure the qubit we will find it with probability $|\alpha|^2$ to carry the value "0" and with probability $|\beta|^2$ to carry the value "1";

$$p(\text{``0''}) = |\alpha|^2\,, \quad p(\text{``1''}) = |\beta|^2\,. \tag{1.3}$$

While by the definition of the qubit we seem to lose certainty about its properties, it is important to know that (1.2) describes a *coherent* superposition rather than an incoherent mixture between "0" and "1". The essential point here is that for a coherent superposition there is always a basis in which the value of the qubit is well defined, while for an incoherent mixture it is a mixture whatever way we choose to describe it. For simplicity consider the specific state

$$|Q'\rangle = \frac{1}{\sqrt{2}}(|0\rangle + |1\rangle)\,. \tag{1.4}$$

This clearly means that with 50% probability the qubit will be found to be either in "0" or "1". But interestingly, in a basis rotated by 45° in Hilbert space the value of the qubit is well-defined. We might simply study this by applying the proper transformation to the qubit. One of the most basic transformations in quantum information science is the so-called Hadamard transformation whose actions on a qubit are

$$H|0\rangle \rightarrow \frac{1}{\sqrt{2}}(|0\rangle + |1\rangle)\,, \quad H|1\rangle \rightarrow \frac{1}{\sqrt{2}}(|0\rangle - |1\rangle)\,. \tag{1.5}$$

Applying this to the qubit $|Q'\rangle$ above, results in

$$H|Q'\rangle = |0\rangle \,. \tag{1.6}$$

that is, a well-defined value of the qubit. This is never possible with an incoherent mixture.

1.3 Single-Qubit Transformations

Insight in some of the most basic experimental procedures in quantum information physics can be gained by investigating the action of a simple 50/50 beamsplitter. Such beamsplitters have been realised for many different types of particles, not only for photons. For a general beamsplitter, as shown in Fig. 1.2, let us investigate the case of just two incoming modes and two outgoing modes which are arranged as shown in the figure.

For a 50/50 beamsplitter, a particle incident either from above or from below has the same probability of 50% of emerging in either output beam, above or below. Then quantum unitarity, that is, the requirement that no particles are lost if the beamsplitter is non-absorbing, implies certain phase conditions on the action of the beamsplitter [7] with one free phase. A very simple way to describe the action of a beamsplitter is to fix the phase relations such that the beamsplitter is described by the Hadamard transformation of (1.5).

Let us again assume that the incident state is the general qubit

$$|Q\rangle_{in} = \alpha|0\rangle_{in} + \beta|1\rangle_{in} \,. \tag{1.7}$$

For a single incident particle this means that α is the probability amplitude to find the particle incident from above and β is the probability amplitude for

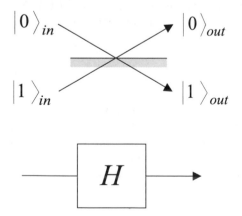

Fig. 1.2. The 50/50 beamsplitter (top) and the corresponding diagram using the Hadamard transform H (below).

finding the particle incident from below. Then the action of the beamsplitter results in the final state

$$|Q\rangle_{out} = H|Q\rangle_{in} = \frac{1}{\sqrt{2}} \left((\alpha + \beta)|0\rangle_{out} + (\alpha - \beta)|1\rangle_{out} \right), \tag{1.8}$$

where $(\alpha + \beta)$ is now the probability amplitude for finding the particle in the outgoing upper beam and $(\alpha - \beta)$ is the probability amplitude for finding it in the outgoing lower beam. For the specific case of either $\alpha = 0$ or $\beta = 0$, we find that the particle will be found with equal probability in either of the outgoing beams. For another specific case, $\alpha = \beta$, we find that the particle will definitely be found in the upper beam and never in the lower beam.

It is interesting and instructive to consider sequences of such beamsplitters because they realise sequences of Hadamard transformations. For two successive transformations the Mach–Zehnder interferometer (Fig. 1.3) with two identical beamsplitters results.

Furthermore, the mirrors shown only serve to redirect the beams; they are assumed to have identical action on the two beams and therefore can be omitted in the analysis. The full action of the interferometer can now simply be described as two successive Hadamard transformations acting on the general incoming state of (1.7):

$$|Q\rangle_{out} = HH|Q\rangle_{in} = |Q\rangle_{in}. \tag{1.9}$$

This results from the simple fact that double application of the Hadamard transformation of (1.5) is the identity operation. It means that the Mach–Zehnder interferometer as sketched in Fig. 1.3, with beamsplitters realising the Hadamard transformation at its output, reproduces a state identical to the input. Let us consider again the extreme case where the input consists of one beam only, that is, without loss of generality, let us assume $\alpha = 1$, the lower beam being empty. Then, according to (1.9), the particle will def-

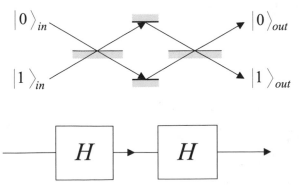

Fig. 1.3. A Mach–Zehnder interferometer (top) is a sequence of two Hadamard transformations (bottom).

initely be found in the upper output. Most interestingly, this is because between the two beamsplitters the particle would have been found (with the correct relative phase) with equal probability in both beam paths. It is the interference of the two amplitudes incident on the final beamsplitter which results in the particle ending up with certainty in one of the outgoing beams and never in the other.

In quantum information language, the output qubit of the empty Mach–Zehnder interferometer will have a definite value if the input qubit also has a definite value, and this only because between the two Hadamard transformations the value of the qubit was maximally undefined.

Another important quantum gate besides the Hadamard gate is the phase shifter, which is introduced additionally in Fig. 1.4 into the Mach–Zehnder interferometer. Its operation is simply to introduce a phase change φ to the amplitude of one of the two beams (without loss of generality we can assume this to be the upper beam because only relative phases are relevant). In our notation, the action of the phase shifter can be described by the unitary transformation

$$\Phi|0\rangle = e^{i\varphi}|0\rangle\,, \quad \Phi|1\rangle = |1\rangle\,. \tag{1.10}$$

Therefore the output qubit can be calculated by successive application of all proper transformations to the input qubit:

$$|Q\rangle_{out} = H\Phi H|Q\rangle_{in}\,. \tag{1.11}$$

We leave it to the reader to calculate the general expression for arbitrary input qubits. We will restrict our discussion again to the case where we have only one input namely $\alpha = 1$ and $\beta = 0$, i.e., $|Q\rangle_{in} = |0\rangle$. The final state then becomes

$$H\Phi H|0\rangle = \frac{1}{2}\left((e^{i\varphi} + 1)|0\rangle + (e^{i\varphi} - 1)|1\rangle\right)\,. \tag{1.12}$$

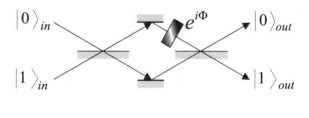

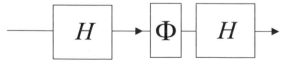

Fig. 1.4. Top: Mach–Zehnder interferometer including a phase shifter φ in one of the two beams. This completely changes the output. Bottom: The equivalent representation with Hadamard transformations and a phase shifter gate.

This has a very simple interpretation. First we observe by inspection of (1.12) that for $\varphi = 0$ the value of the qubit is definitely "0". On the other hand, for $\varphi = \pi$ the value of the qubit is definitely "1". This indicates that the phase shift φ is able to switch the output qubit between 0 and 1. In general, the probability that the output qubit has the value "0" is $P_0 = \cos^2(\varphi/2)$, and the probability that the qubit carries the value "1" is $P_1 = \sin^2(\varphi/2)$.

In the present section we have discussed some of the basic notions of linear transformation of qubits. We will now turn to entangled qubits.

1.4 Entanglement

Consider a source which emits a pair of particles such that one particle emerges to the left and the other one to the right (see source S in Fig. 1.5). The source is such that the particles are emitted with opposite momenta. If the particle emerging to the left, which we call particle 1, is found in the upper beam, then particle 2 travelling to the right is always found in the lower beam. Conversely, if particle 1 is found in the lower beam, then particle 2 is always found in the upper beam. In our qubit language we would say that the two particles carry different bit values. Either particle 1 carries "0" and then particle 2 definitely carries "1", or vice versa. Quantum mechanically this is a two-particle superposition state of the form

$$\frac{1}{\sqrt{2}} \left(|0\rangle_1 |1\rangle_2 + e^{i\chi} |1\rangle_1 |0\rangle_2 \right) . \tag{1.13}$$

The phase χ is just determined by the internal properties of the source and we assume for simplicity $\chi = 0$. Equation (1.13) describes what is called an entangled state [8] [1]. The interesting property is that neither of the two qubits carries a definite value, but what is known from the quantum state is that as soon as one of the two qubits is subject to a measurement, the result of this measurement being completely random, the other one will immediately be found to carry the opposite value. In a nutshell this is the conundrum of quantum non-locality, since the two qubits could be separated by arbitrary distances at the time of the measurement.

A most interesting situation arises when both qubits are subject to a phase shift and to a Hadamard transformation as shown in Fig. 1.5. Then, for detection events after both Hadamard transformations, that is, for the case of the two-particle interferometer verification [10] for detections behind the beamsplitters, interesting non-local correlations result which violate Bell's inequalities [11]. Without going into the theoretical and formal details here (for more information see Sect. 1.7), the essence of such a violation is that

---

[1] The word *Entanglement* is a (free) translation of the word *Verschränkung* that was introduced in 1935 by Schrödinger to characterise this special feature of composite quantum systems [9].

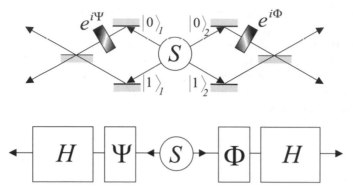

Fig. 1.5. A source emits two qubits in an entangled state. Top: A two-particle interferometer verification. Bottom: The principle in terms of one-photon gates

there is no possibility to explain the correlations between the two sides on the basis of local properties of the qubits alone. The quantum correlations between the two sides cannot be understood by assuming that the specific detector on one given side which registers the particle is not influenced by the parameter setting, that is, by the choice of the phase for the other particle. There are many ways to express precisely the meaning of Bell's inequalities, and there are many formal presentations. Some of this discussion will be presented in Sect. 1.7, and for the remainder we refer the reader to the appropriate literature (e.g., Ref. [12] and references therein).

A very interesting, and for quantum computation quite relevant generalisation follows if entanglement is studied for more than two qubits. For example, consider the simple case of entanglement between three qubits, as shown in Fig. 1.6. We assume that a source emits three particles, one into each of the apparatuses shown, in the specific superposition, a so-called Greenberger–Horne–Zeilinger (GHZ) state [13] (see also Sect. 6.3),

$$\frac{1}{\sqrt{2}} \left(|0\rangle_1 |0\rangle_2 |0\rangle_3 + |1\rangle_1 |1\rangle_2 |1\rangle_3 \right). \tag{1.14}$$

This quantum state has some very peculiar properties. Again, as in two-particle entanglement, none of the three qubits carries any information on its own, none of them has a defined bit value. But, as soon as one of the three is measured, the other two will assume a well-defined value as long as the measurement is performed in the chosen 0-1 basis. This conclusion holds independent of the spatial separation between the three measurements.

Most interestingly, if one looks at the relations predicted by the GHZ state (1.14) between the three measurements after passing the phase shifters and the Hadamard transforms, a number of perfect correlations still result for certain joint settings of the three parameters [14], the interesting property now being that it is not possible to understand even the perfect correlations with a local model. This shows that quantum mechanics is at variance with

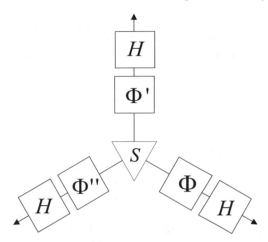

Fig. 1.6. Three-particle entanglement in a so-called GHZ state. Here we show only the representation in terms of our elementary gates, it will be straightforward for the reader to consider the physical realisation in a three-particle interferometer.

a classical local world view not only for the sector of statistical predictions of the theory but also for predictions which can be made with certainty.

1.5 Entanglement and Quantum Indistinguishability

In order to understand both the nature of entanglement and ways of producing it, one has to realise that in states of the general form (1.13) and (1.14), we have a superposition between product states. We recall from the discussion of the double-slit diffraction phenomenon (Sect. 1.1) that superposition means that there is no way to tell which of the two possibilities forming the superposition actually pertains. This rule must also be applied to the understanding of quantum entanglement. For example, in the state

$$|\Psi\rangle_{12} = \frac{1}{\sqrt{2}}(|0\rangle_1|1\rangle_2 + |1\rangle_1|0\rangle_2) \tag{1.15}$$

there is no way of telling whether qubit 1 carries the value "0" or "1", and likewise whether qubit 2 carries the value "0" or "1". Yet, if one qubit is measured the other one immediately assumes a well-defined quantum state. These observations lead us directly to the conditions of how to produce and observe entangled quantum states.

To produce entangled quantum states, one has various possibilities. Firstly, one can create a source which, through its physical construction, is such that the quantum states emerging already have the indistinguishability feature discussed above. This is realised, for example, by the decay of a spin-0 particle into two spin-1/2 particles under conservation of the internal angular momentum [15]. In this case, the two spins of the emerging particles have to be opposite, and, if no further mechanisms exist which permit us to distinguish the possibilities right at the source, the emerging quantum state is

$$|\Psi\rangle_{12} = \frac{1}{\sqrt{2}}(|\uparrow\rangle_1|\downarrow\rangle_2 - |\downarrow\rangle_1|\uparrow\rangle_2),\tag{1.16}$$

where, e.g. $|\uparrow\rangle_1$ means particle 1 with spin up. The state (1.16) has the remarkable property that it is rotationally invariant, i.e., the two spins are anti-parallel along whichever direction we choose to measure.

A second possibility is that a source might actually produce quantum states of the form of the individual components in the superposition of (1.15), but the states might still be distinguishable in some way. This happens, for example, in type-II parametric down-conversion [16] (Sect. 3.4.4), where along a certain chosen direction the two emerging photon states are

$$|H\rangle_1|V\rangle_2 \quad\text{and}\quad |V\rangle_1|H\rangle_2.\tag{1.17}$$

That means that either photon 1 is horizontally polarised and photon 2 is vertically polarised, or photon 1 is vertically polarised and photon 2 is horizontally polarised. Yet because of the different speeds of light for the H and V polarised photons inside the down-conversion crystal, the time correlation between the two photons is different in the two cases. Therefore, the two terms in (1.17) can be distinguished by a time measurement and no entangled state results because of this potential to distinguish the two cases. However, in this case too one can still produce entanglement by shifting the two photon-wave packets after their production relative to each other such that they become indistinguishable on the basis of their positions in time. What this means is the application of a quantum eraser technique [17] where a marker, in this case the relative time ordering, is erased such that we obtain quantum indistinguishability resulting in the state

$$|\Psi\rangle_{12} = \frac{1}{\sqrt{2}}(|H\rangle_1|V\rangle_2 + e^{i\chi}|V\rangle_1|H\rangle_2),\tag{1.18}$$

which is entangled.

A third means of producing entangled states is to project a non-entangled state onto an entangled one. We remark, for example, that an entangled state is never orthogonal to any of its components. Specifically, consider a source producing the non-entangled state

$$|0\rangle_1|1\rangle_2.\tag{1.19}$$

Suppose this state is now sent through a filter described by the projection operator

$$P = |\Psi\rangle_{12}\langle\Psi|_{12},\tag{1.20}$$

where $|\Psi\rangle_{12}$ is the state of (1.15). Then the following entangled state results:

$$\frac{1}{2}(|0\rangle_1|1\rangle_2 + |1\rangle_1|0\rangle_2)((\langle 0|_1\langle 1|_2 + \langle 1|_1\langle 0|_2)|0\rangle_1|1\rangle_2 = \frac{1}{2}(|0\rangle_1|1\rangle_2 + |1\rangle_1|0\rangle_2);$$

(1.21)

it is no longer normalised to unity because the projection procedure implies a loss of qubits.

While each of the three methods discussed above can in principle be used to produce outgoing entangled states, a further possibility exists to produce entanglement upon observation of a state. In general, this means that we have an unentangled or partially entangled state of some form and the measurement procedure itself is such that it projects onto an entangled state, in much the same way as discussed just above. This procedure was used, for example, in the first experimental demonstration of GHZ entanglement of three photons (see Sect. 6.3) [18].

1.6 The Controlled NOT Gate

Thus far, we have discussed only single-qubit gates, that is, gates which involve one qubit only. Of greatest importance for quantum computation applications are two-qubit gates, where the evolution of one qubit is conditional upon the state of the other qubit. The simplest of these gates is the quantum controlled NOT gate illustrated in Fig. 1.7. The essence of the controlled NOT gate is that the value of the so-called target qubit is negated if and only if the control qubit has the logical value "1". The logical value of the control qubit does not change. The action of the quantum controlled NOT gate can be described by the transformations

$$|0\rangle_c|0\rangle_t \rightarrow |0\rangle_c|0\rangle_t \qquad |0\rangle_c|1\rangle_t \rightarrow |0\rangle_c|1\rangle_t$$
$$|1\rangle_c|0\rangle_t \rightarrow |1\rangle_c|1\rangle_t \qquad |1\rangle_c|1\rangle_t \rightarrow |1\rangle_c|0\rangle_t$$

(1.22)

where $|0\rangle_c$ and $|1\rangle_c$ refer to the control qubit and $|0\rangle_t$ and $|1\rangle_t$ refer to the target qubit. Together with the single-qubit transformations described in

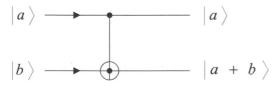

Fig. 1.7. The controlled NOT gate is a transformation involving two qubits. The value of the control qubit (the upper one in the figure) influences the lower one, whose value is flipped if the upper qubit carries "1", and not flipped if the upper qubit carries "0". This is equivalent to addition modulo 2.

Sect. 1.3 the quantum controlled NOT gate can be used to realise quantum computation networks. One interesting explicit application is the production of two-qubit or multi-qubit entangled states using these gates [19].

1.7 The EPR Argument and Bell's Inequality

Immediately after the discovery of modern quantum mechanics, it was realised that it contains novel, counterintuitive features, as witnessed most remarkably in the famous dialogue between Niels Bohr and Albert Einstein [20]. While Einstein initially tried to argue that quantum mechanics is inconsistent, he later reformulated his argument towards demonstrating that quantum mechanics is incomplete. In the seminal paper [21], Einstein, Podolsky and Rosen (EPR) consider quantum systems consisting of two particles such that, while neither position nor momentum of either particle is well defined, the sum of their positions, that is their centre of mass, and the difference of their momenta, that is their individual momenta in the center of mass system, are both precisely defined. It then follows that a measurement of either position or momentum performed on, say, particle 1 immediately implies a precise position or momentum, respectively, for particle 2, without interacting with that particle. Assuming that the two particles can be separated by arbitrary distances, EPR suggest that a measurement on particle 1 cannot have any actual influence on particle 2 (locality condition); thus the property of particle 2 must be independent of the measurement performed on particle 1. To them, it then follows that both position and momentum can simultaneously be well defined properties of a quantum system.

In his famous reply [22], Niels Bohr argues that the two particles in the EPR case are always parts of one quantum system and thus measurement on one particle changes the possible predictions that can be made for the whole system and therefore for the other particle.

While the EPR–Bohr discussion was considered for a long time to be merely philosophical, in 1951 David Bohm [15] introduced spin-entangled systems and in 1964 John Bell [23] showed that, for such entangled systems, measurements of correlated quantities should yield different results in the quantum mechanical case to those expected if one assumes that the properties of the system measured are present prior to, and independent of, the observation. Even though a number of experiments have now confirmed the quantum predictions [24]–[26], from a strictly logical point of view the problem is not closed yet as some loopholes in the existing experiments still make it logically possible, at least in principle, to uphold a local realist world view [27].

Let us briefly present the line of reasoning that leads to an inequality equivalent to the original Bell inequality. Consider a source emitting two qubits (Fig. 1.8) in the entangled state

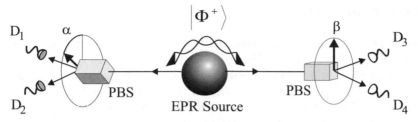

Fig. 1.8. Correlation measurements between Alice's and Bob's detection events for different choices for the detection bases (indicated by the angles α and β for the orientation of their polarising beamsplitters, PBS) lead to the violation of Bell's inequalities.

$$|\Phi^+\rangle_{12} = \frac{1}{\sqrt{2}}(|H\rangle_1|H\rangle_2 + |V\rangle_1|V\rangle_2). \tag{1.23}$$

One qubit is sent to Alice (to the left in Fig. 1.8), the other one to Bob (to the right). Alice and Bob will perform polarisation measurements using a polarising beamsplitter with two single-photon detectors in the output ports. Alice will obtain the measurement result "0" or "1", corresponding to the detection of a qubit by detector 1 or 2 respectively, each with equal probability. This statement is valid in whatever polarisation basis she decides to perform the measurement, the actual results being completely random. Yet, if Bob chooses the same basis, he will always obtain the same result. Thus, following the first step of the EPR reasoning, Alice can predict with certainty what Bob's result will be. The second step employs the locality hypothesis, that is, the assumption that no physical influence can instantly go from Alice's apparatus to Bob's and therefore Bob's measured result should only depend on the properties of his qubit and on the apparatus he chose. Combining the two steps, John Bell investigated possible correlations for the case that Alice and Bob choose detection bases which are at oblique angles. For three arbitrary angular orientations α, β, γ, one can see [28] that the following inequality must be fulfilled:

$$N(1_\alpha, 1_\beta) \le N(1_\alpha, 1_\gamma) + N(1_\beta, 0_\gamma), \tag{1.24}$$

where

$$N(1_\alpha, 1_\beta) = \frac{N_0}{2} \cos^2(\alpha - \beta) \tag{1.25}$$

is the quantum-mechanical prediction for the number of cases where Alice obtains "1" with her apparatus at orientation α and Bob achieves "1" with orientation β, and N_0 is the number of pairs emitted by the source. The inequality is violated by the quantum-mechanical prediction if we choose, for example, the angles $(\alpha - \beta) = (\beta - \gamma) = 30°$. The violation implies that at least one of the assumptions entering Bell's inequality must be in conflict with quantum mechanics. This is usually viewed as evidence for non-locality, though that is by no means the only possible explanation.

1.8 Comments

As recently as a decade ago, the issues discussed here were mainly considered
to be of a philosophical nature, though very relevant ones in our attempts
to understand the world around us and our role in it. In the last few years,
very much to the surprise of most of the early researchers in the field, the
basic concepts of superposition and quantum entanglement have turned out
to be key ingredients in novel quantum communication and quantum computation schemes. Here we have given only a condensed introduction. More
details are contained in the various chapters of this book. Further information can also be found on the world wide web, for example at www.qubit.org
or www.quantum.at with many links to other relevant sites.

2. Quantum Cryptography

A. Ekert, N. Gisin, B. Huttner, H. Inamori, H. Weinfurter

2.1 What is Wrong with Classical Cryptography?

2.1.1 From SCYTALE to ENIGMA

Human desire to communicate secretly is at least as old as writing itself and goes back to the beginnings of our civilisation. Methods of secret communication were developed by many ancient societies, including those of Mesopotamia, Egypt, India, and China, but details regarding the origins of cryptology[1] remain unknown [29].

We know that it was the Spartans, the most warlike of the Greeks, who pioneered military cryptography in Europe. Around 400 BC they employed a device known as the SCYTALE. The device, used for communication between military commanders, consisted of a tapered baton around which was wrapped a spiral strip of parchment or leather containing the message. Words were then written lengthwise along the baton, one letter on each revolution of the strip. When unwrapped, the letters of the message appeared scrambled and the parchment was sent on its way. The receiver wrapped the parchment around another baton of the same shape and the original message reappeared as shown in Fig. 2.1.

Julius Caesar allegedly used, in his correspondence, a simple letter substitution method. Each letter of Caesar's message was replaced by the letter that followed it alphabetically by three places. The letter A was replaced by D, the letter B by E, and so on. For example, the English word COLD after the Caesar substitution appears as FROG. This method is still called the Caesar cipher, regardless the size of the shift used for the substitution.

These two simple examples already contain the two basic methods of encryption which are still employed by cryptographers today namely *transposition* and *substitution*. In transposition (e.g. scytale) the letters of the

---

[1] The science of secure communication is called cryptology from Greek *kryptos* hidden and *logos* word. Cryptology embodies cryptography, the art of code-making, and cryptanalysis, the art of code-breaking.

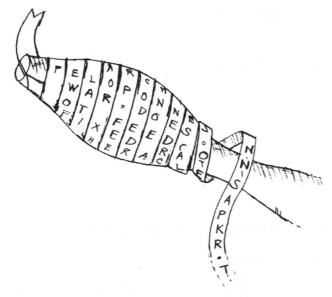

Fig. 2.1. The first cryptographic machine – a Scytale.

plaintext, the technical term for the message to be transmitted, are rearranged by a special permutation. In substitution (e.g. Caesar's cipher) the letters of the plaintext are replaced by other letters, numbers or arbitrary symbols. In general the two techniques can be combined.

Until some years ago, sophisticated cryptography was restricted primarily to the military world. Only the military had sufficient resources to produce sophisticated mechanical devices, such as the famous ENIGMA which was widely used by Germans during World War II or its American counterpart the M-209. ENIGMA ciphers were broken before the war in Poland and during the war at Bletchley Park in England. The Bletchley Park team, which included Alan Turing, had to develop the electromechanical tools to break these ciphers, which resulted in building the first digital computer called COLOSSUS. Thus modern cryptology (for an introduction see, for example, [30]–[32]) was born together with computer science. As expressed by R.L. Rivest (codiscoverer of the popular RSA public key system), cryptanalysis was "the midwife of computer science".

2.1.2 Keys and Their Distribution

Originally the security of a cryptotext depended on the secrecy of the entire encrypting and decrypting procedures; however, today we use ciphers for which the algorithm for encrypting and decrypting could be revealed to anybody without compromising the security of a particular cryptogram. In such ciphers a set of specific parameters, called a *key*, is supplied together with the plaintext as an input to the encrypting algorithm, and together with the cryptogram as an input to the decrypting algorithm. This can be written as

$$\hat{E}_k(P) = C, \text{ and conversely, } \hat{D}_k(C) = P, \tag{2.1}$$

where P stands for plaintext, C for cryptotext or cryptogram, k for cryptographic key, and $\hat{E}$ and $\hat{D}$ denote an encryption and a decryption operation respectively.

The encrypting and decrypting algorithms are publicly known; the security of the cryptogram depends entirely on the secrecy of the key, and this key must consist of a *randomly chosen*, sufficiently long string of bits. Probably the best way to explain this procedure is to have a quick look at the Vernam cipher, also known as the one-time pad pad.

If we choose a very simple digital alphabet, in which we use only capital letters and some punctuation marks, such as

A	B	C	D	E	...	...	X	Y	Z	?	,	.
00	01	02	03	04	...	...	23	24	25	26	27	28	29

we can illustrate the secret-key encrypting procedure by the following simple example (we refer to the dietary requirements of 007): In order to obtain

S	H	A	K	E	N		N	O	T		S	T	I	R	R	E	D
18	07	00	10	04	13	26	13	14	19	26	18	19	08	17	17	04	03
15	04	28	13	14	06	21	11	23	18	09	11	14	01	19	05	22	07
03	11	28	23	18	19	17	24	07	07	05	29	03	09	06	22	26	10

the cryptogram (sequence of digits in the bottom row) we add the plaintext numbers (the top row of digits) to the key numbers (the middle row), which are randomly selected from between 0 and 29, and take the remainder after division of the sum by 30, that is we perform addition modulo 30. For example, the first letter of the message "S" becomes a number "18" in the plaintext, then we add $18 + 15 = 33$; $33 = 1 \times 30 + 3$, therefore we get 03 in the cryptogram. The encryption and decryption can be written as $P + k \pmod{30} = C$ and $C - k \pmod{30} = P$ respectively.

The cipher was invented in 1917 by the American AT&T engineer Gilbert Vernam. It was later shown, by Claude Shannon [33], that as long as the key is truly random, has the same length as the message, and is never reused then the one-time pad is perfectly secure. So, if we have a truly unbreakable system, what is wrong with classical cryptography?

There is a snag. It is called *key distribution*. Once the key is established, subsequent communication involves sending cryptograms over a channel, even one which is vulnerable to total passive eavesdropping (e.g. public announcement in mass-media). This stage is indeed secure. However in order to establish the key, two users, who share no secret information initially, must at a certain stage of communication use a reliable and a very secure channel. Since the interception is a set of measurements performed by an eavesdropper on this channel, however difficult this might be from a technological point of view, *in principle* any classical key distribution can always be passively monitored, without the legitimate users being aware that any eavesdropping has taken place. This would not be such a problem if the key were established once and for all. In this case, the users may spend enough resources (such as strong safes and protection) to ensure that the key arrives safely to its addressee. But since the key has to be renewed for every message, key distribution would become prohibitively expensive. For this reason, in most applications, one does not require this absolute secrecy, but rather settles for less expensive and less secure systems.

For more mundane transmissions, the system of choice is the Data Encryption Standard (DES), which was announced in 1977, and is still in use for sensitive but non-secret information, especially for commercial transactions. This system only requires a short key, 64 bits of which 56 bits are used directly by the algorithm and 8 bits are used for error detection. It encrypts blocks of 64 bits of the plaintext. In the easiest implementation, a long plaintext is cut into blocks, and the key is then used to encrypt each of them. In more sophisticated (and safer) systems, the message is further protected by making each enciphered block depend on the previous ones. Frequent rumours that DES has been broken have never been substantiated and it seems that DES was designed using excellent criteria; given the short key length it is a very good algorithm. Further discussion of the numerous possibilities of DES are outside the scope of this review, and can be found in the literature or in the internet. As explained above, none of these are totally secure: since the same key is used many times, there is information about the plaintext in the cryptogram. The goal of the encryption methods is to hide it as well as possible. A dedicated cryptanalyst will be able to break the cipher and obtain the message, but if it takes too long the information may become obsolete. In most applications, it is recommended to use one key for only a few days, before discarding it for a new one. Of course, the problem of transmitting the key to the receiver remains, but, for all practical purposes, is made less critical, as the amount of key required is much smaller.

Thus a pretty good security is possible, but what about a perfect security? It follows from our brief discussion above that in principle we can achieve a perfect security in communication via one-time pads provided we solve the key distribution problem. The question is: can we solve the key distribution problem? The answer to this question is basically "yes". There are two very interesting solutions, one mathematical and one physical. The mathematical one is known as *public-key cryptography* and the physical one is referred to as *quantum cryptography*.

2.1.3 Public Keys and Quantum Cryptography

Before we proceed any further let us introduce our three main characters: Alice and Bob, two individuals who want to communicate secretly, and Eve, an eavesdropper. The scenario is: Alice and Bob want to establish a secret key and Eve wants to gain at least partial information about the key.

Cryptologists have tried hard to give Alice and Bob the edge and to solve the key distribution problem. The 1970s, for example, brought a clever mathematical discovery in the shape of "public key" systems. The two main public key cryptography techniques in use today are the Diffie–Hellman key exchange protocol [34] and the RSA encryption system [35]. They were discovered in the academic community in 1976 and 1978, respectively. However, these techniques were known to the British government agencies prior to these dates, although this was not officially confirmed until recently. In fact the techniques were first discovered at CESG in the early 1970s by James Ellis, who called them "Non-Secret Encryption". In 1973, building on Ellis' idea, C. Cocks designed what we now call RSA, and in 1974 M. Williamson proposed what is essentially known today as the Diffie–Hellman key exchange protocol.

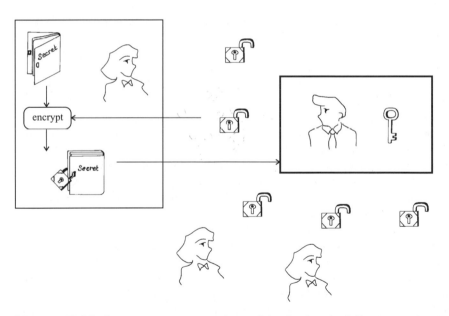

Fig. 2.2. Public key cryptosystem can be explained using the following mechanical analogy. Imagine Bob who can produce many padlocks and anybody who wants to send secret messages to Bob can receive an open padlock manufactured by Bob. An open padlock can be viewed as a public key. In particular Alice gets one too. Once the padlock is locked by Alice only Bob can open it because only Bob has the key – the private key. Thus Alice can lock any data she wants to send to Bob with this padlock. Once the data is locked, only Bob can access it thanks to his private key.

In the public-key systems users do not need to agree on a secret key before they send the message. They work on the principle of a safe with two keys, one public key to lock it, and another private one to open it. Everyone has a key to lock the safe but only one person has a key that will open it again, so anyone can put a message in the safe but only one person can take it out. Another analogy is the padlock example shown in Fig. 2.2. These systems exploit the fact that certain mathematical operations are easier to do in one direction than the other. The systems avoid the key distribution problem but unfortunately their security depends on unproven mathematical assumptions, such as the difficulty of factoring large integers. That is, it is perfectly possible to figure out the private key from the public one but it is difficult. For example, RSA – a very popular public key cryptosystem named after the three inventors, Ron Rivest, Adi Shamir, and Leonard Adleman [35] – gets its security from the difficulty of factoring large numbers. Mathematicians believe (firmly, though they have not actually proved it) that in order to factorise a number with N decimal digits, any classical computer needs a number of steps that grows exponentially with N: that is to say, adding one extra digit to the number to be factorised generally multiplies the time required by a fixed factor. Thus, as we increase the number of digits, the task rapidly becomes intractable.

This means that if and when mathematicians or computer scientists come up with fast and clever procedures for factoring large integers, the whole privacy and discretion of public-key cryptosystems could vanish overnight. Indeed, recent work in quantum computation shows that quantum computers can, at least in principle, factor much faster than classical computers [36]! This means that in one sense public key cryptosystems are already insecure: any RSA-encrypted message that is recorded today will become readable moments after the first quantum computer is switched on, and therefore RSA cannot be used for encrypting any information that will still need to be secret on that happy day. Admittedly, that day is probably decades away, but can anyone prove, or give any reliable assurance, that it is? Confidence in the slowness of technological progress is all that the security of the RSA system now rests on.

Quantum cryptography brings an entirely new way of solving the key distribution problem. What quantum computation takes away with one hand, it returns, at least partially, with the other. One of the simplest types of quantum computation — a type which is now routinely carried out in the laboratory and may soon be a commercial proposition — is quantum cryptography. It provides perfectly secure key distribution because, unlike all classical cryptography, it relies on the laws of physics rather than on ensuring that successful eavesdropping would require excessive computational effort.

Before we discuss quantum cryptography (QC) in detail let us mention briefly yet another difficulty in the business of secure communication, namely *authentication*.

2.1.4 Authentication: How to Recognise Cinderella ?

So far, we trusted the integrity of the communication channel: we allowed Eve to eavesdrop on messages exchanged between Alice and Bob, but we took for granted that Eve could not forge or modify them. That is we assumed that Alice and Bob have access to a perfect public channel, that is a channel that can be freely monitored by anybody; however, it should be impossible to modify the information sent through such a channel, e.g., a radio broadcast. This may be a risky assumption in many realistic scenarios. In some cases, a cunning Eve may interfere in the Alice–Bob communication channel by cutting it in two and impersonating Alice to Bob and vice-versa.

Under this condition, she can, for example, generate two pairs of public-private keys and give one public key to Alice and one to Bob informing Alice that she has been given Bob's public key and informing Bob that he now has Alice's public key. Eve keeps the corresponding private keys and from now on any subsequent communication between Alice and Bob would be under her complete control.

Likewise, a private key cryptosystem such as the one-time pad is vulnerable to tampering if the enemy knows the message being sent. Suppose an embassy is using the previously described Vernam cipher to communicate with its country. If Eve knows exactly the message being sent, such as names of some individuals, she could then intercept the encrypted message and prevent it from reaching its destination. Meanwhile, she gets the corresponding Vernam key by performing the subtraction modulo 30 of the ciphertext by the message. Afterwards she may use this key at her mercy, for interesting purposes like disinformation. This example shows that even perfectly secure cryptosystems should not be used blindly.

"Certifying" a public key or "authenticating" a message is a cryptographic technique to counter the kind of attacks described above, called man-in-the-middle or separate worlds attacks.

Once Alice and Bob truly share a secret key then convenient and efficient methods of authentication exist. However, so far there is no convenient way to certify a public key. The only reliable way to check a key's authenticity is to meet face-to-face with its owner. Unfortunately, quantum key distribution does not provide any more convenient ways to authenticate, to counter a man-in-the-middle attack. Alice and Bob should meet at least once to exchange an authentication key[2].

In the following we assume that Alice and Bob do have access to a perfect public channel but we will return, very briefly though, to the authentication problem.

---

[2] In both situations, Alice and Bob can rely on a third party, a trusted arbitrator, who is in charge of certifying digital keys.

2.2 Quantum Key Distribution

Let us start our discussion of the quantum key distribution with an overview of some general principles. This will be followed by a more detailed description and experimental considerations in Sect. 2.6.

2.2.1 Preliminaria

Quantum key distribution begins with the transmission of single or entangled quanta between Alice and Bob. Eavesdropping, from a physical point of view, is based on a set of measurements performed by an eavesdropper on carriers of information, in this case on the transmitted quanta. According to the rules of quantum mechanics, in general, any measurement performed by Eve unavoidably modifies the state of the transmitted quanta and this can be discovered by Alice and Bob in a subsequent public communication [3]. Thus the main ingredients of the quantum key distributing system are: a quantum channel for the exchange of quanta and the so-called public channel, which is used to test whether or not the transmission through the quantum channel is distorted (see Fig. 2.3). Let us repeat that any public channel can be freely monitored by anybody; however, it should be impossible to modify the information sent through such a channel.

During the quantum transmission the key is either encoded using a prescribed set of non-orthogonal quantum states of a single particle or is obtained from a prescribed set of measurements performed on entangled particles after the transmission (in this case the key does not even exist during the transmission).

2.2.2 Security in Non-orthogonal States: No-Cloning Theorem

The idea of using non-orthogonal quantum states to encode secret information is due to Stephen Wiesner who proposed "quantum money" [37] which cannot be forged by copying. This is because one cannot clone non-orthogonal quantum states (or any unknown quantum state). To see this, consider two

---

[3] A legitimate question here is: how can we be sure that the rules of quantum mechanics are correct? The answer is that quantum mechanics has been tested repeatedly to a very high degree of accuracy and it is the best theory we have at the moment. It does not make much sense to ask physicists to prove the laws of physics in general and of quantum mechanics in particular. Of course, no body of experimental evidence confirming quantum mechanics makes it more "correct" but one single experiment may refute the theory. The growth of our scientific knowledge is based on conjectures and refutations and most likely quantum mechanics will eventually be superseded by a new theory but it seems unlikely that this new theory will give new results in the present realm of application of quantum mechanics. Rather, new effects will be found in extreme situations as encountered, for example, in strong gravitational fields.

Alice

Public Channel

Bob

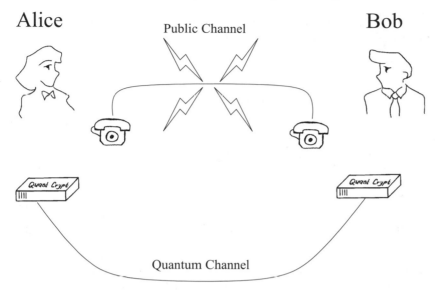

Quantum Channel

Fig. 2.3. Quantum key distribution scenario. Alice and Bob are linked by two channels, a quantum channel and a classical public channel.

normalised states $|0\rangle$ and $|1\rangle$ such that $\langle 0|1\rangle \neq 0$. Suppose there exists a cloning machine which operates as follows

$$|0\rangle|\text{blank}\rangle|\text{machine}\rangle \to |0\rangle|0\rangle|\text{machine}_0\rangle \tag{2.2}$$

$$|1\rangle|\text{blank}\rangle|\text{machine}\rangle \to |1\rangle|1\rangle|\text{machine}_1\rangle , \tag{2.3}$$

where "blank" is an initial state of a particle which after the operation becomes the clone and all the states are properly normalised. This operation must be unitary and should preserve the inner product, thus we require

$$\langle 0|1\rangle = \langle 0|1\rangle\langle 0|1\rangle\langle\text{machine}_0|\text{machine}_1\rangle , \tag{2.4}$$

which is only possible when $\langle 0|1\rangle = 0$ (the two states are orthogonal) or when $\langle 0|1\rangle = 1$ (the two states are indistinguishable and therefore cannot be used to encode two different bit values), which contradicts our initial assumption. Thus if somebody secretly prepares a random sequence of states of the type $|1\rangle|0\rangle|1\rangle|1\rangle$ ..., where $|0\rangle$ and $|1\rangle$ are chosen randomly, it is impossible to reproduce this sequence faithfully. Wiesner's money with such unclonable quantum signatures would require storing non-orthogonal quantum states on the banknotes which is way more difficult than sending non-orthogonal quantum states from one place to another. That is why Wiesner's idea was adapted to the key distribution. Charles Bennett and Gilles Brassard proposed to use non-orthogonal states of polarised photons to distribute cryptographic keys [38]. Any eavesdropper trying to distinguish between nonorthogonal $|0\rangle$ and $|1\rangle$ during the quantum transmission has a problem. Suppose Eve prepares her measuring device initially in a normalised state $|m\rangle$ and wants to tcll $|0\rangle$ from $|1\rangle$ without disturbing the two states, i.e., she wants to implement the following unitary operation

$$|0\rangle|m\rangle \rightarrow |0\rangle|m_0\rangle \qquad (2.5)$$

$$|1\rangle|m\rangle \rightarrow |1\rangle|m_1\rangle. \qquad (2.6)$$

The unitarity condition implies $\langle 0|1\rangle\langle m|m\rangle = \langle 0|1\rangle\langle m_0|m_1\rangle$, i.e., $\langle m_0|m_1\rangle = 1$, the final state of the measuring device is the same in both cases. The two states are not disturbed but Eve gained no information about the encoded bit value. A more general measurement (but still not the most general one), which disturbs the original states so that $|0\rangle \rightarrow |0'\rangle$ and $|1\rangle \rightarrow |1'\rangle$ is of the form

$$|0\rangle|m\rangle \rightarrow |0'\rangle|m_0\rangle \qquad (2.7)$$

$$|1\rangle|m\rangle \rightarrow |1'\rangle|m_1\rangle. \qquad (2.8)$$

The unitarity condition gives $\langle 0|1\rangle = \langle 0'|1'\rangle\langle m_0|m_1\rangle$. The minimum of $\langle m_0|m_1\rangle$, which corresponds to the situation where Eve has the best chance to distinguish the two states, is obtained for $\langle 0'|1'\rangle = 1$, i.e., the two states $|0\rangle$ and $|1\rangle$ become the same state after the interaction. Although the measurement just described is not the most general one it gives a good illustration of the trade-off between the information gained in the measurement and the disturbance of the original states. The key distribution protocol which employs this trade-off is described in detail later.

2.2.3 Security in Entanglement

The conceptual foundation for entanglement-based quantum cryptography is of a different nature and involves the Einstein–Podolsky–Rosen paradox. In 1935 Einstein together with Boris Podolsky and Nathan Rosen (EPR) published a paper in which they outlined how a "proper" fundamental theory of nature should look [21]. The EPR programme required completeness ("In a complete theory there is an element corresponding to each element of reality"), locality ("The real factual situation of the system A is independent of what is done with the system B, which is spatially separated from the former"), and defined the element of physical reality as "If, without in any way disturbing a system, we can predict with certainty the value of a physical quantity, then there exists an element of physical reality corresponding to this physical quantity". EPR then considered a thought experiment on two entangled particles which showed that quantum states cannot in all situations be complete descriptions of physical reality. The EPR argument, as subsequently modified by David Bohm [15], goes as follows. Imagine the singlet-spin state of two spin-$\frac{1}{2}$ particles

$$|\Psi\rangle = \frac{1}{\sqrt{2}}\left(|\uparrow\rangle|\downarrow\rangle - |\downarrow\rangle|\uparrow\rangle\right), \qquad (2.9)$$

where the single particle kets $|\uparrow\rangle$ and $|\downarrow\rangle$ denote spin up and spin down with respect to some chosen direction. This state is spherically symmetric and the choice of the direction does not matter. The two particles, which we label A and B, are emitted from a source and fly apart. After they are sufficiently separated so that they do not interact with each other we can predict with certainty the x component of spin of particle A by measuring the x component of spin of particle B. This is because the total spin of the two particles is zero and the spin components of the two particles must have opposite values. The measurement performed on particle B does not disturb particle A (by locality) therefore the x component of spin is an element of reality according to the EPR criterion. By the same argument and by the spherical symmetry of state $|\Psi\rangle$ the y, z, or any other spin components are also elements of reality. However, since there is no quantum state of a spin-$\frac{1}{2}$ particle in which all components of spin have definite values the quantum description of reality is not complete.

The EPR programme asked for a different description of quantum reality but until John Bell's (1964) theorem it was not clear whether such a description was possible and if so whether it would lead to different experimental predictions. Bell showed that the EPR propositions about locality, reality, and completeness are incompatible with some quantum mechanical predictions involving entangled particles [23]. The contradiction is revealed by deriving from the EPR programme an experimentally testable inequality which is violated by certain quantum mechanical predictions. In Sect. 1.7 a brief derivation of the inequality is given. Extension of Bell's original theorem by John Clauser and Michael Horne (1974) made experimental tests of the EPR programme feasible [39] and quite a few of them have been performed. The experiments have supported quantum mechanical predictions.

What does all this have to do with data security? Surprisingly, a lot! It turns out that the very trick used by Bell to test the conceptual foundations of quantum theory can protect data transmission from eavesdroppers! Perhaps it sounds less surprising when one recalls again the EPR definition of an element of reality: "If, without in any way disturbing a system, we can predict with certainty the value of a physical quantity, then there exists an element of physical reality corresponding to this physical quantity". If this particular physical quantity is used to encode binary values of a cryptographic key then all an eavesdropper wants is an element of reality corresponding to the encoding observable. This way the entanglement-based quantum cryptography made a practical use of quantum entanglement and of the Bell theorem, showing that a border between blue sky and down-to-earth research is quite blurred. The protocol is described in detail later on.

2.2.4 What About Noisy Quantum Channels?

Regardless of the type of the quantum transmission, the bottom line is: a perfect quantum channel (i.e., a channel with no noise) is secure. Any disturbance in the channel is the signature that an eavesdropper tried to break into the channel. Thus noisy transmissions should be discarded. Unfortunately, quantum channels are very fragile and in practice it is impossible to avoid a certain amount of innocent noise due to interaction with the environment rather than with an eavesdropper. So, instead of discarding any noisy transmission, the legitimate users have to find a procedure to extract a secret key, even in the presence of some noise. To start with Alice and Bob have to estimate how much information may have leaked to an eavesdropper, as a function of parameters that they can measure. This amount of information could be either acceptable, tolerable, or intolerable. By tolerable we mean that by some subsequent procedures such as privacy amplification or quantum privacy amplification (see Sect. 8.4) it can be reduced to any desired acceptable level, at the expense of shortening the key. There exists, however, a threshold and if too much information has leaked to an eavesdropper no further privacy amplification is possible and the transmission should be discarded. The need for more precise security criteria was originally emphasised by Huttner and Ekert [40]; since then quantum eavesdropping has evolved into a field of its own.

If the quantum transmission over noisy channels is based on distributing entangled particles, then the quantum privacy amplification specifies the criteria of security, taking into account the most general attack an eavesdropper can mount. The quantum privacy amplification transforms partially entangled particles (due to eavesdropping or any external disturbance) into completely entangled ones and it is known when such a purification of quantum entanglement is possible. However, on the practical side, the technology required to perform quantum purification is similar to that required for the quantum computer, and is therefore not yet available.

The literature about security in single particle transmission is considerable. At the beginning, only security against so-called "incoherent attacks" – in which Eve deals with Alice's particles individually – were discussed. But quantum mechanics allows more general and more powerful attacks, known as "coherent attacks", in which Eve is allowed to use a quantum computer. Proofs of security against such attacks have been proposed recently. However, the more powerful the considered attacks are, the more stringent are the necessary security conditions. The same applies to the optimisation of the entire protocol, which is crucial for practical applications.

2.2.5 Practicalities

Quantum Cryptography (QC) is plagues by several other problems. The first one, which is common to most implementations, except the ones with entangled pairs of photons (Sect. 2.4), is that we still do not know how to create purely single-photon pulses. The usual source of light for QC is merely an attenuated laser. For this type of light, the number of photons in the pulse is a random variable, with a Poisson distribution. This means that some pulses may contain no photon at all, while others contain 1, 2 or even more photons. Pulses with more than one photon per pulse should be avoided, since they may leak information to an eavesdropper. In order to make the probability of more than one photon per pulse low enough, one needs to use very weak pulses, which in turns reduces the signal to noise ratio. The value generally adopted is 0.1 photon per pulse on average (this really means that only one pulse out of 10 contains a photon), which gives a probability of more than one photon of 5×10^{-3}. This still means that 5 % of the usable pulses (with at least one photon), contain two or more photons, and could leak information to an eavesdropper. Development of a good single photon source seems technologically possible, but has not been achieved yet.

The second, more serious problem for practical applications of QC is that a quantum channel cannot be amplified without losing its quantum properties. Therefore, due to losses in the transmission, QC can operate only over limited distances. For all existing systems, which are based on infrared photons in silica fibres, the minimum loss rate is about 0.2 dB/km. So it seems that QC systems with a range of more than 100 km (with losses of 20 dB, or a transmission rate of 0.01) are not possible for the foreseeable future. Therefore, a transatlantic cable with QC secrecy remains a complete utopia for the time being.

The third problem is that QC is well adapted to point-to-point exchanges, but not so well to other types of networks. Recent proposals suggested some improvements in this direction [41], but these are still limited to one-to-a-few users. QC access for home-to-home transactions is still impractical. However, a kind of Local Area Network, with a central broadcasting station (e.g. the main branch of a bank) and a number of receivers (e.g. the local branches of the bank), is certainly conceivable.

2.3 Quantum Key Distribution with Single Particles

2.3.1 Polarised Photons

Quantum key distribution with polarised photons, as originally proposed by C.H. Bennett and G.Brassard [38, 42], employed pulses of green light in free space, over a distance of 40 cm, and we shall discuss it in some detail. This experiment was obviously not useful for actual key transmission, but represented the first experimental steps of QC. The first implementation of this particular protocol with optical fibres (over a distance of about 1 km) was done at the university of Geneva [43]. Nowadays, distances have reached the tens of kilometers range. In this section, we shall present the principles of QC with polarised photons, leaving the experimental implementations to Sect. 2.6

Let us consider pulses of polarised light, each pulse containing a single photon. We shall begin with polarisation either horizontal or vertical, denoted

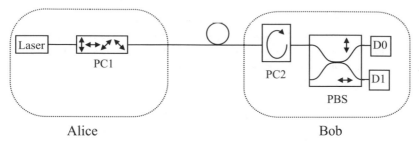

Fig. 2.4. Polarisation scheme: The sender, Alice, sends very weak pulses of polarised light to Bob. The polarisation is controlled by a Pockels cell (PC1), which enables Alice to choose between the four possible polarisations: $|\updownarrow\rangle$, $|\leftrightarrow\rangle$, $|\nearrow\rangle$, $|\nwarrow\rangle$. On Bob's side, a second Pockels cell (PC2) controls the rotation of the setup: $0°$ corresponds to a measurement in basis $\oplus$, while $45°$ corresponds to a measurement in basis $\otimes$. The polarisation beamsplitter (PBS) separates the beam into two orthogonal components, which are detected by either D0 or D1 (the setup chosen corresponds to a measurement in $\oplus$).

in the quantum mechanical Dirac notation by $|\leftrightarrow\rangle$ and $|\updownarrow\rangle$ respectively. To transmit information we need a coding system, say $|\updownarrow\rangle$ codes for 0, while $|\leftrightarrow\rangle$ codes for 1. Using this system, the sender, known as Alice, can send any message to the receiver, known as Bob. For example, if Alice sends a series of pulses: $|\leftrightarrow\rangle$, $|\updownarrow\rangle$, $|\leftrightarrow\rangle$, $|\leftrightarrow\rangle$, $|\updownarrow\rangle$; the corresponding binary number is 10110. When she sends either $|\leftrightarrow\rangle$ or $|\updownarrow\rangle$ only, we shall say that Alice sends her photons in the $\oplus$ basis. As the required key needs to be random, Alice will send 0 or 1 with equal probability. In order to detect the message, Bob uses a Polarisation Beamsplitter (PBS) transmitting the vertical polarisation while deflecting the horizontal one. This is followed by single-photon detectors in each arm of the set-up, as shown in Fig. 2.4. Detection in detector D0 (D1) means that Alice sent a 0 (1). In this case, we shall say that Bob detects in the $\oplus$ basis as well. As detectors are not perfect, and also due to possible losses in the transmission, both detectors will often fail to register any photon. In this case, Bob shall tell Alice that he failed to register anything, and the corresponding bit shall be discarded. Therefore, only a fraction of the original bits will be actually used, but the remaining ones should be shared by Alice and Bob. This system is thus useless for sending a given message, but it will be useful to send a cryptographic key, where the only requirements are randomness and confidentiality.

Up to this point, our setup is totally insecure. The eavesdropper, known as Eve, could also measure the pulses with a setup similar to Bob's, and re-send similar pulses to Bob. Eve would then know all the bits shared by Alice and Bob. To obtain confidentiality, Alice adds another random choice: she shall now use either the previous horizontal-vertical polarisations (the $\oplus$ basis); or one of the two linear diagonal polarisations, with $|\nearrow\rangle$ denoting a 0 and $|\nwarrow\rangle$ denoting a 1. Here again, Alice shall send a 0 or 1 with equal probability. This corresponds to the $\otimes$ basis. By rotating his setup by $45°$,

Table 2.1. Example of a polarisation protocol. Alice chooses at random a basis (⊕ or ⊗) and a bit value (0 or 1), and sends the corresponding polarisation state to Bob. Bob chooses also at random the reception basis, and obtains a given bit. The ensemble of these bits is the raw key. Alice and Bob then tell each other the basis used over the public channel, and keep only the bits corresponding to the same basis. This is the sifted key. They choose at random some of the remaining bits to test for Eve, then discard them. In this case, there are no errors, which indicates that the transmission is secure. The remaining bits form the shared key.

A basis	⊗	⊕	⊕	⊗	⊕	⊗	⊗	⊕	⊗	⊗	⊕
A bit value	0	1	0	1	1	0	1	0	0	0	0
A sends	$\lvert\swarrow\rangle$	$\lvert\leftrightarrow\rangle$	$\lvert\updownarrow\rangle$	$\lvert\searrow\rangle$	$\lvert\leftrightarrow\rangle$	$\lvert\nearrow\rangle$	$\lvert\searrow\rangle$	$\lvert\updownarrow\rangle$	$\lvert\nearrow\rangle$	$\lvert\nearrow\rangle$	$\lvert\updownarrow\rangle$
B basis	⊗	⊕	⊗	⊕	⊕	⊗	⊗	⊗	⊕	⊕	⊕
B bit	0	1	0	0	1	0	1	1	0	1	0
Same basis?	y	y	n	n	y	y	y	n	n	n	y
A keeps	0	1			1	0	1				0
B keeps	0	1			1	0	1				0
Test Eve?	y	n			y	n	n				n
Key		1				0	1				0

Bob can also choose to measure in the ⊗ basis. Safety is obtained thanks to a fundamental property of quantum mechanics: indeterminism. A single photon pulse prepared in the ⊗ basis and measured in the ⊕ basis has probability $\frac{1}{2}$ of going towards either detector, D0 or D1. And this choice is purely random: there is nothing in the photon to reveal which way it will go. So if Alice prepares a photon in, say state $\lvert\nearrow\rangle$, and Bob (or anybody else) attempts to measure it in the ⊕ basis, he may get a count in either detector, D0 or D1, with equal probability. Let us emphasise that this does not mean at all that half of the photons in a beam of $\lvert\nearrow\rangle$ are polarised vertically and half horizontally. This would be inconsistent with the fact that, when Bob uses the ⊗ basis, he always gets a 0. In fact, the systems behaves as if, when it is measured, it chooses randomly which way to go.

Obviously, the above applies equally well to Eve. As Alice uses either basis at random, there is no way for Eve to decide which measurement basis to use. Whenever she uses the wrong basis, she gets a random result, which is not correlated to Alice's choice. Another important point is that Eve cannot know that she got a wrong result: a count in D0 may mean that the photon was prepared in the $\lvert\updownarrow\rangle$ state, but it may also mean that it was in the $\lvert\nearrow\rangle$ or in the $\lvert\searrow\rangle$ state, and simply "choose" to go towards D0. This is why we do need single-photon pulses: a pulse with more than one photon sent in the wrong basis may give a count in both D0 and D1, thus telling Eve that she used the wrong basis. She could then simply discard the transmission, thus avoiding creating any error. However, when she receives only one photon, Eve has no other choice but to send it on to Bob, in the state that she measured. This will unavoidably create errors in the string received by Bob. The above eavesdropping strategy, known as the intercept-resend strategy is only one of the possibilities available to Eve.

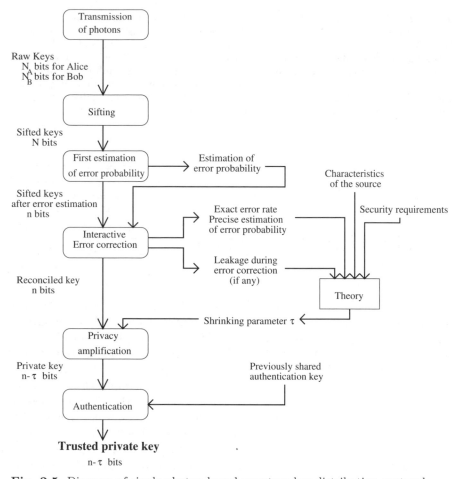

Fig. 2.5. Diagram of single-photon based quantum key distribution protocol

We now have the basic blocks for the polarisation cryptograpy protocol, an example of which is given in Table 2.1. The whole protocol is illustrated in Fig. 2.5 and is summarised as follows:

1. Alice chooses at random both the basis and the polarisation of her single-photon pulses, and sends them to Bob.
2. For each pulse, Bob chooses also at random which basis he will use, and measures the pulse. He either registers the count in D0 or D1, or fails to register anything, due to losses in the detection or in the transmission. The ensemble of all the received bits is the raw key.
3. Bob uses the public channel to tell Alice which photons were registered, and which basis was used. Of course, Bob does not tell the result of the measurement (count in D0 or D1). Alice answers back by telling

which basis she used. Whenever Alice and Bob used the same basis, either $\oplus$ or $\otimes$, they should get perfectly correlated bits. However, due to imperfections in the setup, and to a potential eavesdropper, there will be some errors. The ensemble of these bits is the sifted key.

4. To transform their partly corrupted and maybe not entirely secret strings into a usable shared and secret key, Alice and Bob now need some processing. The processing stage is in fact common to all implementations of QC with single particles. The main steps are: to estimate the error rate of the transmission; to infer the maximum information that may have leaked to an eavesdropper; and then to correct all the errors, while reducing the information potentially available to Eve to any level required. The remaining string of bits is the secret key.

Polarisation schemes are very appealing in free space, where polarisation is conserved, but are more complicated to implement in optical fibres, due to depolarisation and randomly fluctuating birefringence. Depolarisation is not a major problem: its effects can be suppressed by means of a sufficiently coherent source. The timescale of the fluctuations of the birefringence in stable conditions is quite slow (1 hour). However, during an experiment on an installed cable, we have also observed much shorter timescales, which rendered transmission impossible. An electronic compensation system, enabling continuous tracking and correction of the polarisation is certainly possible, but requires an alignment procedure between Alice and Bob. This may make the scheme a bit too cumbersome for potential users.

2.3.2 Phase Encoded Systems

Instead of relying on polarisation, which is not easy to control in optical fibres, one can base a QC system on phase encoding. Originally the phase encoding, with optical fibres and the Mach–Zehnder interferometers, was introduced in the context of the entanglement-based quantum cryptography [44], but it can also be used with the single-particle schemes [45]. The theoretical setup is shown in Fig. 2.6. This is an extended Mach–Zehnder interferometer, with Alice on the left, and Bob on the right, with two connecting fibres. Both Alice and Bob have a phase modulator (PM) on their side to enable the coding and decoding. Let us assume for the moment that Bob does not use his PM, and that the interferometer is aligned to have a constructive interference in D0, and a destructive one on D1. If Alice uses her PM to get either 0 or π phase shift (corresponding to bit value 0 and 1), Bob will either get a count in D0 or in D1. This is the equivalent of the previous scheme with two polarisations only. To obtain confidentiality, we add the random choice of basis. Here, this means that Alice shall choose between four phase shifts: 0, π (corresponding to the $\oplus$ basis), and $\frac{\pi}{2}$, $\frac{3\pi}{2}$ (corresponding to the $\otimes$ basis). On his side, Bob will also choose between 0 phase shift, i.e. measuring in the $\oplus$ basis, and

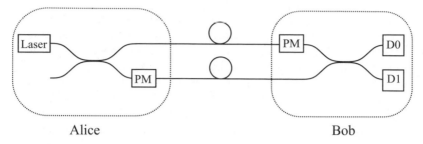

Fig. 2.6. Phase setup with an extended Mach–Zehnder interferometer. The relative choice of phase in the two phase modulators (PM) gives the interference pattern. Alice chooses between four possibilities: 0 or π corresponding to basis $\oplus$; $\frac{\pi}{2}$ or $\frac{3\pi}{2}$ corresponding to basis $\otimes$. Bob chooses between 0 (corresponding to a measurement in basis $\oplus$) and $\frac{\pi}{2}$ (corresponding to $\otimes$). When Alice and Bob use the same basis, a count in D0 means 0, and a count in D1 means 1. When the two bases are different, there are no correlations between the bit sent by Alice and the one received by Bob.

$\frac{\pi}{2}$ phase shift, i.e. measuring in the $\otimes$ basis. This is the equivalent to the previous polarisation scheme.

Unfortunately, keeping the phase difference in such an extended interferometer (each arm should be about 20 km long) is very difficult. Therefore a better practical setup is to collapse the interferometer, as shown in Fig. 2.7. One pulse entering Alice's side of the MZ is split into two. The two pulses propagating one after the other along the single transmission fibre are denoted by S (for short path) and L (for long path). After travelling through Bob's side of the MZ, these create three output pulses. Two of them, noted SS (for short-short) and LL (for long-long) are not relevant, as they show no interference effect. The central one however corresponds to two possible paths: SL or LS, which are indistinguishable and therefore interfere. The choice of the phase shifts by Alice and Bob gives the encoding-decoding, as in the previous paragraph. This setup is much more stable than the previous one, since

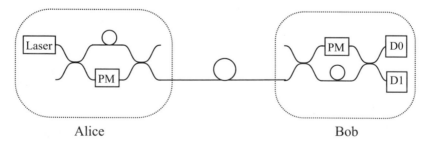

Fig. 2.7. Phase setup with a collapsed Mach–Zehnder interferometer: Instead of having the two pulses propagating through different paths, they now propagate through the same optical fibre, but with a time-delay. This increases the stability of the interferometer, but adds 3 dB of losses in Bob's setup.

the pulses actually follow the same path for most of the interferometer. The drawback is that we lose half of the signal in the two SS and LL paths.

The scheme proposed by C. Bennett [45], used only two phases for Alice. We refer the reader to the original article for a detailed explanation. The main advantage of this type of systems is that, in principle, it does not require polarisation control. In practice, however, due to some polarisation dependence in the components, it seems preferable to control the polarisation. Moreover, these schemes still need careful path length adjustment and control between the two sides of the interferometer.

2.4 Quantum Key Distribution with Entangled States

2.4.1 Transmission of the Raw Key

The key distribution is performed via a quantum channel which consists of a source that emits pairs of photons in the singlet state of polarisations:

$$| \psi \rangle = \frac{1}{\sqrt{2}} \left(|\updownarrow\rangle|\leftrightarrow\rangle - |\leftrightarrow\rangle|\updownarrow\rangle \right) \tag{2.10}$$

The photons fly apart along the z-axis towards the two legitimate users of the channel, Alice and Bob, who, after the photons have separated, perform measurements and register the outcome of the measurements in one of three bases, obtained by rotating the $\oplus$ basis around the z-axis by angles $\phi_1^a = 0, \phi_2^a = \frac{1}{4}\pi, \phi_3^a = \frac{1}{8}\pi$ for Alice and by angles $\phi_1^b = 0, \phi_2^b = -\frac{1}{8}\pi, \phi_3^b = \frac{1}{8}\pi$ for Bob.

Superscripts "a" and "b" refer to Alice's and Bob's analysers respectively. The users choose their bases randomly and independently for each pair of the incoming particles. Each measurement yield two possible results, +1 (the photon is measured in the first polarisation state of the chosen basis) and −1 (it is measured in the other polarisation state of the chosen basis), and can potentially reveal one bit of information.

The quantity

$$E(\phi_i^a, \phi_j^b) = P_{++}(\phi_i^a, \phi_j^b) + P_{--}(\phi_i^a, \phi_j^b) - P_{+-}(\phi_i^a, \phi_j^b) - P_{-+}(\phi_i^a, \phi_j^b) \tag{2.11}$$

is the correlation coefficient of the measurements performed by Alice in the basis rotated by ϕ_i^a and by Bob in the basis rotated by ϕ_j^b. Here $P_{++}(\phi_i^a, \phi_j^b)$ denotes the probability that the result ± 1 has been obtained in the basis defined by ϕ_i^a and ± 1 in the basis defined by ϕ_j^b. According to the quantum rules

$$E(\phi_i^a, \phi_j^b) = -\cos\left[2(\phi_i^a - \phi_j^b)\right]. \tag{2.12}$$

For the two pairs of bases of the same orientation (ϕ_1^a, ϕ_1^b and ϕ_3^a, ϕ_3^b) quantum mechanics predicts total anticorrelation of the results obtained by Alice and Bob: $E(\phi_1^a, \phi_1^b) = E(\phi_3^a, \phi_3^b) = -1$.

One can define the quantity S composed of the correlation coefficients for which Alice and Bob used analysers of different orientation

$$S = E(\phi_1^a, \phi_3^b) + E(\phi_1^a, \phi_2^b) + E(\phi_2^a, \phi_3^b) - E(\phi_2^a, \phi_2^b). \qquad (2.13)$$

This is the same S as in the generalised Bell theorem proposed by Clauser, Horne, Shimony, and Holt, and known as the CHSH inequality [12]. Quantum mechanics requires

$$S = -2\sqrt{2}. \qquad (2.14)$$

After the transmission has taken place, Alice and Bob can announce in public the orientations of the analysers they have chosen for each particular measurement and divide the measurements into two separate groups: a first group for which they used different orientation of the analysers, and a second group for which they used the same orientation of the analysers. They discard all measurements in which either or both of them failed to register a particle at all. Subsequently Alice and Bob can reveal publicly the results they obtained but within the first group of measurements only. This allows them to establish the value of S, which if the particles were not directly or indirectly "disturbed" should reproduce the result of (2.14). This assures the legitimate users that the results they obtained within the second group of measurements are anticorrelated and can be converted into a secret string of bits — the key.

An eavesdropper, Eve, cannot elicit any information from the particles while in transit from the source to the legitimate users, simply because there is no information encoded there! The information "comes into being" only after the legitimate users perform measurements and communicate in public afterwards. Eve may try to substitute her own prepared data for Alice and Bob to misguide them, but as she does not know which orientation of the analysers will be chosen for a given pair of particles there is no good strategy to escape being detected. In this case her intervention will be equivalent to introducing elements of *physical reality* to the polarisation directions and will lower S below its 'quantum' value. Thus the Bell theorem can indeed expose eavesdroppers.

2.4.2 Security Criteria

The best way to analyse eavesdropping in the system is to adopt the scenario that is most favourable for eavesdropping, namely where Eve herself is allowed to prepare all the pairs that Alice and Bob will subsequently use to establish a key. This way we take the most conservative view which attributes all disturbance in the channel to eavesdropping even though most of it (if not all) may be due to an innocent environmental noise.

Let us start our analysis of eavesdropping in the spirit of the Bell theorem and consider a simple case in which Eve knows precisely which particle is in which state. Following [46] let us assume that Eve prepares each particle in the EPR pairs separately so that each individual particle in the pair has a well defined polarisation in some direction. These directions may vary from pair to pair so we can say that she prepares with probability $p(\theta_a, \theta_b)$ Alice's particle in state $|\theta_a\rangle$ and Bob's particle in state $|\theta_b\rangle$, where θ_a and θ_b are two angles measured from the vertical axis describing the polarisations. This kind of preparation gives Eve total control over the state of *individual* particles. This is the case where Eve will always have the edge and Alice and Bob should abandon establishing the key; they will learn about it by estimating $|S|$ which in this case will always be smaller than $\sqrt{2}$. To see this let us write the density operator for each pair as

$$\rho = \int_{-\pi/2}^{\pi/2} p(\theta_a, \theta_b) \, |\theta_a\rangle \, \langle\theta_a| \otimes |\theta_b\rangle \, \langle\theta_b| \; d\theta_a d\theta_b. \tag{2.15}$$

Equation (2.13) with appropriately modified correlation coefficients reads

$$S = \int_{-\pi/2}^{\pi/2} p(\theta_a, \theta_b) d\theta_a d\theta_b \; \{ \; \cos[2(\phi_1^a - \theta_a)] \cos[2(\phi_3^b - \theta_b)]$$
$$+ \cos[2(\phi_1^a - \theta_a)] \cos[2(\phi_2^b - \theta_b)]$$
$$+ \cos[2(\phi_2^a - \theta_a)] \cos[2(\phi_3^b - \theta_b)]$$
$$- \cos[2(\phi_2^a - \theta_a)] \cos[2(\phi_2^b - \theta_b)] \; \}, \tag{2.16}$$

and leads to

$$S - \int_{-\pi/2}^{\pi/2} p(\theta_a, \theta_b) d\theta_a d\theta_b \sqrt{2} \cos[2(\theta_a - \theta_b)], \tag{2.17}$$

which implies

$$-\sqrt{2} \leq S \leq \sqrt{2}, \tag{2.18}$$

for any state preparation described by the probability distribution $p(\theta_a, \theta_b)$.

Clearly Eve can give up her perfect control of quantum states of individual particles in the pairs and entangle at least some of them. If she were to prepare all the pairs in perfectly entangled singlet states she would lose all her control and knowledge about Alice's and Bob's data who can then easily establish a secret key. This case is unrealistic because, in practice, Alice and Bob will never register $|S| = 2\sqrt{2}$. However, if Eve prepares only partially entangled pairs then it is still possible for Alice and Bob to establish the key with absolute security, provided they use a *Quantum Privacy Amplification* algorithm (QPA) [47]. The case of partially entangled pairs, $\sqrt{2} \leq |S| \leq 2\sqrt{2}$, is the most important one and in order to claim that we have an operational key distribution scheme we have to prove that the key can be established in this particular case. Skipping technical details we will present only the main idea behind the QPA; details can be found in [47] and in Sect. 8.4.

Firstly, note that any two particles that are jointly in a pure state cannot be entangled with any third physical object. Therefore, any procedure that delivers EPR pairs in pure states must also have eliminated the entanglement between any of those pairs and any other system. The QPA scheme is based on an iterative quantum algorithm which, if performed with perfect accuracy, starting with a collection of EPR-pairs in mixed states, would discard some of them and leave the remaining ones in states converging to the pure singlet state. If (as must be the case realistically) the algorithm is performed imperfectly, the density operator of the pairs remaining after each iteration will not converge on the singlet but on a state close to it; however, the degree of entanglement with any eavesdropper will nevertheless continue to fall, and can be brought to an arbitrary low value. The QPA can be performed by Alice and Bob at distant locations by a sequence of local unitary operations and measurements which are agreed upon by communication over a public channel and could be implemented using technology that is currently being developed (c.f. [48]).

The essential element of the QPA procedure is the "entanglement purification" scheme [49] (see Chap. 8). It has been shown recently that any partially entangled states of two-state particles can be purified [50]. Thus, as long as the density operator cannot be written as a mixture of product states, i.e., is not of the form (2.15), then Alice and Bob can outsmart Eve!

2.5 Quantum Eavesdropping

The QPA procedure requires technology which is not quite available today. Therefore, let us discuss techniques which are much closer to experimental implementations. They are important because we want to build the key distribution prototypes with the current technology and we need to specify the conditions under which they are really secure. Our discussion below is of a general nature and can be applied both to the single-particle and the entanglement-based key distribution. Our description, however, for purely pedagogical reasons, assumes the single-particle scheme where Alice sends photons to Bob.

2.5.1 Error Correction

Since it is essential that Alice and Bob share an identical string of bits, they must correct the discrepancies in their sifted keys. This step, called reconciliation or error correction may use the public channel, but it should disclose as little information as possible to Eve about the reconciled key (or use as few private bits as possible if they decide to encrypt the critical part of their public communication with a previously shared private key). The minimum number r of bits that Alice and Bob have to exchange publicly to correct their data is given by Shannon's Coding theorem [32]: In our case, in which each bit is transmitted incorrectly with an error probability ϵ independently for each bit transmitted, the theorem asserts that

$$r = n \left(-\epsilon \log_2 \epsilon - (1 - \epsilon) \log_2 (1 - \epsilon)\right), \tag{2.19}$$

where n is the length of the sifted key.

Shannon's theorem has a non-constructive proof, which means that we know there exists a correction scheme disclosing only r bits of private data, but the theorem does not provide an explicit procedure. The usual linear error-correcting codes turn out to be rather inefficient in this regard. However, Brassard and Salvail [51] devised a practical interactive correction scheme that gets close to Shannon's limit. The scheme works as follows:

Alice and Bob group their bits into blocks of a given size, which has to be optimised as a function of the error rate. They exchange information about the parity of each block over the public channel. If their parities agree then they proceed to the next block. If their parities disagree, they deduce that there was an odd number of errors in the corresponding block, and search one of them recursively by cutting the block into two sub-blocks and comparing the parities of the first sub-block: if the parities agree then the second sub-block has an odd number of errors and if they do not, then the first sub-block has an odd number of errors. This procedure is continued recursively on the sub block with an odd number of errors.

After this first step, every considered block has either an even number of errors or none. Alice and Bob then shuffle the positions of their bits and repeat the same procedure with blocks of bigger size (this size being optimised as well). However, when an error is corrected, Alice and Bob might deduce that some blocks treated previously now have an odd number of errors. They choose the smallest block amongst them and correct one error recursively, as before. They proceed until every previously treated block has an even number of errors, or none.

Similar steps follow, and the interactive error correction terminates after a specified number of steps. This number is to be optimised in order to maximise the probability that no discrepancies remain and, at the same time, minimise the leakage of private data. Unlike the correction scheme used originally in [42], this correction scheme does not discard any bit from the sifted key.

2.5.2 Privacy Amplification

At this point Alice and Bob share, with high probability, an identical reconciled key. They also know the exact error rate $\bar{\epsilon}$, which gives a very good estimation of the error probability ϵ. Alice and Bob assume that all the errors were caused by the potential eavesdropper, Eve. They also take into account the leakage during the error correction step, if any. Then they deduce τ, the number of bits by which the reconciled key has to be shortened so that Eve's information about the final key is lower than a specified value. More precisely, in most quantum key distribution protocols, given the integer τ, Alice picks randomly a $(n - \tau) \times n$ binary matrix K (a matrix whose entries are 0 or 1) and publicly transmits K to Bob (without encrypting it). The final private key is then:

$$\mathbf{k}_{\text{final}} = K \cdot \mathbf{k}_{\text{reconciled}} \quad (\text{mod } 2) \tag{2.20}$$

where $\mathbf{k}_{\text{reconciled}} = (k_1, k_2, \dots, k_n)$, $k_i \in \{0, 1\}$, is the reconciled key.

Implementation of privacy amplification is easy, but proving security of the entire quantum key distribution protocol is a hard theoretical task in quantum cryptography. Therefore, proofs of security have been proposed gradually, against more and more powerful attacks. Usually we divide those attacks in two categories:

1. Incoherent attacks (Fig. 2.8): In incoherent attacks, or individual particle attacks, Eve is limited to entangling a quantum probe $\mathcal{P}_i$ with one photon at a time. She may keep $\mathcal{P}_i$ until the entangled photon is measured by Bob and all public discussions between Alice and Bob are completed. Indeed, Alice and Bob cannot tell whether Eve measures her probes before or after Bob measures his photons. Therefore the best strategy for Eve is to wait until measurement bases are announced publicly by Alice and Bob and then cleverly measure her probes to extract as much information as possible. However, in incoherent attacks, Eve is limited to measuring her probes $\mathcal{P}_i$ individually.

In more detail, taking into account the scenario presented in Sect. 2.3.1 and denoting by $|E\rangle_i$ the initial state of Eve's probe, the most general unitary transformation $\mathcal{U}$ entangling $\mathcal{P}_i$ to Alice's photon reads (in the $\oplus$ basis):

$$|E\rangle_i \, |\updownarrow\rangle \xmapsto{\mathcal{U}} |E_{00}^{\oplus}\rangle \, |\updownarrow\rangle + |E_{01}^{\oplus}\rangle \, |\leftrightarrow\rangle \tag{2.21}$$

$$|E\rangle_i \, |\leftrightarrow\rangle \xmapsto{\mathcal{U}} |E_{10}^{\oplus}\rangle \, |\updownarrow\rangle + |E_{11}^{\oplus}\rangle \, |\leftrightarrow\rangle \tag{2.22}$$

where $|E_{ij}^{\oplus}\rangle$ are unnormalised states of $\mathcal{P}_i$. Since $|E\rangle_i$ can be chosen to lie in the span of $\{|E_{ij}^{\oplus}\rangle\}_{i,j}$, we can assume that $\mathcal{P}_i$ is described with a 4-dimensional Hilbert space, i.e. each probe is described by 2 qubits.

The action of $\mathcal{U}$, if Alice sends her photon in the $\otimes$ basis, is derived from (2.21, 2.22) using linearity:

$$|E\rangle_i \, |\nearrow\rangle \xmapsto{\mathcal{U}} |E_{00}^{\otimes}\rangle \, |\nearrow\rangle + |E_{01}^{\otimes}\rangle \, |\searrow\rangle \tag{2.23}$$

$$|E\rangle_i \, |\searrow\rangle \xmapsto{\mathcal{U}} |E_{10}^{\otimes}\rangle \, |\nearrow\rangle + |E_{11}^{\otimes}\rangle \, |\searrow\rangle, \tag{2.24}$$

where

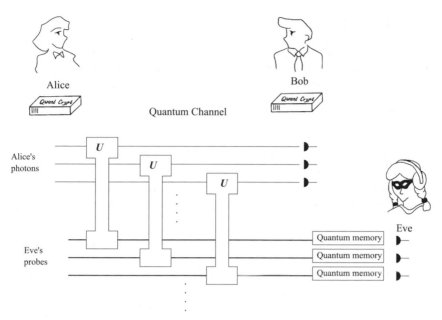

Fig. 2.8. Incoherent attacks: each photon is entangled independently to a 2-qubit probe. The probes are stored in a quantum memory until measurement bases are announced. Then each probe is measured independently.

$$\big| E_{00}^{\otimes} \big\rangle = \frac{\big| E_{00}^{\oplus} \big\rangle + \big| E_{10}^{\oplus} \big\rangle + \big| E_{01}^{\oplus} \big\rangle + F_{11}^{\oplus} \big\rangle}{2} \tag{2.25}$$

$$\big| E_{01}^{\otimes} \big\rangle = \frac{\big| E_{00}^{\oplus} \big\rangle + \big| E_{10}^{\oplus} \big\rangle - \big| E_{01}^{\oplus} \big\rangle - \big| E_{11}^{\oplus} \big\rangle}{2} \tag{2.26}$$

$$\big| E_{10}^{\otimes} \big\rangle = \frac{\big| E_{00}^{\oplus} \big\rangle - \big| E_{10}^{\oplus} \big\rangle + \big| E_{01}^{\oplus} \big\rangle - \big| E_{11}^{\oplus} \big\rangle}{2} \tag{2.27}$$

$$\big| E_{11}^{\otimes} \big\rangle = \frac{\big| E_{00}^{\oplus} \big\rangle - \big| E_{10}^{\oplus} \big\rangle - \big| E_{01}^{\oplus} \big\rangle + \big| E_{11}^{\oplus} \big\rangle}{2} \; . \tag{2.28}$$

Eve has to choose $\mathcal{U}$ so that:

1. the eavesdropping is discreet, i.e. for instance, the probability that Bob measures $| \updownarrow \rangle$ while Alice sent $| \leftrightarrow \rangle$ should be lower than the tolerated error rate. We can see that this is equivalent to requiring that the norms $\langle E_{ij}^{\oplus} | E_{ij}^{\oplus} \rangle$ and $\langle E_{ij}^{\otimes} | E_{ij}^{\otimes} \rangle$, $i \neq j$, should be small (those probabilities are usually called disturbances).
2. the eavesdropping is efficient, i.e. Eve should maximise the probability of guessing the correct bit value knowing the used basis (she learned from the public channel), and measuring her probe accordingly. For instance, suppose Eve learns that ith photon was sent in the $\oplus$ basis. She then knows that if Alice's corresponding bit value is 0, then Eve's probe $\mathcal{P}_i$ should be in the mixed state:

$$\rho_0 = \text{Tr}_{\text{photon}} \left[(\mathcal{U} \,|\, E \rangle_i \,|\, \updownarrow \rangle)(\mathcal{U} \,|\, E \rangle_i \,|\, \updownarrow \rangle)^\dagger \right] \tag{2.29}$$

$$= |\, E_{00}^\oplus \rangle \langle E_{00}^\oplus \,| + |\, E_{01}^\oplus \rangle \langle E_{01}^\oplus \,| . \tag{2.30}$$

Likewise, if Alice sent her photon in the $|\leftrightarrow\rangle$ state (corresponding to the bit value 1), Eve's probe should be in the mixed state:

$$\rho_1 = \text{Tr}_{\text{photon}} \left[(\mathcal{U} \,|\, E \rangle_i \,|\, \leftrightarrow \rangle)(\mathcal{U} \,|\, E \rangle_i \,|\, \leftrightarrow \rangle)^\dagger \right] \tag{2.31}$$

$$= |\, E_{10}^\oplus \rangle \langle E_{10}^\oplus \,| + |\, E_{11}^\oplus \rangle \langle E_{11}^\oplus \,| . \tag{2.32}$$

Eve's goal is therefore to decide, as reliably as possible, whether her probe $\mathcal{P}_i$ is in the state ρ_0 or in the state ρ_1. It is known [52, 53] that this is achieved by performing a measurement on $\mathcal{P}_i$. The measured observable is determined by its eigenvectors which, in this case, coincide with the eigenvectors of $\rho_0 - \rho_1$.

The optimisation of this entanglement has been thoroughly discussed in Refs. [52]–[56] for various single-photon quantum key distribution protocols. Their results link the error probability of the quantum channel (or disturbance) to the maximum information Eve could have gained. Knowing this value (more precisely, a related value called the Renyi information) the generalised privacy amplification theorem [57] can be used to compute the shrinking parameter τ which guarantees expected confidentiality. The leakage of information is considered tolerable if τ is reasonably small compared to the size of the reconciled key.

2. Coherent attacks (Fig. 2.9): In coherent or joint attacks, Eve can entangle in any unitary manner a probe of any dimension and in any state (mixed or not) with the *whole sequence* of transmitted photons. She keeps this big probe until public discussions are over and then performs the most general measurement of her choice. The most general class of measurements is known as positive operator valued measures (POVM), for more details see for example [58].

Collective attacks (Fig. 2.10) form a subclass of the coherent attacks where Alice's photon i is entangled individually to a separate probe $\mathcal{P}_i$. Therefore, Eve gets the probes in the same states as in incoherent attacks. However, after public discussions are completed, Eve is allowed to carry out any POVM on all the probes considered as a single big quantum system. Note that in a collective attack, before this POVM, the individual probes $\mathcal{P}_i$ are unentangled and independent of each other. Claims of security against coherent attacks are difficult to prove. So far, only protocols using linear error correcting codes rather than interactive error correction have been considered. Proof of the security of such protocols against collective attacks can be found in [59], and against general coherent attacks in [60].

Authentication: As we mentioned earlier, Alice and Bob should authenticate their communication in order to counter a possible man-in-the-middle

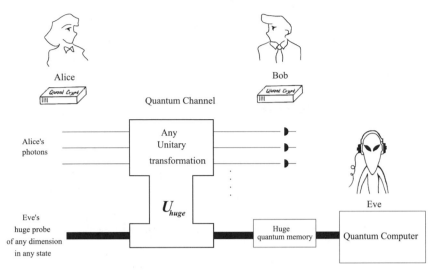

Fig. 2.9. Coherent attacks: Eve is allowed to use a probe of any dimension in any initial state and to entangle it with every photon sent by Alice in any unitary manner. This probe is stored until bases are announced.

attack. They should also ensure that they effectively share a new private key. Fortunately, there exist classical cryptographic techniques to achieve these tasks with arbitrarily high probability. We provide a concise description of an authentication algorithm and refer the reader to [61] for further details. General discussion about authentication can be found in [30].

We assumed that Alice and Bob shared an authentication key $\mathbf{A}$ which is a secret string of binary digits. This key is shorter than the new private key generated by quantum key distribution, but we assume that it is long enough for authentication purposes.

An integer t is chosen; it is a security parameter. Suppose Alice wants to authenticate the data $\mathbf{M_0}$ to Bob. The binary string $\mathbf{M_0}$ contains, for instance, predefined parts of their public discussions. The string $\mathbf{M_0}$, of length m, is then broken into sub-blocks P_i of length $2s$ where $s = t + \log_2 \log_2 m$ (the last sub-block is padded with zeros if necessary). Alice and Bob take the first $2s$ bits of $\mathbf{A}$ to define a number a. The next $2s$ bits of $\mathbf{A}$ define a number b. These $4s$ bits are discarded from $\mathbf{A}$. Then they compute, for each sub-block P_i,

$$p_i' = a p_i + b \pmod{2^s}, \tag{2.33}$$

where p_i is the number represented by the binary string P_i.

The resulting numbers p_i' are converted into bit-streams of length s and concatenated to form $\mathbf{M_1}$. The same operation is repeated (s remains unchanged) r times until the length of $\mathbf{M_r}$ is s. The low-order t bits of $\mathbf{M_r}$ constitute the tag T. The used part of $\mathbf{A}$ is discarded and never reused.

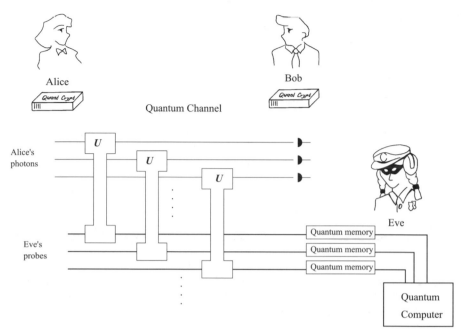

Fig. 2.10. Collective attacks: similar to incoherent attacks, but Eve is now allowed to make global generalised measurement on all probes considered as a single quantum system.

Finally the tag T is sent to Bob, who checks the authenticity of $\mathbf{M_0}$ by doing the same calculations and comparing their results.

The authentication in the quantum key distribution protocol could be implemented as follows. Alice authenticates predefined parts of the public communication. Bob does the same, but with other predefined parts. If this authentication succeeds, the quantum key distribution is considered to be successful and a small part of the new private key can be used as an authentication key for a next session of key distribution. This way, Alice and Bob do not need to meet again to share another authentication key. Suppose a man-in-the-middle attack was performed by Eve. Eve shares a private key with Alice, and another private key with Bob. She knows the data $\mathbf{M_0}$ authenticated by Alice, since Eve was impersonating Bob to Alice during the whole protocol. However, receiving T and knowing $\mathbf{M_0}$, it can be shown that Eve has negligible probability of guessing the authentication key. Therefore, Eve will not be able to pass the authentication test.

2.6 Experimental Realisations

After the first proof-of-the-principle experiments by the IBM-Montreal group
[42] (key distribution using polarised photons and free space propagation)
and the Oxford-DERA group [44] (entangled photons, propagation in optical
fibres, phase encoding) the development of quantum cryptography has continued in two distinct directions: On the one hand it aims to optimise the
systems with respect to transmission length, key generation rate and quantum
bit error rate (QBER), but on the other hand efforts are simultaneously made
to make the systems more stable and easier to use for some potential end-user
interested in secure communication, rather than in quantum mechanics and
optical alignment. As shown in the previous sections, the general idea behind
the various implementations is similar, except for the EPR-based schemes,
differing mainly in the type of modulation or analysis used. In the following
we describe some of the key developments that constitute the current state
of the art in quantum cryptography.

Besides achieving a maximum of reliability for the transmitter and receiver modules of Alice and Bob, a key issue is to increase the transmission
length. Generally, there are two ways: the first is to establish direct free optical path between Alice and Bob and to transmit the light through free space
by using telescopes. The other approach uses optical fibres to guide the light
between the two points. The choice of the transmission method more or less
dictates the wavelength used. Optical fibres have very low absorption in the
so-called telecom windows around 1300nm (0.35 dB/km) and around 1550nm
(0.2 dB/km). However, for this regime the single photon detectors needed are
not that well developed yet [62]. Free space cryptography via satellites in near
earth orbits might bridge arbitrary distances and initial tests on earth indicate that such quantum cryptography transmission is in principle possible,
at least for low bit rates.

2.6.1 Polarisation Encoding

The first quantum cryptography set-up used different polarisation states for
the key distribution protocol. On a standard optical bench of 1m length, Alice
first generated the faint light pulses with a simple light emitting diode (LED)
and passed the collimated light through an interference filter (550 ± 20nm) and
a polarising filter. Using two Pockels cells, she could set one of four polarisation directions (here horizontal, vertical, left and right circular). The Pockels
cell uses the change of the birefringence of certain crystals depending on some
applied electrical field. Usually one needs quite high voltages, on the order of
2–4kV, to generate a rotation of the polarisation by $90°$, say from horizontal
to vertical. (This limits the switching rate for practical applications.) At the
end of a quantum channel of 32 cm, Bob could analyse the polarisation in the
basis set with his Pockels cell by detecting a photon with photomultipliers
behind a Wollaston prism.

Even if, according to the authors, an eavesdropper could have broken the system by listening to the noise of the Pockels cell switches, this first demonstration experiment already has many of the appealing features of quantum cryptography. It was shown from the very beginning how simple experimental quantum cryptography can be – and should be, in order to increase the usability and acceptance for the quantum communication end-user. Moreover, an error rate of only ∼4.4% was reached allowing one to distribute, after error correction, a key of 219 secure bits within a time of 85s.

In order to provide a larger distance between Alice and Bob, a fibre transmission line of 1 km was used in an experiment by Muller et al. [43]. However, a fibre based polarisation encoding system has to overcome several drawbacks. On the one hand, Bob's analyser has to be kept aligned with respect to the polarisation sent by Alice; on the other hand, the polarisation of light will be changed when transported along a fibre cable. Due to the geometry of the light path, topological effects will influence the resulting polarisation at Bob's end of the fibre [63]. Moreover, stress induced birefringence causes both fluctuations in the resulting polarisation and a reduction of the polarisation due to polarisation-mode dispersion. This necessitates the use of single mode lasers to obtain a large enough coherence time and active polarisation stabilisation between Alice and Bob. Finally, careful selection of the various optical components of the transmitter and receiver modules is necessary to minimise any intrinsic polarisation dependence.

More recently, free space systems have begun to utilise the higher stability of the polarisation encoding modules. Since atmosphere is essentially non-birefringent, one does not have to worry about the fluctuations of the relative alignment between Alice's and Bob's modules. Quantum cryptography over outdoor optical paths [64] mainly faces the problem of transmitting light through turbulent media and detecting single photons against a high background. Combining narrow bandwidth and spatial filtering with nanosecond timing should enable key generation with reasonable error rates. A recent experiment in Los Alamos achieved a 14% coupling efficiency over a 950m free space path length, resulting in a bit rate of 50Hz (starting with 20kHz pulse rate at Alice's transmitter) with an error of about 1.5 [65]. This experiment shows the feasibility of establishing a secret key with a low orbit satellite, at least at night-time, with reasonable bit rate.

2.6.2 Phase Encoding

As pointed out in Sect. 2.3.2 phase encoding can be performed analogously to polarisation encoding. The extreme sensitivity to any external influences of a Mach–Zehnder set up shown in Fig. 2.6 can be overcome with the unbalanced Mach–Zehnder configuration proposed by Bennett [45]. Since the two coherent contributions are then separated by only a few nanoseconds but propagating along the same fibre, there are essentially no temperature or stress induced fluctuations. The path length difference of Bob's unbalanced interferometer has to be the same as in Alice's interferometer and has to be kept stable on the sub-wavelength scale. However, this simply requires careful local temperature stabilisation of the two interferometers.

Phase modulators are commercially available for the two telecom wavelengths which seemingly makes the standard phase encoding scheme the best choice for fibre implementations. However, polarisation also places stringent alignment conditions on such a scheme. Of course, in the two unbalanced Mach–Zehnder interferometers the polarisation has to be controlled such that the interfering components have the same polarisation at Bob's output beamsplitter. After an initial alignment of Alice' and Bob's modules, this should be stable and cause no further trouble. A more severe problem comes from the fact that phase modulators are made of electro-optic crystals with preferred guiding only for one of the two polarisation components. In order to avoid intensity fluctuations at Bob's output, only one well defined polarisation can be sent through the modulators. This in turn again makes control of the transmitted polarisation necessary.

In their experimental realisation Townsend et al. [66] first split the incoming laser pulse (1.3 μm, 80 ps) along the two paths of Alice's unbalanced Mach–Zehnder interferometer. In one arm, the phase modulator causes one of the four possible phase shifts according to the BB84 protocol. In the other arm, the polarisation is rotated such that, at Alice's output beamsplitter, the two contributions have *orthogonal* polarisation. Bob's input beamsplitter is replaced by a polarising beamsplitter to ensure correct polarisation in the arm going to Bob's phase modulator. A polarisation controller at the end of the transmission line is set such that these two polarisation directions agree with the axes of Bob's input polarisation splitter. Although polarisation stabilisation becomes necessary again, the specifications are not so strict in such a set-up, since small deviations cause only negligible fluctuations in the final intensity. Error rates of less than 4% were achieved even for a pulse rate of 1 MHz. Further improvements with transmission over 48 km underground fibre cable were achieved by the Los Alamos group [67] with about 1% error at a pulse rate of 30 kHz.

No continuous polarisation alignment of the fibre transmission line is necessary for the so called "plug & play" system. The idea behind this is that the light pulse is emitted not at Alice's station, but by Bob, then first propagates to Alice, where it is modulated and reflected back to Bob. If the reflections in this scheme are done by *Faraday mirrors*, the polarisation of the interfering components at Bob's output are always aligned with each other.

A Faraday mirror, i.e. a 45° Faraday rotator and a back-reflecting mirror, render the back reflected light orthogonal to the light sent into the fibre, thus any polarisation changes along the transmission line or along the interferometer arms are effectively undone.

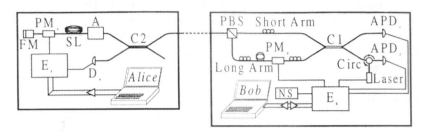

Fig. 2.11. Principle of plug&play quantum cryptography: Bob sends a light pulse through a circulator. This pulse splits at the coupler $C1$. The first half travels through the short arm. A polarisation controller is set so that this pulse is completely transmitted at the polarising beamsplitter PBS. It then propagates to Alice, where it splits again at coupler $C2$ to provide a timing signal. It then travels through Alice's equipment and is reflected back to Bob. Thanks to the Faraday mirror, the birefringence of the optical link is compensated, and the pulse comes back orthogonally polarised. It is then reflected by the PBS and takes the long arm, where Bob applies a phase shift ϕ_B with the modulator PM. The second pulse propagates through the two arms in reverse order. Alice applies to it a phase shift ϕ_A. Since both pulses travel exactly the same optical path, they reach the coupler $C1$ simultaneously with identical polarisation, giving rise to interference. A storage line SL is introduced in Alice's system to avoid problems due to Rayleigh backscaterring.

The system implementing a 4-state BB84 protocol using this idea is depicted in Fig. 2.11 and in [68]. In this experiment Alice and Bob were separated by 23 km using standard telecom fibre cable as the transmission line. Without any continuous active stabilisation an error as low as 1% was achieved while a net key creation rate of 210 Hz was obtained. In all these experiments at the telecom wavelengths of 1300 nm most of the noise is due to the high dark count rate of the single photon detectors (InGaAs/InP-avalanche photo-diodes cooled to only 173 K, i.e. within the reach of Peltier cooling). Currently, clever timing and gated detection electronics help to reduce the noise level, but further improvements of the detectors will tremendously influence the subsequent applicability of quantum cryptography.

2.6.3 Entanglement-Based Quantum Cryptography

A number of new features in cryptography become possible when utilising the non-classical properties of entangled pairs of particles (see Sect. 2.4). However, with the current technology, such schemes are more difficult to realise than the single particle approaches described so far, mostly because one has to generate a high degree of entanglement. Imperfect entanglement between the photons delivered to Alice and Bob could be improved only with techniques such as entanglement purification, which are not realisable with current technology. Thus any noise in the entanglement directly determines the performance of the system. Since the first demonstration [44], the main goal has thus been to further develop the source of entangled photon pairs. Today, parametric down-conversion is used as a source of photon pairs. Due to the low efficiency of this process broad band light has to be used to obtain a sufficient bit rate. Here a compromise has to be found in order to avoid problems when transmitting the photon pairs through dispersive optical fibre.

Most approaches use the time–energy entanglement (for details see [69, 70]). If a photon pair is produced by the process of parametric down-conversion, non-local interference can occur between the outputs of two un-balanced, but otherwise identical Mach–Zehnder or Michelson interferome-ters, provided the path length difference of each of the interferometers is less than the coherence time of the down-conversion pump laser. In order to discriminate between interfering and non-interfering contributions, time selection of the detection events is required. The minimum time resolution of the single photon detectors of about 300 ps makes a corresponding path length difference of about 30 cm necessary. Experiments on the EPR–Bell problem performed in Geneva demonstrate that it is possible to distribute entangled pairs along standard telecom lines and to observe a high degree of entanglement over a physical distance between the detectors of 10 km (the actual length of two optical fibres between the source and detectors was 8 km and 9 km) [71].

Polarisation entanglement can be also obtained in the process of para-metric down-conversion (type II, [16]). In a recent experiment, violation of a Bell inequality was observed also for independent observers [72]. In this experiment the two observers, Alice and Bob, are separated by about 400 m (connected by 1 km optical fibre). But here all their measurements, from generating a random orientation for analysis until detection of the photon, are performed within times (~ 80 ns) much shorter than the time it takes to send information between them (~ 1300 ns). The fast electro-optic modula-tion system and detection electronics developed for this experiment can be directly used to perform quantum cryptography both with true single photon states as well as with a violation of a Bell inequality as an assurance of secure communication.

2.7 Concluding Remarks

Research in quantum cryptography in all its possible variations has become very active and any comprehensive review of the field would quickly be over-taken by events. Hence we have decided to provide here only some very basic knowledge, hoping that this will serve as a good starting point for entering the field. The basic message is: quantum cryptography today is a viable al-ternative to conventional methods of encryption and in the not-too-distant future we may have to rely on quantum mechanics rather than number theory in our confidential communication.

The reader should be warned that we have barely scratched the surface of the current activities, neglecting topics such as secure two-party computation, details of quantum authentication, detailed analysis of eavesdropping techniques and security criteria, and some alternative key distribution techniques (e.g. Vaidman and Goldenberg scheme based on sending orthogonal states in two parts). Many interesting papers on these and other related topics can be found at the Los Alamos National Laboratory e-print archive (http://xxx.lanl.gov/archive/quant-ph) and on other WWW servers such as http://www.qubit.org.

3. Quantum Dense Coding
and Quantum Teleportation

3.1 Introduction

D. Bouwmeester, H. Weinfurter, A. Zeilinger

In Chap. 2 it was shown how quantum entanglement can be used to distribute secret keys. In this chapter we will address other primitives of quantum communication employing entanglement. Section 3.2 describes "Quantum Dense Coding" which is a way to transmit two bits of information through the manipulation of only one of two entangled particles, each of which individually can carry only 1 bit of information [73]. The "Quantum Teleportation" scheme as originally proposed by Bennett, Brassard, Crépeau, Jozsa, Peres, and Wootters [74] is explained in Sect. 3.3. The basic idea of quantum teleportation is to transfer the state of a quantum system to another quantum system at a distant location.

Quantum optics has proven very successful for the implementation of quantum dense coding and quantum teleportation. Two crucial ingredients for the optical implementations are the source of entangled photons, described in Sect. 3.4, and the Bell-state analyser, described in Sect. 3.5. In Sect. 3.6 the experimental demonstration of quantum dense coding is presented [75]. Section 3.7 describes the quantum teleportation experiment performed in Innsbruck [76] in which the polarisation state of a single photon is teleported using an auxiliary pair of entangled photons. Section 3.8 describes the experiment, proposed by Popescu [77] and performed in Rome [78], in which the polarisation state prepared on one of a pair of momentum entangled photons is transferred to its partner at a distant location. Section 3.9 explains the teleportation of continuous quantum variables, which was initially proposed by Vaidman [79], further elaborated upon by Braunstein and Kimble [80], and experimentally demonstrated at Caltech [81]. Each experiment has its own advantages and disadvantages and we refer to the literature for a comparison between the various methods [82]–[84].

If the initial quantum state of the teleportation protocol is part of an entangled state, the result of the teleportation process is that two systems that did not directly interact with one another become entangled. This process, referred to as "entanglement swapping", will be described in Sect. 3.10 and applications [85]–[87] are presented in Sect. 3.11.

3.2 Quantum Dense Coding Protocol

The scheme for quantum dense coding, theoretically proposed by Bennett and Wiesner [73], utilises entanglement between two qubits, each of which individually has two orthogonal states, $|0\rangle$ and $|1\rangle$. Classically, there are four possible polarisation combinations for a pair of such particles; 00, 01, 10, and 11. Identifying each combination with different information implies that we can encode two bits of information by manipulating *both* particles.

Quantum mechanics also allows one to encode the information in superpositions of the classical combinations. Such superpositions of states of two (or more) particles are called entangled states (see Sect. 1.4) and a convenient basis in which to represent such states for two particles, labeled 1 and 2, is formed by the maximally entangled Bell states

$$|\Psi^+\rangle_{12} = (|0\rangle_1|1\rangle_2 + |1\rangle_1|0\rangle_2)/\sqrt{2} \tag{3.1}$$

$$|\Psi^-\rangle_{12} = (|0\rangle_1|1\rangle_2 - |1\rangle_1|0\rangle_2)/\sqrt{2} \tag{3.2}$$

$$|\Phi^+\rangle_{12} = (|0\rangle_1|0\rangle_2 + |1\rangle_1|1\rangle_2)/\sqrt{2} \tag{3.3}$$

$$|\Phi^-\rangle_{12} = (|0\rangle_1|0\rangle_2 - |1\rangle_1|1\rangle_2)/\sqrt{2}. \tag{3.4}$$

Identifying each Bell state with different information we can again encode two bits of information, yet, now by manipulating only *one* of the two particles.

This is achieved in the following quantum communication scheme. Initially, Alice and Bob each obtain one particle of an entangled pair, say, in the state $|\Psi^+\rangle_{12}$ given in (3.1). Bob then performs one out of four possible unitary transformations on his particle (particle 2) alone. The four such transformations are

1. Identity operation (not changing the original two-particle state $|\Psi^+\rangle_{12}$)
2. State exchange ($|0\rangle_2 \rightarrow |1\rangle_2$ and $|1\rangle_2 \rightarrow |0\rangle_2$, changing the two-particle state to $|\Phi^+\rangle_{12}$)
3 State-dependent phase shift (differing by π for $|0\rangle_2$ and $|1\rangle_2$ and transforming to $|\Psi^-\rangle_{12}$)
4. State exchange and phase shift together (giving the state $|\Phi^-\rangle_{12}$).

Since the four manipulations result in the four orthogonal Bell states, four distinguishable messages, i.e. 2 bits of information, can be sent via Bob's two-state particle to Alice, who finally reads the encoded information by determining the Bell state of the two-particle system. This scheme enhances the information capacity of the transmission channel to two bits compared to the classical maximum of one bit.[1]

---

[1] While it is clear that this scheme enhances the information capacity of the transmission channel accessed by Bob to two bits, we have to notice that the channel

3.3 Quantum Teleportation Protocol

In this section we will review the quantum teleportation scheme as proposed by Bennett, Brassard, Crépeau, Jozsa, Peres, and Wootters [74]. The scheme is illustrated in the Fig. 3.1.

The idea is that Alice has particle 1 in a certain quantum state, the qubit $|\Psi\rangle_1 = \alpha|0\rangle_1 + \beta|1\rangle_1$, where $|0\rangle$ and $|1\rangle$ represent two orthogonal states with complex amplitudes α and β satisfying $|\alpha|^2 + |\beta|^2 = 1$. She wishes to transfer this quantum state to Bob but suppose she cannot deliver the particle directly to him. According to the projection postulate of quantum mechanics we know that any quantum measurement performed by Alice on her particle will destroy the quantum state at hand without revealing all the necessary information for Bob to reconstruct the quantum state. So how can she provide Bob with the quantum state? The answer is to use an ancillary pair of entangled particles 2 and 3 (EPR pair), where particle 2 is given to Alice and particle 3 is given to Bob. Let us consider the case in which the entangled pair of particles 2 and 3 shared by Alice and Bob is in the state

$$|\Psi^-\rangle_{23} = \frac{1}{\sqrt{2}}(|0\rangle_2|1\rangle_3 - |1\rangle_2|0\rangle_3)\,. \tag{3.5}$$

The important property of this entangled state is that as soon as a measurement on one of the particles projects it onto a certain state, which can be any normalised linear superposition of $|0\rangle$ and $|1\rangle$, the other particle has to be in the orthogonal state. The specific phase relation between the two terms on the right hand side of (3.5) (here the phase difference is π, which results in the minus sign) implies that the statement of orthogonality is independent of the basis chosen for the polarisation measurement.

Although initially particles 1 and 2 are not entangled, their joint polarisation state can always be expressed as a superposition of the four maximally entangled Bell states, given by (3.1)–(3.4), since these states form a complete orthogonal basis. The total state of the 3 particles can be written as:

$$\begin{aligned}
|\Psi\rangle_{123} = |\Psi\rangle_1 \otimes |\Psi\rangle_{23} = \frac{1}{2} \big[\; &|\Psi^-\rangle_{12}\,(-\alpha|0\rangle_3 - \beta|1\rangle_3) \\
+ &|\Psi^+\rangle_{12}\,(-\alpha|0\rangle_3 + \beta|1\rangle_3) \\
+ &|\Phi^-\rangle_{12}\,(\alpha|1\rangle_3 + \beta|0\rangle_3) \\
+ &|\Phi^+\rangle_{12}\,(\alpha|1\rangle_3 - \beta|0\rangle_3) \big]\,.
\end{aligned} \tag{3.6}$$

Alice now performs a Bell state measurement (BSM) on particles 1 and 2, that is, she projects her two particles onto one of the four Bell states. As a result of the measurement Bob's particle will be found in a state that is directly related to the initial state. For example, if the result of Alice's Bell state measurement is $|\Phi^-\rangle_{12}$ then particle 3 in the hands of Bob is in the

---

carrying the other photon transmits 0 bits of information, thus the total transmitted information does not exceed 2 bits.

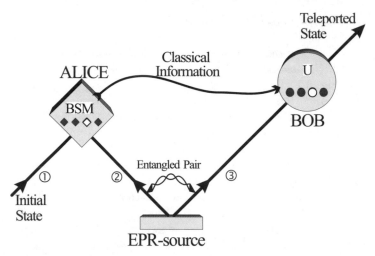

Fig. 3.1. Principle of quantum teleportation: Alice has a quantum system, particle 1, in an initial state which she wants to teleport to Bob. Alice and Bob also share an ancillary entangled pair of particles 2 and 3 emitted by an Einstein-Podolsky-Rosen(EPR) source. Alice then performs a joint Bell state measurement (BSM) on the initial particle and one of the ancillaries, projecting them also onto an entangled state. After she has sent the result of her measurement as classical information to Bob, he can perform a unitary transformation (U) on the other ancillary particle resulting in it being in the state of the original particle. In the case of quantum teleportation of a qubit, Alice makes a projection measurement onto four orthogonal entangled states (the Bell states) that form a complete basis. Sending the outcome of her measurement, i.e. two bits of classical information, to Bob will enable Bob to reconstruct the initial qubit.

state $\alpha|1\rangle_3 + \beta|0\rangle_3$. All that Alice has to do is to inform Bob via a classical communication channel on her measurement result and Bob can perform the appropriate unitary transformation (U) on particle 3 in order to obtain the initial state of particle 1. This completes the teleportation protocol.

Note that, during the teleportation procedure, the values of α and β remain unknown. By her Bell state measurement Alice does not obtain any information whatsoever about the teleported state. All that is achieved by the Bell state measurement is a transfer of the quantum state. Note also that during the Bell state measurement particle 1 loses its initial quantum state because it becomes entangled with particle 2. Therefore the state $|\Psi\rangle_1$ is destroyed on Alice's side during teleportation, thus obeying the no-cloning theorem of quantum mechanics [88]. Furthermore, the initial state of particle 1 can be completely unknown not only to Alice but to anyone. It could even be quantum mechanically completely undefined at the time the Bell state measurement takes place. This is the case when, as already remarked by Bennett et al. [74], particle 1 itself is a member of an entangled pair and therefore has no well-defined properties on its own. This ultimately leads to entanglement swapping which will be discussed in Sect. 3.10 [85, 87].

The experimental implementation of quantum teleportation or of quantum dense coding and entanglement swapping requires the generation of entangled particles and the construction of a Bell state analyser. The following two sections describe experimental techniques in quantum optics by which entangled photons and a (partial) Bell state analyser can be realised.

3.4 Sources of Entangled Photons

N. Gisin, J.G. Rarity, G. Weihs

There exist several sources of entangled quantum systems. A source of entangled atoms based on cavity quantum electrodynamics will be described in Sect. 5.2.3. Entangled ions have been prepared in electromagnetic Paul traps, see Sect. 5.2.11. Controlled entanglement between nuclear spins within a single molecule can be achieved by the technique of nuclear magnetic resonance and is presented in Sect. 5.3. Sources of entanglement in solid state physics are also being studied; however, it is still too early to see whether controlled entanglement in solid state physics is realisable. Here we will describe the sources of entanglement using quantum optics, which have been proven to be most successful, up to now, in generating high-quality entanglement.

In quantum optics there are two classes in which entanglement can be established (for a general view on creating entanglement see Sect. 1.5). One class is characterised by entanglement between single photons and will be described in this section. The other way is to establish entanglement between the quadrature components (i.e. the in- and out-of-phase electric-field components with respect to a local oscillator) of light beams or between two orthogonal polarisation components of light beams (see Sect. 3.9.2).

3.4.1 Parametric Down-Conversion

Nonlinear optical processes have been utilised for many experiments in quantum optics. Nonlinear optics is the part of classical electrodynamics which deals with strong fields that are scattered inelastically in various media. Inelastic scattering in the optical domain means that not only the direction but also the frequency of light is being changed by the interaction with the material, which is described by its electromagnetic susceptibility. During such interactions in most cases new fields are created. A power expansion of the susceptibility gives the lowest order nonlinear processes; three-wave-mixing (parametric interactions) and four-wave-mixing. The individual components P_i of the electromagnetic polarisation $\mathbf{P}$ inside a material are given by

$$P_i = \chi_{ij}^{(1)}\, E_j + \chi_{ijk}^{(2)}\, E_j\, E_k + \chi_{ijkl}^{(3)}\, E_j\, E_k\, E_l + \dots, \tag{3.7}$$

where the E_i are the components of the electric field.

In order to be able to observe nonlinear interactions from an interaction volume that is large compared to the wavelengths involved, we have to consider contributions from the whole volume. Interference between these contributions leads to the so-called phase-matching relations, which are relations between the wavevectors of the respective electromagnetic fields.

If we look at these processes from a quantum electrodynamical viewpoint, we find that there are not only the stimulated but also the spontaneous processes just as in the interactions of the electromagnetic field with an atom. The spontaneous creation of photons in nonlinear interactions was first investigated theoretically by Klyshko [89] and experimentally by Burnham and Weinberg [90]. A special case of such a process is spontaneous parametric down-conversion, a $\chi^{(2)}$-nonlinear process, in which only one of the fields is initially excited with a frequency ω_p. Due to the nonlinear interaction and this pump field, photons will be created spontaneously in the other two fields at frequencies ω_1 and ω_2. As energy is conserved in the interaction we will find that

$$\omega_1 + \omega_2 = \omega_p. \tag{3.8}$$

Together with the phase-matching condition

$$\mathbf{k}_1 + \mathbf{k}_2 = \mathbf{k}_p, \tag{3.9}$$

this leads to various solutions of the interaction dynamics, depending on the material used and on the frequencies that are being observed. The rate of conversion is governed by the modulus of the corresponding components of $\chi^{(2)}$ and is in general very low. If, for example, we pump a material with a high nonlinearity (e.g. potassium di-deuterium phosphate, β-barium borate) with 100 mW (UV), we can observe of the order of 10^{10} photons per second of converted light from a small (a few mm long) piece of crystal. Symmetry considerations tell us further that $\chi^{(2)}$-nonlinearities are only possessed by materials which are non-centrosymmetric, a property that belongs only to certain crystals.

In parametric down-conversion in the visible range of the spectrum, we distinguish two possible phase-matching schemes. "Type-I" phase-matching is the case where the two down-conversion photons have parallel polarisations whereas in "type-II" phase-matching they have orthogonal polarisations in the basis distinguished by the crystal orientation. It is the simultaneous production of the two photons in the conversion process and the phase-matching relations, together with proper spatial and temporal selection of the observed light, which are responsible for the creation and observation of entanglement.

3.4.2 Time Entanglement

There are various properties of photon pairs emerging from a down-conversion process that can be correlated. In type-I and type-II down-conversion we can observe what is sometimes called time entanglement, which only relies on fact that the two photons in a pair are created simultaneously and that they satisfy the energy conservation rule stated above. This latter criterion means that the emission time of any pair is uncertain within the coherence time of the pump laser. The simultaneity criterion arises because the individual photons of the pair are broadband (nanometre bandwidth) with coherence times of order 100 fs. This kind of entanglement has been used for so-called two-photon Franson–interferometry (see Fig. 3.2), where both photons pass separate unbalanced Mach–Zehnder interferometers [91]. The two interferometers are constructed in the same way and such that the coherence length of an individual photon is shorter than the path-length difference. As a result no interference can be seen in the direct count rates of detectors at the outputs of the interferometers. If, however, we look at the coincidences in the outputs of the two interferometers, we will observe oscillations of the coincidence count rates as we vary the phases between the arms of the interferometers. The state within the interferometers can be represented by

$$|\Psi\rangle = \frac{1}{2}\left[|S\rangle_1|S\rangle_2 + e^{i(\phi_1+\phi_2)}|L\rangle_1|L\rangle_2\right.$$
$$\left. + e^{i\phi_2}|S\rangle_1|L\rangle_2 + e^{i\phi_1}|L\rangle_1|S\rangle_2\right], \qquad (3.10)$$

where the subscripts 1 and 2 refer to the photon moving to the left and to the right respectively in Fig. 3.2. State (3.10) is in fact a product state. However only long–long (L-L) and short–short (S-S) detections are truly coincident at the detectors and other events can be discarded by suitable coincidence gating. Initial experiments [91] did not use this time gating and were limited to maximum interference visibility of 50%. Later experiments using narrow coincidence gates to post-select only the entangled state show interference visibilities greater than 90% [92].

An interesting elaboration of time-entanglement should be mentioned. One can replace the cw pump laser by a pulsed laser followed by an unbalanced interferometer with pulses shorter than the arm length difference of the interferometer [93], see Fig. 3.3. Thus, if a pump photon is split into a

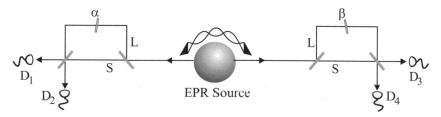

Fig. 3.2. Schematic of a Franson–type experiment testing the interference of time-entangled photon pairs by measuring them with two remote unbalanced Mach–Zehnder-interferometers. The phase of each interferometer can be changed by a phase shifter in the long (L) paths.

twin-photon inside the crystal after the first interferometer, the time of creation of the latter is undefined. More precisely, the unbalanced interferometer transforms the state of the pump photon in a superposition $\alpha|\text{short}\rangle_{\text{pump}} + \beta|\text{long}\rangle_{\text{pump}}$ and the down-conversion process in the crystal transforms this state into

$$\alpha|\text{short}\rangle_s \otimes |\text{short}\rangle_i + \beta|\text{long}\rangle_s \otimes |\text{long}\rangle_i . \qquad (3.11)$$

Contrary to time entangled photons produced with a cw pump laser, the coherence of the pulsed pump laser is of no importance, as the necessary coherence is built by the unbalanced interferometer. In other words, the uncertainty of the pump photon's arrival time at the crystal (within the coherence length of the pump laser) is replaced by the two sharp values corresponding to $|\text{short}\rangle$ and $|\text{long}\rangle$ which form the basis of our qubit space. Hence, any standard laser diode, for instance, can be used as pump. Moreover, the basic states can be distinguished by their time of arrival, without any optical

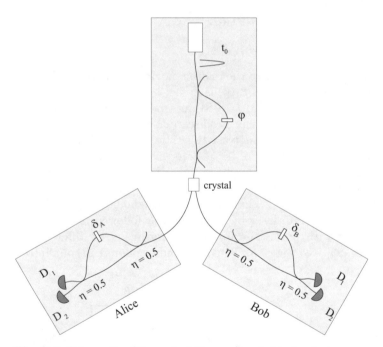

Fig. 3.3. Schematic of the pulsed time-entangled twin-photon source and a possible application for quantum cryptography. The twin-photons created by a pump photon passing through the short and the long arm of the first interferometer are coherent. Alice and Bob detect photons at 3 different times (relative to the emission time): short, medium, long. Short and long counts are 100% correlated. Medium counts correspond to the complementary basis, $|\text{short}\rangle \pm |\text{long}\rangle$, and are also perfectly correlated (assuming $\varphi + \delta_A + \delta_B = 0$). Note that no random generator is necessary, nor any active optical element.

circuit. By varying the coupling ratio and phase of the unbalanced interferometer, all 2-qubit entangled states can be produced. Hence all of the 2-qubit quantum communication protocols can be implemented.

3.4.3 Momentum Entanglement

Another kind of entanglement that is present in non-collinear down-conversion is momentum entanglement. This is induced by the phase-matching relation which governs the emission of different wavelengths into different directions. Using apertures A (see Fig. 3.4) two individual mode pairs (directions) from the emission of a down-conversion source are selected [94]. The selection is such that each pair consists of one photon with colour a (slightly above half of the pump frequency) and one photon with colour b (slightly below half of the pump frequency). The pairs are emitted into either modes $a1$, $b1$ or modes $a2$, $b1$ as shown in Fig. 3.4. Before the beam-splitter we thus have the state

$$|\Psi\rangle = \frac{1}{\sqrt{2}} \left[e^{i\phi_b}|a\rangle_1|b\rangle_2 + e^{i\phi_a}|a\rangle_2|b\rangle_1 \right] , \tag{3.12}$$

which is entangled although the modes at this stage are clearly distinguishable. The entanglement manifests itself when the a-modes and b-modes are recombined in a beam-splitter. From behind the beamsplitter upper and lower paths cannot be distinguished leading to interference. The 50/50 beam-splitter transforms the incoming fields through

$$|\text{in}\rangle_1 \rightarrow \frac{1}{\sqrt{2}} \left[|\text{out}\rangle_3 + i|\text{out}\rangle_4 \right] , \tag{3.13}$$

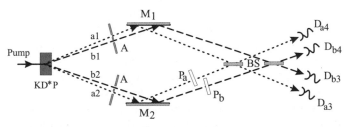

Fig. 3.4. Schematic of the Rarity–Tapster experiment on momentum entanglement from a type-I down-conversion source. Two correlated pairs of modes are selected from the emission spectrum of a type-I down-conversion source using two double apertures A. The different wavelengths are recombined on two beam-splitters BS. The detectors D_{a3}, D_{b3}, D_{a4}, and D_{b4} are used to measure the outputs from the beam-splitters.

$$|\text{in}\rangle_2 \rightarrow \frac{1}{\sqrt{2}} \left[|\text{out}\rangle_4 + i|\text{out}\rangle_3 \right].$$

The state before the detectors is thus

$$|\Psi\rangle = \frac{1}{2} \left[(e^{i\phi_a} - e^{i\phi_b})|a\rangle_4|b\rangle_3 + (e^{i\phi_b} - e^{i\phi_a})|a\rangle_3|b\rangle_4 \right. \tag{3.14}$$
$$\left. + i(e^{i\phi_a} + e^{i\phi_b})|a\rangle_4|b\rangle_4 + i(e^{i\phi_a} + e^{i\phi_b})|a\rangle_3|b\rangle_3 \right].$$

The four terms now show the probability amplitudes for coincident detections in each of the four possible detector pairs. Taking the modulus square of these amplitudes provides the probability of coincident detections between the a- and b-detectors which varies cosinusoidally on changing interferometer phase difference $\phi = \phi_a - \phi_b$. First order interference effects between the combined a- and b-modes are not seen because there is no phase conservation for individual photons of each pair. The phase conservation in parametric down-conversion arises in the energy conservation stated above; it is the sum of the phases in the a- and b-modes that are locked to that of the pump beam.

The a-mode (b-mode) interferometer measures a 'phase' between the two possible emissions in a basis fixed by the offset phase ϕ_a (ϕ_b). The 100% correlation (anticorrelation) in the binary measurement of this phase whenever $\phi = \phi_a - \phi_b = 0$ ($\pi/2$) confirms the non-local nature of the effect. This result cannot be reproduced if there is a local realistic phase (satisfying the sum phase condition above) associated with each photon pair as it leaves the crystal. In the experiment [94] an interference visibility of 82% was measured, beyond the maximum predicted for any local realistic model of the experiment. However the interference visibility is low compared to polarisation based entanglement experiments due to the difficulties of alignment and overlap of the four beams.

3.4.4 Polarisation Entanglement

More recently a new type of down-conversion source was found, which relies on non-collinear type-II phase matching [16]. At certain angles between the pump-beam and the optic axis of the conversion crystal the phase-matching conditions will be such that the photons are emitted along cones, which do not have a common axis, as is illustrated in Fig. 3.5 and Fig. 3.6. One of the cones is ordinarily polarised the other one extraordinarily. These cones will in general intersect along two directions. If we now remember that in type-II down-conversion the two photons in a pair are always polarised orthogonally, we will find that along the two directions of intersection the emitted light is unpolarised, because we cannot distinguish whether a certain photon belongs to one or the other cone. This is not yet exactly true, because in the birefringent crystal the ordinary and extraordinary photons will propagate at different velocities and so we could at least in principle distinguish the two cases by the order of their detection times. It is, however possible to compensate for that "walkoff", by inserting identical crystals of half the thickness

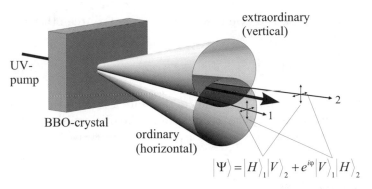

extraordinary
(vertical)

UV-
pump

BBO-crystal

ordinary
(horizontal)

$$|\Psi\rangle = |H\rangle_1|V\rangle_2 + e^{i\varphi}|V\rangle_1|H\rangle_2$$

Fig. 3.5. Non-collinear type-II down-conversion can produce two tilted cones of light of a certain wavelength. At same time other wavelengths are emitted, but in order to observe polarisation entanglement only we cut out a certain wavelength using narrow-band optical filters.

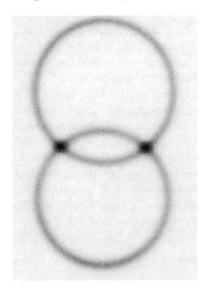

Fig. 3.6. Type-II down-conversion light as seen through a narrow-band filter. The two rings are the ordinary and extraordinary cones of light rays. Along the intersecting directions we observe unpolarised light.

rotated by 90° in each of the two beams. This procedure completely erases any such information and we have a true polarisation-entangled state which can be described by

$$|\Psi\rangle = \frac{1}{\sqrt{2}} \left[|V\rangle_1|H\rangle_2 + e^{i\varphi}|H\rangle_1|V\rangle_2 \right]. \tag{3.15}$$

Furthermore we can use these compensator crystals to change the phase φ between the two components of the entangled state. If we use an additional

half-wave plate in one of the two beams we can also produce the other two
of the four Bell-states.

$$|\Phi^{\pm}\rangle = \frac{1}{\sqrt{2}} \left[|V\rangle_1 |V\rangle_2 \pm |H\rangle_1 |H\rangle_2 \right]. \tag{3.16}$$

Again in order to see the interference effects the state is studied in a basis
where the vertical and horizontal polarisations cannot be distinguished. This
can be done simply by mixing the states in a polariser rotated to 45°.

3.5 Bell-State Analyser

D. Bouwmeester, H. Weinfurter, A. Zeilinger

Formally speaking, a Bell-state analysis, required for quantum dense coding
and for quantum teleportation (see Sects. 3.2 and 3.3), is not a problem.
All you have to do is project any incoming state onto the Bell state basis,
(3.1)–(3.4), and you will find out by repeating this experiment with which
probability the original state can be found in one of the Bell states. The
Bell states depend, of course, on the type of entanglement that is present.
In the case of entanglement between the polarisation and the momentum
degree of freedom of a single photon, the projection onto a complete Bell-
state basis is possible (see Sect. 3.8) with simple linear optical elements. In
the case of polarisation entanglement between two photons, the situation is
more complicated and, so far, only the projection onto two Bell states has
been achieved, leaving the other two states degenerate in their detection. This
partial Bell-state analysis will be explained in the next section.

3.5.1 Photon Statistics at a Beamsplitter

The partial Bell-state analysis of polarisation entanglement exploits the
statistics of two qubits at a beamsplitter. The basic principle of that Bell-
state analyser rests on the observation that of the four Bell states (3.1)–(3.4)
only one state is antisymmetric under exchange of the two particles. This is
the $|\Psi^-\rangle_{12}$ state (3.2), which clearly changes sign upon exchange of labels 1
and 2. The other three states are symmetric. We thus observe that the qubit
obeys fermionic symmetry in the case of $|\Psi^-\rangle_{12}$ and bosonic symmetry in
case of the other three states. Thus far we have not specified whether the
particles carrying the qubits are bosons or fermions. In fact, the four Bell
states could equally well be those of fermions or those of bosons. This is
because the states written in (3.1)–(3.4) are not the complete states of the
particles but describe only the internal (two-level) state of the particles. The
total state can be obtained by adding the spatial state of the particles which

could also be symmetric or antisymmetric. Then, in the case of bosons, the spatial part of the wave function has to be antisymmetric for the $|\Psi^-\rangle_{12}$ state and symmetric for the other three, while for fermions this has to be just the reverse.

Let us first consider two photons, which are bosons, and assume that the Bell states above describe the polarisation of the photons, that is, an internal degree of freedom. Then, clearly, the total state of the two photons has to be symmetric. For the case of the two particles incident symmetrically onto a beamsplitter, i.e., one entering from each input mode $|a\rangle$ and $|b\rangle$, the possible external (spatial) states are

$$|\Psi_A\rangle_{12} = \frac{1}{\sqrt{2}}(|a\rangle_1|b\rangle_2 - |b\rangle_1|a\rangle_2) \tag{3.17}$$

$$|\Psi_S\rangle_{12} = \frac{1}{\sqrt{2}}(|a\rangle_1|b\rangle_2 + |b\rangle_1|a\rangle_2), \tag{3.18}$$

where $|\Psi_A\rangle_{12}$ and $|\Psi_S\rangle_{12}$ are antisymmetric and symmetric, respectively. Because of the requirement of symmetry, the total two-photon states are

$$|\Psi^+\rangle|\Psi_S\rangle, \quad |\Psi^-\rangle|\Psi_A\rangle, \quad |\Phi^+\rangle|\Psi_S\rangle, \text{ and } |\Phi^-\rangle|\Psi_S\rangle. \tag{3.19}$$

We note that only the state antisymmetric in external variables is also antisymmetric in internal variables. It is this state which also emerges from the beamsplitter in an external antisymmetric state. This can easily be found by assuming that the beamsplitter does not influence the internal state and by applying the beamsplitter operator (Hadamard transformation) on the external (spatial) state. Using

$$H|a\rangle = \frac{1}{\sqrt{2}}(|c\rangle + |d\rangle) \tag{3.20}$$

$$H|b\rangle = \frac{1}{\sqrt{2}}(|c\rangle - |d\rangle) \tag{3.21}$$

it can now easily be seen that

$$H|\Psi_A\rangle_{12} = \frac{1}{\sqrt{2}}(|c\rangle_1|d\rangle_2 - |d\rangle_1|c\rangle_2) = |\Psi_A\rangle_{12}. \tag{3.22}$$

Therefore the spatially antisymmetric state is an eigenstate of the beamsplitter operator [95, 96]. In contrast, in all three cases of the symmetric external state $|\Psi_S\rangle$, the two photons emerge together in one of the two outputs of the beamsplitter. It is therefore evident that the state $|\Psi^-\rangle$ can be clearly discriminated from all the other states. It is the only one of the four Bell states which leads to coincidences between detectors placed on each side after a beamsplitter [97]–[99]. How can we then identify the other three states? It turns out that distinction between $|\Psi^+\rangle$ on the one hand and $|\Phi^+\rangle$ and $|\Phi^-\rangle$ on the other hand can be based on the fact that only in $|\Psi^+\rangle$ do the two photons have different polarisation while in the other two they have the same polarisation. Thus performing polarisation measurements and observing the photons on the same side of the beamsplitter distinguishes the state $|\Psi^+\rangle$ from the states $|\Phi^+\rangle$ and $|\Phi^-\rangle$. It should be remarked that a simple generalisation of this procedure implies that any two orthogonal maximally entangled states can be distinguished from each other in the same way, because by local unitary transformations one can perform rotations in the two-dimensional Hilbert space.

Consider now the same experiment with fermions [100] where again the Bell states describe the internal states, for example if the two qubits are entangled in spin, we find that the four possible states now are

$$|\Psi^+\rangle|\Psi_A\rangle, \quad |\Psi^-\rangle|\Psi_S\rangle, \quad |\Phi^+\rangle|\Psi_A\rangle, \text{ and } |\Phi^-\rangle|\Psi_A\rangle. \tag{3.23}$$

because of the antisymmetry requirement of the total state. For fermions, therefore, only one of the states is spatially symmetric, the other three are spatially anti-symmetric. Thus in only one of the cases, namely for $|\Psi^-\rangle$, will both fermions emerge together from the beamsplitter. In the other three cases they will emerge from different sides. Yet, remarkably, it is again this state which can immediately be distinguished from the other three because of its distinct symmetry properties.

3.6 Experimental Dense Coding with Qubits

A quantum-optical demonstration of the quantum dense coding scheme [75], described in Sect. 3.2, requires three distinct parts (Fig. 3.7): the EPR-source generating entangled photons, Bob's station for encoding the messages by a unitary transformation of his particle, and Alice's Bell-state analyser to read the signal sent by Bob. The polarisation-entangled photons can be produced by type-II parametric down-conversion (Sect. 3.4.4). A UV-beam ($\lambda = 351$ nm) from an argon-ion laser is down-converted into pairs of photons ($\lambda = 702$ nm) with orthogonal polarisation.

The entangled state $|\Psi^+\rangle$ is obtained after compensation of birefringence in the BBO crystal along two distinct emission directions (carefully selected by 2 mm irises, 1.5 m away from the crystal). One beam was first directed to Bob's encoding station, the other directly to Alice's Bell-state analyser; in the alignment procedure an optical trombone was employed to equalise the path lengths to well within the coherence length of the down-converted photons ($\ell_c \approx 100\,\mu$m), in order to enable Alice to perform a (partial) Bell-state analysis.

For polarisation encoding, the necessary transformations of Bob's particle were performed using a half-wave retardation plate for changing the polarisation and a quarter-wave plate to generate the polarisation dependent phase

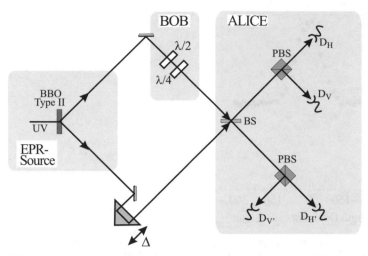

Fig. 3.7. Experimental set-up for quantum dense coding [75].

shift[2]. The beam manipulated in this way in Bob's encoding station was then combined with the other beam at Alice's Bell-state analyser. It consisted of a single beamsplitter followed by two-channel polarisers in each of its outputs and proper coincidence analysis between four single photon detectors.

Since only the state $|\Psi^-\rangle$ has an antisymmetric spatial part, only this state will be registered by coincidence detection between the different outputs of the beamsplitter (i.e. coincidence between detectors D_H and $D_{V'}$ or between $D_{H'}$ and D_V). For the remaining three states both photons exit into the same output port of the beamsplitter. The state $|\Psi^+\rangle$ can easily be distinguished from the other two due to the different polarisations of the two photons, giving, behind the two-channel polariser, a coincidence between detectors D_H and D_V or between $D_{H'}$ and $D_{V'}$. The two states $|\Phi^+\rangle$ and $|\Phi^-\rangle$ both result in a two-photon state being absorbed by a single detector and thus cannot

Table 3.1. Overview of possible manipulations and detection events of the quantum dense coding experiment with correlated photons.

Bob's setting		State sent	Alice's registration events
$\lambda/2$	$\lambda/4$		
$0°$	$0°$	$|\Psi^+\rangle$	coinc. between D_H and D_V or $D_{H'}$ and $D_{V'}$
$0°$	$90°$	$|\Psi^-\rangle$	coinc. between D_H and $D_{V'}$ or $D_{H'}$ and D_V
$45°$	$0°$	$|\Phi^+\rangle$	2 photons in either D_H, D_V, $D_{H'}$ or $D_{V'}$
$45°$	$90°$	$|\Phi^-\rangle$	2 photons in either D_H, D_V, $D_{H'}$ or $D_{V'}$

---

[2] The component polarised along the axis of the quarter-wave plate is advanced only by $\pi/2$ relative to the other. Reorienting the optical axis from vertical to horizontal causes a net phase change of π between $|H\rangle$ and $|V\rangle$.

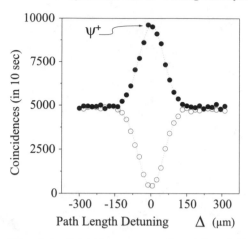

Fig. 3.8. Coincidence rates C_{HV} ($\bullet$) and $C_{HV'}$ ($\circ$) as functions of the path length difference Δ when the state $|\Psi^+\rangle$ is transmitted. For perfect tuning ($\Delta = 0$) constructive interference occurs for C_{HV}, allowing identification of the state sent.

be distinguished. Table 3.1 gives an overview of the different manipulations and detection probabilities of Bob's encoder and Alice's receiver.

The experiments were performed by first setting the output state of the source such that the state $|\Psi^+\rangle$ left Bob's encoder when both retardation plates are set to vertical orientation; the other Bell-states could then be generated with the respective settings (Table 3.1). To characterize the interference observable at Alice's Bell-state analyser, we varied the path length difference Δ of the two beams with the optical trombone. For $\Delta \gg \ell_c$ no interference occurs and one obtains classical statistics for the coincidence count rates at the detectors. For optimal path-length tuning ($\Delta = 0$), interference enables one to read the encoded information.

Figures 3.8 and 3.9 show the dependence of the coincidence rates C_{HV}($\bullet$) and $C_{HV'}$($\circ$) on the path length difference for $|\Psi^+\rangle$ and $|\Psi^-\rangle$, respectively (the rates $C_{H'V'}$ and $C_{H'V}$ display analogous behaviour; we use the notation C_{AB} for the coincidence rate between detectors D_A and D_B). At $\Delta = 0$, C_{HV} reaches its maximum for $|\Psi^+\rangle$ (Fig. 3.8) and vanishes (aside from noise) for $|\Psi^-\rangle$ (Fig. 3.10). $C_{HV'}$ displays the opposite dependence and clearly signifies $|\Psi^-\rangle$. The results of these measurements imply that if both photons are detected, we can identify the state $|\Psi^+\rangle$ with a reliability of 95%, and the state $|\Psi^-\rangle$ with 93%.

When using Si-avalanche diodes in the Geiger-mode for single photon detection, a modification of the Bell-state analyser is necessary, since then one also has to register the two photons leaving the Bell-state analyser for the states $|\Phi^+\rangle$ or $|\Phi^-\rangle$ via a coincidence detection.[3]

---

[3] A special identification of the two-photon state is necessary: Si-avalanche photodiodes give the same output pulse for one or more photons, thus only a coin-

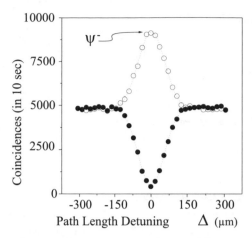

Fig. 3.9. Coincidence rates C_{HV} (•) and $C_{HV'}$ (∘) depending on the path length difference Δ, for transmission of the state $|\Psi^-\rangle$. The constructive interference for the rate $C_{HV'}$ enables one to read the information associated with that state.

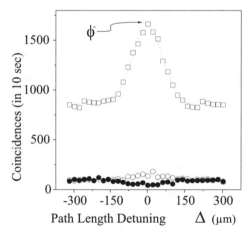

Fig. 3.10. Coincidence rates $C_{H\overline{H}}$ (□), C_{HV} (•), and $C_{HV'}$ (∘) as functions of the path length detuning Δ. The maximum in the rate $C_{H\overline{H}}$ signifies the transmission of a third state $|\Phi^-\rangle$ encoded in a two-state particle. $C_{H\overline{H}}$ is smaller by a factor of 4 compared to the rates of Figures 3.8 and 3.9 due to a further reduced registration probability of $|\Phi^-\rangle$, see text.

One possibility is to avoid interference for these states completely by introducing polarisation-dependent delays $\gg \ell_c$ before Alice's beamsplitter, e.g., using thick quartz plates, retarding $|H\rangle$ in one beam and $|V\rangle$ in the other. Another approach is to split the incoming two-photon state at an additional

---

cidence detection allows the registration of the two-photon state. Special photo-multipliers can distinguish between one- and two-photon absorption, but are too inefficient at present.

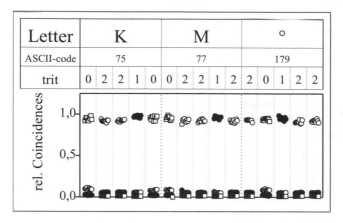

Fig. 3.11. "1.58 bit per photon" quantum dense coding : The ASCII-codes for the letters "KM°" (i.e. 75, 77, 179) are encoded in 15 trits (with "0"≡ $|\Phi^-\rangle \hat{=} \Box$, "1"≡ $|\Psi^+\rangle \hat{=} \bullet$, "2"≡ $|\Psi^-\rangle \hat{=} \circ$) instead of the 24 bits usually necessary. The data for each type of encoded state are normalised to the maximum coincidence rate for that state.

beamsplitter and to detect it (with 50% likelihood) by a coincidence count between detectors in each output. For the purpose of this proof-of-principle demonstration, we put such a configuration only in place of detector D_H. Figure 3.10 shows the increase of the coincidence rate $C_{H\overline{H}}(\Box)$ at path length difference $\Delta = 0$, with the rates C_{HV} and $C_{HV'}$ at the background level, when Bob sends the state $|\Phi^-\rangle$.

Note, however, that for both methods half of the time both photons still are absorbed by one detector; therefore, and since we inserted only one such configuration, the maximum rate for $C_{H\overline{H}}$ is about a quarter of that of C_{HV} or $C_{HV'}$ in Figs. 3.8 and 3.9.

Since we now can distinguish the three different messages, the stage is set for the quantum dense coding transmission. Figure 3.11 shows the various coincidence rates (normalised to the respective maximum rate of the transmitted state) when sending the ASCII codes of "KM°" (i.e. codes 75, 77, 179) in only 15 trits instead of 24 classical bits. From this measurement one also obtains a signal-to-noise ratio by comparing the rates signifying the actual state with the sum of the two other registered rates. The ratios for the transmission of the three states varied due to the different visibilities of the respective interferences and were $S/N_{|\Psi+\rangle} = 14.8$, $S/N_{|\Psi-\rangle} = 13.0$, and $S/N_{|\Phi-\rangle} = 8.5$.

3.7 Experimental Quantum Teleportation of Qubits

D. Bouwmeester, J.-W. Pan, H. Weinfurter, A. Zeilinger

In this section an experimental demonstration of quantum teleportation of qubits, encoded in the polarisation state of single photons, will be given [76]. During teleportation, an initial photon which carries the polarisation that is to be transferred and one of a pair of entangled photons are subjected to a measurement such that the second photon of the entangled pair acquires the polarisation of the initial photon. Figure 3.12 is a schematic drawing of the experimental setup. As explained in Sect. 3.3, an experimental realisation of quantum teleportation necessitates both creation and measurement of entangled states, indicated in Fig. 3.12 by the Einstein–Podolski–Rosen (EPR) source and the Bell-state measurement (BSM) respectively. The EPR source of polarisation entangled photons was described in Sect. 3.4 and the $|\Psi^-\rangle_{12}$ Bell-state analyser was described in Sect. 3.5.

The experimental realisation of the quantum teleportation of a qubit presented in this section is restricted to use the $|\Psi^-\rangle_{12}$ Bell-state projection only.[4] The unitary transformation that Bob has to perform when Alice measures photon 1 and 2 in $|\Psi^-\rangle_{12}$ is simply the identity transformation, i.e. Bob should detect a photon in the same state as photon 1.

To avoid photons 1 and 2, which are created independently, being distinguished by their arrival times at the detectors, which would eliminate the possibility of performing the Bell-state measurement, the following technique is used. Photon 2, together with its entangled partner photon 3, is produced by pulsed parametric down-conversion. The pump pulse, generated by a frequency-doubled mode-locked titanium-sapphire laser, is 200 fs long. The pulse is reflected back through the crystal (see Fig. 3.12) to create a second pair of photons, photons 1 and 4. Photon 4 is used as a trigger to indicate the presence of photon 1. Photons 1 and 2 are now located within 200 fs long pulses, which can be tuned by a variable delay such that maximal spatial overlap of the photons at the detectors is obtained. However, this does not yet guarantee indistinguishability upon detection since the entangled down-converted photons typically have a coherence length corresponding to about a 50 fs long wavepacket, which is shorter than the pulses from the pump laser. Therefore, coincidence detection of photons 1 and 2 with their partners 3 and 4 with a time resolution better than 50 fs could identify which photons were created together. To achieve indistinguishability upon detection, the photon wavepackets should be stretched to a length substantially longer than that of the pump pulse. In the experiment this was done by placing 4 nm narrow interference filters in front of the detectors. These filter out pho-

---

[4] It is possible to extent the Bell-state analyser into an analyser that can uniquely identify both the $|\Psi^-\rangle_{12}$ state and the $|\Psi^+\rangle_{12}$ (see Sect. 3.5).

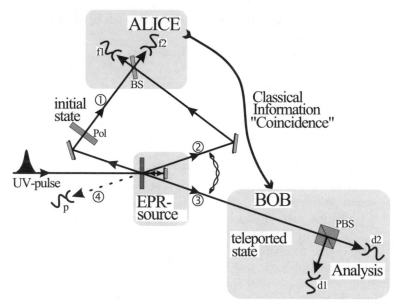

Fig. 3.12. Schematic drawing of the experimental setup for quantum teleportation of a qubit. A pulse of ultraviolet (UV) light passing through a nonlinear crystal creates the ancillary pair of entangled photons 2 and 3. After retroflection during its second passage through the crystal, the ultraviolet pulse can create another pair of photons, one of which will be prepared in the initial state of photon 1 to be tele-ported, the other one serving as a trigger indicating that a photon to be teleported is underway. Alice then looks for coincidences after a beamsplitter (BS) where the initial photon and one of the ancillaries are superposed. Bob, after receiving the classical information that Alice obtained a coincidence count in detectors f1 and f2 identifying the $|\Psi^-\rangle_{12}$ Bell-state, knows that his photon 3 is in the initial state of photon 1 which he then can check using polarisation analysis with the polaris-ing beamsplitter (PBS) and the detectors d1 and d2. The detector P provides the information that photon 1 is underway.

ton wavepackets with a time duration of the order of 500 fs, which yields a maximum indistinguishability of photons 1 and 2 of about 85% [101].

All the important experimental components of the teleportation setup have now been discussed. This brings us to the question of how to prove experimentally that an unknown quantum state can be teleported with the above setup? For this, one has to show that teleportation works for a set of known non-orthogonal states. The test for non-orthogonal states is necessary to demonstrate the crucial role of quantum entanglement in the teleportation scheme.[5]

---

[5] The reason for this is essentially the same as the reason why non-orthogonal states are used in constructing Bell's inequality (see Sect. 1.7 and references therein).

3.7.1 Experimental Results

In the first experiment photon 1, which has encoded the initial qubit, is prepared with a linear polarisation at 45°. Teleportation should work as soon as photons 1 and 2 are detected in the $|\Psi^-\rangle_{12}$ state. This implies that if a coincidence between detectors f1 and f2 (Fig. 3.12) is recorded, i.e. photons 1 and 2 are projected onto the $|\Psi^-_{12}\rangle$ state, then photon 3 should be polarised at 45° (to within an irrelevant overall minus sign, see (3.6)). The polarisation of photon 3 is analysed by passing it through a polarising beamsplitter selecting +45° and −45° polarisation. To demonstrate teleportation, only detector d2 at the +45° output of the polarising beamsplitter should detect a photon once f1 and f2 record a coincidence detection. Detector d1 at the −45° output of the polarising beamsplitter should not detect a photon. Therefore, recording a three-fold coincidence d2f1f2 (+45° analysis) together with the absence of a three-fold coincidence d1f1f2 (−45° analysis) is a proof that the polarisation of photon 1, which represents the initial qubit, has been transferred to photon 3.

To meet the condition of indistiguishability of photons 1 and 2 (see previous subsection), the arrival time of photon 2 is varied by changing the delay between the first and second down-conversion by translating the retroflection mirror (see Fig. 3.12). Within the region of temporal overlap of photons 1 and 2 at the detectors the teleportation should occur.

Outside the region of teleportation photons 1 and 2 will each go to either f1 or to f2 independently of one another. The probability of obtaining a coincidence between f1 and f2 is therefore 50%. This is twice as high as the probability inside the region of teleportation since only the $|\Psi^-\rangle$ component of the two-photon state entering the beamsplitter will give a coincidence recording. Since photon 2 is part of an entangled state it does not have a well-defined polarisation on its own, and the joint state of photons 1 and 2 is an equal superposition of all four Bell states, irrespective of the state of photon 1. Photon 3 should also have no well-defined polarisation because it is entangled with photon 2. Therefore, d1 and d2 both have a 50% chance of receiving photon 3. This simple argument yields a 25% probability both for the −45° analysis (d1f1f2 coincidences) and for the +45° analysis (d2f1f2 coincidences) outside the region of teleportation.

Figure 3.13 summarises the predictions as a function of the delay. Successful teleportation of the +45° polarisation state is then characterized by a decrease to zero in the −45° analysis, see Fig. 3.13a, and by a constant value for the +45° analysis, see Fig. 3.13b. Note that the above arguments are conditional upon the detection of a trigger photon by detector p (see Fig. 3.12).

The experimental results for teleportation of photons polarised at +45° are shown in the first panel of Fig. 3.14. Figure 3.14a and 3.14b should be compared with the theoretical predictions shown in Fig. 3.13.

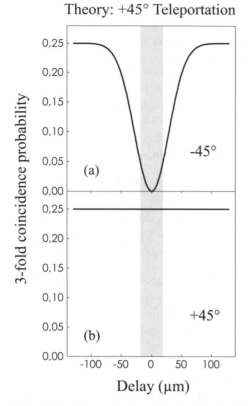

Fig. 3.13. Theoretical prediction for the three-fold coincidence probability between the two Bell-state detectors (f1, f2) and one of the detectors analysing the teleported state. The signature of teleportation of a photon polarisation state at +45° is a dip to zero at zero delay in the three-fold coincidence rate with the detector analysing −45° (d1f1f2) (**a**) and a constant value for the detector analysis +45° (d2f1f2) (**b**). The shaded area indicates the region of teleportation.

The strong decrease in the −45° analysis, and the constant signal for the +45° analysis, indicate that photon 3 is polarised along the direction of photon 1, consistent with the quantum teleportation protocol. Note again that a four-fold coincidence detection has been used where the fourth photon is a trigger that indicates the presence of photon 1.

To rule out any classical explanation for the experimental results, a four-fold coincidence measurement for the case of teleportation of the +90° polarisation states, that is, for a state non-orthogonal to the +45° state, has been performed. The experimental results are shown in Fig. 3.14c and 3.14d. Visibilities of 70% ± 3% are obtained for the dips in the orthogonal polarisation states.

From Fig. 3.14 one can directly obtain the measured fidelity of teleportation of a qubit encoded in the polarisation of a single-photon state. The

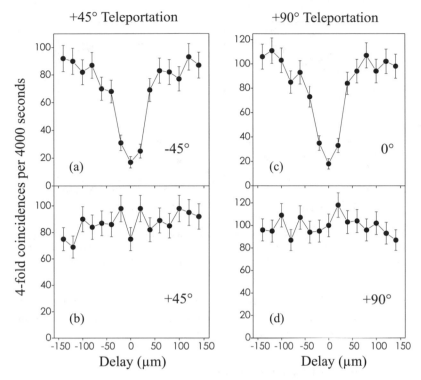

Fig. 3.14. Experimental demonstration of the teleportation of qubits: Measured coincidence rates d1f1f2 ($-45°$) and d2f1f2 ($+45°$) in the case where the photon state to be teleported is polarised at $+45°$ (**a**) and (**b**) or at $+90°$ (**c**) and (**d**), and conditional upon the detection of the trigger photon by detector p. The four-fold coincidence rates are plotted as a function of the delay (in μm) between the arrival of photons 1 and 2 at Alice's beamsplitter (see Fig. 3.12). These data, in cunjunction with with Fig. 3.13, confirm teleportation for an arbitrary qubit state.

fidelity is defined as the overlap of the input qubit with the teleported qubit and is plotted in Fig. 3.15. In the experiment, the detection of the teleported photons played the double role of filtering out the experimental runs in which there is a single input qubit present and of measuring the fidelity of the teleportation procedure. With respect to the filtering, note that two detection events at Alice's Bell-state analyser could have been due to two pairs of photons both created during the return passage of the pump pulse. Then no photon will be observed by Bob [83], but two photons will travel towards detector p. This situation can be identified and therefore eliminated by using a detector p that can discriminate between a one-photon and a two-photon impact [102].

Whether or not such a modified detection is used, the measured fidelity will be the same [84] and is primarily determined by the degree of indistinguishability of the photons detected in Alice's Bell-state analyser. The

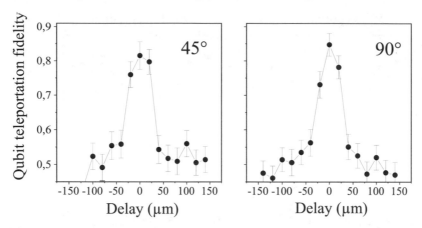

Fig. 3.15. Fidelity of teleportation of a qubit encoded in the polarisation of a single-photon state: The overlap of the input qubit with the teleported qubit has been determined via a four-fold coincidence technique to be as high as 80%.

amount of indistinguishability is directly related to the ratio of the bandwidth of the pump pulse and the interference filters. The larger this ratio the higher the fidelity but the lower the countrates.

3.7.2 Teleportation of Entanglement

Instead of using the fourth photon in the experiment described above as a mere trigger to indicate that photon 1 is underway, one can explore the fact that photon 1 and 4 can also be produced in an entangled state, say in the $|\Psi^-\rangle_{14}$ state, as illustrated in Fig. 3.16.

The state of photon 1 is therefore completely undetermined and all the information is stored in joint properties of photons 1 and 4. If photon 1 is now subjected to quantum teleportation as described in the previous section, photon 3 obtains the properties of photon 1 and therefore becomes entangled with photon 4 (see Fig. 3.16). Interestingly, photon 4 and photon 3 originate from different sources and never interacted directly with one another, yet they form an entangled pair after the quantum teleportation procedure. The experimental verification of this process of transferring entanglement [86], known as entanglement swapping, and several possible applications [85, 87] will be described in Sects. 3.10 and 3.11.

3.7.3 Concluding Remarks and Prospects

Pairs of polarisation entangled photons and two-photon interferometric methods have been used to transfer one qubit encoded in the polarisation state of one photon onto another one. Teleportation has also been addressed in other

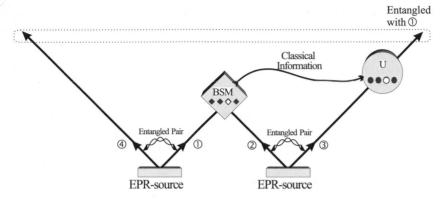

Fig. 3.16. Principle of entanglement swapping: Two EPR sources produce two pairs of entangled photons, pair 1-4 and pair 2-3. Two photons, one from each pair (photons 1 and 2) are subjected to a Bell-state measurement(BSM). This results in projecting the other two outgoing photons 3 and 4 onto an entangled state.

optical systems, which will be discussed in the following two sections. However, quantum teleportation is by no means restricted to optical experiments. In addition to pairs of entangled photons one can employ entangled atoms [103], and one can, in principle, entangle photons with atoms or phonons with ions, and so on. Then teleportation would allow the transfer of the state of, for example, fast-decohering, short-lived particles onto some more stable systems. This opens up the possibility of quantum memories, where the information of incoming photons is stored on trapped ions/atoms, carefully shielded from the environment.

Furthermore, with entanglement purification [49] (see Chap. 8), a scheme for improving the quality of entanglement when it has been degraded by decoherence during storage or transmission of the particles over noisy channels, it becomes possible to send the quantum state of a particle to some place, even if the available quantum channels are of limited quality and thus sending the particle itself might destroy the fragile quantum state. If the distance over which one wants to send the quantum state through a noisy quantum channel becomes too long, the fidelity of transmission becomes too low for the application of the standard purification method. In this situation the quantum repeater method allows one to divide the quantum channel into shorter segments that are purified separately and then connected by entanglement swapping [104] (Sect. 8.7). The feasibility of preserving quantum states in a hostile environment will have great advantages in the realm of quantum communication and quantum computation.

3.8 A Two-Particle Scheme for Quantum Teleportation

D. Bouwmeester

The teleportation scheme, as described in Sect. 3.3, presents two new concepts. First, it shows how entanglement can be used as part of a quantum communication channel. Second, it shows that the information associated with the state of a quantum particle can be physically decomposed into, and reconstructed from a classical component and a genuine quantum one. Alone, neither of these two components contain any information whatsoever about the quantum state; put together, they determine it completely.

In the previous section these concepts were demonstrated using three- and four-photon experiments. A limitation of these experiments was that Alice could not perform a full Bell-state measurement, which reduced the efficiency of the quantum state teleportation. A full Bell-state measurement would imply a controlled interaction between two photons, which is extremely difficult to implement in practice. The scheme described here, which was proposed by S. Popescu [77] and experimentally realised in Rome [78], avoids this problem but does place restrictions on the quantum states that can be transferred.

The original teleportation scheme involves three particles. Two of the particles, one sent to Alice and one sent to Bob are in an entangled state (singlet) and constitute the "non-local communication channel". The third particle is initially in the state Ψ which Alice has to transmit. One might imagine that the particle was prepared in this state by a third party, the Preparer, or that Alice acquired it herself directly from nature. The scheme considered here involves only two particles, namely the ones which form the non-local channel. The Preparer has to help Alice by encoding Ψ directly into her member of the singlet pair instead of encoding it into a third particle. To this end, the Preparer uses some other degree of freedom of Alice's particle, different from the degree of freedom by which it is entangled with Bob's particle. This doesn't change the problem facing Alice – Alice cannot find out what Ψ is. So if she were limited to the use of classical channels she couldn't help Bob prepare his particle in the state Ψ. However, by using the nonlocal quantum channel she is able to accomplish the task, transferring the quantum state to Bob.

In this two-particle scheme Alice's actions are simpler than in the three-particle scheme, since to make different degrees of freedom of the same particle interact is often easier than to make two different particles interact.

We will describe the two-particle protocol for quantum teleportation by going step by step through the optical experimental setup proposed in Ref. [77]. The first step is to produce two photons entangled in their direction of propagation, i.e. entangled in momentum, but each with a well-defined

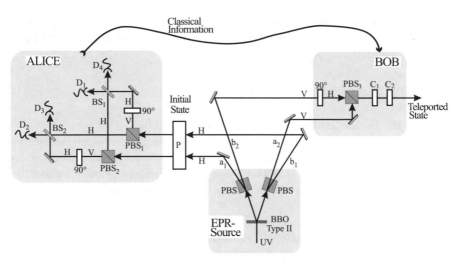

Fig. 3.17. Experimental scheme for the two-particle protocol for quantum teleportation. The setup consists of a type-II (BBO) down-conversion source for polarisation entangled photons, polarising beamsplitters (PBS), 50/50 beamsplitters (PB), single-photon detectors (D), 90° polarisation rotation plates, the Preparer (P) of the initial quantum state, and polarisation transformers (C).

polarisation. The box representing the EPR source in Fig. 3.17 shows how this can be achieved [78]. Using type-II parametric down-conversion, one first creates the polarisation entangled state

$$|\Psi^+\rangle = \frac{1}{\sqrt{2}}\left(|H\rangle_1|V\rangle_2 + |V\rangle_1|H\rangle_2\right),\tag{3.24}$$

where 1 and 2 label the two output directions of the correlated photons. Following this, both photons are passed through polarising beamsplitters which deflect/transmit horizontal/vertical photons. This transfers the polarisation entanglement into momentum entanglement resulting in the state

$$\frac{1}{\sqrt{2}}\left(|a_1\rangle|a_2\rangle + |b_1\rangle|b_2\rangle\right)|H\rangle_1|V\rangle_2.\tag{3.25}$$

Labels 1 and 2 now indicate the double channels that lead to Alice and Bob respectively. Photons with label 1 are necessarily H polarised and photons with label 2 necessarily V polarised. The momentum entangled photons form the nonlocal transmission channel.

On the way to Alice photon 1 is intercepted by the Preparer P who changes the polarisation from H to an arbitrary quantum superposition

$$|\Psi\rangle_1 = \alpha|H\rangle_1 + \beta|V\rangle_1.\tag{3.26}$$

The Prepare affects the polarisation in both paths a_1 and b_1 in the same way. The state $|\Psi\rangle_1$ is the quantum state that Alice wants to transmit to

Bob. Note that it is crucial that both the spatial and polarisation degrees of freedom of the quantum particles are being used.[6] The total state $|\Phi\rangle$ of the two photons after the preparation is

$$|\Phi\rangle = \frac{1}{\sqrt{2}} \left(|a_1\rangle |a_2\rangle + |b_1\rangle |b_2\rangle \right) |\Psi\rangle_1 |V\rangle_2 , \qquad (3.27)$$

which is the formal analogue of the state Ψ_{123} in (3.6).

The next step in the protocol is that Alice performs a joint (Bell-state) measurement on the initial state $|\Psi\rangle_1$ and on her part of the momentum entangled state. Assuming that there is a way to project photon 1 onto the four Bell states for its polarisation and momentum, we obtain the equivalent of (3.6):

$$\begin{aligned}
|\Phi\rangle = \frac{1}{2} \Big[\; &(|a_1\rangle |V\rangle_1 + |b_1\rangle |H\rangle_1)(\beta |a_2\rangle + \alpha |b_2\rangle) |V\rangle_2 \\
+ &(|a_1\rangle |V\rangle_1 - |b_1\rangle |H\rangle_1)(\beta |a_2\rangle - \alpha |b_2\rangle) |V\rangle_2 \\
+ &(|a_1\rangle |H\rangle_1 + |b_1\rangle |V\rangle_1)(\alpha |a_2\rangle + \beta |b_2\rangle) |V\rangle_2 \\
+ &(|a_1\rangle |H\rangle_1 - |b_1\rangle |V\rangle_1)(\alpha |a_2\rangle - \beta |b_2\rangle) |V\rangle_2 \; \Big] .
\end{aligned} \qquad (3.28)$$

The first part of each term corresponds to a Bell state for photon 1 and the second part to the corresponding state of photon 2. In contrast to the case of the three-particle protocol, the projection of particle 1 onto the Bell-state basis does not pose a serious problem, and can be achieved with almost 100% efficiency. For the projection we have to entangle the polarisation and directional properties of photon 1. This can be done by using polarising beamsplitters in paths a_1 and b_1, and by combining the V component coming from a_1 ($|a_1\rangle |V\rangle_1$) with the H component coming from b_1 ($|b_1\rangle |H\rangle_1$), and vice versa. The combination, sensitive to the relative phase, is obtained by rotating the photons to the same polarisation and letting them interfere on a normal beamsplitter. A photon detection by D_1, D_2, D_3, or D_4 now corresponds directly to a projection onto one of the four Bell states.

The final step of the protocol is that Alice informs Bob which detector registered a photon. With this information Bob can reproduce the inital polarisation state as follows. He first transforms the momentum superposition of photon 2 (see (3.28)) into the same superposition in polarisation by simply using a 90° rotation plate in paths b_2 (or a_2) and a polarising beamsplitter to combine the paths. After this, he just switches two optical elements on or off, depending on the information obtained from Alice, to interchange H and V and to provide a relative phase shift of π between H and V. This transforms the polarisation state of photon 2 into the polarisation state prepared on photon 1, and thus completes the transmission.

---

[6] M. Zukowski proposed to use both the spatial and polarisation degrees of freedom of particles for generating "three-particle" GHZ entanglement using only two particles [105].

An advantage of the present scheme is that it uses a full Bell-state measurement and only two particles in demonstrating two basic concepts of teleportation: it proves that quantum information can be decomposed into the classical and the genuine quantum part, and it displays the nonlocal transmission. Furthermore it has a high efficiency compared to the three-particle scheme described in the previous section.

A drawback of the scheme is that it does not allow Alice to teleport the state of an outside particle. Therefore it requires the Preparer's help: the initial polarisation state given to Alice has to be prepared on a particle which is momentum entangled with the one given to Bob. Also the state Ψ has to be pure, implying that it cannot be part of an entangled state.

We refer to Ref. [78] for details about the experimental realisation of the setup described above and for the experimental data confirming the transfer of the quantum state from Alice to Bob.

Acknowledgement: We are very grateful to S. Popescu for his help in preparing this section.

3.9 Teleportation of Continuous Quantum Variables

D. Bouwmeester

3.9.1 Employing Position and Momentum Entanglement

In this section we outline the basic idea of another scheme for quantum teleportation, proposed by L. Vaidman [79], further elaborated on by Braunstein and Kimble [80], and experimentally realised at Caltech [81]. This scheme uses position and momentum entanglement instead of polarisation entanglement. The result of this quantum teleportation scheme is that the position and momentum (defining the external state) of a quantum system are transferred to a distant quantum system, in contrast to the schemes discussed in Sects. 3.7 and 3.8 where the internal state (polarisation) was transferred. An important difference between position and momentum compared to polarisation is their representation in terms of superpositions of certain basis states. Position and momentum both require an infinite number of basis states since, to any two different positions or momenta there correspond two different eigenstates which are orthogonal (position eigenstates and momentum eigenstates form an infinite-dimensional Hilbert space). The polarisation of a particle can however be expressed as the superposition of only two basis states (polarisation has a two-dimensional Hilbert space).

Consider the case in which Alice has a quantum particle with a certain position x_1 and momentum p_1 (see Fig. 3.18), and she wishes to send this

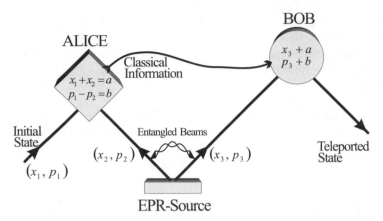

Fig. 3.18. Schematic drawing of quantum teleportation of continuous variables.

quantum information to Bob who is at a distant location. Due to the Heisenberg uncertainty relation between x and p, which follows from the fact that the operators for position and momentum do not commute, $[\hat{x}, \hat{p}] = i\hbar$, Alice cannot measure both x_1 and p_1 with arbitrary precision. Therefore, quantum mechanics forbids Alice to obtain the information she wishes to transfer. The way out of this dilemma is conceptually the same as the protocol described in Sect. 3.3. In the same manner an auxiliary pair of entangled particles, produced by the EPR source in Fig. 3.18, has to be distributed between Alice and Bob. However, the auxiliary particles should now be entangled in their position and momentum. Let us consider the case in which the entanglement of particles 2 and 3 is described by the conditions:

$$x_2 + x_3 = 0, \text{and } p_2 - p_3 = 0. \tag{3.29}$$

The properties of the individual particles, x_2, x_3, p_2, and p_3 are completely undetermined by (3.29). Instead, their joint properties are defined. Note that, although the operators $\hat{x}$ and $\hat{p}$ do not commute for each particle, the operators for $(x_2 + x_3)$ and $(p_2 - p_3)$ do commute as a result of the relative minus sign between the addition of the positions and the addition of momenta. Therefore, for the entangled state the joint properties, $(x_2 + x_3)$ and $(p_2 - p_3)$, can both be measured with an arbitrary accuracy.

The next step in the protocol is that Alice performs the equivalent of a Bell-state measurement on particles 1 and 2. That is, the state of particles 1 and 2 is projected onto an entangled state. In the case of teleportation of the internal (polarisation) state of a particle, there are only 4 possible outcomes for the Bell-state measurement since the polarisation entanglement between two particles, each individually with a two-dimensional Hilbert space, can be represented as a superposition of 4 basis states. In the present case the measurement by Alice yields

$$x_1 + x_2 = a\,, \text{ and } p_1 - p_2 = b\,, \tag{3.30}$$

where a and b are two real numbers which both have a continuous range of possible values. This indicates that the measurement of the sum of positions and the difference in momenta of the two particles requires the projection onto an (∞)-dim Hilbert space.

As a result of the initial entanglement (3.29) and of Alice's measurement (3.30), the information obtained about the quantum state in the hands of Bob is

$$x_3 = x_1 - a\,, \text{ and } p_3 = p_1 - b\,. \tag{3.31}$$

To complete the quantum teleportation protocol, all Alice has to do is to send Bob via a classical channel the results of her measurements, i.e. the measured values a and b, and then Bob just displaces the position and momentum of his particle by a and b, respectively. The final result is that Bob has particle 3 in the initial quantum state of particle 1.

3.9.2 Quantum Optical Implementation

The experimental implementation of quantum teleportation of continuous quantum variables has been performed at Caltech, California [81]. This implementation does not use the position x and momentum p of particles but uses light beams that can be characterized by parameters obeying the same commutation relations as $\hat{x}$ and $\hat{p}$. The analogy is based on the fact that a single (transversal) mode of the quantized radiation field can be characterized by a quantum harmonic oscillator [106]–[109].

The classical harmonic oscillator of mass m, frequency ω, displacement x, and momentum p is described by the Hamiltonian

$$H = \frac{p^2}{2m} + \frac{m}{2}\omega^2 x^2\,. \tag{3.32}$$

To obtain the quantum-mechanical Hamiltonian, x and p should be interpreted as operators ($x \to \hat{x}$, and $p \to \hat{p} = i\hbar\partial/\partial x$) which obey the commutation relation $[\hat{x}, \hat{p}] = i\hbar$. If we define

$$\hat{x} = \sqrt{\frac{\hbar}{2m\omega}}\left(\hat{a}^\dagger + \hat{a}\right)\,, \tag{3.33}$$

$$\hat{p} = i\sqrt{\frac{\hbar m\omega}{2}}\left(\hat{a}^\dagger - \hat{a}\right)\,, \tag{3.34}$$

then the Hamiltonian for the quantized harmonic oscillator takes the natural form

$$\hat{H} = \hbar\omega\left(\hat{a}^\dagger\hat{a} + \frac{1}{2}\right)\,. \tag{3.35}$$

The most important relations for $\hat{a}$ and $\hat{a}^\dagger$ are

$$\hat{a}|n\rangle = \sqrt{n}|n-1\rangle\,, \qquad \hat{a}|0\rangle = 0\,, \tag{3.36}$$

$$\hat{a}^\dagger|n\rangle = \sqrt{n+1}|n+1\rangle\,, \tag{3.37}$$

$$[\hat{a},\hat{a}^\dagger] = 1\,, \qquad [\hat{a},\hat{a}] = [\hat{a}^\dagger,\hat{a}^\dagger] = 0\,, \tag{3.38}$$

$$\hat{a}^\dagger\hat{a} = \hat{N}\,, \tag{3.39}$$

with $|n\rangle$ the nth-excited state of the quantum harmonic oscillator and $\hat{N}$ the number operator. According to (3.36) and (3.37), $\hat{a}$ and $\hat{a}^\dagger$ can be interpreted as the annihilation (lowering) and creation (raising) operators for the harmonic oscillator.

A single transversal mode (frequency ω) of the quantized radiation field can be expressed in terms of the operators $\hat{a}$ and $\hat{a}^\dagger$. In its most basic form, i.e. including all prefactors into a single constant E_0 and considering one polarisation direction, the electric field vector operator at a fixed position is given by

$$\hat{\vec{E}}(t) = E_0\left(\hat{a}e^{-i\omega t} - \hat{a}^\dagger e^{+i\omega t}\right)\,, \tag{3.40}$$

where $\hat{a}^\dagger$ and $\hat{a}$ are now interpreted as the photon-creation and photon-annihilation operators. In analogy to the harmonic oscillator, we can define operators $\hat{X}$ and $\hat{P}$ via

$$\hat{X} = \left(\hat{a}^\dagger + \hat{a}\right)\,, \tag{3.41}$$

$$\hat{P} = i\left(\hat{a}^\dagger - \hat{a}\right)\,. \tag{3.42}$$

The electric field operator can now be expressed in terms of $\hat{X}$ and $\hat{P}$ as

$$\hat{\vec{E}}(t) = E_0\left(\hat{X}\cos(\omega t) + \hat{P}\sin(\omega t)\right)\,. \tag{3.43}$$

The eigenvalues of $\hat{X}$ and $\hat{P}$, referred to as the quadrature field amplitudes, can be interpreted as the amplitudes of the in- and out-of-phase components of the electric field (with respect to a local oscillator). From the commutation relation $[\hat{X},\hat{P}] = 2i$ it follows that $\Delta X\Delta P = 1$ $(\langle\Delta A\rangle^2 = \langle A^2\rangle - \langle A\rangle^2)$, which means that the in- and out-of-phase amplitudes cannot be simultaneously measured with arbitrary accuracy, in close analogy to the position x and momentum p of a quantum particle. Hence we have now established the mapping of x and p for a particle to X and P for a single-mode light field.

The next step towards an implementation of the quantum teleportation scheme with continuous parameters is to construct entangled light fields. To achieve this we need to introduce the notion of squeezed light [108]. It is instructive to visualise the quantum state of a single-mode light field in the X, Y plane. The vacuum state is represented by disc 1 around the origin in Fig. 3.19. Disc 2 in Fig. 3.19 represents a "coherent field" which is defined as a displaced vacuum field.

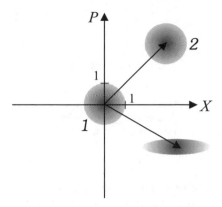

Fig. 3.19. Representation of single-mode light fields in the X (in-phase amplitude) and P (out-of-phase amplitude) plane. Disc 1, around the origin, indicates the symmetric minimum-uncertainty vacuum state. Disc 2 represents a coherent state which is defined as a displaced vacuum state. The ellipse represents a squeezed state (squeezed in the P direction.

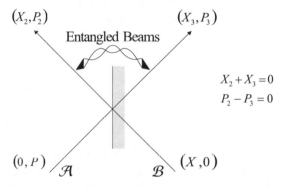

Fig. 3.20. Production of entangled light fields. Two light fields, $\mathcal{A}$ and $\mathcal{B}$, maximally squeezed in X and Y, entering a 50/50 beamsplitter produce at the output of the beamsplitter a pair of entangled light beams.

The discs indicate the minimum uncertainty in the values for X and P. The uncertainty is symmetric in X and P, however this symmetry is not necessary in order to fulfill the relation $\Delta X \Delta P = 1$. The ellipse in Fig. 3.19 represents a squeezed state for which $(\Delta Y)^2 < 1$ and necessarily $(\Delta X)^2 > 1$.

Consider now the case of two light fields $\mathcal{A}$ and $\mathcal{B}$ maximally squeezed in X and Y, respectively, and let these beams enter the two input ports of a 50/50 beamsplitter as illustrated in Fig. 3.20. Behind the beamsplitter the fields labeled with 2 and 3 are characterized by the relations

$$X_2 + X_3 = 0 \text{ , and } P_2 - P_3 = 0 \,, \tag{3.44}$$

which specify precisely the desired entangled state [81]. (For polarisation entangled light fields see Refs. [110]–[112].)

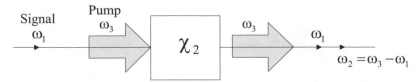

Fig. 3.21. Parametric amplification. An incoming signal field with frequency ω_1 is combined inside a nonlinear crystal (χ_2 material) with a strong pump field with frequency ω_3. As a result of the nonlinear interaction, the signal field will be amplified and a third field will be created with the frequency $\omega_2 = \omega_3 - \omega_1$.

The production of squeezed states, as required for the generation of entangled light fields, is based on parametric amplification inside a nonlinear crystal [107, 112, 113]. An incoming signal field with frequency ω_1 will be combined inside a nonlinear crystal with a strong pump field with frequency ω_3 (see Fig. 3.21). As a result of the nonlinear interaction, the signal field will be amplified and a third field will be created with the frequency $\omega_2 = \omega_3 - \omega_1$. We consider the simplest case involving only one polarisation direction, assuming collinear phase matching, that is all fields propagate in the same direction, and taking the degenerate case of $\omega_1 = \omega_2 \equiv \omega$ and $\omega_3 = 2\omega$.

The evolution of the radiation field with frequency ω, interacting inside the crystal with the strong field at frequency 2ω, is described by the following Hamiltonian,

$$\hat{H} = \hbar\omega \left(\hat{a}^\dagger \hat{a} + \frac{1}{2} \right) + S \cos(2\omega t) \left(\hat{a}^\dagger - \hat{a} \right)^2 . \tag{3.45}$$

The second term on the right-hand side of (3.45) describes the interaction between the pump field, which is described classically, and the two fields at degenerate frequency ω. S is the coupling strength which depends on the nonlinearity inside the crystal and on the pump intensity. The principle of energy conservation reduces this interaction term to

$$S \left((\hat{a})^2 e^{i2\omega t} - (\hat{a}^\dagger)^2 e^{-i2\omega t} \right) . \tag{3.46}$$

The time evolution of the radiation field operator (we work in the Heisenberg representation in which the operators evolve as a function of time) is determined by the evolution equations for $\hat{a}$ and $\hat{a}^\dagger$:

$$\frac{d\hat{a}}{dt} = -\frac{i}{\hbar} \left[\hat{a}, \hat{H} \right] = -i\omega\hat{a} - iS\hat{a}^\dagger e^{-i2\omega t} , \tag{3.47}$$

$$\frac{d\hat{a}^\dagger}{dt} = -\frac{i}{\hbar} \left[\hat{a}^\dagger, \hat{H} \right] = i\omega\hat{a}^\dagger + iS\hat{a} e^{+i2\omega t} . \tag{3.48}$$

This set of coupled equations decouples if we use the operators $\hat{X}$ and $\hat{P}$ as defined in (3.41) and (3.42). The evolution equations for the quadrature field-amplitude operators are simply

$$\frac{d\hat{X}}{dt} = S\hat{X}, \qquad \frac{d\hat{P}}{dt} = -S\hat{P}, \qquad (3.49)$$

which have the solutions

$$\hat{X}(t) = \hat{X}(0)e^{St}, \qquad \hat{P}(t) = \hat{P}(0)e^{-St}. \qquad (3.50)$$

As a function of the interaction time, t, the in-phase amplitude operator $\hat{X}$ grows exponentially whereas the out-of-phase amplitude operator $\hat{P}$ decreases exponentially. Degenerate parametric amplification thus acts as a phase-sensitive amplifier, providing gain to in-phase ($\varphi = 0 \bmod \pi$) signals and damping to out-of-phase ($\varphi = (\pi/2)\bmod\pi$) signals. In other words, the parametric amplification of a signal will squeeze the P component of the light field.

To enhance the interaction time, and hence the amount of squeezing, the nonlinear crystal is usually placed inside an optical cavity which is resonant with ω. Such a device is called an optical parametric oscillator (OPO). The cavity losses are kept slightly larger than the parametric amplification to prevent laser operation and hence the build up of very high intensity light fields which would introduce saturation effects (mixing of higher order nonlinearities) inside the crystal. In the experiment reported in Ref. [81] there was no external field at frequency ω injected in the OPO, so that only the vacuum is amplified.

Having described the production of EPR light fields using two squeezed light fields and a beamsplitter, we now turn to the problem of performing a Bell-state-like measurement. Whereas the Bell-state analyser for polarisation entangled states posed experimental problems, see Sect. 3.5, here the projection onto an entangled state is straightforward. Mixing the initial beam, characterized by (X_1, P_1), with one beam coming from the EPR source, represented by (X_2, P_2), onto a 50/50 beamsplitter, yields in the two output ports beams characterized by

$$(X_{\mathcal{C}}, P_{\mathcal{C}}) = (X_1 - X_2, P_1 - P_2), \text{ and } (X_{\mathcal{D}}, P_{\mathcal{D}}) = (X_1 + X_2, P_1 + P_2). \qquad (3.51)$$

Using the balanced homodyne detection method (see e.g. Ref. [107]), Alice can now measure the X component of beam $\mathcal{D}$ and the P component of $\mathcal{C}$, providing her with the values $a = X_1 + X_2$, and $b = P_1 - P_2$, respectively, as required for the quantum teleportation protocol. The balanced homodyne detection method is based on mixing of the signal field with a local oscillator on a 50/50 beamsplitter and the recording of the difference in the photocurrent (proportional to the field intensity) between two detectors in the output arms of the beamsplitter. The difference in measured intensity as a function of the phase φ of the local oscillator is given by [107]

$$I(\varphi) = C\left(X\sin\varphi + P\cos\varphi\right), \qquad (3.52)$$

where C is an overall constant depending on the intensity of the local oscillator and on the properties of the detectors. Tuning the phase φ of the local oscillator, one can measure any superposition of the quadrature components.

Following the quantum teleportation scheme, Alice sends to Bob the measured values a and b and Bob has to displace the light field at his side accordingly. Bob can achieve the displacement experimentally by reflecting his light field from a partially reflecting mirror (say 99% reflection and 1% transmission) and adding through the mirror a field that has been phase and amplitude modulated according to the values a and b. In principle, Bob ends up with an almost perfect replica of the light field that was initially in the hands of Alice.

The actual experiment, reported in Ref. [81], requires several sophisticated experimental techniques, such as the generation of highly squeezed states and the precise alignment in positions and phases of the light fields. Imperfections in these techniques limited the quality, defined here as the measured overlap of the input state at Alice and the teleported state at Bob, to 0.58 ± 0.02. This quality is, however, higher than the limit of 0.5 which can be obtained (under the assumption that the output state falls in the class of coherent states) by only classical communication between Alice and Bob.

Acknowledgement: We are very grateful to H.J. Kimble and E.S. Polzik for their useful comments on this section.

3.10 Entanglement Swapping: Teleportation of Entanglement

D. Bouwmeester, J-W. Pan, H. Weinfurter, A. Zeilinger

Entanglement can be realised by having two entangled particles emerge from a common source [94, 114] (Sect. 3.4), or by allowing two particles to interact with each other [103, 115] (Sects. 4.3, 5.2.4 and 5.2.11). Yet, another possibility to obtain entanglement is to make use of a projection of the state of two particles onto an entangled state. This projection measurement does not necessarily require a direct interaction between the two particles: When each of the particles is entangled with one other partner particle, an appropriate measurement, for example, a Bell-state measurement, of the partner particles will automatically collapse the state of the remaining two particles into an entangled state. This striking application of the projection postulate is referred to as entanglement swapping [74, 85, 87].

Consider two EPR sources, each simultaneously emitting a pair of entangled particles (Fig. 3.22). In anticipation of the experiments described below, we assume that these are polarisation entangled photons in the state

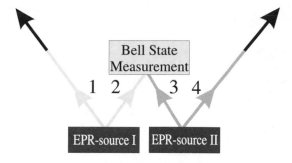

Fig. 3.22. Principle of entanglement swapping. Two EPR sources produce two pairs of entangled photons, pair 1-2 and pair 3-4. One photon from each pair (photons 2 and 3) is subjected to a Bell-state measurement. This results in a projection the other two outgoing photons, 1 and 4, onto an entangled state. Change of shading of the lines indicates the change in the set of possible predictions that can be made.

$$|\Psi\rangle_{1234} = \frac{1}{2} \left(|H\rangle_1 |V\rangle_2 - |V\rangle_1 |H\rangle_2 \right) \left(|H\rangle_3 |V\rangle_4 - |V\rangle_3 |H\rangle_4 \right) . \tag{3.53}$$

The total state describes the fact that photons 1 and 2 (3 and 4) are entangled in an antisymmetric polarisation state. Yet, the state of pair 1-2 is factorisable from the state of pair 3-4, that is, there is no entanglement of either of the photons 1 or 2 with either of the photons 3 or 4.

We now perform a joint Bell-state measurement on photons 2 and 3, that is, photons 2 and 3 are projected onto one of the four Bell states (see Sect. 3.5). This measurement also projects photons 1 and 4 onto a Bell state, one that depends on the result of the Bell-state measurement for photons 2 and 3. Close inspection shows that for the initial state given in (3.53) the emerging state of photons 1 and 4 will be identical to the one onto which photons 2 and 3 are projected. This is a consequence of the fact that the state of (3.53) can be rewritten as

$$\begin{aligned} |\Psi\rangle_{1234} = \frac{1}{2} \big(& \left|\Psi^+\right\rangle_{14} \left|\Psi^+\right\rangle_{23} - \left|\Psi^-\right\rangle_{14} \left|\Psi^-\right\rangle_{23} \\ & - \left|\Phi^+\right\rangle_{14} \left|\Phi^+\right\rangle_{23} + \left|\Phi^-\right\rangle_{14} \left|\Phi^-\right\rangle_{23} \big) . \end{aligned} \tag{3.54}$$

In all cases photons 1 and 4 emerge entangled, despite the fact that they never interacted in the past. After projection of particles 2 and 3 one knows about the entanglement between particles 1 and 4.

As already noted in Sect. 3.7.2, entanglement swapping can also be viewed as the teleportation of an entangled state, and the experimental setup (Fig. 3.23) used for its demonstration is similar to the teleportation setup shown in Fig. 3.12. We refer to Sect. 3.7 for a description of the common features of the setups. The essential difference between the two experiments is that in the teleportation scheme for single qubits (Fig. 3.12) photon 4 played the role of a trigger, indicating the presence of photon 1, whereas here (Fig. 3.23) the entanglement between each pair of photons is fully utilised.

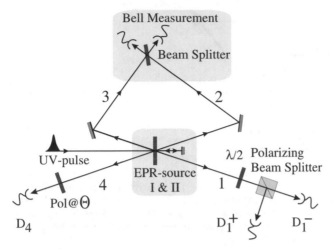

Fig. 3.23. Experimental setup. A UV pulse passing through a nonlinear crystal creates pair 1-2 of entangled photons. Photon 2 is directed to the beamsplitter. After reflection, during its second passage through the crystal the UV pulse creates a second pair 3-4 of entangled photons. Photon 3 will also be directed to the beamsplitter. When photons 2 and 3 yield a coincidence click at the two detectors behind the beamsplitter they are projected into the $|\Psi^-\rangle_{23}$ state. As a consequence of this Bell-state measurement the two remaining photons 1 and 4 will also be projected into an entangled state. To analyse their entanglement one looks at coincidences between detectors D1$^+$ and D4, and between detectors D1$^-$ and D4, for different polarisation angles Θ. By rotating the $\lambda/2$ plate in front of the polarising beamsplitter one can analyse photon 1 in any linear polarisation basis. Note that, since the detection of coincidences between detectors D1$^+$ and D4, and D1$^-$ and D4 are conditional on the detection of the Ψ^- state, one looks at 4-fold coincidences.

Entanglement swapping can be seen as teleportation either of the state of photon 2 over to photon 4 or the state of photon 3 over to photon 1. Those viewpoints are completely equivalent. The remarkable feature of the scheme is that the state actually teleported is a photon state which is not well defined. As is well known, the state of a particle which is maximally entangled to another has to be described by a maximally mixed density matrix. Therefore, what is teleported in such a situation is not the quantum state of the photon but just the way in which it was entangled with another photon.

According to the entanglement swapping scheme, upon projection of photons 2 and 3 onto the $|\Psi^-\rangle_{23}$ state, photons 1 and 4 should be projected onto the $|\Psi^-\rangle_{14}$ state. To verify that this entangled state is obtained we have to analyse the polarisation correlations between photons 1 and 4 conditional on coincidences between the detectors of the Bell-state analyser. If photons 1 and 4 are in the $|\Psi^-\rangle_{14}$ state their polarisations should be orthogonal upon measurement in any polarisation basis. Using a $\lambda/2$ retardation plate at 22.5° and two detectors (D1$^+$ and D1$^-$) behind a polarising beamsplitter, one can analyse the polarisation of photon 1 along the $+45°$ axis (D1$^+$) and the $-45°$

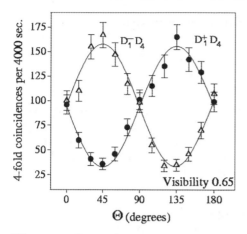

Fig. 3.24. Entanglement verification. Four-fold coincidences, resulting from two-fold coincidences D1$^+$D4 and D1$^-$D4 conditional on the two-fold coincidences at the Bell-state measurement, when varying the polariser angle Θ. The two complementary sine curves with a visibility of 0.65 ± 0.02 demonstrate that photons 1 and 4 are polarisation entangled.

axis (D1$^-$). Photon 4 is analysed by detector D4 at the variable polarisation direction Θ.

If entanglement swapping occurs, then the two-fold coincidences between D1$^+$ and D4, and between D1$^-$ and D4, conditional on the $|\Psi^-\rangle_{23}$ detection, should show two sine curves as a function of Θ which are 90° out of phase. The D1$^+$D4 curve should, in principle, go to zero for $\Theta = 45°$ whereas the D1 D4 curve should show a maximum at this position. Figure 3.24 shows the experimental results for the coincidences between D1$^+$ and D4, and between D1$^-$ and D4, given that photons 2 and 3 have been registered by the two detectors in the Bell-state analyser.

Note that this method requires four-fold coincidences. The result clearly demonstrates the expected sine curves, complementary for the two detectors (D1$^+$ and D1$^-$), registering photon 1 along orthogonal polarisations. By additional measurements it was verified that the sine curves are independent (up to the corresponding shift in Θ) of the detection basis of photon 1, that is, independent of the rotation angle of the $\lambda/2$ retardation plate. The observed visibility of 0.65 clearly surpasses the 0.5 limit of a classical wave theory. Note that this result is a realisation of quantum teleportation in a clear quantum situation, since entanglement between two particles that did not share a common origin nor interacted with one another in the past is the very result of the procedure. In the following section several applications of entanglement swapping will be presented.

3.11 Applications of Entanglement Swapping

S. Bose, V. Vedral and P.L. Knight

Entanglement swapping can be used for a number of practical purposes: constructing a *quantum telephone exchange*, to *speed up* the distribution of entangled particles between two parties, in a sort of *series purification* and for the *construction of entangled states involving higher number of particles* [87]. We describe these applications in some detail below.

3.11.1 Quantum Telephone Exchange

Suppose there are N users in a communication network. To begin with, each user of the network needs to share entangled pairs of particles (in a Bell state) with a central exchange. Consider Fig. 3.25 : A, B, C and D are users who share the Bell pairs (1,2), (3,4), (5,6) and (7,8) respectively with a central exchange O. Now suppose that A, B and C wish to share a GHZ triplet. Then a measurement which projects particles 2, 3 and 5 to GHZ states will have to be performed at O. Immediately, particles 1, 4 and 6 belonging to A, B and C respectively will be reduced to a GHZ state. In a similar manner one can entangle particles belonging to any N users of the network and create a N-particle cat state.

The main advantages of using this technique for establishing entanglement over the simple generation of N-particle entangled states at a source and their subsequent distribution are as follows.

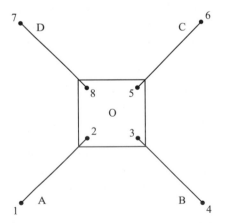

Fig. 3.25. The configuration used for the distribution of entanglement. Initially users A,B,C and D share Bell pairs with the central exchange O. Subsequently, a local measurement at O is sufficient to entangle particles belonging to any subset of users chosen from A, B, C and D .

(A) Firstly, each user can at first purify a large number of partially deco-hered Bell pairs shared with the central exchange to obtain a smaller number of pure shared Bell pairs. These can then be used as the starting point for the generation of any types of multiparticle cat states of the particles possessed by the users. The problems of decoherence during propagation of the parti-cles can thus be avoided (at least in principle). Also the necessity of having to purify N-particle cat states can be totally avoided. Purification of singlets followed by our scheme will generate N-particle cats in their purest form.

(B) Secondly, our method allows a certain degree of freedom to entangle particles belonging to any set of users only if the necessity arises. It may not be known in advance exactly which set of users will need to share an N-particle cat state. To arrange for all possibilities in an a priori fashion would require selecting all possible combinations of users and distributing particles in multiparticle entangled states among them. That is very uneconomical. On the other hand, generating entangled N-tuplets at the time of need and supplying them to the users who wish to communicate is definitely time consuming.

Biham, Huttner and Mor [116] have developed a similar scheme of cryp-tographic network with exchanges using a time reversed EPR scheme for setting up the connections.

3.11.2 Speeding up the Distribution of Entanglement

We now explain how standard entanglement swapping helps to save a sig-nificant amount of time when one wants to supply two distant users with a pair of atoms or electrons (or any particle possessing mass) in a Bell state from some central source. The trick is to place several Bell-state-producing and Bell-state-measuring substations in the route between them. Consider Fig. 3.26a: A and B are two users separated by a distance L; O, which is sit-uated midway between A and B is a source of Bell pairs. The time needed for the particles to reach A and B is at least $t_1 = L/2v$ where $v < c$ (the speed of light) is the speed of the particles. Now consider Fig.3.26b in which two Bell pair producing stations C and D are introduced halfway between AO and BO, respectively, and O is now just a Bell state measuring station. At $t = 0$, both C and D send off Bell pairs (1,2) and (3,4) respectively. 2 and 3 arrive at O, 1 reaches A and 4 reaches B. They all arrive at their destinations exactly at $t = L/4v$. At this instant a Bell state measurement is performed on particles 2 and 3 at O. This measurement immediately reduces the particles 1 and 4 reaching A and B respectively, to a Bell state. If the time of measurement is denoted by t_m, then the time needed to supply a Bell pair to A and B with the two extra substations C and D on the path is $t_2 = L/4v + t_m$. It is evident that t_2 is less than t_1 if $t_m < L/4v$. Of course, to this time one must add the time needed to classically communicate between the station O and the users A and B the particular Bell state to which particles 1 and 4 are projected. So for photons in Bell states, this procedure does not really (a)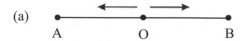

(b)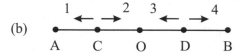

Fig. 3.26. A method of increasing the speed of distributing an entangled pair of particles (with nonzero mass) between two distant users A and B is illustrated. Extra Bell-state-generating substations C and D are inserted between A and B and a Bell-state projection is performed at O to speed up the distribution of a Bell pair between A and B.

save any time. But for particles possessing mass, this is definitely one way to reduce the time needed to supply two distant users with a Bell pair. In this way one can reduce the time needed to supply two distant users with a Bell pair even further by including more and more Bell pair producing and measuring substations on the way.

3.11.3 Correction of Amplitude Errors Developed due to Propagation

We would like to show that entanglement swapping can be used, with some probability which we quantify, to correct amplitude errors that might develop in maximally entangled states during propagation. Assume that in Fig. 3.26b, the Bell pairs emitted from C and D acquire amplitude errors and become less entangled states of the type

$$|\Psi\rangle = \cos\theta|01\rangle + \sin\theta|10\rangle. \tag{3.55}$$

Thus, the combined state of the two entangled pairs, when particles 2 and 3 reach O is given by,

$$|\Phi\rangle = \cos^2\theta|0101\rangle + \sin\theta\cos\theta(|1001\rangle$$
$$+ |0110\rangle) + \sin^2\theta|1010\rangle. \tag{3.56}$$

If a Bell state measurement is now performed on particles 2 and 3 that reach O, then the probability of them being projected onto the Bell states $|00\rangle + |11\rangle$ or $|00\rangle - |11\rangle$ is $\sin^2 2\theta/2$, while the probability of them being projected onto any of the other two Bell states is $(1 + \cos^2 2\theta)/2$. In the first case (i.e when 2 and 3 get projected to $|00\rangle + |11\rangle$ or $|00\rangle - |11\rangle$), the distant particles 1 and 4 are projected onto the Bell states $|00\rangle + |11\rangle$ or $|00\rangle - |11\rangle$. In this way in spite of amplitude errors due to propagation of the particles, A and B may finally share a Bell state. Of course in case of the other two outcomes of the state of particles 2 and 3, particles 1 and

4 go to states even less entangled than that of (3.55). That is why we can consider entanglement swapping suitable for correction of amplitude errors only probabilistically. The probability of success in this case ($\sin^2 2\theta/2$), is lower than the probability of failure $((1 + \cos^2 2\theta)/2)$. However, from the outcome of the Bell-state measurement, one knows when the correction has been successful. This may be regarded as a kind of purification in series, in contrast to the standard purifications [47, 117] (see Sect. 8.2) which occur in parallel. It can be shown that there is a measure of entanglement which is conserved in this type of purification process [118] (see also Sect. 6.4 for measures of entanglement).

3.11.4 Entangled States of Increasing Numbers of Particles

Entangled states involving higher numbers of particles can be generated from entangled states involving lower numbers of particles by employing our scheme. The basic ingredients which we need are GHZ (three particle maximally entangled) states and a Bell state measuring device. Let us describe how to proceed from an N-particle maximally entangled state to an $N + 1$-particle maximally entangled state. One has to take one particle from the N-particle maximally entangled state and another particle from a GHZ state and perform a Bell state measurement on these two particles. The result will be to put these two particles in a Bell state and the remaining $N+1$ particles in a maximally entangled state. Symbolically, the way to proceed from an N-particle maximally entangled state to a $N + 1$-particle maximally entangled state is given by

$$|E(N)\rangle \otimes |E(3)\rangle \xrightarrow{\text{Bell State Meas.}} |E(N + 1)\rangle \otimes |E(2)\rangle.$$

An example of proceeding from a 4 particle maximally entangled state to a 5 particle maximally entangled state by the above procedure is shown in Fig.3.27.

As far as the question of generating the GHZ state, which is a basic ingredient, is concerned, one can perhaps use the method suggested by Zeilinger et al. [119] (see also Sect. 6.3.4 for the generation of three-photon entanglement) Alternatively, one can generate GHZ states using our method by starting from three Bell pairs and performing a GHZ state measurement, taking one particle from each pair. An explicit scheme, for producing 3-particle GHZ states from 3 entangled pairs was suggested earlier by Zukowski et al. [101].

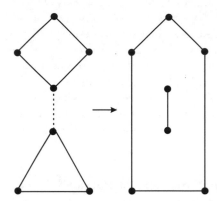

Fig. 3.27. Building of a 5 particle entangled state from a 4 particle entangled state using a GHZ state and a Bell state measurement

4. Concepts of Quantum Computation

There are many ways and levels of explaining quantum computation. This chapter is intended to reflect this fact. It is composed of the three self-contained sections. The first one gives a very basic introduction to the subject stressing the fundamental issues and avoiding mathematical formalism. Many may find this level of explanation adequate for their purposes. Those who want to become familiar with details are encouraged to proceed to the second section. It takes the reader from the very first quantum algorithms, through the discussion of computational complexity, to more advanced topics, such as quantum factoring. Last but not least, the third section provides a proposal for converting esoteric theoretical ideas into working devices. Chapter 5 presents experimental achievements to date and continuing efforts to make further progress in quantum computation.

4.1 Introduction to Quantum Computation

D. Deutsch and A. Ekert

4.1.1 A New Way of Harnessing Nature

Many milestones in the history of technology have involved the discovery of new ways of harnessing nature — exploiting various physical resources such as materials, forces, and sources of energy. In the twentieth century *information* was added to this list when the invention of computers allowed complex information processing to be performed outside human brains. The history of computer technology has itself involved a sequence of changes from one type of physical realisation to another — from gears to relays to valves to transistors, integrated circuits and so on. Today's advanced lithographic techniques can etch logic gates and wires less than a micron across onto the surfaces of silicon chips. Soon they will yield even smaller components, until we reach the point where logic gates are so small that they consist of only a few atoms each.

On the scale of human perception and above, classical (non-quantum) laws of physics are good phenomenological approximations, but on the atomic scale the laws of quantum mechanics become dominant, and they have quite a different character. If computers are to continue to become faster (and therefore smaller), new, *quantum* technology must replace or supplement what we have now, but it turns out that such technology can offer much more than smaller and faster microprocessors. It can support entirely new modes of computation, with new quantum algorithms that do not have classical analogues. And more: the quantum theory of computation plays an even more fundamental role in the scheme of things than its classical predecessor did, so that anyone seeking a fundamental understanding of either physics or information processing must incorporate its new insights into their world view.

4.1.2 From Bits to Qubits

What makes quantum computers so different from their classical counterparts? Let us take a closer look at the basic unit of information: the *bit*. Although bits and qubits have already been explained in Chap.1, we have decided, for the completeness and consistency of this exposition, to mention them again.

From a physical point of view a bit is a two-state system: it can be prepared in one of two distinguishable states representing two logical values — no or yes, false or true, or simply 0 or 1. For example, in digital computers, the voltage between the plates of a capacitor can represent a bit of information: a charge on the capacitor denotes 1 and the absence of charge denotes 0. One bit of information can also be encoded using, for instance, two different polarisations of light or two different electronic states of an atom. Now, quantum mechanics tells us that if a bit can exist in either of two distinguishable states, it can also exist in *coherent superpositions* of them. These are further states, which in general have no classical analogues, in which the atom represents *both* values, 0 and 1, simultaneously. To get used to the idea that a physical quantity can have two values at once, it is helpful to consider the experiment in Fig. 4.1.

A half–silvered mirror is one that reflects half the light that impinges upon it, while allowing the remaining half to pass through unaffected. Let us aim a single photon at such a mirror, as in Fig. 4.1. What happens? One thing we know is that the photon doesn't split in two: we can place photodetectors wherever we like in the apparatus, fire in a photon, and verify that if any of the photodetectors registers a hit, none of the others do. In particular, if we place a photodetector behind the mirror in each of the two possible exit beams, the photon is detected with equal probability at either detector. So does the photon leave the first mirror in one of the two possible directions, at random? It does not! It may seem obvious that at the very least, the photon

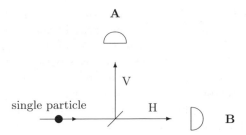

Fig. 4.1. A half-silvered mirror reflects half the light that impinges upon it. But a single photon doesn't split: when we send a photon towards such a mirror it is detected, with equal probability, either at detector A or B. This does not, however, mean that the photon leaves the mirror in either the horizontal (H) or the vertical (V) direction at random. In fact the photon takes both paths at once! This can be demonstrated with the help of a slightly more complicated experiment shown in Fig. 4.2.

is *either* in the transmitted beam H *or* in the reflected beam V during any one run of this experiment. But that is not so either. In fact the photon takes both paths at once, as can be demonstrated with the help of the apparatus shown in Fig. 4.2. Two normal mirrors are placed so that both paths intersect at a second half–silvered mirror. With this setup we can observe the astonishing, purely quantum phenomenon of *single-particle interference.*

Suppose that a particular photon followed the horizontal path marked H in Fig. 4.2 after striking the mirror. Then (by comparison with Fig. 4.1) we should find that the two detectors registered hits with equal probability.

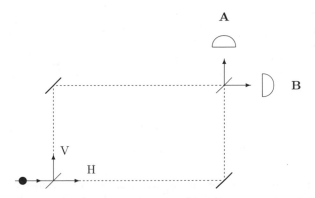

Fig. 4.2. Single-particle interference. A photon which enters the interferometer always strikes detector A and never detector B. Any explanation which assumes that the photon takes exactly one path through the interferometer — either H or V — leads to the conclusion that detectors A and B should on average each fire on half the occasions when the experiment is performed. But experiment shows otherwise.

Exactly the same would be observed if the photon were on the vertical path V. Hence if it were really the case that the photon takes exactly one path through the apparatus — no matter which one — detectors A and B would on average each fire on half the occasions when the experiment is performed. However, that is not what happens. It turns out that in the arrangement shown, the photon *always* strikes detector A and *never* detector B.

The inescapable conclusion is that the photon must, in some sense, have travelled both routes at once — for if either of the two paths is blocked by an absorbing screen, it immediately becomes equally probable that A or B is struck. In other words, blocking off either of the paths illuminates B; with both paths open, the photon somehow receives information that prevents it from reaching B, information that travels along the other path at the speed of light, bouncing off the mirror, exactly as a photon would. This property of quantum interference — that there seem to be invisible counterparts affecting the motion of particles that we detect — applies not only to photons but to all particles and all physical systems. Thus quantum theory describes an enormously larger reality than the universe we observe around us. It turns out that this reality has the approximate structure of multiple variants of that universe, co-existing and affecting each other only through interference phenomena — but for the purposes of this article, all we need of this "parallel universes" ontology is the fact that what we see as a single particle is actually only one tiny aspect of a tremendously complex entity, the rest of which we cannot detect directly. Quantum computation is all about making the invisible aspects of the particle — its counterparts in other universes — work for us.

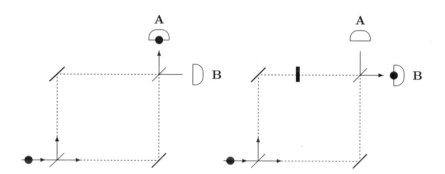

Fig. 4.3. A sliver of glass inserted into one of the two paths in the interferometer can redirect photons from one detector to another. All photons that enter the left interferometer strike detector A. In the right interferometer, the interference is modified by the presence of the sliver of glass on the vertical path, and as a result all photons end up in detector B. Thus something that has happened on only one of the paths has, with certainty, changed the final outcome of the experiment. This effect is especially useful in quantum computation.

One effect that is especially useful in quantum computation can be demonstrated if we delay the photon on one of the paths H or V. This can be done by inserting a sliver of glass into that path, as illustrated in Fig. 4.3. Since the interference between the photon and its invisible counterpart depends on their exact arrival times, we can, for instance, choose the thickness of the glass, and hence the delay time, in such a way that the photon will certainly (i.e. in all universes) emerge at detector B instead of detector A. Thus something that has happened on only one of the paths (and hence in only one of the universes) has affected both of them. We shall return to this point below.

Just as the photon can be in a coherent superposition of being on the path H and on the path V, any quantum bit, or *qubit*, can be prepared in a superposition of its two logical states 0 and 1. That is the sense in which a qubit can store both 0 and 1 simultaneously, in arbitrary proportions. But note that just as the photon, if measured, will be detected on only one of the two paths, likewise if the qubit is measured, only one of the two numbers it holds will be detected, at random: not a very useful property in itself.

But now let us push the idea of superpositions of numbers a little further. Consider a register composed of three physical bits. A classical 3-bit register can store exactly one of eight different numbers i.e the register can be in one of the eight possible configurations 000, 001, 010, ..., 111, representing the numbers 0 to 7. But a quantum register composed of three qubits can simultaneously store up to eight numbers in a quantum superposition. It is quite remarkable that eight different numbers can be physically present in the same register; but it should be no more surprising than the numbers 0 and 1 both being present in the same qubit. If we add more qubits to the register its capacity for storing quantum information increases exponentially: four qubits can store 16 different numbers at once, and in general L qubits can store up to 2^L numbers at once. A 250-qubit register — essentially made of 250 atoms, say — would be capable of holding more numbers simultaneously than there are atoms in the known universe. (If anything, this *understates* the amount of quantum information that they hold, for in general, the elements of a superposition are present in continuously variable proportions, each with its own phase angle as well.) Even so, if we measure the register's contents, we will see only one of those numbers. However, now we can start doing some non-trivial quantum computation, for once the register is prepared in a superposition of many different numbers, we can perform mathematical operations on all of them at once.

For example, if the qubits are atoms then suitably tuned laser pulses affect their electronic states and cause initial superpositions of encoded numbers to evolve into different superpositions. During such an evolution each number in the superposition is affected, so we are performing a massive parallel computation. Thus a quantum computer can in a single computational step perform the same mathematical operation on, say, 2^L different input numbers, and the result will be a superposition of all the corresponding outputs. In order to accomplish the same task any classical computer has to repeat the computation 2^L times, or has to use 2^L different processors working in parallel. In this way a quantum computer offers an enormous gain in the use of computational resources such as time and memory — though only in certain types of computation.

4.1.3 Quantum Algorithms

What types? As we have said, ordinary information storage is not one of them, for although the computer now holds all the outcomes of 2^L computations, the laws of physics only allow us to see one of them. However, just as the single answer "A" in the experiment of Fig. 4.2 depends on information that travelled along each of two paths, quantum interference now allows us to obtain a single, final result that depends logically on all 2^L of the intermediate results.

This is how a remarkable quantum algorithm recently discovered by Lov Grover of AT&T's Bell Laboratories in New Jersey [120] achieves the mind-boggling feat of searching an unsorted list of N items in only $\sqrt{N}$ or so steps. Consider, for example, searching for a specific telephone number in a directory containing a million entries, stored in the computer's memory in alphabetical order of names. It is easily proved (and obvious) that no classical algorithm can improve on the brute-force method of simply scanning the entries one by one until the given number is found, which will, on average, require 500,000 memory accesses. A quantum computer can examine all the entries simultaneously, in the time of a single access. However, if it is merely programmed to print out the result at that point, there is no improvement over the classical algorithm: only one of the million computational paths (i.e. one in a million universes) would have checked the entry we are looking for, so there would be a probability of only one in a million that we would obtain that information if we measured the computer's state. But if we leave that quantum information in the computer, unmeasured, a further quantum operation can cause that information to affect other paths, just as in the simple interference experiment described above. In this way the information about the desired entry is spread, through quantum interference, to more universes. It turns out that if this interference-generating operation is repeated about 1000 times, (in general, $\sqrt{N}$ times) the information about which entry contains the desired number will be accessible to measurement with probability 0.5 — i.e. it will have spread to more than half the universes. Therefore repeating the entire algorithm a few more times will find the desired entry with a probability overwhelmingly close to 1.

In addition to finding the entry with a given property, variations on Grover's search algorithm can also find the largest or smallest value in a list, or the modal value, and so on, so it is a very versatile searching tool. However, in practice, searching a physical database is unlikely to become a major application of Grover's algorithm — at least so long as classical memory remains cheaper than quantum memory. For since the operation of transferring a database from classical to quantum memory (bits to qubits) would itself require $O(N)$ steps, Grover's algorithm would improve search times by at best a constant factor, which could also be achieved by classical parallel processing. Where Grover's algorithm would really come into its own is in *algorithmic* searches — that is, searches of lists that are not stored in memory but are themselves generated on the fly by a computer program. For instance, a chess-playing quantum computer could use it to investigate a trillion possible continuations from a given position in roughly the number of steps that a classical computer (using blind "brute-force" searching) would need to investigate a mere million. Despite the greater scope for "tree-pruning" in classical chess-playing algorithms, this is likely to provide a very significant improvement.

As Gilles Brassard of the Université de Montréal has recently pointed out [121], another important application of Grover's algorithm will be in cryptanalysis, to attack classical cryptographic schemes such as DES (the Data Encryption Standard, see Chap. 2 on quantum cryptography). Cracking DES essentially requires a search among $2^{56} = 7 \times 10^{16}$ possible keys. If these can be checked at a rate of, say, one million keys per second, a classical computer would need over a thousand years to discover the correct key while a quantum computer using Grover's algorithm would do it in less than four minutes!

By some strange coincidence, several of the superior features of quantum computers have applications in cryptography. One of them is Grover's algorithm. Another is the quantum algorithm discovered in 1994 by Peter Shor, also of AT&T's Bell Laboratories in New Jersey, for factorising large integers efficiently [36]. Here the difference in performance between the quantum and classical algorithms is even more spectacular. Mathematicians believe (firmly, though they have not actually proved it) that in order to factorise a number with N decimal digits, any classical computer needs a number of steps that grows exponentially with N: that is to say, adding one extra digit to the number to be factorised generally *multiplies* the time required by a fixed factor (see Sect. 4.2). Thus, as we increase the number of digits, the task rapidly becomes intractable. The largest number that has been factorised as a mathematical challenge, i.e. a number whose factors were secretly chosen by mathematicians in order to present a challenge to other mathematicians, had 129 digits. No one can even conceive of how one might factorise, say, thousand-digit numbers by classical means; the computation would take many times as long the estimated age of the universe. In contrast, quantum computers could factor thousand-digit numbers in a fraction of a second — and the execution time would grow only as the cube of the number of digits.

Now, the intractability of factorisation underpins the security of what are currently the most trusted methods of encryption, in particular of the RSA (Rivest, Shamir and Adleman) system, which is often used to protect electronic bank accounts [122] (for details see Chap. 2). Once a quantum factorisation engine (a special-purpose quantum computer for factorising large numbers) is built, all such cryptographic systems will become insecure.

The potential power of quantum phenomena to perform computations was first adumbrated in a talk given by Richard Feynman at the First Conference on the Physics of Computation, held at MIT in 1981. He observed that it appeared to be impossible in general to simulate the evolution of a quantum system on a classical computer in an efficient way [123]. The computer simulation of quantum evolution typically involves an exponential slowdown in time, compared with the natural evolution, essentially because the amount of classical information required to describe the evolving quantum state is exponentially larger than that required to describe the corresponding classical system with a similar accuracy. (To predict interference effects, one has to describe all the system's exponentially many counterparts in parallel universes.) However, instead of viewing this intractability as an obstacle, Feynman regarded it as an opportunity. He pointed out that if it requires that much computation to work out what will happen in a multi-particle interference experiment, then the very act of setting up such an experiment and measuring the outcome is equivalent to performing a complex computation.

Quantum computation has already been used, in simple cases, to predict the behaviour of quantum systems. At some point in the foreseeable future, they will take on a new and irreplaceable role in the structure of science, for the ability of science to make predictions will then depend on quantum computation.

The foundations of the quantum theory of computation (which must now be regarded as *the* theory of computation — Turing's classical theory being only an approximation) were laid down in 1985 when David Deutsch of the University of Oxford published a crucial theoretical paper in which he described a *universal quantum computer* [124]. Since then, the hunt has been on for interesting things for quantum computers to do, and at the same time, for the scientific and technological advances that could allow us to build quantum computers.

4.1.4 Building Quantum Computers

In principle we know how to build a quantum computer; we start with simple quantum logic gates (see Chap. 1) and connect them up into quantum networks.

A quantum logic gate, like a classical gate, is a very simple computing device that performs one elementary quantum operation, usually on two qubits, in a given time [125]. Of course, quantum logic gates differ from their classical counterparts in that they can create, and perform operations, on quantum superpositions. However as the number of quantum gates in a network increases, we quickly run into some serious practical problems. The more interacting qubits are involved, the harder it tends to be to engineer the interaction that would display the quantum interference. Apart from the technical difficulties of working at single-atom and single-photon scales, one of the most important problems is that of preventing the surrounding environment from being affected by the interactions that generate quantum superpositions. The more components there are, the more likely it is that quantum information will spread outside the quantum computer and be lost into the environment, thus spoiling the computation. This process is called *decoherence* and is discussed in detail in Chap. 7. Thus our task is to engineer sub-microscopic systems in which qubits affect each other but not the environment.

Some physicists are pessimistic about the prospects of substantial further progress in quantum computer technology. They believe that decoherence will in practice never be reduced to the point where more than a few consecutive quantum computational steps can be performed. (This, incidentally, would already allow for some very useful devices — see Table 4.1 below.) Other, more optimistic researchers believe that practical quantum computers will appear in a matter of years rather than decades. We tend towards the optimistic end of the scale, partly because theory tells us that there is now no *fundamental* obstacle in the way and that quantum error correction and fault tolerant computation (see Chap. 7) are possible, partly thanks to the astonishing talents and problem-solving abilities of the experimental physicists now working on this project, and partly because optimism makes things happen.

However, the problems will not be solved in one fell swoop. The current challenge is not to build a fully-fledged universal quantum computer right away, but rather to move from the experiments in which we merely observe quantum phenomena to experiments in which we can control those phenomena in the necessary ways. Simple quantum logic gates involving two qubits are being realised in laboratories in Europe and U.S.A. The next decade should bring control over several qubits and, without any doubt, we shall already begin to benefit from our new way of harnessing nature. It is known, for instance, that simple quantum networks can offer better frequency standards [126] (see Sect. 7.6). Some possible milestones in the development of quantum computer technology are shown in Table 4.1.

4.1.5 Deeper Implications

When the physics of computation was first investigated systematically in the 1970s, the main fear was that quantum-mechanical effects might place fundamental bounds on the accuracy with which physical objects could realise the properties of bits, logic gates, the composition of operations, and so on, which appear in the abstract and mathematically sophisticated theory of computation. Thus it was feared that the power and elegance of that theory, its deep concepts such as computational universality, its deep results such as Turing's halting theorem, and the more modern theory of complexity, might

Table 4.1. Milestones in the development of quantum computer technology

Type of hardware	No. of qubits needed	No. of steps before decoherence	Status
Quantum Cryptography	1	1	implemented
Entanglement based quantum cryptography	2	1	demonstrated
Quantum C-NOT gate	2	1	demonstrated
Composition of gates	2	2	demonstrated
Deutsch's algorithm	2	3	demonstrated
Channel capacity doubling	2	2	imminent
Teleportation	3	2	demonstrated
Entanglement swapping	4	1	demonstrated
Repeating station for quantum cryptography	a few	a few	theory still incomplete
Quantum simulations	a few	a few	simple demos
Grover's algorithm with toy data	3+	6+	demonstrated with NMR
Ultra-precise frequency standards	a few	a few	foreseeable
Entanglement purification	a few	a few	foreseeable
Shor's algorithm with toy data ...	16+ ...	hundreds + ...	
Quantum factoring engine	hundreds	hundreds	
Universal quantum computer	thousands +	thousands +	

all be mere figments of pure mathematics, not really relevant to anything in nature.

Those fears have not only been proved groundless by the research we have been describing, but also, in each case, the underlying aspiration has been wonderfully vindicated to an extent that no one even dreamed of just twenty years ago. As we have explained, quantum mechanics, far from placing limits on what classical computations can be performed in nature, permits them all, and in addition provides whole new modes of computation, including algorithms that perform tasks (such as perfectly secure public-key cryptography) that no classical computer can perform at all. As far as the elegance of the theory goes, researchers in the field have now become accustomed to the fact that the real theory of computation hangs together better, and fits in far more naturally with fundamental theories in other fields, than its classical approximation could ever have been expected to. Even at the simplest level, the very word "quantum" means the same as the word "bit" — an elementary chunk — and this reflects the fact that fully classical physical systems, being subject to the generic instability known as "chaos", would not support digital computation at all (so even Turing machines, the theoretical prototype of all classical computers, were secretly quantum-mechanical all along!). The Church–Turing hypothesis in the classical theory (that all "natural" models of computation are essentially equivalent to each other), was never proved. Its analogue in the quantum theory of computation (the Turing Principle, that the universal quantum computer can simulate the behaviour of any finite physical system) was straightforwardly proved in Deutsch's 1985 paper [124]. A stronger result (also conjectured but never proved in the classical case), namely that such simulations can always be performed in a time that is at most a polynomial function of the time taken for the physical evolution, has since been proved in the quantum case.

Among the many ramifications of quantum computation for apparently distant fields of study are its implications for both the philosophy and the practice of mathematical proof. Performing any computation that provides a definite output is tantamount to *proving* that the observed output is one of the possible results of the given computation. Since we can describe the computer's operations mathematically, we can always translate such a proof into the proof of some mathematical theorem. This was the case classically too, but in the absence of interference effects it is always possible to note down the steps of the computation, and thereby produce a proof that satisfies the classical definition: a sequence of propositions each of which is either an axiom or follows from earlier propositions in the sequence by the standards rules of inference. Now we must leave that definition behind. Henceforward, a proof must be regarded as a process — the computation itself, not a record of all its steps — for we must accept that in future, quantum computers will prove theorems by methods that neither a human brain nor any other arbiter will ever be able to check step-by-step, since if the "sequence of propositions" corresponding to such a proof were printed out, the paper would fill the observable universe many times over. A more comprehensive discussion of the deeper implications of quantum computation can be found in [127].

4.1.6 Concluding Remarks

Experimental and theoretical research in quantum computation is now attracting increasing attention from both academic researchers and industry worldwide. The idea that nature can be controlled and manipulated at the quantum level is a powerful stimulus to the imagination of physicists and engineers. There is almost daily progress in developing ever more promising technologies for realising quantum computation and new quantum algorithms with various advantages over their classical counterparts. There is potential here for truly revolutionary innovation.

This contribution is a revised version of the introductory paper on quantum computation which originally appeared in the March 1998 issue of the Physics World [128].

4.2 Quantum Algorithms

R. Jozsa

4.2.1 Introduction

A quantum algorithm is any physical process which utilises characteristically quantum effects to perform useful computational tasks. It is convenient to formalise the description of these quantum computational processes in terms of a model which closely parallels the formalism of classical computation. In essence, the memory bits of the computer are qubits rather than bits and the elementary operations are unitary transformations, each operating on a fixed finite number of qubits, rather than the Boolean operations of classical computation. It may be argued [124] that a model of this type suffices to describe any general quantum physical process. Any computer is required to operate by "finite means" i.e. it is equipped only with the possibility of applying any operation of some finite fixed set of basic unitary operations. Any other unitary operation that we may need in an algorithm must be built (or rather approximated to sufficient accuracy) out of these basic building blocks by concatenating their action on selected qubits. It may be shown [129, 130] that various quite small collections of unitary operations (so-called "universal sets" of operations) suffice to approximate any unitary operation on any number of qubits to arbitrary accuracy.

One of the most useful and significant consequences of this formalism is that it provides a way of assessing the complexity of a computational task (again by paralleling concepts from classical computational complexity theory). We will be particularly concerned with the time complexity, i.e. assessing the number of elementary operations required to complete a computational task as a function of the size of the input.

If two computers A and B are equipped with different (universal) sets of basic operations then the time complexity of any computational task will in general be different. However, B may first program each of A's basic operations in terms of its own set and hence run any program which is written in terms of A's set of operations. Let k be the maximum number of steps that B requires to mimic any one of A's basic operations. Then the time complexity on B for any computational task will be at most k times the time complexity relative to A, i.e. a change in the set of basic operations results in at most a constant slowdown (independent of input size) for any computational task. In computational complexity theory we are generally not interested in the exact number of steps in a computation but rather, only in the characteristic rate of growth of the number of steps with increasing input size. Indeed we generally only ask whether the number of steps is bounded by a polynomial function of the input size (giving so-called polynomial-time algorithms or efficient algorithms) or whether it grows exponentially (or super-polynomially) with input size. According to the above remarks this distinction will be independent of the choice of computer and it is an intrinsic property of the computational task itself.

In the study of quantum algorithms it is of paramount interest to find polynomial-time algorithms for problems where no classical polynomial-time algorithm is known, i.e. we wish to demonstrate that quantum effects may give rise to an exponential speedup in running time over classical information processing. We will describe various situations in which this occurs – the algorithms of Deutsch, Simon and Shor. We will also describe the quantum searching algorithm of Grover which provides a square root speedup over any classical algorithm, rather than an exponential speedup. This is still of considerable practical interest and Grover's algorithm also has much theoretical interest because of its relation to the classical complexity class called NP [131, 132].

We will see in Chap. 5 that the prospective implementation of any extended quantum algorithm currently presents a very considerable experimental challenge. However the existence of interesting quantum algorithms, merely at the level of theoretical constructs, is of great value in itself as it points to new essential differences between the fundamental structure classical physics compared to quantum physics. From our point of view of information processing, time evolution in quantum physics is seen to be intrinsically more complex than classical time evolution, in a way that can be quantified using the conceptual framework of computational complexity theory.

The essential quantum mechanical effects giving rise to the computational speedup in the quantum algorithms listed above, may be traced to various properties of quantum *entanglement*. We begin by discussing two such effects which feature predominantly; we refer to them as "quantum parallel computation" (Sect. 4.2.2) and "the principle of local operations" (Sect. 4.2.3).

4.2.2 Quantum Parallel Computation

Consider a function $f : A \to B$ where A and B are finite sets. Typically A and B may be the collection of all 2^n n-bit strings (for some n), as in the algorithms of Deutsch and Simon, or $\mathcal{Z}_N$, the set of integers mod N (for some N) as in Shor's algorithm. In our applications A and B will also be Abelian groups. Let $\mathcal{H}_A$ (respectively $\mathcal{H}_B$) be a Hilbert space with an orthonormal basis labelled by the elements of A (respectively B). In the context of quantum computation the computation of f corresponds to a unitary evolution U_f which is customarily taken as an operation on $\mathcal{H}_A \otimes \mathcal{H}_B$ transforming $|a\rangle |b\rangle$ into $|a\rangle |b \oplus f(a)\rangle$ (c.f. Fig. 4.4). Here $\oplus$ denotes the Abelian group operation in B.

$\mathcal{H}_A$ is the state space of the input register and $\mathcal{H}_B$ is the state space of the output register. The input $|a\rangle$ is carried through to ensure that U_f is

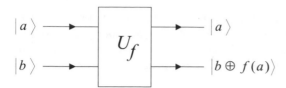

Fig. 4.4. Quantum gate picture of the unitary transformation U_f corresponding to the evaluation of the function f. The upper and lower lines represent the input and output registers respectively.

unitary for every possible f. If b is initially set to 0 then $f(a)$ may be read directly from the output register by a standard measurement in the given basis.

Suppose now that the input register is set up as a superposition of values, say the equal superposition $\sum_{a \in A} |a\rangle$ (where we have omitted the normalisation factor). Then applying U_f with $b = 0$ we get, by the linearity of quantum evolution, the output superposition $\sum |a\rangle |f(a)\rangle$ (c.f. Fig. 4.5).

By running U_f just *once* we have computed *all* values of f in superposition. This is the process of quantum parallel computation, introduced by Deutsch in [124]. Note that the output state $\sum |a\rangle |f(a)\rangle$ is generally an entangled state of the input and output registers. Indeed the phenomenon of superposition is a feature also of *classical* linear systems and any effect depending on superposition alone can readily be implemented in a classical system. However the phenomenon of quantum entanglement has no classical analogue and its fundamental role in quantum computation has been emphasised and elaborated in [133, 134].

Let $B = \{0, 1\}$ denote the additive group of integers mod 2 and denote by $\mathcal{B}$ the Hilbert space of one qubit i.e. a two dimensional Hilbert space equipped with a standard basis denoted by $\{|0\rangle, |1\rangle\}$. $\mathcal{B}^n$ will denote the 2^n-dimensional Hilbert space $\mathcal{B} \otimes \ldots \otimes \mathcal{B}$ of n qubits with a basis $\{|x\rangle : x \in B^n\}$ labelled by all n-bit strings. Let H denote the fundamental one-qubit unitary operation

$$H = \frac{1}{\sqrt{2}} \begin{pmatrix} 1 & 1 \\ 1 & -1 \end{pmatrix}. \tag{4.1}$$

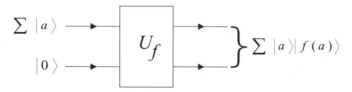

Fig. 4.5. Quantum parallel computation.

Thus

$$H\,|\,0\rangle = \frac{1}{\sqrt{2}}(|\,0\rangle + |\,1\rangle) \quad \text{and} \quad H\,|\,1\rangle = \frac{1}{\sqrt{2}}(|\,0\rangle - |\,1\rangle)\,. \tag{4.2}$$

Consider a function $f\,:\,B^n \to B$. As an example of computation by quantum parallelism, we may set up a superposition of all input values and compute all values of f in superposition as follows:

(i) Start with the standard state $|\,0\rangle \ldots |\,0\rangle$ of n (input) qubits and apply H separately to each qubit. This will result in the state:

$$\frac{1}{2^{n/2}}(|\,0\rangle + |\,1\rangle)\ldots(|\,0\rangle + |\,1\rangle) = \frac{1}{2^{n/2}}\sum_{x\in B^n}|\,x\rangle\,. \tag{4.3}$$

(ii) Adjoin a further single (output) qubit in state $|\,0\rangle$ and apply U_f giving the state:

$$|\,f\rangle = \frac{1}{2^{n/2}}\sum_{x\in B^n}|\,x\rangle\,|\,f(x)\rangle\,. \tag{4.4}$$

Note that (i) requires only $O(n)$ operations, which is polynomial in n, yet it leads to a superposition of *exponentially* many values of f in (4.4).

Quantum entanglement also plays another important role in the representation of superpositions. If we wish to build a general superposition of 2^n modes classically, we would need a *single* system capable of supporting each mode, e.g. 2^n modes of vibration of a vibrating string. These modes will correspond to higher and higher levels of some physical resource, e.g. energy in the vibrating string, and a general superposition of 2^n modes would then require an exponential (in n) amount of the physical resource to represent it. In contrast, in quantum theory, we can represent a superposition of 2^n states using n 2-level systems – *because of the phenomenon of entanglement*. A general such superposition now requires only a *linear* amount of physical resources to represent it, since at most each of the n systems needs to be separately excited. Hence, although superposition occurs in classical systems, the phenomenon of quantum entanglement leads to an exponential saving of physical resources needed to represent large superpositions.

4.2.3 The Principle of Local Operations

In all computation, be it classical or quantum, the information which is being processed is embodied in the identity of the physical state of (part of) the computer. Let us compare the description of the identity of a state of n classical bits with its quantum analogue, a state of n qubits. Although n bits can be in any one of exponentially many states, each state can be fully described by giving just n bits of information. In contrast, a general (entangled) state of n qubits may involve exponentially many superposition components which need to be listed. In this sense a quantum system can embody exponentially more information than its classical counterpart. This is not a consequence of the fact that quantum amplitudes can take a continuous range of values – it persists even if we limit amplitudes to some simple basic set of numbers. For example the $(n+1)$-qubit state $|f\rangle$ in (4.4) embodies the information of all the exponentially many zero/one values of the function f. Note that the information needed to describe an unentangled (product) state of n qubits grows only linearly with n, being n times the information needed to describe a single qubit state.

The formalism of quantum mechanics allows the vast information content of a quantum state to be efficiently processed, at a rate that cannot be matched in real time by any classical means. This remarkable feature of quantum theory was first noted by Feynman in [123]. Suppose that we have a physical system of n qubits in some entangled state $|\psi\rangle$ and we apply a 1-qubit operation U to the first qubit. This would count as one step in a quantum computation (or rather a constant number of steps independent of n, if U needs to be fabricated from other basic operations provided by the computer). Consider now the classical computation corresponding to this processing of information in the state. $|\psi\rangle$ may be described in components (relative to the product basis of the n qubits) by $a_{i_1\cdots i_n}$ where each subscript is 0 or 1, and U is represented by a 2×2 unitary matrix U_i^j. The application of U corresponds to the matrix multiplication

$$a_{i_1\cdots i_n}^{(\text{new})} = \sum_j U_{i_1}^j a_{ji_2\cdots i_n} .$$ (4.5)

Thus the 2×2 matrix multiplication needs to be performed 2^{n-1} times, once for each possible value of the string $i_2 \cdots i_n$, requiring a computing effort which grows *exponentially* with n. On a quantum computer, because of entanglement, this 2^{n-1} repetition is unnecessary. This is our "principle of local operations": a single local unitary operation on a subsystem of a large entangled system processes the embodied information by an amount which would generally require an exponential effort to represent in classical computational terms.

In the sense noted above, n qubits have an exponentially larger capacity to represent information than n classical bits. However the potentially vast information embodied in a quantum state has a further remarkable feature – most of it is *inaccessible* to being read by any possible means! Indeed quantum measurement theory places severe restrictions on the amount of information that we can obtain about the identity of a given unknown quantum state. This intrinsic inaccessibility of the information may be quantified [135, 136] in terms of Shannon's information theory [137]. In the case of a general state of n qubits, with its $O(2^n)$ information content, it turns out that at most n classical bits of information about its identity may be extracted from a single copy of the state by any physical means whatsoever. This coincides with the maximum information capacity of n classical bits.

The full (largely inaccessible) information content of a given unknown quantum state is called quantum information. Natural quantum physical evolution may be thought of as the processing of quantum information. Thus the viewpoint of computational complexity reveals a new bizarre distinction between classical and quantum physics: to perform natural quantum physical evolution, Nature must process vast amounts of information at a rate that cannot be matched in real time by any classical means, yet at the same time, most of this processed information is kept hidden from us! However it is important to point out that the inherent inaccessibility of quantum information does *not* cancel out the possibility of exploiting this massive information processing capability for useful computational purposes. Indeed, small amounts of information may be extracted about the overall identity of the final state which would still require an exponential effort to obtain by classical means. The technique of quantum parallel computation described above, provides an example: the full quantum information of the state $|f\rangle$ in (4.4) incorporates the information of all the individual function values $f(x)$ but this is not accessible to any measurement. However certain global properties of the collection of all the function values *may* be determined by suitable measurements on $|f\rangle$ which are not diagonal in the standard basis $\{|x\rangle|y\rangle\}$. For example, if f is a periodic function, we may determine the value of the period which falls far short of characterising the individual function values but would generally still require an exponential number of function evaluations to obtain reliably by classical means. This will be a key fact in the workings of Shor's efficient quantum factoring algorithm (Sect. 4.2.6).

Having discussed some basic computational benefits of quantum theory in general terms we will now describe the workings of various fundamental quantum algorithms.

4.2.4 Oracles and Deutsch's Algorithm

Deutsch's algorithm [124, 138] was the first explicit example of a computational task which could be performed exponentially faster using quantum effects than by any classical means. It was subsequently improved in [139] and we will describe here its most up-to-date form.

Consider first the four possible one-bit functions $f : B \to B$. We have two constant functions:

$$\begin{array}{ccc} f(0) = 0 & & f(0) = 1 \\ & \text{or} & \\ f(1) = 0 & & f(1) = 1 \end{array} \tag{4.6}$$

and two "balanced" functions (balanced in the sense that the output values 0 and 1 occur equally often):

$$\begin{array}{ccc} f(0) = 0 & & f(0) = 1 \\ & \text{or} & \\ f(1) = 1 & & f(1) = 0 \end{array} . \tag{4.7}$$

Suppose now that we are given a "black box" or "oracle" which computes an (unknown) one of these functions. The oracle may be pictured as a sealed box (c.f. Fig. 4.4) providing the value of the function for any given input value (or input superposition as in Fig. 4.5). Alternatively we may think of the oracle as a computer subroutine which we may run but whose text or internal workings we are not allowed to examine. (Later we will give a discussion of the significance of this limitation on our access to the evaluation of f.) Our problem is to determine whether the function computed by the oracle is balanced or constant.

In the context of classical computation we clearly need to query the oracle twice to solve the problem with certainty. Indeed if we know only one value of the function (i.e. either $f(0)$ or $f(1)$) then we have no information at all about whether the function is balanced or constant! We will now show that on a quantum computer the problem may be solved with certainty with just one query to the oracle.

We exploit the possibility of quantum parallel computation (as described above) but with an extra twist – of first setting the output register to $\frac{1}{\sqrt{2}}(|0\rangle - |1\rangle)$. The quantum computation runs as follows. Starting from the standard state $|0\rangle |0\rangle$ of the input and output registers we apply the NOT operation to the output and then H to both registers giving

$$|0\rangle |0\rangle \rightarrow |0\rangle |1\rangle \rightarrow \left(\frac{|0\rangle + |1\rangle}{\sqrt{2}}\right)\left(\frac{|0\rangle - |1\rangle}{\sqrt{2}}\right)$$

$$= \frac{1}{\sqrt{2}}\sum_{x \in B} |x\rangle \left(\frac{|0\rangle - |1\rangle}{\sqrt{2}}\right). \tag{4.8}$$

Next we present this state to the oracle, i.e. we apply U_f. Recalling that U_f transforms $|x\rangle |y\rangle$ into $|x\rangle |y \oplus f(x)\rangle$ we see that

$$U_f : |x\rangle (|0\rangle - |1\rangle) \longrightarrow \begin{cases} |x\rangle (|0\rangle - |1\rangle) \text{ if } f(x) = 0 \\ -|x\rangle (|0\rangle - |1\rangle) \text{ if } f(x) = 1 \end{cases}.$$

Thus

$$U_f : \frac{1}{\sqrt{2}}\sum_{x \in B} |x\rangle \left(\frac{|0\rangle - |1\rangle}{\sqrt{2}}\right) \longrightarrow \left(\frac{1}{\sqrt{2}}\sum_{x \in B}(-1)^{f(x)} |x\rangle\right)\left(\frac{|0\rangle - |1\rangle}{\sqrt{2}}\right). \tag{4.9}$$

Throughout this process the output register has remained in state $\frac{1}{\sqrt{2}}(|0\rangle - |1\rangle)$. The input register is left in state $\frac{1}{\sqrt{2}}\sum_{x \in B}(-1)^{f(x)} |x\rangle$. If f is a constant function we get $\pm\frac{1}{\sqrt{2}}(|0\rangle + |1\rangle)$ and if f is balanced we get $\pm\frac{1}{\sqrt{2}}(|0\rangle - |1\rangle)$. Now it is easy to verify directly that H is its own inverse, i.e. that $HH = I$. Thus finally applying H to the input register (and noting (4.2)) the state of this register will be $\pm|0\rangle$ if f was constant and $\pm|1\rangle$ if f was balanced. These may be reliably distinguished by a measurement in the standard basis, thus distinguishing balanced from constant functions with certainty after just one

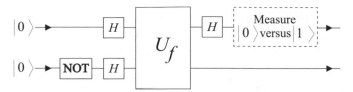

Fig. 4.6. Deutsch's algorithm for 1-bit functions. A measured value of 0 (respectively 1) signals that f is constant (respectively balanced).

query to the oracle. The overall sequence of operations is summarised in the network diagram shown in Fig. 4.6.

The above distinction between one and two calls to the oracle has no direct significance for formal complexity considerations but we may readily generalise the idea of the above process to a situation which *does* exhibit an *exponential* separation between the classical and quantum solutions.

Instead of having functions from one bit to one bit suppose we are given an oracle which computes some function from n bits to one bit:

$$f : B^n \to B$$

(and we also know the value of n). It is promised that the function is either constant (i.e. the 2^n values are either all 0 or all 1) or balanced, where balanced means that exactly half (i.e. 2^{n-1}) of the values are 0 and half are 1. Note that for $n > 1$ a general function from n bits to 1 bit is neither balanced nor constant but there are a large number of possible balanced functions. Our problem is again to determine (with certainty) whether f is balanced or constant. The case of $n = 1$ is precisely the problem considered previously.

In a classical scenario, if we query the oracle 2^{n-1} times to obtain 2^{n-1} values of f, in any way whatever with later queries possibly depending on the outcome of earlier ones, then we will still not be able to solve the problem in *every* case. Indeed suppose that the 2^{n-1} values come out to be all the same (which is always possible although very unlikely if the function is really balanced). Then regardless of the choice of input arguments there will always be a constant and a balanced function which is consistent with the totality of the information gained. Hence any classical solution to the problem must query the oracle more than 2^{n-1} times i.e. at least an exponential (in n) number of times. In fact it is easy to see that $2^{n-1} + 1$ queries will always suffice. In a quantum scenario the problem may be solved with certainty in every case with just *one* call to the oracle. The method is a straightforward generalisation of the one bit case.

We start with a row of n (input) qubits and one (output) qubit all in standard state $|0\rangle$. We apply H to each of the input qubits. As given in (4.3) this results in an equal superposition of all inputs in the first n qubits. We prepare the last (output) qubit in state $\frac{1}{\sqrt{2}}(|0\rangle - |1\rangle)$ exactly as previously.

Next we offer the resulting $n + 1$ qubit state to the oracle. This is formally the same as (4.9) except that now x ranges over B^n rather than just B. After processing by the oracle the first n qubits will be in state

$$| \xi_f \rangle = \frac{1}{\sqrt{2^n}} \sum_{x \in 2^n} (-1)^{f(x)} | x \rangle . \tag{4.10}$$

(In passing we note here that in the original 1992 version of the Deutsch algorithm [138] the output register was initialised in state $|0\rangle$ and two calls to the oracle were needed to produce the state $| \xi_f \rangle$). Now if f was a constant function then $| \xi_f \rangle$ will be just an equal superposition of all the $| x \rangle$'s with an overall plus or minus sign whereas if f was a balanced function then $| \xi_f \rangle$ will be an equally weighted superposition with exactly half of the $| x \rangle$'s having minus signs. Thus these two possibilities are orthogonal and so there exists a suitable measurement on $| \xi_f \rangle$ which will distinguish balanced from constant functions with certainty.

We need to describe explicitly how this measurement can be performed. In any quantum algorithm we cannot assume that any measurement can be performed by fiat as one step of computation (just as we cannot assume the application of complicated unitary operations as one step). To assess the complexity of any measurement we assume that the only possible measurement available to us is an elementary $|0\rangle$ versus $|1\rangle$ measurement of any one qubit in the computational basis and this counts as one step. Any general measurement may be reduced to a sequence of these standard measurements by first unitarily rotating the eigenbasis of the measurement into the computational basis and then successively reading the bits. The complexity of the measurement is then measured by the number of steps required to implement this unitary rotation plus the number of qubits that need to be read.

In our case the measurement that distinguishes balanced from constant $| \xi_f \rangle$'s may be implemented simply as follows. Recalling that H is its own inverse (i.e. $HH = I$) and that H applied to each qubit of $|0\rangle |0\rangle \ldots |0\rangle$ results in an equal superposition of all $| x \rangle$'s (c.f. (4.3)), it follows that if H is again applied to each qubit of this equal superposition then the resulting state will be $|0\rangle |0\rangle \ldots |0\rangle$. Hence we apply H to each qubit of $| \xi_f \rangle$ (involving n steps). If f was constant then the resulting state is $\pm |0\rangle |0\rangle \ldots |0\rangle$. If f was balanced then the resulting state will be orthogonal to this i.e. a superposition of $| x \rangle$'s with $x \neq 00 \ldots 0$. Thus we read each of the n qubits to see if they are all 0 or not (a further n steps) which completes the measurement. Overall, Deutsch's quantum algorithm requires $O(n)$ steps (including one call to the oracle) to distinguish balanced from constant functions with certainty whereas any classical algorithm requires $O(2^n)$ steps to achieve the same task.

Deutsch's algorithm is a so-called "oracle result" or "relativised" separation result (relative to an oracle). It does not provide an *absolute* exponential separation between quantum and classical computation but gives this separation only if we make some further (plausible but unproven) computational assumptions related to the fact that we are forbidden access to the internal workings of the oracle. In effect we have assumed that, if we are given a program which computes f, there is no mechanical way of using the syntax of a general such program to determine whether f is constant or balanced, more quickly than by just running the program a sufficient number of times. Of course, a constant function for example, may have a very short program which may be recognised immediately as computing a constant function but an adversary may also provide a very complicated disguised program which still computes a constant function, and this may be very hard to see by reading the syntax. Although this assumption is very plausible it remains unproven as it is very difficult to analyse algorithms which operate on the syntax of a program as input! We remark that if an *absolute* exponential separation between classical and quantum computation could be proved it would resolve some long standing fundamental open questions in classical complexity theory (e.g. it would imply that $P \neq PSPACE$; see [131] for a definition of these terms). Thus it is likely to be very difficult to formally prove that quantum computation is exponentially more powerful than classical computation.

Another significant feature of Deutsch's algorithm is that if the algorithm is not required to work perfectly, i.e. if we tolerate some (arbitrarily small) error in the answer, then the displayed exponential separation between classical and quantum computation collapses. Indeed given any $\epsilon > 0$ there is a classical (probabilistic) algorithm running for a *constant* number of steps (independent of n!), which will distinguish balanced from constant functions, providing an answer that is correct with probability $(1 - \epsilon)$ for any given choice of f. This algorithm runs simply as follows. We evaluate f on some K *randomly* chosen inputs. If the answers are all the same then f is deemed to be constant. Otherwise it is deemed to be balanced. A little thought shows that the answer 'balanced' is always correct and the answer 'constant' will be correct with probability of error less than $1/2^K$. Thus for any given $\epsilon > 0$ we choose K large enough to have $\frac{1}{2^K} < \epsilon$. Note that K is independent of n so the K evaluations count as a constant number of steps in the algorithm.

It is only in the limiting case of $\epsilon = 0$ that the exponential separation between quantum and classical computation occurs. One may argue that this limiting situation is actually unphysical because any computer, being a physical device, can never be perfectly isolated from its environment. Thus it always has some (generally very small) probability of functioning incorrectly, e.g. a memory bit may be flipped by a cosmic ray at any time. Hence it is of great interest to exhibit a computational task whose computational complexity separates quantum from classical computation by an exponential amount even if a small error in the result is tolerated. The first such example was given by Bernstein and Vazirani [140]. Using a recursive construction they described a computational task involving an oracle which could be solved on a quantum computer in polynomial time but which required $O(n^{\log n})$

time on a classical computer. Then Simon [141] described a simpler oracle problem which could be solved in $O(n^2)$ time on a quantum computer but required fully exponential time (i.e. $O(2^n)$ time) on a classical computer. The apotheosis of this line of development was the algorithm of Shor [36] for factorisation which also eliminated the dependence on an oracle. Shor's algorithm provides a method for factorising an integer N in a number of steps which is polynomial (less than cubic) in the number of digits $(\log N)$ of N and returns a correct result with probability $1 - \epsilon$ for any prescribed $\epsilon > 0$. Despite a great deal of effort for some hundreds of years (by eminent mathematicians such as Gauss, Legendre, Fermat and others) there is no known *classical* probabilistic polynomial time algorithm for this problem. Unlike the algorithms of Deutsch and Simon, Shor's algorithm does not involve an oracle. However this does not provide a proof of an absolute exponential benefit of quantum computation over classical computation because there is also no known *proof* that a classical polynomial time factoring algorithm does not exist (only an immense wealth of unsuccessful attempts at constructing such an algorithm!)

4.2.5 The Fourier Transform and Periodicities

Shor's quantum factoring algorithm and Simon's algorithm will depend in an essential way on a quantum computer's remarkable ability to efficiently determine the periodicity of a given periodic function. We illustrate the ideas involved with the following basic example. Suppose that we have a black box which computes a function $f : \mathcal{Z}_N \to \mathcal{Z}$ that is guaranteed to be periodic with some period r:

$$f(x + r) = f(x) \qquad \text{for all } x. \tag{4.11}$$

Recall that $\mathcal{Z}_N$ denotes the group of integers modulo N and addition here is modulo N. We also assume that f does not take the same value twice within any single period. Note that (4.11) can hold only if r divides N exactly.

Our aim is to determine r. Classically (in the absence of any further information about f) we can merely try different values of x in the black box hoping for two equal results which will then give information about r. Generally we will require $O(N)$ random tries to hit two equal values with high probability. Using quantum effects we will be able to find r using only $O((\log N)^2)$ steps, which represents an exponential speedup over any classical algorithm.

We begin by using quantum parallel computation to compute all values of f in equal superposition, resulting in the state

$$|f\rangle = \frac{1}{\sqrt{N}} \sum_{x=0}^{N-1} |x\rangle |f(x)\rangle. \tag{4.12}$$

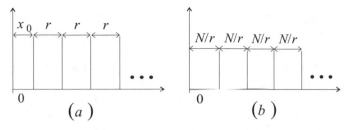

Fig. 4.7. Graphical representation of the periodic amplitudes of (a) the state $|\psi\rangle$ and (b) its Fourier transform. In passing to $\mathcal{F}|\psi\rangle$ the periodicity r has been inverted to N/r and the random shift x_0 has been eliminated.

Although this state embodies the periodicity of f it is not immediately clear how to extract the information of r! If we measure the value in the second register, giving a value y_0 say, then the state of the first register will be reduced to an equal superposition of all those $|x\rangle$'s such that $f(x) = y_0$. If x_0 is the least such x and $N = Kr$ then we will obtain in the first register the periodic state

$$|\psi\rangle = \frac{1}{\sqrt{K}} \sum_{k=0}^{K-1} |x_0 + kr\rangle .$$ (4.13)

It is important to note here that $0 \leq x_0 \leq r-1$ has been generated at random, corresponding to having seen any value y_0 of f with equal probability. So if we now measure the value in this register, the overall result is merely to produce a number between 0 and $N-1$ uniformly at random, giving no information at all about the value of r!

The resolution of this difficulty is to use the Fourier transform which, even for classical data, is known to be able to pick out periodic patterns in a set of data regardless of how the whole pattern is shifted. The discrete Fourier transform $\mathcal{F}$ for integers modulo N is the N by N unitary matrix with entries

$$\mathcal{F}_{ab} = \frac{1}{\sqrt{N}} e^{2\pi i \frac{ab}{N}} .$$ (4.14)

If we apply this unitary transform to the state $|\psi\rangle$ above then we obtain [144]

$$\mathcal{F}|\psi\rangle = \frac{1}{\sqrt{r}} \sum_{j=0}^{r-1} e^{2\pi i \frac{x_0 j}{r}} \left| j \frac{N}{r} \right\rangle .$$ (4.15)

The important point to note here is that the random shift x_0 no longer appears in the ket labels (see Fig. 4.7).

If we now read the label we will obtain a value c say, which is necessarily a multiple of N/r, i.e. $c = \lambda N/r$. Thus we can write

$$\frac{c}{N} = \frac{\lambda}{r} ,$$ (4.16)

where c and N are known numbers and and $0 \leq \lambda \leq r - 1$ has been chosen uniformly at random by the measurement (as all amplitudes in $\mathcal{F} | \psi \rangle$ have equal size.) Now if the randomly chosen λ is fortuitously coprime to r (i.e. λ and r have no common factors) we can determine r by cancelling c/N down to an irreducible fraction. What is the probability that a randomly chosen r actually *is* coprime to r? According to the prime number theorem (c.f. [142, 143] and appendix A of [144]), the number of prime numbers less than or equal to r goes as $r/\log r$ for large r. Thus the probability that our randomly chosen λ is coprime to r is at least $1/\log r$ which exceeds $1/\log N$. Hence if we repeat the above procedure $O(\log N)$ times we can succeed in determining r with any prescribed probability $1 - \epsilon$ as close to 1 as desired.

We noted above that we want our quantum algorithm for determining r to run in time poly$(\log N)$, i.e. in a number of steps which is polynomial in $\log N$ rather than N itself, to achieve an exponential speed up over any known classical algorithm for determining periodicity. We showed above that $O(\log N)$ repetitions suffice to determine r but there is still a significant gap in our argument: the Fourier transform $\mathcal{F}$ that we used is a large non-trivial unitary operation, of size $N \times N$, and we cannot *ab initio* just assume that it can be implemented using only poly $(\log N)$ basic computational operations. Indeed it may be shown that any $d \times d$ unitary operation may be implemented on a quantum computer (equipped with any universal set of operations) in $O(d^2)$ steps [124, 144]. This is also the number of steps needed for the classical computation of multiplying a $d \times d$ matrix into a d dimensional column vector. For our use of $\mathcal{F}$ this bound of $O(N^2)$ does not suffice. Fortunately the Fourier transform has extra special properties which enable it to be implemented in $O((\log N)^2)$ steps. These properties stem from the classical theory of the fast Fourier transform (FFT) [145] which shows how to reduce the $O(N^2)$ steps of classical matrix multiplication to $O(N \log N)$ steps. If the same ideas are implemented in a quantum setting then the principle of local operations may be seen [134, 144] to reduce the number of steps to $O((\log N)^2)$ giving our desired implementation. Having made this important point we will omit the considerable technical details of the FFT construction and its implementation in a quantum setting. These details are elaborated in [134] to which we refer the interested reader. Note also that according to (4.14) we have

$$\mathcal{F} | 0 \rangle = \frac{1}{\sqrt{n}} \sum_{x=0}^{N-1} | x \rangle \,, \qquad (4.17)$$

so that once we have an efficient implementation of $\mathcal{F}$ we will be able to efficiently produce the uniform large superposition necessary to get $| f \rangle$ in (4.12).

In summary, the quantum algorithm for determining the periodicity of a given function f, with N inputs, begins with an application of quantum parallel computation to compute all values of f in superposition using $O(\log N)$ steps. The the Fourier transform is applied to pick out the periodic structure of the resulting state. The principle of local operations applied to the quantum implementation of the FFT algorithm guarantees that the Fourier transform may be implemented in poly($\log N$) steps. An analogous classical computation would require $O(N)$ invocations of f to compute a column vector of all the function values and then $O(N \log N)$ steps to perform the FFT. Thus the quantum algorithm represents an exponential speedup.

It is interesting to observe that the concept of periodicity and the construction of the Fourier transform may be extended to apply to *any* finite group G. Our discussion above pertains simply to the special case of the additive group of integers modulo N. The generalised viewpoint provides considerable insight into the workings of the Fourier transform. We will now briefly outline some of the essential ideas involved, restricting attention to the case of finite Abelian groups. (The remainder of this section may be omitted, if desired, without any loss of continuity with the following sections.)

Let G be any finite Abelian group. Let $f : G \to X$ be a function on the group (taking values in some set X) and consider

$$K = \{k \in G : f(k + g) = f(g) \text{ for all } g \in G\}. \tag{4.18}$$

(Note that we write the group operation in additive notation). K is necessarily a subgroup of G called the stabiliser or symmetry group of f. It characterises the periodicity of f with respect to the group operation of G. In our previous example G was $\mathcal{Z}_N$ and K was the cyclic subgroup of all multiples of r. Given a device that computes f, our aim is to determine K. More precisely we wish to determine K in time $O(\text{poly}(\log |G|))$ where $|G|$ is the size of the group and the evaluation of f on an input counts as one computational step. (Note that we may easily determine K in time $O(\text{poly}(|G|))$ by simply evaluating and examining all the values of f). We begin as in our example by constructing the state

$$|f\rangle = \frac{1}{\sqrt{|G|}} \sum_{g \in G} |g\rangle |f(g)\rangle \tag{4.19}$$

and read the second register. Assuming that f is suitably non-degenerate – in the sense that $f(g_1) = f(g_2)$ iff $g_1 - g_2 \in K$, i.e. that f is one-to-one within each period – we will obtain in the first register

$$|\psi(g_0)\rangle = \frac{1}{\sqrt{|K|}} \sum_{k \in K} |g_0 + k\rangle, \tag{4.20}$$

corresponding to seeing $f(g_0)$ in the second register and g_0 has been chosen at random. In (4.20) we have an equal superposition of labels corresponding to a randomly chosen coset of K in G. Now G is the disjoint union of all the cosets so that if we read the label in (4.20) we will see a random element of a random coset, i.e. a label chosen equiprobably from all of G, yielding no information at all about K.

The general construction of a "Fourier transform on G" will provide a way of eliminating g_0 from the labels (just as in our example) and the resulting state will then provide direct information about K. Let $\mathcal{H}$ be a Hilbert space with a basis $\{|g\rangle : g \in G\}$ labelled by the elements of G. Each group element $g_1 \in G$ gives rise to a unitary "shifting" operator $U(g_1)$ on $\mathcal{H}$ defined by

$$U(g_1)|g\rangle = |g + g_1\rangle \qquad \text{for all } g. \tag{4.21}$$

Note that the state in (4.20) may be written as a g_0-shifted state:

$$\sum_{k \in K} |g_0 + k\rangle = U(g_0)\left(\sum_{k \in K} |k\rangle\right). \tag{4.22}$$

Our basic idea now is to introduce into $\mathcal{H}$ a new basis $\{|\chi_g\rangle : g \in G\}$ of special states which are *shift-invariant* in the sense that

$$U(g_1)|\chi_{g_2}\rangle = e^{i\phi(g_1, g_2)}|\chi_{g_2}\rangle \qquad \text{for all } g_1, g_2, \tag{4.23}$$

i.e. the $|\chi_g\rangle$'s are the common eigenstates of all the shifting operations $U(g)$. Note that the $U(g)$'s all commute so such a basis of common eigenstates is guaranteed to exist. Then according to (4.22) if we view $|\psi(g_0)\rangle$ in the new basis then $\sum_{k \in K}|k\rangle$ and $\sum_{k \in K}|g_0 + k\rangle$ will contain the same pattern of labels, determined by the subgroup K only. Reading the label in the new basis will then directly provide information about the constituent elements of K.

The Fourier transform $\mathcal{F}$ on G is defined to simply be the unitary transformation which takes the shift-invariant basis back to the standard basis:

$$\mathcal{F}|\chi_g\rangle = |g\rangle \qquad \text{for all } g. \tag{4.24}$$

Hence to read $|\psi(g_0)\rangle$ in the new basis we just apply $\mathcal{F}$ and read in the standard basis.

To give an explicit construction of $\mathcal{F}$ it suffices to give the states $|\chi_g\rangle$ written as components in the standard basis. There is a standard way of calculating these components based on constructions from group representation theory. We omit the details here but the interested reader will find an introduction in [134] and [146]. For the group $\mathcal{Z}_N$ we get

$$|\chi_k\rangle = \frac{1}{\sqrt{N}}\sum_{j=0}^{N-1} e^{2\pi i \frac{jk}{N}}|j\rangle \tag{4.25}$$

leading to the Fourier transform formula given in (4.14).

The above group-theoretic framework serves to generalise and extend the applicability of the quantum algorithm for periodicity determination. For example, Simon's quantum algorithm [134, 141, 146, 147] turns out to be just a periodicity determination on the group $(\mathcal{Z}_2)^n$, the group of all n-bit strings with componentwise addition modulo 2. Simon considered the following problem: suppose that we have a black box which computes a function f from n-bit strings to n-bit strings. It is also promised that the function is "two-to-one" in the sense that there is a fixed n-bit string ξ such that

$$f(x + \xi) = f(x) \qquad \text{for all } n\text{-bit strings } x. \tag{4.26}$$

Our problem is to determine ξ.

To see that this is just a generalised periodicity determination, note that in the group $(\mathcal{Z}_2)^n$ of n-bit strings, every element satisfies $x + x = 0$. Hence (4.26) states just that f is periodic on the group with periodicity subgroup $K = \{0, \xi\}$. Thus to determine ξ we construct the Fourier transform on the group of n-bit strings and apply the standard algorithm above. The relevant Hilbert space $\mathcal{H}$ with a basis labelled by n-bit strings is just a row of n qubits. Using the general constructions of group representation theory, the Fourier transform may be seen [134] to be the application of H (from (4.1)) to each of the n qubits. The quantum algorithm determines ξ in $O(n^2)$ steps whereas it may be argued [141] that any classical algorithm must evaluate f at least $O(2^n)$ times. A full description of the algorithm may be found in [141, 146, 147].

The Fourier transform formalism has emerged as the most important ingredient in the quantum algorithms discovered so far. Some interesting further developments of it, including the extension to non-Abelian groups, may be found in [148, 149].

4.2.6 Shor's Quantum Algorithm for Factorisation

The most celebrated quantum algorithm devised to date is Shor's efficient algorithm for factorisation [36, 144, 146]. Given a number N we wish to determine a number k (not equal to 1 or N) which divides N exactly. In this section we will outline how this problem may be reduced to a problem of periodicity determination for a suitable periodic function f. Then the quantum algorithm described in the preceding section will achieve the factorisation of N in poly($\log N$) time, i.e. polynomial in the number of digits of N.

We note first that there is no known classical algorithm which will factorise any given N in a time polynomial in the number of digits of N. For example the most naive factoring algorithm involves test-dividing N by each number from 1 to $\sqrt{N}$ (as any composite N must have a factor in this range). This requires at least $\sqrt{N}$ steps (at least one step for each trial factor) and $\sqrt{N} = 2^{\frac{1}{2}\log N}$ is exponential in $\log N$. In fact using all the ingenuity of modern mathematics, the fastest known classical factoring algorithm runs in a time of order $\exp((\log N)^{\frac{1}{3}}(\log\log N)^{\frac{2}{3}})$.

To reduce the problem of factoring N to a problem of periodicity we will need to use some basic results from number theory. These are further described in the appendix of [144] and complete expositions may be found in most standard texts on number theory such as [142, 143]. We begin by selecting a number $a < N$ at random. Using Euclid's algorithm, we compute in poly$(\log N)$ time, the highest common factor of a and N. If this is larger than 1, we will have found a factor of N and we are finished! However it is overwhelmingly likely that a randomly chosen a will be coprime to N. The prime number theorem (mentioned in the last section) implies that this probability will be exceed $1/\log N$ for large N. If a is coprime to N, then Euler's theorem of number theory guarantees that there is a power of a which has remainder 1 when divided by N. Let r be the smallest such power:

$$a^r \equiv 1 \mod N \qquad \text{and } r \text{ is the least such power.} \tag{4.27}$$

(If a is not coprime to N, then no power of a has remainder 1). r is called the *order* of a modulo N. Next we show that the information of r can provide a factor of N.

Suppose that we have a method for determining r (see below) and suppose further that r comes out to be an *even* number. Then we can rewrite (4.27) as $a^r - 1 \equiv 0 \mod N$ and factorise as a difference of squares:

$$(a^{r/2} - 1)(a^{r/2} + 1) \equiv 0 \mod N. \tag{4.28}$$

Let $\alpha = a^{r/2} - 1$ and $\beta = a^{r/2} + 1$. Then N exactly divides the product $\alpha\beta$. If neither α nor β is a multiple of N then N must divide partly into α and partly into β. Thus computing the highest common factor of N with α and β (again using Euclid's algorithm) will generate a non-trivial factor of N.

As an example take $N = 15$ and choose the coprime number $a = 7$. By computing the powers of 7 modulo 15 we find that $7^4 \equiv 1 \mod 15$, i.e. the order of 7 modulo 15 is 4. Thus 15 must exactly divide the product $(7^{4/2} - 1)(7^{4/2} + 1) = (48)(50)$. Computing the highest common factor of 15 with 50 and 48 gives 5 and 3 respectively, which are indeed nontrivial factors of 15.

Our method will give a factor of N provided that r comes out to be even and that neither of $(a^{r/2} \pm 1)$ are exact multiples of N. To guarantee that these conditions occur often enough (for randomly chosen a's) we have
Theorem: Let N be odd and suppose that $a < N$ coprime to N is chosen at random. Let r be the order of a modulo N. Then the probability that r is even and $a^{r/2} \pm 1$ are not exact multiples of N is always $\geq \frac{1}{2}$. $\square$
The (somewhat lengthy) proof of this theorem may be found in appendix B of [144], to which we refer the reader for details.

Overall, our method will produce a factor of N with probability at least half in every case. This success probability may be amplified as close as desired to 1, since K repetitions of the procedure (with K constant independent of N) will succeed in factorising N with probability exceeding $1 - \frac{1}{2^K}$.

All steps in the procedure, such as applying Euclid's algorithm and the arithmetic manipulation of numbers, can be done in poly$(\log N)$ time. The only remaining outstanding ingredient is a method for determining r in poly($\log N$) time. Consider the exponential function:

$$f(x) = a^x \mod N. \tag{4.29}$$

Now (4.27) says precisely that f is periodic with period r, i.e. that $f(x+r)$ $= f(x)$. Thus we use the quantum algorithm for periodicity determination, described in the previous section, to find r. To apply the algorithm as stated, we need to restrict the scope of x values in (4.29) to a *finite* range $0 \leq x \leq q$ for some q. If q is not an exact multiple of (the unknown) r, i.e. $q = Ar + t$ for some $0 < t < r$, then the resulting function will not be exactly periodic – the single final period over the last t values will be incomplete. However if q is chosen large enough, giving sufficiently many intact periods of f, then the single corrupted period will have negligible effect on the use of the $q \times q$ Fourier transform to determine r, as we might intuitively expect. In fact it may be shown that if q is chosen to have size $O(N^2)$ then we get a reliable efficient determination of r. For the technical analysis of this imperfect periodicity (involving the theory of continued fractions) we refer the reader to [36, 144]. q is also generally chosen to be a power of 2 which fits in particularly well with the formalism of *fast* Fourier transforms (c.f. [134, 145]).

4.2.7 Quantum Searching and NP

Suppose that we have a database consisting of an unsorted unstructured list of N records and at most one of the records satisfies a given property of interest. We want to locate the special record. Any classical method which locates the record with some constant probability (independent of N) will require $O(N)$ steps. Indeed elementary probability theory shows that if we examine k of the records then we have probability k/N of finding the special record. This probability tends to 0 with increasing N unless k is at least of order N. Grover's quantum searching algorithm [120, 150] solves the problem with only $O(\sqrt{N})$ steps. Thus quantum effects can provide a square root speedup in this problem which should be contrasted to the much greater exponential speedup exhibited by the previously discussed quantum algorithms. In Grover's algorithm we will require the ability to examine different records in superposition just as our previous algorithms evaluated functions on superpositions of input values.

The assumption of unstructuredness of the database is very important for the result. For example if the database consisted of N random numbers which are *sorted* in ascending order then we would need only $O(\log N)$ steps classically (using a standard bisection method) to locate any given one of the numbers. Similarly any prior known structure of the database might be exploited to reduce the search time. The unstructuredness assumption is analogous to our previous use of oracles (or black boxes) whose internal structure we were unable to access. In fact the database searching problem

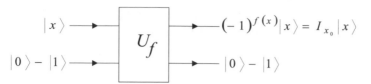

Fig. 4.8. The construction of I_{x_0} from U_f. Here f is the oracle which marks x_0.

may be more accurately re-phrased in terms of an oracle as follows: we are given a black box which computes a function of N inputs, with output values 0 or 1. Furthermore it is promised that $f(x) = 1$ for exactly one input value x_0 (all other values of f being 0). Our task is to find x_0.

We will now outline Grover's quantum searching algorithm for finding x_0 in $O(\sqrt{N})$ steps. (The following technical details may be omitted if preferred at first reading, without essential loss of continuity, noting the features of the algorithm already described above.) As in our discussion of Deutsch's algorithm and quantum parallel computation, we will assume that the oracle is given as a unitary transformation U_f which transforms $|x\rangle|j\rangle$ into $|x\rangle|j \oplus f(x)\rangle$. Here $1 \le x \le N$, $j = 0$ or 1 and $\oplus$ is addition modulo 2. It will also be convenient to restrict attention to the case where $N = 2^n$ i.e. N is a power of 2 so that f is a function from n bits to one bit. Let $\mathcal{B}^n$ be the Hilbert space of n qubits (i.e. the input register) with a standard basis $\{|x\rangle\}$ labelled by all n-bit strings x. The original form of Grover's algorithm is based on two unitary operations I_{x_0} and D, each acting on $\mathcal{B}^n$. I_{x_0} is the operation which merely inverts the amplitude of $|x_0\rangle$:

$$I_{x_0}|x\rangle = \begin{cases} |x\rangle & \text{if } x \ne x_0 \\ -|x\rangle & \text{if } x = x_0 \end{cases} . \tag{4.30}$$

This is easily constructed from U_f by first setting its output register (the last of $n + 1$ qubits) to $\frac{1}{\sqrt{2}}(|0\rangle - |1\rangle)$ just as we did in Deutsch's algorithm. The action of U_f then effects I_{x_0} on the input register while leaving the output register in state $\frac{1}{\sqrt{2}}(|0\rangle - |1\rangle)$ (see Fig. 4.8).

The operator D is defined as follows. Let H_n be the application of H (c.f. (4.1)) to each of the n qubits and let I_0 be the operator I_{x_0} with $x = 00\ldots0$. Then D is defined by

$$D = -H_n I_0 H_n . \tag{4.31}$$

A direct computation of the matrix elements of D [120, 150] shows that all off-diagonal elements are $\frac{2}{N}$ and all diagonal elements are $-1 + \frac{2}{N}$ (recalling that $N = 2^n$ here). Hence

$$D|x\rangle = -|x\rangle + \frac{2}{N}\sum_y |y\rangle . \tag{4.32}$$

D has a simple geometrical interpretation as being "inversion about the mean". For any state $|\psi\rangle = \sum a_x |x\rangle$ let $D|\psi\rangle = \sum a'_x |x\rangle$ and let $\bar{a} = \frac{1}{N} \sum a_x$ denote the average amplitude for the state $|\psi\rangle$. Using (4.32) we get

$$a'_x = -a_x + \frac{2}{N} \sum_y a_y = \bar{a} - (a_x - \bar{a}). \tag{4.33}$$

Writing $\Delta a_x = a_x - \bar{a}$ we have that $a_x = \bar{a} + \Delta a_x$ and $a'_x = \bar{a} - \Delta a_x$ so that the values of the amplitudes are just reflected in the mean $\bar{a}$.

To perform Grover's algorithm we begin with an equal superposition $|\psi_0\rangle = \frac{1}{\sqrt{N}} \sum |x\rangle$ which may be prepared, for example, by applying H_n to $|0\ldots 0\rangle$. This state corresponds to examining the database at all positions in equal superposition. Our aim is to modify $|\psi_0\rangle$ to concentrate the amplitude at $x = x_0$. The algorithm consists of repeatedly applying the operator DI_{x_0} giving a sequence of states $|\psi_k\rangle$:

$$\begin{aligned} |\psi_0\rangle &= \tfrac{1}{\sqrt{N}} \sum |x\rangle \\ |\psi_{k+1}\rangle &= DI_{x_0} |\psi_k\rangle \,. \end{aligned} \tag{4.34}$$

Using our expressions for D and I_{x_0} it is easy to see that the amplitudes of all $|x\rangle$'s with $x \neq x_0$ remain equal to each other so that each $|\psi_k\rangle$ has the form

$$|\psi_k\rangle = \alpha_k \sum_{x \neq x_0} |x\rangle + \beta_k |x_0\rangle \,, \tag{4.35}$$

where α_k and β_k are also real. Using the matrix elements of D and I_{x_0} we can derive the recurrence relations:

$$\begin{aligned} \alpha_0 &= \beta_0 = \tfrac{1}{\sqrt{N}} \\ \alpha_{k+1} &= (1 - \tfrac{2}{N})\alpha_k - \tfrac{2}{N}\beta_k \\ \beta_{k+1} &= (1 - \tfrac{2}{N})\beta_k + (N - 1)\tfrac{2}{N}\alpha_k \,. \end{aligned} \tag{4.36}$$

Normalisation gives

$$\beta_k^2 + (N - 1)\alpha_k^2 = 1 \,, \tag{4.37}$$

which suggests that we write $\alpha_k = \frac{1}{\sqrt{N-1}} \cos\theta_k$ and $\beta_k = \sin\theta_k$. It is then straightforward to verify [151] that the recurrence relations in (4.36) are satisfied by

$$\alpha_k = \frac{1}{\sqrt{N-1}} \cos(2k+1)\theta \,, \qquad \beta_k = \sin(2k+1)\theta \,, \tag{4.38}$$

where θ is the angle given by $\sin\theta = \frac{1}{\sqrt{N}}$.

Thus β_k varies sinusoidally with the number of iterations k. We will have $\beta_k = 1$ if $(2k+1)\theta = \pi/2$ i.e. if $k = \frac{\pi-2\theta}{4\theta}$. For large N, we have $\sin\theta = \frac{1}{\sqrt{N}} \approx \theta$ and then $k = \frac{\pi}{4}\sqrt{N} - \frac{1}{2}$ which is of order $\sqrt{N}$. Thus if we iterate the process for a number of steps given by the whole number nearest to this value of k, then x_0 may be obtained with a high probability (independent of N) by reading the final state in the standard basis (c.f. [151] for a further analysis of the probabilities involved.) This completes the algorithm.

Since Grover's original work, the basic ideas involved in the above algorithm have been extended to a variety of further applications such as estimating the mean and median of a database of N given numbers [152] and the analysis of the case of more than one marked item in a database [151, 153]. Using an ingenious combination of Grover's algorithm and Shor's algorithm, Brassard, Hoyer and Tapp have shown [153] that it is also possible to estimate the *number* of such marked items (rather than locating their positions). The underlying idea, broadly speaking, is to note that the amplitudes α_k and β_k above vary periodically with a period that is determined by the number of marked items. The periodicity is then estimated using the quantum Fourier transform, as described in preceding sections. It has also been shown [151, 153, 154] that, somewhat surprisingly at first sight, the unitary operation H_n in the definition of D may be replaced by almost any unitary operator U and the algorithm with the modified D still succeeds in finding x_0 in $O(\sqrt{N})$ steps.

Grover's algorithm provides a means of searching an exponentially large space of possibilities. Exponential searches in general are of fundamental importance in many branches of mathematics and computer science. Of particular interest is the situation in which the desired property (for which we are searching) can be verified to hold for any proposed item in *polynomial* time, i.e. intuitively the property itself is "computationally simple" to verify but we need to determine whether an example exists amongst an exponentially large number of candidates. As an illustrative example, suppose we are given a graph, described as a set of vertices and edges connecting selected vertices. A graph with n vertices may be coded as an $n \times n$ matrix of 0's and 1's with entry 1 in position ij if and only if there is an edge connecting vertex i to vertex j. We want to decide whether it is possible to find a closed path through the graph which visits each vertex once and only once. This is the so-called Hamiltonian circuit problem which has many important applications. Now given a graph, there is generally an exponential number of possible circuits (i.e. exponentially many as a function of the size of the description of the graph) but given any circuit it is easy to check in polynomial time whether it satisfies the required condition or not (i.e. just go around the circuit and see if it visits each vertex exactly once or not). In the theory of computation the class of all decision problems of this sort is called NP (c.f. [131, 132] for an extensive discussion). Intuitively for NP properties, it is "hard" to find a satisfying instance but given a proposed instance, it is "easy" to check whether the property holds or not.

Many computational problems of great mathematical and practical interest lie in NP (c.f. [132] for a long and varied list of examples). Perhaps the most famous unsolved problem of classical complexity theory, the so-called $P \neq NP$ problem, is to establish whether every computational task in NP can in fact be solved in polynomial time or not. The motivating idea here is that if a property is "computationally simple" to verify then maybe the question of whether or not it held in a given structure, should also be able to be decided in polynomial time. Note that here we are not thinking of an exhaustive search amongst exponentially many candidates (which certainly must take exponential time) but of some clever analysis of the structure itself that generated the exponentially many possibilities. For example in the Hamiltonian circuit problem, is there a way of examining the description of the graph itself to see if it has a Hamiltonian circuit or not, instead of just unintelligently testing each circuit in turn?

Considering the intricacy and wide-ranging scope of some problems in NP [132] it would appear unlikely that they can be solved in polynomial time but this issue so far remains unproven, despite a great deal of attention! Note that some special mathematical properties of the particular structure of the problem would need to be invoked, e.g. in the Hamiltonian circuit problem the solution would be tantamount to developing some deep new theorem of graph theory.

Let us now return to the scenario of Grover's search algorithm. Here the database was required to be *unstructured* (in contrast to the above remark) yet by quantum methods, we achieved a square root speed up over a direct exhaustive classical search. This speed up can be applied to a blind search in any NP problem. The crucial question now is this: can a search through an *unstructured* space of exponentially many candidates be *further* speeded up using quantum effects in some even more ingenious way? Indeed we have seen that exponentially large superpositions can be generated in linear time (4.3) and that these large superpositions can then be used to probe exponentially many values of a function using only a single query (c.f. (4.4)). In the early days of quantum computation, it was hoped that this effect might lead to a method of searching an exponentially large unstructured space of possibilities in polynomial time leading possibly to a quantum method of solving NP problems in polynomial time. For example given a graph we can look at all possible circuits in superposition but can we use this effect to determine, with high probability, whether there is a Hamiltonian circuit or not? This hope was dashed by Bennett, Bernstein, Brassard and Vazirani [155] who proved rigorously that no quantum process can speedup an unstructured search beyond the square root speed up exhibited in Grover's algorithm. Roughly speaking the intuitive idea is that, although we can examine exponentially many candidates in superposition in one query, the registering of the desired property will generally occur only with an exponentially small amplitude because of the exponential number of components in the superposition. Hence the process will have to be repeated an exponential number of times to register the property with any constant level of probability.

Thus in the context of quantum computation, just as in classical computation, if we are to solve NP problems in polynomial time, it will be essential to exploit the structure of the problem in some intelligent way. For example the exponential speedup in the algorithms of Simon and Shor makes use of special mathematical properties of the theory of periodicity via the techniques of Fourier analysis. Unfortunately the important question of the relation of the whole class NP to polynomial time computability, appears on the face of it to be no easier to resolve in the quantum context than in the context of classical computational complexity theory.

4.3 Quantum Gates and Quantum Computation with Trapped Ions

J.I. Cirac, P. Zoller, J.F. Poyatos

4.3.1 Introduction

It is clear from the preceding discussion in this chapter that quantum computation can offer amazing power. The question is: can we implement basic elements of quantum computation, such as quantum logic gates, and if so, how and in what kind of physical systems. Instead of a general discussion we will focus on one particular example. We will describe in some detail proposals related to the implementation of a quantum computer with trapped ions [156, 157]. In this scheme, each qubit is implemented as a superposition of the ground electronic state ($|0\rangle$) and the excited (metastable) state ($|1\rangle$) of an ion (see Fig. 4.9). It will be shown that a set of ions interacting with laser light and moving in a linear trap provides a realistic physical system to realise a quantum computer.

4.3.2 Quantum Gates with Trapped Ions

We will consider the situation where N ions are confined in a linear Paul trap, which is able to trap and confine the ions by means of a combination of static and ac electric fields (see Chap. 5). The ions basically move in only

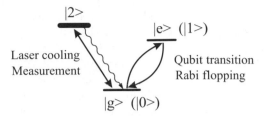

Fig. 4.9. Double resonance structure of the internal levels of a single ion. Those levels associated with the weak transition act as a qubit ($|0\rangle, |1\rangle$), while the third level, $|2\rangle$, connected to the $|0\rangle$ state by a dipole allowed transition is used for cooling and detection, by means of the quantum jump technique.

one dimension, the axial–direction, because in this direction the trapping potential is rather weak, and interact with different laser fields (Fig. 4.10).

The coupling of the motion of the ions is provided by the Coulomb repulsion which is much stronger than any other interaction for typical separation between the ions of a few optical wavelengths.

One of the initial advantages of the trapped ion system is that many of the required techniques to prepare and manipulate quantum states have already been developed for the purpose of high precision spectroscopy and frequency standards. Thus, Rabi floppings and measurements of the electronic states are both well developed tools, that will constitute basic parts of the computation. While Rabi flopping, i.e. coherent transitions between the internal states, are performed by applying a laser pulse for a fixed time (for example, a π pulse inverts completely the population from the excited to the ground state or vice versa), measurements of the internal quantum state are performed using the so-called quantum jump technique. Considering a double resonance situation, where one transition is strongly resonant, the other one being weaker, it is possible to measure the state of the selected levels chosen as qubits. This is done by using two laser beams tuned to each transition respectively. The state of the qubit will be measured by the presence or absence of spontaneously emitted light from the (dipole-allowed) strong transition, see Fig. 4.9. This scheme for detection has been proved to be of almost unit efficiency. On the other hand, we will also make use of laser cooling techniques to reduce the movement of the ions to small oscillations around their equilibrium position. In brief, laser cooling is based on the efficient use of radiation pressure, the momentum associated with every light beam. Such a momentum, negligible on a macroscopic scale, can nevertheless exert big enough forces on the atoms to considerably reduce their velocities (this force can be as big as $10^4 g$, where g is the acceleration due to gravity). An efficient way of using such forces is by means of the Doppler effect: in this way, ions moving opposite to the direction of propagation of the laser beam will experience a force able to considerably slow their motion.

Let us assume that the ions have been laser cooled in all three dimensions so that they merely undergo very small oscillations around the equilibrium position. In this case, the motion of the ions is described in terms of normal modes, being equivalent to a collection of uncoupled harmonic oscillators that can be quantized independently in the usual way. As a requirement, it is necessary to fulfill the so-called Lamb–Dicke limit for each mode, which physically means that the ion is confined in a region much smaller than the wavelength of the applied radiation.

The task of implementing a quantum computer will be equivalent to finding ways to implement single and two–qubit gates. Single qubit gates will be simple, since all we need is to induce Rabi flopping between the internal states of the qubit. As we already mentioned, this is a well known technique in the case of the trapped ions. Two-qubit gates will be more difficult to realise. The main difficulty is to find a way to connect quantum mechanically, i.e. maintaining the coherent superpositions, two qubits. To do this, we will consider the external degrees of freedom associated with the string of ions. In particular, we make use of the lowest quantized mode, the centre-of-mass (CM) motion describing the motion of all ions as if they were a joined single mass. The challenge is to swap information from the internal qubit onto the *quantum wire*, the CM motion. Once this is achieved, it will be possible to transfer the information from the *quantum wire* onto another selected qubit, realising in this way a coherent interaction between two qubits.

4.3.3 N Cold Ions Interacting with Laser Light

This section will be a little bit more technical, showing in more detail how to describe the system of ions and lasers and its ability to realise quantum computation. We consider the interaction of a given ion i with a standing laser wave (a travelling wave could be studied in the same way). The Hamiltonian describing this situation, in a frame rotating with the laser frequency, is given by $H = H_{\mathrm{ex}} + H_{\mathrm{int}} + H_{\mathrm{las}}$, where $(\hbar = 1)$

$$H_{\mathrm{ex}} = \sum_{k=1}^{N} \nu_k a_k^\dagger a_k,$$

$$H_{\mathrm{int}}^i = -\frac{\delta_i}{2} \sigma_z^i,$$

$$H_{\mathrm{las}}^i = \frac{\Omega_i}{2} \sin(k_{\mathrm{L}} r_i + \phi_i)(\sigma_i^+ + \sigma_i^-). \tag{4.39}$$

Here, $\delta_i = \omega_{\mathrm{L}}^i - \omega_0^i$ is the laser detuning (ω_{L}^i being the frequency of the laser and ω_0^i the frequency associated with the qubit transition), ν_k is the frequency of the different normal modes, Ω_i is the Rabi frequency[1] (the rate of coherent

---

[1] This name is due to I. I. Rabi who developed the initial idea of using an oscillator-driven magnetic field to induce transitions between internal levels of atoms and molecules.

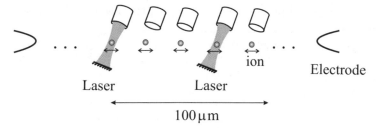

Fig. 4.10. N ions in a linear trap interacting with laser light. The motion of the ions is used as a data bus among qubits.

evolution induced by the applied laser field), k_L the laser wave vector (the laser beam is normally applied in a direction oblique to the trap axis, in this case k_L will be given by $k_\theta = k_L \cos(\theta)$, see Fig 4.10), ϕ_i is the phase describing the situation of the ion with respect to the standing wave and r_i is the position of the ion (expressed in general as a linear combination of the normal modes). In addition, we have used the Pauli operators associated with a two-level (spin 1/2) atom, and the creation (annihilation) operators associated with the quantized harmonic oscillator.

When a laser beam acts on one of the ions it will induce transitions between the (internal) ground and excited levels and can change the state of the collective normal modes. However, within the Lamb–Dicke limit, and considering weak enough laser intensities, only the CM motion will be modified. Under these limits the interaction with the laser will take the form

$$H^i_{\text{las}} \approx H^i_a + H^i_b$$
$$= \frac{\Omega^a_i}{2}(\sigma^+_i + \sigma^-_i) + \frac{\Omega^b_i}{2} \frac{\eta_{\text{cm}}}{\sqrt{N}}(a_{\text{cm}}\sigma^+_i + a^\dagger_{\text{cm}}\sigma^-_i), \qquad (4.40)$$

where η_{cm} is the Lamb–Dicke parameter associated with ν_z, the confinement frequency in the axial direction which coincides with the frequency of the CM mode. The above Hamiltonian is only valid when either $\Omega^a_1 \neq 0$ ($\delta_a = 0$) or $\Omega^b_1 \neq 0$ ($\delta_b \approx -\nu_1$). This means that we will find two available interactions modifying (b), or not modifying (a), the motion of the ions.

We show now how to realise quantum gates between one or two qubits making use of the above described interactions. Single-qubit quantum gates are easy to implement, since they imply only individual rotations of a single ion, without modifying its motional state. They can be realised using a laser at resonance with the internal transition frequency ($\delta_i = 0$) with the ion localised at the antinode of the standing wave laser beam. We have seen that the evolution in this case is given by the Hamiltonian H^i_a, inducing the following rotation

$$|g\rangle_i \rightarrow \cos(k_L\pi/2)|g\rangle_i - ie^{i\phi}\sin(k_L\pi/2)|e\rangle_i,$$
$$|e\rangle_i \rightarrow \cos(k_L\pi/2)|e\rangle_i - ie^{-i\phi}\sin(k_L\pi/2)|g\rangle_i.$$

On the other hand, two qubit gates will be more difficult to implement. We consider first the laser frequency to be chosen in such a way that $\delta_i = -\nu_z$, i.e. it excites only the CM mode, and the ion localised at the node of the standing wave laser beam. The interaction with the laser is now given by the above H_b^i Hamiltonian. Applying a laser for a fixed time $t = k\pi/(\Omega_i^b \eta_z/\sqrt{N})$ (a $k\pi$ pulse) the states will evolve in the following way

$$|g\rangle_i|1\rangle \to \cos(k_L\pi/2)|g\rangle_i|1\rangle - ie^{i\phi}\sin(k_L\pi/2)|e'\rangle_i|0\rangle,$$
$$|e'\rangle_i|0\rangle \to \cos(k_L\pi/2)|e'\rangle_i|0\rangle - ie^{-i\phi}\sin(k_L\pi/2)|g\rangle_i|1\rangle,$$
$$|g\rangle|0\rangle \to |g\rangle|0\rangle, \tag{4.41}$$

where $|0\rangle$ ($|1\rangle$) denotes of the CM mode with zero (one) phonon, ϕ is the phase of the laser and $|e'\rangle$ can be either the state $|1\rangle$ of the qubit considered (denoted $|e\rangle$) or an auxiliary electronic state selectively excited. (This selective excitation can be realised by means of different polarisations or frequencies. Experimentally frequencies seem to be better controlled than polarisations). A two-qubit logic quantum gate can be implemented as follows: (i) using a π pulse focused on the first ion, we swap the internal state of the first ion to the motional state of the CM mode, (ii) introduce a conditional sign flip by means of a 2π pulse on the second ion using the auxiliary level $|e'\rangle_i$, and (iii) a π pulse will swap back the quantum state of the CM mode to the internal state of the first ion. The complete evolution will be given by

$$
\begin{array}{cccc}
(i) & (ii) & (iii) & \\
|g\rangle_1|g\rangle_2|0\rangle \longrightarrow & |g\rangle_1|g\rangle_2|0\rangle \longrightarrow & |g\rangle_1|g\rangle_2|0\rangle \longrightarrow & |g\rangle_1|g\rangle_2|0\rangle, \\
|g\rangle_1|e\rangle_2|0\rangle \longrightarrow & |g\rangle_1|e\rangle_2|0\rangle \longrightarrow & |g\rangle_1|e\rangle_2|0\rangle \longrightarrow & |g\rangle_1|e\rangle_2|0\rangle, \\
|e\rangle_1|g\rangle_2|0\rangle \longrightarrow & -i|g\rangle_1|g\rangle_2|1\rangle \longrightarrow & i|g\rangle_1|g\rangle_2|1\rangle \longrightarrow & |e\rangle_1|g\rangle_2|0\rangle, \\
|e\rangle_1|e_0\rangle_2|0\rangle \longrightarrow & -i|g\rangle_1|e\rangle_2|1\rangle \longrightarrow & -i|g\rangle_1|e\rangle_2|1\rangle \longrightarrow & -|e\rangle_1|e\rangle_2|0\rangle.
\end{array}
\tag{4.42}
$$

In this way, the net effect of the interaction will be a sign flip only when both ions are in the (internal) excited state. Note that before and after the gate the CM mode is in the vacuum state $|0\rangle$. Finally, making use of these operations we can realise logical gates employing n-qubits among every set of ions.

4.3.4 Quantum Gates at Non–zero Temperature

We have seen in the previous section how the system consisting of a set of ions in a linear trap appears to be a promising candidate for realistic implementations of quantum computations in the lab. The basic requirements for computing with laser cooled trapped ions seem to be precise control of the Hamiltonian operations, a high degree of decoherence and cooling of ions to the vibrational ground state to prepare a pure initial state for the collective phonon mode. We will not enter into the first two problems, since these are more related to the issues of error correction and decoherence that will be discussed in Chap. 7, but we will show now how the restriction of cooling to the zero temperature limit can be overcome.

Let us consider the case of two ions in a linear trap. The novel idea is to use the movement of one of the ions' motional wave packet to the right or to the left depending on the absorption or emission of a laser induced photon, after which, the position of a second ion in the trap will be conditioned to the dynamics experienced by the first one. In this way one can enforce a position-dependent change of the internal state of the second ion. The result is a logic quantum gate essential for computation, i.e., the final internal state of the second ion depends on the initial internal state of the first one.

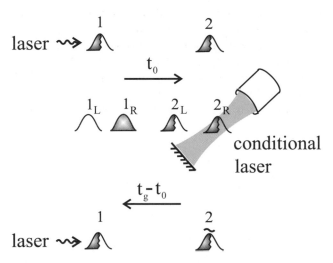

Fig. 4.11. Lasers and wave packet configuration for a two-qubit gate at non zero-zero temperature. After the realisation of the gate, the internal state of the target qubit (ion 2), will change or not (denoted with the tilde), depending on the internal state of the control qubit (ion 1), i.e. kick right or left due to stimulated photon absorption or emission. Here, the dark (light) filling of the wave packets stands for the internal excited (ground) states. See text for more details.

In some sense, we borrow ideas from atom interferometry, where atom wave packets are usually split into different parts, each one undergoing different dynamics, and joined at the end of the process to study the experienced evolution, as a kind of optical interference analysis.

We will show in particular how the two-qubit gate operation can be implemented. Firstly, by means of a laser beam, ion 1 is kicked left or right depending on its internal state due to photon absorption (emission). Thus, the other ion will experience a kick via the Coulomb repulsion conditional on the internal state of the ion 1. The corresponding wave packet would evolve into two possible spatial wavepackets which are entangled to the internal state of the control ion (denoted 1_R, 1_L, ... standing for ion 1 to the right, to the left, etc). Provided the spatial splitting of these wave packets issufficiently large (at a given time t_0), we can manipulate the internal state of the target ion, ion 2, depending on its spatial position, i.e depending on the state of the control ion (ion 1), and thus implement a gate operation on the qubits. With time, these atomic wave packets will oscillate in the trap, and with a proper sequence of laser pulses this momentum transferred to the two ions can be undone to restore the original motional state (at time t_g), see Fig. 4.11. The motional state of the ion will then factorise from the internal atomic state before and after the gate, independent of whether it is in a mixed or a pure state, i.e. independent of the temperature.

In summary, in this section we have introduced a promising system to implement quantum computation. We have discussed proposals of conditional dynamics with ions considering two completely different situations, namely at zero and non-zero temperature. A proof of principle of the zero–temperature proposal was already reported by the group of D. Wineland at NIST [158] which indicates the building of small scale ion trap quantum computers will become feasible in the very near future. In the following chapter several aspects of the experimental realisation of quantum logic gates will be presented.

5. Experiments Leading Towards Quantum Computation

5.1 Introduction

The basic theoretical ideas of quantum computation have been explained in the previous chapter. But how feasible is it to actually construct a quantum computer? Realising that even a single quantum gate requires two strongly interacting quantum systems highly isolated from environmental disturbances, forces us to temper our optimism. This chapter presents several experimental techniques and results which indicate that a small number of highly controlled, strongly interacting, quantum systems are conceivable. However, whether or not it is possible to scale up to practical quantum computation remains to be seen.

Three experimental methods have succeeded in realising the proper experimental conditions for small-scale quantum-logic operations. They are based on cavity quantum electrodynamics (cavity QED), trapped ions, and nuclear magnetic resonances (NMR). The first two methods implement one of the simplest coupled quantum-mechanical systems: a two-level system coupled to a quantum oscillator. To stress this common feature, Sect. 5.2 presents the cavity QED experiments in parallel with the corresponding experiments on trapped ions.

The cavity QED experiments have been particularly successful in demonstrating fundamental features of quantum mechanics, like the quantum Rabi oscillation, presented in Sect. 5.2.3, Schrödinger's cat states and quantum decoherence, presented in Sect. 5.2.4. These experiments demonstrate in a beautiful way basic quantum logic operations; however, it seems very difficult to perform a large number of such operations with these techniques.

With respect to the scaling-up problem, trapped ion experiments seem more promising since it is possible to store and cool a string of ions in a linear trap. This string can be considered as a register of qubits where each qubit (stored on a single ion) can be addressed by tightly focused laser beams. In Sects. 5.2.5 to 5.2.12 it is demonstrated that quantum logic on the level of single ions can be performed and Sect. 5.3 provides a general overview of the experiments aimed towards quantum computation with strings of ions.

The third method under investigation for quantum computation, based on nuclear magnetic resonances (NMR), has already demonstrated a small sequence of simple quantum-logic operations. NMR involves transitions between the Zeeman sub-levels of an atomic nucleus in a magnetic field. The frequencies of NMR signals from nuclei inside molecules depend on the precise chemical environment of the nucleus. This allows one to address different nuclear spins inside single molecules. The spins play the role of qubits, and via the strong spin-coupling interactions inside molecules they interact with one another. This provides the basic ingredients for quantum computation. Section 5.4 describes the principles of NMR quantum computation.

More speculative routes to performing quantum logic are based on solid state devices. Although a breakthrough in the fabrication of such devices would be extremely important, this field of research has not yet developed enough to be included here.

5.2 Cavity QED-Experiments: Atoms in Cavities and Trapped Ions

H.C. Nägerl, D. Leibfried, F. Schmidt-Kaler, J. Eschner, R. Blatt, M. Brune, J.M. Raimond, S. Haroche

5.2.1 A Two-Level System Coupled to a Quantum Oscillator

An atom in an optical cavity or ions in a trap can, to a good approximation, be considered as a two-level system coupled to a quantum harmonic oscillator. In the former case, a two-level atom is coupled to the cavity resonant mode. In the latter case, two internal states of one ion (hyperfine or metastable energy levels) are coupled to the vibrational degrees of freedom of the ions in the trap. Both systems can thus be characterized by the same interaction. The interaction (Jaynes–Cummings) Hamiltonian [159] can be written as:

$$H_{\text{int}} = -\hbar \frac{\Omega}{2} (a\sigma^+ + a^\dagger \sigma^-) , \tag{5.1}$$

where a and $a^\dagger$ are the annihilation and creation operators for the quantum oscillator, σ^+ and σ^- are the raising and lowering operators for the two-level system, and Ω is the coupling amplitude. This Hamiltonian describes emission or absorption of photons (in the case of cavity QED experiments) or phonons (in the case of trapped ion experiments) associated to an atomic or ionic transition. When the harmonic oscillator mode is exactly at resonance with the two-level system, the interaction term describes real energy exchange. When the systems are off resonance, the energy transfer processes are virtual and the interaction results in a phase shift of the atomic levels.

The key point is to realise the strong coupling regime, where the simple interaction of (5.1) dominates all relaxation processes, such as atomic spontaneous emission, photon/phonon damping, and decoherence caused by thermal noise. A convincing experimental realisation of the simplest matter–field system demonstrates elementary quantum logic operations. At the same time, it provides severe tests of our understanding of the least intuitive aspects of quantum theory, such as non-local entanglement and mesoscopic state superpositions.

Cavity QED developed both in the optical and the microwave domains, the basic principles of the experiments being extremely similar. For a review of these two classes of experiments, see [160]. In the optical domain, optical atomic transitions are coupled to very high finesse cavities. The strong coupling regime has been realised and investigated. This section will focus on the microwave domain. Long-lived, easily detected, circular Rydberg atoms are strongly coupled to the millimeter-wave radiation contained in a high-Q superconducting cavity. Atoms traveling at thermal velocities across the cavity get entangled with the field mode. The lifetimes of both the cavity field and the atomic two-level system are much longer than the interaction time. Therefore, the field and atom remain entangled even after the atom has left the cavity. The joint quantum state of the field and atom may thus be further investigated or manipulated at will.

The second class of experiments described in this section involves ions that are confined in an electromagnetic harmonic trap. The quantum oscillator is a specific mode of vibration of the ions. It is coupled, by laser pulses, to the internal state of the ionic two-level system. With well chosen pulses of laser light, the interaction of the ion motion with the internal state is, to an excellent approximation, described by the Jaynes–Cummings type of Hamiltonians. Long coherence times of both the ionic two-level system and the vibration mode are achieved with techniques developed for ionic frequency standards.

In spite of a completely different experimental environment, the atom–cavity and trapped-ion experiments implement the same simple model. Therefore, any experiment designed for cavity QED can be translated in the context of ion traps, and vice versa. Moreover, the achievements of these two techniques are quite comparable. The next sections review cavity QED experiments in the microwave domain and trapped-ion experiments involving a Jaynes–Cummings interaction, followed by a comparison of the possible perspectives for quantum computation for both techniques.

5.2.2 Cavity QED with Atoms and Cavities

The general scheme of cavity QED experiments with atoms in microwave resonators is presented in this section. Experimental and theoretical details can be found elsewhere [160, 161].

Circular Rydberg atoms offer unprecedented tools for the realisation of cavity QED experiments. These atoms with their high-lying energy levels [162, 163], having principal quantum numbers n of the order of 50 and maximum orbital and magnetic quantum numbers, behave as huge antennae strongly coupled to millimetre-wave radiation. The dipole-matrix element on the transition between the circular states $n = 51$ ($|e\rangle$) and $n = 50$ ($|g\rangle$) at 51.099 GHz is as high as 1250 atomic units. When placed in a weak directing electric field, which avoids mixing with other levels in the hydrogenic multiplicity, these levels have a long lifetime, of the order of 30 ms, and behave as a true two-level system. Furthermore, they can be detected in a selective and sensitive way by the field-ionization method.

In the millimetre-wave domain, superconducting materials allow very high quality cavities. Centimetre-sized Fabry–Perot type cavities with niobium mirrors are used in the experiments. At low temperatures such as 0.6 K, the quality factor is in the range of 10^8 to 10^9, corresponding to a photon storage time T_r of a few hundred microseconds up to a few milliseconds. This is much longer than the atom–cavity interaction time which is a few tens of microseconds for atoms at thermal velocities. At these low temperatures, the thermal field is quite negligible and the probability of finding the cavity in its ground state is above 98%.

The experimental set-up used in Ecole Normale, Paris [164]–[168], is sketched in Fig. 5.1. Its core is cooled to 0.6 K by a ^{3}He-^{4}He cryostat. The atoms, initially effusing from an oven O, are velocity selected with the help of a laser beam at an angle with respect to the atomic beam propagation by velocity-selective optical pumping in zone V. The velocity-selected atoms are then prepared in box B in one of the states $|e\rangle$ or $|g\rangle$ by a succession of laser pulses and adiabatic radiofrequency transitions [163]. The preparation is pulsed and produces bursts of circular atoms at well defined times, with well controlled velocities between 200 and 400 m/s with a ± 2 m/s precision. The position of the atoms is known at any time with a ± 1 mm precision. Selective transformations can thus be applied on different atoms crossing the apparatus. The average number of atoms in each burst is kept below one, so that the probability of preparing two atoms at the same time remains small.

The superconducting cavity C is made of two spherical niobium mirrors, 2.7 cm apart. It sustains a transversal electromagnetic Gaussian mode with a 6 mm waist. When required, the cavity can be filled either by the atoms themselves through the process of resonant atom–field coupling or by a microwave source S injecting a coherent field. The cavity can be tuned in and out of resonance with the atomic transition by adjusting the mirrors' distance or by modifying the atomic transition frequency through an electric field applied across the mirrors.

Before entering C, the atoms cross a low-Q auxiliary cavity R_1 in which a classical microwave pulse can mix levels $|e\rangle$ and $|g\rangle$. Each atom crosses C in a few 10 μs during which there is a strong interaction between the atom and the

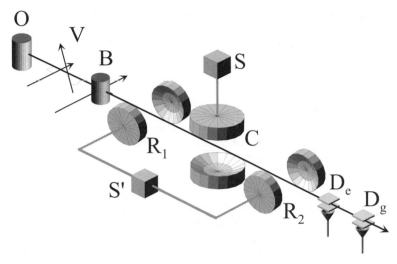

Fig. 5.1. Scheme of the atom–cavity experimental set-up.

cavity field. The atom–field coupling amplitude (Ω in the Jaynes–Cummings interaction) is $\Omega/2\pi = 50$ kHz for an atom at the centre of the cavity. This corresponds to the exchange rate of a single photon between an atom and the cavity mode. When the atom moves across the cavity, the coupling $\Omega(\mathbf{r})$ is a Gaussian function of its position. After C, a pulse of classical, resonant microwave may mix $|e\rangle$ and $|g\rangle$ again in the auxiliary cavity R_2. Finally, the atoms reach two state-selective field-ionization detectors D_e and D_g, which count atoms in states $|e\rangle$ and $|g\rangle$ with a 40% efficiency.

An experimental sequence consists in sending one or two atoms, separated by a well defined interval, across the system and detecting them in D_e or D_g. The same sequence is repeated many times, with a repetition period of 1.5 ms which is longer than the cavity damping time, so that the field in C is in the same initial state at the beginning of each sequence. Statistics from repeated sequences are then extracted. Samples for joint two-atom probabilities correspond typically to 15000 events, recorded in about two hours. Two types of experiments have been performed. In the first one, presented in Sect. 5.2.3, the atoms and the cavity mode are at exact resonance which leads, via energy exchange, to entanglement of the atomic and field energies. In the second, presented in Sect. 5.2.4, the atoms and cavity are not at resonance and therefore the interaction produces atomic or cavity energy shifts, resulting in a phase entanglement.

5.2.3 Resonant Coupling: Rabi Oscillations and Entangled Atoms

Consider the case in which the cavity is tuned in resonance with the $|e\rangle \rightarrow |g\rangle$ atomic transition. Single photons can be emitted or absorbed by the single atom in C [161]–[169] with a continuous stream of atoms, such cumulative emissions lead to the micromaser operation [170]. Such a single-photon single-atom interaction system has been used to demonstrate the quantum Rabi oscillation [171], direct evidence for field quantisation, a quantum memory [167], entanglement between two atoms [168], and single photon absorption-free detection [169].

The simplest experiment is performed by sending an atom in level $|e\rangle$ into the cavity and measuring the probability that it flips from $|e\rangle$ to $|g\rangle$ (zones R_1 and R_2 are not used) [165]. The measurement is repeated for various atom–cavity interaction times t, obtained either by changing the atomic velocity, or by Stark tuning the atomic transition into resonance with the cavity for a fraction of the crossing time.

Figure 5.2(A) shows the Rabi oscillation signal versus effective interaction time t in the case that the cavity field is initially in the vacuum state. The points are experimental and the line is a theoretical fit. The effective interaction time t, calculated from the experimental parameters, takes into account the Gaussian variation of the coupling inside the cavity. Four complete Rabi oscillations are observed, at a frequency close to $\Omega/2\pi =50$ kHz. They correspond to the basic Jaynes–Cummings process: the reversible evolution of the atom between $|e\rangle$ and $|g\rangle$, correlated to the emission and absorption of one photon. The damping of the oscillations is caused by experimental imperfections. This vacuum Rabi oscillation signal is the time domain counterpart of the vacuum Rabi splitting observed in the spectrum of the atom–empty cavity system [172, 173].

Figures 5.2(B–D) show the oscillation signal when the cavity initially contains a coherent field with an average photon number equal, respectively for each figure, to $n = 0.40(\pm0.02), 0.85(\pm0.04)$ and $1.77(\pm0.15)$. The oscillation involves several frequency components, corresponding to the various photon numbers present in the field. The beating between them gives rise to a collapse and a revival of the oscillations [171]. The Fourier transforms of the Rabi signals, shown in Fig. 5.2(a–d), exhibit peaks at the frequencies $\Omega\sqrt{n+1}$ corresponding to the Rabi frequency in the field of n photons ($n = 0$ to 3). The Rabi frequency, proportional to the amplitude for a classical field, is thus a discrete quantity. This provides a *direct evidence of field quantization in a box*. Figures 5.2(α–δ) show the Fourier components amplitudes, which give directly the photon number distribution. The small peak at $\Omega\sqrt{2}$ in Fig. 5.2(a)is due to the residual thermal field, which has an average photon number at 0.8 K of 0.06.

Besides providing a visceral evidence of field energy quantization, this experiment demonstrates that the atom–cavity resonant interaction dominates the relaxation processes. The resulting atom–field entanglement can be used to create or manipulate quantum entanglement, thus providing the basis for elementary quantum computation operations.

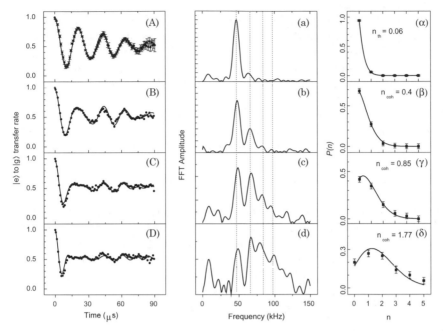

Fig. 5.2. Quantum Rabi oscillations. (A), (B), (C) and (D): Rabi nutation signals (A): no injected field and 0.06 (±0.01) thermal photon on average; (B), (C) and (D): coherent fields with 0.40 (±0.02), 0.85 (±0.04) and 1.77 (±0.15) photons on average. The points are experimental; the solid lines are theoretical fits. (a), (b), (c), (d): corresponding Fourier transforms. Frequencies ranging as the square roots of successive integers are indicated by vertical lines. (α), (β), (γ), (δ): photon number distribution inferred from experimental signals (points). Solid lines: theoretical thermal (α) or coherent((β), (γ), (δ)) distributions.

Atom–field entanglement has first been used to realise a very simple device: a quantum memory holding a single qubit in the cavity. This memory is written by a first atom and read by a second. In the simplest situation, the first atom enters the empty cavity in state $|e\rangle$. The effective interaction time t is such that $\Omega t = \pi$. Therefore, the atom exits C in $|g\rangle$, leaving a one-photon state in C. The second atom, entering the cavity in state $|g\rangle$ after a delay T, absorbs this photon, provided it has not spontaneously decayed, and ends up in state $|e\rangle$. The decay of the probability of finding the second atom in $|g\rangle$ versus T measures the lifetime of a single photon in the cavity. Not surprisingly, it is equal to the classical field energy damping time T_r [167].

One can also send into the empty cavity an atom prepared in a superposition of $|e\rangle$ and $|g\rangle$ states with equal weights by a microwave $\pi/2$ pulse in R_1 (frequency ν). The $|e\rangle$ component of the atomic state emits, with unit probability, a photon in C, while the $|g\rangle$ component remains unaltered. The atomic state superposition is thus mapped onto the field as a superposition of 0 and 1 photon states, and the atom exits C in state $|g\rangle$. The field in C

has an average photon number equal to $1/2$ and a well defined phase, directly related to that of the microwave fields in R_1. The phase information has been carried by the atom from R_1 to C.

The field is read out by a second atom, prepared in state $|g\rangle$ after a delay T, which again undergoes a π pulse in C. The quantum coherence is then mapped onto this atom, as a superposition of $|e\rangle$ and $|g\rangle$ states, leaving the cavity empty. A $\pi/2$ pulse is applied to the second atom in R_2, with the same frequency ν and phase as the one applied on the first atom in R_1. The cavity R_2 followed by D_e and D_g thus acts as a detector of the superposition state of the second atom, including phase information. The probability of detecting this atom in $|e\rangle$ or $|g\rangle$ oscillates versus ν, as in the usual Ramsey fringes situation. At variance with the usual situation, the two pulses are acting on two different atoms and the coherence is transferred between them via the cavity field in C. Figures 5.3(a–c) show the fringe signals indicating the coherence transfer for three different time intervals between atoms. When this time increases, the fringe period and the fringe amplitude decrease. The contrast reduction reveals the field decay in C. The decay time is twice as long as T_r, since this experiment involves a superposition of the $|1\rangle$ and $|0\rangle$ Fock (photon-number) states, the second being undamped.

In this experiment, a qubit is transferred between two atoms via a one-photon field. In the intermediate state, the cavity field is a highly non-classical superposition of one- and zero-photon states. Such an atom-to-field mapping process is essential in a proposed implementation of a cavity QED quantum gate [174].

The same scheme, under slightly different conditions, may be used to prepare and manipulate non-local atom–field or atom–atom entanglement [175]. A first atom sent into the empty cavity in state $|e\rangle$ undergoes a $\pi/2$ pulse ($\Omega t = \pi/2$). The atom and the cavity are then in the entangled state $|e, 0\rangle + |g, 1\rangle$. Atom–atom entanglement can be produced by sending a second atom prepared in state $|g\rangle$ across C with an interaction time such that $\Omega t = \pi$. The photon left by the first atom is absorbed by the second with unit probability, leaving the cavity empty and the atoms in the entangled state:

$$|\Psi_{\mathrm{EPR}}\rangle = \frac{1}{\sqrt{2}} \left(|e_1, g_2\rangle - |g_1, e_2\rangle \right), \tag{5.2}$$

where the indices label the first and the second atom respectively.

This is an Einstein–Podolsky–Rosen pair of entangled particles [21]. The atoms can be represented by a spin one-half particle, the $|e\rangle$ and $|g\rangle$ states corresponding to the $+1/2$ and $-1/2$ states quantized along a direction Oz. $|\Psi_{\mathrm{EPR}}\rangle$ is then the rotationally invariant "spin-zero" state, which means that the two spins should be anti-correlated in the sense that they will always be detected with opposite projections along any quantization axis. To illustrate this, choose an axis in the xOy plane in a direction making an angle ϕ with Ox. The spin eigenvectors along this axis are of the form $|e\rangle \pm e^{i\phi}|g\rangle$ and the state $|\Psi_{\mathrm{EPR}}\rangle$ can be written (within an overall phase factor) as:

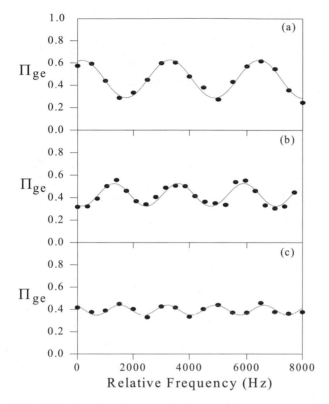

Fig. 5.3. Transfer of coherence between two atoms: conditional probability $\Pi_{ge}(\nu)$ of detecting the second atom in $|e\rangle$ provided the first one is detected in $|g\rangle$, versus the frequency ν of the microwave pulses applied to the first atom in R_1 and to the second in R_2. The delays between the two microwave pulses in R_1 and R_2 are 301, 436 and 581 μs respectively from (a) to (c).

$$|\Psi_{EPR}\rangle = (|e_1\rangle + e^{i\phi}|g_1\rangle)(|e_2\rangle - e^{i\phi}|g_2\rangle) - (|e_1\rangle - e^{i\phi}|g_1\rangle)(|e_2\rangle + e^{i\phi}|g_2\rangle)$$
$$(5.3)$$

depicting the anti-correlation.

To analyse the entanglement in the energy basis (Oz axis), we detect the state of the atoms after they leave C. Ideally, the joint probabilities of detecting the atoms in the various combinations of $|e\rangle$ and $|g\rangle$ should be $P_{eg} = P_{ge} = 1/2$, $P_{ee} = P_{gg} = 0$. We find instead $P_{eg} = 0.44, P_{ge} = 0.27, P_{ee} = 0.06, P_{gg} = 0.23$. The difference is due to the decay of the photon stored in C between the passage of the two atoms, and to various other imperfections. A quantitative analysis shows that EPR pairs of atoms have been produced with a purity of 63% [168].

The anti-correlation property expressed by Eq. (5.3) is analysed by applying to both atoms a $\pi/2$ pulse in R_2. The spin rotation in R_2, followed by a detection along the Oz direction, is equivalent to a detection along a

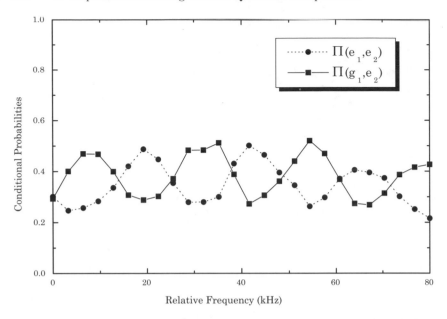

Fig. 5.4. EPR atomic entanglement: conditional probabilities $\Pi(e_1, e_2)$ (circles) and $\Pi(g_1, e_2)$ (squares) of measuring the second atom in state $|e\rangle$ when the first one has been found in $|e\rangle$ or $|g\rangle$ respectively, plotted versus the frequency ν of the pulses in R_2. The lines connecting the experimental points have been added for visual convenience.

quantization axis in the horizontal plane. To be more specific, a detection in $|e\rangle$ or $|g\rangle$ after R_2, corresponds to an atomic superposition $|e\rangle \pm e^{i\phi}|g\rangle$ before R_2, where ϕ is the phase of the pulse applied in R_2 (+ sign for $|e\rangle$). According to the anti-correlation, the second atom should thus be projected by this measurement on the superposition pointing in the direction opposite the measured direction of the first atom. If both atoms were crossing R_2 simultaneously, a perfect anti-correlation between $|e\rangle$ and $|g\rangle$ detectors should be observed. In fact, the coherence of the second atom, delayed by time T, and the field in R_2 precess during the time interval T. The final probability of detecting the second atom in $|e\rangle$ or $|g\rangle$ depends upon the phase accumulated between the atomic coherence and the microwave in R_2. This phase slip is proportional to the atom/Ramsey field frequency difference and to the flight time T. This is again a Ramsey fringes situation. However, the two microwave pulses are applied to different atoms and the phase is transferred between them through a non-local quantum correlation.

Figure 5.4 shows the conditional probabilities Π_{e_1,e_2} (Π_{g_1,e_2}) of detecting the second atom in $|e\rangle$, when the first is in $|e\rangle$ ($|g\rangle$) versus the frequency ν in the Ramsey zones. The modulations reveal the coherence of the state of the second atom. They are out of phase since the phase of the second atom changes by π when the first atom is detected in $|g\rangle$ instead of $|e\rangle$.

The experimental data demonstrate the preparation of controlled entanglement of two qubits (here, two atoms separated by approx. 1.5 cm). By combining resonant and dispersive interactions, this scheme can be extended to prepare triplets of atoms of the form $|e, e, e\rangle - |g, g, g\rangle$ [175]-[177].

The resonant atom–field interaction has also been used to perform the absorption-free detection of a single photon stored in the cavity [169]. The heart of the method is the conditional phase shift experienced by an atom crossing the cavity in level g and undergoing a 2π Rabi rotation in a single photon field. When the atom crosses an empty cavity (initial state $|g, 0\rangle$), it is unaffected by the interaction. When the cavity contains one photon, the atom–cavity system undergoes the transformation $|g, 1\rangle \rightarrow -|g, 1\rangle$. The π phase shift of the global wavefunction is similar to the one of a spin 1/2 undergoing a 2π rotation in real space. This conditional phase shift can be tested by Ramsey interferometry on a transition connecting g to a reference level i uncoupled to the cavity field. The observation of the phase shift amounts to detecting the photon in the cavity. At variance with most photo-detectors, the photon is left in the cavity after the interaction with the "meter" atom. This experiment is thus equivalent to a quantum non-demolition measurement of a single photon field, restricted to the subspace spanned by the zero and one photon states. Moreover, the conditional dynamics at the heart of the method can be viewed as a quantum logic gate.

5.2.4 Dispersive Coupling: Schrödinger's Cat and Decoherence

Consider now the case in which the atomic transition frequency ω_0 and the field mode frequency ω differ by δ, where δ is large compared to Ω and to the cavity linewidth. Under this condition, energy conservation prevents the emission or absorption of photons by the atoms and the interaction with the cavity is purely dispersive. The atom–field energy entanglement, as described in the previous section, is replaced by an entanglement of the atomic state with the phase of the radiation field, which can be considered to be classical. A microscopic degree of freedom controls thus a "macroscopic" quantity. This entanglement is a prototype of a quantum measurement and allows us to explore the weirdness of quantum mechanics at an unusual scale.

Let a circular Rydberg atom interact with a small coherent field in C, with cavity-field amplitude α and an average photon number $|\alpha|^2$, typically between 0 and 10. Since the vacuum Rabi frequency is a Gaussian function of the atomic position inside the cavity, the interaction is turned on and off adiabatically. This makes photon exchange between the atom and the cavity field very unlikely, even at small atom–cavity detunings ($\delta/2\pi = 100$ to 700 kHz). Therefore, the interaction results only in line shifts. The cavity mode is shifted by $\pm\Omega^2/4\delta$ for the atom at the centre of the cavity. This shift, resulting from the effect of the index of refraction of a single atom, takes the opposite value for an atom in states $|e\rangle$ or $|g\rangle$ [161]. It can reach up to

(a)   (b)

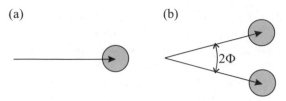

Fig. 5.5. (a): Pictorial representation in phase space of a coherent field state. (b) Components of the field in (5.4) correlated to the atomic states $|e\rangle$ and $|g\rangle$.

± 6 kHz for $\delta/2\pi = 100$ kHz, corresponding to an index per atom 15 orders of magnitudes larger than the ones of "ordinary atoms".

The frequency shift, produced by the passage of a single atom through the cavity, results in a phase shift of the coherent cavity field by $\pm\Phi = \pm\Omega^2 t/4\delta$, where t is the effective interaction time. The phase shift is typically of the order of one radian. This atom–field interaction can be used to generate a non-classical superposition of field states with different phases. The atom is prepared in a superposition of $|e\rangle$ and $|g\rangle$ by a $\pi/2$ pulse in R_1. When it crosses C, it simultaneously imparts to the field two opposite phase shifts, $\pm\Phi$. The combined atom–field system thus becomes

$$|\Psi\rangle = \frac{1}{\sqrt{2}}\left(|e, \alpha e^{i\Phi}\rangle + |g, \alpha e^{-i\Phi}\rangle\right). \tag{5.4}$$

This is an entangled state, the energy of the atom being correlated to the phase of the cavity field. The coherent field can be represented as an arrow in phase space whose length and direction are associated to the amplitude and phase, as illustrated in Fig. 5.5(a). The tip of the arrow lies in a circle of unit radius describing the quantum uncertainties of the field. Equation (5.4) allows to see this arrow as a "meter needle" assuming two different directions correlated to the atomic state, as shown in Fig. 5.5(b). The interaction realises a "measurement" in which the "field arrow" is used to determine the energy of the atom. One can also adopt Schrödinger's metaphor [178]: the $+\Phi$ and $-\Phi$ field components are then analogous to the "live" and "dead" states of the famous cat entangled to an atom in a superposition of excited and ground states.

After leaving the cavity and before detection, the atom undergoes another $\pi/2$ pulse in R_2, phase coherent with the one in R_1. The probability P_g of detecting the atom in $|g\rangle$ is measured as function of the frequency ν applied in R_1 and R_2. Figure 5.6(a) shows the experimental result for the case of no photons in the cavity field and for a detuning $\delta/2\pi = 712$ kHz. The atomic state can be transferred from $|e\rangle$ to $|g\rangle$ either in R_1 (crossing C in state $|g\rangle$) or in R_2 (crossing C in state $|e\rangle$). Since the atom does not leave any trace of its presence inside the cavity, these two paths cannot be distinguished and the corresponding amplitudes interfere, leading to oscillations (Ramsey fringes) in P_g.

Figures 5.6(b–d) show the experimental results for a coherent cavity field with an average of 9.5 photons and for decreasing atom–cavity detunings. The smaller the detuning, the larger the separation of the field components in C will be. The inserts in Fig. 5.6(b–d) illustrate the phase information of the field which is a record of the atomic state. Such Welcher-Weg (which-way) information, even unread, must destroy the interference effect according to the complementarity principle. A quantitative analysis shows that the fringe signal is ruled by the overlap integral between the two field components, its modulus yielding the fringe contrast and its phase the one of the Ramsey fringes. For large Φ, the overlap is small and the fringes disappear. For small Φ, fringes are observed, albeit with a reduced contrast. The signals show convincingly that the cavity acts as a meter for the atomic state. Moreover, the phase shift of the fringes for large detunings provide a precise determination of the photon number.

The quantum superposition of the mesoscopic field, resulting from the above preparation and detection scheme of the atom passing the cavity, is fragile and subject to decoherence, especially when $|\alpha|^2$ and/or Φ become large [179]–[186]. In order to monitor the evolution from a quantum superposition to a statistical mixture, the "cat state" of the field is probed with a second atom, crossing the cavity after a delay T [166, 186]. The probe produces the same phase shifts as the first atom. It splits each of the two field components, caused by the first atom, into two parts. This means that the final field state exhibits four components, two of which coincide at zero phase. Whenever the two atoms crossed C in the $|e\rangle, |g\rangle$ or in the $|g\rangle, |e\rangle$ combination, the phase returns to its initial value. After the atomic states mixing in R_2, there is no information left on the path followed ($|e\rangle, |g\rangle$ or $|g\rangle, |e\rangle$), since the second atom has partially erased [187] the information left in the field by the first one. The contributions of these two paths thus lead, in the joint probabilities P_{ee}, P_{eg}, P_{ge} and P_{gg}, and in the correlation signal $\eta = P_{ee}/(P_{ee} + P_{eg}) - P_{ge}/(P_{ge} + P_{gg})$, to the presence of interference terms.

If the state superposition survives during T, η ideally takes the value 1/2, whereas it vanishes when the field state is a mere statistical mixture. The experimental values of η versus T are shown in Fig. 5.7 for two different "cat" states (depicted in the inserts). The points are experimental and the curves theoretical [188]. The maximum value is 0.18 only, due to the limited contrast of the Ramsey interferometer. Decoherence occurs within a time much shorter than the cavity damping time and is more efficient when the separation between the cat components is increased. It shows that we observe a non-trivial relaxation mechanism, whose time constants drastically depend upon the initial state.

Decoherence is due to the loss of photons out of the cavity. Each "escaping" photon can be described as a small "Schrödinger kitten" copying in the environment the phase information contained in C. The mere fact that this "leaking" information could be read out is enough to wash out the interfer-

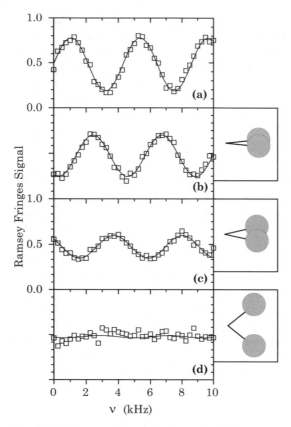

Fig. 5.6. Ramsey fringes in the probability versus ν of detecting the atom in level $|g\rangle$: (a) C empty, $\delta/2\pi = 712$ kHz; (b) to (d) C stores a coherent field with $|\alpha| = \sqrt{9.5} = 3.1$, $\delta/2\pi = 712$, 347 and 104 kHz respectively. Points are experimental and curves are sinusoidal fits. Inserts show the phase space representation of the field components left in C.

ence effects related to the quantum coherence of the "cat". In this respect, decoherence is a complementarity phenomenon. The short decoherence time of the Schrödinger cat states presented above, about T_{cav}/n, is explained by this approach. The larger the photon number, the shorter is the time required to leak a single "photon-copy" into the environment. This experiment verifies the basic features of decoherence and vividly exhibits the fragility of quantum coherences in large systems. Extrapolation of quantum mechanical superposition states to macroscopic scale leads to an almost instantaneous decoherence, validating the Copenhagen interpretation of quantum measurement for any practical purpose. This experiment also provides interesting insight into the difficulties which have to be overcome in order to produce and control large-scale quantum entanglement, namely that quantum decoherence appears to be the major limitation to large scale quantum information processing.

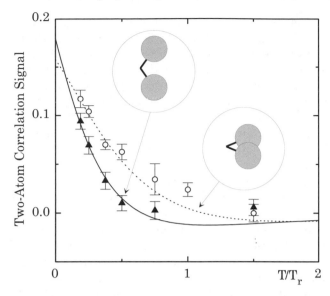

Fig. 5.7. Decoherence of a Schrödinger cat: two-atom correlation signal η versus T/T_r for $\delta/2\pi = 170$ kHz (circles) and $\delta/2\pi = 70$ kHz (triangles). Dashed and solid lines are theoretical. Inserts: pictorial representations of corresponding field components separated by 2Φ.

A further discussion of the limits to quantum computation, without quantum error correction schemes, is given in Sect. 7.3.

5.2.5 Trapped-Ion Experiments

One or a few ions stored in radio-frequency Paul traps offer an ideal environment to study the dynamics of simple quantum systems, and, with the aid of laser pulses, the investigator can tailor the interaction of those simple systems almost at will. An especially interesting scenario is created by substituting the photon field of cavity QED, as described in the previous sections, by the harmonic oscillator describing the motion of the ion(s) in the external trapping potential. A suitable light field can couple two internal electronic levels of the ion(s), $|g\rangle$ and $|e\rangle$, to the external vibrational motion at frequency ω with an interaction Hamiltonian of the form [189]–[192]:

$$H_{\text{int}} = -\hbar G \left(\sigma^+ e^{i\eta(a^\dagger + a) - i\delta t} + \sigma^- e^{-i\eta(a^\dagger + a) + i\delta t} \right), \qquad (5.5)$$

where $\eta = \delta k \sqrt{\hbar/(2m\omega)}$ is the Lamb–Dicke parameter with the modulus δk of the wavevector (or a wavevector difference if the systems are coupled by Raman transitions), $(a^\dagger + a)$ the position operator in terms of the harmonic oscillator ladder operators and G is a coupling strength, proportional to the amplitude of the coupling light field. This interaction Hamiltonian is inherently richer than the Jaynes–Cummings Hamiltonian, (5.1), but reduces to the latter by choosing the detuning of the light field with respect to the energy difference of the two internal states to be $\delta = -\omega$ and in the limit $\eta\sqrt{\langle(a^\dagger + a)^2\rangle} << 1$. In general any detuning with $\delta = (n' - n)\omega$ (n, n' integer numbers) will resonantly drive transitions between the states $|g, n\rangle$ and $|e, n'\rangle$, and thus lead to another effective interaction Hamiltonian. In addition, the coupling strength G is not fixed by dipole matrix elements and the mode volume of the cavity, as is the case in the experiments presented in the previous sections, but can be varied by an appropriate choice of the light intensity.

The techniques to realise the situation described above in a laboratory have grown out of the efforts to build frequency standards with trapped and cooled ions [193]–[195]. Dynamical trapping of charged particles in radiofrequency (rf) traps was first proposed and experimentally verified by W. Paul in 1958 [196]. A rf electric field, generated by an appropriate electrode structure, creates a pseudo-potential confining a charged particle [197]. For the trapping of *single* atomic ions the electrodes have typical dimensions of a few millimetres down to about 100 μm. The rf fields are in the 10–300 MHz range, with a peak to peak voltage of hundreds of Volts. The motion of a particle confined in such a field involves a fast component synchronous to the applied driving frequency (micro motion) and the slow (secular) motion in the dynamically created pseudo-potential. For a quadrupole (rf) field geometry, the pseudo-potential is harmonic and the quantized secular motion of the trapped ion is very accurately described by a quantum harmonic oscillator. For a more detailed description of different types of Paul traps and their special properties we refer to Sect. 5.3.2.

For frequency standards, the trapped ions should offer at least one long lived, narrow transition that can be either in the microwave (for example, a ground state hyperfine transition) or the optical range (for example a transition to a metastable excited state). To reduce Doppler shifts and other adverse effects related to the motion, laser cooling of the ions is a very convenient tool. This cooling mechanism was proposed in 1975 by Wineland and Dehmelt [198] and experimentally observed in 1978 [199]. For experiments with fundamental quantum systems and quantum logic applications the requirements are almost identical. The narrow transition now forms the well isolated two-level system, while laser cooling is the key tool to initialise the harmonic oscillator of the motion in a well defined state.

5.2.6 Choice of Ions and Doppler Cooling

Although an ion trap is very deep (several eV potential well depth) and will hold almost every ion, only a few ions are suitable for cavity QED-like experiments. They should exhibit energy levels appropriate for the realisation of a two-level system with negligible decoherence by spontaneous decay, and should also allow for optical cooling and detection. The ions of choice have

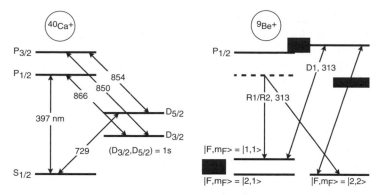

Fig. 5.8. ^{40}Ca$^+$ and ^{9}Be$^+$ level scheme. The wavelengths of the different transitions are indicated. For ^{40}Ca$^+$, the lifetimes of the excited states are indicated too.

typically one electron in the outermost shell (hydrogenic ions) and a correspondingly simple electronic level structure. The two-level system can either be provided by two hyperfine ground states or by a long-lived metastable electronic state [200]. Most of the relevant experiments have been done with ^{9}Be$^+$ by the NIST ion storage group in Boulder [201], but other groups are also gearing up to work on quantum logic and coherent control, as e.g. IBM Almaden (^{138}Ba$^+$), JPL in Los Angeles [202] (^{199}Hg$^+$), the MPQ in Garching [203] (^{25}Mg$^+$), Los Alamos National Laboratory [204] (^{40}Ca$^+$) and the Universities of Mainz [205] (^{40}Ca$^+$), Hamburg [206] (^{138}Ba$^+$, ^{171}Yb$^+$) and Innsbruck [207] (^{40}Ca$^+$, ^{138}Ba$^+$). The following discussion will concentrate on ^{9}Be$^+$, where hyperfine ground states form the two-level system, and on ^{40}Ca$^+$, where an optically excited metastable level is used. The level schemes of ^{40}Ca$^+$ and ^{9}Be$^+$ are shown in Fig. 5.8.

Cooling is required to realise a well defined initial state of vibration for the trapped ions. The most obvious choice is the ground state [208], but trapping states have also been proposed [209]. Most of the kinetic energy can already be extracted by Doppler cooling. This technique is based on the fact that atoms moving towards a laser source can be excited if the laser frequency is slightly detuned to the red (Doppler shift) with respect to the optical transition. The motion of the atoms will slow down due to scattering of photons. The momentum transfer due to absorption constantly adds up while it averages to zero for spontaneous emission which is spread over a 4π solid angle. Thus, the motional energy or equivalently the temperature of the ions is reduced. The mean final energy which can be reached by this technique is given by the Doppler cooling limit $E_D = \hbar\Gamma/2$ where Γ denotes the natural width of the excited state of the cooling transition. The same procedure is applied for trapped ions if the vibrational frequency (the secular frequency ω_i along the respective axis) is smaller than the natural line width Γ. Here, the required motion towards the laser source is provided by the periodic vibration of the ions in the trap and, as in the case of free atoms, the final temperature for this cooling process is $T_D = E_D/k_B$ [210] (typically on the order of a few milliKelvin).

For most ions the optical transition used for Doppler cooling is in the ultra violet. For $^9\text{Be}^+$, the $^2\text{S}_{1/2}$ to $^2\text{P}_{3/2}$ transition at 313 nm is used, while for $^{40}\text{Ca}^+$ the corresponding transition is at 397 nm. Coincidentally, the linewidth is about 20 MHz in both Be^+ and Ca^+. The cooling light is generated by frequency doubling a dye or a Ti:Sapphire laser respectively. In Ca^+ the $\text{P}_{1/2}$ level may decay to a metastable $D_{3/2}$ level and one needs an additional laser diode at 866 nm to repump the ions. In both cases Doppler cooling leads to a thermal state of motion with a temperature of about 1 mK, but $\langle n_D \rangle$ the corresponding mean number of vibrational quanta in the harmonic oscillator depends on the trap stiffness. For the trap used in the Be^+ experiments at NIST $\omega/2\pi$ was 11.2 MHz leading to $\langle n_D \rangle \simeq 1.3$ [211], while for the much weaker symmetry axis of the linear trap used for Ca^+ in Innsbruck ($\omega/2\pi \simeq 100$–180 kHz) $\langle n_D \rangle \simeq 50$ [212]. The design of traps is determined by a tradeoff between the spacing between the ions, which one wishes to be large enough to address each ion by single laser beams [213], and the cooling schemes which one wishes to keep as simple as possible. The Innsbruck ion trap has an ion spacing of about 15 micrometres whereas the NIST ion trap has a spacing of 1–2 micrometres.

For a single ion the notion of temperature is used in an ergodic sense, i.e. the average over repeated measurements will eventually reveal the final energy (or temperature). For motional frequencies ω_i larger than Γ it is more appropriate to consider the spectral structure of the cooling transition. Due to the vibrational motion of a trapped ion, the absorption spectrum acquires sidebands at $(\omega_0 \pm n\omega)$ where ω_0 denotes the transition frequency. The strength of these sidebands is given by the vibrational energy. It is possible to use these sidebands to obtain optical cooling below the Doppler limit. This method will be explained in the next section.

5.2.7 Sideband Cooling

To a good approximation a trapped ion can be treated as a quantum mechanical harmonic oscillator. As indicated in Fig. 5.9 for motion along one axis, the internal states of a single two-level atom are dressed with a harmonic oscillator level structure similar to a molecular structure, where the vibrational states are given by the trap frequency along this axis. These levels can then be conveniently labeled by the internal degrees of freedom $|e\rangle, |g\rangle$ (describing electronic excitation) and the external degrees of freedom $|n\rangle$ (i.e., motional excitation of the harmonic oscillator). For ions in a string the spectral structure is much richer , but the procedures and techniques outlined in this section are applicable, after some modification, to ion strings as well (see Sect. 5.3.3).

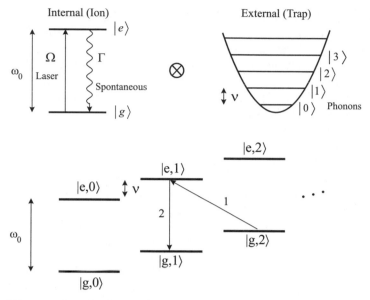

Fig. 5.9. Level scheme of a single two-level ion trapped in a harmonic potential. Sideband cooling is achieved by a photon absorption inducing the transition $|g,n\rangle \to |e,n-1\rangle$ indicated by arrow 1, and the subsequent decay (via spontaneous emission or an additional optical pump process) dominantly into $|g,n-1\rangle$ (see arrow 2).

Very efficient cooling is obtained by tuning the laser frequency such that absorption occurs on the lower sideband of the vibrational motion. This absorption is due to the transition $|g,n\rangle \to |e,n-1\rangle$ (e.g. arrow 1 in Fig. 5.9). Subsequent spontaneous emission appears predominantly on the carrier frequency, i.e. $|e,n-1\rangle \to |g,n-1\rangle$ (arrow 2 in Fig. 5.9) and thus the average excitation of the mechanical oscillation is effectively damped by one vibrational quantum. One can also actively repump to $|g,n-1\rangle$ via a fast decaying third level. If the photon recoil energy E_{rec} in the decay is much smaller than an oscillator energy quantum, the motional state changes only with probability $E_{rec}/(\hbar\omega)$. On average the recoil is not absorbed by the ion's motion, but rather by the whole trap structure. When these steps are repeated a sufficient number of times, the ion is finally left in the ground state with high probability, since once $|g,0\rangle$ is reached, it decouples from both laser fields (dark state).

In the experiments performed on Be$^+$, Raman transitions, that is transitions induced by two laser beams R1 and R2 indicated by R1/R2 in Fig. 5.8, couple two (hyperfine ground) states with a frequency difference of $\omega_{HF}/(2\pi) \simeq 1.25$ GHz via a virtual third level. The Raman beams are produced by detuning a frequency doubled dye laser from the $^2S_{1/2}$-$^2P_{3/2}$ transition by approx. 12 GHz and splitting it into two components about 1.25 GHz apart with an acousto-optical modulator (AOM). In this way the frequency difference and relative phase of the two components can be controlled with rf-accuracy, and not too high demands are put on the absolute stability of the laser. In the NIST experiment no special precautions are taken to spectrally narrow the dye laser which has a linewidth of approximately 1 MHz. For resolved sideband cooling, the frequency difference is tuned to $\omega_{HF} - \omega$ (red sideband). The cooling cycle then proceeds as described above, with the repumping induced by excitation on the $^2S_{1/2}$ to $^2P_{3/2}$ dipole transition also used for Doppler cooling [211].

For Ca^+, the metastable $D_{5/2}$ level, indicated in Fig. 5.8, with a spontaneous lifetime of approx. 1 second, can be used together with the ground state for resolved sideband cooling techniques. Again, motional quanta are removed by inducing transitions with the exciting laser detuned by ω to the red of the narrow resonance. In contrast to Raman transitions, the laser has to exhibit a good absolute frequency stability to resolve motional sidebands, so care has to be taken in the stabilisation. The setup used at Innsbruck University consists of a Ti:Sapphire laser at 729 nm, stabilised to a thermally and acoustically insulated reference cavity suspended in vacuum. The finesse of the cavity is 250 000 and preliminary tests suggest a laser linewidth of better than 1 kHz. In principle the recoilless return to the ground state could serve as a means of repumping, but the 1 second lifetime of the metastable state would make cooling very slow. To speed up the cooling cycle the ions are repumped to the ground state via the quickly decaying $P_{3/2}$ level. In this manner a single Hg^+ ion was cooled to the ground state in one dimension by the NIST group in 1989 [214]. In Ca^+, the repumping transition can be driven by a laser diode at 854 nm. Ground-state cooling of a single ion, and recently the ground-state cooling of various modes of vibration for two ions, has been observed in a spherical Paul trap at the University of Innsbruck [215]. The first cooling to the ground state of collective modes of motion of two trapped $^9Be^+$ ions has been reported in Ref. [216].

Obviously, ground state cooling is easier if Doppler cooling results in a low mean oscillator quantum number. In this case, only few resolved sideband cooling cycles are necessary to reach the vibrational ground state. For the stiff NIST trap, 5 Raman cooling cycles are enough to end up in the ground state 98% of the time [211]. In the case of Ca^+ in the spherical Innsbruck trap, 99.9% motional ground-state occupation (at a 4.5 MHz trap frequency) was measured after a cooling period of 6.4 ms [215]. Here the cooling rate was a few kHz. In the case of the linear Innsbruck trap, which has a lower trap frequency and consequently higher vibrational quantum numbers after Doppler cooling, the difficulty of ground-state cooling is enforced. However, the advantage of the linear trap, as mentioned above, is a wider ion-to-ion spacing, which simplifies individual addressing for quantum gate operations. Furthermore, low heating, as low as one phonon per 190 ms, has been observed which is related to the relatively large trap dimensions of 1.4 mm [215].

5.2.8 Electron Shelving and Detection of Vibrational Motion

The quantized motion of a small number of ions couples only very weakly to the environment and it is hard to detect it directly. In contrast, the internal electronic state can be detected in a very convenient way by the so-called "electron shelving" method proposed by Dehmelt [217]. This situation is quite similar to the "classical" cavity QED experiments, where the photon field is confined inside the superconducting cavity and hard to access, but can be inferred indirectly by measurements on the Rydberg atoms after their interaction with the oscillator mode.

The basic idea of the "electron shelving" method is very simple. A three-level system is needed consisting of a ground state $|g\rangle$, a metastable excited state $|e\rangle$, and a short lived excited state $|p\rangle$. The ground state is now coupled to the excited state $|e\rangle$ for some time, leaving the system in some superposition $\alpha|g\rangle + \beta|e\rangle$. If the $|g\rangle \to |p\rangle$ transition is now driven, the short-lived state $|p\rangle$ will be excited and decay if, and only if, the system collapses into $|g\rangle$. The fact that a photon is emitted with the decay of $|p\rangle$, that could, in principle, be observed, constitutes a measurement on the superposition. The measurement yields the result $|g\rangle$ with probability $|\alpha|^2$, corresponding to the excitation and decay of $|p\rangle$, and the result $|e\rangle$ with probability $|\beta|^2$, corresponding to the absence of excitation and decay of $|p\rangle$. Even if the efficiency for detecting the photon from one decay of $|p\rangle$ is very low (typically 10^{-3}), one can keep re-exciting the system and scatter millions of photons, eventually detecting a few of them provided the state is reduced to $|g\rangle$. If the state is "shelved" in the metastable state $|e\rangle$ no scattering will happen. In every single experiment the answer will be either $|g\rangle$ (scattered photons detected) or $|e\rangle$ (no scattered photons detected), thus measuring these states with almost 100 % detection efficiency and destroying all coherences between $|g\rangle$ and $|e\rangle$.

Averaged over many experiments, the number of tries where scattered photons are observed will be proportional to $|\alpha|^2$. As an example of the efficiency of this method, Fig. 5.10 shows the light scattered from a single Ca$^+$ ion into a photomultiplier during continuous excitation on the S$_{1/2} \to$ P$_{1/2}$ transition at 397 nm. When the Ca$^+$ ion is in the S$_{1/2}$ state it scatters about 2000 photons in 100 ms into the photomultiplier. At certain times, for example around $t =$20 s, the ion is excited into the D$_{5/2}$ state with a weak beam at 729 nm and the rate drops to about 150 events in 100 ms, given by the number of dark counts of the imperfect photomultiplier and some 397 nm light directly scattered from the exciting beam into the detector. Obviously, the two states can be well discriminated with good precision within 1 ms, and the average dark time is about 1 second, the radiative lifetime of the D$_{5/2}$ state.

With minor modifications the quantum shelving method can also be applied to distinguish between hyperfine ground states, as is necessary in experiments with ^{9}Be$^+$. Since $|g\rangle$ is chosen to be the state with maximum m_F

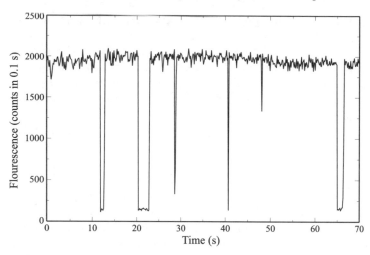

Fig. 5.10. Quantum jumps of a single ^{40}Ca$^+$ ion. If the ion makes the transition to the metastable D$_{5/2}$ state, the fluorescence drops. After a mean time equal to the lifetime of the excited state ($\tau \simeq 1$ s), a spontaneous transition returns the ion to the ground state and the fluorescence returns to the higher level.

($F = 2, m_F = 2$), one can excite a cycling transition to the ^{2}P$_{3/2}$ ($F = 3$, $m_F = 3$) state using σ^+ circular polarised laser light (D2 in Fig. 5.8) leaving the ion no other decay channel but the one back to $|g\rangle$. A combination of experimental imperfections in producing the polarised light σ^+ and off resonant excitations can lead to optical pumping into non-scattering states, reducing the detection efficiency [218].

5.2.9 Coherent States of Motion

The production of coherent states of light using cavity QED has been discussed in Sect. 5.2.3. Here we describe the production of coherent states of motion for a ion(s) in a trap. Starting from the ground state, coherent states of motion can be produced by coupling the ion(s) to a classical force resonant with the oscillation frequency. The most convenient way is to expose the ions to an electric driving field at ω. Depending on the magnitude, phase and duration of the drive the emerging coherent states are described by a complex parameter α with $|\alpha|^2 = \bar{n}$, the mean quantum number of the oscillator.

With more than one ion, normal modes can be excited by dialing in their resonant frequencies. Care has to be taken that the exciting field has the correct geometry. The centre-of-mass mode will be driven by a homogenous field, the stretch mode needs some field curvature, and higher order modes will need higher moments of the field. A couple of movies taken of large coherent states ($\bar{n} \simeq 100000$) in a string of up to seven ions can be seen on the home page of the Innsbruck group [207] and are also displayed in Fig. 5.11. The field inhomogeneity in this experiment was large enough to excite the

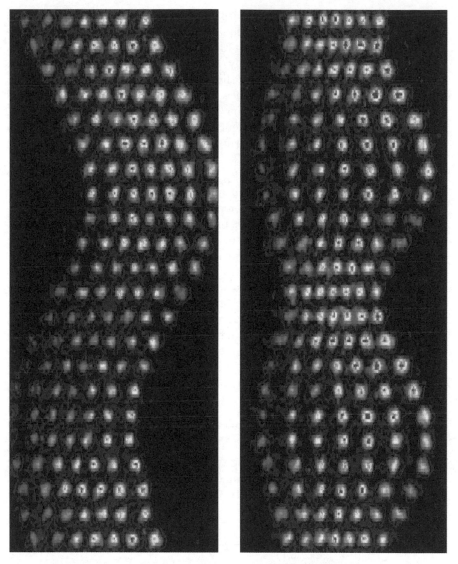

Fig. 5.11. Experimental demonstration of (**a**) the breathing mode and (**b**) the centre-of-mass motion of a string of 7 ions. The figures are compilations of snapshots take of the string of ions at fixed time intervals (short compared to the time scale of the vibrational motion).

lowest two normal modes. Figure 5.11(a) shows the stretch or breathing mode and Fig. 5.11(b) shows the centre-of-mass motion. The pictures were taken stroboscopically with a slow scan CCD camera.

Instead of using the electric charge of the ions and electric external fields to induce the coherent excitation of vibrational modes one can use the internal state of the ions interacting with laser light fields. Two laser (Raman) beams with a frequency difference equal to ω will not induce internal state transitions, but will coherently excite higher and higher vibrational modes. As a result the ion(s) will (collectively) oscillate with the harmonic oscillator frequency ω, driven by the beating of the two light fields. Since each of the two laser (Raman) beams is near resonance with the $^2S_{1/2}$ to $^2P_{1/2}$ transition, an oscillating dipole force acts on the ion. By polarising the Raman beams σ^+, one can even make this force dependent on the internal state: For $|g\rangle$ there is no coupling state in the $^2P_{1/2}$ hyperfine manifold, so only the $|e\rangle$ state will feel the dipole force. This point will be crucial for creating Schrödinger's cat type states as described in Sect. 5.2.11. Both techniques to produce coherent states have been used by the NIST group on a single trapped Be^+ ion.

For coherent states with a small mean vibrational quantum number the amplitude of the vibrational motion is too small to be resolved with a camera, and it is very difficult to detect the motion of the ion directly. Instead, one can couple the vibrational motion to the internal two-state system.

To measure the vibrational motion, that is, to determine the populations of phonon-number states $|n\rangle$, we first induce "blue sideband" transitions by laser light, frequency-detuned to the blue by $\delta = +\omega$. These transitions between $|g, n\rangle$ and $|e, n + 1\rangle$ are indicated in Fig. 5.12. By using continuous laser light, Rabi oscillations will be induced between the levels indicated by the arrows in Fig. 5.12.

With the blue-detuned laser on, the probability $P_g(t)$ that an ion originally in internal state $|g\rangle$ is still there after time t is given by

$$P_g(t) = \frac{1}{2}\left[1 + \sum_{n=0}^{\infty} P_n \cos\left(2\Omega_{n,n+1}t\right)e^{-\gamma_n t}\right],\tag{5.6}$$

where P_n is the probability of finding the atom in the nth motional number state and $\Omega_{n,n+1}$ is the exchange frequency between $|g, n\rangle$ and $|e, n + 1\rangle$. In the limit discussed in connection with (5.5), $\Omega_{n,n+1} = \Omega_0\eta\sqrt{n+1}$. The key

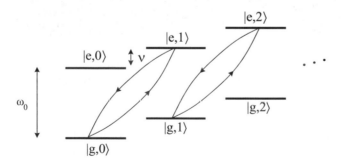

Fig. 5.12. Level scheme of a single two-level ion trapped in a harmonic potential. The arrows indicate Rabi oscillations between the levels $|g, n\rangle$ and $|e, n + 1\rangle$. The Rabi frequency depends on n.

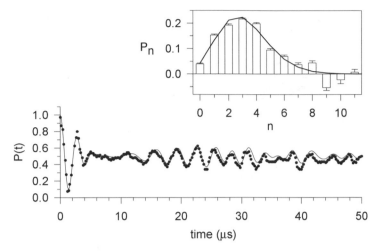

Fig. 5.13. P_g for a coherent state. The solid line is a fit of the data (dots) to a sum of number states having a coherent state distribution. The fitted value for the mean quantum number is $\bar{n} = 3.1\pm0.1$. The inset shows the amplitudes of the number state components (bars) with a fit to a Poisson distribution, corresponding to $\bar{n} = 2.9+0.1$ (line).(Reproduced from Ref. [220])

point is that the frequencies are different for all pairs $(n, n+1)$, thus a Fourier transform of $P_g(t)$ will yield all probabilities P_n. Data points are taken by shining in the blue sideband radiation for time t and then measuring the internal state of the ion with the "shelving" technique as discussed in the previous section. In the limit of many experiments for each time t (1000 experiments in practice) one can deduce $P_g(t)$. The time traces can then be Fourier transformed to get the probability distribution of motional levels P_n. The experimentally determined signal $P_g(t)$ and its Fourier transform for a $\bar{n} = 3.1$ coherent state of a single Be^+ ion are shown in Fig. 5.13. The trace is very similar to the cavity-QED results shown in Fig.5.2. After a quick collapse around 6 μs, the signal revives at $t \simeq 12$ μs. Another collapse and revival is visible from 32 μs to 45 μs before the signal is finally washed out by decoherence.

5.2.10 Wigner Function of the One-Phonon State

The P_n, as determined in the previous section, correspond directly to the diagonal elements ρ_{nn} of the density matrix ρ and at first glance this seems to be all one can determine. But one can circumvent this problem by coherently shifting the initial motional state. Experimentally this is done exactly as creating coherent states. Instead of shifting the ground state, $|\alpha\rangle = U(\alpha)|0\rangle$, the initial state of motion is now shifted, $|\Psi_{\mathrm{mot}}, \alpha\rangle = U(\alpha)|\Psi_{\mathrm{mot}}\rangle$. Then the occupation of the different number states $|\langle n|U(\alpha)|\Psi_{\mathrm{mot}}\rangle|^2$ is measured as described in Sect. 5.2.9. By doing that with a sufficient number of different

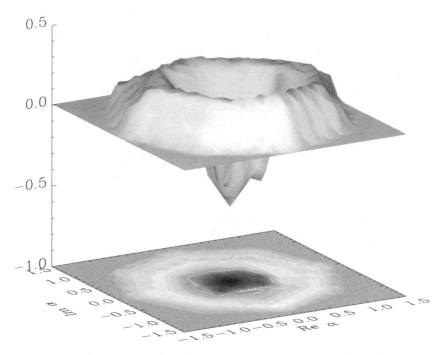

Fig. 5.14. Surface and contour plots of the reconstructed Wigner function $W(\alpha)$ of an approximate $n = 1$ number state. The negative values of $W(\alpha)$ around the origin highlight the non-classical nature of this state. (Reproduced from Ref. [219])

shift parameters α, one can reconstruct the off-diagonal elements of the density matrix in the number state basis or the Wigner function of the initial motional state [219].

Starting from the ground state of motion and with the tools at hand that are offered by the Hamiltonian given in (5.5), motional states can almost be created at will. In practice thermal states, number (Fock) states, squeezed states, Schrödinger cat type and other superpositions of number states of a single ion [219]–[221] have all been created and analysed by the NIST group.

Number states are created from the ground state by alternating π-pulses on the blue and red sideband. This sequence makes the ion climb the following ladder: $|g, 0\rangle \rightarrow |e, 1\rangle \rightarrow |g, 2\rangle \rightarrow$... and so forth. Number states up to $n = 16$ have been created this way. Their signal $P_g(t)$ is a simple sinusoid whose frequency increases roughly proportional to $\sqrt{n+1}$ with deviations caused by the fact that η is nonzero ($\eta = 0.202$, see Fig. 1 in [220]). More interesting is the Wigner function which exhibits negative regions for number states when n is odd. The experimentally determined Wigner function of the $|n\rangle = |1\rangle$ number state is depicted in Fig. 5.14. The experimentally determined Wigner function is negative around the origin, in good agreement with theory.

5.2.11 Squeezed States and Schrödinger Cats with Ions

Squeezed vacuum states can be produced analogously to an optical parametric oscillator by driving the ion at 2ω either with an electric field or with
two Raman beams detuned accordingly. Squeezed vacuum states with a ratio of quadrature variances of 40 (16 dB noise suppression in the squeezed
quadrature) [220] have been created experimentally. Unfortunately in contrast to squeezed light, there is no sensitive measurement application so far
that could make use of this astonishing degree of squeezing.

Schrödinger's cat type states of the exact same form as (5.4) but involving
the motion of the ion instead of a photon field have been created in Be^+ [221].
After laser cooling to the $|g, n = 0\rangle$ state, represented by Fig. 5.15 (a), the
Schrödinger cat state is created by applying several sequential pulses of the
Raman beams.

A $\pi/2$-pulse on the carrier frequency splits the wave function into an
equal superposition of states $|g, 0\rangle$ and $|e, 0\rangle$ as indicated in Fig. 5.15 (b).
Then polarised Raman beams detuned relative to one another by ω excite
only the motion correlated with the $|e\rangle$ component to a coherent state $|\alpha\rangle$
as described in Sect. 5.2.9 and indicated in Fig. 5.15 (c). Figure 5.15 (d)
illustrates how a π-pulse on the carrier then swaps the internal states of
the superposition. Figure 5.15 (e) indicates how a second pulse of polarised
Raman beams excites the motion correlated with the new $|e\rangle$ component to
a second coherent state $|\alpha e^{i\phi}\rangle$. After this step the state has the desired form

$$|\Psi\rangle = \frac{1}{\sqrt{2}} \left(|e\rangle |\alpha e^{i\phi}\rangle + |g\rangle |\alpha e^{-i\phi}\rangle \right) . \tag{5.7}$$

The relative phase ϕ is determined by the phases of the rf difference frequencies of the Raman beams, which is easily controlled by phase-locking
the rf sources. In examining the decoherence properties of this state, one has

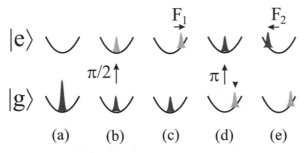

Fig. 5.15. Creation of Schrödinger cat states with ions. (a) Initial state $|g, n = 0\rangle$.
(b) A $\pi/2$-pulse creates the state $|g, 0\rangle$ and $|e, 0\rangle$. (c) Excitation of a coherent state
of vibrational motion via optical interaction between polarised Raman beams and
$|e\rangle$. (d) A π-pulse interchanges the internal state populations. (e) Finally another
coherent state is excited for the new $|e\rangle$ component, creating the Schrödinger cat
state.

to live with the drawback that it is not as well characterized and modeled as the decay of a cavity mode. On the other hand, the variety of possible interactions may enable the experimentalist to engineer a reservoir at will [222]. This artificial reservoir will largely determine the decoherence as long as the coupling is adjusted in a way that the induced dissipation timescales are much shorter than those of the dissipation observed without reservoir.

5.2.12 Quantum Logic with a Single Trapped ^{9}Be$^+$ Ion

Trapped and cooled ions interacting with laser fields are strong candidates for the experimental implementation of quantum gates as described in Sect. 4.3. This was first pointed out by Cirac and Zoller [156]. The quantum information is stored in the qubits made up by the internal levels of the ions, while the normal modes of external motion, shared by all ions in the trap, can serve as the "data bus" to entangle the internal states (see Sect. 5.3.7). Up to now, several groups have cooled ions in a linear trap to the point where they form crystalline strings (see e.g. Fig. 5.11). Cooling to the ground state of motion for two ions has been achieved and work is in progress to demonstrate ground-state cooling for strings containing higher numbers of ions.

In an experiment performed in 1995, the NIST group created a quantum controlled-NOT gate between the internal two-state system of one ion ($|g\rangle$ and $|e\rangle$, target bit) and its motion in the trap ($|n = 0\rangle$ and $|n = 1\rangle$, control bit), thus demonstrating that it is possible to read from the "data bus" the harmonic motion [223]. A sequence of three laser pulses was applied to perform the gate:

1. A $\pi/2$ pulse on the carrier generated a linear superposition of $|g\rangle$ and $|e\rangle$.
2. A 2π pulse on the blue sideband of an auxiliary transition connecting $|e\rangle$ and $|aux\rangle$ introduced a conditional phase shift on the $|e\rangle$ part of the superposition. This sideband only couples $|e\rangle$ and $|aux\rangle$ if the motion is in $|n = 1\rangle$, then the phase of the $|e\rangle$-part is reversed.
3. Finally a $-\pi/2$ pulse on the carrier led to constructive or destructive interference for one of the states, depending on whether or not the conditional phase shift was acquired by the $|e\rangle$-part.

To get a more intuitive picture one can think of the whole sequence as a Ramsey experiment on resonance. Starting in $|g\rangle$ the first $\pi/2$-pulse creates the superposition $|g\rangle + |e\rangle$. Then, depending on whether or not $n = 0$, the superposition remains untouched or a phase shift is introduced for the excited part (i.e., $|g\rangle - |e\rangle$, only if $n = 1$). The last step is a $-\pi/2$ pulse. Hence without the phase shift the internal state returns to $|g\rangle$, but if the phase shift occured ($n = 1$) it will be flipped to $|e\rangle$. The control qubit remains unchanged during the process. The NIST group measured the truth table for the controlled-NOT operation implemented in this way and also demonstrated the coherence of the gate (see Figs. 2 and 3 in Ref. [223]).

5.2.13 Comparison and Perspectives

In the preceding sections experiments on quantum information and quantum computing based on cavity QED and trapped ions have been described. Even if cavity QED and ion-trap experiments basically implement Jaynes–Cummings type Hamiltonians and thus the same dynamics, each technique has its own assets and drawbacks. The essential differences between the two techniques are presented in this section.

The initial state preparation involves standard technology for microwave cavity QED since the ground state of the cavity may be reached by cryogenic cooling to ^{3}He temperature. The generation of a velocity-selected beam of long-lived circular Rydberg atoms involves an excitation by some standard infrared diode lasers and a radiofrequency field. Laser cooling of ions mostly involves ultraviolet light sources. Cavity QED experiments realise rigorously the Jaynes–Cummings interaction, while the coupling for ions in a trap is only an approximation of the Jaynes–Cummings Hamiltonian in the limit of small Lamb–Dicke parameter. On the other hand, the coupling of trapped ions with the oscillator mode provides more freedom and can be tailored at will to realise more sophisticated functions than the basic Jaynes–Cummings interaction. The atomic/ionic decoherence is practically negligible for both Rydberg states of atoms and hyperfine/metastable states of ions. Concerning the harmonic oscillator mode, the losses of the superconducting cavity are fairly well understood and can be modeled. The only adjustable parameter of decoherence, the cavity quality factor, is determined independently by classical microwave techniques. For ions in traps, the sources of vibrational decoherence are not yet fully understood. The calculation of "fundamental" sources of decoherence such as damping induced by the image charge of the ion in the electrode structure or background gas collisions, result in order of magnitude lower heating rates than observed experimentally [215, 218]. This "anomalous" heating will be further studied and may eventually be overcome since there are no known fundamental reasons for it.

To perform interesting operations for quantum information, it is necessary to manipulate at least a few quantum bits. Using present techniques, cavity QED experiments relying on a beam of circular Rydberg atoms crossing a cavity turn out to be quite difficult with more than two or three consecutive atoms. As discussed above, the average number of atoms per pulse has to be kept well below one to avoid two-atom events. Three or four atom coincidences are very rare and the acquisition time increases exponentially with the number of atoms. This limitation does not affect ion trap experiments. Trapping a few ions in a linear trap is relatively easy. Individual addressing of single ions with well-focused laser pulses is feasible. Provided the collection of ions is cooled to the vibrational ground state, quantum logic operations involving a few qubits can be realised.

Another major asset of the ion trap experiments is the possibility of detecting the ion's state with almost 100% quantum efficiency, using the quantum shelving methods. Experiments testing the Bell inequalities on entangled trapped ions, for instance, could very easily close the detection efficiency loophole which is still open in the other experiments involving photons or even atoms (in cavity QED it seems that there is no prospect of increasing the detection efficiency far above 90%).

It thus seems that "classical" cavity QED experiments are more suited for investigations of decoherence and entanglement with a limited number of atoms involved (up to about four) in a very well controlled system. The preparation of an entangled triplet of atoms of the GHZ type is currently being performed. Further studies of decoherence will also be undertaken. In particular, it is possible to directly determine the Wigner function of the cavity field [224]. This would allow an in-depth understanding of the decoherence of a Schrödinger cat state. Finally, experiments with two separate superconducting cavities could yield non-local mesoscopic states, combining two most intriguing features of the quantum world.

In ion traps the reconstruction of the Wigner function has already been demonstrated, but the absence of theoretical models and the unclear nature of the decoherence process in ion traps complicates its understanding. Ion traps are also promising as a tool to investigate quantum logic on a moderate scale, involving perhaps up to a dozen qubits and a few hundred operations. However the implementation of the Shor factorisation algorithm (see Sect. 4.2) with "interesting" numbers to break classical cryptographic codes requires at least 400 qubits which seems out of reach with current knowledge and technology [225].

New ways have to be found to overcome fundamental limits such as spontaneous emission, but the implementation of error correction and code stabilisation techniques (Chap. 7) might offer a way of tackling these issues. En route, there are many interesting quantum information processing operations already accessible with a few qubits, for example entanglement purification. These "information-enriched" states could also be used to improve the performance of frequency standards using ions in traps (Sect. 7.6).

Beyond all possible applications, experiments on simple fundamental systems interacting in a well controlled environment will give us a glimpse of the most intimate features of quantum mechanics.

5.3 Linear Ion Traps for Quantum Computation

H.C. Nägerl, F. Schmidt-Kaler, J. Eschner, R. Blatt,
W. Lange, H. Baldauf, H. Walther

5.3.1 Introduction

Having achieved almost perfect control of the quantum state of a single ion, as shown in Sect. 5.2, attention has turned to systems of several ions with well controlled interactions between them [226]. Manipulations of their overall quantum state include the preparation of entangled states that have no classical counterpart. Moreover, the possibility of entangling massive particles offers prospects for new experiments including measurements with Bell states and GHZ states [176] which would allow new tests of quantum mechanics. Entanglement of particles offers the possibility to study the process of quantum measurement in detail and to investigate the phenomenon of decoherence [183, 221].

Due to its unique properties, a string of ions in a linear trap has been proposed for the realisation of quantum logic gates [156], the basic building blocks of a quantum computer. This device operates with quantum registers made up of quantum bits (qubits) which can be manipulated analogously to classical bits by using gate operations. Ion trap quantum gates rely on the entanglement of internal degrees of freedom of the ions (electronic excitation) and the collective motion (vibrational excitation) of the trapped string to logically combine the qubits. The quantum mechanical analogue of a classical XOR-gate is the so-called controlled-NOT operation which can be realised using a well defined series of laser pulses to address two different ions in the string. It has been shown that a controlled-NOT gate is a universal quantum gate, so that in principle arbitrary computations can be carried out using just this two-ion quantum gate and one-bit rotations [227]. The realisation of these gate operations based on a string of ions is of fundamental interest since all basic algorithms could be tested using just a string of trapped ions.

In this section, the specific properties of linear ion traps are summarised and their use for quantum computation is discussed. In Sect. 5.3.2 we review the operation of ion traps and various realisations of linear traps are described. In Sect. 5.3.3 we present the techniques required to achieve cooling to the ground state of motion, a necessary prerequisite for realising quantum gates with strings of ions. Ordered structures of ions are briefly discussed in Sect. 5.3.4. In Sects. 5.3.5 to 5.3.9 the specific techniques needed for the operation of quantum gates for, e.g., state preparation and manipulation, common mode excitations and the readout of the internal electronic state with unit detection efficiency are reviewed and discussed.

5.3.2 Ion Confinement in a Linear Paul Trap

Charged particles, such as atomic ions, can be confined by electromagnetic fields, either by using a combination of a static electric and magnetic field (Penning trap) or a time dependent inhomogeneous electric field (Paul trap) [197]. For the application of trapped ions as quantum bits and registers, the Paul trap, and especially its linear variant, seem favorable [228].

In order to confine a particle a restoring force F is required, for example, $F \propto -r$ where r is the distance from the origin of the trap. Such forces may be obtained with a quadrupole potential $\Phi = \Phi_0(\alpha x^2 + \beta y^2 + \gamma z^2)/r_0^2$, where Φ_0 denotes a voltage applied to a quadrupole electrode configuration, r_0 is the characteristic trap size and the constants α, β, γ determine the shape of the potential. For example, the three-dimensional confinement in a Paul trap is described by $\alpha = \beta = -2\gamma$, while for $\alpha = -\beta, \gamma = 0$ the quadrupole mass filter is obtained. The three-dimensional Paul trap provides a confining force with respect to a single point in space and therefore is mostly used for single ion experiments or for the confinement of large centro-symmetric ion clouds. In order to realise a quantum register with trapped ions, linear arrays of ions, i.e. ion strings, are required. Therefore, in most cases one employs the linear variant of the Paul trap, which is based on the quadrupole mass filter potential. The latter potential provides confining forces in the two directions perpendicular to the z-axis, but the motion along the z-axis is not affected. For axial confinement, additional electrodes must be employed. Radial confinement of the ions requires a dc-voltage U_{dc} and an ac-voltage $V_{ac}\cos(\Omega t)$ applied to the electrodes. Near the trap axis this creates a potential of the form

$$\Phi = \frac{U_{dc} + V_{ac}\cos(\Omega t)}{2r_0^2}(x^2 - y^2), \tag{5.8}$$

where r_0 denotes the distance from the trap axis to the surface of one of the electrodes. If only a dc-voltage is applied, (5.8) represents a saddle potential which leads to stable confinement in one direction only, as shown in Fig. 5.16. However, with the time dependent (ac) voltage, trapping is obtained. As can be seen from Fig. 5.16, reversing the sign of the ac-voltage leads to confinement in the previously unstable direction. With an appropriately chosen frequency Ω, particles can be trapped indefinitely. As is inferred from (5.8), the potential is ideally created using hyperbolically shaped electrodes (see Fig. 5.17a). For simplicity they are usually approximated by cylindrical rods as in Fig. 5.17b, or more elaborate shapes (Fig. 5.17c), depending on the requirements for laser access and diagnostics. Axial confinement is provided by an additional static potential U_{cap} applied along the z-axis using additional ring electrodes (Fig. 5.17b) or segmented parts of the rod electrodes (Fig. 5.17c). This creates a static harmonic well in the z direction which is characterized by the longitudinal trap frequency

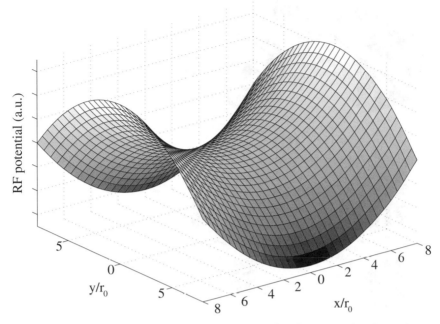

RF potential (a.u.)

y/r_0

x/r_0

Fig. 5.16. Saddle potential of the rf-Paul trap. Confinement of a charged particle near $x = y = 0$ is achieved by rapid alternation of the sign of the potential

$$\omega_z = \sqrt{2\kappa q U_{\mathrm{cap}}/m z_0^2}\,. \tag{5.9}$$

Here, m and q denote the ion mass and charge, z_0 is half the length between the axially confining electrodes, and κ is an empirically determined geometric factor of order unity which accounts for the particular electrode configuration. In principle, exact values of κ can be obtained either numerically or, in some cases, analytically. From a practical point of view, however, using a measured value of κ suffices to describe the experimental data. In the x and y directions, the equations of motion resulting from (5.8) are given by the Mathieu equations [228]

$$\frac{d^2 u_x}{d\tau^2} + (a_x + 2q_x \cos(2\tau))u_x = 0 \tag{5.10}$$

$$\frac{d^2 u_y}{d\tau^2} + (a_y + 2q_y \cos(2\tau))u_y = 0\,, \tag{5.11}$$

where

(a)   **(b)**

(c)   **(d)**

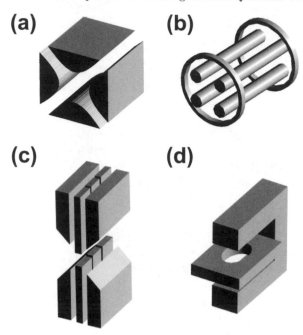

Fig. 5.17. Various realisations of the linear ion trap. (**a**) Linear quadrupole trap; (**b**) four rod trap; (**c**) linear end cap trap; (**d**) Paul trap with elongated ring electrode.

$$a_x = \frac{4q}{m\Omega^2} \left(\frac{U_{dc}}{r_0^2} - \frac{\kappa U_{cap}}{z_0^2} \right) \tag{5.12}$$

$$a_y = -\frac{4q}{m\Omega^2} \left(\frac{U_{dc}}{r_0^2} + \frac{\kappa U_{cap}}{z_0^2} \right) \tag{5.13}$$

$$q_x = -q_y = \frac{2qV_{ac}}{m\Omega^2 r_0^2} \tag{5.14}$$

$$\tau = \frac{\Omega t}{2}. \tag{5.15}$$

The general solution of (5.10,5.11) can be found as an infinite series of harmonics of the trap frequency Ω [197]. In practice, the condition that $a_i < q_i^2 \ll 1, i = x, y$ is usually fulfilled, allowing for an analytical approximate solution to the equations of motion. It consists of a harmonic secular motion (macromotion) at frequencies ω_i with a superimposed micromotion at the trap's driving frequency Ω,

$$u_i(t) = A_i \cos(\omega_i t + \varphi_i) \left[1 + \frac{q_i}{2} \cos(\Omega t) \right], i = x, y. \tag{5.16}$$

The amplitude A_i and the phases φ_i depend on the initial conditions, and the secular frequencies are given by

$$\omega_i = \beta_i \frac{\Omega}{2}, \qquad \beta_i \approx \left[a_i + \frac{q_i^2}{2} \right].$$ (5.17)

In this limit and for $U_{dc} = 0$ (which is usually chosen), the micromotion is negligibly small and a confined ion oscillates as if trapped in a harmonic pseudopotential Ψ in the radial direction, given by

$$q\Psi = q \frac{|\nabla \Phi|^2}{4m\Omega^2} = \frac{1}{2} m \omega_r^2 (x^2 + y^2)$$ (5.18)

with the radial secular frequency $\omega_r \approx q V_{ac} / (\sqrt{2} m \Omega r_0^2)$.

A major advantage of a linear Paul trap (compared with a three-dimensional Paul trap used for the storage of single ions) is that the micromotion completely vanishes for ions confined to the z-axis. The motion is then a pure harmonic oscillation in the static potential providing axial confinement.

Although the use of linear traps for quantum registers with ions seems favorable, an elongated version of the three-dimensional Paul trap can be used as well to provide strings of two and three ions [216]. Such a device consists of an elliptically shaped ring electrode and two end cap electrodes (Fig. 5.17d) and the ion string is oriented along the long axis of the ring electrode. With this geometry, much higher trap frequencies are possible than with a linear trap, which is an advantage for optical cooling (see Sects. 5.2.7 and 5.3.3). On the other hand, there is always residual micromotion which may cause rf-heating of the string.

5.3.3 Laser Cooling and Quantum Motion

In order to store quantum information in a well-defined way, the quantum state of each single ion in a string of ions has to be carefully prepared. This is achieved with laser cooling techniques in a way similar to that described in Sect. 5.2.7 for a single trapped ion. The final stage of cooling will also be a sideband cooling technique which eventually prepares the ion string in the motional ground state. However, the appearance of distinct modes of vibration of the string, with different frequencies, modifies the cooling process. In particular, the picture of sideband cooling as described in Sect. 5.2.7 does not generally hold for two or more ions. The important difference is that the incommensurate frequencies of the vibrational modes lead to a quasi-continuous energy spectrum rather than a spectrum of discrete equidistant levels, as for one single mode of vibration. The energy levels of the system are now labeled by the internal state $|g\rangle$ or $|e\rangle$ and the motional state $|\mathbf{n}\rangle$ where $\mathbf{n} = (n_1, n_2, ...)$ is the vector of quantum numbers of the modes of vibration with frequencies $\omega = (\omega_1, \omega_2, ...)$. Correspondingly, the resonance spectrum for transitions $|g, \mathbf{n}\rangle$ to $|e, \mathbf{m}\rangle$ exhibits sidebands which are much more densely spaced than for a single ion, and by tuning the laser to one specific frequency, all sideband transitions around that frequency, in an interval of the linewidth γ of the transition, are excited simultaneously.

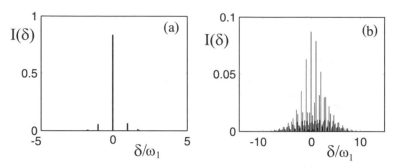

Fig. 5.18. Resonance spectrum of two trapped ions inside (**a**) and outside (**b**) the Lamb–Dicke regime. The optical transition without change of the motional state, at detuning zero, is shown together with its vibrational sidebands at their respective detunings. Inside the Lamb–Dicke regime (**a**) only the fundamental sidebands at $\delta = \omega_{1,2}$ are significant, which involve the exchange of just one vibrational quantum. Outside the Lamb-Dicke regime (**b**), many sidebands appear which involve changes in the excitation of both modes by one or more quanta. Taken from [229].

More precisely, two cases have to be distinguished [229]. If the sideband cooling happens in the Lamb–Dicke regime, i.e. if only vibrational states n_j and $n_{j\pm1}$ are appreciably coupled by the recoil of the light interaction, only first-order sidebands contribute, while the exchange of more than one vibrational quantum is suppressed. The sideband spectrum is simple, see Fig. 5.18a, and tuning to one of the sidebands leads to cooling of the respective mode, as for a single ion. Yet the situation is not exactly the same because the other modes, which do not interact with the laser, are heated due to spontaneous emission, so that different settings of the detuning, or a sufficiently large linewidth γ, are required to reach the ground state for all modes.

The other case, i.e. sideband cooling outside the Lamb–Dicke regime, applies to most of the currently pursued implementations of quantum logic with linear ion traps. An example of a sideband spectrum for this case with a string of two ions is shown in Fig. 5.18b. Obviously, if the laser is tuned to a certain frequency below resonance, a set of transitions is excited which involve changes in the excitation of both modes by one or more quanta. In this case, in contrast to the Lamb–Dicke regime, both modes are cooled simultaneously. Furthermore, there appears a new dependence of the cooling rate on the linewidth γ of the transition: The cooling rate increases nonlinearly with the linewidth because first the rate for absorption emission cycles is proportional to γ, and second the number of levels to which an initial state is coupled, and hence the number of channels through which the ion string is cooled, also increases with γ. Consideration of the cooling rate, i.e. the total cooling time, is important if, after Doppler cooling, many vibrational quanta are still excited. This is typically the case in linear ion-trap experiments.

It has been shown by numerical calculations [229] that both inside and outside the Lamb–Dicke regime, sideband cooling can be used to bring two ions to their motional ground state. Outside of the Lamb–Dicke regime, the strong dependence of the cooling rate on the linewidth γ of the transition can be exploited to optimise the cooling time, by adjusting γ in the course of the cooling process.

The ion species employed for the cooling does not necessarily have to be the same as that used for the desired quantum calculation. At the Max-Planck Institute for Quantum Optics in Garching, an experiment is set up in which a linear string containing magnesium and indium ions is employed. Indium can be sideband cooled to the ground state very efficiently [230], while magnesium would be used to carry the quantum information. The separation of cooling and computation allows the continuous cooling of all normal modes without disturbing the contents of the quantum register.

As a last experimental consideration for laser cooling to the vibrational ground state in Paul traps, we mention that any residual stray electric fields have to be carefully compensated. Such fields may be caused by patch fields on the electrodes and will result in ions being pushed away from the trap axis. Consequently, ions undergo residual micromotion which can prevent proper optical cooling. Stray fields are compensated by the application of dc-potentials to additional electrodes in order to push the ions back to the trap axis. This is routinely done in all three spatial dimensions with single trapped ions in ordinary Paul traps. A similar technique can be applied in linear ion traps. In the case of a string of ions, careful alignment of all electrodes is an important precondition for the cancellation of micromotion.

5.3.4 Ion Strings and Normal Modes

In a linear ion trap, ions can be confined and optically cooled such that they form ordered structures [212, 231]. If the radial confinement is strong enough, ions arrange themselves in a linear pattern along the trap axis at distances determined by the equilibrium of the Coulomb repulsion and the potential providing axial confinement. Figure 5.19 shows an example of a string of Ca^+ ions in a linear trap.

The equilibrium positions of the ions may be numerically determined. If the trap potential is sufficiently harmonic, the positions can be described by a single parameter, the axial frequency ω_z (5.9) [212, 232]. Small displacements of the ions from their equilibrium positions cannot be described in terms of the motion of individual ions since the Coulomb interaction couples the charged particles. Instead, the motion of the ion string must be described in terms of normal modes of the entire chain vibrating at distinct frequencies [156, 232]. As an example, consider two ions confined in a linear ion trap. The first normal mode corresponds to an oscillation of the entire chain of ions moving back and forth as if they were rigidly joined. This oscillation is referred to as the *centre-of-mass mode* (COM) of the string [232]. The second

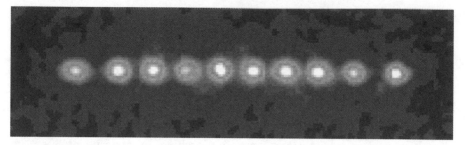

Fig. 5.19. Example of a string of ions in a linear Paul trap. The average distance between two ions is about 10 μm. The exposure time for the CCD camera was 1 s. The measured resolution of the imaging system consisting of lens and CCD camera is better than 4 μm. See also Ref. [231] for comparison.

normal mode corresponds to an oscillation where the ions move in opposite directions. More generally, this so-called *breathing mode* describes a string of N ions moving with an amplitude proportional to their mean distance from the trap center. Figure 5.11a and b in Sect. 5.2.9 shows the stroboscopic observation made at the university of Innsbruck of the breathing mode and the centre-of-mass motion for a string of 7 ions.

Explicit calculation of the normal modes (eigenmodes) and the respective eigenfrequencies of an ion string yield the following simple results [200, 232]: (i) for a one-dimensional string consisting of N ions there are exactly N normal modes and normal frequencies; (ii) the center of mass mode has a frequency which is exactly equal to the frequency of a single ion; (iii) higher order frequencies are nearly independent of the ion number N, and are given by $(1, 1.732, 2.4, 3.05(2), 3.67(2), 4.28(2), 4.88(2), ...) \omega_z$, where the numbers in brackets indicate the maximum frequency deviation as N is increased from 1 to 10 ions, (iv) the relative amplitudes of the normal modes have to be evaluated numerically (at least for strings with more than 3 ions, see equation (28) in Ref. [232]).

After loading the trap with a string of ions, normal modes can be excited by applying additional ac-voltages to either one of the ring electrodes or to the compensation electrodes [212]. The normal mode excitation can be observed as an increase of the spot width on the CCD camera long before there is a dip in the fluorescence collected by the photomultiplier. The frequency measured for the breathing mode agrees (to within 1%) with the expected frequency of $\sqrt{3}$ times the centre-of-mass frequency. Figure 5.20 shows the excitation of the centre-of-mass mode (158.5 kHz) for two excitation amplitudes and the excitation of the breathing mode (276.0 kHz) for 5 ions. In order to excite the breathing mode it was necessary to apply voltages which are typically about 300 times higher than the ones needed for excitation of the centre-of-mass mode (3 V compared to 0.01 V). Excitations of higher order modes were not observed with the ac-voltages available in the setup of [212]. This is due to the fact that the exciting field is nearly uniform along the ion string, meaning

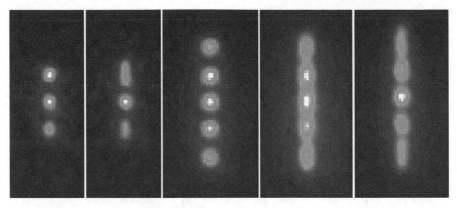

Fig. 5.20. Vibrational excitation of a string of five ions by an externally applied ac-voltage. From left to right: no excitation, weak and strong excitation of the COM-mode (158.5 kHz), excitation of the breathing mode (276.0 kHz).

that the higher modes which need field gradients across the ions are much less efficiently excited.

The COM vibration is excited with a uniform field and therefore is very susceptible to field fluctuations whose spatial variation is usually small on a length scale given by the ion distance. In contrast, the excitation of higher order modes requires large field gradients. Therefore, unwanted excitation occurs much less frequently for higher order modes. Note that during a quantum computation, vibrational quanta in the ion chain are generated by Raman sideband transitions induced by laser interaction with a single ion.

5.3.5 Ions as Quantum Register

Quantum information may be stored in an ion by preparing it in either one of two distinct electronic states $|g\rangle$, $|e\rangle$ or in any superposition of them. An obvious requirement for the choice of these states is that both should have a radiative lifetime sufficiently long for the computation to finish before coherence is destroyed by spontaneous decay. One possibility is to use the ground state of the ion and a metastable excited state, or even two metastable states. Lifetimes can be on the order of seconds (an example being the ^{2}D levels in ^{40}Ca$^+$, Fig. 5.21b), which should be sufficient for simple quantum calculations. Even longer lifetimes are possible if one uses two hyperfine components of the ground state, which are stable with respect to electric dipole decay [216, 228]. Examples include ^{9}Be$^+$, ^{25}Mg$^+$ and ^{43}Ca$^+$, with beryllium being shown in Fig. 5.21c. Also, in the case of ions which do not possess hyperfine structure, information may be stored in the ground state by exploiting its Zeeman substructure. Note that since ions usually have two Zeeman ground states, this approach precludes qubit operations which use auxiliary ionic levels like the phase gate described below. Together the internal states of N

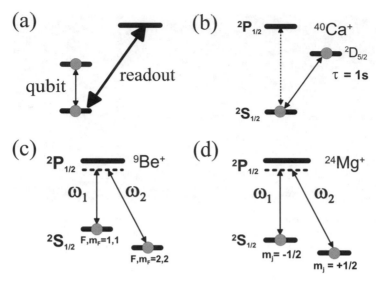

Fig. 5.21. Level scheme of trapped ions used for quantum computation. (**a**) Three level scheme with slow qubit transition and fast transition for efficient readout; (**b**) qubit stored in ground state and a metastable state; (**c**) qubit stored in hyperfine ground states; (**d**) qubit stored in Zeeman sublevels.

ions in the trap span the $2N$ dimensional Hilbert space in which the quantum computation evolves.

5.3.6 Single-Qubit Preparation and Manipulation

Prior to performing a quantum calculation, input data must be loaded into the quantum register. This process corresponds to the excitation of each of the N ions to a certain electronic quantum state. This is most conveniently achieved by laser manipulation of the internal states of the ions. A prerequisite is that each of the ions can be addressed individually by a laser beam. The separation of neighbouring ions in the trap is on the order of 10 μm, so that the laser must be focused to this size in order to avoid cross-excitation of the ions. A suitable scheme for addressing the ions is to deflect a single laser beam by means of the acousto-optic or electro-optic effect, sequentially pointing it to each ion in the chain. This has been experimentally demonstrated by the Innsbruck group [213].

Preparation of the input state of a given qubit proceeds in two steps. First the qubit is erased by transferring the ion to one of the two basis states ($|g\rangle$ or $|e\rangle$), for example by optical pumping. From this well-determined initial state an arbitrary superposition state ($\alpha|g\rangle + \beta|e\rangle$) of the qubit may be excited by using a resonant laser pulse of variable length to drive a Rabi oscillation between the two qubit-states. If a π-pulse is used, the qubit is flipped to the orthogonal state, and for shorter pulses a superposition state of the qubit is prepared. The technique of Rabi flopping is also used if unconditional single-qubit rotations are required during a quantum calculation to coherently modify the contents of a quantum register.

The details of how the Rabi flopping is accomplished depend on the level structure used. If the qubit states are separated by optical frequencies, a single-photon transition is employed. In the case of hyperfine states, or Zeeman substates of the same electronic level, two Raman beams are used connecting the qubit states through an intermediate virtual level close to an excited state of the ion.

5.3.7 Vibrational Mode as a Quantum Data Bus

The operations described so far manipulate single qubits independently of each other. For useful computations (logic operations) however, it is necessary to provide a strong coupling between the qubits, so that the dynamics of any ion in the chain may be conditional on the state of other ions. By far the strongest interaction between ions in a trap is their Coulomb repulsion, which in equilibrium is balanced by the external trapping potential. As was indicated in Sect. 5.3.4, the ions perform oscillations around this equilibrium position, which are highly correlated. Of particular interest for coupling ions in different positions of a linear trap is the centre-of-mass (COM) mode of oscillation, in which all the ions oscillate in phase in the direction of the trap axis. Cirac and Zoller [156] have shown how the COM-mode may be used to transfer quantum information between ions which can possibly be at widely separated positions of the chain.

Initially, the COM-vibration must be cooled to its quantum mechanical ground state, which may be accomplished with the technique of resolved sideband cooling described in Sect. 5.3.3. Quantum information may then be transferred from any ion in the string to the COM-mode by the following procedure: One ion is selectively illuminated by a focused laser beam and through a π-pulse on the first red-detuned vibrational sideband of the ionic resonance, the internal state of this ion is mapped to an external (vibrational) state of the ion chain (see Fig. 5.22a). As a result, the ground state and the first excited state of the COM-vibration are found in a superposition corresponding to the superposition of the lower and upper qubit state that was originally present in the ion. Due to the correlated COM-motion, all ions in the chain undergo the same oscillatory motion and hence have access to the same quantum information. The task of performing a quantum gate, i.e., of changing the state of an ion conditional on the state of another ion is therefore reduced to the task of changing the ionic state conditional on the vibrational state of the COM-mode (see Fig. 5.22b), as explained in the following section. The oscillation of the ions acts like a quantum bus, linking the qubit registers along the chain. After the operation on the second ion has been performed, step (a) must be reversed in order to restore the vibrational

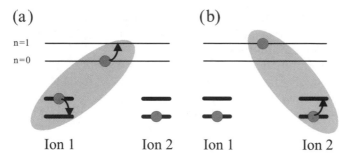

(a)   **(b)**

n=1

n=0

Ion 1   Ion 2   Ion 1   Ion 2

Fig. 5.22. Vibrational mode of an ion as a quantum data bus. (a) With the first laser pulse the state of ion 1 is mapped to the COM mode; (b) the state of ion 2 is changed conditional on the state of the COM mode.

mode to its ground state and at the same time return the first ion to its initial state.

5.3.8 Two-Bit Gates in an Ion-Trap Quantum Computer

The essential step of the Cirac–Zoller proposal for an ion-trap quantum computer is the realisation of a two-bit quantum gate, with the vibrational state of the COM-mode and the internal state of one ion as input qubits. In the following, we will describe gates in which the vibrational mode acts as the control bit, conditioning the state change in the target ion.

The most straightforward gate is one in which only one combination of basis states will lead to a modification of the output. This is the case for the so-called phase gate, in which the wavefunction of the system acquires a phase shift of π (change of sign) if both input qubits are in the upper state and is left unchanged in all other cases. To realise the change of sign of the wavefunction it is sufficient to apply a 2π-pulse to the ion. In order to obtain the required conditional dynamics, the pulse should be on a transition which couples only to the upper internal state of the ion. This requires the presence of an auxiliary electronic level, which could be another Zeeman substate or a different electronic level. Conditioning on the vibrational state is achieved by tuning to the first blue COM-sideband, which only leads to a transition if at least one vibrational quantum is present. Note that by construction, no more than one vibrational quantum may be excited in this scheme.

Other gates are possible by combining the phase gate with single qubit rotations. An example is the controlled NOT (CNOT) gate (see Sect. 5.2.12), in which the target bit is flipped depending on the state of the control bit. This may be realised by applying a (resonant) $\pi/2$-pulse before and after the phase gate, corresponding to a temporary change of the computational basis to $|g\rangle \pm |e\rangle$. A CNOT gate for a single qubit using its vibrational mode as the control bit has been experimentally demonstrated [211].

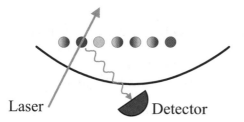

Fig. 5.23. State measurements on ion qubits. Each ion is individually addressed with a laser beam tuned to the readout transition (cf. Fig. 5.21a) and the fluorescence monitored.

In some cases it may be useful to obtain the CNOT directly, for example when no suitable auxiliary levels are available in the ion's level scheme. To do this one can exploit the fact that the coupling between internal and external degrees of freedom depends nonlinearly on the number of excited vibrational quanta [233]. For a suitable choice of parameters, a resonant pulse will act as a 2π-pulse if the system is in its lowest vibrational state, but as a π-pulse if one vibrational quantum is present, so that only in the latter case will the ion's state be flipped.

5.3.9 Readout of the Qubits

At the end of the quantum computation it is necessary to read out the result of the calculation, i.e., determine the state of the qubit register. Clearly this involves a projection of the state of the ions onto the basis states used for the detection.

The ion trap quantum computer has the advantage that the readout can be achieved with nearly 100% detection efficiency by applying a method first demonstrated for the detection of quantum jumps in single ions [234] (see Sect. 5.2.8). Each ion is subsequently illuminated by a laser tuned to a fast transition which is coupled to only one of the qubit states and the emitted fluorescent light is detected (Fig. 5.23). The presence of scattered light indicates occupation of the coupled state, its absence occupation of the orthogonal basis state. Superposition states may be probed by rotating the qubit prior to detection.

5.3.10 Conclusion

In the above sections we have outlined the principle of operation of an ion trap and its application to the task of performing quantum computations. Currently, a string of ions in a linear trap seems to be a most promising candidate for demonstrating the basic concept of a quantum computer. The principal benefits of the system are the long decoherence times of the internal states of the ions and the ability to prepare, coherently control and read out the states of the qubits by means of laser pulses. Among the quantum computation schemes implemented experimentally so far, ion traps have, at least theoretically, the largest potential for being scaled up to provide qubit registers long enough to run useful quantum algorithms.

In a realistic ion trap quantum computer, practical issues limit the size of calculations that may be implemented. Electromagnetic field fluctuations and collisions with background gas in the vacuum chamber may lead to decoherence rates larger than the radiative decay rates of the internal states of the ion. Even more restrictive is decoherence of the vibrational states of the ion string. For a single $^{198}Hg^+$ ion, a transition out of the zero-point vibrational level occurred in 0.15 s [214], while in the case of $^9Be^+$ a lifetime of 1 ms [211] was measured. For experimental data on $^{40}Ca^+$ see Ref. [215]. These processes put an upper limit on the number of operations that may be performed with a quantum computer before coherence is lost. However, in view of the recent experimental results [212, 216], some of the more technical limitations may be overcome using a breathing mode as the quantum data bus.

Additional problems affect the performance of a quantum computer during logic operations. Processes compromising the fidelity of the system evolution are inaccurate timing of the laser pulses, errors in the detunings, intensities and phases of the laser beams, and deviations between the laser focus and the ion positions. However, such errors may be taken care of eventually by an implementation of error correcting codes and protocols.

Although the number of ions that may be stored in the trap should only be limited by the size of the trap and the laser power available for cooling, only a string of two ions has been successfully cooled to the ground state of motion so far [216]. This number is likely to increase in the near future to a few tens of ions, but the thousands of qubits and billions of laser pulses needed, for example, to implement Shor's algorithm for factorising nontrivial numbers seems to be beyond experimental reach at present. However, ion traps offer the best prospects for testing small networks of quantum gates as well as schemes for quantum error correction. In this way the ion trap provides an ideal environment for synthesizing, manipulating and probing highly entangled quantum states of a string of ions.

5.4 Nuclear Magnetic Resonance Experiments

J.A Jones

5.4.1 Introduction

Nuclear magnetic resonance (NMR) is the study of transitions between the Zeeman levels of an atomic nucleus in a magnetic field. Described so simply, it is hard to see why anyone would be interested in it, but NMR is in fact one of the most important spectroscopic techniques available in the molecular sciences [235, 236]. This is because the frequencies of NMR signals depend subtly on the precise chemical environment of the nucleus, and so careful study of a molecule's NMR spectrum allows its structure to be determined.

NMR has long been considered as a possible technology for implementing quantum computers. Superficially the idea is attractive, as nuclear spins provide a good source of qubits, and it is fairly simple to construct quantum logic gates. There is, however, one major problem: it is difficult to place an NMR quantum computer in a well defined initial state, which appears essential for any interesting computation. This problem was solved recently by two separate approaches [237]–[239], and since then progress has been rapid.

Because of the importance of NMR in the molecular sciences, there has been extensive technical development of NMR spectrometers. Huge sums of money have been spent on optimising every component, and commercial spectrometers are widely available with performances close to the theoretical limits. Modern spectrometers are extremely complex devices, but they are easily controlled, and with a little assistance even the most nervous theoretician should be able to perform simple NMR experiments.

5.4.2 The NMR Hamiltonian

The NMR Hamiltonian can in the worst case be rather complex [236, 240, 241], but in many cases much of this complexity can be ignored. Firstly I will only consider spin-$\frac{1}{2}$ nuclei (such as ^{1}H, ^{13}C, ^{15}N, ^{19}F, and ^{31}P), as these nuclei do not experience many of the interactions which occur in high-spin nuclei. These nuclei are also the most important for current implementations of NMR quantum computers, as the two spin states of a spin-$\frac{1}{2}$ nucleus provide a natural two-level system for implementing a qubit. Secondly I shall assume that the NMR sample is a fluid (normally either a pure liquid or a solution). Rapid molecular motion in fluids greatly simplifies the NMR Hamiltonian, as anisotropic interactions can be replaced by their isotropic average, which is often zero. NMR signals from spin-$\frac{1}{2}$ nuclei in fluids are typically rather narrow, and so such studies are often referred to as "high resolution" NMR [242].

Two interactions are particularly important in high resolution NMR. The first of these is of course the Zeeman interaction. In the presence of a magnetic field B_z, directed along the z-axis, the degeneracy of the two spin states ($I_z = \pm\frac{1}{2}\hbar$) is lifted by the Zeeman interaction

$$\mathcal{H} = -\gamma I_z B_z, \tag{5.19}$$

where γ (the gyromagnetic ratio) is a constant characteristic of the nucleus. The Zeeman splitting corresponds to a frequency of around 500 MHz for ^{1}H nuclei in typical NMR magnets, and so NMR experiments are performed using radio frequency (RF) radiation.

It is not practical to use conventional spatial localisation techniques to pick out individual molecules, as the spacing between molecules (a few Å) is small compared with the wavelength of the RF radiation, and in any case the individual molecules are undergoing rapid motion. Instead, the combined signal from all the molecules is detected. This has important consequences for NMR experiments, as they are implemented not on individual spin systems but on statistical ensembles of such systems. It is, however, possible to distinguish between different nuclei in the same molecule. Electrons surrounding the nuclei act to shield them from the magnetic field, thus modifying the apparent gyromagnetic ratio. The extent of this shielding depends on the chemical environment of the nucleus, and thus nuclei in different environments have slightly different transition frequencies.

The second important interaction in high resolution NMR is scalar coupling (J-coupling). This is not simple dipole–dipole coupling, which is averaged out by rapid molecular tumbling, but a more subtle effect related to the Fermi contact interaction. When the coupling between two nuclei, I and S, is small compared with the difference between their NMR frequencies (weak coupling) the coupling Hamiltonian takes the simple form

$$\mathcal{H} = J_{IS} I_z S_z, \tag{5.20}$$

where J_{IS}, the spin–spin coupling constant, depends on details of the molecular structure. This coupling is directly observable in NMR spectra as a splitting (of size J_{IS}) in the NMR signals corresponding to each nucleus.

A simple example: Figure 5.24 shows the chemical structure of deuterated cytosine. Cytosine is one of the four "bases" which are used to encode information in DNA, and has recently been used to implement an NMR quantum computer [243]. For this purpose three of the hydrogen nuclei in the molecule were replaced by deuterium, which can be easily achieved by dissolving it in D_2O. The ^{1}H spectrum of this molecule on a 500 MHz NMR spectrometer is shown in Fig. 5.25. Each of the two ^{1}H nuclei gives rise to a pair of signals, called a doublet. The two doublets occur at a frequency of about 500 MHz,

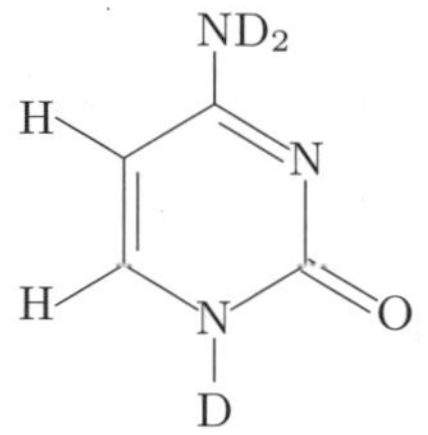

ND$_2$

H

N

H

N

O

D

Fig. 5.24. The structure of partially deuterated cytosine obtained by dissolving cytosine in D$_2$O; the three protons bound to nitrogen nuclei exchange with solvent deuterons, leaving two ^{1}H nuclei as an isolated two spin system (all other nuclei can be ignored).

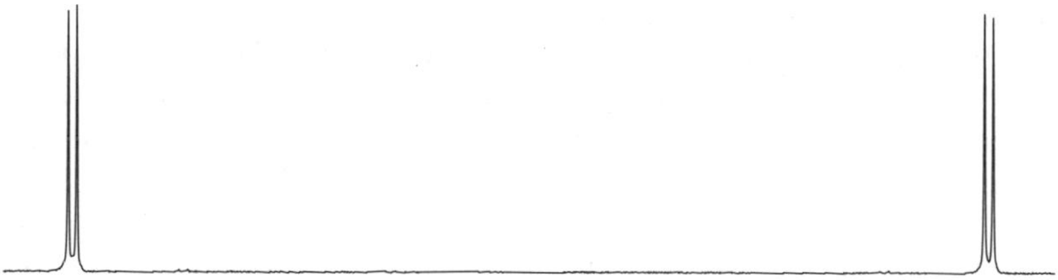

Fig. 5.25. The ^{1}H NMR spectrum of partially deuterated cytosine. Each pair of lines is the NMR signal from one of the two ^{1}H nuclei.

with a separation between them of 763 Hz; the small splitting within each doublet (7.2 Hz) is due to spin–spin coupling between the nuclei.

5.4.3 Building an NMR Quantum Computer

While several different models of quantum computing have been considered, the most common approach is based on quantum logic circuits. Such a quantum computer has four main elements which must be implemented. The first of these, qubits, is easy, as the two spin states of a spin-$\frac{1}{2}$ nucleus provide an ideal two-level system. The remaining elements are slightly more complex.

Quantum gates: Quantum logic circuits are constructed by interconnecting qubits with quantum gates. While many different gates are possible it is well known that any gate can be constructed using a suitable combination of one qubit and two qubit gates [244]. One qubit gates correspond to rotations of a single spin within its own Hilbert space, and these can be readily achieved using RF fields. Two qubit gates, such as the controlled-NOT gate, are more complex as they involve conditional dynamics, and thus require an interaction between the two qubits. In NMR the scalar coupling (J-coupling) is well suited to this purpose: while scalar coupling does not have exactly the form required to construct traditional controlled gates it can be easily combined with one qubit gates to make them [245]. For example the controlled-NOT gate can be achieved by placing a controlled phase shift gate (which performs the transformation $|11\rangle \rightarrow -|11\rangle$, while leaving the other basis states unchanged) between a pair of one qubit Hadamard gates applied to the target qubit. The controlled phase shift can itself be achieved by combining evolution under the scalar coupling, which results in a two qubit phase rotation, with single qubit phase shift gates [245].

The CLEAR operator: Quantum logic gates transform qubits from one state to another. Clearly this is only useful if the qubits start off in some well defined input state. In practice it is sufficient to have some method for reaching any single state, as other initial states can then be reached by applying one bit gates. The obvious choice of initial state is to have all qubits in the $|0\rangle$ state, corresponding to a CLEAR operation.

In principle CLEAR should be easy to implement as it takes the quantum computer to its energetic ground state, which can be achieved by some cooling process. Unfortunately this approach is not practical in NMR as the energy gap between Zeeman levels is small compared with the Boltzmann energy at any reasonable temperature. At room temperature the energy gap is so small compared to kT that the population of all the states will be almost equal, with only small deviations (around one part in 10^4) from the average. No NMR signal will be observed from the average population, as the signals from different molecules will cancel out, but a small signal can be seen which arises from the deviations away from the average.

For a molecule containing a single isolated nucleus, that is a computer with a single qubit, it is easy to reach an effective $|0\rangle$ state: at thermodynamic equilibrium the deviation from equal populations is just a slight excess in the (low energy) $|0\rangle$ state compared with the (slightly higher energy) $|1\rangle$ state. Unfortunately this simple approach does not work for larger systems, as the pattern of population deviations is more complicated, and does not have the desired form. This apparent inability to implement CLEAR made NMR an impractical quantum computing technology for many years.

Towards the end of 1996 two separate approaches were discovered for solving this problem. The first approach, due to Cory and coworkers [237, 238], uses complex NMR pulse sequences to modify the populations of different spin states, eventually creating the desired pattern, and thus a state equivalent to the desired initial state. An alternative approach, due to Chuang and Gershenfeld, works by separating the spin system into many different subsystems [239, 246]. Within these subsystems the equilibrium pattern of populations has the desired form, and so the desired starting state is accessible. While this approach is theoretically elegant, it is complicated to apply in practice, and has not been widely used. More recent approaches, such as temporal averaging [247], are conceptually related to that of Cory et al., and will not be described further. A detailed comparison of the various methods has been made by Havel and coworkers [248].

Output: Finally it is necessary to have some method for reading out the final answer. Typically this is obtained by reading the values of one or more qubits which finish the calculation in eigenstates. In an NMR quantum computer this corresponds to determining whether the population of the $|0\rangle$ state is higher than that of the $|1\rangle$ state, or vice versa. It is not practical to determine these populations directly, but an equivalent measurement is easily made by applying a $90°$ excitation RF pulse. This creates a coherent superposition of $|0\rangle$ and $|1\rangle$ which then oscillates in the magnetic field. The relative populations can then be determined by observing the size and phase of this oscillatory signal. The absolute phase of the signal is meaningless, but it is possible to incorporate a reference signal, so that only relative phases need be measured.

Some quantum algorithms produce a result occupying two or more qubits, and in this case two different approaches are possible. The first approach is to excite only one of the corresponding spins; in this case the states of the other spins can be monitored by examining the multiplet structure of the observed spin. Alternatively it is possible to excite all the spins and observe them simultaneously; in this case the state of each spin can be determined directly from the phase of its NMR signal.

NMR quantum computers have a potential advantage over other designs in that it is not necessary for the answer to be stored as an eigenstate. It is instead possible to observe some superpositions directly. This possibility arises because of the ensemble average implicit in any NMR measurement. While measurements on a single spin system cause superpositions to collapse, the equivalent effect is not seen in ensemble averages. Thus it is possible, for example, to monitor two complementary observables continuously and simultaneously. This mode of operation could be useful in future experiments.

5.4.4 Deutsch's Problem

The concepts described above can be illustrated using an NMR quantum computer designed to implement an algorithm to solve Deutsch's problem [138, 249] . This problem is described in detail in Sect. 4.2.4, and only a brief summary will be given here. Consider a binary function

$$f(x) : B \mapsto B, \tag{5.21}$$

and suppose we have a corresponding operator U_f, such that

$$|x\rangle |y\rangle \xrightarrow{U_f} |x\rangle |y \oplus f(x)\rangle . \tag{5.22}$$

Clearly it is possible to build quantum circuits to determine $f(0)$ and $f(1)$, as shown in Fig. 5.26a. Deutsch's problem is the determination of $f(0) \oplus f(1)$ with only a single application of U_f (corresponding to a single evaluation of f). This is impossible on a classical computer, but can be achieved on a quantum computer using the circuit shown in Fig. 5.26b.

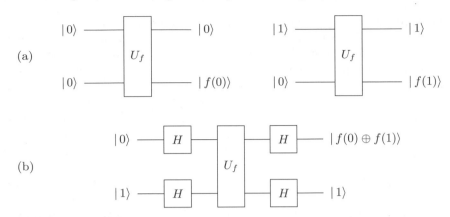

Fig. 5.26. (a) Quantum circuits to determine $f(0)$ and $f(1)$ for a binary function. (b) A quantum circuit to determine $f(0) \oplus f(1)$ with a single application of U_f (Deutsch's problem). H represents the single qubit Hadamard gate.

This circuit has been implemented on our two qubit NMR quantum computer based on partially deuterated cytosine [243] (similar results have also been obtained by Chuang et al. using a two qubit NMR quantum computer based on chloroform [250]). In our NMR quantum computer each doublet corresponds to the signal from one qubit. The value of the qubit can be determined from the phase of the corresponding signal: a positive signal corresponds to a qubit in the $|0\rangle$ state, while a negative signal corresponds to a qubit in the $|1\rangle$ state.

As mentioned above, the absolute phase of an NMR signal is not meaningful, as it depends on a variety of experimental factors. Relative phases are, however, meaningful, and so it is possible to obtain "absolute" phases by adjusting the spectrum so that the phase of a reference signal is correct. The relative phases of signals in two different experiments can also be meaningful if the two experiments are acquired in an identical fashion, and so it is possible to use a reference signal from one experiment to correct signals from another experiment. This is the approach adopted in the results discussed below.

Experimental results from a classical algorithm to determine $f(0)$ are shown in Fig. 5.27. In this algorithm the left hand pair of lines (corresponding to the first qubit) indicates the input value, while the right hand pair of lines (corresponding to the second qubit) indicate the output value. Results are shown for the four possible binary functions, listed in Table 5.1. As expected

Table 5.1. The four possible binary functions mapping one bit to another.

x	$f_{00}(x)$	$f_{01}(x)$	$f_{10}(x)$	$f_{11}(x)$
0	0	0	1	1
1	0	1	0	1

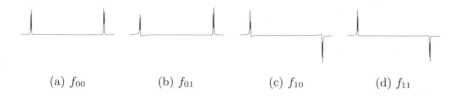

(a) f_{00} (b) f_{01} (c) f_{10} (d) f_{11}

Fig. 5.27. Experimental results from an NMR quantum computer determining $f(0)$; the result is shown for each of the four possible binary functions, f.

(a) f_{00} (b) f_{01} (c) f_{10} (d) f_{11}

Fig. 5.28. Experimental results from an NMR quantum computer determining $f(1)$; the result is shown for each of the four possible binary functions, f.

the left hand signals are always positive, indicating the input value (0), while the right hand signals are positive when $f(0) = 0$ (for f_{00} and f_{01}) and negative when $f(0) = 1$ (for f_{10} and f_{11}). The absolute phase of these spectra is unknown, but this was solved by adjusting the phase of spectrum (a) such that the left hand signal was positive, and then applying the same phase correction to all the other spectra.

These plots do not clearly show the fine structure within each doublet, but this is not particularly important as within this implementation of a quantum computer all the lines in the multiplet should have the same sign, as is indeed observed. Ideally this sign would be simply positive or negative, but in practice the lineshapes observed are slightly more complex. Similarly all the lines should have the same height, while the experimental results show substantial variations. These lineshape and height distortions arise from errors in the computer. For the most part these errors are systematic, in that they arise because the computer does not implement quantum gates perfectly correctly. It should be possible to reduce these errors by careful optimisation of the NMR pulse sequences used to implement gates.

The same algorithm can be used to determine $f(1)$: all that is needed is to change the input value. The results of this approach are shown in Fig. 5.28. In this case the left hand signals are always negative, indicating the new input value (1), while the right hand signals can be either negative or positive. As expected this signal is positive when $f(1) = 0$ (for f_{00} and f_{10}) and negative when $f(1) = 1$ (for f_{01} and f_{11}). Note that the same phase correction was used

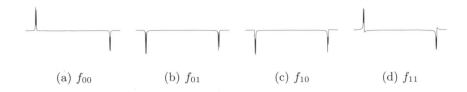

(a) f_{00} (b) f_{01} (c) f_{10} (d) f_{11}

Fig. 5.29. Experimental results from an NMR quantum computer determining $f(0) \oplus f(1)$ (Deutsch's problem); the result is shown for each of the four possible binary functions, f.

for these spectra as for those in Fig. 5.27, showing that relative phases can be defined for two different experiments performed under identical conditions.

Finally, this quantum computer can also be used to implement an algorithm to solve Deutsch's problem (determining $f(0) \oplus f(1)$). The results are shown in Fig. 5.29. In this case there is no input bit, as the quantum computer uses a superposition of the two possible inputs, and the answer is encoded as the phase of the left hand signals. The second qubit is simply a working bit, and both starts and ends the computation in state $|1\rangle$. As expected the right hand signals are always negative, while the left hand signals are positive for f_{00} and f_{11} (for which $f(0) \oplus f(1) = 0$), and negative for f_{01} and f_{10} (for which $f(0) \oplus f(1) = 1$).

5.4.5 Quantum Searching and Other Algorithms

Since the discovery that it is possible to generate effectively pure starting states in NMR quantum computers progress has been extremely rapid. Two qubit computers have been used to implement Grover's quantum search algorithm with a two qubit search space [251]–[253]. This allows a single item to be located in a search over four items with a single query; the algorithm begins with the quantum computer in the state $|00\rangle$ and ends in the state corresponding to the matching item ($|00\rangle$, $|01\rangle$, $|10\rangle$, or $|11\rangle$). This algorithm has been implemented on our cytosine quantum computer [252], and the results are shown in Fig. 5.30. The results shown are slightly better than those published earlier [252]; they were acquired using modified pulse sequences as described in [254].

While NMR quantum computers are capable of performing a simple Grover search, for which there is only one item to be found, difficulties arise in the general case when more than one item matches the search criteria. In this case a conventional quantum computer will return one of the matching items at random, while an NMR implementation will return some sort of ensemble average over all the matches, and it is difficult or impossible to deduce anything useful from this ensemble result. It is, however, possible to overcome this problem by using a closely related approach, approximate quantum counting [254].

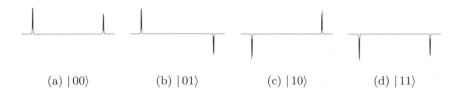

(a) $|00\rangle$ (b) $|01\rangle$ (c) $|10\rangle$ (d) $|11\rangle$

Fig. 5.30. Experimental results from an NMR quantum computer implementing Grover's quantum search over a two qubit search space; the result is shown for each of the four possible matching items.

Three qubit systems have been studied, but have largely been used to demonstrate interesting quantum phenomena, such as GHZ states [255, 256], simple error correction protocols [257, 258], and teleportation [259]. They have also been used, however, to implement the three qubit Deutsch–Jozsa algorithm [260]. A partial demonstration of the Deutsch–Jozsa algorithm on a five-qubit system has also been given [261].

5.4.6 Prospects for the Future

There are several major problems which might act to limit the size of real NMR quantum computers based on the current approach. The most widely discussed problems are the exponential loss of signal intensity with increasing numbers of qubits, followed by the effects of decoherence. In fact these effects are unlikely to be very important as other problems are likely to become visible first. Nevertheless it is useful to discuss these issues and how they might be tackled.

Exponential signal loss: The exponential loss in signal with increasing numbers of qubits arises as a result of the need to distill an effective pure state from the thermal equilibrium density matrix. Adding an additional qubit means adding an additional spin, doubling the number of spin states in the system and thus doubling the number of ways in which a flip of the state of any one spin can occur. Distilling out an effective pure state is equivalent to selecting only one of these possible transitions, with a consequent loss in signal intensity [262]. Note that this problem is not confined to NMR, but will also arise in *any* ensemble quantum computation working in the high temperature regime ($\Delta E \ll kT$).

Clearly this exponential fall off in signal is a potential limit, but in practice its importance has been overstated. NMR spectra can be acquired with a fairly high signal-to-noise ratio (the spectrum in Fig. 5.25 has a ratio of about 800), and thus the signal loss will only be a serious problem for NMR computers containing ten qubits or more. It is possible to increase the signal-to-noise ratio by a variety of simple means, such as signal averaging or increasing the sample size, or by more subtle approaches such as optical pumping [263].

A different approach, suggested by Schulman and Vazirani [264] is to use computational methods to purify a collection of low fidelity qubits. It is not practical to apply this approach directly to a thermal ensemble, but if used in combination with other methods for increasing the initial polarisation, such as optical pumping, it may prove useful.

Decoherence: Decoherence (that is, the conversion of coherent superpositions into incoherent mixtures by random processes) is another potential problem, which is common to all implementations of quantum computers. Any quantum superposition has a characteristic decoherence time, and it is necessary to ensure that any calculations are completed in a time which is not too long compared with the decoherence time (although error correction techniques allow this time scale to be extended). In NMR quantum computers this time is generally related to the spin–spin relaxation time, T_2, although this is a simplification as T_2 is the decoherence time of a single spin coherence, and the decoherence times for multi-spin coherences can be quite different. Nevertheless T_2 does give a very approximate idea of the appropriate time scale, which for the NMR computers currently being investigated (based on small molecules in solution) is of the order of a few seconds.

The relevant parameter for a quantum computer is not the decoherence time itself, but the ratio of the decoherence time to the time taken to execute a quantum gate. For simple two-bit gates, such as the controlled-NOT, this time is comparable to the inverse of the scalar spin–spin coupling (around 5–150 ms), suggesting that it should be possible to implement tens or hundreds of gates. It is true that systems with much larger values of T_2 are known, but such systems cannot be used to build NMR quantum computers of the current design as they do not have the spin–spin interactions necessary to build quantum gates.

Other problems: Far more important than either of the problems discussed above are two other problems: the problem of selectively addressing spins, and the problem of the growth in the complexity of gates with increasing numbers of spins.

The problem of selectively addressing different spins is simple to understand. In conventional quantum computers individual qubits are distinguished by the spatial locations of the corresponding physical systems, but this approach cannot be used in NMR. Instead qubits are distinguished by the different NMR transition frequencies of their corresponding spins. Unfortunately this frequency range is rather narrow (typically only a few thousand Hz), and it is difficult to perform completely selective excitations on spins whose frequencies are close together [265]. This is one major source of the distortions clearly visible in the experimental spectra (Figs. 5.27–5.30). Clearly this problem will be more serious in systems with more spins, as it will be harder to ensure that all the spins are separated by substantial frequency gaps.

Because of this most authors have preferred to study heteronuclear spin systems, such as NMR computers based on the ^{1}H–^{13}C spin pair in chloroform. This is much simpler than the corresponding homonuclear problem, as the transition frequencies of the two spins now differ by hundreds of MHz, and spin selective excitation is essentially trivial. This approach has allowed rapid progress with two spin and three spin systems, but it cannot be extended indefinitely as there are only a small number of different nuclei which are suitable, and in any event most NMR spectrometers are not capable of dealing with more than two or three different nuclei at the same time. Thus any NMR quantum computer involving more than a few qubits will have to face the problems of selectively addressing spins.

A second, more subtle, problem is the increasing complexity of quantum logic gates in multispin systems. Ideally it would be possible to take a two qubit gate, developed for a two qubit computer, and use it in a three or four qubit computer without major modification. With NMR quantum computers this may prove tricky. The interactions which form the basis of gates, in particular spin–spin coupling, are part of the background NMR Hamiltonian, under which the spin system evolves in the absence of specific excitation. Quantum logic gates are formed by modulating the intensity of different elements of this background Hamiltonian, to give an effective Hamiltonian which has the desired form. This process, however, becomes more difficult in the presence of additional qubits, as it is necessary not only to modulate the interactions between the spins involved in the gate, but also to modulate any interactions with the additional spins so as to effectively remove them [266]. In the worst case a system of N spins has a total of $\frac{1}{2}N(N+1)$ one and two-spin interactions in the background Hamiltonian, of which only three are relevant to forming any particular two qubit gate. Although this problem is not quite as serious as it might initially appear [267]–[269] cancelling out all these irrelevant interactions may prove to be the hardest aspect of building NMR quantum computers with more than a handful of qubits.

Alternative approaches: Mindful of the potential problems outlined above, some researchers have begun to think about radically different approaches to building quantum computers with NMR systems. So far none of these ideas have been demonstrated, and they bear little resemblance to "conventional" NMR quantum computers.

One feature common to many of these speculative schemes is the use of solid samples instead of fluids. This has many significant consequences for NMR studies, both helpful and unhelpful. Individual molecules will remain approximately stationary in a sold sample, and so spatial localisation techniques could in principle be used to selectively excite particular spins. The long wavelength of RF radiation precludes direct approaches, but techniques developed for NMR imaging [270] do allow spatial discrimination between spins. It will be difficult to achieve atomic resolution with this approach, however, partly because of the difficulty of constructing sufficiently powerful field gradients, but also because the low sensitivity of NMR makes it impractical to directly detect single spins [270]. Calculations suggest a limiting resolution of about 1μm, so it will be necessary to use clusters of spins rather than individual nuclei.

A second consequence of moving to the solid state is a substantial change in the NMR Hamiltonian, as anisotropic interactions are no longer averaged to their isotropic values. In particular the direct dipole–dipole coupling between spins is the largest spin–spin interaction. This coupling is much larger than scalar coupling, allowing the implementation of more rapid logic gates, but has the disadvantage that every spin is coupled to all other nearby spins. This makes it difficult to use the coupling in the selective manner needed for logic gates, and can also lead to rapid decoherence.

A recent proposal due to Kane [271] confronts these problems in a most ingenious way, combing solid state NMR with conventional silicon microchip technology. It envisages the use of isolated ^{31}P atoms in a silicon matrix, with electrostatic gates, both to control the excitation of individual spins and to modulate couplings between them. Single spin detection would be achieved by using the nuclear spin to control a single electron transfer process. While this proposal is well beyond the scope of current technology, it is likely that many of the requirements will have been attained within the next ten years.

5.4.7 Entanglement and Mixed States

It has recently been suggested that NMR might not be a quantum mechanical technique at all! When assessing this claim, it should be remembered that "quantum mechanical" is used here with a technical meaning of "provably non-classical". As NMR experiments are conducted in the high temperature regime (kT is large compared with the splitting between energy levels), the density matrix describing a nuclear spin system is always close to the maximally mixed state, and such states can always be decomposed [272] as a mixture of product states (that is, states containing no entanglement between different nuclei). As NMR states are describable without invoking entanglement, they can therefore be described using classical models (although these classical models may be somewhat contrived). However, while classical models can be used to describe an individual NMR state, it is not clear that such models can be used to describe the evolution of the state during an NMR experiment [273]. The significance of these conclusions remains controversial and unclear.

5.4.8 The Next Few Years

NMR provides the most powerful technology for implementing quantum computers currently available, and is likely to remain so for several more years. Several small NMR quantum computers have been built, and quantum algorithms have been implemented upon them.

In the next few years it seems likely that NMR computers with three to five qubits will become routine, and that larger systems will be under investigation. It seems unlikely, however, that NMR systems with many more than ten qubits will be built without a major change in approach. In the longer term, approaches such as Kane's solid state NMR computer may prove extremely promising.

6. Quantum Networks and Multi-Particle Entanglement

6.1 Introduction

The basic concepts of quantum entanglement have been presented in previous chapters. In this chapter various advanced topics of quantum entanglement will be discussed. Section 6.2 describes a scheme for establishing entanglement between atoms at spatially separated nodes through the exchange of photons. In this way a quantum network can be built combining the virtues of trapped atom/ion systems, i.e. long storage times and local quantum state processing, with the advantages of quantum optics, i.e. flexible and reliable quantum communication over long distances.

Section 6.3 addresses entangled states of more than two particles. Such states are not only important in the field of quantum information but were initially introduced by Greenberger, Horne and Zeilinger (GHZ) to address the Einstein–Podolsky–Rosen (EPR) conflict of local realism with quantum mechanics in a most conclusive way. It is shown how three-photon GHZ entanglement can be generated and why entanglement between more than two particles illustrates quantum properties that are completely incomprehensible from any classical local-realistic viewpoint.

In Sect. 6.4 it is shown that entanglement between more than two particles is a very delicate concept. In fact, entanglement between more than two particles cannot be defined in a unique way. Measures are introduced to quantify the entanglement, and related topics such as entanglement distillation and the relative entropy of entanglement will be explained.

6.2 Quantum Networks I:
Entangling Particles at Separate Locations

H.-J. Briegel, S. J. van Enk, J. I. Cirac, and P. Zoller

6.2.1 Interfacing Atoms and Photons

Quantum networks consist of spatially separated nodes where qubits are stored and locally manipulated, and quantum communication channels connecting the nodes. Exchange of information within the network is accomplished by sending qubits through the channels. A physical implementation of such a network could consist e.g. of clusters of trapped atoms or ions representing the nodes, with optical fibres or similar photon "conduits" providing the quantum channels, as shown in Fig. 6.1.

Atoms and ions are particularly well suited for storing qubits in long-lived internal states, and recently proposed schemes for performing quantum gates between trapped atoms or ions provide an attractive method for local processing within an atom/ion node [156, 274, 275]. On the other hand, photons clearly represent the best qubit-carrier for fast and reliable communication over long distances [276, 277]. In this section, we describe a scheme [278] to implement an interface between the atoms and the photons, i.e. between the nodes and the communication channels of the network. This scheme allows quantum transmission with (in principle) unit efficiency between distant atoms 1 and 2. The possibility of combining local quantum processing with quantum transmission between the nodes of the network opens the possibility for a variety of novel applications ranging from entangled-state cryptography [279] and teleportation [280] to more complex activities such as multi-particle communication and distributed quantum computing [281, 282].

The basic idea of the scheme is to utilise strong coupling between a high-Q optical cavity and the atoms [276] forming a given node of the quantum network. By applying laser beams, one first transfers the internal state of

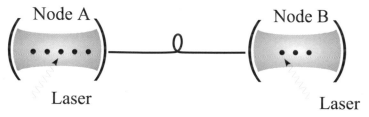

Fig. 6.1. Element of a quantum network. Atoms in high-Q cavities are used to locally store and process quantum information; photons are used to transfer quantum information between spatially separated "nodes" of the network.

an atom at the first node to the optical state of the cavity mode. The generated photons leak out of the cavity, propagate as a wavepacket along the transmission line, and enter an optical cavity at the second node. Finally, the optical state of the second cavity is transferred to the internal state of an atom. Multiple-qubit transmissions can be achieved by sequentially addressing pairs of atoms (one at each node), as entanglements between arbitrarily located atoms are preserved by the state-mapping process. The distinguishing feature of the protocol is that, by controlling the atom-cavity interaction, one can avoid the reflection of the wavepackets from the second cavity, effectively switching off the dominant loss channel that would be responsible for decoherence in the communication process.

6.2.2 Model of Quantum State Transmission

A simple configuration of quantum transmission between two nodes consists of two atoms 1 and 2 which are strongly coupled to their respective cavity modes, see Fig. 6.2.

The Hamiltonian describing the interaction of each atom with the corresponding cavity mode is ($\hbar = 1$):

$$\hat{H}_i = \omega_c \hat{a}_i^\dagger \hat{a}_i + \omega_0 |r\rangle_{i\,i}\langle r| + g(|r\rangle_{i\,i}\langle g|\hat{a}_i + \text{h.c.})$$
$$+ \frac{1}{2}\Omega_i(t)\left[e^{-i[\omega_L t + \phi_i(t)]}|r\rangle_{i\,i}\langle e| + \text{h.c.}\right] \quad (i = 1, 2). \tag{6.1}$$

Here, $\hat{a}_i$ and $\hat{a}_i^\dagger$ are the annihilation and creation operators for cavity mode i with frequency ω_c. The states $|g\rangle, |r\rangle$, and $|e\rangle$ form a three-level system of excitation frequency ω_0 (Fig. 6.2), and the qubit is stored in a superposition of the two degenerate ground states. The states $|e\rangle$ and $|g\rangle$ are coupled by a Raman transition [274, 275, 283], where a laser of frequency ω_L excites the atom from $|e\rangle$ to $|r\rangle$ with a time-dependent Rabi frequency $\Omega_i(t)$ and phase $\phi_i(t)$, followed by a transition $|r\rangle \to |e\rangle$ which is accompanied by emission of a photon into the corresponding cavity mode, with coupling constant g. In order to suppress spontaneous emission from the excited state during the Raman process, we assume that the laser is strongly detuned from the atomic

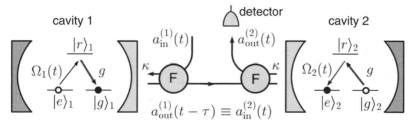

Fig. 6.2. Schematic representation of unidirectional quantum transmission between two atoms in optical cavities connected by a quantized transmission line.

transition $|\Delta| \gg \Omega_{1,2}(t), g, |\dot{\phi}_{1,2}|$ (with $\Delta = \omega_L - \omega_0$). In such a case, one can eliminate adiabatically the excited states $|r\rangle_i$. The new Hamiltonian for the dynamics of the two ground states becomes, in a rotating frame for the cavity modes at the laser frequency,

$$\hat{H}_i = -\delta \hat{a}_i^\dagger \hat{a}_i + \frac{g^2}{\Delta} \hat{a}_i^\dagger \hat{a}_i |g\rangle_i\ _i\langle g| + \delta\omega_i(t)|e\rangle_i\ _i\langle e|$$

$$-ig_i(t)\left[e^{i\phi_i(t)}|e\rangle_i\ _i\langle g|\hat{a}_i - \text{h.c.}\right]. \quad (i = 1, 2) \quad (6.2)$$

The first term involves the Raman detuning $\delta = \omega_L - \omega_c$. The next two terms are AC–Stark shifts of the ground states $|g\rangle$ and $|e\rangle$ due to the cavity mode and laser field, respectively, with $\delta\omega_i(t) = \Omega_i(t)^2/(4\Delta)$. The last term is the familiar Jaynes–Cummings interaction, with an effective coupling constant $g_i(t) = g\Omega_i(t)/(2\Delta)$. Here we ignore for the moment the small effects produced by spontaneous emission during the Raman process. The notation $|e\rangle$ as "excited" and $|g\rangle$ as "ground" state is motivated by this analogy with the Jaynes–Cummings Model.

The aim is to select the time-dependent Rabi frequencies and laser phases[1] to accomplish the *ideal quantum transmission*

$$(c_g|g\rangle_1 + c_e|e\rangle_1)|g\rangle_2 \otimes |0\rangle_1|0\rangle_2|\text{vac}\rangle$$

$$\rightarrow |g\rangle_1(c_g|g\rangle_2 + c_e|e\rangle_2) \otimes |0\rangle_1|0\rangle_2|\text{vac}\rangle, \quad (6.3)$$

where $c_{g,e}$ are complex numbers; in general, they have to be replaced by unnormalised states of other "spectator" atoms in the network. In (6.3), $|0\rangle_i$ and $|\text{vac}\rangle$ represent the vacuum state of the cavity modes and the free electromagnetic modes connecting the cavities. Transmission will occur by photon exchange via these modes.

In the present context, it is convenient to formulate the problem in the language of quantum trajectories [284, 285]. Let us consider a fictitious experiment where the output field of the second cavity is continuously monitored by a photodetector (see Fig. 6.2). The evolution of the quantum system under continuous observation, conditional upon observing a particular trajectory of counts, can be described by a pure state wavefunction $|\Psi_c(t)\rangle$ in the system Hilbert space (where the radiation modes outside the cavity have been eliminated). During the time intervals when no count is detected, this wavefunction evolves according to a Schrödinger equation with non-hermitian effective Hamiltonian

$$\hat{H}_{\text{eff}}(t) = \hat{H}_1(t) + \hat{H}_2(t) - i\kappa\left(\hat{a}_1^\dagger \hat{a}_1 + \hat{a}_2^\dagger \hat{a}_2 + 2\hat{a}_2^\dagger \hat{a}_1\right). \quad (6.4)$$

Here, κ is the cavity loss rate, which is assumed to be the same for the first and the second cavity. The detection of a count at time t_r is associated with a quantum jump according to $|\Psi_c(t_r + dt)\rangle \propto \hat{c}|\Psi_c(t_r)\rangle$, where $\hat{c} = \hat{a}_1 + \hat{a}_2$

---

[1] One could also modulate the cavity transmission, but this is technically more difficult.

[285, 286]. The probability density for a jump (detector click) to occur during the time interval from t to $t + dt$ is $\langle \Psi_c(t) | \hat{c}^\dagger \hat{c} | \Psi_c(t) \rangle dt$ [285, 286].

6.2.3 Laser Pulses for Ideal Transmission

We wish to design the laser pulses in both cavities in such a way that ideal quantum transmission condition (6.3) is satisfied. A necessary condition for the time evolution is that a quantum jump (detector click, see Fig. 6.2) never occurs, i.e. $\hat{c} | \Psi_c(t) \rangle = 0 \; \forall t$, and thus the effective Hamiltonian will become a hermitian operator. In other words, the system will remain in a *dark* state of the cascaded quantum system. Physically, this means that the wavepacket is not reflected from the second cavity. We expand the state of the system as

$$|\Psi_c(t)\rangle = |c_g|gg\rangle|00\rangle$$
$$+ |c_e\Big[\alpha_1(t)e^{-i\phi_1(t)}|eg\rangle|00\rangle + \alpha_2(t)e^{-i\phi_2(t)}|ge\rangle|00\rangle$$
$$+ \beta_1(t)|gg\rangle|10\rangle + \beta_2(t)|gg\rangle|01\rangle\Big]. \tag{6.5}$$

Ideal quantum transmission (6.3) will occur for

$$\alpha_1(-\infty) = \alpha_2(+\infty) = 1, \quad \phi_1(-\infty) = \phi_2(+\infty) = 0. \tag{6.6}$$

The first term on the RHS of (6.5) does not change under the time evolution generated by H_{eff}. Defining symmetric and antisymmetric coefficients $\beta_{1,2} = (\beta_s \mp \beta_a)/\sqrt{2}$, we find the following *evolution equations*

$$\dot{\alpha}_1(t) = g_1(t)\beta_a(t)/\sqrt{2}, \tag{6.7}$$
$$\dot{\alpha}_2(t) = -g_2(t)\beta_a(t)/\sqrt{2}, \tag{6.8}$$
$$\dot{\beta}_a(t) = -g_1(t)\alpha_1(t)/\sqrt{2} + g_2(t)\alpha_2(t)/\sqrt{2}, \tag{6.9}$$

where we have chosen the laser frequencies $\omega_L + \dot{\phi}_{1,2}(t)$ so that $\delta = g^2/\Delta$ and

$$\dot{\phi}_{1,2}(t) = \delta\omega_i(t) \tag{6.10}$$

in order to compensate the AC–stark shifts; thus (6.7–6.9) are decoupled from the phases. The *dark state condition* implies $\beta_s(t) = 0$, and therefore

$$\dot{\beta}_s(t) = g_1(t)\alpha_1(t)/\sqrt{2} + g_2(t)\alpha_2(t)/\sqrt{2} + \kappa\beta_a(t) \equiv 0, \tag{6.11}$$

as well as the normalisation condition

$$|\alpha_1(t)|^2 + |\alpha_2(t)|^2 + |\beta_a(t)|^2 = 1. \tag{6.12}$$

We note that the coefficients $\alpha_{1,2}(t)$ and $\beta_s(t)$ are real.

The mathematical problem is now to find pulse shapes $\Omega_{1,2}(t) \propto g_{1,2}(t)$ such that the conditions (6.6–6.9, 6.11) are fulfilled. In general this is a difficult problem, as imposing conditions (6.6, 6.11) on the solutions of the differential equations (6.7–6.9) gives functional relations for the pulse shape whose solution are not obvious. We shall construct a class of solutions guided by the following physical idea. Let us consider that a photon leaks out of an optical cavity and propagates away as a wavepacket. Imagine that we were able to "time reverse" this wavepacket and send it back into the cavity; then this would restore the original (unknown) superposition state of the atom, provided we would also reverse the timing of the laser pulses. If, on the other hand, we are able to drive the atom in a transmitting cavity in such a way that the outgoing pulse were already symmetric in time, the wavepacket entering a receiving cavity would "mimic" this time reversed process, thus "restoring" the state of the first atom in the second one. Thus, we look for solutions satisfying the *symmetric pulse condition*

$$g_2(t) = g_1(-t) \quad (\forall t). \tag{6.13}$$

This implies $\alpha_1(t) = \alpha_2(-t)$, and $\beta_a(t) = \beta_a(-t)$. The latter relation leads to a symmetric shape of the photon wavepacket propagating between the cavities.

Suppose that we specify a pulse shape $\Omega_1(t) \propto g_1(t)$ for the second half of the pulse in the first cavity $(t \geq 0)$ [2]. We wish to determine the first half $\Omega_1(-t) \propto g_1(-t)$ (for $t > 0$), such that the conditions for ideal transmission (6.3) are satisfied. From (6.6, 6.11) we have

$$g_1(-t) = -\frac{\sqrt{2}\kappa\beta_a(t) + g_1(t)\alpha_1(t)}{\alpha_2(t)}, \quad (t > 0). \tag{6.14}$$

Thus, the pulse shape is completely determined provided we know the system evolution for $t \geq 0$. However, a difficulty arises when we try to find this evolution, since it depends on the yet unknown $g_2(t) = g_1(-t)$ for $t > 0$ [see (6.7–6.9)]. In order to circumvent this problem, we use (6.11) to eliminate this dependence in (6.7, 6.9). This gives

$$\dot{\alpha}_1(t) = g_1(t)\beta_a(t)/\sqrt{2}, \tag{6.15}$$
$$\dot{\beta}_a(t) = -\kappa\beta_a(t) - \sqrt{2}g_1(t)\alpha_1(t) \tag{6.16}$$

for $t \geq 0$. These equations have to be integrated with the initial conditions

$$\alpha_1(0) = \left[\frac{2\kappa^2}{g_1(0)^2 + \kappa^2}\right]^{\frac{1}{2}} \tag{6.17}$$

$$\beta_a(0) = [1 - 2\alpha_1(0)^2]^{\frac{1}{2}} \tag{6.18}$$

which follow immediately from $\alpha_1(0) = \alpha_2(0)$, and (6.11, 6.12) at $t = 0$. Given the solution of (6.15, 6.16), we can determine $\alpha_2(t)$ from the normalisation

---

[2] $\Omega_1(t)$ has to be such that $\alpha_1(\infty) = 0$. This is fulfilled if $\Omega_1(\infty) > 0$, which also guarantees that the denominator in (6.14) does not vanish for $t > 0$.

(6.12). In this way, the problem is solved since all the quantities appearing on the RHS of (6.14) are known for $t \geq 0$. It is straightforward to find analytical expressions for the pulse shapes, for example by specifying $\Omega_1(t) = \text{const}$ for $t > 0$.

6.2.4 Imperfect Operations and Error Correction

We have assumed that all operations involved in the transmission process, e.g. the state mapping from the atom to the cavity field via laser pulses, are perfect and did not pay special attention to absorption losses and decoherence in the communication channel. In reality, of course, such processes will always occur with a certain probability. The optical cavity–fibre system, together with the Raman pulses, is an example of a *noisy quantum channel.* Generally speaking, quantum noise tends to diminish the fidelity of the transmission and to destroy the quantum correlations that are ideally established between the nodes. This effect becomes particularly dominant if the nodes are separated by a long distance, where long is defined in comparison with the coherence length and/or absorption length of the channel. Fortunately, since the advent of quantum error correction [287] and entanglement purification [288], there are some tools to fight the effects of quantum noise and decoherence. In Sect. 8.6, we will describe how an efficient error correction can be implemented in above quantum network, correcting transmission errors to all orders. This will allow communication with high fidelity over a short distance. For long distance communication, where the error probability grows exponentially with the length of the channel, we develop a concept of a quantum repeater that plays a role analogous to amplifiers in classical communication.

6.3 Multi-Particle Entanglement

D. Bouwmeeester, J.-W. Pan, M. Daniell, H. Weinfurter, A. Zeilinger

6.3.1 Greenberger–Horne–Zeilinger states

Entanglement between many particles is essential for most quantum communication schemes, e.g. error-correction schemes and secret key distribution networks, and for quantum computation. However, the original motivation for the discussion and the generation of entangled states for more than two particles, so called Greenberger–Horne–Zeilinger (GHZ) states, stems from a different direction [289, 290]. Namely from the debate about whether or not quantum mechanics is a complete theory. Although it is not the intention to give a detailed exposure of this fundamental philosophical discussion here, a brief presentation will be given in order for the reader to obtain a better understanding of the quantum information stored in many-particle entangled system and why their quantum properties are in strong conflict with Einstein's notion of locality. The presentation is structured around an experimental realisation of three-photon entanglement, which, in its own right, is important for the field of quantum information [291].

6.3.2 The Conflict with Local Realism

Greenberger, Horne and Zeilinger showed that quantum-mechanical predictions for certain measurement results on three entangled particles are in conflict with local realism in cases where quantum theory makes definite, i.e. non-statistical, predictions [289]–[294]. This is in contrast to the case of Einstein–Podolsky–Rosen experiments with two entangled particles testing Bell's inequality, where the conflict with local realism only arises for statistical predictions [21, 23, 295, 296, 297].

How are the quantum predictions of a three-photon GHZ-state in stronger conflict with local realism than the conflict for two-photon states?[3] To answer this, consider the state

$$\frac{1}{\sqrt{2}}(|H\rangle_1 |H\rangle_2 |H\rangle_3 + |V\rangle_1 |V\rangle_2 |V\rangle_3), \tag{6.19}$$

where H and V denote horizontal and vertical polarisations. This state indicates that the three photons are in a quantum superposition of the state $|H\rangle_1 |H\rangle_2 |H\rangle_3$ (all three photons are horizontally polarised) and the state $|V\rangle_1 |V\rangle_2 |V\rangle_3$ (all three photons are vertically polarised). This specific state is symmetric with respect to the interchange of all photons which simplifies the arguments below, however the line of reasoning holds for any other maximally entangled three-photon state.

Consider now some specific predictions following from state (6.19) for polarisation measurements on each photon in either a basis rotated through $45°$ with respect to the original H/V basis, denoted by H'/V', or in a circular polarisation basis denoted by L/R (left-handed, right-handed). These new polarisation bases can be expressed in terms of the original ones as

$$|H'\rangle = \frac{1}{\sqrt{2}}(|H\rangle + |V\rangle), \quad |V'\rangle = \frac{1}{\sqrt{2}}(|H\rangle - |V\rangle), \tag{6.20}$$

$$|R\rangle = \frac{1}{\sqrt{2}}(|H\rangle + i|V\rangle), \quad |L\rangle = \frac{1}{\sqrt{2}}(|H\rangle - i|V\rangle). \tag{6.21}$$

Let us denote $|H\rangle$ by the vector $(1,0)$ and $|V\rangle$ by the vector $(0,1)$; they are thus the two eigenstates of Pauli operator σ_z, with the corresponding

---

[3] For two-photon states Hardy [298] has found situations where local realism predicts that a specific result occurs *sometimes* and quantum mechanics predicts that the same result *never* occurs [299].

eigenvalues $+1$ and -1. One can also easily verify that $|H'\rangle$ and $|V'\rangle$ or $|R\rangle$ and $|L\rangle$ are two eigenstates for Pauli operator σ_x or σ_y with the values $+1$ and -1, respectively. We will refer to a measurement in the H'/V' basis as an x measurement and in the L/R basis as a y measurement.

Representing state (6.19) in the new bases one obtains predictions for measurements of these new polarisations. For example, in the case of measurement of circular polarisation on, say, both photon 1 and 2, and measurement of linear polarisation H' and V' on photon 3, denoted as a yyx measurement, the state becomes

$$\frac{1}{2} \left(|R\rangle_1 |L\rangle_2 |H'\rangle_3 + |L\rangle_1 |R\rangle_2 |H'\rangle_3 \right.$$
$$\left. + |R\rangle_1 |R\rangle_2 |V'\rangle_3 + |L\rangle_1 |L\rangle_2 |V'\rangle_3 \right). \tag{6.22}$$

This expression has a number of significant implications. Firstly, a specific result that is obtained in any individual or two-photon joint measurement is maximally random. For example, photon 1 will exhibit polarisation R or L with the same probability of 50%.

Secondly, because only those terms yielding a -1 product for a yyx measurement appear in the expression, one realises that, given the results of measurements on two photons, it is possible to predict with certainty what the result of a corresponding measurement performed on the third photon will be. For example, suppose photon 1 and 2 are both found to exhibit right-handed (R) circular polarisation (i.e., both having the value $+1$). By the third term in the expression above, photon 3 will definitely be V' polarised (i.e., having the value -1).

By cyclic permutation, analogous expressions are obtained for any case of the measurement of circular polarisation on two photons and V'-H' polarisation on the remaining one. Again, only those terms which give a -1 product are the possible outcomes in a yxy or an xyy measurement. Thus, the measurement result both for circular polarisation and for linear H', V' polarisation can be predicted with certainty for any one of these photons given the result of appropriate measurements on the other two.

Now let us analyse the implications of these predictions from the point of view of local realism. First note that the predictions are independent of the spatial separation of the photons and independent of the relative time order of the measurements. Let us thus consider the experiment to be performed such that the three measurements are performed simultaneously in a given reference frame, say, for conceptual simplicity, in the reference frame of the source. Employing the notion of Einstein locality implies that no information can travel faster than the speed of light. Hence the specific measurement result obtained for any photon must not depend on which specific measurement is performed simultaneously on the other two nor on the outcome of these measurements. The only way then to explain from a local realist point of view the perfect correlations discussed above is to assume that each photon carries elements of reality for all the measurements considered and that these elements of reality determine the specific measurement result [289, 290, 294].

Let us now consider a measurement of linear H', V' polarisation on all three photons, i.e. an xxx measurement. What outcomes are possible here if elements of reality exist? State (6.19) and its permutations imply that whenever the result H' [V'] is obtained for any one photon, the other two photons must carry opposite [identical] circular polarisations. Suppose that for three specific photons, one finds, say, the result V' for photons 2 and 3. Because photon 3 is a V', both photon 1 and 2 must carry identical circular polarisations; and because photon 2 is a V', both photons 1 and 3 must carry identical circular polarisations. Clearly, if these circular polarisations are elements of reality, then all three photons must carry identical circular polarisations. Thus, if photons 2 and 3 have identical circular polarisations, then photon 1 must necessarily carry linear polarisation V'. Thus the existence of elements of reality leads to the conclusion that the result $|V_1'\rangle|V_2'\rangle|V_3'\rangle$ is one possible outcome if one elects to measure H', V' polarisations of all three particles, i.e. if an xxx measurement is performed. By parallel constructions, one can verify that the only four possible outcomes are

$$|V_1'\rangle|V_2'\rangle|V_3'\rangle, \ |H_1'\rangle|H_2'\rangle|V_3'\rangle, \ |H_1'\rangle|V_2'\rangle|H_3'\rangle, \text{ and } |V_1'\rangle|H_2'\rangle|H_3'\rangle. \quad (6.23)$$

How do these predictions of local realism compare with those of quantum physics? Expressing the state given in (6.19) in terms of H', V' polarisation yields

$$\frac{1}{2} \ (\ |H'\rangle_1|H'\rangle_2|H'\rangle_3 + |H'\rangle_1|V'\rangle_2|V'\rangle_3$$
$$+ |V'\rangle_1|H'\rangle_2|V'\rangle_3 + |V'\rangle_1|V'\rangle_2|H'\rangle_3). \quad (6.24)$$

Comparing the terms given in (6.23) with the terms in (6.24) one observes that whenever local realism predicts that a specific result definitely occurs for a measurement on one of the photons given the results for the other two, quantum physics definitely predicts the opposite result. Thus, while in the case of Bell's inequalities for two photons the difference between local realism and quantum physics happens for statistical predictions of the theory, here any statistics is only due to inevitable measurement errors occurring in any and every experiment of classical or quantum physics.

6.3.3 A Source for Three-Photon GHZ Entanglement

Proposals for the creation of entanglement between more than two particles have been made for experiments with photons [300], atoms [301] and ions (see Sect. 4.3), and three nuclear spins within a single molecule have been prepared such that they locally exhibit three-particle correlations [302]. In this section the first experimental observation of polarisation entanglement of three spatially separated photons is described [291]. The method used for

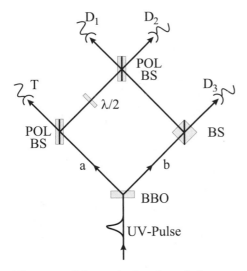

Fig. 6.3. Schematic drawing of the experimental setup for the demonstration of Greenberger–Horne–Zeilinger entanglement for spatially separated photons. Conditional on the registration of one photon at the trigger detector T, the three photons registered at D_1, D_2, and D_3 exhibit the desired GHZ correlations.

the experiment is a further development of the techniques that have been used in experiments on quantum teleportation [76] (Sect. 3.7) and entanglement swapping [86] (Sect. 3.10).

As proposed in Ref. [300], the main idea is to transform two pairs of polarisation entangled photons into three entangled photons and a fourth independent photon.[4] Figure 6.3 is a schematic drawing of the experimental setup. Pairs of polarisation entangled photons are generated by a 200 fs pulse of UV-light which passes through a BBO crystal (see Sect. 3.4.4). The pair creation is such that the following polarisation entangled state is obtained [26]:

$$\frac{1}{\sqrt{2}}(\,|\,H\rangle_a\,|\,V\rangle_b + e^{i\chi}\,|\,V\rangle_a\,|\,H\rangle_b).\tag{6.25}$$

This state represents a superposition of the possibility that the photon in arm a is horizontally polarised and the one in arm b is vertically polarised $|\,H\rangle_a\,|\,V\rangle_b$, with the opposite possibility $|\,V\rangle_a\,|\,H\rangle_b$.

In the rare event that two such pairs are created by the passage of a single UV pulse through the crystal the setup is designed such that detection of one photon at each of the four detectors (four-fold coincidence) corresponds to the observation of the state

---

[4] The method developed to obtain three-particle entanglement from a source of pairs of entangled particles can be extended to obtain entanglement between many more particles [303].

$$\frac{1}{\sqrt{2}} \left(|H\rangle_1 |H\rangle_2 |V\rangle_3 + |V\rangle_1 |V\rangle_2 |H\rangle_3 \right) , \tag{6.26}$$

by the detectors D1, D2 and D3. This can be understood in the following way. When a four-fold coincidence recording is obtained, one photon in path a must have been transmitted by the polarising beamsplitter (Pol BS) in path a and therefore must have had horizontal polarisation upon detection by the trigger detector T. Its companion photon in path b must then be vertically polarised, and it has 50% chance of being transmitted by the beamsplitter (see Fig. 6.3) towards detector D_3 and 50% chance of being reflected by the beamsplitter towards the final polarising beamsplitter where it will be reflected to D_2. In the former case, the counts at detectors D_1 and D_2 are due to the second pair. One photon of this second pair travels via path a and must necessarily be V polarised in order to be reflected by the polarising beamsplitter in path a; thus its companion, taking path b, must be H polarised and after reflection at the beamsplitter in path b (with a 50% probability) it will be transmitted by the final polarising beamsplitter and arrive at detector D_1. The photon detected by D_2 therefore must be H polarised since it came via path a and had to transit the last polarising beamsplitter. Note that this latter photon was initially V polarised but after passing the $\lambda/2$ plate (at 22.5°) it became polarised at 45° which gave it a 50% chance of arriving as an H polarised photon at detector D_2. Thus one concludes that if the photon detected by D_3 is the companion of the T photon, then the coincidence detection by D_1, D_2, and D_3 corresponds to the detection of the state

$$|H\rangle_1 |H\rangle_2 |V\rangle_3 . \tag{6.27}$$

By a similar argument one can show that if the photon detected by D_2 is the companion of the T photon, the coincidence detection by D_1, D_2, and D_3 corresponds to the detection of the state

$$|V\rangle_1 |V\rangle_2 |H\rangle_3 . \tag{6.28}$$

In general, the two possible states (6.27) and (6.28) corresponding to a four-fold coincidence recording will not form a coherent superposition, i.e. a GHZ state, because they could, in principle, be distinguishable. Besides possible lack of mode overlap at the detectors, the exact detection time of each photon can reveal which state is present. For example, state (6.27) is identified by noting that T and D_3, or D_1 and D_2, fire nearly simultaneously. To erase this information it is necessary that the coherence time of the photons is substantially longer than the duration of the UV pulse (approx. 200 fs) [304]. This can be achieved by detecting the photons behind narrow band-width filters (3.6 nm bandwidth) which yield a coherence time of approx. 500 fs. Thus, the potential to distinguish between states (6.27) and (6.28) largely vanishes, and, by a basic rule of quantum mechanics, the state detected by a coincidence recording of D_1, D_2, and D_3, conditional on the trigger T, is the quantum superposition given in (6.26). Rigorously speaking, this erasure technique is perfect, hence produces a pure GHZ state, only in the limit of infinitesimal pulse duration and infinitesimal filter bandwidth, but detailed calculations [305] reveal that the experimental parameters given above are sufficient to create a clearly observable entanglement, up to about 80% purity, consistent with the experimental data given below. The plus sign in (6.26) follows from the following more formal derivation. Consider two down-conversions producing the product state

$$\frac{1}{2}\left(|H\rangle_a\,|V\rangle_b - |V\rangle_a\,|H\rangle_b\right)\left(|H\rangle'_a\,|V\rangle'_b - |V\rangle'_a\,|H\rangle'_b\right)\,. \tag{6.29}$$

Here it is initially assumed that the components $|H\rangle_{a,b}$ and $|V\rangle_{a,b}$ created in one down-conversion might be distinguishable from the components $|H\rangle'_{a,b}$ and $|V\rangle'_{a,b}$ created in the other one. The evolution of the individual components of state (6.29) through the apparatus towards the detectors T, D_1, D_2, and D_3 is given by

$$|H\rangle_a \rightarrow |H\rangle_T\,, \qquad\qquad |V\rangle_b \rightarrow \frac{1}{\sqrt{2}}(|V\rangle_2 + |V\rangle_3)\,, \tag{6.30}$$

$$|V\rangle_a \rightarrow \frac{1}{\sqrt{2}}(|V\rangle_1 + |H\rangle_2)\,, \qquad |H\rangle_b \rightarrow \frac{1}{\sqrt{2}}(|H\rangle_1 + |H\rangle_3)\,. \tag{6.31}$$

Identical expressions hold for the primed components. Inserting these expressions into state (6.29) and restricting ourselves to those terms where only one photon is found in each output we obtain

$$-\frac{1}{4\sqrt{2}}\,\{\ |H\rangle_T\left(|V\rangle'_1\,|V\rangle_2\,|H\rangle'_3 + |H\rangle'_1\,|H\rangle'_2\,|V\rangle_3\right)$$
$$+\ |H\rangle'_T\left(|V\rangle_1\,|V\rangle'_2\,|H\rangle_3 + |H\rangle_1\,|H\rangle_2\,|V\rangle'_3\right)\ \}\,. \tag{6.32}$$

If the experiment is now performed such that the photon states from the two down-conversions are indistinguishable, one finally obtains the desired state (up to an overall minus sign)

$$\frac{1}{\sqrt{2}}\,|H\rangle_T\left(|H\rangle_1\,|H\rangle_2\,|V\rangle_3 + |V\rangle_1\,|V\rangle_2\,|H\rangle_3\right)\,. \tag{6.33}$$

Note that the total photon state produced by the setup, i.e., the state before detection, also contains terms in which, for example, two photons enter the same detector. In addition, the total state contains contributions from single down-conversions. The four-fold coincidence detection acts as a projection measurement onto the desired GHZ state (6.33) and filters out the unwanted terms. The efficiency for one UV pump pulse to yield such a four-fold coincidence detection is very low (of the order of 10^{-10}). Fortunately, 7.6×10^7 UV-pulses are generated per second, which yields about one double pair creation and detection per 150 seconds. Triple and multiple pair creations can be completely neglected.

6.3.4 Experimental Proof of GHZ Entanglement

To experimentally demonstrate that GHZ entanglement can be obtained by the method described above, one first has to verify that, conditional on a photon detection by the trigger T, both the $H_1H_2V_3$ and the $V_1V_2H_3$ component are present and no others. This was done by comparing the count rates of the eight possible combinations of polarisation measurements, $H_1H_2H_3$, $H_1H_2V_3$, ..., $V_1V_2V_3$. The observed intensity ratio between the desired and undesired states was 12:1. Existence of the two terms as just demonstrated is a necessary but not yet sufficient condition for demonstrating GHZ entanglement. In fact, there could in principle be just a statistical mixture of those two states. Therefore, one has to prove that the two terms coherently superpose. This was done by a measurement of linear polarisation of photon 1 along $+45°$, bisecting the H and V direction. Such a measurement projects photon 1 into the superposition

$$| +45°\rangle_1 = \frac{1}{\sqrt{2}}(| H\rangle_1 + | V\rangle_1),\tag{6.34}$$

which implies that the state (6.33) is projected into

$$\frac{1}{\sqrt{2}} | H\rangle_T | +45°\rangle_1 (| H\rangle_2 | V\rangle_3 + | V\rangle_2 | H\rangle_3).\tag{6.35}$$

Thus photon 2 and 3 end up entangled as predicted under the notion of "entangled entanglement" [306]. Rewriting the state of photon 2 and 3 in the $45°$ basis results in the state

$$\frac{1}{\sqrt{2}} (| +45°\rangle_2 | +45°\rangle_3 - | -45°\rangle_2 | -45°\rangle_3).\tag{6.36}$$

This means that if photon 2 is found to be polarised along $-45°$, photon 3 is also polarised along the same direction. The absence of the terms $| +45°\rangle_2 | -45°\rangle_3$ and $| -45°\rangle_2 | +45°\rangle_3$ is due to destructive interference and thus indicates the desired coherent superposition of the terms in the GHZ state (6.33). The experiment therefore consisted of measuring four-fold coincidences between the detector T, detector 1 behind a $+45°$ polariser, detector 2 behind a $-45°$ polariser, and measuring photon 3 behind either a $+45°$ polariser or a $-45°$ polariser. In the experiment, the difference in arrival time of the photons at the final polariser, or more specifically, at the detectors D1 and D2, was varied.

The data points in Fig. 6.4a are the experimental results obtained for the polarisation analysis of the photon at D_3, conditioned on the trigger and the detection of two photons polarised at $45°$ and $-45°$ by the two detectors D_1 and D_2, respectively.

The two curves show the four-fold coincidences for a polariser oriented at $-45°$ (squares) and $+45°$ (circles) in front of detector D_3 as function of the

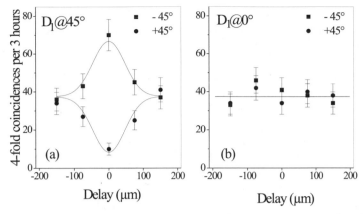

Fig. 6.4. Experimental confirmation of GHZ entanglement. Graph (**a**) shows the results obtained for polarisation analysis of the photon at D_3, conditional on the trigger and the detection of one photon at D_1 polarised at $45°$ and one photon at detector D_2 polarised $-45°$. The two curves show the four-fold coincidences for a polariser oriented at $-45°$ and $45°$ respectively in front of detector D_3 as function of the spatial delay in path a. The difference between the two curves at zero delay confirms the GHZ entanglement. By comparison (graph (**b**)) no such intensity difference is found, as predicted, if the polariser in front of detector D_1 is set at $0°$.

spatial delay in path a. From the two curves it follows that for zero delay the polarisation of the photon at D_3 is oriented along $-45°$, in accordance with the quantum-mechanical predictions for the GHZ state. For non-zero delay, the photons travelling via path a towards the second polarising beamsplitter and those traveling via path b become distinguishable. Therefore increasing the delay gradually destroys the quantum superposition in the three-particle state.

Note that one can equally well conclude from the data that at zero delay, the photons at D_1 and D_3 have been projected onto a two-particle entangled state by the projection of the photon at D_2 onto $-45°$. The two conclusions are only compatible for a genuine GHZ state.

For an additional confirmation of state (6.33) measurements have been performed conditional on the detection of the photon at D_1 under $0°$ polarisation (i.e. V polarisation). For the GHZ state $(1/\sqrt{2})(H_1 H_2 V_3 + V_1 V_2 H_3)$ this implies that the remaining two photons should be in the state $V_2 H_3$ which cannot give rise to any correlation between these two photons in the $45°$ detection basis. The experimental results of these measurement are presented in Fig. 6.4b. The data clearly indicate the absence of two-photon correlations and thereby confirm the observation of GHZ entanglement between three spatially separated photons.

Recall that the GHZ entanglement is only observed under the condition that both the trigger photon and the three entangled photons are detected.

This implies that the four-fold coincidence detection plays the double role both of projecting into the desired GHZ state (6.26) and of performing a specific measurement on the state.

This might raise doubts about whether such a source can be used to test local realism. Actually the same doubts had also been raised for the former Bell-type experiments involving indistinguishability of photons [307, 308]. Although these experiments have successfully produced certain long-distance quantum-mechanical correlations, in the past it was generally believed [309], [310] that they could never, not even their idealised versions, be considered as genuine tests of local realism. However, Popescu, Hardy and Zukowski [311] showed that this general belief is wrong and that the above experiments indeed constitute (modulo the usual detection loopholes) true tests of local realism. Following the same line of reasoning, Zukowski [312] has shown that the above GHZ entanglement source enables one to perform a three-particle test of local realism. In essence, the GHZ argument for testing local realism is based on detection events and knowledge of the underlying quantum state is not even necessary. It is indeed enough to consider only the four-fold coincidences discussed above and ignore totally the contributions by the other terms.

6.3.5 Experimental Test of Local Realism Versus Quantum Mechanics

How can one experimentally address the conflict between local realism and quantum mechanics using the GHZ entanglement source described in the previous section? As explained in Sect. 6.3.2, one first has to perform a set of experiments for yyx, yxy and xyy. Each of the three experiments has in principle 2^3 possible outcomes.

Figure 6.5 indicates the experimentally obtained probabilities for each of the 3×2^3 possible outcomes. Here, in order to compare with the GHZ reasoning for state (6.19) given in Sect. 6.3.2, we have simply redefined the polarisation states of photon 3 in (6.26), that is, the notation $| H \rangle_3$ and $| V \rangle_3$ have been interchanged.

From the values of the maxima and minima in Fig. 6.5 one concludes that with 71%±4% accuracy, i.e. with a visibility of $(\langle \max \rangle - \langle \min \rangle)/(\langle \max \rangle + \langle \min \rangle) = 0.71 \pm 0.04$, the terms that are expected to be present and those that are expected to be absent can be identified. Although the limited visibility is mainly explained by the finite length of the pump-pulse and the finite bandwidth of the frequency filters (see Sect. 6.3.3), it is appropriate, if not compulsory, for a fundamental test of local realism versus quantum mechanics to consider the data shown in Fig. 6.5 as being obtained from measurements on an ensemble of three particles emerging from a black box. In this way no presuppositions about the source of GHZ entanglement are included in the following demonstration of the conflict with local realism. From the data in Fig. 6.5, and taking a local realistic point of view, i.e., assuming that

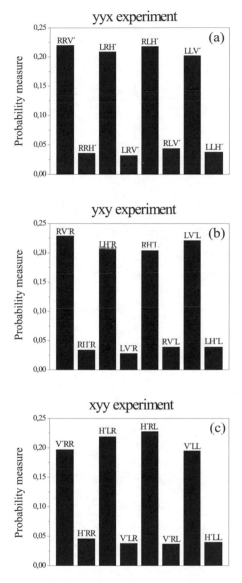

Fig. 6.5. Experimentally determined probabilities of all the possible outcomes of (**a**) a yyx measurement, (**b**) a yxy measurement and (**c**) an xyy measurement.

the outcome of a certain measurement on one particle is independent of the result of any measurement that has been performed on another particle that is specially separated from the former, one can predict (following the arguments given in Sect. 6.3.2) the possible outcomes for an xxx measurement. These predictions are shown in Fig. 6.6a.

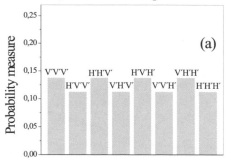

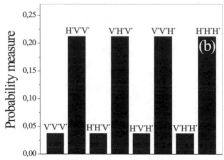

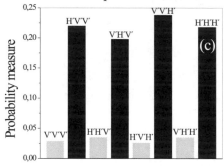

Fig. 6.6. (**a**): Local realistic predictions for the probabilities of the eight three-particle correlations for an xxx measurement (based on data given in Fig. 6.5). (**b**): The corresponding quantum-mechanical predictions. (**c**): The experimental results, which are in strong conflict with the local realistic predictions and in agreement with the quantum-mechanical predictions within experimental accuracy.

The predictions following from quantum mechanics are shown in Fig. 6.6b. These later predictions follow from the argument that the data in Fig. 6.5 indicate the presence of entangled three-particle systems with a purity of about 71%. Finally, Fig. 6.6c shows the experimental results for an xxx measurement.

The results are in strong conflict with the local realism predictions and in full agreement with the quantum mechanical predictions. Actually, within the experimental uncertainty, the experimental data clearly show that only those triple coincidences predicted by quantum mechanics, see (6.24), occur and that those predicted by local realism, see (6.23), are absent. In this sense, the described experiment constitutes the first three-particle test of local realism without inequalities [313].

Since no real experiment can fully fulfill the perfect correlation condition required by the original reasoning of GHZ, a local realist may argue that the GHZ predictions can never be perfectly tested in the laboratory and thus he/she might not be convinced by the above analysis. To face this difficulty, a number of Bell-type inequalities for N-particle GHZ states have been derived [314]–[316]. All these works show that quantum mechanical predictions for GHZ states violate these inequalities by an amount that grows exponentially with N. For instance, the optimal Bell-type inequality for a three-particle GHZ state given by Mermin reads as follows

$$|\langle xyy \rangle + \langle yxy \rangle + \langle yyx \rangle - \langle xxx \rangle| \leq 2, \tag{6.37}$$

where, for example, $\langle xyy \rangle$ denotes the expectation value of the product of the eigenvalues for x, y, and y, measurements on particles 1, 2, and 3, respectively. The necessary visibility to violate this Bell-type inequality for a three-particle GHZ state is 50% [314]. The visibility observed in the above GHZ experiment is about 70% and clearly surpasses the 50% limit. Substituting the experimental results into the left-hand side of inequality (6.37) gives

$$|\langle xxy \rangle + \langle yxy \rangle + \langle yyx \rangle - \langle xxx \rangle| = 2.83 \pm 0.09. \tag{6.38}$$

Therefore, the experimental results violate the inequality (6.37) by over 9 standard deviations, which concludes the demonstration of the conflict with local realism. It should be pointed out that the above test does not provides the final verdict for local realistic theories. Some "loopholes" are still open since the experiments have not been performed with a high-efficiency and space-like separated detection method.

6.4 Entanglement Quantification

V. Vedral, M.B. Plenio, P.L. Knight

6.4.1 Schmidt Decomposition and von Neumann Entropy

A composite quantum system is one that consists of a number of quantum subsystems. When those subsystems are entangled it is impossible to ascribe a definite state vector to any one of them. A simple example of a composite quantum system is a pair of two polarisation entangled photons (see Sect. 3.4.4). The composite system is mathematically described by

$$|\Psi^-\rangle_{12} = \frac{1}{\sqrt{2}}(|H\rangle_1|V\rangle_2 - |V\rangle_1|H\rangle_2)\,. \tag{6.39}$$

The property that is described is that the direction of polarisation of the two photons is orthogonal along any axis. One can immediately see from (6.39) that neither of the photons possesses a definite state (polarisation) vector. The best that one can say is that if a measurement is made on one photon, and it is found, say, to be vertically polarised ($|V\rangle$), then the other photon is certain to be horizontally polarised ($|H\rangle$). This type of description however can not be applied to a general composite system, unless the former is written in a special form. This motivates us to introduce the so called Schmidt decomposition [317], which not only is mathematically convenient, but also gives a deeper insight into correlations between the two subsystems.

The Schmidt decomposition shows that any state of two subsystems A and B (one of dimension N and the other of dimension $M \leq N$) can be written as

$$|\Psi_{AB}\rangle = \sum_{i=1}^{N} c_i|u_i\rangle|v_i\rangle\,, \tag{6.40}$$

where $\{|u_i\rangle\}$ is a basis for subsystem A and $\{|v_i\rangle\}$ is a basis for subsystem B. There are two important observations to be made, which are absolutely fundamental to understanding correlations between the two subsystems in a joint pure state:

- The reduced density matrices of both subsystems, written in the Schmidt basis, are diagonal and have the same positive spectrum. We find the reduced density matrix of the subsystem A by tracing the joint state $\rho_{AB} = |\Psi_{AB}\rangle\langle\Psi_{AB}|$ over all states of the subsystem B, so that

$$\rho_A = \text{Tr}_B\rho_{AB} := \sum_q \langle v_q|\rho|v_q\rangle = \sum_p |c_p|^2|u_p\rangle\langle u_p|\,. \tag{6.41}$$

Analogously we find $\rho_B = \sum_p |c_p|^2|v_p\rangle\langle v_p|$.

- If a subsystem is N dimensional it can be entangled with no more than N orthogonal states of another one.

We would like to point out that the Schmidt decomposition is, in general, impossible for more than two entangled subsystems. Mathematical details of this fact are exposed in [318]. To clarify this, however, we consider three entangled subsystems as an example. Here, our intention would be to write a general state such that by observing the state of the one of the subsystems would instantaneously and with certainty tell us the state of the other two. But this is impossible in general since one can perform a measurement on one of the three subsystems such that the remaining two subsystems are entangled systems (see Sect. 6.3.4). Clearly, involvement of even more subsystems complicates this analysis even further. The same reasoning applies to mixed states of two or more subsystems (i.e. states whose density operator is not idempotent $\rho^2 \neq \rho$), for which we cannot have the Schmidt decomposition in general. This reason alone is responsible for the fact that the entanglement of two subsystems in a pure state is simple to understand and quantify, while for mixed states, or states consisting of more than two subsystems, the question is much more involved.

To quantify entanglement in a pure state of two subsystems we introduce the following "measure of uncertainty" in a state of a quantum system.

Definition. *The von Neumann entropy* of a quantum system described by a density matrix ρ is defined as [319]

$$S_N(\rho) := -\operatorname{Tr}(\rho \ln \rho) . \tag{6.42}$$

(We will drop the subscript N whenever there is no possibility of confusion). So entanglement between A and B can be understood as follows. The uncertainty in the system B before we measured A is $S(\rho_B)$, where ρ_B is the reduced density matrix of system B. After the measurement there is no uncertainty, i.e. if we obtain $\{|u_i\rangle\}$ for A, then we know that the state of B is $\{|v_i\rangle\}$. So the information gained is $S(\rho_B) = S(\rho_A)$. Thus A and B are most entangled when their reduced density matrices are maximally mixed. Specialising to two qubits, a maximally entangled state is e.g. $\frac{1}{\sqrt{2}}(|00\rangle+|11\rangle)$.

There is also another physical interpretation of this measure of entanglement for pure states. Namely it can be shown [117] that the amount of entanglement that can be distilled locally from a pure state of the form $a|00\rangle + b|11\rangle$ is limited by the reduced entropy of that pure state. On the other hand, if we want to create, by local operations, an ensemble of systems each in the state $a|00\rangle + b|11\rangle$ then the average amount of entanglement per pair that we need to share initially is again given by the reduced entropy of that pure state.

For mixed states the Schmidt decomposition no longer exists, so that the reduced entropy is no longer a good measure of entanglement. A way to proceed in quantifying entanglement turns out to be via entanglement

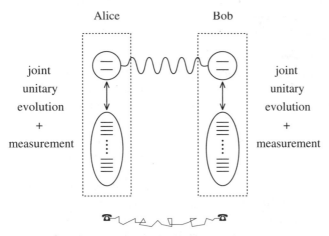

Fig. 6.7. Quantum state purification methods allow local general measurements as indicated by the dashed boxes. An additional multilevel system interacts with our qubit and subsequently the multilevel system is measured. This is the most general form of measurement. Also allowed is classical communication, here symbolised by the telephones.

purification procedures. We first formalise general purification procedures and then, based on that, show three different ways of quantifying entanglement.

6.4.2 Purification Procedures

There are three different ingredients involved in procedures aiming at distilling locally a subensemble of highly entangled states from an original ensemble of less entangled states.

1. *Local general measurements* (LGM): these are performed by the two parties A and B separately and are described by two sets of operators satisfying the completeness relations $\sum_i A_i^\dagger A_i = \mathbf{I}$ and $\sum_j B_j^\dagger B_j = \mathbf{I}$. The joint action of the two is described by $\sum_{ij} A_i \otimes B_j = \sum_i A_i \otimes \sum_j B_j$, which is again a complete general measurement, and obviously local. Any local general measurement on a system can be implemented by letting it interact with an additional system and then measuring this additional system. The situation is depicted in Fig. 6.7.
2. *Classical communication* (CC): this means that the actions of A and B can be correlated. This can be described by a *complete measurement* on the whole space $A + B$ and is not necessarily decomposable into a sum of direct products of individual operators (as in LGM). If ρ_{AB} describes the initial state shared between A and B then the transformation involving 'LGM+CC' would look like

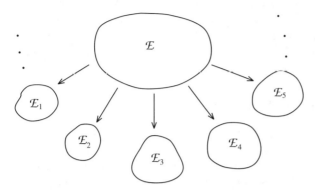

Fig. 6.8. Subselection according to the result of local measurements is the key ingredient of a quantum state purification procedure. The initial ensemble $\mathcal{E}$ is decomposed into subensembles $\mathcal{E}_i$. Some of these subensembles may have a higher entanglement per pair than the original ensemble.

$$\rho_{AB} \longrightarrow \sum_i A_i \otimes B_i \; \rho_{AB} \; A_i^\dagger \otimes B_i^\dagger \; , \tag{6.43}$$

i.e. the actions of A and B are 'correlated'.

3. *Post-selection* (PS) is performed on the *final ensemble* according to the above two procedures (Illustrated in Fig. 6.8). Mathematically this amounts to the general measurement not being complete, i.e. we leave out some operations. The density matrix describing the newly obtained ensemble (the subensemble of the original one) has to be renormalised accordingly. Suppose that we kept only the pairs where we had an outcome corresponding to the operators A_i and B_j, then the state of the chosen subensemble would be

$$\hat{\rho}_{AB} \longrightarrow \frac{A_i \otimes B_j \; \rho_{AB} \; A_i^\dagger \otimes B_j^\dagger}{\mathrm{Tr}(A_i \otimes B_j \; \rho_{AB} \; A_i^\dagger \otimes B_j^\dagger)} \; , \tag{6.44}$$

where the denominator provides the necessary normalisation.

Any manipulation involving either of the above three elements or their combination is called a *purification procedure*. It should be noted that the three operations described above are local. This implies that the entanglement of the total ensemble cannot increase under these operations. However, classical correlations between the two subsystems *can* be increased, even for the whole ensemble, if we allow classical communication.

We assume the following definition: a state ρ_{AB} is disentangled (also called separable) if and only if

$$\rho_{AB} = \sum_i p_i \rho_A^i \otimes \rho_B^i \; , \tag{6.45}$$

where $\sum_i p_i = 1$ and $p_i \geq 0$ for all i. Otherwise it is said to be entangled. Note that all the states in the above expansion can be pure. This is because each ρ^i can be expanded in terms of its eigenvectors. So, in the above sum we can in addition require that $\rho_A^i{}^2 = \rho_A^i$ and $\rho_B^i{}^2 = \rho_B^i$ for all i. This fact will be used later in this section.

6.4.3 Conditions for Entanglement Measures

It can be proven that, out of certain states, it is possible to distill maximally entangled states by means of LGM+CC+PS a subensemble of maximally entangled states [50]. The disentangled states, of course, yield no entanglement through purification, but the converse is not true in general; namely, if a state is entangled then this does not necessarily imply that it can be purified [320]. The question remains open as to how much entanglement a certain state contains. This question is not entirely well defined unless we state what physical circumstances characterise the amount of entanglement. This immediately implies that a measure of entanglement is non–unique, as will be seen shortly. Before we define three different measures of entanglement we state four conditions that every measure of entanglement has to satisfy [321, 322].

E1. $E(\sigma) = 0$ iff σ is separable.

E2. Local unitary operations leave $E(\sigma)$ invariant, i.e. $E(\sigma) = E(U_A \otimes U_B \sigma U_A^\dagger \otimes U_B^\dagger)$.

E3. The expected entanglement cannot increase under LGM+CC+PS given by $\sum V_i^\dagger V_i = I$, i.e.

$$\sum tr(\sigma_i) \, E(\sigma_i/tr(\sigma_i)) \leq E(\sigma) \; , \tag{6.46}$$

where $\sigma_i = V_i \sigma V_i^\dagger$.

E4. For pure states the measure of entanglement has to reduce to the entropy of the reduced density operator.

Condition E1 ensures that disentangled and only disentangled states have a zero value of entanglement. Condition E2 ensures that a local change of basis has no effect on the amount of entanglement. Condition E3 is intended to abolish the possibility of increasing entanglement by performing local measurements aided by classical communication. It takes into account the fact that we have a certain knowledge of the final state. Namely, when we start with n states σ we know exactly which $m_i = n \times \text{Tr}(\sigma_i)$ pairs will end up in the state σ_i after performing a purification procedure. Therefore we can separately access the entanglement in each of the possible subensembles described by σ_i. Clearly the total entanglement at the end should not exceed the original entanglement, which is stated in E3. This, of course, does not exclude the possibility that we can select a subensemble whose entanglement per pair is higher than the original entanglement per pair. The fourth condition has been introduced as a consistency criterion because the measure of entanglement for pure states is unique. We now introduce three different measures of entanglement which obey E1–E4. Note that we might wish to relax condition E4. This would allow us more possible measures of entanglement which might have applications in special situations. We will give an example later in this section.

First we discuss the entanglement of formation (sometimes also called the entanglement of creation) [323]. Bennett et al. define the entanglement of creation of a state $\hat{\rho}$ by

$$E_c(\rho) := \min \sum_i p_i S(\rho_A^i) \tag{6.47}$$

where $S(\rho_A) = -\mathrm{Tr}\rho_A \ln \rho_A$ is the von Neumann entropy and the minimum is taken over all the possible realisations of the state, $\hat{\rho}_{AB} = \sum_j p_j |\psi_j\rangle\langle\psi_j|$ with $\hat{\rho}_A^i = \mathrm{Tr}_B(|\psi_i\rangle\langle\psi_i|)$. The entanglement of creation cannot be increased by the combined action of LGM+CC and therefore satisfies all the four conditions E1–E4 [323]. The physical basis of this measure presents the number of singlets that must be invested in order to create a given entangled state. It should also be added that a closed form of this measure has been found recently [324].

Related to this measure is the entanglement of distillation [323]. It defines an amount of entanglement of a state σ as a proportion of singlets that can be distilled using a purification procedure. As such it is dependent on the efficiency of a particular purification procedure and can be made more general only by introducing some sort of universal purification procedure. Unlike the entanglement of formation there is no closed form analytical expression for the entanglement of distillation. However, some upper bounds can be provided and we come back to this later.

We now introduce a third measure of entanglement which may actually give rise to a whole family of good entanglement measures. It can be seen that this measure is intimately related to the entanglement of distillation by providing an upper bound for it [322].

If $\mathcal{D}$ is the set of all disentangled states (see Fig. 6.9), the measure of entanglement for a state σ is then defined as

$$E(\sigma) := \min_{\rho \in \mathcal{D}} \ D(\sigma||\rho), \tag{6.48}$$

where D is any measure of *distance* (not necessarily a metric) between the two density matrices ρ and σ such that $E(\sigma)$ satisfies the above conditions E1–E4.

Now an important question is what condition a candidate for $D(\sigma||\rho)$ has to satisfy in order for E1–E4 to hold for the entanglement measure? Necessary and sufficient conditions are not known, although a set of sufficient conditions exists [321]. Without going into any mathematical detail (see [322] if necessary) we present one measure that satisfies E1–E4 and one measure that only satisfies E1–E3.

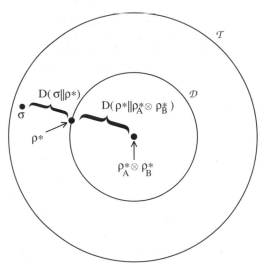

Fig. 6.9. The set of all density matrices, $\mathcal{T}$ is represented by the outer circle. Its subset, a set of disentangled states $\mathcal{D}$ is represented by the inner circle. A state σ belongs to the entangled states, and ρ^* is the disentangled state that minimises the distance $D(\sigma||\rho)$, thus representing the amount of quantum correlations in σ. State $\rho_A^* \otimes \rho_B^*$ is obtained by tracing ρ^* over A and B. $D(\rho^*||\rho_A^* \otimes \rho_B^*)$ represent the classical part of the correlations in the state σ.

6.4.4 Two Measures of Distance Between Density Matrices

We first state that E1–E4 hold for the quantum relative entropy, i.e. when $D(\sigma||\rho) = S(\sigma||\rho) := \text{Tr}\,\{\sigma(\ln\sigma - \ln\rho)\}$ [322]. Note that the quantum relative entropy is not a true metric, as it is not symmetric and does not satisfy the triangle inequality. In the next subsection the reasons for this will become clear. A question arises as to why the entanglement is not defined as $E(\sigma) = \min_{\rho \in \mathcal{D}} S(\rho||\sigma)$. Since the quantum relative entropy is asymmetric this gives a different result to the original definition. However, the major problem with this convention is that for maximally entangled states this measure is infinite. Although this does have a sound statistical interpretation (see the next section) it is hard to relate it to any physically reasonable scheme (e.g. a purification procedure). This is the prime reason for excluding this convention from any further considerations. The measure of entanglement generated by the quantum relative entropy will hereafter be referred to as the relative entropy of entanglement. An important result is that (for a proof see [322])

Theorem. For pure states the relative entropy of entanglement is equal to the von Neumann reduced entropy.

This is physically a very satisfying property of an entanglement measure, because it is already known that for pure states the von Neumann reduced entropy is a good measure of entanglement.

We also state an important result, that the entanglement of creation E_c is never smaller than the relative entropy measure of entanglement E. We will show later that this property has the important implication that the amount of entanglement that we have to invest to create a given quantum state is usually larger than the entanglement that one can recover using quantum state distillation methods.

Theorem. $E_c(\sigma) \leq E(\sigma) = \min_{\rho \in \mathcal{D}} S(\sigma||\rho)$.

We add that both the entanglement of creation and the relative entropy of entanglement can be calculated easily for the Bell diagonal states [321]. It turns out that for these states the entanglement of formation is substantially larger than the relative entropy of entanglement.

A "closed form" for the relative entropy of entanglement is not yet known, and a computer search is necessary to find the minimum ρ^*, for each given σ. However, we can numerically find the amount of entanglement for two spin-1/2 particles very efficiently using methods described in the next section.

An example of a measure of entanglement that satisfies conditions E1–E3 but not E4 is given by the (modified) Bures metric, i.e. when $D(\sigma||\rho) = D_B(\sigma||\rho) := 2 - 2F(\sigma, \rho)$, where $F(\sigma, \rho) := \left[\text{Tr}\{\sqrt{\sqrt{\rho}\sigma\sqrt{\rho}}\}^{1/2}\right]^2$ is the so-called fidelity (or Uhlmann's transition probability). We can, as in the case of the quantum relative entropy, calculate the measure of entanglement in this case for some simple states. For example, for maximally entangled states we obtain $E = 1$. Following the lines of the above proof it can be shown that for a general pure state $\alpha|00\rangle + \beta|11\rangle$[5] the entanglement is $4\alpha^2\beta^2$. In general, a computer search is necessary, as in the previous case. We now turn to describing this general computer calculation of a relative entropy of entanglement.

6.4.5 Numerics for Two Spin 1/2 Particles

As there is no closed analytical formula for the relative entropy of entanglement, we have to resort to a numerical search to find the entanglement of a general quantum state σ. Such a search can be performed efficiently using some results from convex analysis [325]. In the following we introduce one basic definition and one important result from convex analysis [325]. From this point onwards we concentrate on the quantum relative entropy as a measure of entanglement although most of the considerations are of a more general nature. The following theorem is crucial for our minimisation problem as it shows that we do not have to have an infinite number of parameters in the decomposition of a disentangled state in (6.45) to search over.

Caratheodory's theorem. Let $A \subset \mathbf{R}^N$. Then any $x \in \text{co}(A)$ has an expression of the form $x = \sum_{n=1}^{N+1} p_n a_n$ where $\sum_{n=1}^{N+1} p_n = 1$, and, for $n = 1, \ldots, N + 1$, $p_n \geq 0$ and $a_n \in A$.

---

[5] That this is, indeed, the most general form can be seen for the Schmidt decomposition [317].

A direct consequence of Caratheodory's theorem is that any state in $\mathcal{D}$ can be decomposed into a sum of at most $(\dim(H_1) \times \dim(H_2))^2$ products of pure states. So, for two spin-1/2 particles there are at most 16 terms in the expansion of any disentangled state in (6.45). In addition, each pure state can be described using two real numbers, so that there are altogether at most $15 + 16 \times 4 = 79$ real parameters needed to completely characterize a disentangled state in this case.

We note that this efficient computer search provides an alternative criterion for deciding when a given state σ of two spin-1/2 systems is disentangled, i.e. of the form given in (6.45). The already existing criterion is the one given by Peres and the Horodecki family. It states that a state is disentangled iff its partial trace is a negative operator (see the second and third references in [326]). This criterion is only valid for two spin 1/2, or one spin 1/2 and one spin 1 systems. In the absence of a more general analytical criterion, our computational method provides a way of deciding this question.

At the end of this section we mention *additivity* as an important property desired from a measure of entanglement, i.e. we would like to have

$$E(\sigma_{12} \otimes \sigma_{34}) = E(\sigma_{12}) + E(\sigma_{34}) \ , \tag{6.49}$$

where systems $1 + 2$ and systems $3 + 4$ are entangled separately from each other. The exact definition of the left hand side is

$$E(\sigma_{12} \otimes \sigma_{34}) = \min_{p_i, \rho_{13}, \rho_{24}} S(\sigma_{12} \otimes \sigma_{34} || \sum_i p_i \rho_{13}^i \otimes \rho_{24}^i) \ . \tag{6.50}$$

Why should we choose this form? One would originally assume that $\sigma_{12} \otimes \sigma_{34}$ should be minimised by the states of the form $(\sum_i p_i \rho_1 \otimes \rho_2^i) \otimes (\sum_j p_j \rho_3 \otimes \rho_4^i)$. However, Alice and Bob can also perform arbitrary unitary operation on their subsystems (i.e. locally). This obviously leads to the creation of entanglement between 1 and 2 and between 3 and 4 and hence the form in (6.50). Additivity is, of course, already true for the pure states as can be seen from the proof above, when our measure reduces to the von Neumann entropy. For a more general case we have not been able to provide any analytical proof, so that the above property remains a conjecture. However, for two spin-1/2 systems, our program has not found any counter-example. We will therefore assume this property to hold. A direct consequence of this and E3 is that the relative entropy of entanglement is an upper bound on the efficiency of any purification procedure. Namely if we start with n pairs in the state σ and obtain m singlets as a result of a purification procedure then

$$n \times E(\sigma) \geq m \ln 2 \ , \tag{6.51}$$

i.e. the efficiency m/n is always bounded by $E(\sigma)$. Since $E(\sigma)$ can be smaller than the entanglement of creation, this implies that the entanglement of creation and distillation are not necessarily equal.

6.4.6 Statistical Basis of Entanglement Measure

Let us see how we can interpret our entanglement measure in the light of experiments, i.e. statistically [327]. We first show how the notion of relative entropy arises in classical information theory as a measure of distinguishability of two probability distributions. We then generalise this idea to the quantum case, i.e. to distinguishing between two quantum states (for a discussion of distinguishability of pure quantum states see e.g. [328]). We will see that this naturally leads to the notion of the quantum relative entropy. It is then straightforward to extend this concept to explain the relative entropy of entanglement. Suppose we would like to check if a given coin is "fair", i.e. if it generates a "head–tail" distribution of $f = (1/2, 1/2)$. If the coin is biased then it will produce some other distribution, say $uf = (1/3, 2/3)$. So, our question of the coin fairness boils down to how well we can differentiate between two given probability distributions given a finite number, n, of experiments to perform on one of the two distributions. In the case of a coin we would toss it n times and record the number of 0's and 1's. What is the probability that a fair coin will be mistaken for an unfair one with the distribution of $(1/3, 2/3)$ given n trials on the fair coin? For large n the answer is [327, 329] (Sanov's theorem)

$$p(\text{fair} \to \text{unfair}) = e^{-nS_{cl}(uf||f)} , \tag{6.52}$$

where $S_{cl}(uf||f) = 1/3 \ln 1/3 + 2/3 \ln 2/3 - 1/3 \ln 1/2 - 2/3 \ln 1/2$ is the classical relative entropy for the two distributions. So,

$$p(\text{fair} \to \text{unfair}) = 3^n 2^{-\frac{5}{3}n} , \tag{6.53}$$

which tends exponentially to zero with $n \to \infty$. In fact we see that already after ~ 20 trials the probability of mistaking the two distributions is vanishingly small, $\leq 10^{-10}$.

In quantum theory we therefore state a law analogous to Sanov's theorem (see also [327]),

Theorem. (Quantum Sanov's Theorem). The probability of *not* distinguishing two quantum states (i.e. density matrices) σ and ρ after n measurements is

$$p(\rho \to \sigma) = e^{-nS(\sigma||\rho)} . \tag{6.54}$$

It can be claimed with certainty that the above presents the lower limit to the probability of confusing ρ with σ after performing n measurements on ρ [327]. In fact, this bound is reached asymptotically as proved in [330], and the measurements achieving this are projectors independent of the state σ [331]. Now the interpretation of the relative entropy of entanglement becomes immediately transparent [327]. The probability of mistaking an entangled state σ for a closest, disentangled state, ρ, is $e^{-n \times min_{\rho \in \mathcal{D}} S(\sigma, \rho)} = e^{-nE(\sigma)}$. If entanglement of σ is greater, then it takes fewer measurements to distinguish it from a disentangled state (or, fixing n, there is a smaller probability of confusing it with some disentangled state). Let us give an example. Consider a state $(|00\rangle+|11\rangle)/\sqrt{2}$, known to be a maximally entangled state. The closest to it is the disentangled state $(|00\rangle\langle00|+|11\rangle\langle11|)/2$ [321]. To distinguish these states it is enough to perform projections onto $(|00\rangle + |11\rangle)/\sqrt{2}$. If the state that we are measuring is the above mixture, then the sequence of results (1 for a successful projection, and 0 for an unsuccessful projection) will contain on average an equal number of 0's and 1's. For this to be mistaken for the above pure state the sequence has to contain all n 1's. The probability for that is 2^{-n}, which also comes from using (6.54). If, on the other hand, we performed projections onto the pure state itself, we would then never confuse it with a mixture, and from (6.54) the probability is seen to be $e^{-\infty} = 0$.

We see that the above treatment does not refer to the number (or indeed dimensionality) of the entangled systems. This is a desired property as it makes our measure of entanglement universal. The extensions to three or more systems are straightforward [322, 327]. (See also Sect. 8.5 on multiparticle entanglement purification).

7. Decoherence and Quantum Error Correction

7.1 Introduction

The main obstacle for the experimental implementations of quantum state processing is quantum decoherence. In Sect. 7.2 it is shown that decoherence of the state of a quantum system can be viewed as the consequence of entanglement between the quantum system and its environment. Section 7.3 illustrates the seemingly devastating effect of decoherence due to spontaneous decay for an ion-trap quantum computer.

One of the most important achievements in the field of quantum information is the discovery of methods to overcome the problem of decoherence. These methods are called quantum error correction schemes and are introduced in Sect. 7.4. The methods make use of the fact that the state of a single qubit can be encoded on entangled states of several qubits. Symmetry properties of these entangled states, together with the fact that quantum noise can be digitized by projection measurements, enables the detection and correction of quantum errors. Since entangled states are themselves more vulnerable to decoherence than single-qubit states, there is a trade-off between correcting and inducing quantum errors for such schemes. The general theory of quantum error correction and the issue of fault tolerance will be addressed in Sect. 7.5. A good illustration of a realistic error correction procedure is the problem of creating a frequency standard using Ramsey spectroscopy and this is presented in Sect. 7.6.

Another route to overcome decoherences is to distill from a large set of entangled particles, that has been degraded in purity by decoherence, a subset of particles with enhanced entanglement purity. Entanglement purification is the topic of Chap. 8.

7.2 Decoherence

A.K. Ekert, G.M. Palma, K.A. Suominen

7.2.1 Decoherence: Entanglement Between Qubits and Environment

As described in Chap. 4 of this book a quantum computer can be viewed as a sort of "programmable interferometer" where different computational paths are designed in such a way as to interfere constructively on the desired result. In order for such interference to take place the evolution of the computer must be coherent, i.e. unitary. Any deviation from unitarity due to decoherence would spoil the interference visibility.

Decoherence appears whenever our qubits are coupled with their environment. To illustrate the origin of decoherence mechanisms let us assume that the qubit–environment coupling induces a joint unitary time evolution of the following form

$$|0\rangle|E\rangle \xrightarrow{U(t)} |0\rangle|E_0(t)\rangle \qquad\qquad |1\rangle|E\rangle \xrightarrow{U(t)} |1\rangle|E_1(t)\rangle\,, \qquad (7.1)$$

where $|E\rangle$ is some fixed initial state of the environment, and $U(t)$ is the joint unitary time evolution operator. In (7.1) the environment acts as a measuring apparatus which acquires information on the states of our qubit [332]. When the initial state of the qubit is a linear superposition of states $|0\rangle$ and $|1\rangle$, $U(t)$ will introduce entanglement between qubit and environment:

$$(a_0|0\rangle + a_1|1\rangle) \otimes |E\rangle \xrightarrow{U(t)} a_0|0\rangle|E_0(t)\rangle + a_1|1\rangle|E_1(t)\rangle\,. \qquad (7.2)$$

Decoherence is due exactly to such entanglement, since nonunitarity emerges once we trace over the environment degrees of freedom. The reduced density matrix of the qubit corresponding to state (7.2) is given by

$$\rho_q(t) = \text{Tr}_E \varrho_{q+E} = \begin{bmatrix} |a_0|^2 & a_0 a_1^* \langle E_1|E_0\rangle \\ a_1 a_0^* \langle E_0|E_1\rangle & |a_0|^2 \end{bmatrix}\,. \qquad (7.3)$$

In most cases states $|E_0(t)\rangle, |E_1(t)\rangle$ become more orthogonal in time (i.e. more and more information on the qubit state leaks into the environment) and we can conveniently write

$$\langle E_0(t)|E_1(t)\rangle = e^{-\Gamma(t)}\,, \qquad (7.4)$$

where $\Gamma(t)$ is a function of time whose specific form will depend on the details of the coupling between qubit and environment [333]. Its value depends on the type of qubits and their interaction with the environment and can vary from 10^4 s for nuclear spins in a paramagnetic atom to 10^{-12} s for electron–hole excitations in the bulk of a semiconductor [334]. As a consequence the particular kind of entanglement described by (7.2) kills the off-diagonal matrix elements of the density matrix – the so-called "coherences" – while leaving the diagonal ones, known as "populations" unaffected. This effect is known as dephasing. We will describe later the effects of other kind of qubit–environment entanglement. From the complexity viewpoint it is important to know how the characteristic decoherence time scales with the size of our quantum computer. To this end let us introduce a model of qubit–environment coupling which generates a time evolution of the kind described in (7.1). We will model our environment as a bath of harmonic oscillators [333, 335] and we will assume that the interaction Hamiltonian between a single qubit and its environment is of the form

$$H = \frac{1}{2}\sigma_z\omega_0 + \sum_{\mathbf{k}} b_{\mathbf{k}}^\dagger b_{\mathbf{k}}\omega_k + \sum_{\mathbf{k}} \sigma_z(g_{\mathbf{k}}b_{\mathbf{k}}^\dagger + g_{\mathbf{k}}^* b_{\mathbf{k}}), \tag{7.5}$$

where $\omega_k, b_{\mathbf{k}}^\dagger, b_{\mathbf{k}}$ are, respectively, the frequency and the creation and annihilation bosonic operators of the $\mathbf{k}$ mode of our bath of harmonic oscillators, and σ_z is a Pauli pseudospin operator. The first and the second term on the r.h.s. of (7.5) describe, respectively, the free evolution of the qubit and of the environment, and the third term describes the interaction between the two. The state of the combined system (qubit + environment) is described by a density operator $\varrho(t)$ which at time $t = 0$ is assumed to be

$$\varrho(0) = |\psi\rangle\langle\psi| \otimes \prod_{\mathbf{k},\mathbf{k'}} |0_{\mathbf{k}}\rangle\langle 0_{\mathbf{k'}}| = \rho(0) \otimes |vac\rangle\langle vac|, \tag{7.6}$$

where $|\psi\rangle$ is the initial state of our qubit and $|vac\rangle = \prod_{\mathbf{k}}|0_{\mathbf{k}}\rangle$ is the vacuum state of all the bath modes. Since $[\sigma_z, H] = 0$, the populations of the qubit density matrix, $\rho(t) = \mathrm{Tr}_R\varrho(t)$ are not affected by the environment, which in our model simply erodes quantum coherence as anticipated. This model is *exactly* soluble and allows a clear analysis of the mechanism of entanglement between qubit and environment which, as we have discussed, is believed to be at the core of most decoherence processes.

It can be easily shown that the time evolution operator $U(t)$ in the interaction picture is a conditional displacement operator for the field [333], the sign of the displacement being dependent on the logical value of the qubit. $U(t)$ will therefore induce a dynamics of the kind described in (7.2) with

$$|E_0\rangle = \prod_{\mathbf{k}} |-\phi_{\mathbf{k}}\rangle \qquad\qquad |E_1\rangle = \prod_{\mathbf{k}} |\phi_{\mathbf{k}}\rangle, \tag{7.7}$$

where the states $|\phi_{\mathbf{k}}\rangle$ are coherent states of amplitude $\phi_{\mathbf{k}} = g_{\mathbf{k}}(1 - e^{\omega_k t})/\omega_k$. A detailed calculation of $\Gamma(t)$ and an extension of the analysis to the finite temperature case can be found in [333, 335].

7.2.2 Collective Interaction and Scaling

We now have all the ingredients to analyse the decoherence of a register on n qubits [333]. The Hamiltonian in this case will read

$$H = \frac{1}{2} \sum_i \sigma_{z,i} \omega_0 + \sum_{\mathbf{k}} b_{\mathbf{k}}^\dagger b_{\mathbf{k}} \omega_k + \sum_{i,\mathbf{k}} \sigma_z (g_{i,\mathbf{k}} b_{\mathbf{k}}^\dagger + g_{i,\mathbf{k}}^* b_{\mathbf{k}}), \qquad (7.8)$$

where the coupling constants $g_{i,\mathbf{k}}$ will now depend on the position of the ith qubit. The entanglement induced by this Hamiltonian will be of the form

$$\left(\sum_{i_1 \ldots i_n} c_{i_1 \ldots i_n} |i_1 \ldots i_n\rangle \right) \otimes |vac\rangle \overset{U(t)}{\longmapsto} \sum_{i_1 \ldots i_n} c_{i_1 \ldots i_n} |i_1 \ldots i_n\rangle |E_{i_1, i_2 \ldots i_n}\rangle, \qquad (7.9)$$

where i_n labels the logical value of the nth qubit. The bath of harmonic oscillators will be characterized by a coherence length λ_c over which its fluctuations are correlated. The form of states $|E_{i_1 \ldots i_n}\rangle$ can be instructively obtained in two limiting cases of physical relevance, depending on the ratio between the physical size of our register and λ_c.

Short λ_c: In this case each qubit will feel its own independent environment and will decohere individually. We will have

$$|E_{i_1, i_2 .. i_n}\rangle = |E_{i_1}\rangle |E_{i_2}\rangle \cdots |E_{i_n}\rangle, \qquad (7.10)$$

where the $|E_{i_n}\rangle$ are the same as in (7.7) and the density operator matrix elements will decay as

$$\rho_{i_1 \ldots i_n, j_1 \ldots j_n}(t) = \rho_{i_1 \ldots i_n, j_1 \ldots j_n}(0) \langle E_{i_1} | E_{j_1}\rangle \langle E_{i_2} | E_{j_2}\rangle \cdots \langle E_{i_n} | E_{j_n}\rangle. \qquad (7.11)$$

The fastest decay will occur for

$$\rho_{11 \ldots 1, 00 \ldots 0}(t) = \rho_{11 \ldots 1, 00 \ldots 0}(0) \langle E_1 | E_0\rangle^n = \rho_{11 \ldots 1, 00 \ldots 0}(0) e^{-n\Gamma(t)}. \qquad (7.12)$$

Long λ_c: When λ_c is sufficiently long we can assume that all the qubits collectively interact with the same environment, i.e. we can assume $g_{i,\mathbf{k}} = g_{\mathbf{k}}$ for all qubits. $U(t)$ will then be a conditional displacement operator of amplitude depending on the logical value of *all* qubits in our register. More explicitly

$$|E_{i_1 \ldots i_n}\rangle = \prod_{\mathbf{k}} | - \{(-1)^{i_1} + (-1)^{i_2} \cdots (-1)^{i_n}\} \phi_{\mathbf{k}}\rangle. \qquad (7.13)$$

The fastest decay will occur for

$$\rho_{11 \ldots 1, 00 \ldots 0}(t) = \rho_{11 \ldots 1, 00 \ldots 0}(0) \langle E_{11 \ldots 1} | E_{00 \ldots 0}\rangle = \rho_{11 \ldots 1, 00 \ldots 0}(0) e^{-n^2 \Gamma(t)}. \qquad (7.14)$$

The physical origin of the n^2 in the exponent can be easily understood by noting that $|E_{00\cdots0}\rangle, |E_{11\cdots1}\rangle$ are the tensor product on coherent states of amplitude $n\phi_{\mathbf{k}}$.

The above discussion shows how the decay of coherences of a register of n qubits scales as $\exp[-Poly(n)\gamma(t)]$, with $Poly(n)\sim n$ for independent interaction with the environment and $Poly(n)\sim n^2$ for collective interaction.

7.2.3 Subspace Decoupled From Environment

If collective interactions lead to faster decay rates it should be noted that it also leads to the appearance of subspaces decoupled from the environment. As (7.13) clearly shows, states with an equal number of 0 and 1 do not get entangled with the environment and therefore are not prone to decoherence. In other words the interaction does not displace the amplitude of the field modes. This suggests the possibility of using this decoupled subspace to implement a simple form of redundant coding. Let us suppose that we can manufacture in our laboratory a quantum register of 2L qubits composed of pairs of qubits close enough to each other so that each pair is effectively interacting with the same reservoir. Different pairs can interact with different reservoirs, although the results we are going to illustrate are not modified if all the qubits interact with the same reservoir. We could then encode the logical states as follows

$$|\tilde{0}\rangle = |0, 1\rangle, \qquad\qquad |\tilde{1}\rangle = |1, 0\rangle. \qquad\qquad (7.15)$$

The idea is that if we use a pair of qubits to encode a bit we might effectively decouple the register from the environment.

Several problems remain open with this kind of coding. First of all we should make sure that such states are also robust also with respect to other channels of decoherence (we will come to this question in the next section). Secondly the problem remains of how to prepare such states (states which are decoupled from the environment are often also decoupled from external probes) and how to read them (this will imply collective measurements). Finally, it is not yet clear how to perform quantum computation confined within such subsystems. Qubit–qubit controllable interactions might turn out to be useful tools for implementing gate operation [336, 337].

7.2.4 Other Find of Couplings

In the remainder of this section we would like to discuss which of the results obtained survives once we take into account more realistic mechanisms for qubit–environment interaction. The model we will briefly analyse is one commonly used to describe a broad range of physical phenomena, like the exchange of photons between the electromagnetic field and a two-level atom in quantum optics [338]. In this model the Hamiltonian of a system of n identical qubits coupled with the reservoir of harmonic oscillators will be

$$H = \frac{1}{2}\sum_i \sigma_{z,i}\omega_0 + \sum_{\mathbf{k}} b_{\mathbf{k}}^\dagger b_{\mathbf{k}}\omega_k + \sum_{i,\mathbf{k}}(g_{i,\mathbf{k}}\sigma_{-,i}b_{\mathbf{k}}^\dagger + g_{i,\mathbf{k}}^*\sigma_{+,i}b_{\mathbf{k}}), \qquad (7.16)$$

where $\sigma_{-,i}$ and $\sigma_{+,i}$ are the lowering and raising operators for qubit i.

The dynamics generated by (7.16) cannot be solved exactly. However, under the so called Born–Markov approximation, the time evolution of the qubit reduced density operator can be described by a master equation [338, 339]. If the spacing between the qubits is smaller than the wavelength of the resonant modes it reasonable to assume $g_{i,\mathbf{k}} \sim g_0$, and the desired master equation will be:

$$\frac{d\rho}{dt} = i\omega_0\rho - \frac{\gamma}{2}(S_+S_-\rho + \rho S_+S_- - 2S_-\rho S_+), \qquad (7.17)$$

where we have introduced the collective operators $S_z = \sum_i \sigma_{z,i}, S_\pm = \sum_{\pm i} \sigma_\pm$ and the decay constant $\gamma \propto |g_0|^2\delta(\omega_k - \omega_0)$.

The dynamics described by (7.17) is clearly nonunitary. The nonunitarity is again due to entanglement between qubit and environment, although this is less evident than in the exactly soluble model analysed in the previous section.

In the case of dissipation of a single qubit the reduced density at time t will be

$$\rho(t) = \begin{pmatrix} (1 - \rho_{11})e^{-\gamma t} & \rho_{10}e^{-\frac{\gamma}{2}t} \\ \rho_{01}e^{-\frac{\gamma}{2}t} & \rho_{11}e^{-\gamma t} \end{pmatrix}, \qquad (7.18)$$

which shows clearly that this model of coupling induces decoherence *and* decay of the populations.

In order to illustrate the characteristics of collective interaction in this new scenario it is instructive to discuss the decay of the entangled Bell states $|\Psi_\pm\rangle = \frac{1}{\sqrt{2}}\{|01\rangle \pm |10\rangle\}$. The probability amplitude for the decay into state $|00\rangle$ is proportional to the matrix element of operator S_+

$$\langle\Psi_\pm|S_+|00\rangle = \frac{1}{\sqrt{2}}\{\langle 01|\sigma_{+2}|00\rangle \pm \langle 10|\sigma_{+1}|00\rangle. \qquad (7.19)$$

This shows clearly how the probability *amplitudes* for the decay of the $|\Psi_+\rangle$ state interfere constructively leading to a decay rate twice the decay rate of a single qubit while they interfere destructively for the $|\Psi_-\rangle$ state. For a large number n on qubits the collective decay will lead to decay constants scaling from $n\gamma$ to $n^2\gamma$, while the singlet collective state will be decoupled from the environment. This is the well known phenomenon of superradiance vs. subradiance [339, 340]. Again this suggests the possibility of using the subradiant subspaces of a register of n qubits [341]. Of course also in this case all the difficulties we have mentioned in the previous section remain.

To conclude, we would like to point out that, although different models will lead to different physical decay mechanisms and will need different techniques for their treatment, many of the qualitative features of decoherence processes do not depend on the specific model of coupling. In particular all decoherence processes will lead to a nonunitary time evolution of the quantum register. Furthermore collective interaction will enhance the decay of some register subspaces and will inhibit the decay of other. Therefore our considerations on the scaling of the decoherence time with the size of our quantum computer and on collective encoding remain valid regardless of the details of the coupling with the environment.

7.3 Limits to Quantum Computation
Due to Decoherence

M.B. Plenio, P.L. Knight

The previous section presented models to describe decoherence and dissipation of an array of qubits, implemented e.g. on a string of ions (see Chap. 5). After these general considerations we will now estimate how serious the impact of noise will be on a quantum computer. In particular we would like to see how many quantum operations we can possibly perform for example with an ion trap quantum computer of which the principles have been described in Sect. 4.3 and Chap. 5 [156]. We will not discuss here many of the other potential implementations of a quantum computer such as nuclear magnetic resonance schemes [342, 343] (see also Sect. 5.4).

There are many possible mechanisms that produce noise in a quantum computer. In this subsection we will discuss only the effect of spontaneous emission from the ions [344]–[347] because the analysis is quite instructive. Other mechanisms such as noise in the centre-of-mass mode [348], laser instabilities and cross-talking between different ions due to their small spatial separation [349] will not be discussed here. For these effects we refer the reader to the cited literature.

Now we want to estimate the effect of spontaneous emission on a quantum computer. To do this we use as a benchmark the algorithm for the factorisation of large numbers [350]. The discussion can easily be generalised to other algorithms. As was shown in Sect. 4.2, finding factors of a large number on a classical computer is a hard problem and cannot be done efficiently. On a quantum computer, however, an efficient algorithm has been found. Under ideal conditions this algorithm would allow a quantum computer to find factors of a large number exponentially faster than on a classical computer.

We will now discuss what the largest number is that one can factorise on a quantum computer if we assume that the only source of error is spontaneous emission from ions. To simplify the analysis, we do not consider the possibility of quantum error correction here but refer the reader to literature [346] and to the next section of this chapter.

Consider the following experimental setup: A string of ions is placed in a linear ion trap and cooled to the motional ground state. Each qubit is represented by a metastable optical transition in the ion. The internal structure of the ions we are considering is shown in Fig. 7.1). The qubit is represented by the atomic levels 0 and 1. Transitions are driven by a laser with Rabi frequency Ω_{0i} and spontaneous emissions from level i can occur at a rate $2\Gamma_{ii}$. The existence of the additional level 2 is important and will be discussed later. Of course more sophisticated methods for the representation of the qubit are possible, e.g. in Zeeman sub-levels, but the analysis becomes more complicated while the conclusions are similar. Therefore we refer the reader to the literature [346].

Our aim is the factorisation of an L-bit number, which means a number which is not larger than 2^L. From Shors' algorithm [350], we know that this task can be performed using ϵL^3 elementary operations such as one-bit gates, CNOT gates and Toffoli gates. Networks that perform this task have been designed [351] and it turns out that the algorithm requires of order $5L$ qubits to factorise an L bit number.

How long does it take to perform all the necessary gates? It takes 1.5 times as long to implement a Toffoli gate than it takes to make a CNOT gate [156]. Therefore it is enough to calculate the time required to perform a CNOT gate. Single bit gates will not be considered because they can be implemented much faster. The reason is that, unlike for a CNOT gate, the implementation of a single bit gate does not require an excitation of the centre-of-mass mode (see Sect. 5.2.9).

The implementation of a CNOT gate requires

$$\tau_{el} = 4\pi \frac{\sqrt{5L}}{\eta \Omega_{01}} \ . \tag{7.20}$$

Here $5L$ is the number of ions in the trap, Ω_{01} is the Rabi frequency of the laser that drives the qubit transition and η is the Lamb–Dicke parameter (see Chap. 5 for experimental details). Therefore the total time required to perform the factorisation of an L bit number is the number of required CNOT gates multiplied by τ_{el}. We find

$$T = \frac{4\pi\sqrt{5L}}{\eta \Omega} \epsilon L^3 \ . \tag{7.21}$$

Obviously there are free parameters in this expression. In particular we could imagine that we could increase the Rabi frequency as much as we like to permit a very rapid calculation. This would allow us to avoid spontaneous

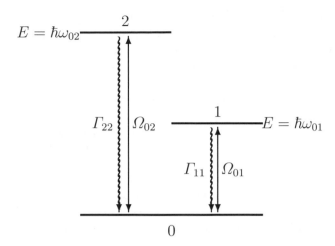

$E = \hbar\omega_{02}$ ——— 2 ———

Γ_{22} Ω_{02} ——— 1 ———$E = \hbar\omega_{01}$

Γ_{11} Ω_{01}

0

Fig. 7.1. Schematic level scheme of the ions used in quantum computation. The $0 \leftrightarrow 1$ transition represents the qubit. It is driven by a laser of Rabi frequency Ω_{01}. Level 1 has a spontaneous decay rate $2\Gamma_{11}$ which is assumed to be small. The laser which is resonant with the $0 \leftrightarrow 1$ transition inevitably couples level 0 also to other non-resonant levels such as level 2. The Rabi frequency on that transition is then Ω_{02} and the decay rate $2\Gamma_{22}$ is usually much larger than $2\Gamma_{11}$. The effective Rabi frequency on the $0 \leftrightarrow 2$ transition is very small as the laser is detuned by $\Delta_{02} \gg \Omega_{02}$.

emission from the upper level of the qubit. However, this is not so easy. The reason for this is the fact that the Rabi frequency of a transition and the decay constant of that transition are related to each other by

$$\frac{\Omega^2}{\Gamma} = \frac{6\pi c^3 \epsilon_0}{\hbar \omega_{01}^3} E^2 \ , \tag{7.22}$$

where E is the electric field strength of the laser, c is the speed of light, ϵ_0 is the permittivity of free space, and ω_{01} the transition frequency. Still one could imagine increasing the electric field strength of the laser E arbitrarily. Obviously there are some upper limits to that process. If E is so strong that it exceeds the electric field between the electron and the nucleus then the ion will ionize immediately. This limit, however, is quite high and other effects are more relevant. In fact at high field strengths of the laser we cannot continue to assume that the ion has only two relevant energy levels. Other energy levels will contribute to the dynamics, as they might obtain some small population due to off-resonant transitions to them. This situation is presented in Fig. 7.1. In addition to the qubit levels 0 and 1 there are other, far detuned levels around. We summarise the effect of all existing auxiliary levels by assuming one additional energy level 2 that couples to the lower qubit state 0. Because the laser is far detuned from the $0 \leftrightarrow 2$ transition the population in the upper level will be small. Nevertheless, spontaneous emission from that level may take place, especially because this auxiliary level could well have a very short lifetime. The stronger the electric field of the applied laser, the larger the population in this auxiliary level. Therefore we have a trade-off between spontaneous emission from the upper qubit level and spontaneous emission from the auxiliary level. The faster the computation, the lower the spontaneous emissions from the upper qubit state 1 but the greater the spontaneous emissions from the auxiliary level.

In the following we calculate the probability p_{tot} of an emission from either level 1 or level 2. The aim is to minimise this probability. This minimisation then leads to an intensity-independent limit to the size of the number that can be factorised by a quantum computer in the presence of spontaneous emission.

During all the quantum computation, on average half of the qubits are in the upper state. Therefore the probability of a spontaneous emission occurring from the upper level during the whole computation is given by

$$p_1 = \frac{1}{2} 2 \, \Gamma_{11} \, 5LT \ . \tag{7.23}$$

On the other hand, the auxiliary level is populated only during the interaction of the ion with the laser. Therefore the probability of suffering a spontaneous emission from an auxiliary level is given by

$$p_2 = \frac{\Omega_{02}^2}{8 \, \Delta_{02}} 2\Gamma_{22}T \ . \tag{7.24}$$

If we now use (7.22), which gives

$$\frac{\Omega_{01}^2}{\Gamma_{11}} = \frac{\omega_{02}^3}{\omega_{01}^3} \frac{\Omega_{02}^2}{\Gamma_{22}} \ , \tag{7.25}$$

and define

$$x = \sqrt{\frac{\Omega_{01}^2}{\Gamma_{11}}} \ , \tag{7.26}$$

we obtain, using (7.21),

$$p_{tot} = p_1 + p_2 \tag{7.27}$$

$$= \frac{4\pi\sqrt{5L}}{\eta} \epsilon L^4 \sqrt{\Gamma_{11}} \left[\frac{1}{x} + \frac{1}{L} \frac{\omega_{01}^3}{\omega_{02}^3} \frac{\Gamma_{22}^2}{4\Delta_{02}^2 \Gamma_{11}} x \right] \ . \tag{7.28}$$

We can minimise this expression with respect to x and obtain for the minimum

$$p_{min} = \frac{4\pi\sqrt{5}\epsilon L^4}{\eta} \sqrt{\frac{\omega_{01}^3}{\omega_{02}^3}} \sqrt{\frac{\Gamma_{22}^2}{\Delta_{02}^2}} \ . \tag{7.29}$$

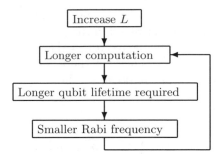

Fig. 7.2. The strong L dependence in (7.30) is due to a positive feedback. If we try to increase L our computation becomes longer. That requires a longer lifetime of the qubit which reduces the achievable Rabi frequency on the qubit transition. This lengthens the computation even more.

To ensure that with a high probability there is no spontaneous emission during the quantum computation, we require $p_{min} \ll 1$. We can therefore transform (7.29) into an upper bound on L which is given by

$$L^8_{max} \approx \frac{\eta^2 \Delta^2_{02}}{80 \Gamma^2_{22} \pi^2 \epsilon^2} \left(\frac{\omega_{02}}{\omega_{01}} \right)^3 . \tag{7.30}$$

The reader might wonder where the power of L^8 in (7.30) originates from. The reason is a positive control loop as shown in Fig. 7.2.

To see whether this is a serious limitation we need to plug some numbers into the equation. We will use values for realistic ions, i.e. ions that are being used in ion trap experiments.

In Table 7.1 (which is taken from [346]) we can see the results for some real atoms. The resulting limits for the factorisable numbers are really small. This

Table 7.1. For several possible systems the upper limit on the bitsize L of the number N that can be factorised on a quantum computer is calculated. A qubit is stored in a metastable optical transition. The atomic levels which are abbreviated in Fig. 7.1 by $0, 1$ and 2 are given. The atomic data are inserted into (7.30) and the result is given in the last row of the table.

Ion	Ca^+	Hg^+	Ba^+
level 0	$4s\,^2S_{1/2}$	$5d^{10}6s^2\,^2S_{1/2}$	$6s\,^2S_{1/2}$
level 1	$3d\,^2D_{5/2}$	$5d^96s^2\,^2D_{5/2}$	$5d\,^2D_{5/2}$
level 2	$4s\,^2P_{3/2}$	$5d^{10}6p^2\,^2P_{1/2}$	$6s\,^2P_{3/2}$
$\omega_{01}\,[s^{-1}]$	$2.61 \cdot 10^{15}$	$6.7 \cdot 10^{15}$	$1.07 \cdot 10^{15}$
$\omega_{02}\,[s^{-1}]$	$4.76 \cdot 10^{15}$	$11.4 \cdot 10^{15}$	$4.14 \cdot 10^{15}$
$\Gamma_{22}\,[s^{-1}]$	$67.5 \cdot 10^6$	$5.26 \cdot 10^8$	$58.8 \cdot 10^6$
$L(\eta = 0.01)$	2.2	1.6	4.5

shows that even noise from spontaneous emission places serious limitations on quantum computation. This is the reason why scientists in this field have been highly motivated to develop methods that are able to correct the errors generated by noise such as spontaneous emission. These methods will be presented in the next section and in fact they can improve the limitations that we have derived in this chapter.

7.4 Error Correction and Fault-Tolerant Computation

C. Macchiavello, G.M. Palma

7.4.1 Symmetrisation Procedures

The first proposed remedy for quantum noise in quantum computation was based on a symmetrisation procedure [352]. We briefly summarise here the basic idea. Suppose you have a quantum system, you prepare it in some initial state $|\Psi_i\rangle$ and you want to implement a prescribed unitary evolution $|\Psi(t)\rangle$ or you simply want to preserve $|\Psi_i\rangle$ for some period of time t. Now, suppose that instead of a single system you can prepare R copies of $|\Psi_i\rangle$ and subsequently you can project the state of the combined system onto the symmetric subspace i.e. the subspace containing all states which are invariant under any permutation of the sub-systems. The claim is that frequent projections on the symmetric subspace will reduce errors induced by the environment. The intuition behind this concept is based on the observation that a prescribed error-free storage or evolution of the R independent copies starts in the symmetric sub-space and should remain in that sub-space. Therefore, since the error-free component of any state always lies in the symmetric subspace, upon successful projection it will be unchanged and part of the error will have been removed. Note, however, that the projected state is generally not error-free since the symmetric subspace contains states which are not of the simple product form $|\psi\rangle|\psi\rangle\ldots|\psi\rangle$. Nevertheless it has been shown that the error probability will be suppressed by a factor of $1/R$ [353].

We illustrate here this effect in the simplest case of two qubits. The projection into the symmetric subspace is performed in this case by introducing the symmetrisation operator

$$S = \frac{1}{2}(P_{12} + P_{21}) , \tag{7.31}$$

where P_{12} represents the identity and P_{21} the permutation operator which exchanges the states of the two qubits. The symmetric projection of a pure state $|\Psi\rangle$ of two qubits is just $S|\Psi\rangle$, which is then renormalised to unity.

It follows that the induced map on mixed states of two qubits (including renormalisation) is

$$\rho_1 \otimes \rho_2 \longrightarrow \frac{S(\rho_1 \otimes \rho_2)S^\dagger}{\text{Tr}S(\rho_1 \otimes \rho_2)S^\dagger} . \tag{7.32}$$

The state of either qubit separately is then obtained by the partial trace over the other qubit.

Let us assume that the two copies are initially prepared in a pure state $\rho_0 = |\Psi\rangle \langle\Psi|$ and that they interact with independent environments. After some short period of time δt the state of the two copies $\rho^{(2)}$ will have undergone an evolution

$$\rho^{(2)}(0) = \rho_0 \otimes \rho_0 \longrightarrow \rho^{(2)}(\delta t) = \rho_1 \otimes \rho_2 , \tag{7.33}$$

where $\rho_i = \rho_0 + \varrho_i$ for some Hermitian traceless ϱ_i. We will retain only terms of first order in the perturbations ϱ_i so that the overall state at time δt is

$$\rho^{(2)} = \rho_0 \otimes \rho_0 + \varrho_1 \otimes \rho_0 + \rho_0 \otimes \varrho_2 + O(\varrho_1 \varrho_2) . \tag{7.34}$$

We can calculate the average purity of the two copies before symmetrisation by calculating the average trace of the squared states:

$$\frac{1}{2} \sum_{i=1}^{2} \text{Tr}((\rho_0 + \varrho_i)^2) = 1 + 2\text{Tr}(\rho_0 \tilde{\varrho}), \tag{7.35}$$

where $\tilde{\varrho} = \frac{1}{2}(\varrho_1 + \varrho_2)$. Note that $\text{Tr}(\rho_0 \tilde{\varrho})$ is negative, so that the expression above does not exceed 1. After symmetrisation each qubit is in state

$$\rho_s = [1 - \text{Tr}(\rho_0 \tilde{\varrho})]\rho_0 + \frac{1}{2}\tilde{\varrho} + \frac{1}{2}(\rho_0 \tilde{\varrho} + \tilde{\varrho}\rho_0) \tag{7.36}$$

and has purity

$$\text{Tr}(\rho_s^2) = 1 + \text{Tr}(\rho_0 \tilde{\varrho}). \tag{7.37}$$

Since $\text{Tr}\rho_s^2$ is closer to 1 than (7.35), the resulting symmetrised system ρ_s is left in a purer state.

Let us now see how the fidelity changes by applying the symmetrisation procedure. The average fidelity before symmetrisation is

$$F_{bs} = \frac{1}{2} \sum_i \langle\Psi | \rho_0 + \varrho_i |\Psi\rangle = 1 + \langle\Psi | \tilde{\varrho} |\Psi\rangle , \tag{7.38}$$

while after successful symmetrisation it takes the form

$$F_{as} = \langle\Psi | \rho_s |\Psi\rangle = 1 + \frac{1}{2} \langle\Psi | \tilde{\varrho} |\Psi\rangle . \tag{7.39}$$

The state after symmetrisation is therefore closer to the initial state ρ_0.

For the generic case of R copies the purity of each qubit after symmetrisation is given by [353]

$$\mathrm{Tr}(\rho_s^2) = 1 + 2\frac{1}{R}\mathrm{Tr}(\rho_0\tilde{\varrho}) , \tag{7.40}$$

where now $\tilde{\varrho} = \frac{1}{R}\sum_{i=1}^{R}\varrho_i$, and the fidelity takes the form

$$\langle\Psi\,|\,\rho_s\,|\,\Psi\rangle = 1 + \frac{1}{R}\mathrm{Tr}(\rho_0\tilde{\varrho}) . \tag{7.41}$$

Formulae (7.40) and (7.41) must be compared with the corresponding ones before symmetrisation, i.e. (7.35) and (7.38). As we can see, ρ_s approaches the unperturbed state ρ_0 as R tends to infinity. Thus by choosing R sufficiently large and the rate of symmetric projection sufficiently high, the residual error at the end of a computation can, in principle, be controlled to lie within any desired small tolerance.

7.4.2 Classical Error Correction

A different class of error correcting techniques originates from an extension to the quantum realm of existing classical error correcting codes [354]. Indeed the problem of how to transmit and manipulate information reliably when errors can be induced by noise is present also in classical information theory. Before we begin our analysis of quantum error correcting codes it is therefore appropriate to briefly review how error correction is implemented in a classical scenario. In what follows a code will be a set of c binary sequences $\mathbf{w}_1\cdots\mathbf{w}_c$, called codewords, of length n. During transmission or storage, some bits, due to the action of external noise, can undergo random flips. Bit flips are the only possible kind of classical error. If the channel is a binary symmetric memoryless channel (see Fig. 7.3) the set of possible received sequences $\mathbf{v}_1\cdots\mathbf{v}_{2^n}$ is the set of all the 2^n binary sequences of length n. The task of the receiver is, given a received sequence $\mathbf{v}_0$, to identify the most likely codeword $\mathbf{w}_i$ sent by the transmitter, i.e. to identify the $\mathbf{w}_i$ closest to $\mathbf{v}_0$. In this context the distance between two binary sequences $d(\mathbf{w},\mathbf{v})$, the so called Hamming distance, is measured by the number of digits in which the two strings differ. For a binary symmetric memoryless channel the $\mathbf{w}_i$ with smallest Hamming distance $d(\mathbf{w}_i,\mathbf{v}_0)$ is also the most likely.

Clearly the larger the distance between codewords the better they are distinguishable in the presence of errors and therefore the more the code is robust against noise. If $d(\mathbf{w}_i,\mathbf{w}_j) \geq 2\eta + 1$ for $i \neq j$ then up to η errors can be corrected.

The Hamming bound provides an upper bound to the number of codewords c in a code able to correct up to η errors. Each codeword $\mathbf{w}_i$ is the centre of a sphere of radius η containing all binary sequences $\mathbf{v}$ with $d(\mathbf{w_i},\mathbf{v}) \leq \eta$,

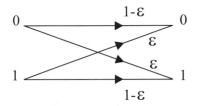

Fig. 7.3. In a binary symmetric channel each bit is transmitted with an error probability ϵ.

i.e. differing from $\mathbf{w}_i$ in up to η locations. Figure 7.4 is an illustration of this situation for $\eta = 4$. If the code can correct the errors, these spheres must be disjoint. Obviously the number of sequences in each sphere times the number of spheres must be smaller than the total number of sequences of length n. Since each sphere contains a codeword $\mathbf{w}$ plus all the sequences differing from it in $1, 2, \cdots \eta$ positions we must have

$$c \left\{ 1 + n + \binom{n}{2} \cdots \binom{n}{\eta} \right\} = c \sum_{i=o}^{\eta} \binom{n}{i} \leq 2^n. \tag{7.42}$$

A family of codes which has proved very efficient is known for historical reasons as parity check codes [354]. In these codes the codewords $\mathbf{w}$ are chosen in such a way as to satisfy a set of linear equations. The receiver tests whether the received sequence $\mathbf{v}$ satisfies this set of linear relations. If $\mathbf{v}$ fails the test the receiver corrects the smallest error which might have produced $\mathbf{v}$. Let's see in more detail how the code works. The set of linear equations the codewords must satisfy is characterized by a parity check matrix $\mathbf{M}$. Codewords $\mathbf{w}$ are chosen to satisfy the relation

$$\mathbf{M} \cdot \mathbf{w} = 0. \tag{7.43}$$

For example codewords

$$\mathbf{w_1} = 0000 \qquad \mathbf{w_2} = 0101 \qquad \mathbf{w_3} = 1110 \qquad \mathbf{w_4} = 1011 \tag{7.44}$$

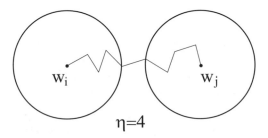

Fig. 7.4. In codes with $d(\mathbf{w}_i, \mathbf{w}_j) \geq 2\eta + 1$ disjoint spheres of radius η centred on each codeword contain all the sequences with up to η errors.

satisfy (7.43), with

$$\mathbf{M} = \begin{pmatrix} 1 & 0 & 1 & 0 \\ 0 & 1 & 1 & 1 \end{pmatrix} \tag{7.45}$$

where all the arithmetic is modulo 2. If the rank of $\mathbf{M}$ is m than $k = n - m$ bits of our codeword can be specified arbitrarily while the remaining m digits are check digits determined by relation (7.43). The number of linearly independent codewords is therefore $c = 2^{n-m} = 2^k$ and the Hamming bound (7.42) can be rewritten as

$$2^k \sum_{i=o}^{\eta} \binom{n}{i} \leq 2^n \longrightarrow 2^{n-k} = 2^m \geq \sum_{i=o}^{\eta} \binom{n}{i}, \tag{7.46}$$

which is a lower bound for the number of check digits. Suppose that the sequence $\mathbf{w}$ is transmitted and that the sequence $\mathbf{v}$ is received. The sequence $\mathbf{z} = \mathbf{w} - \mathbf{v}$, known as the error pattern, is a binary sequence with ones in the positions where an error has occurred and zeros elsewhere. If $\mathbf{z} \neq 0$ than $\mathbf{v}$ fails the parity check: $\mathbf{M} \cdot \mathbf{v} = \mathbf{M} \cdot (\mathbf{w} + \mathbf{z}) = \mathbf{M} \cdot \mathbf{z} = \mathbf{s}$. The vector $\mathbf{s}$, known as error syndrome, is the sum of the columns of the parity check matrix in the location where $\mathbf{z}$ has ones. For example if $\mathbf{w} = 1110$ is transmitted and $\mathbf{v} = 1000$ is received then $\mathbf{z} = 0110$ and, with $\mathbf{M}$ as given by (7.45), $\mathbf{s} = 10$.

The task of the receiver, once an error syndrome $\mathbf{s}$ is detected, is to identify the error patterns $\mathbf{z}$ which might have produced $\mathbf{s}$ and to correct the smallest one, i.e. the one with the smallest number of 1's. It should be noted that if our code can correct a single error the syndrome is simply the column where the error has occurred. If the columns of $\mathbf{M}$ are different the receiver can easily identify the location of the error and correct it.

7.4.3 General Aspects of Quantum Error Correcting Codes

As soon as we try to extend the error correcting techniques illustrated above to the quantum scenario we immediately face two problems:

1. Due to external noise each qubit may not only flip its logical value but also decohere. In general it will get entangled with the environment, as was shown in Sect. 7.2.
2. We are not allowed to read the state of the qubit before the end of the computation. Failure to observe this rule leads to decoherence. We must therefore acquire knowledge on the location and nature of the error without acquiring knowledge on the state of the qubits.

We will show that the way out problem 2 is to use as "codevectors" $|\mathbf{w}\rangle$ entangled states of n qubits. The information we want to protect is therefore spread by the entanglement over all the n qubits. Reading (or decohering) only a few qubits will not lead to an irreversible loss of quantum information.

Codevectors are chosen in such a way that an error will move the $|\mathbf{w}\rangle$ into mutually orthogonal subspaces. Measurement of the syndrome will therefore reveal only which subspace $|\mathbf{w}\rangle$ has moved to. In what follows we will assume that each qubit can undergo an error with probability ϵ and that errors on different qubits are independent. With these assumptions the probability of errors on two qubits is of order $O(\epsilon^2)$. For sufficiently small values of ϵ we can reasonably assume that only one error has occurred. The probability of successful computation is $(1 - \epsilon)$. If we can implement a quantum error correction routine able to correct single errors the probability of success can be increased to $(1 - O(\epsilon^2))$. In general a code able to correct up to t errors increases the probability of successful computation to $(1 - O(\epsilon^{t+1}))$.

7.4.4 The Three Qubit Code

To gain some familiarity with quantum error correcting codes and to illustrate the ideas sketched above we will start by analyzing the three qubit code which can correct phase errors on a single qubit [355]. Suppose that each qubit of the qubit of a codeword can independently undergo an entanglement with the environment of the form (7.1). We will show that we can undo the effects of phase entanglement if we can correct phase errors, defined as

$$|0\rangle \longrightarrow |0\rangle \qquad\qquad\qquad |1\rangle \longrightarrow -|1\rangle \qquad (7.47)$$

due to the error operator σ_z. To this goal let us choose as codewords the following entangled states of three qubits:

$$|\mathbf{w}_0\rangle = |000\rangle + |011\rangle + |101\rangle + |110\rangle ,$$
$$|\mathbf{w}_1\rangle = |111\rangle + |100\rangle + |010\rangle + |001\rangle . \qquad (7.48)$$

If only one qubit gets entangled with the environment, an arbitrary linear superposition of $|\mathbf{w}_0\rangle, |\mathbf{w}_1\rangle$ will become

$$
\begin{aligned}
(a_0|\mathbf{w}_0\rangle + a_1|\mathbf{w}_1\rangle)|E\rangle \longrightarrow \; & (a_0|\mathbf{w}_0\rangle_0 + a_1|\mathbf{w}_1\rangle_0)|E_0\rangle \\
& + \; (a_0|\mathbf{w}_0\rangle_1 + a_1|\mathbf{w}_1\rangle_1)|E_1\rangle \\
& + \; (a_0|\mathbf{w}_0\rangle_2 + a_1|\mathbf{w}_1\rangle_2)|E_2\rangle \\
& + \; (a_0|\mathbf{w}_0\rangle_3 + a_1|\mathbf{w}_1\rangle_3)|E_3\rangle , \qquad (7.49)
\end{aligned}
$$

where the error state $|\mathbf{w}_j\rangle_k$ is codeword $j, (j = 0, 1)$ with a phase error on his k^{th} qubit ($k = 0$ labels no error). For example $|\mathbf{w}_0\rangle_2 = |000\rangle - |011\rangle + |101\rangle - |110\rangle$. The $|E_k\rangle$ are the corresponding environment states. Note that the error states are orthogonal:

$$_k\langle \mathbf{w}_j|\mathbf{w}_l\rangle_i = \delta_{jl}\delta_{ki} . \qquad (7.50)$$

Codes in which error states are orthogonal are called non-degenerate. The error correction procedure is therefore the following:

- Project the code space onto the error subspaces spanned by $|\mathbf{w}_0\rangle_i|\mathbf{w}_1\rangle_i$
- Depending on the outcome of the measurement correct the appropriate qubit with a phase error applying σ_z. More explicitly, if the result of the above projection measurement is i, apply σ_z to the ith qubit (when $i = 0$ the state is not modified).

Note that at the end of the procedure the codevector and the environment are disentangled and that the amplitudes a_0, a_1 are not modified.

7.4.5 The Quantum Hamming Bound

We can now turn our attention to codes able to correct the most general kind of qubit–environment entanglement, which is of the form

$$|0\rangle|E\rangle \longrightarrow |0\rangle|E_{00}\rangle + |1\rangle|E_{01}\rangle \qquad |1\rangle|E\rangle \longrightarrow |0\rangle|E_{10}\rangle + |1\rangle|E_{11}\rangle . \tag{7.51}$$

For a linear superposition of qubit states this can be conveniently written as

$$
\begin{aligned}
(a_0|0\rangle + a_1|1\rangle)|E\rangle \longrightarrow \ & (\ a_0|0\rangle + a_1|1\rangle\ )|E_0\rangle \\
& + [\sigma_x(a_0|1\rangle + a_1|0\rangle)]|E_x\rangle \\
& + [\sigma_z(a_0|0\rangle - a_1|1\rangle)]|E_z\rangle \\
& + [\sigma_y(a_0|1\rangle - a_1|0\rangle)]|E_y\rangle ,
\end{aligned}
\tag{7.52}
$$

where σ_x is the error operator for bit flips, σ_z the error operator for phase flips defined in the previous paragraph and $\sigma_y = -i\sigma_z\sigma_x$ is the operator for both errors. As we can see from (7.52), a general qubit–environment interaction can be expressed as a superposition of unity and Pauli operators σ_x, σ_y and σ_z acting on the qubit. This means that the qubit state evolves into a superposition of an error-free component and three erroneous components, with errors of the σ_x, σ_y and σ_z type.

We can now easily translate into the quantum language the arguments which led us to the Hamming bound for "non-degenerate codes" [355] (less restrictive conditions hold for general quantum codes, see for example [323]). If a code with 2^q codevectors can correct up to η errors the codesvectors $|\mathbf{w}\rangle$ and all the states which can be obtained from the $|\mathbf{w}\rangle$ with the action of up to η error operators must form a set of orthogonal states. The interaction with the entanglement will evolve each codevector as

$$
\begin{aligned}
|\mathbf{w}\rangle|E\rangle \longrightarrow |\mathbf{w}\rangle|E_0\rangle + \sum_{i,k_i} |\mathbf{w}_i^{k_i}\rangle|E_i^{k_i}\rangle \\
+ \sum_{ij,k_jk_j} |\mathbf{w}_{ij}^{k_ik_j}\rangle|E_{ij}^{k_ik_j}\rangle + \sum_{ijl,k_ik_jk_l} |\mathbf{w}_{ijl}^{k_ik_jk_l}\rangle|E_{ijl}^{k_ik_jk_l}\rangle \cdots ,
\end{aligned}
\tag{7.53}
$$

where indices $i, j, \cdots$ label the qubits of the codevectors and the $k_i, k_j, \cdots = x, y, z$ label the error on the corresponding qubit. If the code corrects up to

η errors, all the states with up to η errors which originate for each of the 2^q codevectors must be orthogonal. The number of orthogonal states must be smaller than the dimension of the Hilbert space of n qubits, and we have

$$2^q \sum_{i=0}^{\eta} 3^i \binom{n}{i} < 2^n \longrightarrow 2^{n-q} \geq \sum_{i=0}^{\eta} 3^i \binom{n}{i,} \tag{7.54}$$

which puts a lower bound on the number of check qubits $n-q$ of a quantum error correcting code able to correct up to η errors. The factor 3^i in (7.54) comes from the fact that in the quantum case three independent errors can occur for each qubit, at variance with the classical case, where the only kind of possible errors are bit flips.

7.4.6 The Seven Qubit Code

We are now ready to illustrate a quantum code which can correct any general error on a single qubit. Although five qubit codes exist [323, 356] with this property, as predicted by the quantum Hamming bound, for pedagogical reasons we will describe the seven qubit code introduced by Steane [357, 358]. First of all let us introduce the following parity check matrix:

$$\mathbf{M} = \begin{pmatrix} 0\,0\,0\,1\,1\,1\,1 \\ 0\,1\,1\,0\,0\,1\,1 \\ 1\,0\,1\,0\,1\,0\,1 \end{pmatrix}. \tag{7.55}$$

As all the columns of $\mathbf{M}$ are different, if only one bit flip occurs the measurement of the syndrome will reveal the position of the qubit in error. We will use as starting ingredients to build the codevectors the (classical) sequences $\mathbf{u}$ which satisfy the parity check $\mathbf{Mu} = 0$ and the corresponding states of seven qubits $|\mathbf{u}\rangle$ such that the logical value of the qubits corresponds to sequence $\mathbf{u}$. The codevectors $|\mathbf{w}_0\rangle, |\mathbf{w}_1\rangle$ are then defined as entangled superposition of states $|\mathbf{u}\rangle$ with an even and an odd number of 1's, respectively:

$$|\mathbf{w}_0\rangle = \sum_{even} |\mathbf{u}\rangle_e \qquad |\mathbf{w}_1\rangle = \sum_{odd} |\mathbf{u}\rangle_0. \tag{7.56}$$

The final ingredient is a procedure to measure the syndrome. To this goal let us add three ancillary qubits, one for each bit of the syndrome, i.e. one for each row of $\mathbf{M}$ (see Fig. 7.5). When matrix element $\mathbf{M}_{i,j} = 1$ than a CNOT gate is introduced, whose target is the ancillary qubit i and whose control is qubit j of the codevector.

If the initial codevector is $|\mathbf{v}\rangle$ and the initial vector of the ancillary qubits is $|0\rangle$ then the final vector of the ancillary qubits, the ancilla, will be $|\mathbf{s}\rangle = |\mathbf{Mv}\rangle$ corresponding to the value of the syndrome:

$$|\mathbf{v}\rangle \otimes |0\rangle_{anc.} \longrightarrow |\mathbf{v}\rangle \otimes |\mathbf{Mv}\rangle_{anc.} \tag{7.57}$$

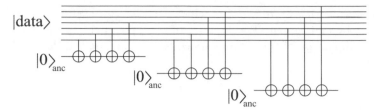

Fig. 7.5. Measurement of the bit-flip syndrome in the seven qubit code.

If only one error has occurred, a measurement of the ancilla will project the codevector either in the correct state or in a state with one bit flip. Furthermore the logical value of the ancilla will reveal the location of the qubit in error, which can then be corrected by applying operator σ_x.

The technique described above can easily be extended to correct also phase flips once we note that phase flips in base $|0\rangle, |1\rangle$ become bit flips in the Hadamard rotated basis. The problem therefore reduces to the correction of bit flips in the rotated basis. If we apply bitwise the Hadamard rotation each qubit will transform as

$$|0\rangle \longrightarrow |\tilde{0}\rangle \frac{1}{\sqrt{2}} \equiv (|0\rangle + |1\rangle), \qquad |1\rangle \longrightarrow |\tilde{1}\rangle \frac{1}{\sqrt{2}} \equiv (|0\rangle + |1\rangle), \qquad (7.58)$$

and the codevectors as

$$|\mathbf{w}_0\rangle \longrightarrow |\tilde{\mathbf{w}}_0\rangle \equiv \frac{1}{\sqrt{2}}(|\mathbf{w}_0\rangle + |\mathbf{w}_1\rangle), \quad |\mathbf{w}_1\rangle \longrightarrow |\tilde{\mathbf{w}}_1\rangle \equiv \frac{1}{\sqrt{2}}(|\mathbf{w}_0\rangle + |\mathbf{w}_1\rangle).$$
$$(7.59)$$

Note that $|\tilde{\mathbf{w}}_0\rangle, |\tilde{\mathbf{w}}_1\rangle$ satisfy the parity check. The procedure to correct phase errors is therefore the following: Apply a bitwise Hadamard rotation to the codevectors, correct the bit flips in the rotated basis, and rotate back to return to the original basis $|0\rangle, |1\rangle$ (see Fig. 7.6). The phase error will automatically be corrected. This shows that the seven qubit code can therefore correct any arbitrary phase and/or amplitude error in a single qubit.

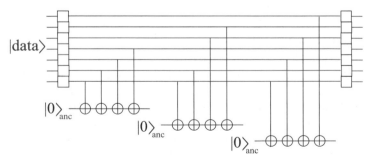

Fig. 7.6. Measurement of the phase-flip syndrome in the seven qubit code.

7.4.7 Fault-Tolerant Computation

So far, computational steps have been assumed to be error-free. In practice gate operations are themselves prone to errors. Furthermore, coding, decoding and error correction are also computational operations. The problem then arises of how to implement reliable computation using faulty circuits. We will illustrate in the remainder of this section the basic ideas behind fault-tolerant quantum computation [359]. As an example of how faulty gate operation can infect the quantum data beyond the recovery ability of our quantum error correcting codes, consider the measurement of the syndrome with the help of an ancillary qubit. The ancillary qubit is the target of several CNOT gates. Since, in a quantum CNOT, phase errors in the target act back on the control qubit, any phase error in the ancillary qubit can propagate to more than one data qubit. Note, however, that our code can correct only one error. Therefore, if the ancillary qubit contaminates two data qubits corruption is beyond recovery.

A way to confine the spreading of infection is to use separate ancillary qubits as targets of separate data qubits. The syndrome bit will then be inferred from a collective measurement of the ancillary qubits. Care must be taken however to make sure that such a procedure will give us information only on the errors and not on the state of the data qubits. The solution to this problem has been found by Shor. In his scheme the ancillary qubits are prepared in a linear superposition of states with an even number of 1's:

$$|Shor\rangle = \sum_{even} |\mathbf{x}\rangle \qquad (7.60)$$

For instance the ancillary qubits – four for each syndrome bit – are prepared in state

$$|Shor\rangle = \frac{1}{\sqrt{8}} \; (\; |0000\rangle + |0011\rangle + |0101\rangle + |1001\rangle + |0110\rangle$$
$$+ \; |1010\rangle + |1100\rangle + |1111\rangle \;) \, . \qquad (7.61)$$

Each ancillary qubit will be the target of a different data qubit. At the end the value of the syndrome bit is inferred by measuring the parity of the bits in the ancillary state. This procedure ensures that measurement of the ancilla provides us with information only on the errors. Furthermore it guarantees that errors in the ancillary qubits will not spread in the data.

Our ambition, however, is not only to store data but also to perform computations on them. The easiest thing to do would be to decode the data, perform the desired computation and then to encode again. While decoded, however, data are vulnerable to external noise. Therefore, in order to protect our qubits we would like to perform computation directly on codevectors. Furthermore we would like to perform this computation in a fault-tolerant way in order to avoid propagation of errors. This is automatically achieved

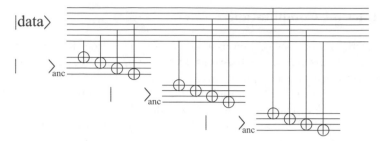

Fig. 7.7. Fault-tolerant measurement of the syndrome in the seven qubit code.

whenever we can construct gate operations on codevectors as bitwise operations on the single encoded qubits. We have shown in (7.58) that this is possible for the Hadamard rotation. It is also possible to implement the CNOT gate on codevectors pairwise on the code qubits of the control and target codevectors. These two gates alone, however, do not constitute a universal set. They can however be supplemented with a fault-tolerant version of the Toffoli gate in order to form such a universal set.

7.5 General Theory of Quantum Error Correction and Fault Tolerance

A. Steane

Introductory material and examples of quantum error correction (QEC) methods were given in the previous section. Here we will give a summary of the simplest aspects of the more general theory.

QEC is based on three central ideas: digitisation of noise, the manipulation of error operators and syndromes, and quantum error correcting code (QECC) construction. The degree of success of QEC relies on the physics of noise; we will turn to this after discussing the three central ideas.

7.5.1 Digitisation of Noise

"Digitisation of noise" is based on the observation that *any* interaction between a set of qubits and another system (such as the environment) can be expressed by a generalisation of (7.52):

$$|\phi\rangle |\psi\rangle_e \rightarrow \sum_i (E_i |\phi\rangle) |\psi_i\rangle_e \tag{7.62}$$

where each "error operator" E_i is a tensor product of Pauli operators acting on the qubits, $|\phi\rangle$ is the initial state of the qubits, and $|\psi\rangle_e$ are states of the environment, not necessarily orthogonal or normalised. We thus express general noise and/or decoherence in terms of Pauli operators $\sigma_x, \sigma_y, \sigma_z$ acting on the qubits. These will be written $X \equiv \sigma_x$, $Z \equiv \sigma_z$, $Y \equiv -i\sigma_y = XZ$.

To write tensor products of Pauli matrices acting on n qubits, we introduce the notation $X_u Z_v$ where u and v are n-bit binary vectors. The non-zero coordinates of u and v indicate where X and Z operators appear in the product. For example,

$$X \otimes I \otimes Z \otimes Y \otimes X \equiv X_{10011} Z_{00110}. \tag{7.63}$$

Error correction is a process which takes a state such as $E_i |\phi\rangle$ to $|\phi\rangle$. Correction of X errors takes $X_u Z_v |\phi\rangle$ to $Z_v |\phi\rangle$; correction of Z errors takes $X_u Z_v |\phi\rangle$ to $X_v |\phi\rangle$. Putting all this together, we discover the highly significant fact that to correct *the most general possible* noise (7.62), it is sufficient to correct just X and Z errors.

7.5.2 Error Operators, Stabiliser, and Syndrome Extraction

We will now examine the mathematics of error operators and syndromes, using the insightful approach put forward by Gottesman [360] and Calderbank et. al. [361, 362], building on the first discoveries of Steane [357, 358] and Calderbank and Shor [363, 364].

Consider the set $\{I, X, Y, Z\}$ consisting of the identity plus the three Pauli operators. The Pauli operators all square to I: $X^2 = Y^2 = Z^2 = I$, and have eigenvalues ± 1. Two members of the set only ever commute ($XI = IX$) or anticommute: $XZ = -ZX$. Tensor products of Pauli operators, i.e. error operators, also square to one and either commute or anticommute. N.B. the term 'error operator' is here just a shorthand for 'product of Pauli operators'; such an operator will sometimes play the role of an error, sometimes of a parity check, c.f. classical coding theory, Sect. 7.4.2.

If there are n qubits in the quantum system, then error operators will be of *length* n. The *weight* of an error operator is the number of terms not equal to I. For example $X_{10011} Z_{00110}$ has length 5, weight 4.

Let $\mathcal{H} = \{M\}$ be a set of commuting error operators. Since the operators all commute, they can have simultaneous eigenstates. Let $\mathcal{C} = \{|u\rangle\}$ be the orthonormal set of simultaneous eigenstates all having eigenvalue $+1$:

$$M |u\rangle = |u\rangle \quad \forall |u\rangle \in \mathcal{C}, \forall M \in \mathcal{H}. \tag{7.64}$$

The set $\mathcal{C}$ is a quantum error correcting code, and $\mathcal{H}$ is its *stabiliser*. The orthonormal states $|u\rangle$ are termed *code vectors* or *quantum codewords*. In what follows, we will restrict attention to the case in which $\mathcal{H}$ is a group. Its size is 2^{n-k}, and it is spanned by $n - k$ linearly independent members of $\mathcal{H}$. In this case $\mathcal{C}$ has 2^k members, so it encodes k qubits, since its members span a 2^k dimensional subspace of the 2^n-dimensional Hilbert space of the whole system. A general state in this subspace, called an *encoded state* or *logical state*, can be expressed as a superposition of the code vectors:

$$|\phi\rangle_L = \sum_{|u\rangle \in \mathcal{C}} a_u |u\rangle . \qquad (7.65)$$

Naturally, a given QECC does not allow correction of all possible errors. Each code allows correction of a particular set $\mathcal{S} = \{E\}$ of *correctable errors*. The task of code construction consists of finding codes whose correctable set includes the errors most likely to occur in a given physical situation. We will turn to this important topic in the next section. First, let us show how the correctable set is related to the stabiliser, and demonstrate how the error correction is actually achieved.

First, error operators in the stabiliser are all correctable, $E \in \mathcal{S} \; \forall \; E \in \mathcal{H}$, since these operators actually have no effect on a general logical state (7.65). If these error operators are themselves the only terms in the noise of the system under consideration, then the QECC is a noise-free subspace, also called decoherence-free subspace of the system.

There is a large set of further errors which do change encoded states but are nevertheless correctable by a process of extracting an error syndrome, and then acting on the system depending on what syndrome is obtained. We will show that $\mathcal{S}$ can be any set of errors $\{E_i\}$ such that every product $E_1 E_2$ of two members is either in $\mathcal{H}$, or anticommutes with a member of $\mathcal{H}$. To see this, take the second case first:

$$E_1 E_2 M = -M E_1 E_2 \text{ for some } M \in \mathcal{H}. \qquad (7.66)$$

We say that the combined error operator $E_1 E_2$ is *detectable*. This can only happen if

$$\begin{aligned} \text{either} \quad & \{M E_1 = -E_1 M, \;\; M E_2 = E_2 M\} \\ \text{or} \quad & \{M E_1 = E_1 M, \;\; M E_2 = -E_2 M\} . \end{aligned} \qquad (7.67)$$

To extract the syndrome we measure all the observables in the stabiliser. To do this, it is sufficient to measure any set of $n - k$ linearly independent M in $\mathcal{H}$. Note that such a measurement has no effect on a state in the encoded subspace, since such a state is already an eigenstate of all these observables. The measurement projects a noisy state onto an eigenstate of each M, with eigenvalue ± 1. The string of $n - k$ eigenvalues is the syndrome. Equations (7.67) guarantee that E_1 and E_2 have different syndromes, and so can be distinguished from each other. For, when the observable M is measured on the corrupted state $E |\phi\rangle_L$, (7.67) means a different eigenvalue will be obtained when $E = E_1$ than when $E = E_2$. Therefore, the error can be deduced from the syndrome, and reversed by re-applying the deduced error to the system (taking advantage of the fact that error operators square to 1).

Let us see how this whole process looks when applied to a general noisy encoded state. The noisy state is

$$\sum_i (E_i \, | \, \phi \rangle_L) \, | \, \psi_i \rangle_e \, . \tag{7.68}$$

The syndrome extraction can be done most simply by attaching an $n-k$ qubit ancilla a to the system, and storing in it the eigenvalues by a sequence of CNOT gates and Hadamard rotations. The exact network can be constructed either by thinking in terms of parity check information stored in the ancilla (c.f. Fig. 7.5), or by the following standard eigenvalue measurement method. To extract the $\lambda = \pm 1$ eigenvalue of operator M, prepare an ancilla in $(| \, 0 \rangle + | \, 1 \rangle)/\sqrt{2}$. Operate controlled-$M$ with ancilla as control, system as target, then Hadamard rotate the ancilla. The final state of the ancilla is $[(1 + \lambda) \, | \, 0 \rangle + (1 - \lambda) \, | \, 1 \rangle]/2$. Carrying out this process for the $n - k$ operators M which span $\mathcal{H}$, the effect is to couple system and environment with the ancilla as follows:

$$| \, 0 \rangle_a \sum_i (E_i \, | \, \phi \rangle_L) \, | \, \psi_i \rangle_e \rightarrow \sum_i | \, s_i \rangle_a \, (E_i \, | \, \phi \rangle_L) \, | \, \psi_i \rangle_e \, . \tag{7.69}$$

The s_i are $(n - k)$-bit binary strings, all different if the E_i all have different syndromes. A projective measurement of the ancilla will collapse the sum to a single term taken at random: $| \, s_i \rangle_a \, (E_i \, | \, \phi \rangle_L) \, | \, \psi_i \rangle_e$, and will yield s_i as the measurement result. Since there is only one E_i with this syndrome, we can deduce the operator E_i which should now be applied to correct the error!

This remarkable process can be understood as first forcing the general noisy state to 'choose' among a discrete set of errors, via a projective measurement, and then reversing the particular discrete error 'chosen' using the fact that the measurement result tells us which one it was. Alternatively, the correction can be accomplished by a unitary evolution consisting of controlled gates with ancilla as control, system as target, effectively transferring the noise (including entanglement with the environment) from system to ancilla.

We left out of the above the other possibility mentioned just before (7.66), namely that

$$E_1 E_2 \in \mathcal{H}. \tag{7.70}$$

In this case E_1 and E_2 will have the same syndrome, so are indistinguishable in the syndrome extraction process. However, this does not matter! We simply interpret the common syndrome of these two errors as an indication that the corrective operation E_1 should be applied. If it was E_1 that occurred, this is obviously fine, while if in fact E_2 occurred, the final state is $E_1 E_2 \, | \, \phi \rangle_L$ which is also correct! This situation has no analogue in classical coding theory. The quantum codes which take advantage of it are termed *degenerate* and are not constrained by the quantum Hamming bound, (7.54).

The discussion based on the stabiliser is useful because it focuses attention on operators rather than states. Quantum codewords are nevertheless very interesting states, having a lot of symmetry and interesting forms of entanglement. The codewords in the QECC can readily be shown to allow correction of the set $\mathcal{S}$ if and only if [323, 365]

$$\langle u \,|\, E_1 E_2 \,|\, v \rangle = 0 \tag{7.71}$$

$$\langle u \,|\, E_1 E_2 \,|\, u \rangle = \langle v \,|\, E_1 E_2 \,|\, v \rangle \tag{7.72}$$

for all $E_1, E_2 \in \mathcal{S}$ and $|u\rangle, |v\rangle \in \mathcal{C}, |u\rangle \neq |v\rangle$. In the case that $E_1 E_2$ always anticommutes with a member of the stabiliser, we have $\langle u \,|\, E_1 E_2 \,|\, u \rangle = \langle u \,|\, E_1 E_2 M \,|\, u \rangle = - \langle u \,|\, M E_1 E_2 \,|\, u \rangle = - \langle u \,|\, E_1 E_2 \,|\, u \rangle$, therefore $\langle u \,|\, E_1 E_2 \,|\, u \rangle = 0$. This is a nondegenerate code; all the code vectors and their erroneous versions are mutually orthogonal, and the quantum Hamming bound must be satisfied.

7.5.3 Code Construction

The power of QEC results from the physical insights and mathematical techniques already discussed, combined with the fact that useful QECCs can actually be found. Code construction is itself a subtle and interesting area, which we will merely introduce here.

First, recall that we require the members of the stabiliser all to commute. It is easy to show that $X_u Z_v = (-1)^{u \cdot v} Z_v X_u$, where $u \cdot v$ is the binary parity check operation, or inner product between binary vectors, evaluated in $GF(2)$. From this, $M = X_u Z_v$ and $M' = X_{u'} Z_{v'}$ commute if and only if

$$u \cdot v' + v \cdot u' = 0 \,. \tag{7.73}$$

The stabiliser is completely specified by writing down the $n - k$ linearly independent error operators which span it. It is convenient to write these error operators by giving the binary strings u and v which indicate the X and Z parts, in the form of two $(n - k) \times n$ binary matrices H_x, H_z. The whole stabiliser is then uniquely specified by the $(n - k) \times 2n$ binary matrix

$$H = (H_x |\, H_z) \tag{7.74}$$

and the requirement that the operators all commute (i.e. that $\mathcal{H}$ is an abelian group) is expressed by

$$H_x H_z^T + H_z H_x^T = 0 \,, \tag{7.75}$$

where ^{T} indicates the matrix transpose.

The matrix H is the analogue of the parity check matrix for a classical error correcting code. The analogue of the generator matrix is the matrix $G = (G_x | G_z)$ satisfying

$$H_x G_z^T + H_z G_x^T = 0. \tag{7.76}$$

In other words, H and G are duals with respect to the inner product defined by (7.73). G has $n + k$ rows. H may be obtained directly from G by swapping the X and Z parts and extracting the usual binary dual of the resulting $(n + k) \times 2n$ binary matrix.

Note that (7.76) and (7.75) imply that G contains H. Let $\mathcal{G}$ be the set of error operators generated by G, then also $\mathcal{G}$ contains $\mathcal{H}$.

Since by definition (7.76), all the members of $\mathcal{G}$ commute with all the members of $\mathcal{H}$, and since (by counting) there can be no further error operators which commute with all of $\mathcal{H}$, we deduce that all error operators not in $\mathcal{G}$ anticommute with at least one member of H. This leads us to a powerful observation: if all members of $\mathcal{G}$ (other than the identity) have weight at least d, then all error operators (other than the identity) of weight less than d anticommute with a member of $\mathcal{H}$, and so are detectable. Such a code can therefore correct all error operators of weight less than $d/2$.

What if the only members of $\mathcal{G}$ having weight less than d are also members of $\mathcal{H}$? Then the code can still correct all error operators of weight less than $d/2$, using property (7.70) (a degenerate code). The weight d is called the minimum distance of the code.

The problem of code construction is thus reduced to a problem of finding binary matrices H which satisfy (7.75), and whose duals G, defined by (7.76), have large weights. We will now write down such a code by combining well-chosen classical binary error correcting codes:

$$ H = \left(\begin{array}{c|c} H_2 & 0 \\ \hline 0 & H_1 \end{array} \right), \qquad G = \left(\begin{array}{c|c} G_1 & 0 \\ \hline 0 & G_2 \end{array} \right). \tag{7.77} $$

Here H_i, $i = 1, 2$, is the check matrix of the classical code C_i generated by G_i. Therefore $H_i G_i^T = 0$ and (7.76) is satisfied. To satisfy commutativity, (7.75), we force $H_1 H_2^T = 0$, in other words, $C_2^\perp \subset C_1$. By construction, if the classical codes have size k_1, k_2, then the quantum code has size $k = k_1 + k_2 - n$. The quantum codewords are

$$ |u\rangle_L = \sum_{x \in C_2^\perp} |x + u \cdot D\rangle, \tag{7.78} $$

where u is a k-bit binary word, x is an n-bit binary word, and D is a $(k \times n)$ matrix of coset leaders. These are the CSS (Calderbank–Shor–Steane) codes. Their significance is first that they can be efficient, and second that they are useful in fault-tolerant computing (see below).

By "efficient" we mean that there exist codes of given d/n whose rate k/n remains above a finite lower bound, as $k, n, d \to \infty$. The CSS codes have $d = \min(d_1, d_2)$. If we choose the pair of classical codes in the construction to be the same, $C_1 = C_2 = C$, then we are considering a classical code which contains its dual. A finite lower bound for the rate of such codes can be shown to exist [364]. This is highly significant: it means that QEC can be a very powerful method to suppress noise (see next section).

There exist QECCs more efficient than CSS codes. Good codes can be found by extending CSS codes, and by other methods. For illustration, we finish this section with the stabiliser and generator of the $[[n, k, d]] = [[5, 1, 3]]$ perfect code. It encodes a single qubit ($k = 1$), and corrects all errors of weight 1 (since $d/2 = 1.5$).

$$H = \begin{pmatrix} 11000 & 00101 \\ 01100 & 10010 \\ 00110 & 01001 \\ 00011 & 10100 \end{pmatrix}, \quad G = \begin{pmatrix} H_x & H_z \\ 11111 & 00000 \\ 00000 & 11111 \end{pmatrix}. \tag{7.79}$$

7.5.4 The Physics of Noise

Noise and decoherence are themselves a large subject. Here we will simply introduce a few basic ideas, in order to clarify what QEC can and cannot do. By 'noise' we mean simply any unknown or unwanted change in the density matrix of our system.

The statement (7.62) about digitisation of noise is equivalent to the statement that any interaction between a system of qubits and its environment has the form

$$H_I = \sum_i E_i \otimes H_i^e , \tag{7.80}$$

where the operators H_i^e act on the environment. Under the action of this coupling, the density matrix of the system (after tracing over the environment) evolves from ρ_0 to $\sum_i a_i E_i \rho_0 E_i$. QEC returns all terms of this sum having correctable E_i to ρ_0. Therefore, the fidelity of the corrected state, compared to the noise-free state ρ_0, is determined by the sum of all coefficients a_i associated with uncorrectable errors.

For a mathematically thorough analysis of this problem, see [365, 366]. The essential ideas are as follows. Noise is typically a continuous process affecting all qubits all the time. However, when we discuss QEC, we can always adopt the model that the syndrome is extracted by a projective measurement. Any statement such as 'the probability that error E_i occurs' is just a short-hand for 'the probability that the syndrome extraction projects the state onto one which differs from the noise-free state by error operator E_i'. We would like to calculate such probabilities.

To do so, it is useful to divide up (7.80) into a sum of terms having error operators of different weight:

$$H_I = \sum_{\text{wt}(E)=1} E \otimes H_E^e + \sum_{\text{wt}(E)=2} E \otimes H_E^e + \sum_{\text{wt}(E)=3} E \otimes H_E^e + \ldots . \tag{7.81}$$

There are $3n$ terms in the first sum, $3^2 n!/(2!(n-2)!)$ terms in the second, and so on. The strength of the system–environment coupling is expressed by coupling constants which appear in the H_E^e operators. In the case where only the weight 1 terms are present, we say the environment acts independently on the qubits: it does not directly produce correlated errors across two or more qubits. In this case, errors of all weights will still appear in the density matrix of the noisy system, but the size of the terms corresponding to errors of weight w will be $O(\epsilon^{2w})$, where ϵ is a parameter giving the system–environment coupling strength.

Since QEC restores all terms in the density matrix whose errors are of weight $\leq t = d/2$, the fidelity of the corrected state, in the uncorrelated noise model, can be estimated as one minus the probability $P(t+1)$ for the noise to generate an error of weight $t+1$. This is probability is approximately

$$ P(t+1) \simeq \left(3^{t+1} \binom{n}{t+1} \epsilon^{t+1} \right)^2 \tag{7.82} $$

when all the single-qubit error amplitudes can add coherently (i.e. the qubits share a common environment), or

$$ P(t+1) \simeq 3^{t+1} \binom{n}{t+1} \epsilon^{2(t+1)} \tag{7.83} $$

when the errors add incoherently (i.e. either seperate environments, or a common environment with couplings of randomly changing phase). The significance of (7.82) and (7.83) is that they imply QEC works extremely well when t is large and $\epsilon^2 < t/3n$. Since good codes exist, t can in fact tend to infinity while t/n and k/n remain fixed. Therefore, as long as the noise per qubit is below a threshold around $t/3n$, almost perfect recovery of the state is possible. The ratio t/n constrains the rate of the code through the quantum Hamming bound or its cousins.

Such uncorrelated noise is a reasonable approximation in many physical situations, but we need to be careful about the degree of approximation, since we are concerned with very small terms of order ϵ^d. If we relax the approximation of completely uncorrelated noise, (7.82) and (7.83) remain approximately unchanged, if and only if the coupling constants in (7.81) for errors of weight t are themselves of order $\epsilon^t/t!$.

A very different case in which QEC is also highly successful is when a set of correlated errors, also called burst errors, dominate the system–environment coupling, but we can find a QEC whose stabiliser includes all these correlated errors. This is sometimes called 'error avoiding' rather than 'error correction' since by using such a code, we don't even need to correct the logical state: it is already decoupled from the environment. The general lesson is that the more we know about the environment, and the more structure there exists in the system–environment coupling, the better able we are to find good codes.

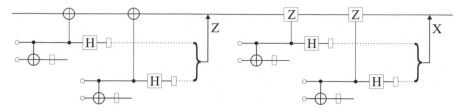

Fig. 7.8. Fault-tolerant syndrome extraction network

7.5.5 Fault-Tolerant Quantum Computation

The above discussion of QEC is relevant to high-fidelity communication down noisy quantum channels, but it is not yet clear how relevant it may be to quantum computing. This is because so far we have assumed the quantum operations involved in syndrome extraction are themselves noise-free. Therefore we are using processing power to combat noise, but it is not clear what degree of precision of the processing is necessary in order to gain something.

Fault-tolerant computation is concerned with processing information reliably even when every elementary operation, and every period of free evolution, is itself noisy. One way to approach this is to use QEC repeatedly, but with the syndrome extraction procedure carefully constructed in such a way that it corrects more noise than it introduces. Most of the essential new insights which permit us to do this were introduced by Shor [367] and helpfully discussed by Preskill [359]; see also [368]–[370]. Here we will adopt Shor's general approach, but with significant improvements introduced by Steane [371, 372]. Note that this subject is much less mature than QEC; many avenues remain unexplored. Here we will concentrate on explaining one method to extract syndromes in the right way.

A complete fault-tolerant syndrome extraction network is shown in Fig. 7.8. For brevity, we consider the simplest case of a single-error correcting code; the ideas can be generalised to codes correcting many errors. The fundamental 2-state entities in the computer are called physical qubits. Each horizontal line in the network represents not a single physical qubit, but a block of n such qubits. Operators such as Hadamard and CNOT are applied across the relevant block or blocks, i.e. n operations, one for each qubit or pair of qubits.

The method relies on the careful use of repetition, on the fact that X and Z errors propagate differently, and on useful properties of CSS codes. Define an *error location* to be any 1 or 2-qubit gate on physical qubits (including preparation and measurement operations), or the free evolution of any single physical qubit during one timestep. The noise is assumed to be uncorrelated and stochastic, so that failures occur independently with probability $\sim \gamma$. The aim of the whole network is to achieve a single-error correction of the computer block, in such a way that no failure at a single location can result in an error of weight ≥ 2 in the computer block. The idea is that while the syndrome extraction must make single-qubit errors in the computer more likely, these are the very ones which are correctable. The important thing is not to generate uncorrectable errors with $O(\gamma)$ probability.

We begin by introducing 2 ancilla blocks, and preparing each in the logical zero state $|0\rangle_L$. Each preparation is not fault tolerant, it will fail in such a way that the prepared state can have any error of any weight with probability $O(\gamma)$. Operate CNOT blockwise between the two ancillas, and measure all the bits of one of them in the computational basis. Here we are trying to verify that the correct state was prepared, using the fact that blockwise physical CNOT acts as a logical CNOT for a CSS code. Therefore, the measurement result should be a member of the classical code $C_2^\perp$ (7.78). If it is not, then reprepare the pair of ancillas and repeat until it is. At this stage, the probability for the remaining unmeasured ancilla to have X errors of weight ≥ 2 is $O(\gamma^2)$, because it can only happen if failures occur in at least two locations. Note that the ancilla might still have Z errors of any weight.

Now couple the verified ancilla to the computer by blockwise physical CNOT. Once again, we use the fact that this acts as logical CNOT, so there should be no effect! In fact something does happen: X errors propagate from ancilla to computer, and Z errors propagate from computer to ancilla. This is a sneaky, and fault tolerant, way to gather the Z-error syndrome into the ancilla. We read it out by Hadamard transforming the ancilla (to convert Z errors to bit flips) and measuring all the bits of the ancilla in the computational basis. Here we have used the property, valid for a certain class of CSS codes, that blockwise physical H acts as logical H, so will keep the ancilla state in the encoded subspace, except for the Z errors which become X errors.

There is still no single error location which can produce a weight-2 error in the computer, but now we are in danger, since there are many locations where a single failure would lead to an incorrect syndrome. If we were to 'correct' the computer on the basis of the wrong syndrome, we would actually introduce more errors. Therefore, the whole of the process described up till now is repeated. We finally end up with two syndromes. If they agree, then the only way they can be wrong is if failures occurred at two different locations, an $O(\gamma^2)$ process, so we go ahead and believe them. If they disagree, a third syndrome must be extracted, and we act on the majority vote.

We have now completed the correction of Z errors in the computer (while generating further Z errors, which will be caught in the next round of correction). The second half of the network acts similarly, but now gathers up and corrects the X errors in the computer.

Note that the whole process depends on the fact that X and Z errors propagate differently. We can fault-tolerantly verify the ancilla against X errors, but only by accepting the risk of having high-weight Z errors in the ancilla. This is OK because those Z errors stay put; they don't propagate up to the computer, they just make the syndrome wrong. We subsequently check for their presence by generating the syndrome again. Note also the heavy reliance on useful properties of CSS codes, such as their behaviour under blockwise gates.

In a repeated series of error recoveries, each round of recovery corrects not just the errors developed in the computer during that round, but also the errors caused by the previous round (as long as they are correctable). It leaves uncorrected the errors it itself caused. The noise level accumulated after R rounds is therefore suppressed from $O(R\gamma)$ to $O(R\gamma^2 + \gamma)$, which is beneficial for large R and sufficiently small γ.

To complete the task of fault tolerant *computation*, not just memory storage, we need to be able to evolve the computer state through the desired quantum algorithm. We already saw how to perform logical Hadamard and CNOT operations on the state encoded by a CSS code: operate blockwise on the qubits. This is fault tolerant since each physical gate only connects to one physical qubit per block. To obtain a complete set of operations, we use the fact that the members of the continuous set of all gates can be approximated efficiently by using members of a discrete set. To complete the set, it is sufficient to have a fault-tolerant Toffoli gate, or one of a set of closely related gates, among which is the controlled-$\pi/2$ rotation. Shor [367] proposed a (somewhat obscure) network for Toffoli. It is possible to understand the construction as related to teleportation. Teleportation can be understood as a form of fault tolerant swap operation, and it is useful for moving information around fault-tolerantly in a quantum computer [372, 373]. These and other methods are under active investigation.

At the time of writing, fault-tolerant computation based on repeated QEC seems to be the most promising way to realise large quantum algorithms, though the requirements on the physical hardware, both in terms of computer size and noise level, remain formidable.

7.6 Frequency Standards

S.F. Huelga, C. Macchiavello, M.B. Plenio, A.K. Ekert

In this section the precision of frequency measurements based on trapped ions in the presence of decoherence is analysed. Different preparations of n two-level systems are considered as well as different measurements procedures. We show in particular that standard Ramsey spectroscopy on uncorrelated ions and optimal measurements on maximally entangled states provide the same resolution. We suggest the use of symmetrisation procedures to reduce the undesired effects of decoherence and show that these allow one to exceed even the optimal precision achievable with optimised initial preparation of the n-ions state and optimised measurement scheme.

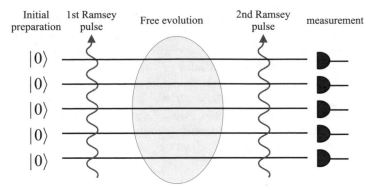

| Initial preparation | 1st Ramsey pulse | Free evolution | 2nd Ramsey pulse | measurement |

Fig. 7.9. Schematic representation of Ramsey-type spectroscopy with uncorrelated particles.

The aim of a frequency standard is to stabilise a reference oscillator to a given atomic frequency. The implementation of an optical frequency standard in an atomic trap according to standard Ramsey interferometry is illustrated in Fig. 7.9.

The ion trap is loaded with n ions initially prepared in the same internal state $|0\rangle$ (we denote by $|0\rangle$ and $|1\rangle$ the ground and the excited states of each ion). A Ramsey pulse of frequency ω is applied to all ions. The pulse shape and duration are carefully chosen so that it drives the atomic transition $|0\rangle \leftrightarrow |1\rangle$ of natural frequency ω_0 and prepares an equally weighted superposition of the two internal states $|0\rangle$ and $|1\rangle$ for each ion.

$$|0\rangle \to \frac{|0\rangle + |1\rangle}{\sqrt{2}} \quad |1\rangle \to \frac{-|0\rangle + |1\rangle}{\sqrt{2}} \, . \tag{7.84}$$

Next the system evolves freely for a time t. In a reference frame rotating at the oscillator frequency ω, the free evolution is governed by the Hamiltonian

$$H = -\hbar\Delta|1\rangle\langle 1| \, , \tag{7.85}$$

where $\Delta = \omega - \omega_0$ denotes the detuning between the classical driving field and the atomic transition. The evolution of the basis atomic states can then be represented as follows:

$$|0\rangle \to |0\rangle \quad |1\rangle \to e^{i\Delta t}|1\rangle \, , \tag{7.86}$$

and the frequency difference between the atomic transition and the reference oscillator leads to the accumulation of a relative phase. If we now apply a second Ramsey pulse, the probability that an ion is found in the state $|1\rangle$ is given by

$$P = \frac{1 + \cos(\Delta t)}{2} \, . \tag{7.87}$$

When this basic scheme is repeated yielding a total duration T of the experiment, the resulting interference curve of the measured population in the upper state allows us to deduce the oscillator detuning and subsequently to adjust the frequency of the reference oscillator. At this point, one question arises. What is the best precision that can be achieved in the measurement of the atomic frequency? More precisely, given T and a fixed given number of ions n, what is the ultimate limit to the resolution of our frequency standard?

The statistical fluctuations associated with a finite sample yield an uncertainty ΔP in the estimated value of P given by

$$\Delta P = \sqrt{P(1 - P)/N} , \tag{7.88}$$

where $N = nT/t$ denotes the actual number of experimental data (we assume that N is large). Hence the uncertainty in the estimated value of ω_0 is given by

$$|\delta\omega_0| = \frac{\sqrt{P(1 - P)/N}}{|dP/d\omega|} = \frac{1}{\sqrt{nTt}}. \tag{7.89}$$

This value is often referred to as the *shot noise limit* [374]. We should stress that this limit comes from the intrinsically statistical character of quantum mechanics, in contrast to other possible sources of technical noise. While the latter may eventually be reduced, the shot noise poses a fundamental limit to the achievable resolution in precision spectroscopy with n independent particles.

The theoretical possibility of overcoming this limit has been put forward recently [375, 376]. The basic idea is to prepare the ions initially in an entangled state. To see the advantage of this approach, let us consider the case of two ions prepared in the maximally entangled state

$$|\Psi\rangle = (|00\rangle + |11\rangle)/\sqrt{2}. \tag{7.90}$$

This state can be generated, for example, by the initial part of the network illustrated in Fig. 7.10. A Ramsey pulse on the first ion is followed by a controlled–NOT gate. After a free evolution period of time t the state of the composite system in the interaction picture rotating at the driving frequency ω reads

$$|\Psi\rangle = (|00\rangle + e^{2i\Delta t}|11\rangle)/\sqrt{2} . \tag{7.91}$$

The second part of the network allows to disentangle the ions after the free evolution period. The population in state $|1\rangle$ of the first ion will now oscillate at a frequency 2Δ:

$$P_2 = \frac{1 + \cos(2\Delta t)}{2}. \tag{7.92}$$

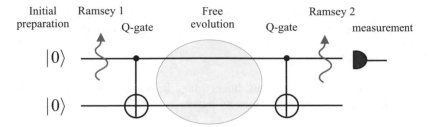

Initial preparation   Ramsey 1   Free evolution   Ramsey 2   measurement

Q-gate   Q-gate

$|0\rangle$

$|0\rangle$

Fig. 7.10. Spectroscopy with two maximally entangled particles. The particles are entangled and disentangled by means of "controlled–NOT" gates.

This scheme can be easily generalised to the n-ion case by a sequence of controlled–NOT gates linking the first ion with each of the remaining ones. In this way, a maximally entangled state of n ions of the form

$$|\Psi\rangle = (|00...0\rangle + |11...1\rangle)/\sqrt{2} \qquad (7.93)$$

is generated. The final measurement on the first ion, after the free evolution period and the second set of controlled–NOT gates, gives the signal

$$P_n = \frac{1 + \cos(n\Delta t)}{2} . \qquad (7.94)$$

The advantage of this scheme is that the oscillation frequency of the signal is now amplified by a factor n with respect to the case of uncorrelated ions and the corresponding frequency uncertainty is

$$|\delta\omega_0| - \frac{1}{n\sqrt{Tt}} . \qquad (7.95)$$

Note that this result represents an improvement of a factor $1/\sqrt{n}$ over the shot noise limit (7.89) by using the same number of ions n and the same total duration of the experiment T and it was argued that this is the best precision possible [377].
Let us now examine the same situation in a realistic experimental scenario, where decoherence effects are inevitably present. The main type of decoherence in an ion trap is dephasing due to processes that cause random changes in the relative phase of quantum states while preserving the population in the atomic levels. Important mechanisms that result in dephasing effects are collisions, stray fields and laser instabilities. We model the time evolution of the reduced density operator for a single ion ρ in the presence of decoherence by the following master equation [378]:

$$\frac{d\rho}{dt} = -i\Delta\left(\rho|1\rangle\langle 1| - |1\rangle\langle 1|\rho\right) + \gamma\left(\sigma_z\rho\sigma_z - \rho\right) . \qquad (7.96)$$

Equation (7.96) is written in a frame rotating at the frequency ω. By $\sigma_z = |0\rangle\langle 0| - |1\rangle\langle 1|$ we denote a Pauli spin operator. Here we have introduced the decay rate $\gamma = 1/\tau_{dec}$, where τ_{dec} is the decoherence time. For the case of independent particles this will give rise to a broadening of signal (7.87):

$$P = (1 + \cos \Delta t e^{-\gamma t})/2. \tag{7.97}$$

As a consequence the corresponding uncertainty in the atomic frequency is no longer detuning-independent. We now have

$$|\delta\omega_0| = \sqrt{\frac{1 - \cos^2(\Delta t)e^{-2\gamma t}}{nTte^{-2\gamma t}\sin^2(\Delta t)}} . \tag{7.98}$$

In order to obtain the best precision it is necessary to optimise this expression as a function of the duration of each single measurement t. The minimal value is attained for

$$\Delta t = k\pi/2 \ (k \ \text{odd}) \quad t = \tau_{dec}/2 \tag{7.99}$$

provided that $T > \tau_{dec}/2$. Thus the minimum frequency uncertainty reads

$$|\delta\omega_0|_{opt} = \sqrt{\frac{2\gamma e}{nT}} = \sqrt{\frac{2e}{n\tau_{dec}T}}. \tag{7.100}$$

For maximally entangled preparation, the signal (7.94) in the presence of dephasing is modified as follows:

$$P_n = \frac{1 + \cos(n\Delta t)e^{-n\gamma t}}{2} \tag{7.101}$$

and the resulting uncertainty for the estimated value of the atomic frequency is now minimal when

$$\Delta t = k\pi/2n \ (k \ \text{odd}) \quad t = \tau_{dec}/2n \ . \tag{7.102}$$

Interestingly, we recover exactly the same minimal uncertainty as for standard Ramsey spectroscopy (7.100). This effect is illustrated in Fig.7.11. The modulus of the frequency uncertainty $|\delta\omega_0|$ is plotted as a function of the duration of each single experiment t for standard Ramsey spectroscopy with n uncorrelated particles and for a maximally entangled state with n particles.

In the presence of decoherence both preparations reach the same precision. This result can be intuitively understood by considering that maximally entangled states are much more fragile in the presence of decoherence: their decoherence time is reduced by a factor n and therefore the duration of each single measurement t has also to be reduced by the same amount. The previous conclusions hold whenever the total duration of the experiment exceeds the typical decoherence time. Hence, maximally entangled states are only advantageous for short term stabilisations. As far as long term experiments

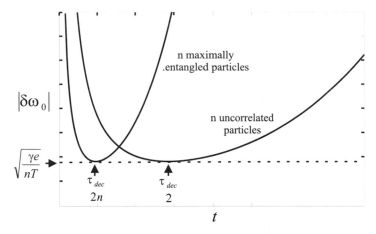

Fig. 7.11. Frequency uncertainty $|\delta\omega_0|$ as a function of the duration of a single shot t for maximally entangled and uncorrelated particles. Note that the minimum uncertainty is exactly the same for both configurations.

are concerned, it has been shown recently [379] that the best resolution is achieved using partially entangled preparations with a high degree of symmetry. The procedure involves both an optimisation of the initial preparation of the state of the n ions and the final measurement after the free evolution region. However, from a practical point of view, the expected improvement is modest. The optimal percentual improvement in the precision relative to the limit (7.100) is of the order of 10% for $n = 7$. Asymptotic limits for large n are still under investigation.

A very different approach to improving the resolution of a frequency standard by means of quantum entanglement is making use of error correction. As it has been shown in previous sections, these procedures can effectively reduce the amount of decoherence and dissipation in quantum systems. However, when established error correction protocols for phase-type errors are applied to this particular problem, difficulties arise. The use of error correction not only corrects phase errors due to environmental noise but also interferes with the desired change of relative phase in the atomic states that appears for a detuned oscillator, which is the quantity we want to estimate. This reduces the sensitivity of the frequency standard. Nevertheless, as will be shown, it is possible to *stabilise* the system against decoherence and overcoming the optimal resolution achievable in the spectroscopy of uncorrelated particles.

The key point is to realise that during the free evolution region, in the absence of decoherence, the state of n particles initially prepared in a state which is invariant under any permutation of the n ions always lies in the symmetric subspace of the Hilbert space of the composite system of the n ions (by symmetric subspace we mean the subspace which includes all the possible

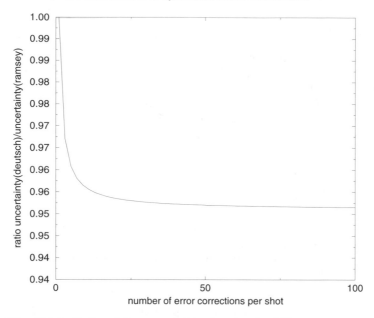

Fig. 7.12. Ratio of the uncertainty for standard Ramsey spectroscopy with and without symmetrisation for $n = 2$ as a function of the number of symmetrisation steps performed during the free evolution region.

states which are invariant under any permutation of the n ions). A projection of the global state into the symmetric subspace [380] would then yield a partial removal of events affected by environmental phase errors. Figure 7.12 shows the percentual precision improvement achievable with this technique for $n = 2$. In this case a standard Ramsey scheme with initially uncorrelated ions has been considered and repeated symmetrisation steps are applied during the free evolution region. After each symmetrisation step the ions are kept only if the symmetrisation is successful, otherwise they are discarded and reset to state $|0\rangle$ to start the scheme from the beginning. Although this reduces the number of experimental data available for statistics, Fig. 7.12 shows that it is a convenient strategy to improve the overall precision of the experiment.

The limits to the precision achievable with symmetrisation procedures for generic n and a generic initial preparation of the state of the ions are still under investigation.

It should be noted that the symmetrization method is an error detection method rather than an error correction method. The symmetrization method simply removes erroneous states instead of correcting them. Although the remaining ensemble contains less errors the statistics of the experiment becomes worse due to the smaller number of systems that remain in the symmetric subspace. Overall a small improvement results. The application of true quantum error correction codes in frequency standards is currently being investigated. Progress in this direction could potentially lead to substantially improved frequency standards. But even a proof that quantum error correction and entanglement cannot improve the precision of frequency standards significantly would be very interesting.

In this section we have presented the application of entanglement and quantum error correction in frequency standards. The motivation for this is that it is an application of the ideas of quantum information theory that requires only small quantum resources. One direction of future research in quantum information theory is certainly the development of other applications that require only small resources. Such applications could then be realised experimentally in the near future.

8. Entanglement Purification

8.1 Introduction

In Chap. 7 the theory of quantum error correction was presented. The present chapter describes an alternative method of overcoming decoherence which is particularly useful for quantum state communication. The main idea is to distill from a large set of (pairs of) entangled particles, possibly degraded in entanglement purity by decoherence, a subset of particles with enhanced entanglement purity. Section 8.2 describes the general principles of entanglement purification. Specific examples are local filtering (Sect. 8.3), suitable for increasing the entanglement for pure states, and quantum privacy amplification (Sect. 8.4), designed to increase the security of quantum cryptography over noisy quantum channels. The generalisation of purification to multi-particle entanglement will be addressed in Sect. 8.5. Section 8.6 shows how to create maximally entangled EPR pairs between spatially distant atoms, each of them inside a high-Q optical cavity, by sending photons through a noisy channel, such as a standard optical fibre. As the absorption probability of photons during the transmission grows exponentially with the distance, so will the required number of repetitions for a successful transmission. Section 8.7 presents the quantum repeater method, which reduces the growth of the required number of operations as function of the transmission distance from exponential to polynomial.

8.2 Principles of Entanglement Purification

H.-J. Briegel

A central problem of quantum communication is the faithful transmission of quantum information from a party A (Alice) to some other party B (Bob) when the communication channel that connects A with B is noisy. The fidelity with which a quantum state is transmitted through a noisy quantum channel decreases, in general, exponentially with its length, so faithful transmission will be restricted to very short distances. This problem can be solved, in principle, by the method of teleportation, which requires that A and B share a certain supply of pairs of particles in a maximally entangled state (EPR pairs). The question remains then, how can A and B create such entangled states if they can only communicate through noisy channels? Since entanglement cannot be created by local operations alone, A and B will have to send quantum bits through the channel at some point, to build up non-local quantum correlations. As these qubits interact with the channel, they are subject to decoherence and the resulting EPR pairs will not be maximally entangled, but instead be described by some mixed state with a certain entanglement fidelity. The idea of *entanglement purification* is to extract from a large ensemble of such low-fidelity EPR pairs a smaller sub-ensemble with sufficiently high fidelity, which may then be used for faithful teleportation [49, 74] (Chap. 3) or for quantum cryptography [46, 47] (Chap. 2).

From the quantum communication perspective, there is a natural connection between entanglement purification and quantum error correction. The theory of quantum error correction has primarily been developed to make quantum computation possible despite the effects of decoherence and imperfect apparatus, but it can, of course, also be used to correct transmission errors.[1] Entanglement purification, on the other hand, is a more specific but powerful tool for quantum communication purposes. By exploiting classical communication between the parties, it allows highly efficient two-way protocols that cannot be realised with quantum error correction techniques. Furthermore, the method is remarkably robust with respect to imperfect apparatus, which makes it very attractive for more advanced applications such as quantum repeaters [381]. A quantitative analysis of the connection between entanglement purification and quantum error correction is given in Ref. [323].

It should be emphasised that the issue of purifying (and quantifying) entanglement is of fundamental interest, regardless of the specific communicational applications that we have in mind *today*. We are likely to learn many more aspects of (multi-)particle entanglement in the future than we are presently aware of, and its applications might not be restricted to computational and communicational tasks. In any case, it will be good to have entangled states in our laboratory, and we need to know how to generate and to purify them efficiently.

So what is entanglement purification?

To illustrate the main ideas we first consider an ensemble of spin 1/2 particles that are partially polarised along a certain direction (z say). For simplicity, we may assume that we are dealing with an incoherent mixture of particles in state $|\uparrow\rangle \equiv |\text{spin up}\rangle$ and $|\downarrow\rangle \equiv |\text{spin down}\rangle$, respectively, represented by the density matrix

$$\rho = f|\uparrow\rangle\langle\uparrow| + (1-f)|\downarrow\rangle\langle\downarrow|, \tag{8.1}$$

---

[1] In fact, *classical* error correction was originally developed for just that purpose [32].

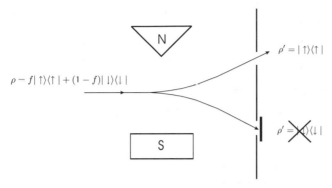

Fig. 8.1. Selection of spin-polarised atoms with Stern-Gerlach magnets: An inhomogeneous magnetic field in z direction, generated by two magnets (S and N), is used to spatially separate particles with different spin. For brevity, we call this arrangement a "Stern-Gerlach apparatus."

although this restriction is not essential for the following argument. We can easily select the subensemble of particles in state $|\uparrow\rangle$ by measuring the particles' spin along the z axis, e.g. by sending them through a Stern–Gerlach (SG) apparatus as shown in Fig. 8.1. By selecting only those particles that leave the apparatus along the upper path (which will be the case for a fraction f of all particles, on average), we will obviously create a subensemble of particles in the pure state $\rho' = |\uparrow\rangle\langle\uparrow|$. We could say that we have "purified" the whole ensemble by "distilling" the particles with the desired polarisation, although this terminology would sound rather forced, at this point.

For reasons that will become clear, imagine a slightly more complicated situation where, by some unknown mechanism, the particles are destroyed (e.g. absorbed) after they have passed through the SG apparatus! We only assume that the apparatus delivers us with a click if a particle goes through the upper hole in Fig. 8.1 and nothing otherwise, absorbing all of the particles. How could we use such a deficient apparatus to purify our ensemble? A possibility would be to not send the particles themselves through the SG apparatus but a *copy* of them, instead. Although it is impossible to copy a general quantum state (no-cloning theory, Sect. 2.2.2 [88]) it is possible to copy the selected *basis* states using an auxiliary particle C and the *measurement gate* (or CNOT gate). The measurement gate has been described in Sect. 1.6: If the initial state of the particle C is $|\uparrow\rangle_C$, its effect is to copy the

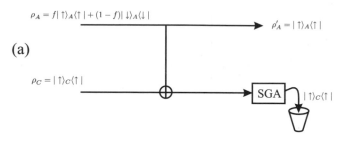

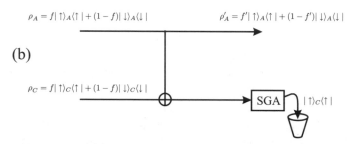

Fig. 8.2. Selection of spin-polarised atoms with a fictitious Stern–Gerlach (SG) apparatus that absorbs an atom upon measuring its state. The state of an atom of the impure ensemble (upper line) is copied (symbol $\oplus$) onto an auxiliary atom C (lower line), on which the destructive measurement is performed. The auxiliary atoms used in (**a**) are polarised in state $|\uparrow\rangle_C$; in (**b**) they are taken from the impure ensemble itself.

basis states $|\uparrow\rangle_A$ and $|\downarrow\rangle_A$ of particle A onto particle C,[2] [3]

$$|\uparrow\rangle_A|\uparrow\rangle_C \longrightarrow |\uparrow\rangle_A|\uparrow\rangle_C$$
$$|\downarrow\rangle_A|\uparrow\rangle_C \longrightarrow |\downarrow\rangle_A|\downarrow\rangle_C \,. \qquad (8.2)$$

Applied to the ensemble (8.1), the measurement gate creates two (classically) correlated ensembles of the form[4]

$$\rho_{AC} = f|\uparrow\rangle_A\langle\uparrow| \otimes |\uparrow\rangle_C\langle\uparrow| + (1-f)|\downarrow\rangle_A\langle\downarrow| \otimes |\downarrow\rangle_C\langle\downarrow| \,. \qquad (8.3)$$

---

[2] This means that any superposition $(\alpha|\uparrow\rangle_A + \beta|\downarrow\rangle_A)$ will be transformed by this gate according to

$$(\alpha|\uparrow\rangle_A + \beta|\downarrow\rangle_A)|\uparrow\rangle_C \rightarrow \alpha|\uparrow\uparrow\rangle_{AC} + \beta|\downarrow\downarrow\rangle_{AC}$$
$$\neq (\alpha|\uparrow\rangle_A + \beta|\downarrow\rangle_A)(\alpha|\uparrow\rangle_C + \beta|\downarrow\rangle_C) \,.$$

The no-cloning principle [88] is therefore not violated.

[3] More generally, the spin of the particle C is flipped under the condition that particle A is in state $|\downarrow\rangle_A$. That is, (8.2) together with the transformations $|\uparrow\rangle_A|\downarrow\rangle_C \longrightarrow |\uparrow\rangle_A|\downarrow\rangle_C$ and $|\downarrow\rangle_A|\downarrow\rangle_C \longrightarrow |\downarrow\rangle_A|\uparrow\rangle_C$ describe the full CNOT gate.

[4] This is true if the auxiliary particles C are initially in the state $|\uparrow\rangle_C$.

If we now measure the spin value of an auxiliary particle, we still destroy *that* particle, but a click will indicate that the corresponding left-behind particle A is in the pure state $\rho'_A = |\uparrow\rangle_A\langle\uparrow|$ (see Fig. 8.2a). By measuring the copy of every particle, we simply check which of the particles are in the right state and can therefore select a purified subensemble.

Obviously, there is a catch: By assuming that we have auxiliary particles in the *pure* state $|\uparrow\rangle_C$ available, the whole purification idea seems to be pointless, since we could have used those auxiliary particles from the beginning, instead of our impure ensemble.

So what can we do if we do not have perfectly polarised spins for copying? The important point is that we may as well use particles taken from the impure ensemble itself, for this purpose. As long as $f > 1/2$, it is more likely that some randomly selected particle (for copying) is in the correct internal state $|\uparrow\rangle_C$ and can thus be used to check the unknown state of some other particle of the ensemble. To see this quantitatively, imagine that we divide the initial ensemble, which we want to purify, into two subensembles ρ_A and ρ_C of the same size (we write two different indices A and C to distinguish their roles in the measurement gate). Both subensembles will be described by the same density matrix (8.6), see also Fig. 8.2b. Now for every atom in the ensemble A, we pick an atom from the ensemble C and copy the state of A onto C with the aid of the measurement gate. After this procedure has been done for all particles, we obtain the following ensemble,

$$\rho_{AC} = \left(f^2|\uparrow\rangle_A\langle\uparrow| + (1-f)^2|\downarrow\rangle_A\langle\downarrow|\right) \otimes |\uparrow\rangle_C\langle\uparrow|$$
$$+ f(1-f)\left(|\uparrow\rangle_A\langle\uparrow| + |\downarrow\rangle_A\langle\downarrow|\right) \otimes |\downarrow\rangle_C\langle\downarrow|. \tag{8.4}$$

We now measure the state of the particles C and collect all those particles of the ensemble A, whose copy is found in state $|\uparrow\rangle_C$ ("click"), into a new ensemble. This new ensemble is then described by the density operator

$$\rho'_A = f'|\uparrow\rangle_A\langle\uparrow| + (1-f')|\downarrow\rangle_A\langle\downarrow| \tag{8.5}$$

with $f' = f^2/(f^2 + (1-f)^2)$. The simple function $f'(f)$ is identical to the one plotted in Fig. 8.4, where we will discuss the purification of mixed entangled states. For $f > 1/2$, we thus obtain a *purified ensemble* with a larger fraction $f' > f$ of particles in the state $|\uparrow\rangle_A$. If we iterate this procedure, as indicated by the staircase in Fig. 8.4, we are able to *distill* particles with a state arbitrarily close to the pure state $|\uparrow\rangle_A$, as long as the initial ensemble is sufficiently large.[5]

We are now ready to discuss the purification of mixed entangled states. Imagine that Alice and Bob want to purify an ensemble of *two*-particle entangled states ρ_{AB}, where their particles A and B are kept at different locations. Consider the following simple example

---

[5] Strictly speaking, to distill pure states by this method, the initial ensemble has to be infinitely large.

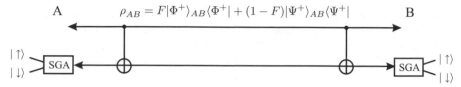

Fig. 8.3. Purification of a mixed-state ensemble of entangled states by local unitary operations, measurements, and classical communication.

$$\rho_{AB} = f|\Phi^+\rangle_{AB}\langle\Phi^+| + (1-f)|\Psi^+\rangle_{AB}\langle\Psi^+| \qquad (8.6)$$

with the Bell states

$$|\Phi^+\rangle_{AB} = \{|\uparrow\uparrow\rangle_{AB} + |\downarrow\downarrow\rangle_{AB}\}/\sqrt{2}$$

and

$$|\Psi^+\rangle_{AB} = \{|\uparrow\downarrow\rangle_{AB} + |\downarrow\uparrow\rangle_{AB}\}/\sqrt{2}$$

and $1/2 < f < 1$. Unless $f = 1/2$, the state (8.6) is inseparable. We may regard (8.6) as a classical mixture of two ensembles of (pure) Bell states $|\Phi^+\rangle_{AB}$ and $|\Psi^+\rangle_{AB}$ of size f and $(1-f)$, respectively.[6] Clearly, by sending both particles through a corresponding SG apparatus on each side, Alice and Bob can distinguish the two subensembles: For pairs in the state $|\Phi^+\rangle_{AB}$, both particles will leave the apparatus on similar paths ("up-up" or "down-down") while for pairs in state $|\Psi^+\rangle_{AB}$ they will leave the apparatus along different paths ("up-down" or "down-up"), assuming that both Alice and Bob have aligned their SG apparatuses in the z-direction. On the other hand, this measurement will *destroy* any previously existing entanglement, and the particles will leave the apparatuses in a product state. The problem is therefore: How can Alice and Bob select the subensemble described by $|\Phi^+\rangle_{AB}$ if, by a local measurement, they destroy the entanglement?

To solve this problem, we may use our insights from the previous discussion of one-particle purification. Can Alice and Bob apply the trick with the measurement gate and send "copies" of A and B through the SG apparatuses, instead of the particles themselves? They can, in fact, if the initial state of the particles used for the copying is itself entangled. To see this, consider the situation where Alice and Bob share two pairs, one pair AB from the ensemble (8.6) and a second pair A'B' in the pure state $|\Phi^+\rangle_{A'B'}$. Now they copy the state of the pair AB onto the pair A'B' by applying the measurement gate of (8.2) on both sides, that is, between particles A and A', and B and B', respectively. The result of this operation can be summarised as follows:

---

[6] The fraction $f = \langle\Phi^+|\rho_{AB}|\Phi^+\rangle_{AB}$ in (8.6) is also called the "entanglement fidelity" (or simply fidelity) of the mixed state ρ_{AB} with respect to the Bell state $|\Phi^+\rangle_{AB}$.

$$|\Phi^+\rangle_{AB}|\Phi^+\rangle_{A'B'} \longrightarrow |\Phi^+\rangle_{AB}|\Phi^+\rangle_{A'B'}$$
$$|\Psi^+\rangle_{AB}|\Phi^+\rangle_{A'B'} \longrightarrow |\Psi^+\rangle_{AB}|\Psi^+\rangle_{A'B'}\,. \tag{8.7}$$

This bi-lateral (CNOT) operation obviously acts like a measurement gate for *pairs* where the states $|\Phi^+\rangle$ and $|\Psi^+\rangle$ play the analogs of $|\uparrow\rangle$ and $|\downarrow\rangle$ in (8.2). This means that, if Alice and Bob share some pairs in the state $|\Phi^+\rangle_{A'B'}$, they can use them to check the state of randomly chosen pairs of the ensemble (8.6) and thereby select the desired subensemble. The problem is, of course, that they do not have auxiliary pairs in the state $|\Phi^+\rangle_{AB}$! (otherwise there would be no need for purification). But – remember the previous discussion for single-particle states – Alice and Bob may equally well use pairs from the mixed ensemble itself, as long as the majority of them is in the right initial state $|\Phi^+\rangle$ (i.e. $f > 1/2$). So the protocol is very similar to that for the one-particle purification (see Fig. 8.3):

1. Alice and Bob pick randomly two pairs of the ensemble (8.6) and use one of the pairs to measure the state of the other pair; i.e.
2. they apply the CNOT gate between corresponding particles on each side;
3. they measure the state of the auxiliary pair, e.g with two SG apparatuses as in Fig. 8.3 (and thus destroy its entanglement).

By keeping only those pairs for which the measurement results give the same spin value, (up-up or down-down) they can select a new ensemble that is described by the density operator

$$\rho'_{AB} = f'|\Phi^+\rangle_{AB}\langle\Phi^+| + (1 - f')|\Psi^+\rangle_{AB}\langle\Psi^+|\,, \tag{8.8}$$

with a larger fraction $f' = f^2/(f^2+(1-f)^2) > f$ (for $f > 1/2$) of pairs in the state $|\Phi^+\rangle_{AB}$ (see Fig. 8.4). Note that, in order to compare the outcomes of their measurements and thus to decide which pairs to keep or to discard, Alice and Bob have to communicate and exchange classical information, which is an integral part of any purification protocol. By iterating this procedure as indicated by the staircase in Fig. 8.4, Alice and Bob can *distill* an ensemble of pairs with entanglement fidelity f arbitrary close to unity.

It seems that with (8.6), we have discussed a rather special case of a mixed two-particle state, but the method also works for general states ρ_{AB}, as long as they contain a sufficiently large fraction $f = \langle\Phi_{\mathrm{me}}|\rho_{AB}|\Phi_{\mathrm{me}}\rangle > 1/2$ of particles in a maximally entangled state $|\Phi_{\mathrm{me}}\rangle$.[7] The first entanglement purification protocol for general mixed entangled states was given by Bennett et al. [49]. It allows one to distill from a large ensemble of entangled states with fidelity $f > 1/2$ a smaller ensemble of pairs with fidelity f arbitrarily close to unity. These pairs can then be used for faithful teleportation through

---

[7] By this we mean any state that is, up to local unitary transformations on Alice's and Bob's particle, equivalent to one of the four (and thus to all) Bell states. Typically, at some point of a protocol that works with general mixed states ρ_{AB}, the dominant component $|\Phi_{\mathrm{me}}\rangle$ of ρ_{AB} is transformed into the Bell state $|\Phi^+\rangle$ before the bilateral CNOT operation is applied.

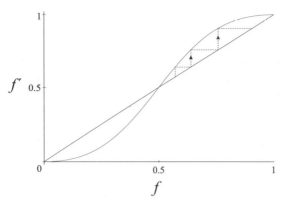

Fig. 8.4. Purification of mixed entangled states. For $f > 1/2$, the fidelity of the pairs (8.6) is increased to the value f' in (8.8). By iteration (staircase), one can distill high fidelity pairs from a large initial ensemble of low-fidelity pairs. Note that for this simple (so-called recurrence) method, more than 50% of all pairs are sacrificed in each step.

a noisy quantum channel. A second protocol, called "quantum privacy amplification," (QPA) was given by Deutsch et al. [47]. Apart from differences in the details (such as the efficiency in producing singlets), both protocols use the measurement gate as a central ingredient to perform measurements on non-local entangled states without destroying their entanglement. The prime motivation of QPA lies in its application to entanglement-based quantum cryptography [46], by establishing a procedure that allows Alice and Bob, in principle, to *disentangle* a potential eavesdropper from a selected subset of pairs, which may subsequently be used for quantum key distribution. This method of quantum privacy amplification will be reviewed in Sect. 8.4

It should be emphasised that the method which we have described above to illustrate the idea of entanglement purification is not the only way of purifying entangled states. There are more sophisticated methods (using e.g. multi-particle measurements) that exploit ideas from classical information theory such as random hashing [49, 323] to increase the efficiency of the protocols. Another interesting and simple method, which is particularly suited for increasing the entanglement of *pure* states, is *local filtering* [117, 382], which will be described in more detail in Sect. 8.3. There have also been a series of further developments in the theory of entanglement purification since the first ideas where formulated a few years ago, but we cannot discuss these in this elementary introduction. Examples include the important notion of "bound entanglement" [383], the discussion of optimal purification protocols [322, 323, 384, 385], and the efficiency and the robustness of purification protocols under imperfect local operations [381, 386, 387]. A generalisation of entanglement purification for multi-particle entangled states is discussed in Sect. 8.5.

8.3 Local Filtering

B. Huttner, N. Gisin

For entanglement purification one considers an unlimited number of pairs of quantum systems, all in the same (possibly mixed) state ρ_{in}. The task is to extract from this a fraction of maximally entangled pure states, by using only local operations and classical communication. Let us first consider the case of a pure entangled state of two quantum systems $\rho_{\text{in}} = |\psi_{\text{in}}\rangle\langle\psi_{\text{in}}|$. We shall show that it can always be "purified" by local filtering to the 2-qubits singlet state $\frac{1}{\sqrt{2}}(|01\rangle - |10\rangle)$. This introduces the concept of local filtering, a particularly simple example of entanglement purification, and shows that for entanglement purification in general it suffices to consider purification towards singlet states [382].

Using the Schmidt decomposition, ψ_{in} can always be written as:

$$\psi_{\text{in}} = \sum_{j=1}^{N} c_j \alpha_j \otimes \beta_j \tag{8.9}$$

where $\{\alpha_j\}$ and $\{\beta_j\}$ are orthonormal bases of the Hilbert spaces of the 2 entangled quantum systems. Since the state ψ_{in} is assumed entangled, there are at least 2 non-vanishing c_j, hence we may assume $c_1 \neq 0$ and $c_2 \neq 0$. To purify ψ_{in} Alice, who holds the system in states α_j, and Bob, who holds the β_j, first measure the projectors $P_{\alpha_1} + P_{\alpha_2}$ and $P_{\beta_1} + P_{\beta_2}$, respectively. By classical communication, Alice and Bob keep only the pairs that give positive outputs to the measurements. These pairs are in the following state:

$$\psi_1 = c_1 \alpha_1 \otimes \beta_1 + c_2 \alpha_2 \otimes \beta_2 . \tag{8.10}$$

Hence each subsystem involves only two orthogonal states, like qubits. Let us assume that $|c_1|^2 \geq |c_2|^2$, then Alice and Bob apply locally 2 filters F_A and F_B that attenuate α_1 and β_1 while letting α_2 and β_2 through unaffected. These filters are represented by the following positive operators:

$$F_A = \sqrt{\frac{|c_2|}{|c_1|}} P_{\alpha_1} + P_{\alpha_2} \quad \text{and} \quad F_B = \sqrt{\frac{|c_2|}{|c_1|}} P_{\beta_1} + P_{\beta_2} . \tag{8.11}$$

Using the classical communication channel, Alice and Bob select only those pairs of systems that passed both filters. (Actually, it suffices if only Alice or only Bob measures her (his) operator and act with a filter). Notice that such filters really exist. For example optical elements with polarisation-dependent loss are common. For an experimental example in quantum optics, see for instance [388]. The state of the filtered systems has equal weights on both product states:

$$\psi_2 = F_A \otimes F_B \psi_1 = \frac{|c_2|}{|c_1|} c_1 \alpha_1 \otimes \beta_1 + c_2 \alpha_2 \otimes \beta_2 \,. \tag{8.12}$$

Finally, Alice and Bob only need to fix the relative phase between $\alpha_1 \otimes \beta_1$ and $\alpha_2 \otimes \beta_2$ to obtain the desired singlet state (up to an irrelevant global phase):

$$\psi_{\text{filtered}} = \alpha_1 \otimes \beta_1 - \alpha_2 \otimes \beta_2 \tag{8.13}$$

In full generality, the problem of entanglement purification is more complex (for more than 2 entangled systems, the general solution is not even known). However, the relatively simple filters presented above can also be used to purify some mixed states, as will be shown now. Inspired by the above results, let us consider the following mixture of 2-qubit states:

$$\rho_{\text{in}}(\lambda, c) = \lambda P_{\psi_c} + \frac{1 - \lambda}{2}(P_{\psi_{11}} + P_{\psi_{00}}) \,, \tag{8.14}$$

where λ and c are two real numbers between 0 and 1, and

$$\psi_c = c|10\rangle - \sqrt{1 - c^2}|01\rangle, \quad \psi_{11} = |11\rangle, \quad \psi_{00} = |00\rangle \,. \tag{8.15}$$

Before showing how the state $\rho(\lambda, c)$ can be purified, we would like to prove that this state can never violate the Bell–CHSH inequality [12]. For this purpose, we use a powerful result by the Horodecki family [389], which applied to state $\rho(\lambda, c)$ concludes that for

$$\frac{1}{2 - 2c\sqrt{1 - c^2}} < \lambda \le \frac{1}{1 + c^2(1 - c^2)} \tag{8.16}$$

no violation of the Bell–CHSH inequality can happen. Hence $\rho(\lambda, c)$ is apparently local, though below we show that $\rho(\lambda, c)$ can be purified to singlet states and that consequently $\rho(\lambda, c)$ is in fact nonlocal.

The procedure to purify $\rho(\lambda, c)$ is actually quite similar to the example presented above: Alice and Bob apply the filters (8.11) with $c_1 = c$ and $c_2 = \sqrt{1 - c^2}$. The filtered state reads:

$$\rho_{\text{filtered}}(\lambda, c) = FA \otimes FB \; \rho_{\text{in}}(\lambda, c) \; FA \otimes FB =$$
$$\frac{1}{N}\left(2\lambda c\sqrt{1 - c^2} P_{\text{singlet}} + \frac{1 - \lambda}{2}(P_{\psi_{11}} + P_{\psi_{00}})\right) \tag{8.17}$$

with the normalisation factor $N = 2\lambda c\sqrt{1 - c^2} + (1 - \lambda)$.

Using again Horodeckis theorem [389], one sees that this state violates the Bell–CHSH inequality iff

$$\lambda > \frac{1}{1 + 2c\sqrt{1 - c^2}(\sqrt{2} - 1)} \,. \tag{8.18}$$

The upper and lower bounds on λ defined by the conditions (8.16) and (8.18) are compatible provided $c\sqrt{1-c^2} \leq \sqrt{2}-1$. Hence there are values of λ and c such that the state $\rho(\lambda, c)$ is "local", in the sense that no Bell–CHSH inequality is violated, and such that the corresponding state filtered by the local environments, $\rho_{\text{filtered}}(\lambda, c)$, violates some Bell–CHSH inequality.

Above we have identified "local" $\approx$ "no violation of Bell–CHSH inequality". In this way the results appear somewhat more dramatic! But clearly this identification can and should be criticized. A state that is explicitly nonlocal after some local interactions does not deserve the qualification of local. An open question is whether the states $\rho(\alpha, \lambda)$ satisfying (8.16) and (8.18) admit a local hidden variable model reproducing all correlations. Since it does not violate any Bell–CHSH inequality, it is plausible that such a model exists. However, even if such a local hidden model exists, the state should be called nonlocal, because reproducing all correlations is not enough, as illustrated by the example presented above.

8.4 Quantum Privacy Amplification

C. Macchiavello

The purpose of entanglement purification schemes is to distill a subset of states with enhanced purity from a larger set of non-pure entangled states. The first scheme of this kind was proposed in [49] and it was shown that this allows faithful teleportation of quantum states via noisy channels. A subsequent more efficient purification scheme was presented in [47], named "quantum privacy amplification" (QPA) because it was designed for cryptographic purposes. Actually, it was proved that it leads to security of quantum cryptography over noisy channels (in the entanglement based scheme [46] also presented in Chap. 2). In this section we describe how the QPA scheme works.

Let us assume that pairs of qubits in maximally entangled states are generated and distributed to two users, Alice and Bob, via a noisy quantum channel. Because of the noise along the transmission channel the distributed pairs interacting with the environment get entangled with it, lose their purity and become mixed states. Acting on the received pairs, Alice and Bob want to enhance their purity. Let us assume that many pairs are distributed and the channel acts in the same way on all of them. We will describe the states of the pairs in the Bell basis representation

$$|\phi^\pm\rangle = \frac{1}{\sqrt{2}}(|00\rangle \pm |11\rangle) \tag{8.19}$$

$$|\psi^\pm\rangle = \frac{1}{\sqrt{2}}(|01\rangle \pm |10\rangle), \tag{8.20}$$

where $\{|0\rangle, |1\rangle\}$ represents a basis for each particle belonging to the pairs. We assume that each pair is initially generated in state $|\phi^+\rangle$ and denote by $\{a, b, c, d\}$ the diagonal components of the density operator ρ of the "noisy" pairs that Alice and Bob receive in the basis $\{|\phi^+\rangle, |\psi^-\rangle, |\psi^+\rangle, |\phi^-\rangle\}$. The first diagonal element $a = \langle\phi^+|\hat{\rho}|\phi^+\rangle$, which we call the 'fidelity', is the probability that the pair would pass a test for being in the state $|\phi^+\rangle$. The purpose of QPA is to drive the fidelity to 1 (which implies that the other three diagonal elements go to 0). We note that it is not necessary to specify the whole density matrix of the noisy pairs because in the QPA algorithm the off-diagonal elements do not contribute on average (i.e. averaging over the ensemble of distributed pairs at each step of the procedure) to the evolution of the diagonal ones and therefore they are not significant in the study of the efficiency of the scheme.

In the QPA procedure Alice and Bob divide the received noisy pairs into groups of two pairs each and perform the following operations on each group. Alice performs the unitary operation

$$U_A = \frac{1}{\sqrt{2}} \begin{pmatrix} 1 & -i \\ -i & 1 \end{pmatrix} \tag{8.21}$$

on each of her two qubits; Bob performs the inverse operation

$$U_B = \frac{1}{\sqrt{2}} \begin{pmatrix} 1 & i \\ i & 1 \end{pmatrix} \tag{8.22}$$

on his. Note that if the qubits are spin-$\frac{1}{2}$ particles and the computation basis is that of the eigenstates of the z components of their spins, then the two operations correspond respectively to rotations by $\pi/2$ and $-\pi/2$ about the x axis.

Then Alice and Bob each perform two instances of the quantum Controlled-NOT operation, described in Sect. 1.6,

$$\overset{\text{control}}{|x\rangle} \overset{\text{target}}{|y\rangle} \longrightarrow \overset{\text{control}}{|x\rangle} \overset{\text{target}}{|x \oplus y\rangle} \qquad (x, y) \in \{0, 1\}, \tag{8.23}$$

where one pair comprises the two control qubits and the other one the two target qubits, and $\oplus$ denotes addition modulo two (a useful table describing the action of this bilateral Controlled-NOT operation in the Bell basis can be found in [49]). Alice and Bob then measure the target qubits in the computational basis (e.g. they measure the z components of the targets' spins). If the outcomes coincide (e.g. both spins up or both spins down) they keep the control pair for the next round, and discard the target pair. If the outcomes do not coincide, both pairs are discarded. The basic operations of the QPA procedure are systematically reported in Fig. 8.5.

To see the effect of this procedure, let us assume that each pair is initially in the same state with diagonal elements $\{a, b, c, d\}$. In the case where the control qubits are retained, their density operator will have diagonal elements $\{A, B, C, D\}$ which depend, on average, *only* on the diagonal elements $\{a, b, c, d\}$:

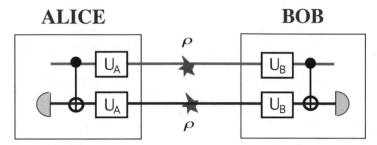

Fig. 8.5. Schematic representation of a QPA step. Alice performs operation U_A on her particles and a Controlled-NOT operation. Bob performs operation U_B and a Controlled-NOT operation. Alice and Bob then measure the target pair and keep the control pair for the next iteration if the results coincide.

$$A = \frac{a^2 + b^2}{p} \tag{8.24}$$

$$B = \frac{2cd}{p} \tag{8.25}$$

$$C = \frac{c^2 + d^2}{p} \tag{8.26}$$

$$D = \frac{2ab}{p}, \tag{8.27}$$

where $p = (a + b)^2 + (c + d)^2$ is the probability that Alice and Bob obtain coinciding outcomes in the measurements on the target pair. Equations (8.24–8.27) describe an elementary step of the QPA algorithm. The procedure is then iterated by applying again the above elementary step to the surviving pairs from the previous iteration. Note that if the average value of the fidelity is driven to 1 then each of the surviving pairs must individually approach the pure state $|\phi^+\rangle\langle\phi^+|$.

In passing we note that if the two input pairs are described by different density operators ρ and ρ' with diagonal elements $\{a, b, c, d\}$ and $\{a', b', c', d'\}$ respectively, then the retained control pairs will, on average, have diagonal elements given by:

$$A = \frac{aa' + bb'}{p} \tag{8.28}$$

$$B = \frac{c'd + cd'}{p} \tag{8.29}$$

$$C = \frac{cc' + dd'}{p} \tag{8.30}$$

$$D = \frac{ab' + a'b}{p}, \tag{8.31}$$

where $p = (a + b)(a' + b') + (c + d)(c' + d')$, which generalises (8.24–8.27).

Several interesting properties of the QPA map (8.24–8.27) can be easily verified. For example if at any stage the fidelity a exceeds $\frac{1}{2}$, then after one more iteration, it still exceeds $\frac{1}{2}$. Although a does not necessarily increase monotonically as a function of the number of iterations, our target point, $A = 1$, $B = C = D = 0$, is a fixed point of the map, and is the only fixed point in the region $a > \frac{1}{2}$. It can be easily seen analytically that it is a local attractor, namely that $A > a$ for a close to 1.

An analytical proof that it is also a global attractor in the region $a > \frac{1}{2}$ has been recently obtained [390]. The proof is based on showing that the function $f(a,b) = (2a - 1)(1 - 2b)$ is monotonic as a function of the number of iterations and asymptotically approaches unity. This implies that if we begin with pairs whose average fidelity exceeds $\frac{1}{2}$, but which are otherwise in an arbitrary state containing arbitrary correlations with the environment, then the states of pairs surviving after successive iterations always converge to the unit-fidelity pure state $|\phi^+\rangle$. It can also be shown [390] that the QPA procedure is always successful for any initial value $b > \frac{1}{2}$ (leading to the pure state $|\phi^+\rangle$) and for any initial value $c > \frac{1}{2}$ or $d > \frac{1}{2}$ (leading in this case to the pure state $|\psi^+\rangle$). In contrast, when none of the diagonal elements of the initial density operator exceeds $1/2$ the procedure does not work.

Notice also that the QPA is capable of purifying a collection of pairs in any state ρ whose average fidelity with respect to at least one maximally entangled state (i.e. a Bell state or a state obtained from a Bell state via local unitary operations) is greater than $\frac{1}{2}$. This is due to the fact that any state of that type can be transformed into $|\phi^+\rangle$ via local unitary operations [73]. If we denote by $\mathcal{B}$ the class of pure, maximally entangled states (the generalised Bell states) then the condition that the state ρ can be purified using the QPA is given by

$$\max_{\phi \in \mathcal{B}} \langle \phi | \rho | \phi \rangle > \frac{1}{2}. \tag{8.32}$$

The speed and the convergence behaviour of the procedure depends on the value of the diagonal elements of the initial density operator. As an example, in Fig. 8.6 we plot the fidelity as a function of the initial fidelity and the number of iterations, in cases where $a > \frac{1}{2}$ and $b = c = d$ initially.

The QPA procedure is rather wasteful in terms of discarded particles: at least one half of the particles (the ones used as targets) is lost at every iteration. Still the efficiency of this scheme compares favourably with the first proposed entanglement purification scheme described in [49] (about 1000 times more efficient for a close to 0.5, i.e. the number of surviving pairs is 1000 times bigger for a prescribed value of final fidelity).

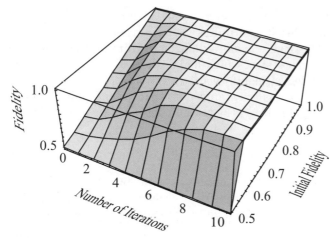

Fig. 8.6. Average fidelity as a function of the initial fidelity and the number of iterations for initial states with $b = c = d$.

8.5 Generalisation of Purification to Multi-Particle Entanglement

M. Murao, M.B. Plenio, S. Popescu, V. Vedral, P.L. Knight

In this section, direct purification protocols proposed in [391] are described for a wide range of mixed diagonal states of N particle entanglement. Although the procedures are not as general as those for two-particle purification of Bennett et al. [49] and Deutsch et al. [47], they are important for our understanding of multi-particle entanglement and have important practical applications. For many spin-1/2 particles, the maximally entangled states are

$$|\phi^{\pm}\rangle = \frac{1}{\sqrt{2}}\left(|00\cdots0\rangle \pm |11\cdots1\rangle\right), \tag{8.33}$$

together with those that are locally unitarily equivalent. The state for each particle is written in the $\{|0\rangle, |1\rangle\}$ basis; for three particles, these are called GHZ states [290].

Purification procedures [47, 49, 117, 382] "distill" from an ensemble of entangled *mixed* states a sub-ensemble of maximally entangled *pure* states by using local operations and classical communications. For two particles, the singlet state $|\psi^-\rangle = (|01\rangle - |10\rangle)/\sqrt{2}$, which is totally antisymmetric, is invariant under any bilateral rotation and plays an important role in these purification schemes.

However, for three or more particles, there is no maximally entangled state which is invariant under trilateral (multi-lateral) rotations (for a classification of entangled states based on invariance under local unitary transformations, see [392]). Local rotations map maximally entangled states into a superposition of maximally entangled states (unless we have trivial rotations by $n\pi$ where n is a integer). This makes it more difficult to transform an *arbitrary* state into one of the Werner states, which makes the search for general purification protocols much less straightforward.

Although there is no maximally entangled state invariant under random bilateral rotations for $N \geq 3$ (where N is the number of entangled particles), we will call the state

$$\rho_W = x \left| \phi^+ \right\rangle \left\langle \phi^+ \right| + \frac{1-x}{2^N} \mathbf{1} \tag{8.34}$$

a "Werner-type state" because of the similarity with the two particle case. Note that we write $\left| \phi^+ \right\rangle$ instead of $\left| \psi^- \right\rangle$ for convenience. The aim of purification is the distillation of a sub-ensemble in the state $\left| \phi^+ \right\rangle$. The fidelity,

$$f = \left\langle \phi^+ \right| \rho_W \left| \phi^+ \right\rangle \tag{8.35}$$

of the Werner-type state is $f = x + (1-x)/2^N$. These Werner-type states are important practically, because mixed entangled states are likely to appear when one has an ensemble of initially maximally entangled states (for example, $\left| \phi^+ \right\rangle$) of N particles, and then transmits the N particles to N different parties via noisy channels (Fig. 8.7).

Consider the effect of a noisy channel, whose action on each particle can be expressed by random rotations about random directions. Each noisy channel causes random rotations (around a random direction and by a random angle) with probability $1 - x$, but leaves the particle unaffected with probability x. The state after transmission through such a channel becomes the Werner-type state given by (8.34).

In the following, a protocol is presented (P1+P2 in Fig. 8.8), which can purify a Werner-type state, provided the fidelity of the initial mixed state is

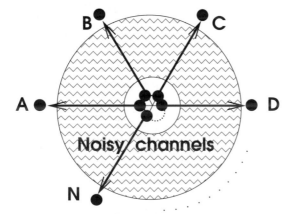

Fig. 8.7. Transmission of N particles in the maximally entangled state to different parties (A, B, C, D, ... N) via noisy channels.

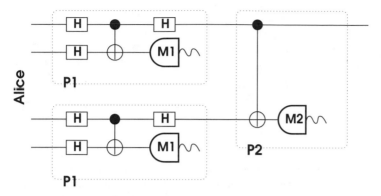

Fig. 8.8. Purification protocol P1+P2. H is a Hadamard transformation, M1 and M2 are local measurement and classical communication. This diagram shows four particles belonging to Alice. Bob and others apply exactly the same procedure.

higher than a certain critical value. The advantage of this protocol is that Werner-type states for *any number of particles* can be *directly* purified.

In the protocol P1+P2, each party (Alice, Bob et al.) perform iterations of the operations P1 followed by P2 on the particles belonging to them.

- The operation P1 consists of a local Hadamard transformation which maps $|0\rangle \to (|0\rangle + |1\rangle)/\sqrt{2}$, $|1\rangle \to (|0\rangle - |1\rangle)/\sqrt{2}$, a local CNOT (Controlled NOT) operation and a measurement M1, and another local Hadamard transformation. In M1, we keep the control qubits if an even number of target qubits are measured to be in the state $|1\rangle$, otherwise the control qubits are discarded. For example when purifying for three particles, we only keep $|000\rangle$, $|011\rangle$, $|101\rangle$, $|110\rangle$.
- The operation P2 consists of a local CNOT operation and a measurement M2 in which we keep the control qubits if all target bits are measured to be in the same state, otherwise the control qubits are discarded. For example, when purifying three particles, we only keep $|000\rangle$ and $|111\rangle$. In this operation, the diagonal and off-diagonal elements of the density matrix are independent of each other, so that the off-diagonal elements do not affect the purification.

The purification scheme, however, is not restricted to Werner-states. There are several types of states which can be purified by the protocol P1 or P2 alone. For example, if the initial mixed state does not have any weight of the pairing state (we call the state $|\phi^-\rangle$ the "pairing state" of $|\phi^+\rangle$) and weights of other states are equal (or even when some weights are zero), iterations of the operation P2 only are sufficient to purify the initial ensemble to the $|\phi^+\rangle$ state (see [391] for more in detail).

In the purification protocols discussed above, many-particle entangled states are *directly* purified. This is necessary for fundamental investigation of characteristic multi-particle entanglement. However, one could imagine

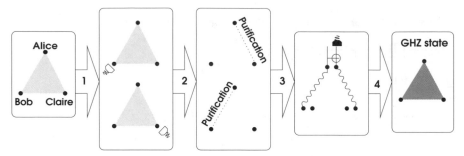

Fig. 8.9. Purification scheme via two-particle purification. The dotted lines represent partial entanglement and the wavy lines represent maximum entanglement. The first measurements (represented by white detector symbols) are in the state $|\chi^{\pm}\rangle = (|0\rangle \pm |1\rangle)/\sqrt{2}$ and the second measurement (represented by a black detector symbol) is, in the state $|0\rangle$ or $|0\rangle$.

schemes which purify many-particle entanglement via two-particle purification: one of these schemes for three particles (of Alice, Bob, and Claire) uses the fact that we know how to purify two particles. So this scheme converts three-particle states into two-particle states, then purifies these two-particle states, and finally re-converts them to three-particle entangled states. The algorithm for this protocol appears more complicated when described in words, so we provide a figure (Fig. 8.9) to help the reader visualise the entire scheme. This involves the following:

1. Divide the entire ensemble of the state for three particles into two equal sub-ensembles.
2. Bob then projects particles of one sub-ensemble onto

$$|\chi^{\pm}\rangle = (|0\rangle \pm |1\rangle)/\sqrt{2}$$

   and Claire performs the same projection using the other sub-ensemble. When Bob or Claire obtain a successful projection onto $|\chi^{-}\rangle$, then they instruct Alice to perform the σ_z operation on her particles. If they obtain a successful projection onto $|\chi^{+}\rangle$, then Alice is instructed to do nothing. The end product of these operations are two sub-ensembles of two-particle entangled states (one pair shared by Alice and Bob, and another pair shared by Alice and Claire).
3. Then Alice and Bob, and separately Alice and Claire perform the two-particle purification protocol in [47, 117] to each of the entangled sub-ensembles of two particles. This results in two maximally entangled ensembles of pairs of particles, shared between Alice and Bob, and between Alice and Claire.
4. Alice now wants to obtain a single GHZ state out of two maximally entangled pairs shared between herself and Bob and Claire. To do this, she chooses one entangled pair from each sub-ensemble and then performs

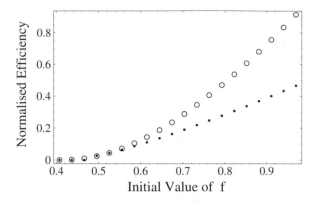

Fig. 8.10. Normalised efficiency of purification of the Werner-type states for three particles against the initial value of fidelity f. The circles are obtained numerically by the purification protocol P1+P2 with a choice of accuracy 10^{-7}. The dots are obtained by the purification scheme via two-particle purification with the same choice of accuracy.

a CNOT operation on her two particles. Then she projects the target particle onto $|0\rangle$ or $|1\rangle$. If Alice obtains a successful projection onto $|1\rangle$, she instructs Claire to perform the σ_x operation on her particle, and otherwise, do nothing. Then we obtain a sub-ensemble containing the maximally entangled GHZ state [300, 303].

We now analyse this indirect scheme and compare it to the direct purification schemes. Any efficient direct three-particle purification scheme should perform better than this indirect method via two particles. We note that we only obtain *one* maximally entangled state of three particles from *two* maximally entangled states of two particles by this scheme (Fig. 8.10, in detail see [391]). For purification of N-particle entangled states, we get one maximally entangled state from $N - 1$ maximally entangled states of two particles. In addition, the number of two-qubit CNOT operations, each of which is difficult in practice to carry out to high accuracy, is greater than in our direct scheme. These "inefficiencies" are the main practical disadvantage of the two-particle scheme.

For two-particle entanglement, an initial fidelity $f > 1/2$ is sufficient for successful purification [47] if we have no knowledge of the initial state. The situation is different if we possess additional information about the state, in which case any entangled state can be purified [50]. However, the sufficiency condition is not as simple for more than three particles. We have found several different criteria, depending on the type of mixed states.

For the Werner-type states of the the form $\rho_W = x\,|\phi^+\rangle\,\langle\phi^+| + \frac{1-x}{2^N}\mathbf{1}$, and purification by the protocol P1+P2, we obtain numerically the results shown in Table 8.1.

Table 8.1. A: Observed fidelity limit of initial states to be purified for N particles of the Werner-type states by the *direct* protocol P1+P2, B: Theoretical fidelity limit of the *indirect* purification scheme via two-particle purification, and C: the theoretical minimum sufficient fidelity for purification.

N	A	B	C
2	$f \geq 0.5395$	$f > 1/2 = 0.5$	$f > 1/2$
3	$f \geq 0.4073$	$f > 5/12 \approx 0.4167$	unknown
4	$f \geq 0.313$	$f > 3/8 = 0.375$	unknown
5	$f \geq 0.245$	$f > 17/48 \approx 0.3542$	unknown
6	$f \geq 0.20$	$f > 11/32 \approx 0.3438$	unknown

The theoretical fidelity limit for the Werner-type states ρ_W of the purification scheme via two-particle purification is determined by the condition that the fidelity f_r of the reduced two-particle states should satisfy $f_r > 1/2$. For example, for three particles, the Werner state having initial fidelity $f = x + (1-x)/8$ is reduced to a two-particle state after the measurement of Bob or Claire as follows

$$\rho_r = x \left| \phi^+ \right\rangle \left\langle \phi^+ \right| + \frac{1-x}{4} \mathbf{1}. \tag{8.36}$$

The fidelity of the reduced two-particle state is now $f_r = (1 + 6f)/7$. For four particles, we have $f_r = (1 + 4f)/5$, for five particles, $f_r = (7 + 24f)/31$, for six particles, $f_r = (5 + 16f)/21$ and so on. We see from Table 8.1 that the protocol P1+P2 is not optimal for two particles. So it may not be optimal for $N > 2$. However, for more than three particles, our observed fidelity limit is lower than that obtained by the purification scheme via two-particle purification.

For states having no weight of $\left| \phi^- \right\rangle \left\langle \phi^- \right|$ and equal weight of all other states except $\left| \phi^+ \right\rangle \left\langle \phi^+ \right|$, the fidelity limit of purification by the protocol P2 is $f > 2^{-(N-1)}$. The fidelity limit obtained by the purification scheme via two-particle purification is $2/5 = 0.4$ for the three-particle case, $65/23 \approx 0.35846$ for the four-particle case, $125/377 \approx 0.328912$ for five-particle case and so on, i.e. worse than that in our protocols.

As we have seen, the fidelity limit of purifiable initial states depends on the distribution of the weight of other diagonal states. This is a condition of a different character from the case of two particles [47]. For two particles, the distribution of weights of other diagonal elements was basically irrelevant for purification, since any distribution of weights of the other diagonal can be transformed into an even distribution by local random rotations of both particles, without changing the amount of entanglement. This suggests that there may be additional structure for many-particle entangled mixed states, which does not exist for two-particle mixed states.

8.6 Quantum Networks II:
Communication over Noisy Channels

H.-J Briegel, W. Dür, S.J. van Enk, J.I. Cirac, P. Zoller

We show how to create maximally entangled EPR pairs between spatially distant atoms, each of them inside a high-Q optical cavity, by sending photons through a general, noisy channel, such as a standard optical fibre. An error correction scheme that uses few auxiliary atoms in each cavity effectively eliminates photon absorption and other transmission errors. For communication over distances much longer than the absorption length or the coherence length of the channel, we describe a novel nested purification protocol, which realises the analogue of a repeater in classical communication.

8.6.1 Introduction

This section continues and generalises the discussion of Sect. 6.2. There, a realisation of a quantum network [278] was proposed, using long-lived states of atoms as the physical basis for storing qubits, and photons as a means for transferring these qubits from one atom to another. To allow for a controlled transfer of the qubit, the atoms are embedded in high finesse optical cavities which are connected by an optical fibre, as shown in Fig. 6.1.

The compound cavity–fibre system, together with the laser pulses constitutes what we abstractly call a *noisy quantum channel*, see Fig. 8.11. When the photons are sent along optical fibres, photon absorption will be a dominant transfer error. Losses will also occur by incoherent scattering on the surface of the cavity mirrors and at the coupling segments between the cavities and the fibre. Another typical transfer error will be caused by imperfectly designed laser pulses for the Raman transition, and an example for a local gate error is spontaneous emission in one of the atoms during the gate operation.

This section shows how high fidelity communication is possible even in the presence of errors due to dissipation and noise, and how one can combat

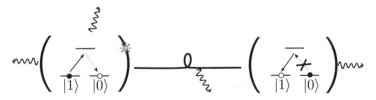

Fig. 8.11. Noisy photon channel: Typical transfer errors include photon absorption, incoherent scattering, and imperfect Raman transitions.

the effects of decoherence. First, we will briefly summarise the arguments of Sect. 6.2, which gives us the opportunity to introduce a notation that is adapted to the language of error correction and quantum information theory. In Sect. 8.6.3 and 8.6.4 we then concentrate on transmission errors that occur during the photon transfer and show how they can be detected and corrected [393]–[395]. For this discussion we assume that local gate operations and measurements can be performed without errors. In Sect. 8.7, we relax this assumption and allow all operations, both local and in the transmission, to be *imperfect*. This reflects the general situation when we have used all means of error correction but cannot exclude the possibility that some errors have escaped our detection and have thus not been corrected, or that the operations and measurements we use are, in some sense, imprecise. In this general context, we study the important problem of 'long-distance' communication and the use of quantum repeaters [381, 387].

From a formal perspective it is advantageous to rephrase quantum communication as the problem of creating distant quantum correlations over a channel, instead of directly propagating an unknown qubit through the channel. Once an EPR pair is created, it *can* be employed for teleportation [74], that is real transmission of information, but also for other purposes such as secret key distribution for quantum cryptography [46]. It is worth pointing out that this approach is different from quantum computation in the sense that, until the full EPR is established, there is no genuine information being processed. All one does is to build up nonlocal quantum correlations which may later be used for transmission purposes. In fact, at that later time, the connecting channel need not even exist any more.

The subject of this chapter is therefore how to create an EPR pair between two parties A and B with the aid of a noisy quantum channel of arbitrary length l that connects A and B.

8.6.2 Ideal Communication

Ideally, the scheme in Sect. 6.2 realises the following transmission

$$\left[\alpha|0\rangle_A + \beta|1\rangle_A\right]|0\rangle_B \longrightarrow |0\rangle_A\left[\alpha|0\rangle_B + \beta|1\rangle_B\right], \qquad (8.37)$$

where an unknown superposition of internal states $|0\rangle = |e\rangle$ and $|1\rangle = |g\rangle$ in atom A in the first cavity is transferred to atom B in the second cavity, see again Fig. 8.12. The cavities may be part of a larger network, so we often refer to them as node A and node B, respectively. The selected internal states $|0\rangle$ and $|1\rangle$ of the atoms define, in the language of quantum information theory, the 'computational basis' for the qubit.

It is important to realise that the atom A may be entangled to other atoms in the same cavity or at other nodes of the network. In that situation, the coefficients α and β in (8.37) are no longer complex numbers but denote unnormalised states of the other atoms. Thus the transmission (8.37) can be

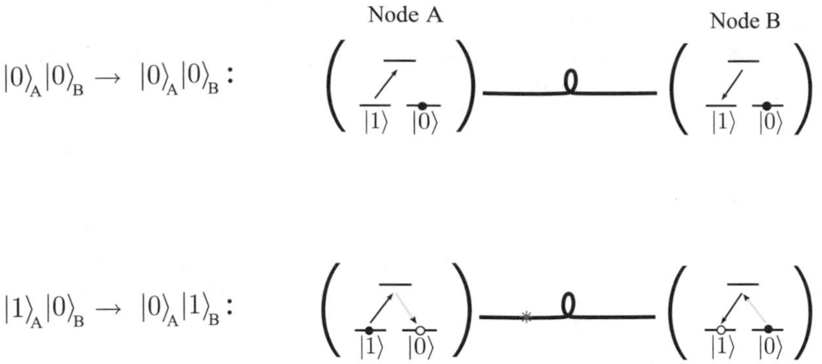

Node A   Node B

$$|0\rangle_A |0\rangle_B \;\rightarrow\; |0\rangle_A |0\rangle_B :$$

$$|1\rangle_A |0\rangle_B \;\rightarrow\; |0\rangle_A |1\rangle_B :$$

Fig. 8.12. Swapping the state of an atom from node A to node B. When the atom at A is in state $|1\rangle_A$, a sequence of Raman transitions as described in Sect. 6.2 can be used to swap its state onto the atom located at node B via photonic transfer. When atom A is in state $|0\rangle_A$, the Raman pulse does not change the state. A superposition of states $|0\rangle_A$ and $|1\rangle_A$ is thereby transferred to node B according to (8.38).

used to transfer single atomic states, but also to transfer *entanglement*. For instance, starting from single particle states, an EPR pair can be created by a two-step process

$$\big[\alpha|0\rangle_A + \beta|1\rangle_A\big]|0\rangle_{A_2}|0\rangle_B \;\longrightarrow\; \big[\alpha|0\rangle_{A_2}|0\rangle_A + \beta|1\rangle_{A_2}|1\rangle_A\big]|0\rangle_B$$
$$\longrightarrow\; |0\rangle_{A_2}\big[\alpha|0\rangle_A|0\rangle_B + \beta|1\rangle_A|1\rangle_B\big]. \qquad (8.38)$$

Here, the first arrow refers to a *local* CNOT operation between two atoms A and A_2 in the first cavity. The second arrow transfers the state of A_2 to B, thereby transferring the entanglement between the atoms A and A_2 to an entanglement between atoms A and B. At the end of this composite transformation, the state of the auxiliary atom A_2 is the same as initially and *factors out*. For $\alpha = \beta$, an ideal EPR pair is created.

8.6.3 Correction of Transfer Errors:
The Photonic Channel

In a realistic model, we have to consider the possibility that the transfer of the atomic state from cavity A to B is imperfect. There is a certain probability that the atom in B will not be excited, even though A was excited. This is due to the interaction of the compound atom–cavity–fibre system with the environment which, even if small, in principle always exists. This results in an entanglement of the atomic states in (8.37) with the environment, i.e. the cavity walls, the fibre, and the radiation field of the free space.

In the following, we assume that photons can be absorbed but not created by the channel. This is a very good approximation for optical photons, where the mean thermal number of photons in the cavities and the fibre is exceedingly small. In this situation, the most general expression for an imperfect transfer operation is of the form

$$|0\rangle_A|0\rangle_B|E\rangle \longrightarrow |0\rangle_A|0\rangle_B|E_0\rangle$$
$$|1\rangle_A|0\rangle_B|E\rangle \longrightarrow |0\rangle_A|1\rangle_B|E_1\rangle + |0\rangle_A|0\rangle_B|E_a\rangle, \qquad (8.39)$$

where $|E\rangle, |E_0\rangle, \dots$ denote unnormalised states of the environment. It is expedient to write $|E_0\rangle = \mathcal{T}_0|E\rangle$, $|E_1\rangle = \mathcal{T}_1|E\rangle$, $|E_a\rangle = \mathcal{T}_a|E\rangle$, thereby introducing operators that entangle the system with the environment. With this notation, (8.39) can be expressed in the compact form[8]

$$|0\rangle_A|0\rangle_B \longrightarrow |0\rangle_A|0\rangle_B\mathcal{T}_0$$
$$|1\rangle_A|0\rangle_B \longrightarrow |0\rangle_A|1\rangle_B\mathcal{T}_1 + |0\rangle_A|0\rangle_B\mathcal{T}_a, \qquad (8.40)$$

which defines the photonic channel [394].

The optical cavities together with the fibre form a compound optical system with a certain resonant structure that defines its spectrum of quasi modes, its relaxation constants, etc. In the special case when only photon absorption plays a role, the operators in (8.40) have a simple form. For optical frequencies, the state of the environment can be very well approximated by the vacuum state, so one can write $\mathcal{T}_0 = 1$, $\mathcal{T}_1 = \alpha(\tau) \sim e^{-\kappa\tau}$, $\mathcal{T}_a = \sum_j \beta_j(\tau)b_j^\dagger$, with $\sum_j |\beta_j(\tau)|^2 \sim 1 - e^{-2\kappa\tau}$ where κ is the damping rate of the total (atom–)cavity–fibre system, and τ is the transfer time. The operators $b_j^\dagger$, b_j are amplitude operators of the j th oscillator mode of the environment.

More generally, the operators $\mathcal{T}_{0,1,a}$ in (8.40) may describe spontaneous emission processes, photon absorption, as well as transitions to and repumping from other internal states of the atoms. Thus, all complicated physics is hidden in the three operators. In this general (non-stationary) situation, the time dependence of the environmental terms has to be taken into account. The operators $\mathcal{T}_{0,1,a}$ then depend on the initial time when the transfer starts. As a consequence, when iterating the channel (8.40), the temporal ordering of the operators becomes important, e.g. $\mathcal{T}_1(t_1)\mathcal{T}_0(t_0) \neq \mathcal{T}_0(t_1)\mathcal{T}_1(t_0)$.

When using (8.40) to create an EPR pair as in (8.38), we obtain

$$[\alpha|0\rangle_A + \beta|1\rangle_A]|0\rangle_B \longrightarrow [\alpha|0\rangle_A|0\rangle_B\mathcal{T}_0 + \beta|1\rangle_A|1\rangle_B\mathcal{T}_1]$$
$$+\beta|1\rangle_A|0\rangle_B\mathcal{T}_a. \qquad (8.41)$$

For $\alpha = \beta$, this expression can be written in the form[9]

---

[8] In expressions of this type, it is understood that both the left- and the right-hand sides are applied to a given state of the environment. Using this compact notation keeps the expressions much more transparent when twofold or more complex applications of the channel are studied.

[9] Throughout this section, normalisation factors are omitted unless they are needed.

$$|\Phi_{AB}^+\rangle\left[\mathcal{T}_0 + \mathcal{T}_1\right] + |\Phi_{AB}^-\rangle\left[\mathcal{T}_0 - \mathcal{T}_1\right] + \left(|\Psi_{AB}^+\rangle + |\Psi_{AB}^-\rangle\right)\mathcal{T}_a \,, \tag{8.42}$$

where we use the Bell basis

$$|\Phi_{AB}^\pm\rangle = \frac{1}{\sqrt{2}}\left(|0\rangle_A|0\rangle_B \pm |1\rangle_A|1\rangle_B\right), \quad |\Psi_{AB}^\pm\rangle = \frac{1}{\sqrt{2}}\left(|0\rangle_A|1\rangle_B \pm |1\rangle_A|0\rangle_B\right).$$

The fidelity of the resulting pair (8.42) can be defined by its overlap with the ideal result $|\Phi_{AB}^+\rangle$. This overlap is given by the norm

$$F = \left\|\frac{[\mathcal{T}_0 + \mathcal{T}_1]|E\rangle}{2}\right\|^2 \sim \left|\frac{1 + e^{-\kappa\tau}}{2}\right|^2. \tag{8.43}$$

The estimate of F in the second term demonstrates how the coupling of the modes of the cavity–fibre system to the environment reduces the attainable fidelity of the EPR pair. In particular, F decreases exponentially with the transfer time and the corresponding length of the fibre.

In order to create an EPR pair over a distance comparable to or larger than the absorption length of the photonic channel, we need to find a method to *detect and correct* a photon loss that may occur during the transfer. Loosely speaking, we are seeking to eliminate the absorption term $\mathcal{T}_a$ in (8.42), and to minimise the other term $\mathcal{T}_0 - \mathcal{T}_1$.

In the following, we outline a method that uses either one or two auxiliary atoms in each cavity. This outline just summarises the essential steps. For details, the reader should consult Refs. [393]–[395].

8.6.4 Purification with Finite Means

The main idea is to entangle the atom in the first cavity with auxiliary (backup) atoms, before transmitting the information. This is reminiscent of a redundant coding scheme, with the fundamental difference that our scheme allows one to correct errors to *all orders* in the photo-absorption probability. By measuring a certain joint state of two atoms in the receiver cavity, one is able to *detect* a photon loss while *maintaining* the initial coherence of the atomic state that was sent. Therefore, the transmission can be repeated as often as necessary until no error is detected.

In detail, this requires three steps:
(1) *Encoding* of the atomic state into a three-particle entangled state

$$\alpha|0\rangle_A + \beta|1\rangle_A \longrightarrow \alpha\left[|0\rangle_A|0\rangle_{A_2}|0\rangle_{A_3} + |1\rangle_A|1\rangle_{A_2}|1\rangle_{A_3}\right]$$
$$+\beta\left[|0\rangle_A|0\rangle_{A_2}|1\rangle_{A_3} + |1\rangle_A|1\rangle_{A_2}|0\rangle_{A_3}\right]. \tag{8.44}$$

This can be realised by applying two CNOT operations between A_3 and A, and A and A_2, respectively.
(2) *Transmission* of a photon *twice* by using (8.40) between atom A_2 and B_2 and then between A_2 and B, applying a local flip operation on A in between.

The result of this operation is a multi-particle entangled state [395] whose explicit form will not be given here.

(3) *Measuring* the states of certain backup atoms in both cavities. Combined with appropriate local unitary transformations, one obtains one of two results.

The effect of this procedure is summarised in the following *absorption-free* (i.e. correcting) channel

$$\left[\alpha|0\rangle_A + \beta|1\rangle_A\right]|0\rangle_B \longrightarrow \alpha|0\rangle_A|0\rangle_B\mathcal{S}_0 + \beta|1\rangle_A|1\rangle_B\mathcal{S}_1$$

$$\underset{\text{error}}{\searrow} \quad \left[\alpha|0\rangle_A + \beta|1\rangle_A\right]|0\rangle_B\mathcal{S}_a . \tag{8.45}$$

Owing to the twofold transmission process, the operators $\mathcal{S}$ appearing in (8.45) are products of the $\mathcal{T}$ operators, e.g. $\mathcal{S}_0 = \mathcal{T}_0\mathcal{T}_1$, $\mathcal{S}_1 = \mathcal{T}_1\mathcal{T}_0$, or in different order. The important feature to notice is that, depending on the results of the measurement in step (3), two outcomes are possible: If an error is detected, the state is projected onto the second line of (8.45) and the transmission can be repeated; if no error is detected, the state is projected onto the first line of (8.45), which completes the channel.

By using (8.45) instead of (8.40) one obtains

$$\left[|0\rangle_A + |1\rangle_A\right]|0\rangle_B \longrightarrow |0\rangle_A|0\rangle_B\mathcal{S}_0 + |1\rangle_A|1\rangle_B\mathcal{S}_1$$

$$= |\Phi^+_{AB}\rangle\frac{1}{2}\left[\mathcal{S}_0 + \mathcal{S}_1\right] + |\Phi^-_{AB}\rangle\frac{1}{2}\left[\mathcal{S}_0 - \mathcal{S}_1\right] . \tag{8.46}$$

For the simple example considered after (8.40), with $\mathcal{T}_0 = 1$ and $\mathcal{T}_1 = e^{-\kappa\tau}$, we have $\mathcal{S}_0 = e^{-\kappa\tau}$ and $\mathcal{S}_1 = e^{-\kappa\tau}$, thus the second term in (8.46) vanishes. In this situation, an ideal EPR pair is established after a *single* use of the channel (8.45). This corresponds to an average number of phototransmissions of $e^{2\kappa\tau}$.

More generally, a similar result is obtained when the state of the environment does not depend on the temporal ordering of the operators $\mathcal{T}_0$ and $\mathcal{T}_1$. Such a *stationary environment* is defined by $\mathcal{T}_1(t_1)\mathcal{T}_0(t_0)|E\rangle = \mathcal{T}_0(t_1)\mathcal{T}_1(t_0)|E\rangle$, i.e. $\mathcal{S}_0|E\rangle = \mathcal{S}_1|E\rangle$. For any system with a stationary environment, an ideal EPR pair is created by a single application of (8.45).

For the discussion of the general, non-stationary case, let us first rewrite the result (8.46) in the form

$$|\Psi^{(1)}\rangle = |\Phi^+_{AB}\rangle|E^{(1)}_+\rangle + |\Phi^-_{AB}\rangle|E^{(1)}_-\rangle , \tag{8.47}$$

where $|E^{(1)}_\pm\rangle = \frac{1}{2}(\mathcal{S}_0 \pm \mathcal{S}_1)|E\rangle$. The norm (square) of the environment $|E^{(1)}_+\rangle$ determines the fidelity of the pair.

At this point, the key advantage of the absorption-free channel (AFC) comes into play, namely that it corrects errors in the transmission process while maintaining the coherence and possible entanglement of the state it is applied to. This allows an iterative purification protocol [394]. At each purification step, the pair is temporarily entangled with two auxiliary atoms,

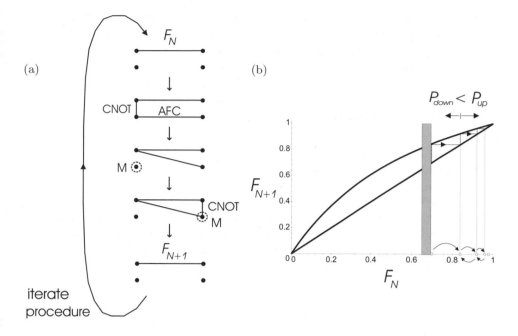

Fig. 8.13. Purification of an EPR pair with finite means. (**a**) Iterative purification protocol. At each purification step, an EPR pair of the form (8.48) with fidelity F_N is temporarily entangled with two auxiliary atoms. This involves two CNOT operations, the absorption-free channel AFC, and measurements M. Furthermore, there are some Hadamard transformations that are not shown in the figure. The value of the new fidelity F_{N+1} depends on the result of the measurements M, as explained in (b). Note that this scheme operates on the *same set of atoms* at each step, thereby realising a 'self-purification process'. (**b**) One-sided random-walk process for fidelity. After each iteration step in (a), the fidelity F_N increases (decreases) with a certain probability P_{up} (P_{down}) that depends on N. If F_N happens to drop below the initial value F_0, we reset the pair to this value by a single use of the AFC, as in (8.46). This is equivalent to a one-sided random walk process with reflections at a lower barrier at F_0, as indicated in the figure. On average, the fidelity thereby approaches unity exponentially fast, $F_N \sim 1 - e^{-\text{const.} \times N}$.

one at each node, using both local CNOT operations and the AFC. In some sense, this creates an auxiliary EPR pair that is used to purify (8.47). The detailed protocol is shown systematically in Fig. 8.13a.

This protocol transforms (8.47) into a sequence of states of the form

$$|\Psi^{(N)}\rangle = |\Phi_{AB}^+\rangle|E_+^{(N)}\rangle + |\Phi_{AB}^-\rangle|E_-^{(N)}\rangle , \tag{8.48}$$

where either

$$|E_\pm^{(N)}\rangle = \frac{1}{2}(\mathcal{S}_0 \pm \mathcal{S}_1)|E_\pm^{(N-1)}\rangle , \text{ or } |E_\pm^{(N)}\rangle = \frac{1}{2}(\mathcal{S}_0 \mp \mathcal{S}_1)|E_\pm^{(N-1)}\rangle ,$$

depending on the result of the measurement. In the first case, which happens with probability $P_{up} = P_{up}^{(N)}$, the fidelity of the pair increases. In the second case, which happens with $P_{down} = 1 - P_{up}$, the fidelity decreases. One can show that this creates a stochastic process corresponding to a one-sided random-walk process as depicted in Fig. 8.13b. On average, the fidelity $F_N = \langle E_+^{(N)} | E_+^{(N)} \rangle$ thereby converges towards unity exponentially fast with the number of purification steps.

8.7 Quantum Repeaters

With the methods discussed in the previous sections, it is possible to create an EPR pair of high fidelity by sending single photons through a dissipative and noisy channel that connects the atoms. There is, however, a limitation to the method when the transmission time through the channel becomes much larger than its relaxation time, i.e. if $\kappa\tau \gg 1$. As the absorption probability grows exponentially with τ, so will the required number of repetitions for one successful transmission.

Absorption losses are well-known in problems of electric signal transmission through classical channels where, at regularly spaced intervals, repeaters are put in the channel. In classical (digital) communication technique such repeaters are used to both amplify and to restore the signal. The distance between the repeaters is then determined by the damping rate of the fibre and the bit rate of the transmission (dispersion effects).

For quantum communication, we cannot use amplifiers. To build up EPR correlations, single qubits (photons) need to be transmitted and these cannot be amplified [88, 396] without destroying the quantum correlations. All we can do here is to detect whether a photon has been absorbed and, whenever that is the case, repeat the transmission.

For the following discussion, let us assume that the dominant transmission error is given by photon absorption, and that the environment is stationary. This corresponds to a photonic channel (8.40) with $\mathcal{T}_0 = 1$ and $\mathcal{T}_1 = e^{-\kappa\tau} = e^{-l/2l_0}$ where $l_0 = c/2\kappa$ defines the half length of the fibre. The probability for a successful transmission of a qubit from A to B, as indicated in Fig. 8.14(top), is then $p(l) = e^{-l/l_0}$ where l is the length of the fibre. Correspondingly, the average number of required repetitions is

$$n(l) = \frac{1}{p(l)} = e^{l/l_0} . \tag{8.49}$$

It is clear that this leads to unrealisticly high numbers for any experiment, if the fibre is much longer than a few half lengths l_0.

Guided by the idea of repeaters in classical communication, we divide the channel into a certain number N of segments, with connection points (nodes) in between, at which it is measured whether a transmission error

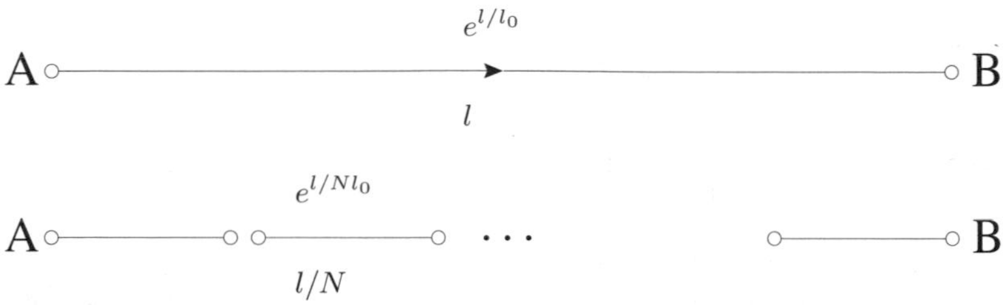

Fig. 8.14. Simple and compound fibre for transmission of single qubits from A to B. As with classical repeaters, to transmit single qubits over long distances, we divide the fibre (channel) into several segments, at the end of which transmission errors are measured.

has occurred (see Fig. 8.14(bottom)). This can be done e.g. with the method explained in Sect. 5.2 by using a few extra ions in a cavity. If an absorption error is detected, the transmission across that segment is repeated. Then a photon is sent through the subsequent segment, and so on. Thereby, ideally, the state of the atom at A can be swapped from one connection point to the next, until one reaches atom B. The average total number of repetitions on each segment is $n(l/N) = e^{l/l_0 N}$. Correspondingly, the total number of transmissions required for successfully sending the qubit across the *compound fibre* is

$$n_{\text{com}} = \frac{N}{p(l/N)} = N e^{l/N l_0} .$$ (8.50)

This is to be compared with (8.49). The compound fibre is thus preferable to the simple fibre if

$$N e^{l/N l_0} < e^{l/l_0} .$$ (8.51)

The optimum number of segments is given by the value of N that minimises the left-hand side of above equation, which is $N_{\text{min}} = l/l_0$. The minimum number of transmissions along the compound fibre is thus given by (8.50) with $N = N_{\text{min}}$, that is

$$n_{\text{min}} = N_{\text{min}} e^{l/N_{\text{min}} l_0} = l/l_0 e^1 .$$ (8.52)

This situation is realised when the connection points are placed along the fibre with a spacing corresponding to the half length l_0.

Up to this point we have assumed that local operations can be performed without errors. There are, in fact, schemes [397] which allow error detection and correction for local 2-bit operations. However, even with these methods, there is the possibility of errors that escape detection, since the detection mechanism itself uses 1-bit operations and measurements which may not be perfect. This has two effects: (i) the local operations at every checkpoint in

A C_1 C_2 C_{N-1} B

Fig. 8.15. Connection of a sequence of N EPR pairs, see text.

Fig. 8.14(bottom) will introduce some noise into the transmission process; (ii) the fidelity of transmission across every segment is already limited to some maximum value $F_{\max}$. This can be seen from the fact that both the absorption free channel (8.45) and the purification protocol of Fig. 8.13a involve local operations that introduce some noise and thereby limit the maximum attainable fidelity. Both effects accumulate (exponentially) with the number of checkpoints and eventually spoil the fidelity of the transmission completely.

To make this point clearer, we consider the following equivalent problem. We first create N elementary EPR pairs of fidelity $F_1 < F_{\max}$ between the nodes $A \& C_1$, $C_1 \& C_2$, ... $C_{N-1} \& B$, as in Fig. 8.15. We then connect these pairs by making Bell measurements at the nodes C_i and classically communicating the results between the nodes as in the schemes for teleportation [74] and entanglement swapping [74, 398]. This will result in a single EPR pair shared between the endpoints A and B in Fig. 8.15. Unfortunately, with every connection the fidelity of the resulting pair will decrease, since the connection process involves imperfect operations that introduce noise. Furthermore, even for perfect connections, the fidelity decreases: Connecting e.g. two Werner states of fidelity F_1 by a Bell measurement, one obtains a new Werner state of fidelity

$$F_2 = \frac{1}{4}\left\{1 + 3\left(\frac{4F-1}{3}\right)^2\right\}, \tag{8.53}$$

so that $F_2 \sim F_1^2$ for $F_1 \sim 1$. Both effects accumulate with every connection and lead to an exponential decrease of the fidelity F_N with N of the final pair shared between $A \& B$. Eventually, the value of F_N drops below a certain threshold value $F_{\min} \geq 1/2$ below which it cannot be purified any more. That means, it will not be possible to increase the fidelity by purification [47, 49].

By dividing the channel into shorter segments, it seems, we have thus eliminated the effect of an exponentially increasing number of required transmissions, at the cost of introducing an exponentially decreasing fidelity!

A possibility to circumvent this limitation is to connect a smaller number $L \ll N$ of pairs so that $F_L > F_{\min}$ and purification becomes possible. The idea is to connect the resulting pairs, purify again, and continue in the same vein. The way in which such alternating sequences of connections and purifications is done has to be properly designed so that the number of required resources does not grow exponentially with N and thus with l.

In the remainder of this section we describe a *nested purification protocol* [381] which consists of connecting and purifying the pairs simultaneously in

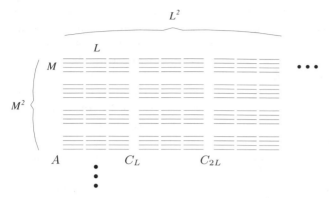

Fig. 8.16. Nested purification with an array of elementary EPR pairs.

the following sense (see Fig. 8.16). For simplicity, assume that $N = L^n$ for some integer n. On the first level, we simultaneously connect the pairs (initial fidelity F_1) at all the connection points except at $C_L, C_{2L}, \ldots, C_{N-L}$. As a result, we have N/L pairs of length L (and fidelity F_L) between A & C_L, C_L & C_{2L} and so on. To purify these pairs, we need a certain number M of copies that we construct in parallel fashion. For keeping track of the resources, it is convenient to arrange them in form of an array of elementary pairs as is done in Fig. 8.16 for $L = 3$ and $M = 4$. We then use these copies on the segments A & C_L, C_L & C_{2L} etc., to purify and (re-)obtain one pair of fidelity F_1 on each segment. This last condition determines the (average) number of copies M that we need, which will depend on the initial fidelity, the degradation of the fidelity under connections, and the efficiency of the purification protocol. The total number of elementary pairs we used up to this point is LM. [In Fig. 8.16, this means that each group of $L \times M = 3 \times 4$ pairs has now been replaced by one single pair of the initial fidelity.] On the second level, we connect L of these larger pairs at every connection point C_{kL} ($k = 1, 2 \ldots$) except at $C_{L^2}, C_{2L^2}, \ldots, C_{N-L^2}$. As a result, we have N/L^2 pairs of length L^2 between A & C_{L^2}, C_{L^2} & C_{2L^2}, and so on of fidelity F_L. Again, we need M parallel copies of these long pairs to repurify up to a fidelity $\geq F_1$. The total number of elementary pairs involved up to this point is $(LM)^2$. [Now, the whole array of $3^2 \times 4^2$ pairs in Fig. 8.16 has been replaced by a single pair of fidelity F_1.] We iterate the procedure to higher and higher levels, until we reach the n-th level. As a result, we have obtained a final pair between A & B of length N and fidelity F_1. In this way, the total number R of elementary pairs will be $(LM)^n$, where M^n alone gives the number of required 'parallel channels' in Fig. 8.16. We can re-express this result in the form

$$R = N^{\log_L M + 1},\tag{8.54}$$

which shows that the resources grow *polynomially* with the distance N.

The idea of nested purification is related to the idea of concatenated coding [399] which has been used in the context of fault-tolerant quantum computing [400]. That scheme allows one, in principle, to transmit a qubit over arbitrarily long distances with a polynomial overhead in the resources. It requires one, however, to encode a single qubit into an entangled state of a large number of qubits which is sent through the channel, and to operate on this code repeatedly during the transmission process. In contrast, in the nested purification scheme, we are not sending an arbitrary qubit through the channel, but creating EPR correlations across the whole channel simultaneously. While creating the correlations, there is no real quantum information being processed (although the EPR pair may subsequently be used for communication via teleportation). As a result, we obtain fidelity requirements on the local operations which are in the few-percent region. In the case of fault-tolerant quantum computing, this number is of the order of 10^{-5} [399].

The array in Fig. 8.16 represents an ensemble of identical (elementary) EPR pairs with which the purification is performed. Alternatively, one can do the purification with the aid of a single auxiliary pair at each level (see [381, 387]). In a sense, the vertical dimension of the diagram in Fig. 8.16 is thereby translated into a temporal axis (number of repetitions). In this case, it is the total *time* needed to create the EPR pair between A and B that scales polynomially in (8.54), whereas the number of backup atoms needed at each connection point grows only logarithmically with $N = l/l_0$. The resulting scheme of a quantum repeater is illustrated schematically in Fig. 8.17. Every connection point in the channel consists of a simple "quantum processor" that stores a small number of atoms on which it performs the gate operations and measurements required for purification. Some of the atoms are used to repeatedly build up EPR pairs between neighbouring connection

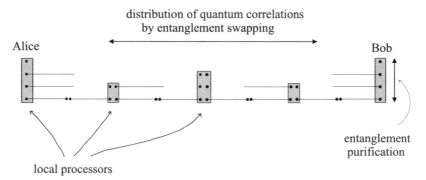

Fig. 8.17. Scheme for the quantum repeater. At every connection point, a small "quantum processor" (consisting of a few qubits only) is used to execute the protocols of entanglement purification and entanglement swapping. The distribution of high-fidelity entanglement across the compound channel is then coordinated by a global protocol called nested entanglement purification [381].

points (here $L=2$), for example by using the methods described in Sect. 8.6. These repeatedly created pairs are used for entanglement purification. More distant pairs are then created by entanglement swapping. To (re-)purify these more distant pairs, one auxiliary atom is needed for storage at each level. The total number that each processor has to store, thus grows only logarithmically with l [381, 387].

In contrast to the case in classical communication, the quantum repeater is not a local amplifier, but it involves both the local checkpoints and global (nested) purification protocol. We have just reported here that our scheme tolerates errors for local operations and measurements that are in the percent region. For more details, the reader should consult Refs. [381, 387].

References

1. R.P. Feynman, R.B. Leighton, and M. Sands, *The Feynman Lectures of Physics, Vol. III, Quantum Mechanics*, Addison-Wesley, Reading (1965).
2. G.I. Taylor, Proc. Camb. Phil. Soc. **15**, 114 (1909).
3. G. Möllenstedt and C. Jönsson, Z. Phys. **155**, 472 (1959); A. Tonomura, J. Endo, T. Matsuda, and T. Kawasaki, Am. J. Phys. **57**, 117 (1989).
4. A. Zeilinger, R. Gähler, C.G. Shull, W. Treimer, and W. Mampe, Rev. Mod. Phys. **60**, 1067 (1988).
5. O. Carnal and J. Mlynek, Phys. Rev. Lett. **66**, 2689 (1991).
6. S.L. Braunstein, A. Mann, and M. Revzen, Phys. Rev. Lett. **68**, 3259 (1992).
7. A. Zeilinger, Am. J. Phys. **49**, 882 (1981).
8. M.P. Silverman, *More than One Mystery: Explorations in Quantum Interference*, Springer, Berlin (1995).
9. E. Schrödinger, "Die gegenwärtige Situation in der Quantenmechanik", Naturwissenschaften, **23**, 807; 823; 844 (1935). English translation, "The Present Situation in Quantum Mechanics", Proc. of the American Philosophical Society, **124**, 323 (1980); reprinted in *Quantum Theory and Measurement* edited by J.A. Wheeler and W.H. Zurek, Princeton, 152 (1983).
10. M.A. Horne and A. Zeilinger, in: *Proceedings of the Symposium Foundations of Modern Physics*, P. Lahti, P. Mittelstaedt (Eds.), World Scientific, Singapore 435 (1985); M.A. Horne and A. Zeilinger, in: *Microphysical Reality and Quantum Formalism*, A. van der Merwe, et al. (Eds.), Kluwer, Dordrecht, 401 (1988).
11. J.S. Bell, Phys. World **3**, 33 (1990).
12. J.F. Clauser, M.A. Horne, A. Shimony, and R.A. Holt, Phys. Rev. Lett. **23**, 880 (1969).
13. D. Greenberger, M.A. Horne, A. Zeilinger, *Going beyond Bell's Theorem, in "Bell's Theorem, Quantum Theory, and Conceptions of the Universe"*, M. Kafatos (Ed.), Kluwer, Dordrecht, 69 (1989).
14. N.D. Mermin, Phys. Today **43**, No. 6, 9 (1990); D.M. Greenberger, M.A. Horne, A. Shimony, and A. Zeilinger, Am. J. Phys. **58**, 1131 (1990).
15. D. Bohm, *Quantum Theory*, Prentice-Hall, Englewood Cliffs, 614 (1951).
16. P.G. Kwiat, H. Weinfurter, T. Herzog, and A. Zeilinger, Phys. Rev. Lett. **74**, 4763 (1995).
17. K.F. Weizsäcker, Z. Phys. **40**, 114 (1931).
18. D. Bouwmeester, J-W. Pan, M. Daniell, H. Weinfurter, and A. Zeilinger, Phys. Rev. Lett. **82**, 1345 (1999).
19. D. Bruss, A. Ekert, F. Huelga, J.-W. Pan, and A. Zeilinger, Phil. Trans. R. Soc. (London) A **355**, 2259 (1997).
20. N. Bohr, "Discussions with Einstein on Epistemological Problems in Atomic Physics" in *Albert Einstein: Philosopher-Scientist*, Edited by P.A. Schilpp, The Library of Living Philosophers, Evanston, 200 (1949).

21. A. Einstein, B. Podolsky, and N. Rosen, Phys. Rev. **47**, 777 (1935).
22. N. Bohr, Phys. Rev. **48**, 696 (1935).
23. J.S. Bell, *On the Einstein-Podolsky-Rosen paradox*, Physics **1**, 195 (1964), reprinted in J.S. Bell, *Speakable and Unspeakable in Quantum Mechanics*, Cambridge U.P., Cambridge (1987).
24. S.J. Freedman and J.S. Clauser, Phys. Rev. Lett. **28**, 938 (1972); A. Aspect, J. Dalibard, and G. Roger, Phys. Rev. Lett. **47**, 1804 (1982); W. Tittel, J. Brendel, H. Zbinden, and N. Gisin, Phys. Rev. Lett. **81**, 3563 (1998); G. Weihs, T. Jennewein, C. Simon, H. Weinfurter, and A. Zeilinger, Phys. Rev. Lett. **81**, 5039 (1998).
25. A. Aspect, P. Grangier, and G. Roger, Phys. Rev. Lett. **47**, 460 (1981); **49**, 91 (1982); A. Aspect, J. Dalibard, and G. Roger, ibid. **49**, 1804 (1982).
26. P.G. Kwiat, K. Mattle, H. Weinfurter, A. Zeilinger, A.V. Sergienko, and Y.H. Shih, Phys. Rev. Lett. **75**, 4337 (1995).
27. P.M. Pearle, Phys. Rev. D **2**, 1418 (1970); J.F. Clauser, A. Shimony, Rep. Prog. Phys. **41**, 1881 (1978).
28. E.P. Wigner, Am. J. Phys. 38, 1005 (1970).
29. D. Kahn, *The Codebreakers: The Story of Secret Writing*, Macmillan, New York (1967).
30. A.J. Menezes, P.C. van Oorschot, and S.A. Vanstone, *Handbook of Applied Cryptography*, CRC Press (1996).
31. B. Schneier, *Applied cryptography: protocols, algorithms, and source code in C*, John Wiley & Sons (1994).
32. D. Welsh, *Codes and Cryptography*, Clarendon Press, Oxford, (1988).
33. C.E. Shannon, Bell Syst. Tech. J, **28**, 656 (1949).
34. W. Diffie, and M.E. Hellman, IEEE Trans. Inf. Theory, **IT-22**, 644 (1976).
35. R. Rivest, A. Shamir, and L. Adleman, *On Digital Signatures and Public-Key Cryptosystems*, MIT Laboratory for Computer Science, Technical Report, MIT/LCS/TR-212 (January 1979).
36. P. Shor, (1994) *Proc. of 35th Annual Symposium on the Foundations of Computer Science*, (IEEE Computer Society, Los Alamitos), p. 124 (Extended Abstract). Full version of this paper appears in S. I. A. M. Journal on Computing, **26** (1997), 1484 and is also available at quant-ph/9508027.
37. S. Wiesner, *SIGACT News*, **15**, 78 (1983); original manuscript written *circa* 1970.
38. C.H. Bennett and G. Brassard, in *"Proc. IEEE Int. Conference on Computers, Systems and Signal Processing"*, IEEE, New York, (1984).
39. J.F. Clauser and M.A. Horne, *Phys. Rev. D* **10**, 526 (1974).
40. B. Huttner and A. Ekert, J. Mod. Opt., **41**, 2455 (1994).
41. P.D. Townsend, Nature **385**, 47 (1997).
42. C.H. Bennett, F. Bessette, G. Brassard, L. Salvail, and J. Smolin, J. Cryptol. **5**, 3 (1992).
43. A. Muller, J. Breguet, and N. Gisin, Europhys. Lett. **23**, 383 (1993).
44. A.K. Ekert, J.G. Rarity, P.R. Tapster, and G.M. Palma, Phys. Rev. Lett. **69** 1293 (1992).
45. C.H. Bennett, Phys. Rev. Lett. **68**, 3121 (1992).
46. A.K. Ekert, Phys. Rev. Lett. **67**, 661 (1991).
47. D. Deutsch, A. Ekert, R. Jozsa, C. Macchiavello, S. Popescu, and A. Sanpera, Phys. Rev. Lett. **77**, 2818 (1996); C. Macchiavello, Phys. Lett. A **246**, 385 (1998).
48. Q.A. Turchette, C.J. Hood, W. Lange, H. Mabuchi, and H.J. Kimble, Phys. Rev. Lett. **75**, 4710 (1995).

49. Bennett, C. H., Brassard, G., Popescu, S., Schumacher, B., Smolin, J. A., Wootters, W. K. Purification of noisy entanglement and faithful teleportation via noisy channels. Phys. Rev. Lett. **76**, 722-725 (1996).

50. M. Horodecki, P. Horodecki, and R. Horodecki, Phys. Rev. Lett. **78** 574 (1997).

51. G. Brassard and L. Salvail, *Eurocrypt '93, Lofthus, Norway* (1993).

52. B.A. Slutsky, R. Rao, P.-C. Sun and Y. Fainman, Phys.Rev.A **57**, 2383 (1998).

53. J.I. Cirac and N. Gisin, Phys. Lett. A **229**, 1 (1997)

54. C.A. Fuchs, N. Gisin, R.B. Griffiths, C.-S. Niu, and A. Peres, Phys. Rev. A **56**, 1163 (1997).

55. H. Bechmann-Pasquinucci and N. Gisin, Phys. Rev. A **59**, 4238 (1999).

56. N. Lütkenhaus, Phys. Rev. A **59**, 3301 (1999).

57. C.H. Bennett, G. Brassard, C. Crépeau, and U. Maurer, *1994 IEEE International Symposium on Information Theory*, Trondheim, Norway, June (1994).

58. A. Peres, *Quantum Theory: Concepts and Methods*, Kluwer Academic Publishers, (1995).

59. E. Biham, M. Boyer, G. Brassard, J. van de Graaf, and T. Mor, *Security of Quantum Key Distribution against all Collective attacks*, quant-ph/9801022 (1998).

60. D. Mayers, *Unconditional security in Quantum Cryptography*, quant-ph/9802025 (1998).

61. M.N. Wegman, J.L. Carter, Journal of Computer and System Sciences **22**, 265-279 (1981).

62. G. Ribordy, J.D. Gautier, H. Zbinden, and N. Gisin, Applied Optics **37**, 2272 (1998).

63. R.Y. Chiao and Y.S. Wu, Phys. Rev. Lett. **57**, 933 (1986).

64. B.C. Jacobs and J.D. Franson, Opt. Lett. **21**, 1854 (1996).

65. W.T. Buttler, R.J. Hughes, P.G. Kwiat, S.K. Lamoreaux, G.G. Luther, G.L. Morgan, J.E. Nordholt, C.G. Peterson, and C.M. Simmons, Los Alamos preprint, quant-ph/9805071.

66. P.D. Townsend, C. Marand, S.J.D. Phoenix, K.J. Blow, and S.M. Barnett, Phil. Trans. Roy. Soc. London A **354**, 805 (1996).

67. R.J. Hughes, G.G. Luther, G.L. Morgan, C.G. Peterson, C.G. and C. Simmons, C. *Quantum cryptography over underground optical fibres*, Advances in Cryptology - Proceedings of Crypto'96, Springer, Berlin, Heidelberg (1996).

68. G. Ribordy, J.-D. Gautier, N. Gisin, O. Guinnard, and H. Zbinden, Electronics Letters **34**, 2116-2117 (1998).

69. J.D. Franson, Phys. Rev. Lett. **62**, 2205 (1989).

70. J.G. Rarity, P.C.M. Owens, and P.R. Tapster, Phys. Rev. Lett. **73**, 1923 (1994).

71. W. Tittel, J. Brendel, B. Gisin, T. Herzog, H. Zbinden and N. Gisin, Phys. Rev. A **57**, 3229 (1998); W. Tittel, J. Brendel, H. Zbinden and N. Gisin, Phys. Rev. Lett. **81**, 3563 (1998).

72. G. Weihs, T. Jennewein, C. Simon, H. Weinfurter, and A. Zeilinger, Phys. Rev. Lett. **81**, 5039 (1998).

73. C.H. Bennett and S.J. Wiesner, Phys. Rev. Lett., **69**, 2881 (1992).

74. C.H. Bennett, G. Brassard, C. Crépeau, R. Jozsa, A. Peres, and W.K. Wootters, Phys. Rev. Lett. **70**, 1895 (1993).

75. K. Mattle, H. Weinfurter, P.G. Kwiat, and A. Zeilinger, Phys. Rev. Lett. **76**, 4656 (1996).

76. D. Bouwmeester, J.-W. Pan, K. Mattle, M. Eible, H. Weinfurter, and A. Zeilinger, Experimental quantum teleportation. Nature **390**, 575-579 (1997).

77. S. Popescu, LANL E-print quant-ph 9501020.

78. D. Boschi, S. Branca, F. De Martini, L. Hardy, and S. Popescu, Phys. Rev. Lett. **80**, 1121 (1998).
79. L. Vaidman, Phys. Rev. A **49**, 1473 (1994).
80. S.L. Braunstein and H.J. Kimble, Phys. Rev. Lett. **80**, 869 (1998).
81. A. Furusawa, J.L. Sørensen, S.L. Braunstein, C.A. Fuchs, H.J. Kimble, and E.S. Polzik, Science Oct23 1998 pp 706-709.
82. Comment by F. De Martini, and Reply by A. Zeilinger, Physics World **11**, nr.3, 23-24 (March 1998).
83. Comment by S.L. Braunstein and H.J. Kimble, and Reply by D. Bouwmeester, J-W. Pan, M. Daniell, H. Weinfurter, M. Zukowski, and A. Zeilinger, Nature (London) **394**, 840-841 (1998).
84. D. Bouwmeester, J.-W. Pan, H. Weinfurter, and A. Zeilinger, High-fidelity teleportation of qubits, J. Mod. Opt. **47**, 279 (2000).
85. M. Zukowski, A. Zeilinger, M.A. Horne, and A. Ekert, Phys. Rev. Lett. **71**, 4287 (1993).
86. J.-W. Pan, D. Bouwmeester, H. Weinfurter, and A. Zeilinger, Experimental entanglement swapping: Entangling photons that never interacted. Phys. Rev. Lett. **80**, 3891-3894 (1998).
87. S. Bose, V. Vedral, and P.L. Knight, *A multiparticle generalisation of entanglement swapping* Phys. Rev. A **57**, 822 (1998).
88. W.K. Wootters and W.H. Zurek, Nature (London) **299**, 802, (1982).
89. D.N. Klyshko, Sov. Phys. JETP **28**, 522 (1969).
90. D.C. Burnham and D.L. Weinberg, Phys. Rev. Lett. **25**, 84 (1970).
91. J.D. Franson and K.A. Potocki, Phys. Rev. A **37**, 2511 (1988).
92. J. Brendel, E. Mohler, and W. Martiennsen, Europhys. Lett. **20**, 575 (1992); P.G. Kwiat, A.M. Steinberg and R.Y. Chiao, Phys. Rev. A **47**, R2472 (1993).
93. J. Brendel, N. Gisin, W. Tittel and H. Zbinden, Phys. Rev. Lett. **82**, 2594 (1999).
94. J.G. Rarity and P.R. Tapster, Phys. Rev. Lett. **64**, 2495 (1990).
95. R. Loudon, *Coherence and Quantum Optics VI*, ed. Eberly, J.H. and Mandel, L. Plenum New York, 703 (1990).
96. A. Zeilinger, H.J. Bernstein, and M.A. Horne, J. Mod. Optics, **41**, 2375, (1994).
97. H. Weinfurter, Europhys. Lett. **25**, 559 (1994).
98. S.L. Braunstein and A. Mann, Phys. Rev. A **51**, R1727 (1995).
99. M. Michler, K. Mattle, H. Weinfurter, and A. Zeilinger, Phys. Rev. A **53**, R1209 (1996).
100. A. Zeilinger, *Proc. of the Nobel Symp. 104* "Modern Studies of Basic Quantum Concepts and Phenomena" E.B. Karlsson and E. Brändes (Eds.), Physica Scripta, T76, 203 (1998).
101. M. Zukowski, A. Zeilinger and H. Weinfurter in *Fundamental Problems in Quantum Theory* vol. 755 Annals of the New York Academy of Sciences (Greenberger and Zeilinger Eds.) p. 91 (1995).
102. J. Kim, S. Takeuchi, Y. Yamamoto, and H.H. Hogue, Appl. Phys. Lett, **74**,902 (1999).
103. E. Hagley, X. Maître, G. Nogues, C. Wunderlich, M. Brune, J.M. Raimond, and S. Haroche, Generation of Einstein-Podolsky-Rosen pairs of atoms. Phys. Rev. Lett. **79**, 1-5 (1997).
104. H-J. Briegel, W. Dür, J.I. Cirac, and P. Zoller, Phys. Rev. Lett. **81**, 5932 (1998).
105. M. Zukowski, Phys. Lett. A 157, 198 (1991).
106. R. Loudon, *The Quantum Theory of Light, second edition.* Clarendon Press, Oxford, (1983).

107. A. Yariv, *Quantum Electronics, third edition.* John Wiley& Sons (1989).
108. D.F. Walls and G.J. Milburn, *Quantum Optics, second edition.* Springer, Berlin, Heidelberg (1994).
109. P.W. Milonni, *The Quantum Vacuum* Academic Press, San Diego, 1994.
110. Z.Y. Ou, S.F. Pereira, H.J. Kimble, and K.C. Peng, Rhys. Rev. Lett. **68**, 3663 (1992).
111. Z.Y. Ou, S.F. Pereira, and H.J. Kimble, Appl. Phys. B **55**, 265 (1992).
112. H.J. Kimble, in *Fundamental Systems in Quantum Optics, Les Houches, 1990*, eds. J. Dalibard, J.M. Raimond, J. Zinn-Justin (Elsevier Science Publishers, Amsterdam, 1992), pp, 549 674.
113. Ling-An Wu, H.J. Kimble, J.L. Hall, and Huifa Wu, Phys. Rev. Lett. **57**, 2520 (1986).
114. See, for example, S.J. Freedman and J.S. Clauser, Phys. Rev. Lett **28**, 938 (1972).
115. M. Lamehi-Rachti and W. Mittig, Phys. Rev. D **14**, 2543 (1976).
116. E. Biham, B. Huttner and T. Mor, Phys. Rev. A **54**, 2651 (1996).
117. C.H Bennett, H.J. Bernstein, S. Popescu, and B. Schumacher, Phys. Rev. A **53**, 2046 (1996).
118. S. Bose, V. Vedral, and P.L. Knight, Phys. Rev. A **60**, 194 (1999).
119. A. Zeilinger, M.A. Horne, H. Weinfurter, and M. Zukowski, Phys. Rev. Lett **78**, 3031 (1997).
120. L. Grover, *Proc. 28 Annual ACM Symposium on the Theory of Computing*, ACM Press New York, 212 (1996).
121. G. Brassard, Science **275**, 627 (1997).
122. R. Rivest, A. Shamir, and L. Adleman, *On Digital Signatures and Public-Key Cryptosystems*, MIT Laboratory for Computer Science, Technical Report, MIT/LCS/TR-212 (January 1979).
123. R. Feynman, Int. J. Theor. Phys. **21**, 467, (1982).
124. D. Deutsch, Proc. R. Soc. London A **400**, 97 (1985).
125. D. Deutsch, Proc. R. Soc. London A: **425**, 73, (1989).
126. S.F. Huelga, C. Macchiavello, T. Pellizzari, A.K. Ekert, M.B. Plenio, and J.I. Cirac, Phys. Rev. Lett. **79**, 3865 (1997).
127. D. Deutsch, *The Fabric of Reality* (Allen Lane, Penguin Press, London).
128. D. Deutsch and A. Ekert, Phys. World **11**, 47 (March 1998).
129. A. Barenco, C.H. Bennett, R. Cleve, D. DiVincenzo, N. Margolus, P. Shor, T. Sleator, J. Smolin, and H. Weinfurter, Phys. Rev. A **52**, 3457 (1995).
130. D. Deutsch, A. Barenco, and A. Ekert, Proc. Roy. Soc. Lond. A **449**, 669 (1995).
131. C.H. Papadimitriou, *Computational Complexity* (Addison-Wesley, Reading, MA, 1994).
132. M. Garey, and D. Johnson, *Computers and Intractability: A Guide to the Theory of NP Completeness* (W. H. Freeman and Co., 1979).
133. R. Jozsa, Entanglement and Quantum Computation in *The Geometric Universe*, 369, eds. S. Huggett, L. Mason, K.P. Tod, S.T. Tsou and N.M.J. Woodhouse (Oxford University Press, 1998).
134. A. Ekert and R. Jozsa, Phil. Trans. Roy. Soc. London Ser A, **356**, 1769 (1998).
135. A.S. Holevo, Probl. Inf. Transm **9**, 177 (1973).
136. C. Fuchs and A. Peres, Phys. Rev. A. **53**, 2038 (1996).
137. T. Cover and J. Thomas, *Elements of Information Theory,* John Wiley and Sons (1991).
138. D. Deutsch and R. Jozsa, Proc. Roy. Soc. Lond. A **439**, 553 (1992).
139. R. Cleve, A. Ekert, C. Macchiavello, and M. Mosca, Proc. Roy. Soc. London Ser A, **454**, 339 (1998) .

140. E. Bernstein and U. Vazirani, *Proc. 25th Annual ACM Symposium on the Theory of Computing*, (ACM Press, New York), p. 11-20 (1993) (Extended Abstract). Full version of this paper appears in S. I. A. M. Journal on Computing, **26**, 1411 (1997).

141. D. Simon, (1994) *Proc. of 35th Annual Symposium on the Foundations of Computer Science*, (IEEE Computer Society, Los Alamitos), p. 116 (Extended Abstract). Full version of this paper appears in S. I. A. M. Journal on Computing, **26**, 1474 (1997).

142. G.H. Hardy and E.M. Wright *An Introduction to the Theory of Numbers* (4th edition, Clarendon, Oxford, 1965).

143. M.R. Schroeder, *Number Theory in Science and Communication* (2nd enlarged edition, Springer, New York, 1990).

144. A. Ekert and R, Jozsa, Rev. Mod. Phys. **68**, 733 (1996).

145. D.K. Maslen and D.N. Rockmore, "Generalised FFT's – A Survey of Some Recent Results", in *Proc. DIMACS Workshop on Groups and Computation – II* (1995).

146. R. Jozsa, Proc. Roy. Soc. London Ser A, **454**, 323 (1998).

147. G. Brassard and P. Hoyer, "An exact polynomial-time algorithm for Simon's problem", *Proc. 5th Israeli Symposium on Theory of Computing and Systems (ISTCS 97)*, 12 (1997), also available at quant-ph/9704027.

148. A. Kitaev, Russian Math. Surveys **52**, 1191 (1997), also available at quant-ph/9511026.

149. R. Beals, *Proc. 29th Annual ACM Symposium on the Theory of Computing – STOC* (ACM Press, New York), 48 (1997).

150. L. Grover, Phys. Rev. Lett.**78**, 325 (1997).

151. M. Boyer, G. Brassard, P. Hoyer, and A. Tapp, *Proc. of fourth workshop on Physics and Computation – PhysComp'96*, 36-43 (1996).

152. L. Grover, "A Framework for Fast Quantum Algorithms", *Proc. 30th ACM Symposium on Theory of Computation (STOC'98)*, 53 (1998), also available at quant-ph/9711043.

153. G. Brassard, P. Hoyer, and A. Tapp, "Quantum Counting", *Proc. 25th ICALP*, Vol 1443, Lecture Notes in Computer Science, 820 (Springer, 1998), also available at quant-ph/9805082.

154. L. Grover, Phys. Rev. Lett. **80**, 4325 (1997).

155. C.H. Bennett, E. Bernstein, G. Brassard, and U. Vazirani, S. I. A. M. Journal on Computing, **26**, 1510 (1997).

156. J.I. Cirac and P. Zoller, Phys. Rev. Lett. **74**, 4091 (1995).

157. J.F. Poyatos, J.I. Cirac, and P. Zoller, Phys. Rev. Lett. **81**, 1322 (1998).

158. C. Monroe, D.M. Meekhof, B.E. King, W.M. Itano, and D. J. Wineland, Phys. Rev. Lett. **75**, 4714 (1995).

159. E.T. Jaynes and F.W. Cummings, Proc. IEEE **51**, 89 (1963).

160. *Cavity Quantum Electrodynamics, Advances in atomic, molecular and optical physics, Supplement 2*, P. Berman editor, Academic Press (1994).

161. S. Haroche, in *Fundamental systems in quantum optics, les Houches summer school session LIII*, J. Dalibard, J.M. Raimond and J. Zinn-Justin eds, North Holland, Amsterdam (1992).

162. D.G. Hulet and D. Kleppner, Phys. Rev. Lett. **51**, 1430 (1983).

163. P. Nussenzveig, F. Bernardot, M. Brune, J. Hare, J.M. Raimond, S. Haroche and W. Gawlik, Phys. Rev. A **48**, 3991 (1993).

164. M. Brune, P. Nussenzveig, F. Schmidt-Kaler, F. Bernardot, A. Maali, J.M. Raimond, and S. Haroche, Phys. Rev. Lett, **72**, 3339 (1994)

165. M. Brune, F. Schmidt-Kaler, A. Maali, J. Dreyer, E. Hagley, J.M. Raimond, and S. Haroche, Phys. Rev. Lett. **76**, 1800 (1996).

166. M. Brune, E. Hagley, J. Dreyer, X. Maître, A. Maali, C. Wunderlich, J.M. Raimond, and S. Haroche, Phys. Rev. Lett.,**77**, 4887 (1996).
167. X. Maître, E. Hagley, G. Nogues, C. Wunderlich, P. Goy, M. Brune, J.M. Raimond and S. Haroche, Phys. Rev. Lett. **79**, 769 (1997).
168. E. Hagley, X. Maître, G. Nogues, C. Wunderlich, M. Brune, J.M. Raimond and S. Haroche, Phys. Rev. Lett. **79**, 1 (1997).
169. G. Nogues, A. Rauschenbeutel, S. Osnaghi, M. Brune, J.M. Raimond and S. Haroche, Nature **400**, 239 (1999).
170. G. Raithel, C. Wagner, H. Walther, L.M. Narducci and M.O. Scully, in *Cavity Quantum Electrodynamics*, P. Berman ed. 57, Academic, New York (1994).
171. J.H. Eberly, N.B. Narozhny and J.J. Sanchez–Mondragon, Phys. Rev. Lett. **44**, 1323 (1980).
172. R.J. Thompson, G. Rempe and H.J. Kimble, Phys. Rev. Lett. **68**, 1132 (1992).
173. F. Bernardot, P. Nussenzveig, M. Brune, J.M. Raimond and S. Haroche , Euro. Phys. Lett. **17**, 33 (1992).
174. P. Domokos, J.M. Raimond, M. Brune and S. Haroche, Phys. Rev. A **52**, 3554 (1995).
175. J.I. Cirac and P. Zoller, Phys. Rev. A **50**, R2799 (1994).
176. D.M. Greenberger, M.A. Horne, A. Shimony, and A. Zeilinger, Am.J.Phys **58**, 1131 (1990). N.D. Mermin, Physics Today (June 9, 1990).
177. S. Haroche in *Fundamental problems in quantum theory*, D. Greenberger and A. Zeilinger Eds, Ann. N.Y. Acad. Sci. **755**, 73 (1995).
178. E. Schrödinger, *Naturwissenschaften* **23**, 807, 823, 844 (1935). Reprinted in english in J.A. Wheeler and W.H. Zurek, *Quantum theory of measurement*, Princeton University Press (1983).
179. W.H. Zurek, Phys. Rev. D **24**, 1516 (1981).
180. W.H. Zurek, Phys. Rev. D **26**, 1862 (1982).
181. A.O. Caldeira and A.J. Leggett Physica A, **121**, 587 (1983).
182. E. Joos and H.D. Zch, Z.Phys.B **59**, 223 (1985).
183. W.H. Zurek, Physics Today **44**, 10 p.36 (1991).
184. R. Omnès, *The Interpretation of Quantum Mechanics*, Princeton University Press (1994).
185. D.F. Walls and G.J. Milburn, Phys. Rev. A **31**, 2403.
186. L. Davidovich, M. Brune, J.M. Raimond and S. Haroche, Phys. Rev. A **53**, 1295 (1996).
187. M.O. Scully and H. Walther, Phys. Rev. A **39**, 5299 (1989).
188. J.M Raimond, M. Brune and S. Haroche, Phys. Rev. Lett. **79**, 1964 (1997).
189. C.A. Blockey, D.F. Walls, and H. Risken, Europhys. Lett. **17**, 509 (1992).
190. J.I. Cirac, R. Blatt, A.S. Parkins, and P. Zoller, Phys. Rev. Lett. **70**, 762 (1993).
191. J.I. Cirac, R. Blatt, A.S. Parkins, and P. Zoller, Phys. Rev. A **49**, 1202 (1994).
192. J.I. Cirac, R. Blatt, and P. Zoller, Phys. Rev. A **49**, R3174 (1994).
193. Proc.5th Symp.Freq.Standards and Metrology, ed. J.C. Bergquist, (World Scientific, 1996).
194. D.J. Berkeland, J.D. Miller, J.C. Bergquist, W.M. Itano, and D.J. Wineland, Phys. Rev. Lett. **80**, 2089 (1998).
195. R. Blatt, in *Atomic Physics* **14**, 219, ed. D.J. Wineland, C. Wieman, S.J. Smith, AIP New York (1995).
196. W. Paul, O. Osberghaus, and E. Fischer, Forschungsberichte des Wirtschafts- und Verkehrsministerium Nordrhein-Westfalen **415** (1958).
197. P.K. Ghosh, Ion traps, Clarendon, Oxford (1995).
198. D.J. Wineland, and H. Dehmelt, Bull. Am. Phys. Soc. **20**, 637 (1975).

199. D.J. Wineland, R.E. Drullinger, and F.L. Walls, Phys. Rev. Lett. **40**, 1639 (1978).
200. A. Steane, Appl. Phys. B **64**, 623 (1997), see Table 1 in which a list of candidate ions is given together with relevant experimental parameters.
201. $http : //www.bldrdoc.gov/timefreq/ion/index.htm$
202. $http : //horology.jpl.nasa.gov/research.html$
203. $http : //mste.laser.physik.uni - muenchen.de/lg/worktop.html$
204. $http : //p23.lanl.gov/Quantum/quantum.html$
205. $http : //dipmza.physik.uni - mainz.de/\ www_werth/calcium/calcium.html$
206. $http : //www - phys.rrz.uni - hamburg.de/home/vms/group_a/index.html$
207. $http : //heart - c704.uibk.ac.at/$
208. D.J. Wineland, W.M. Itano, J.C. Bergquist, and R.G. Hulet, Phys. Rev. A **36**, 2220 (1987).
209. J.I. Cirac, A.S. Parkins, R. Blatt, and P. Zoller, Phys. Rev. Lett. **70**, 556 (1993).
210. S. Stenholm, Rev. Mod. Phys. **58**, 699 (1986).
211. C. Monroe, D.M. Meekhof, B.E. King, S.R. Jeffers, W.M. Itano, D.J. Wineland, and P. Gould, Phys. Rev. Lett. **74**, 4011 (1995).
212. H.C. Nägerl, W. Bechter, J. Eschner, F. Schmidt-Kaler, and R. Blatt, Appl. Phys. B **66**, 603 (1998).
213. H.C. Nägerl, D. Leibfried, H. Rohde, G. Thalhammer, J. Eschner, F. Schmidt-Kaler, and R. Blatt, Phys. Rev. A. **60**, 145 (1999).
214. F. Diedrich, J.C. Bergquist, W.M. Itano, and D.J. Wineland, Phys. Rev. Lett. **62**, 403 (1989).
215. Ch. Roos, Th. Zeiger, H. Rohde, H.C. Nägerl, J. Eschner, D. Leibfried, F. Schmidt-Kaler, and R. Blatt, Phys. Rev. Lett. **83**, 4713 (1999).
216. B.E. King, C.S. Wood, C.J. Myatt, Q.A. Turchette, D. Leibfried, W.M. Itano, C. Monroe, and D.J. Wineland, Phys. Rev. Lett. **81**, 1525 (1998).
217. H. Dehmelt, Bull. Am. Phys. Soc. **20** 60 (1975).
218. D.J. Wineland, C. Monroe, W.M. Itano, D. Leibfried, B. King, and D.M. Meekhof, Journal of Research of the National Institute of Standards and Technology **103**, 259 (1998).
219. D. Leibfried, D.M. Meekhof, B.E. King, C. Monroe, W.M. Itano, and D.J. Wineland, Phys. Rev. Lett **77**, 4281 (1996).
220. D.M. Meekhof, C. Monroe, B.E. King, W.M. Itano, and D.J. Wineland, Phys. Rev. Lett. **76**, 1796 (1996).
221. C. Monroe, D.M. Meekhof, B.E. King, and D.J. Wineland, Science **272**, 1131 (1996)
222. J.F. Poyatos, J.I. Cirac, and P. Zoller, Phys. Rev. Lett. **77**, 4728 (1996).
223. C. Monroe, D.M. Meekhof, B.E. King, W.M. Itano, and D.J. Wineland, Phys. Rev. Lett. **75**, 4714 (1995).
224. L.G. Lutterbach and L. Davidovich, Phys. Rev. Lett. **78**, 2547 (1997).
225. M.B. Plenio and P.L. Knight Phys. Rev. A **53**, 2986 (1996).
226. J.I. Cirac, A.S. Parkins, R. Blatt, and P. Zoller, Adv. At. Molec. Opt. Physics **37**, 238 (1996).
227. D.P. DiVincenzo, Phys. Rev. A **51**, 1015 (1995).
228. D.J. Wineland, C. Monroe, W.M. Itano, D. Leibfried, B. King, and D.M. Meekhof, Rev. Mod. Phys. (1998).
229. G. Morigi, J. Eschner, J.I. Cirac, and P. Zoller, Phys. Rev. A. **59**, 3797 (1999).
230. E. Peik, J. Abel, T. Becker, J. von Zanthier, and H. Walther, Phys. Rev. A **60**, 439 (1999).
231. I. Waki, S. Kassner, G. Birkl, and H. Walther, Phys. Rev. Lett. **68**, 2007 (1992); G. Birkl, S. Kassner, H. Walther, Nature 357, 310 (1992).

232. D.F.V. James, Appl. Phys. B **66** 181 (1998).
233. C. Monroe, D. Leibfried, B.E. King, D.M. Meekhof, W.M. Itano, and D.J. Wineland, Phys. Rev. **A55**, R2489 (1997)
234. W. Nagourney, J. Sandberg, and H. Dehmelt, Phys. Rev. Lett. **56**, 2797 (1986); Th. Sauter, W. Neuhauser, R. Blatt, and P.E. Toschek, Phys. Rev. Lett. **57**, 1696 (1986); J.C. Bergquist, R. Hulet, W.M. Itano, and D.J. Wineland, Phys. Rev. Lett. **57**, 1699 (1986).
235. P.J. Hore, *Nuclear Magnetic Resonance*, Oxford University Press, Oxford (1995).
236. R.R. Ernst, G. Bodenhausen, and A. Wokaun, *Principles of Nuclear Magnetic Resonance in One and Two Dimensions*, Oxford University Press, Oxford (1987).
237. D.G. Cory, A.F. Fahmy, and T.F. Havel, *Proceedings of the Fourth Workshop on Physics and Computation, Nov. 22–24, 1996*, New England Complex Systems Institute, Cambridge, MA (1996).
238. D.G. Cory, A.F. Fahmy, and T.F. Havel, Proc. Natl. Acad. Sci. USA **94**, 1634 (1997).
239. N.A. Gershenfeld and I.L. Chuang, Science **275,** 350 (1997).
240. A. Abragam, *Principles of Nuclear Magnetism*, Clarendon Press, Oxford (1961).
241. C.P. Slichter, *Principles of Magnetic Resonance* 3rd ed. Springer, Berlin, Heidelberg (1990).
242. M. Goldman, *Quantum Description of High-Resolution NMR in Liquids*, Clarendon Press, Oxford (1988).
243. J.A. Jones and M. Mosca, J. Chem. Phys. **109**, 1648 (1998).
244. A. Barenco. C.H. Bennett, R. Cleve, D.P. DiVincenzo, N. Margolus, P. Shor, T. Sleator, J.A. Smolin, and H. Weinfurter, Phys. Rev. A, **52**, 3457 (1995).
245. J.A. Jones, R.H. Hansen, and M. Mosca, J. Magn. Reson. **135**, 353 (1998).
246. L.M.K. Vandersypen, C.S. Yannoni, M.H. Sherwood, and I.L. Chuang, Phys. Rev. Lett. **83**, 3085 (1999).
247. E. Knill, I. Chuang, and R. Laflamme, Phys. Rev. A, **57**, 3348 (1998).
248. T.F. Havel, S.S. Somaroo, C.-H. Tseng, and D.G. Cory, LANL E-print quant-ph/9812026.
249. R. Cleve, A. Ekert, C. Macchiavello, and M. Mosca, Proc. R. Soc. Lond. A **454,** 339 (1998).
250. I.L. Chuang, L.M.K. Vandersypen, X.L. Zhou, D.W. Leung, and S. Lloyd, Nature, **393**, 143 (1998).
251. I.L. Chuang, N. Gershenfeld, and M. Kubinec, Phys. Rev. Lett. **80,** 3408 (1998).
252. J.A. Jones, M. Mosca, and R.H. Hansen, Nature, **393**, 344 (1998).
253. L.K. Grover, Science, **280**, 228 (1998).
254. J.A. Jones and M. Mosca, Phys. Rev. Lett. **83**, 1050 (1999).
255. R. Laflamme, E. Knill, W.H. Zurek, P. Catasti, and S.V.S. Mariappan, Phil. Trans. Roy. Soc. Lond A, **356**, 1941 (1998).
256. R.J. Nelson, D.G. Cory, S. Lloyd, LANL E-print quant-ph/9905028.
257. D.G. Cory, M.D. Price, W. Maas, E. Knill, R. Laflamme, W.H. Zurek, T.F. Havel, and S.S. Somaroo, Phys. Rev. Lett. **81**, 2152 (1998).
258. D. Leung, L. Vandersypen, X. Zhou, M. Sherwood, C. Yannoni, M. Kubinec, and I. Chuang, Phys. Rev. A **60**, 1924 (1999).
259. M.A. Nielsen, E. Knill, and R. Laflamme, Nature, **396**, 52 (1998).
260. N. Linden, H. Barjat, and R. Freeman, Chem. Phys. Lett. **296**, 61 (1998).
261. R. Marx, A. F. Fahmy, J. M. Myers, W. Bermel, and S. J. Glaser, LANL E-print quant-ph/9905087.

262. W.S. Warren, Science, **277**, 1688 (1997).
263. G. Navon, Y.-Q. Song, T. Rõõm, S. Appelt, R.E. Taylor, and A. Pines, Science, **271**, 1848 (1996).
264. L. J. Schulman and U. Vazirani, LANL E-print quant-ph/9804060.
265. R. Freeman, *Spin Choreography*, Spektrum, Oxford, (1997).
266. N. Linden, H. Barjat, R.J. Carbajo, and R. Freeman, Chem. Phys. Lett. **305**, 28 (1999).
267. D.W. Leung, I.L. Chuang, F. Yamaguchi, and Y. Yamamoto, LANL E-print quant-ph/9904100.
268. J.A. Jones and E. Knill, J. Magn. Reson. in press, LANL E-print quant-ph/9905008.
269. N. Linden, Ē. Kupče, and R. Freeman, LANL E-print quant-ph/9907003.
270. P.T. Callaghan, *Principles of Nuclear Magnetic Resonance Microscopy*, Clarendon Press, Oxford (1991).
271. B.E. Kane, Nature **393**, 133 (1998).
272. S.L. Braunstein, C.M. Caves, R. Jozsa, N. Linden, S. Popescu, and R. Schack, Phys. Rev. Lett. **83**, 1054 (1999).
273. R. Schack and C. M. Caves, LANL E-print quant-ph/9903101.
274. T. Pellizzari *et al*, Phys. Rev. Lett. **75** , 3788 (1995).
275. C. Monroe *et al.*, Phys. Rev. Lett. **75**, 4714 (1995).
276. Q. Turchette *et al.*, Phys. Rev. Lett. **75**, 4710 (1995).
277. K. Mattle *at al.*, Phys. Rev. Lett. **76**, 4656 (1996).
278. J. I. Cirac, P. Zoller, H.J. Kimble, and H. Mabuchi, Phys. Rev. Lett. **78**, 3221 (1997).
279. C.H. Bennett, Physics Today **24**, (October 1995) and references cited; A.K. Ekert, Phys. Rev. Lett. **67**, 661 (1991); W. Tittel *et al.*, quant-ph/9707042; W.T. Buttler *et al.*, quant-ph/9801006.
280. C.H. Bennett *et al*, Phys. Rev. Lett. **70**, 1895 (1993); D. Bouwmeester *et al.*, Nature **390**, 575 (1997); D. Boschi *et al.*, Phys. Rev. Lett. **80**, 1121 (1998).
281. L.K. Grover, quant-ph/9704012.
282. A.K. Ekert *et al.*, quant-ph/9803017.
283. C.K. Law and J.H. Eberly, Phys. Rev. Lett. **76**, 1055 (1996).
284. H.J. Carmichael, Phys. Rev. Lett. **70**, 2273 (1993).
285. For a review see P. Zoller and C.W. Gardiner in *Quantum Fluctuations*, Les Houches, ed. E. Giacobino *et al.*, Elsevier, NY, in press.
286. C.W. Gardiner, Phys. Rev. Lett.**70**, 2269 (1993).
287. P.W. Shor, Phys. Rev. A **52**, R2493 (1995); A.M. Steane, Phys. Rev. Lett. **77**, 793 (1996); J.I. Cirac, T. Pellizzari and P. Zoller, Science **273**, 1207 (1996); P. Shor, *Fault–tolerant quantum computation*, quant–ph/9605011; D. DiVincenzo and P.W. Shor, Phys. Rev. Lett. **77**, 3260 (1996).
288. C.H. Bennett *et al.*, Phys. Rev. Lett. **76**, 722 (1996); D. Deutsch *et al.*, Phys. Rev. Lett. **77** , 2818 (1996); N. Gisin, Phys. Lett. A **210**, 151 (1996).
289. D.M. Greenberger, M.A. Horne, A. Zeilinger, A. Going beyond Bell's theorem, in *Bell's Theorem, Quantum Theory, and Conceptions of the Universe*, edited by M. Kafatos, (Kluwer, Dordrecht, 1989) pp. 73-76.
290. D.M. Greenberger, M.A. Horne,A. Shimony, A. Zeilinger, Bell's theorem without inequalities. Am. J. Phys. **58**, 1131 (1990).
291. D. Bouwmeester, J.-W.. Pan, M. Daniell, H. Weinfurter, and A. Zeilinger, Observation of three-photon Greenberger-Horne-Zeilinger entanglement. Phys. Rev. Lett. **82**, 1345 (1999).
292. D.M. Greenberger, M.A. Horne, A. Zeilinger, Multiparticle interferometry and the superposition principle. Physics Today, 22, August 1993.
293. N.D. Mermin, Am. J. Phys. **58**, 731 (1990).

294. N.D. Mermin, What's wrong with these elements of reality? Physics Today, 9, June 1990.
295. S.J. Freedman and J.S. Clauser, Experimental test of local hidden-variable theories. Phys. Rev. Lett. **28**, 938-941 (1972).
296. A. Aspect, J. Dalibard, and G. Roger, Experimental test of Bell's inequalities using time-varying analysers. Phys. Rev. Lett. **47**, 1804-1807 (1982).
297. G. Weihs, T. Jennewein, C. Simon, H. Weinfurter, and A. Zeilinger, Violation of Bell's inequality under strict Einstein locality conditions. Phys. Rev. Lett. **81**, 5039-5043 (1998).
298. L. Hardy, Nonlocality for two particles without inequalities for almost all entagled states. Phys. Rev. Lett. **71**, 1665-1668 (1993).
299. D. Boschi, S. Branca, F. De Martini, and L. Hardy, Ladder proof of nonlocality without inequalities: Theoretical and experimental results. Phys. Rev. Lett. **79**, 2755 (1997).
300. A. Zeilinger, M.A. Horne, H. Weinfurter, and M. Zukowski, Three particle entanglements from two entangled pairs. Phys. Rev. Lett. **78**, 3031-3034 (1997).
301. S. Haroche, Ann. N. Y. Acad. Sci. **755**, 73 (1995); J.I. Cirac, P. Zoller, Phys. Rev. A **50**, R2799 (1994).
302. S. Lloyd, Phys. Rev. A **57**, R1473 (1998); R. Laflamme, E. Knill, W.H. Zurek, P. Catasti, S.V.S. Mariappan, Phil.Trans. R. Soc. Lond. A **356**, 1941 (1998).
303. S. Bose, V. Vedral, P.L. Knight, Phys. Rev. A **57**, 822 (1998).
304. M. Zukowski, A. Zeilinger, H. Weinfurter, Entangling photons radiated by independent pulsed source. Ann. NY Acad. Sci. **755**, 91-102 (1995).
305. M.A. Horne, Fortschr. Phys. **46**, 6 (1998).
306. G. Krenn, A. Zeilinger, Phys. Rev. A. **54**, 1793 (1996).
307. Z.Y. Ou and L. Mandel, Violation of Bell's inequality and classical probability in a two-photon correlation experiment. Phys. Rev. Lett. **61**, 50-53 (1988).
308. Y.H. Shih and C.O. Alley, New type of Einstein-Podolsky-Rosen-Bohm experiment using pairs of light quanta produced by optical parametric down conversion. Phys. Rev. Lett. **61**, 2921-2924 (1988).
309. P. Kwiat, P.E. Eberhard, A.M. Steinberger, and R.Y. Chiao, Proposal for a loophole-free Bell inequality experiment. Phys. Rev. A **49**, 3209-3220 (1994).
310. L. De Caro and A. Garuccio, Reliability of Bell-inequality measurements using polarisation correlations in parametric-down-conversion photons. Phys. Rev. A **50**, R2803-R2805 (1994).
311. S. Popescu, L. Hardy, and M. Zukowski, Revisiting Bell's theorem for a class of down-conversion experiments. Phys. Rev. A. **56**, R4353-4357 (1997).
312. M. Zukowski, Violations of local realism in multiphoton interference experiments. quant-ph/9811013.
313. J.-W. Pan, D. Bouwmeester, M. Daniell, H. Weinfurter, and A. Zeilinger, Experimental test of quantum nonlocality in three-photn Greenberger-Horne-Zeilinger entanglement, Nature **403**, 515 (2000).
314. N.D. Mermin, Extreme quantum entanglement in a superposition of macroscopically distinct states. Phys. Rev. Lett. **65**, 1838-1841 (1990).
315. S.M. Roy and V. Singh,Tests of signal locality and Einstein-Bell locality for multiparticle systems. Phys. Rev. Lett. **67**, 2761-2764 (1991).
316. M. Zukowski and D. Kaszlikowski, Critical visibility for N-particle Greenberger-Horne-Zeilinger correlations to violate local realism. Phys. Rev. A **56**, R1682-1685 (1997).
317. The original reference is E. Schmidt, *Zur Theorie der linearen und nicht linearen Integralgleichungen*, Math. Annalen **63**, 433 (1907), in the context of quantum theory see H. Everett III, in *The Many-World Interpretation of*

Quantum Mechanics, ed. B.S. DeWitt and N. Graham, Princeton University Press, Princeton, 3 (1973), and H. Everett III, Rev. Mod. Phys. **29**, 454 (1957). A graduate level textbook by A. Peres, *Quantum Theory: Concepts and Methods*, Kluwer, Dordrecht, (1993), Chapt. 5 includes a brief description of the Schmidt decomposition; A. Ekert and P.L. Knight, Am. J. Phys., **63**, 415 (1995).

318. A. Peres, "Higher order Schmidt Decompositions", lanl-gov e-print server no. 9504006, 1995.

319. J. von Neumann, "Mathematische Grundlagen der Quantenmechanik" (Springer, Berlin, 1932; English Translation, Princeton University Press, Princeton, 1955).

320. M. Horodecki, P. Horodecki, and R. Horodecki, *Mixed-state entanglement and distillation: is there a "bound" entanglement in nature?*, lanl gov e-print quant-ph/9801069.

321. V. Vedral, M.B. Plenio, M.A. Rippin, and P.L. Knight, Phys. Rev. Lett. **78**, 2275 (1997).

322. V. Vedral and M. B. Plenio, Phys. Rev. A **57**, 1619 (1998).

323. C.H. Bennett, D.P. DiVincenzo, J.A. Smolin, and W.K. Wootters, Phys. Rev. A **54**, 3824 (1996).

324. W.K. Wootters, *Entanglement of Formation of an Arbitrary State of Two Qubits*, lanl e-print server quant-ph/9709029, (1997); S. Hill and W.K. Wootters, Phys. Rev. Lett. **78**, 5022 (1997).

325. T. Rockafeller, *Convex Analysis*, Princeton University Press, New Jersey, (1970).

326. N. Gisin, Phys. Lett. **A 210**, 151 (1996), and references therein; A. Peres, Phys. Rev. A **54**, 2685 (1996); M. Horodecki, P. Horodecki, R. Horodecki, Phys. Lett. A **223**, 1 (1996).

327. V. Vedral, M.B. Plenio, K. Jacobs, and P.L. Knight, Phys. Rev. A **56**, 4452 (1997).

328. W.K. Wootters, Phys. Rev. D **23**, 357 (1981).

329. T.M. Cover and J.A. Thomas, *Elements of Information Theory*, Wiley-Interscience,(1991).

330. F. Hiai and D. Petz, Comm. Math. Phys. **143**, 99 (1991).

331. M. Hayashi, *Asymptotic Attainment for Quantum Relative Entropy*, lanl e-print server: quant-ph/9704040 (1997).

332. W.H. Zurek, Physics Today, 36 (October 1991).

333. G.M. Palma, K.-A. Suominen, and A.K. Ekert, Proc. R. Soc. London A. **452**, 567 (1996).

334. D. DiVincenzo, Phys. Rev. A, **50**, 1015 (1995).

335. W. Unruh, Phys. Rev. A, **51**, 992 (1995).

336. D. Loss and D. DiVincenzo, Phys. Rev. A, **57**, 120 (1998).

337. A. Barenco et.al, Phys. Rev. Lett. **74**, 4083 (1995).

338. C. Cohen-Tannoudji, J. Dupont-Roc, and Grynberg, *Atom Photon Interaction*, John Wiley (1992).

339. M. Gross and S. Haroche, Phys. Rep. **93**, 301 (1982).

340. A. Crubellier, S. Liberman, D. Pavolini, and A. Pillet, J. Phys. B, **18**, 3811 (1985).

341. P. Zanardi and M. Rasetti, Phys. Rev. Lett. **79**, 3306 (1997).

342. D.G. Cory, M.D. Price, T.F. Havel, Physica D **120**, 82 (1998).

343. N.A. Gershenfeld and I.L. Chuang, Science, **275**, 350 (1997).

344. P.L. Knight, M.B. Plenio and V. Vedral, Phil. Trans. Roc. Soc. Lond. A, **355**, 2381 (1997).

345. M.B. Plenio and P.L. Knight, Phys. Rev. A, **53**, 2986 (1996).

346. M.B. Plenio and P.L. Knight, Proc. R. Soc. Lond. A, **453**, 2017 (1997).
347. M.B. Plenio and P.L. Knight, *New Developments on Fundamental Problems in Quantum Physics*, edited by M. Ferrero and A. van der Merwe, Kluwer, Dordrecht, 311 (1997).
348. A. Garg, Phys. Rev. Lett. **77**, 964 (1996).
349. R.J. Hughes, D.F.V. James, E.H. Knill, R. Laflamme, and A.G. Petschek, Phys. Rev. Lett. **77**, 3240 (1996).
350. P.W. Shor, in *Proceedings of the 35th Annual Symposium on the Foundations of Computer Science, Los Alamitos,* CA IEEE Computer Society Press, New York, 124 (1994).
351. V. Vedral, A. Barenco, and A. Ekert, Phys. Rev. A, **54**, 147 (1996).
352. D. Deutsch, (1993) talk presented at the Rank Prize Funds Mini–Symposium on Quantum Communication and Cryptography, Broadway, England; A. Berthiaume, D. Deutsch and R. Jozsa, in *Proceedings of Workshop on Physics and Computation — PhysComp94*, IEEE Computer Society Press, Dallas, Texas, (1994).
353. A. Barenco, A. Berthiaume, D. Deutsch, A. Ekert, R. Jozsa and C. Macchiavello, SIAM J. Comput. **26**, 1541 (1997).
354. Ash, *Information Theory*, Dover (1996).
355. A. Ekert and C. Macchiavello, Phys. Rev. Lett. **77**, 2585 (1996).
356. R. Laflamme, C. Miquel, J.P. Paz and W.H. Zurek, Phys. Rev. Lett. **77**, 198 (1996).
357. A. Steane, Error correcting codes in quantum theory, Phys. Rev. Lett. **77**, 793 (1995).
358. A. Steane, Multiple particle interference and quantum error correction, Proc. R. Soc. Lond. A, **452**, 2551 (1995).
359. J. Preskill, Reliable quantum computers, Proc. Roy. Soc. Lond. A, **454**, 469 (1998).
360. D. Gottesman, Class of quantum error-correcting codes saturating the quantum Hamming bound, Phys. Rev. A, **54**, 1862 (1996).
361. A.R. Calderbank, E.M. Rains, N.J.A. Sloane and P.W. Shor, Quantum error correction and orthogonal geometry, Phys. Rev. Lett. **78** 405 (1997).
362. A.R. Calderbank, E.M. Rains, P.W. Shor and N.J.A. Sloane, Quantum error correction via codes over $GF(4)$, IEEE Trans. Information Theory **44** 1369 (1998).
363. P.W. Shor, Scheme for reducing decoherence in quantum computer memory, Phys. Rev. A, **52**, R2493 (1995).
364. A.R. Calderbank and P.W. Shor, Good quantum error-correcting codes exist, Phys. Rev. A, **54**, 1098 (1996).
365. E. Knill and R. Laflamme, A theory of quantum error correcting codes, Phys. Rev. A, **55**, 900 (1997).
366. E. Knill and R. Laflamme, Concatenated quantum codes, LANL eprint quant-ph/9608012.
367. P.W. Shor, Fault-tolerant quantum computation, in *Proc. 37th Symp. on Foundations of Computer Science*, (Los Alamitos, CA: IEEE Computer Society Press), pp15-65 (1996).
368. A.M. Steane, Space, time, parallelism and noise requirements for reliable quantum computing, Fortschr. Phys. **46**, 443 (1998). (LANL eprint quant-ph/9708021).
369. D. Aharonov and M. Ben-Or, Fault-Tolerant Quantum Computation With Constant Error Rate, LANL eprint quant-ph/9906129.

370. E. Knill, R. Laflamme and W.H. Zurek, Resilient quantum computation: Error Models and Thresholds, Proc. Roy. Soc. Lond A **454**, 365 (1998); Science **279**, 342 (1998). (LANL eprint quant-ph/9702058).

371. A.M. Steane, Active stabilisation, quantum computation and quantum state synthesis, Phys. Rev. Lett. **78**, 2251 (1997).

372. A.M. Steane, Efficient fault-tolerant quantum computing, Nature, vol. **399**, 124-126 (May 1999). (LANL eprint quant-ph/9809054).

373. D. Gottesman, A theory of fault-tolerant quantum computation, Phys. Rev. A **57**, 127 (1998). (LANL eprint quant-ph/9702029).

374. W.H. Itano et al., Phys. Rev. A, **47**, 3554 (1993).

375. W.J. Wineland et al., Phys. Rev. A, **46**, R6797 (1992).

376. D. J. Wineland et al., Phys. Rev. A, **50**, 67 (1994).

377. J.J. Bollinger et al., Phys. Rev. A, **54**, R4649 (1996).

378. C.W. Gardiner, *Quantum Noise*, Springer–Verlag, Berlin (1991).

379. S.F. Huelga, C. Macchiavello, T. Pellizari, A.K. Ekert, M.B. Plenio and J.I. Cirac, Phys. Rev. Lett. **79**, 3865 (1997).

380. A. Barenco, A. Berthiaume, D. Deutsch, A. Ekert, R. Jozsa and C. Macchiavello, SIAM J. Comput. **26**, 1541 (1997).

381. H.-J. Briegel, W. Dür, J.I. Cirac, and P. Zoller, Phys. Rev. Lett. **81**, 5932 (1998).

382. N. Gisin, Phys. Lett. A **210**, 151 (1996).

383. M. Horodecki, P. Horodecki, and R. Horodecki, Phys. Rev. Lett. **80**, 5239 (1998); Phys. Rev. Lett. **82**, 1056 (1999).

384. E.M. Rains, Phys. Rev. A **60**, 173 (1999).

385. A. Kent, N. Linden, and S. Massar, Los Alamos preprint quant-ph/9802022.

386. G. Giedke, H.-J. Briegel, J.I. Cirac, and P. Zoller, Phys. Rev. A **59**, 2641 (1999).

387. W. Dür, H.-J. Briegel, J.I. Cirac, and P. Zoller, Phys. Rev. A **59**, 169 (1999); ibid. **60**, 729 (1999).

388. B. Huttner, J.D. Gautier, A. Muller, H. Zbinden and N. Gisin, Phys. Rev. A, **54**, 3783 (1996).

389. M. Horodecki P. Horodecki and M. Horodecki. Violating bell inequality by mixed spin 1/2 states: necessary and sufficient condition. Phys. Lett. A, **200**, 340 (1995).

390. C. Macchiavello, Phys. Lett. A **246**, 385 (1998).

391. M. Murao, M.B. Plenio, S. Popescu, V. Vedral and P.L. Knight, Phys. Rev. A **57**, R4075 (1998).

392. N. Linden S. Popescu, Fortsch. Phys. **46**, 567 (1998).

393. S.J. van Enk, J.I. Cirac, and P. Zoller, Phys. Rev. Lett., **78**, 4293 (1997).

394. S.J. van Enk, J.I. Cirac, and P. Zoller, Science, **279**, 205 (1998).

395. J.I. Cirac, et al, Physica Scripta, Proceedings of the Nobel Symposium 104, Modern Studies of Basic Quantum Concepts and Phenomena, Uppsala, Sweden, June 13-17 (1997).

396. R.J. Glauber, In *Frontiers in Quantum Optics*, (eds. E.R. Pike and S. Sarkar), 534, Adam Hilger, Bristol (1986).

397. S.J. van Enk, J.I. Cirac, and P. Zoller, Phys. Rev. Lett. **79**, 5178 (1997).

398. M. Zukowski *et al.*, Phys. Rev. Lett. **71**, 4287 (1993); see also S. Bose *et al.*, Phys. Rev. A, **57**, 822 (1998); J.-W. Pan *et al.*, Phys. Rev. Lett. **80**, 3891 (1998).

399. E. Knill and R. Laflamme, quant/ph-9608012. See also A. Yu. Kitaev, Russ. Math. Surv. **52**, 1191 (1997); D. Aharonov and M. Ben-Or, quant-ph/9611025; C. Zalka, quant-ph/ 9612028.

400. P. Shor, quant-ph/9605011; A.M. Steane, Phys. Rev. Lett. **78**, 2252 (1997). D. Gottesman, Phys. Rev. A **57**, 127 (1998); For a review see, for example, J. Preskill, in *Introduction to Quantum Computation*, ed. by H.K. Lo, S. Popescu and T.P. Spiller.

Index

Printing (Computer to Film): Saladruck, Berlin
Binding: Lüderitz & Bauer, Berlin